THE NILE
IN DARKNESS

THE NILE
IN DARKNESS

A Flawed Unity
1863–1899

JOHN O. UDAL

MICHAEL RUSSELL

First published in Great Britain 2005
by Michael Russell (Publishing) Ltd
Wilby Hall, Wilby, Norwich NR16 2JP

Typeset in Sabon by Waveney Typesetters
Wymondham, Norfolk
Printed and bound in Great Britain
by Biddles Ltd, King's Lynn, Norfolk

Index: ed.emery@britishlibrary.net
Maps drawn by J. D. Cartographics
Ashtead, Surrey

TO THE PEOPLES OF THE SUDAN
WITH WHOM, TO OUR GREAT FORTUNE,
THE LIVES OF MY FAMILY
BECAME LINKED

Contents

List of Tables and Illustrations

Maps

Acknowledgements

With the publication of *The Nile in Darkness: A Flawed Unity, 1863–99* I wish to record how much I have again been indebted to my publisher and editor, Michael Russell, for his unfailing patience and good humour in offering wise counsel from which this second volume has enormously benefited. Nor in its preparation do I forget my continuing debt to Andrew and Jackie Best who contributed so much to its predecessor.

Wide-ranging research has been invariably aided by the staffs of various national libraries, notably the British Library; the School of Oriental and African Studies, London University; the Public Record Office, Kew; and the Archives Diplomatiques, Ministère des Affaires Etrangères, Paris. Once again I am especially indebted to the Librarians of the Athenaeum, Kay Walters and Annette Gossage; and to Jane Hogan, Assistant Keeper, Archives and Special Collections of Durham University Library and her staff, whose patient help and courtesy have been much valued.

I gratefully acknowledge a real obligation to the Royal Geographical Society (with the Institute of British Geographers); to Dr Andrew Tatham, its former Keeper, and to Eugène Rae, Librarian, in particular, for permission to consult and to quote extracts from 'The Journals of Sir Samuel White Baker', volumes 3 and 4. Precise details are given in the source notes to chapter 5.

The research, writing and publication of these two volumes of *The Nile in Darkness* has spanned seventeen years, during all of which I have had the unflagging assistance of Lesley Piper in interpreting and rendering legible numberless manuscript drafts, notes and appendices – a matter of despairing frustration for anyone of less equable temperament. Her part has been indispensable and I am deeply grateful.

Another who must unequivocally welcome the completion of this second volume will be my wife Ann who has somehow found inner resources to endure the task of sustaining a husband seemingly committed to a prolonged erosion of family life. Her sacrifice has been wonderful, without which – nothing.

Introduction

To set in context what follows, it will be helpful to encapsulate the main events of the period since the conquest of the Sudan by Mohammed Ali.

When in May 1862 the Regency Council in Cairo, in the absence abroad of the Viceroy Mohammed Sa'id, reinstated the status quo in the Sudan and restored the Governor-Generalship, Turkish-Egyptian rule had been established in the province over forty years. Its Ottoman-style administration had been characterised by brutality and corruption, and the proud peoples of the conquered territories had been tamed by the proven futility of resistance to overwhelming military might. The suppression of the revolts of 1821–2 induced a brooding acquiescence among the populace. The Baqqara, notably the Salim and the Hawazma, were irregularly chastised for withholding tribute, but were not provoked into actual insurrection. Disaffected sections of the Sha'iqiya, however, auxiliaries of the conquerors, did confront their oppressors in 1839; so did the Hadendoa in 1840 and 1844; and the Nuba of Mek Nasir Abu Bakr in the Tegali *jebels* a year later. For the Sha'iqiya the outcome was an honourable surrender, for the Hadendoa a bloody massacre, and for the Nuba successful resistance to a series of military expeditions.

This is not to suggest that life in the kingdom of Sennar before the Turkish conquest of 1820–1 was either tranquil or prosperous. Disintegration had set in following the death of the great military commander Mohammed Abu Keylik in 1774. The prime constituent of the kingdom's cohesion, the alliance between the Fung king at Sennar and the viceregal sheikh of the Abdullab at Gerri, had yielded to recurrent war between kings and regents, and between them and their increasingly nominal viceroys. Kordofan first fell to the Musaba'at, then to the Fur Sultan in 1785, and would remain a province of Darfur until the Turkish conquest of 1821. The Sha'iqiya, independent of Sennar since 1681, had a hundred years later incorporated the mekship of Dongola in their own domain, at least until the arrival of the Mamlouk exiles in 1812;

while the northern Beja – notably the Amarar, Bisharin and Hadendoa – expanded southwards into the more hospitable lands of the Atbara and the Gash. In 1791 the Shukriya Sheikhs in Taka additionally became *manjils* – of the Isle of Meröe – while the murder the previous year of Mohammed el Mismar, the last powerful sheikh of the Abdullab, led to the detachment of the Ja'aliyin district and, in 1801, its severance between two cousins, implacable foes: Sheikhs Nimr at Shendi and Musa'ad at Metemma. The capital town of Sennar had been burned down in 1788 and the last king, Badi VI, reigned from 1792 until 1821 as a sovereign in name only of the old Fung heartland of the Gezira and Fazughli.

After three centuries the kingdom of Sennar had dissolved into the anarchy which preceded its creation. To quote from Alexander Pope's *The Dunciad*:

> Lo! thy dread empire, Chaos! is restored;
> Light dies before thy uncreating word:
> Thy hand, great Anarch, lets the curtain fall;
> And universal darkness buries all.

And yet not quite. The progressive collapse of central government had not of itself generated the spread of terror among the populace. Security may have been diminished but servitude was not imposed. Clashes stemming from the rivalry of neighbouring tribes and of villages would continue to be resolved, if by force of arms, by contestants who knew that in the last resort there would need to be accommodation between local victor and vanquished. Across the territories all were aware of the limitation imposed by relative poverty on sustainable levels of tribute. The inhabitants may not have had the sophistication to ponder the truth or otherwise of Edmund Burke's claim, uttered within a year of Abu Keylik's death, that 'freedom not servitude is the cure of anarchy', but neighbouring factions maintained a basic toleration of each other.

The excesses of violence and cruelty perpetrated by the alien invaders of 1820–1 shocked the Arab peoples of the Sudan. The depravity of the Turkish military excited contempt and disgust, but it was their resort to excessive brutality, whether torture or impalement, which left the local peoples aghast. It was not that the peoples of the Nile were unfamiliar with the face of oppression. The description by Burckhardt of the rough treatment of slaves transported from Shendi to Egypt or Suakin in 1814, and by Cailliaud seven years later of the Shendi slave market, are evidence of that. The Turks however introduced a different dimension of brutality which was unrelieved by any compensating policies of enlightened development. Justice remained subordinate to the whim of the military; initiatives in education and public health were negligible.

Of the original objectives of the Turkish conquest, the Mamlouk threat was quickly eliminated. As to the second, the Ottoman Viceroy Mohammed Ali never abandoned his belief in an El Dorado in the Fazughli mountains, but a chimera it surely proved. The third objective, systematic raiding of the Black peoples of the Fazughli and Nuba mountains to provide a recruitment source for the new model army, was only a qualified success, in that the troops proved vulnerable to the climate and environment of Upper Egypt and of the Levant, and could only be deployed reliably in the Sudan itself. (The notable exception were the men of the Black battalion loaned to the French Emperor in the Mexican campaign 1863–7, a high proportion of whom were now Nilotics.) As to the final strategic objective of the Red Sea littoral and its military significance in regard to Abyssinia, only in 1847 were the Red Sea ports of Suakin and Massawa occupied under lease from the Porte, to be quickly abandoned by Abbas Pasha two years later; indeed not until 1862 was an invasion from Abyssinia a serious threat. Control of the Nile waters themselves did not yet figure in Egyptian strategic interests.

After forty years there was then little to justify or to reward the occupation of a huge territory of the Sudan. There had been some progress in the structure of political administration; marginal economic progress at the cost of onerous taxation; the imposition of government monopolies and a corrupt régime; and virtually no attempt to integrate the conquered territory at all in a civilised polity. A far-sighted Turco-Egyptian initiative might have altered the course of the Sudan's history for the better on three specific occasions, but the opportunity was missed each time.

The first was the visit of the Viceroy Mohammed Ali to Khartoum and Fazughli in 1838–9. At that point the Sudan had enjoyed a dozen years of relative stability and peace thanks to the enlightened and generally conciliatory approach first of Mahu Bey Urfali, then of Ali Khurshid Pasha towards the senior tribal sheikhs of the old kingdom and Kordofan. It was a propitious moment for the announcement of a future policy of cooperation based on friendship and progressive devolution. However, the Viceroy's thoughts were concentrated on his bid for independence from Constantinople and, displeased by the lack of warmth in his reception in Khartoum, he offered no overt encouragement to his subject peoples. Efforts to discover fugitive gold seams

were certainly redoubled, a new town founded in his name in anticipation of success, an expedition of discovery dispatched to the White
Nile source – and that was all. Five thousand purses for expansive
benefaction had accompanied the Viceroy, undistributed, back to
Cairo.

If friendship, humanity and cooperation were not to be the keynotes
of the future relationship, then the resumption of military autocracy, territorial expansion and centralisation was immediately on offer in the
exceptional personality of the contemporary Governor-General,
Mohammed Ali's son-in-law, Ahmed Pasha Widan. He harboured less
than confidential ambitions for the establishment of an independent
province of the Sudan. Such was his generalship, his skilled organisation
of government and taxation, and his ruthless determination that, backed
by the supportive relationships he forged with his Sudanese advisers
from the local communities and granted the tacit connivance of the
Sultan in Constantinople, he might well have forged an autonomous
Sudan. The plot leaked, the Sultan proved wary and the father-in-law
sufficiently enraged to find the strength to reimpose his own relentless
will on his conquered province and his perfidious son-in-law.

Another dozen years, this time of drift and indecision, were to pass
before a Viceroy was drastically to review the long-term future of the
Sudan and provide a third opportunity. When in 1854 Mohammed
Sa'id, younger son of Mohammed Ali, succeeded Abbas Pasha, he
committed himself to visit the Sudan. Having enacted a viceregal decree
to abolish slave trafficking there, he persuaded his younger brother
Mohammed Abdel Halim Pasha to accept the appointment of Governor-General in 1856. European interest had been awakened by the
potential profitability of free trade as much as by the excesses of the
slave raids associated with the annual ivory expeditions to the upper
regions of the White Nile and Gondokoro. Despite Abdel Halim's
initial enthusiasm to eliminate the *razzias* (as the slave raids were
called), at the age of twenty-five, to the detriment of the Sudan, he
found himself physically unequal to the alien environment, and to the
coincident severe outbreak of cholera even before the extreme temper-
atures of summer were established. Quitting on medical advice, he beat
a rapid retreat to Egypt.

The unforeseen abdication of Abdel Halim as *hakimdar* set afoot a
further reappraisal of the future government of the Sudan, in which
doubtless he still exercised some influence. The Viceroy reaffirmed
his personal intent to visit Khartoum but his mind now focused on

devolution of civil power to local tribal notables, with direct Turkish authority to be limited to a centralised army command under the *seraskir*. Notwithstanding the ravages of the cholera epidemic on the first rank of sheikhs, such devolution would seemingly have been the Viceroy's preferred solution had it not been that Arakil Bey el Armani volunteered to assume the position of general-governor of Khartoum and Sennar. Once he was accepted, the provinces of the Sudan became once again directly responsible to Cairo. Mohammed Sa'id may be given good marks for endeavour, but this solution would not survive the predatory intentions of the new Abyssinian Negus. Only the vicere-gal council's eleventh-hour appointment in 1862 of the war-hardened Musa Hamdi as Governor-General – which probably owed little to Mohammed Sa'id – shielded the Sudan from invasion. Life for its discontented people reverted to normal.

Nevertheless, if there was no escape from political oppression, no improvement in living standards or amenities, the traditional routine of life at least outside the towns continued to offer the people some compensation for a harsh environment. Mansfield Parkyns, a percep-tive and articulate traveller of the Sudan, left this account of Arab opin-ion of their conquerors: 'Only when they trust you will they tell you that the Turks are the scourge of God or of the Devil and that the neigh-bouring governors and employees are the quintessence of the scourge, that where a Turk puts his government the grass will not grow (a common saying) and many other little hints of their fondness.' By contrast, the description from his journal en route to Khartoum of an encampment of Rufa'a nomads near the junction of the Rahad and the Blue Nile in 1845 is evocative of traditional Sudanese Arab manners:

This is what I would wish any of my friends to see to persuade them of the pleasure of travelling in these climes. You arrive after a hot fatiguing day's journey completely knocked up: the sun is just setting, the men are not yet returned with the cattle they have been pasturing at a distance in the woods.

The camp is entirely occupied by the women and a few old men; you look out for the largest and best hut or tent and that is where you mark the best spot for tethering your camels. As you pass through the lines you address some kind words of salutation to each party and each one answers you with a friendly welcome. Arrived at your destination while you are 'rubbing' [kneeling] your camels and taking off their saddles and loads, preparations are making for your entertainment under the direction of the old men and the mistress of the house. Couches covered with mats are brought according to the numbers of the party and if the host has not enough to supply your wants they are easily borrowed of the neighbours.

Then when all your baggage is arranged for the night you sit down and a new welcome is given you. Then water with 'abnay' and honey, or sour milk or 'sooridge' is offered to cool your parched lips. You quench your thirst and then having taken a composing whiff of the pipe you look at the scene around you. Before each tent is a large blazing fire round which pretty little girls of from 10 to 15 are stirring their 'bormas' which contain the porridge they are preparing for their fathers' and brothers' supper while their mothers would from time to time give the orders. How pretty they are too, with their beautiful eyes and their long soft hair hanging in tresses over their shoulders, clothed mainly by a sort of petticoat of long thin strips of leather from their waist half way down to their knee, but wearing a garment far superior to all we boast of in Europe – their own native innocence.

You are still contemplating this happy scene when the distant bark of dogs and the lowing of the cattle mixed with the bleating of the goats proclaim the approach of the men. First in come a stately herd of camels and then the others follow, then the former stillness of the camp is a little relieved by the greetings exchanged between the men and their families. And then again the master of the house offers you his welcome and particularly enquires if you have been wanting in anything. Then supper for man and beast is brought, and after a little, quiet homely gossip over sundry bowls of new milk. The stillness returns to the camp and its inmates repose in that quick sleep only to be obtained by a due proportion of bodily labour and the tranquillity of a conscience almost altogether ignorant in even its meaning.

I

A Recentralised Sudan 1862–65

1 THE VICEREGAL ACCESSION OF
ISMAIL PASHA IBRAHIM 1863

When Mohammed Sa'id Pasha, still not yet forty but with his health irreversibly undermined, left in April 1862 for a recuperative tour of Western Europe, the fortunes of both Egypt and the Sudan were at a low ebb. While his predecessor as Viceroy, Abbas (1849–54), a veteran of the latter's uncle Ibrahim Pasha's Syrian campaign of 1839–4, was persuaded of the need to accommodate European Power pressure for free trade and had clipped the wings of his Governor-Generals in Khartoum, Mohammed Sa'id, after his personal visit in January 1857, had still further eroded central authority in the Sudan by substituting an administration of provincial general-governors each responsible to Cairo, and by shrinking the garrisons. The process of erosion had now attracted the notice of the territorially ambitious Emperor Theodore II who had wrested rule of Abyssinia in early 1855.

For Mohammed Sa'id's five-month absence in 1862 a Council of Regency had been established under the presidency of his nephew Ismail, the second of three sons of Ibrahim Pasha (the stepson of Mohammed Ali), older by seven months than his uncle Mohammed Abdel Halim. Ismail, on the death of his elder brother Ahmed Rifaat by drowning in 1858, had become the next eldest surviving male descendant of Mohammed Ali and accordingly, by Ottoman tradition, heir apparent to the Viceroyalty of Egypt. Born in January 1829, like his elder brother he had been educated in France. In the words of J. C. McCoan: 'He possessed much of the inexhaustible energy of his putative grandfather, Mohammed Ali, without the sterner features of his father Ibrahim, and had the advantage over both of receiving a European education which developed an intellectual activity that, soon after his return from Paris in 1849, made him the most prominent figure in Egyptian society.'

At this early age he became rapidly at odds with his cousin Abbas, the new Viceroy, between whom the dislike was mutual. By early 1852

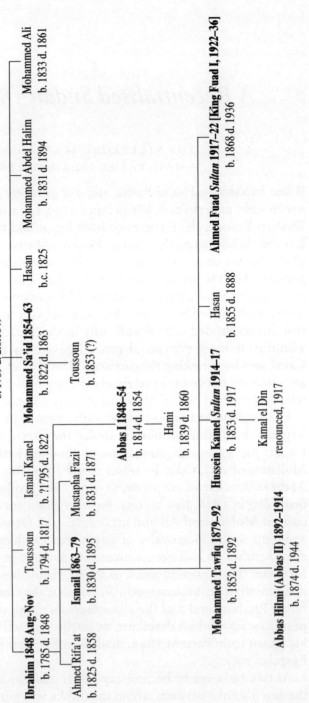

Viceregal Dynasty of Mohammed Ali
1805–1922
[Viceroys in bold type]

Mohammed Ali 1805–48
b. 1769 d. 2.8.1849

Ibrahim 1848 Aug–Nov
b. 1785 d. 1848

Toussoun
b. 1794 d. 1817

Ismail Kamel
b. ?1795 d. 1822

Mohammed Sa'id 1854–63
b. 1822 d. 1863

Hasan
b.c. 1825

Mohammed Abdel Halim
b. 1831 d. 1894

Mohammed Ali
b. 1833 d. 1861

Ahmed Rifa'at
b. 1825 d. 1858

Mustapha Fazil
b. 1831 d. 1871

Abbas I 1848–54
b. 1814 d. 1854

Toussoun
b. 1853 (?)

Ismail 1863–79
b. 1830 d. 1895

Hami
b. 1839 d. 1860

Mohammed Tawfiq 1879–92
b. 1852 d. 1892

Hussein Kamel *Sultan* **1914–17**
b. 1853 d. 1917

Hasan
b. 1855 d. 1888

Ahmed Fuad *Sultan* **1917–22 [King Fuad I, 1922–36]**
b. 1868 d. 1936

Abbas Hilmi (Abbas II) 1892–1914
b. 1874 d. 1944

Kamal el Din
renounced, 1917

both Ismail's elder brother Ahmed Rifa'at and Mohammed Sa'id seem to have become involved in a conspiracy against Abbas with the Porte in Constantinople, and were creating their own armed force in Egypt; while a servant of Ismail was caught spying on the Viceroy, the outcome of which was an unsuccessful public accusation by Abbas against Ismail of murdering one of his viceregal slaves. Ismail's abilities, however, had been quickly recognised by Sultan Abdel Majid I (1839–61), who appointed him to various judicial offices. On Mohammed Sa'id's accession to the viceroyalty, Ismail was made a member of the viceregal council, performing missions to Paris and Rome and, when Mohammed Sa'id made the pilgrimage to Mecca in 1861, acting for the first time as regency president.[1]

Ismail's second discharge of that responsibility, in the summer of 1862, coincided with the discovery of the source of the White Nile in Lake Victoria on 21 July, but it was as Viceroy that he received Speke and Grant the following year when they descended the Nile to Khartoum and Cairo and broke the news of their discovery to the outside world. Of more immediate importance during Ismail's second stint as regency president, in May 1862 reports reached Cairo that Emperor Theodore II of Abyssinia had plans to re-establish the former (Axumite) Ethiopian empire extending down the eastern borders of the Nile as far as Shendi, near ancient Meröe, and encompassing the fertile lands between the Nile and the Atbara. With commendable decision, Ismail at once appointed the tough and very experienced soldier and former provincial governor Musa Bey Hamdi to take over as Governor-General of the Sudan. He was to leave at once with substantial reinforcements for Khartoum – a demonstration of viceregal determination which proved sufficient to deflect Theodore from his invasion of the Sudan.

Mohammed Sa'id Pasha returned to Egypt on 10 October 1862 but lived only until 18 January 1863. His eldest son, Toussoun, was nine years old and Mohammed Sa'id had made no attempt to copy the unsuccessful plans of Ibrahim and Abbas and so to prefer Toussoun's claim to the succession against that of Ismail. Appointing his uncle Abdel Halim Pasha regent in his absence, Ismail left on 20 February for Constantinople to seek the *hatt-i-sharif*, staying there with his younger brother Mustapha Fazil, formerly responsible for finance on Mohammed Sa'id's council and currently Ottoman minister of finance. He returned to Alexandria in early March, his succession confirmed by the new Sultan Abdel Aziz (1861–76), the latter now the richer for

Ismail Pasha Ibrahim, Viceroy and Khedive of Egypt, 1863–79

Ismail's presentation to him of a new British-built steam yacht. It provided a suitable vehicle for the Sultan's return visit to Ismail in early April – the first by an Ottoman Sultan since the conquest by Sultan Selim I in 1517, and the last.

The visit, however, was not an unqualified success. In the weeks before the Sultan's arrival, Ismail was alerted to a plot in Egypt instigated by Mustapha Fazil in Constantinople. Ismail closed his brother's office in Egypt, exiling the agent to Fazughli in the manner of Abbas Pasha. Then the Sultan made it clear that his predecessor's agreement in principle in 1859 to the excavation of the Suez Canal under a 99-year lease granted by Mohammed Sa'id to the Compagnie Universelle of Ferdinand de Lesseps in January 1856 did not extend authority to the Viceroy to negotiate the arrangements with the European Powers. This, on the contrary, was the prerogative of the Sultan who, on visiting Suez, sharply declined to inspect the early excavation works for the Canal.[2]

While de Lesseps, with the support of the French Emperor Napoleon III, had secured the backing of leading European Powers for the Suez Canal project, Britain had persistently opposed it and her government's views were robustly represented to the Sultan by the British Ambassador in Constantinople, Lord Stratford de Redcliffe. So long as Britain and France were allies in the Crimean War, British advice to the Porte was to delay a decision on the Canal by various expedients. The scheme was 'inopportune', but behind that euphemism lay British distrust of French ambitions in Egypt. Britain 'feared that opening the isthmus, by giving too much importance to Egypt, would disturb its relations with Turkey', and if Egyptian independence were the objective, it would also menace British communications with India. Earlier the French promotion of the fortification of the Mediterranean coast and the building of the Delta barrage seemed designed to obstruct a Turkish sea invasion, while the Canal would now interpose a land barrier between Syria and Egypt, colonised moreover by expatriate French technicians. Even if Egypt's dependency on Constantinople were maintained intact, there would be no comparable communications benefit to India from the excavation of the Canal as there had been over the Alexandria-Cairo-Suez railway link. Primitive coal-fired steamships would be uneconomical on the India route, and sailing ship schedules would hardly be helped by four weeks' tacking up the confined waters of the Red Sea.

In January 1856 an International Commission for surveying the isthmus unanimously agreed that the Canal project was 'easy', its construction 'certain', its results for the commerce of the world 'immense'. Further procrastination was unviable and construction began in 1859. Nevertheless Sultan Abdel Aziz, four years later, was only prepared to concede his authority to conduct negotiations with the European Powers to Ismail on condition that the excessive concession to the Canal Company of lands on the banks of the maritime and sweet water canals was substantially reduced in scale; that the neutralisation of the Canal be accepted by the Company; and that forced as opposed to voluntary labour be prohibited. All these conditions were agreed, but the price to Ismail and Egypt was swingeing, the compensation payable to the Company being recklessly referred to the arbitration of Napoleon III, de Lesseps's protector, to be fixed at £E3.36m, payable in 12% Treasury bonds over the period 1864–9. The Canal opened in 1869 in the presence of the French Empress Eugénie and minor European royalty directly invited by Ismail Pasha to the vexation of the Sultan.[3]

Ismail was the first well-educated Viceroy. His initial ambition, inherited from his father and grandfather, was progressively to wrest the independence of Egypt from the Ottoman Empire. To this he now added a second aim: to make of his kingdom and capital an essentially European entity. The Canal project was consonant with these aspirations, as were the expansionist programmes of public works. During his reign 112 additional irrigation canals were constructed – the largest being the Ismailia and the Ibrahimiya (in Upper Egypt) – creating with matching pumping schemes a further one and a quarter million acres of irrigable land especially for cotton. The principal beneficiaries however were the Khedive and also his favoured pashas, with the *fellahin* being increasingly conscripted to labour on their estates under the corvée and the *kurbaj* (whip) and to maintain the perennial canals. Denied the watering of their own fields, they were diverted to water the Khedivial estates by 'superior order'.

The increased cotton-growing programme (350,000 cwt in 1850 and 2m cwt in 1865), initially boosted by the curtailment of American production during the Civil War 1861–5, brought an increase in Egyptian exports from £E4m in 1862 to £E14m in 1864, but there was a fallback to £E10m in 1865. Other public works included bridges, railways, harbour works, telegraph lines and postal services, resulting in improved communications with the Sudan. In the large cities banking facilities were made available but quality was not necessarily the hallmark of new municipal services.

Ismail's expenditure was profligate and was eventually to undo him. Revenue figures for his viceregal reign are elusive but in 1864 may not have exceeded £5m, while in 1875 it was believed that the figure of £E10.5m was inflated by fictitious receipts. Indeed Consul-General Vivian was told by Sharif Pasha in August 1873 that revenue amounted to £E7m –which Lord Cromer thought to be the average sum added annually to the debt over the thirteen years to 1879. To meet the deficit, Ismail turned to public borrowing. He had already inherited in 1863 an overseas loan of £E3.3m contracted by Mohammed Sa'id; in 1864 he borrowed a further £E5.7m from overseas, in 1865 £E4m and in 1867 £E2m. By 1876, when the crash came, Egyptian public debt was £E94m, £E68m funded and £E26m floating.[4]

The Viceroy's personal lifestyle, perhaps as befitted an aspirant European head of state, was lavish. In his quest for independence from Turkey and suspicious of the ambitions of his younger brother Mustapha, currently heir to the viceregal throne, Ismail made overtures to the Sultan on the Sultan's visit to Egypt in April 1863 to grant primogeniture succession to his own heirs, and to bestow on him limited powers to confer honours and to mint his own currency. After three years' negotiation and substantial expenditure in douceurs at the Ottoman court (amounting allegedly to £E3m), Ismail was ultimately successful in May 1866. Tawfik, his eldest, but disliked, son now became heir apparent. Mohammed Abdel Halim, Mohammed Ali's surviving well-loved son, guardian of Mohammed Sa'id's son Toussoun and quite alienated from his nephew, the Viceroy Ismail, was eventually manoeuvred into accepting disinheritance and the surrender of his estates in return for £E1.3m, whereupon he retired to Turkey. Mustapha Fazil was likewise bought out for a similar sum in 1868. The two maintained their intrigues in Constantinople against Ismail, Mustapha Fazil dying in 1871.[5]

Not even the earlier windfall in increased cotton prices during the American Civil War could match Ismail's multi-faceted programme of expenditure. However, a further major concession that he purchased from the Sultan – the permission to increase the size of the Egyptian army – presented him with the opportunity not only to strengthen his forces in Egypt, but to undertake a strategic policy of territorial expansion in the Sudan and eastern Africa. It was the path to eventual bankruptcy. For the while, however, the liabilities were kept at bay and Europe was impressed by the remarkable advance in Egypt's status. In 1867 Queen Victoria conferred upon Ismail the Knight Grand Cross of the Order of the Bath and the next year, in recognition of cooperation over Magdala, the equivalent rank of the Order of the Star of India; while, for a further suitable recompense, the Sultan in 1868 bestowed on him the title of Khedive and, with it, internal freedom in financial, administrative and judicial arrangements and authority to conclude international agreements covering posts, customs and trade transits.[6]

Ismail was at first attentive to the government of the Sudan, recognising that any future territorial expansion in the direction of Syria remained barred to him and must be sought in Africa. Had not his own prompt action as Regent in May 1862 deterred Theodore from invading the Sudan, Ismail would doubtless have welcomed the military defeat of the latter as a legitimate pretext for an Egyptian invasion of Abyssinia. As it was, Theodore's invasion was first delayed, then aborted, while the return to Cairo of the dying Viceroy Mohammed Sa'id led to the dispatch of an unequivocal instruction to Musa Hamdi on 29 October 1862 forbidding war on Abyssinia.

Ismail did not abandon his plans for territorial aggrandisement, but there was little he could do until after Theodore's defeat and death at the hands of the British Magdala expedition in 1868.

Georges Douin identified Mohammed Ali and Ismail as the creators of modern Egypt: 'The first, a genius powerful but rough-hewn, attacked the quarry and with massive blows detached from it a stone block which he fashioned both as to dimension and shape. The second, a more human genius, took up the unfinished work; polishing and chiselling it in his turn, he gave life to its body and suppleness to its limbs, developed its muscles and caused blood to circulate in its arteries. He gave Egypt the face we recognise today.' In respect of the Sudan, however, Ismail's sculpture was a hint metaphysical, in that, unlike his grandfather and immediate predecessor, he never himself visited the country. Like the kings who employed artist scouts to represent the features of potential consorts, Ismail was content to rely on the reports of the governors he posted to the Sudan. And in the end there was no face left to recognise.[7]

2 THE *HAKIMDARIA* OF MUSA PASHA HAMDI 1862–65

The strategy upon which Musa Bey Hamdi embarked on his arrival in Khartoum had been fashioned by recent events. The decision of the former Viceroy Mohammed Sa'id to decentralise the government of the Sudan among four general-governors had proved a failure, and the country in 1862 was under immediate military threat from Abyssinia. While the army had initially been placed under the unified command of Osman Pasha Jarkas, he had died in 1860 and the command had been effectively devolved to the four provinces, little effort being made to ensure that manpower wastage from ill-health and retirement was made good. Musa's first priority then – to defuse the Abyssinian threat – was to reunify the military command under himself and strengthen the military cadres in those Sudan provinces where there was a constant pattern of unrest.

Implicit in the enhanced military requirements of the revived *hakimdaria* was an increase in local revenues, which in turn required an administrative structure competent to ensure that taxes were indeed collected. These objectives, and the upgrading of local agriculture and industry to underpin an increased volume of trade, presupposed an infrastructure of swifter communication over the vast distances between Cairo and the Sudan – initially Wadi Halfa, then Khartoum. If the development of Egypt as a European country would necessarily prove a heavy financial burden, so additionally would this strategy for the Sudan.

Abyssinia: An Aggressive Defence   In tracing the implementation of this strategy, considerable new Turkish documentary evidence from the Abdin Palace archives was researched by Georges Douin and published in volume III of his *Histoire du Règne du Khédive Ismail* in three parts (1936, 1938 and 1941) under the title 'L'Empire Africain' covering 1863–76 – an indispensable aid to the study of this period. It is clear from these records that the reformation and reinforcement of the Sudan army took a full year. Musa had left Cairo in April 1862 with rein- forcements of Egyptian and Sudanese troops – Colquhoun reported two battalions of 400 men each – and some Sha'iqi irregulars, shortly to be followed by 200 *bashi-buzouq* cavalry. He had authority to form a further two Sudan battalions from local recruits, for which he brought with him officer cadres and arms. With the onset of the rains, it was soon clear that no attack from Abyssinia was now in immediate prospect, and having satisfied himself en route of the troop dispositions at Dongola and Berber, Musa allowed himself the best part of four months in Khartoum to muster an expedition to confront Theodore and his rebel Arab chiefs. When he set out on 25 November for Galla- bat via Wad Medani, he had assembled an army of 8,000 men and 5 cannon, of whom 4,500 were regulars, 2,000 horsemen (among them Nur Mohammed Anqara, who would later serve Zubeir, Gordon and the Mahdi) and the remainder local irregular recruits. Notwithstand- ing the arrival of instructions from the Viceroy forbidding him to carry the war into Theodore's territory, Musa was far from satisfied with his overall military capability and on 27 December 1862 he petitioned Cairo for a further two companies of *bashi-buzouqs*, each of 400 men, having already been obliged to dispatch 400 *bashi-buzouqs* and 600 infantry to the defence of Gedaref.[8]

Musa was away for well over five months on his campaign; he returned to Khartoum on 4 May 1863. Proceeding up the River Rahad, he had met and pardoned the rebel Sheikh Ahmed Abu Guenn of Rufa'a before pressing on to occupy Gallabat on 11 February, there to replace Theodore's Sheikh Mohammed Jum'a (Shouma) with his own nominee. He then marched north down the Atbara, planning to ravage Mek Omer Nimr's fastness of Mai Gubba to the east, but the onset of a smallpox

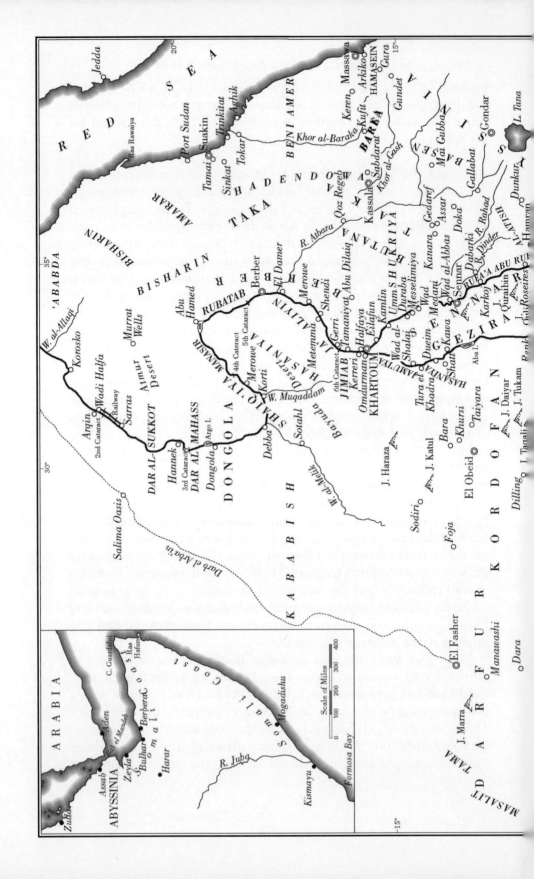

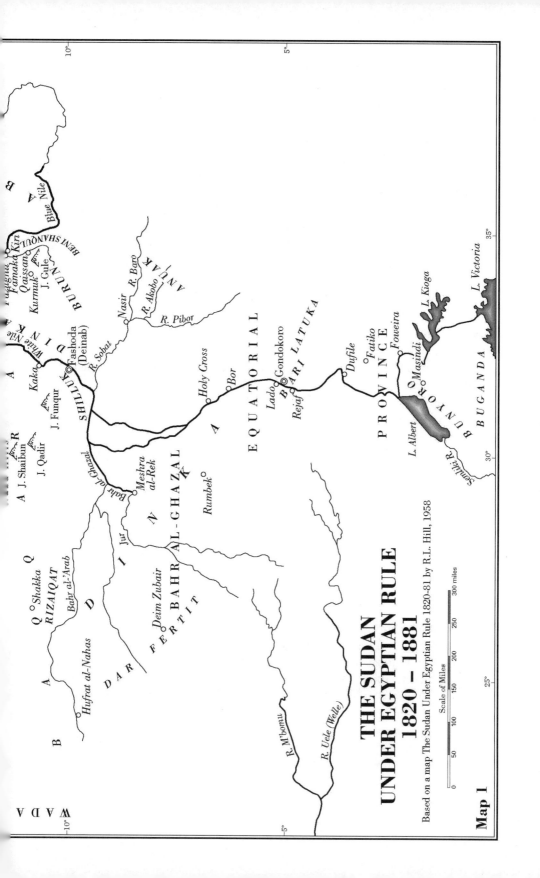

THE SUDAN
UNDER EGYPTIAN RULE
1820 – 1881

Based on a map The Sudan Under Egyptian Rule 1820-81 by R.L. Hill, 1958

Scale of Miles

0   50   100   150   200   250   300 miles

Map 1

epidemic caused him to abort the plan and instead he sent a mounted force to drive Mek Omer back into Abyssinia. Omer was eventually killed in battle against the Makada in July 1865. The show of force had been successful, but the army had scarcely been committed to battle and was numerically far in excess of what was needed. Accordingly, before continuing to Kassala, the province capital of Taka, Musa ordered one battalion each to Sennar and to Mek Ragab Idris Adlan of Fazughli. Their role would be to assist in tribute collection. The remaining three battalions accompanied Musa to Kassala, which he reached on 20 March. He sent a further mounted force to beat up the 'Nimrab', then, after a month, he left for El Damer and Khartoum, detaching at least a further battalion to reinforce the garrison at Kassala.[9]

While on the march the Governor-General was in frequent contact with the Viceroy regarding reinforcements. The two additional companies of *bashi-buzouqs* were sanctioned, as were 4,000 modern rifles, but Musa's request for two further regular battalions of troops from Egypt in addition to his existing eight was refused on the grounds that the manpower did not exist in Egypt, even though the officer cadres would be forthcoming under Miralai Adham Bey. Eventually, by order of the Viceroy dated 2 June 1863, the infantry force of the Sudan was set at four regiments, each of four 600-man battalions – a total of some 10,000 men. Lewa Hasan Ali Bey Arnaut, former Governor of Kordofan, was appointed commander of infantry and Lewa Abdallah Bey el Wanli, former Governor of Dongola, commander of irregulars and *bashi-buzouqs*; while the artillery was increased by a further six cannon in December 1863.

There remained for Musa the task of recruiting the additional other rank cadres. His proposal to revive a practice discontinued by Viceroy Mohammed Sa'id that recruits should be accepted in lieu of tribute – at the rate of 500 piastres per 'volunteer'– was now endorsed by the Viceroy on 2 June in respect of the Fung and Fazughli *jebels* and the Dinka and Shilluk, on condition that the recruits were enlisted not as slaves but on the same basis of service (usually four years) and reward as other volunteers, unless tribute had been withheld by the village sheikh concerned. Musa had in fact already dispatched armed units to assist a tribute collection in the Fung and Fazughli area with the aim of recruitment (and was to do so again in December 1863), and the Viceroy was prepared additionally to authorise the impressing of tribesmen in the Abyssinia mountain border country whose sheikhs refused to submit voluntarily.[10]

Douin quotes a rare eyewitness account of the reality of this policy. In April 1865, visiting the Sudan, F.-B. Garnier, the first dragoman of the French consulate-general, had observed Sha'iqi irregular cavalry and two Black battalions leaving Sennar in order, so the *mudir* Ahmed Bey Abu Sin told him, to encourage Ragab Idris Adlan, Fung Sheikh of Jebel Gule (Quli), to forward his tribute quota. While in Khartoum in July, Garnier happened to witness the arrival by night of the harvest of this démarche: not tribute but some 500 slaves yoked together and consigned to the barracks for enrolment. It was a repeat impressing exercise of that ordered by Musa of Ahmed Bey Abu Sin a year earlier, with a similar yield of recruits.

And if the mountain border people were to be press-ganged, why not the Nilotics in the as yet unannexed undelineated territory of the Upper Nile? Even as Musa had moved off in November 1862 on his Abyssinian expedition, further *razzias* (slave raids) against the Sobat Dinka and of course the Equatoria peoples were already being mounted, necessarily with Musa's knowledge, by the Khartoum trading community. The distinction between recruitment methods sanctioned by the Viceroy and the freelance *razzia* was fine to the point of non-existence.[11]

Ismail Pasha's definition of a sufficient armed force 'in these vast and important regions' of the Sudan was a generous one, but was initially prompted by the continuing threat of invasion by Theodore, whose army - albeit an undisciplined horde armed with spears and ancient matchlock muskets – numbered some 60,000. Since October 1862 Theodore had been waiting on the acceptance by the European powers of his proposed embassy and plea for moral support against Egypt. His angry reaction to the absence of such response was the arrest in chains of the French vice-consul Lejean in April 1863, and then of his British counterpart, Captain Cameron, on the latter's return to Gondar in October. It brought no results from London. For the time being, however, Theodore was occupied with quelling internal rebellions, though still harbouring his territorial ambitions. It seems clear that Ismail also had his mind on expansion, on a scale that would justify such an expensive army.[12]

The autumn of 1863 saw one of the more bizarre happenings in Sudan-Abyssinian relations. Armed with an official letter of introduction, one Comte Raoul du Bisson, a general in the Neapolitan army, arrived in Egypt on 25 September with baggage including 400 rifles, 4 cannon, small arms and 400 kilos of gunpowder. He purported to be setting up a cotton syndicate in Upper Egypt but Ismail Pasha, who at the request of the French Consul-General Tastu granted him an audience, mistakenly supposed he was a clandestine emissary of Napoleon III. Du Bisson encouraged this misapprehension and revealed that his private intent was to establish a military base near the Abyssinian border from which to secure the release of the French vice-consul in Gondar, Guillaume Lejean, under arrest by Theodore since April.

The audience with the Viceroy took place very early in October 1863, shortly after Ismail's meeting in Cairo with Musa Hamdi, now raised to the rank of Pasha in recognition of his services on the Abyssinian border. At the meeting Musa Hamdi had resisted any discussion of invading Abyssinia until at least he had first crushed the rebellious *meks* (tribal kinglets) of the Nuba mountains of southern Kordofan. So for Ismail this new pretext for an expedition against Abyssinia with French backing seemed irresistible, and on 5 October he sent instructions after Musa, now en route to Khartoum, to listen to du Bisson's plans and, if he found them viable, to embark on a joint offensive across the Abyssinian frontier. Du Bisson's force meanwhile was to be backed by viceregal funds and introductions, together with river and desert transport. The force left Cairo three days later.[13]

Musa, alerted by Cairo, left Khartoum by steamer to join du Bisson on the latter's arrival at Berber on 15 November. Events however had by now moved on. Ismail had learned from his private secretary, Nubar Pasha, currently in Paris negotiating details of the Suez Canal agreement, that the Quai d'Orsay had no knowledge of du Bisson. In short his story was fraudulent. By 16 October the Viceroy had been obliged to dispatch new instructions to Musa, with a letter to du Bisson, prohibiting Musa from crossing into Abyssinia, and urging him to prevent du Bisson erecting a fortified base on the frontier. If du Bisson himself insisted on crossing into Abyssinia, he could be provisioned but was not to be accompanied by Turkish troops.

Only then did du Bisson divulge to Musa the origin and purpose of his mission. A missionary priest, possibly Monsignor Biancheri of the Lazarite order at Sennaheit (Keren) in Bogos country, had written to him inviting him to develop 60,000 acres of agricultural land in one of the local valleys. While du Bisson was preparing for this project in Paris, he had been approached by the French Government with a view to rescuing the interned French vice-consul Lejean, and in Cairo had then received the tentative invitation of the Viceroy to undertake a joint venture into Abyssinia. Du Bisson now sought to march from Khartoum to Gallabat to reconnoitre the military positions in that vicinity and to undertake the training of his small force enlisted from the indigent expatriates of Cairo and Alexandria coffee shops.[14]

Musa could not yet know that Lejean had already been expelled by Theodore on the return to Gondar of Bardel, Cameron's secretary, with an unsatisfactory reply to the Emperor from Paris in September 1863. So any excuse for a French territorial incursion was now removed. Musa realised however that du Bisson's personal strategy was coloured by the belief that now he had secured viceregal assent to his Bogos project, he would secure Egyptian funding and, in the case of failure, indemnity. The Bogos agricultural project was likely to provoke a reaction from Theodore, and Musa presently had priority concerns in the Nuba mountains. Accordingly he vetoed the Gallabat objective, escorted du Bisson back from Berber to Khartoum, provisioned du Bisson's Barea expedition and maintained his weapons (du Bisson bought two leather cannons from Petherick). He then directed him to Kassala where Ali Bey Fadli, the deputy Governor-General, and Ibrahim Bey el Mahallawi, governor of Taka, received him on 14 February 1864. Their orders were that du Bisson was only to be defended if Theodore's forces attacked him on Sudanese soil.[15]

Whether or not du Bisson had already been alerted, Father Giovanni Stella and Lejean were already in the locality. The Father apparently urged that the agricultural scheme should be sought in Barea country, not Bogos, and on 31 March du Bisson, with his own small force and a Turkish military escort, left Kassala for the revised site. He arrived at Kufit (between Taka and Bogos) on 12 April. Kufit in Barea was more plausibly Sudanese territory than was Bogos, notwithstanding an edict of Mohammed Sa'id at Khartoum in January 1857 that Bogos was part of the Sudan – a claim doubtless founded on Ahmed Widan's raid of 1842. Kufit was the alternative backed by Stella; but Du Bisson's sojourn there with the trusting Barea people was to be brief. By mid February 1864 Ismail in Cairo had been apprised by Paris that du Bisson was wholly disowned and Musa, now in Kordofan, was instructed that no further help was to be offered him. The forwarded instruction only reached Kassala about 24 April 1864, but by May it had been communicated to du Bisson at Kufit and he, realising he would lose his Turkish contingent, elected to withdraw to Kassala. True to his original strategy, he then sought compensation from Cairo for damages of an alleged 10 million francs, a claim to be dismissed by the authorities with contempt. Significantly, however, the Viceroy, in an instruction to Ja'afar Pasha Sadiq in November 1865, ordered the reoccupation of Kufit, implemented by Ja'afar Pasha Mazhar in January 1867.

There was an extremely serious consequence of this inept adventure. It had been undertaken with the supposed purpose of securing the release of the imprisoned Lejean, who had in the event been released even before du Bisson reached Egypt. By a stroke of irony the report that du Bisson was intending to establish himself in Hamasein (Bogos) gave the Emperor Theodore the excuse to retract a promise, made to his European artisans, to release the British consul Cameron and the Christian missionaries whom he had arrested in October 1863.[16]

In the absence of any sanction from Britain or France, another possible opportunity for Egyptian easterly expansion from the Sudan had to be allowed to slip away. There was no further initiative during Musa Hamdi's time as Governor-General but his Viceroy had not abandoned expansionist ambitions. The only concrete progress to be made came when Musa himself lay dying in early 1865. It related to the reacquisition of the ports of Suakin and Massawa.

Late in 1846, Mohammed Ali Pasha had secured from the Ottoman Sultan the lease of these ports for his lifetime as Viceroy. Possession of Massawa was taken in March 1847 by Ismail Haqqi Abu Jebal, later Governor-General 1852–3, and the wrath of the British Foreign Secretary, Lord Palmerston, was incurred at the alleged intent of the Viceroy to reconnoitre the African Red Sea coast up to the Bab el Mandeb, where Britain had recently acquired the fortress of Aden. Regarding the cession to Egypt of Massawa in January 1848 as a potential threat to British trade relations with Abyssinia (and to the route to India), Palmerston appointed Walter Plowden as British vice-consul to Abyssinia based at Massawa and, in 1849, a treaty of commerce was signed with Gondar. By then the demise of Mohammed Ali and the lack of interest of his successor Abbas Pasha had led to the reversion of the ports to Turkey.

Historically both ports had been a major conduit for the export of slaves from the Sudan. By 1864 increasing knowledge of the White Nile *razzias* and the outcome of the American Civil War concentrated Western public opinion on the abolition of the slave trade. News reached Europe that notwithstanding an interdict from the Porte on the export of slaves from the Arabian ports (and originating from the Sudan), these slaves were being carried from Jedda to Suez in the new viceregal Aziz steamships, having been supposedly granted documents of liberation by the local *qadi*. To stamp this out, Ismail Pasha proposed third party supervision of 'liberated' slaves at Suez but, identifying the real source to be the traffickers of Suakin and Massawa, he advocated and petitioned for the transfer of the latter ports to his jurisdiction. The proposal was predictably resisted by the Porte, but in May 1865, under heavy British pressure, the transfer was agreed for the lifetime of Ismail and a year later, when dynastic primogeniture was conceded to him, for the duration of the dynasty. Suakin was formally possessed by Ja'afar Pasha Mazhar in August 1865 but Massawa not until April 1866, by Lewa Ismail Sadek Pasha. The governors then appointed were respectively Ahmed Mumtaz Bey and Hasan Rifaat Bey.[17]

Provincial Administration   In his first year of office as Governor-General Musa Pasha had been in his capital for five months – 2 August –24 November 1862, and about 10 May–25 June 1863. Then, after seeing the returned ailing British consul, John Petherick, he left for his summer house in Upper Egypt, probably acquired during his spell as governor of Qena ten years earlier. In the extended interval he was absent on his Abyssinian reconnaissance, though like his earlier friend and mentor, Ahmed Pasha Widan, he was kept in regular touch with Sudan events by messengers.

No Turkish ruler had a more extensive knowledge of the Sudan. Having arrived as a *bimbashi* under Ahmed Widan after service in the Syrian campaign, he had taken part in the Taka campaign of 1840, before holding the post of governor of Khartoum and Sennar 1841–3, chief of staff to Ahmed Pasha Manikli in 1844, governor of Dongola 1847–8, and of Kordofan 1849–50, during which time von Heuglin says that he travelled through Bahr el Ghazal country. Removed from the last post by Sultan's firman for gross misconduct and ostensibly recalled in disgrace to Egypt, he yet managed to serve for a while as deputy to Abdel Latif Pasha in Khartoum until appointed as governor of Qena in 1853 (also under Abdel Latif now governor of Upper Egypt) and, later, chief of police in Cairo. No man was better equipped by organisational experience to reintegrate the four general-governor provinces set up by Mohammed Sa'id: Khartoum with Sennar; Berber and Dongola; Kordofan; and Taka.

Musa, in addition to appointing a deputy Governor-General, Ali Bey Fadli, reverted to a subordinate provincial structure. Khartoum remained merged with Sennar, but Mohammed Rasikh Bey, the former general-governor, was dismissed and replaced as governor by the Shukriya Sheikh Ahmed Awad el Karim Abu Sin. Dongola (it is unclear when) was separated from Berber while Taka, under Ibrahim Bey el Mahallawi, and Kordofan, under Mohammed Hilmi Bey, remained territorially unchanged but now subordinate to the Khartoum *hakimdaria*. Various administrative and army officers, previously removed for corruption, were reinstated.

White Nile   Acknowledging that presently the White Nile frontier lay at Kaka, before his departure to the Abyssinia marches Musa had responded positively to the request of two traders appointed honorary *mamurs* – Wad Ibrahim of the Shilluk, and Mohammed Kheir of the Abialang east bank Dinka – that their appointment be strengthened (at British insistence) by a small military detachment on river patrol near Kaka. Musa dispatched a contingent there under Yusuf Hasan el Shallali. When, on the march, Musa on 11 March 1863 acquainted the Viceroy with these dispositions, he sought authority to create a new *muderia* further south at Deinab (Fashoda, modern Kodok) under a *bimbashi* with a garrison of 400 infantry and 100 cavalry. The Viceroy considered that premature and only acceded to the proposal on Musa's visit to Cairo in September 1863, following the strong representations of the British explorers of the White Nile source, Speke and Grant, whom the Viceroy had received that month in Cairo. Four police steamers and six armed sailing boats were then directed to the White Nile.

There is a modicum of confusion as to who was its first governor. Von Heuglin sailed past Deinab on 9 March 1864 but did not stop. Lejean names Muharram Effendi as the first governor early in 1864, while Hill maintains the first was Qa'immaqam Salih Hejazi, previously of Sobat Mouth 1856–7 (?under Deinab), who had been pardoned by Musa after being earlier dismissed for negligence in 1862. However Douin claims that a Qa'immaqam Omer Bey, likewise dismissed from his post as deputy governor of Sennar, was installed as *muhafiz* White Nile to arrest the boats of traders returning from the south after the establishment of the river patrols. He was then transferred to Berber by Ja'afar Pasha Sadiq at the end of 1865 on grounds of ill health, and succeeded as *muhafiz* by Mohammed Hilmi, governor of Kordofan. Already there was a garrison of 1,000 men at Deinab with a detachment at Kaka under Bimbashi Ali Rida el Kurdi, himself to succeed Mohammed Hilmi as governor White Nile at the end of 1866.

Reaching Gondokoro on his return from Albert N'yanza in mid-March 1865, the explorer Samuel Baker learned that at least two of the four steamers based at Khartoum had been established as a patrol of the White Nile, intercepting many slaves and appropriating them for the government. In view of this cruising patrol of the regiment based in the Shilluk country, it was impossible to deliver slaves from Gondokoro to the northern Sudan that season (1864/5); they consequently had to be returned to the inland Equatoria stations. However Baker also heard that, just as Miss Tinné had found near Deinab in March 1864, the White Nile was 'dammed up by a freak of nature', necessitating the crews of thirty boats to spend five weeks cutting a ditch through; and secondly, that the plague was raging at Khartoum and many of the crews 'had died on their passage from Khartoum to Gondokoro of this disease'. It had now broken out at Gondokoro where victims were dying daily. 'Only three boats had arrived from Khartoum' – one *dhahabiyah* (in which Baker descended the river) and two *nuggars* (barges). To resolve this contradiction it would seem probable, despite the patrols and the *werko* tax (see p. 27), that quite a number of boats had set off for Gondokoro in December 1864, but, because of the blockage and the plague, nearly all had returned to Khartoum early in 1865 without their usual cargoes.[18]

Kordofan   On his arrival in Khartoum in August 1862, Musa was well aware that the weak government of Kordofan typified the general plight of the Sudan which encouraged Emperor Theodore's ambitions. The nomad Baqqara remained deeply distrustful of Turkish oppression and tax extortion, their impounded cattle only recoverable at market auction in return for rustled slaves. The most conspicuous affront to the government remained however the rebellious Nuba of the Tegali *jebels*, effectively independent since the successful rising of Mek Nasir in 1845. He had successfully repelled all government attempts to conquer his domain, only to be forcefully deposed himself in 1860 by his nephew Mek Adham. Preoccupied by the Abyssinian threat and du Bisson, Musa was obliged to bide his time before sallying forth from Khartoum in January 1864 with 1,000 infantry and 2,000 cavalry to exact belated revenge on the impudence of the Nuba, and to secure recruits for his expanded army.

By February the deposed Mek Nasir, now confined to four *jebels* (Werne Munzinger two years earlier had described him as 'capricious, cruel, distrustful and ageing'), had surrendered and accepted exile on the White Nile with his supporters. He was then called to Cairo to receive from the Viceroy a ceremonial sword and robe of honour. Musa was not deflected by Mek Adham's willingness to parley over terms of surrender, and on 14 February made a frontal attack on the Tegali leader's force at Jebel Taf. Their bold resistance was adventitiously aided by the onset of torrential early rains lasting three continuous days and Musa, uncharacteristically, was obliged to retire, having sustained 29 dead and lost 579 taken prisoner. He was angered to find the Nuba had many rifles bought from merchants, and petitioned the Viceroy to stop the imports. Nevertheless, on arrival in El Obeid the Governor-General was able from 'conscripts' to bring up to strength his own force as well as the provincial garrison comprising three battalions of the Third Regiment.

While in Kordofan, Musa abolished the Turkish appointment of a *sheikh el masheikh* of the sedentary tribes held originally by Yassin Mohammed Dolabi at Khorsi, and succeeded by the latter's son Mohammed in 1856. The son became *mu'awin* at El Obeid and four *nazirs* were appointed at Khorsi, Bara, Abu Haraz and El Taiara. Two years later the new Kordofan governor, Hasan Hilmi el Juwaisar, had merged the four *nazirates* under Sheikh Abdel Hadi Sabr.

Musa returned to Khartoum on 28 April 1864. Following his departure from El Obeid an event occurred which presaged a grave future problem over the army. A company of irregulars recently sent to El Obeid from Egypt mutinied in protest at arrears of pay and marched back to the Nile at Dongola, sacking villages en route and seizing boats on the Nile until they were intercepted at Abka near the second cataract and overpowered.[19]

Financial Culpability   The reformed provincial structure of the Sudan was perhaps second in importance to the creation within the provinces of tribal districts under the local Sudanese *nazir*, for it was to be these *nazirs* (senior sheikhs), in the riverain areas under the supervision of the reinstated *sheikh al masheikh* Zubeir, son of Sheikh Abdel Qadir appointed nearly forty years earlier by Mahu Bey, who were to be responsible for the collection of taxes. These would be levied no longer on agricultural land as imposed by Arakil Bey on viceregal instruction but, as previously, by way of a poll tax. In that the land tax had removed the incentive of the farmers to maintain, let alone increase, their crop areas, the price of grain in Khartoum had increased by a factor of five within two years, whatever may have been the welcome respite to the nomadic peoples and townsmen of the relief, albeit temporary, from the incidence of poll tax.[20]

In order to secure public endorsement for his intended reforms,

Musa on arrival in the Sudan had at once convened an 'advisory' assembly of notables in the capital. It was to meet in October 1862, after Musa had had time to prepare his intended dispositions. The Chronicler of the *Ta'arikh el Sudan* records that the people rejoiced at Musa's return, 'sure that it meant relief and security… and after its time of trial the *hakimdaria* regained its splendour'. The learned elders were quick to acquiesce in Musa's plan, content with the increased responsibilities delegated to the sheikhs and the shift back to the poll tax. They were initially unable to discern either the extended role of the army in its corrupt collection or the increase in revenue required for the enormously expanded standing army which they were sanctioning. However the truth was dawning upon them when they dispersed, notwithstanding the temporary prosperity from boosted trading activity underpinned by high cotton prices (a cotton ginning factory was erected at Kassala) and by the harvest of the Upper Nile *razzias*.

It is difficult to find reliable figures for incidence of the reinstated poll tax. Du Bisson, who is an unsatisfactory observer, described his voyage from Berber to Khartoum in November 1863, followed by Musa Pasha in his *dhahabiyeh*. All along the Nile's banks people cried for vengeance against the tripling of tax levels. The tribute of the Beni Amer and of the Hadendoa had been raised fourfold, as had been the tax on *saqia* wheels for irrigation. The tax on traders and their employees, however, seems to have been set at 12% of revenue or wages.[21]

As a result of Musa's instructions from the Viceroy to ensure that White Nile commerce should be strictly limited to legitimate trade in ivory, a new tax was devised, the *werko*, under which the employer, foreign or local, should pay 50 piastres or one month's wages (of the anticipated five) in respect of each expedition member. When it was introduced in November 1862, as Musa was leaving for Gallabat, Samuel Baker refused to pay the tax in respect of his expedition about to leave to Gondokoro. A year later, following Musa's visit to the Viceroy in September 1863 and the approval of the enhanced riverain patrols against slave traders on the White Nile, Musa in December doubled the *werko* to 100 piastres for those completing the round trip but trebled it for those disembarked for the year in the Upper Nile trading stations. This action enraged the European community of Khartoum as their boats prepared to leave for the south, the more so when Arab traders were tipped the wink to leave speedily to avoid financial embarrassment. Musa had long been hostile to the European community and to them at least it was clear that his intention was not to stamp

out the slave trade on the White Nile, but to revert to the government
monopoly of the late 1840s – with this difference: Musa – in the name
of the Viceroy – was now claiming that the White Nile constituted
Egyptian territory.[22]

Until Musa Hamdi's rule, detailed and reliable figures for Sudan
revenue and expenditure had been scarce. We have attested estimates
that in the period 1829–38 annual revenues totalled some 28,000
bourses, rising under Ahmed Widan (1838–43) to 40,000 (one bourse
equals £E5) and remaining at that level under his successor. A decade
later, however, a surplus of revenue of 18–20,000 bourses remitted to
Cairo by Abdel Latif Abdullah (1850–2) had by 1854, according to
James Hamilton, been converted into a deficit of 36,000 bourses.
Notwithstanding the economies in expenditure effected by the Viceroy
Mohammed Sa'id (1854–63) through the abolition of the Sudan
hakimdaria and the (hazardous) reduction in the armed forces (16,000
men in 1850 to 4,000 by 1860, as noted by Petherick), such were the
remissions of revenue derived from taxation that it seems there was still
a deficit in 1862 when Musa Hamdi took control. By then revenues had
dropped to £E100,000 (20,000 bourses).[23]

In the budget for Musa's last year of office (1864/5), the only one for
which Douin was able to trace detailed figures, *revenue* was increased
to 46,500 bourses (£E232,500) but this only partially offset the enormous increase in *expenditure* budgeted as follows:

			Bourses	
Civil	Provinces:	Khartoum	2,967.29	
		Kordofan	1,577.36	
		Dongola	1,065.20	
		Taka	867.36	
		White Nile	308.84	
		Berber	1,137.48	
		Hakimdaria	3,538.38	
Total Civil				11,461.91
Military		Regular Army	33,865.43	
		Irregular Forces	39,481.22	
Total Military		73,346.35		
Other			500.00	500.00
Grand Total Expenditure (bourses)				85,308.00 (£E426,540)

Thus Musa was budgeting for a deficit of 38,807 bourses (£E194,035), with armed forces costs (73,346 bourses) 86% of total expenditure.

His resort to payment in kind of a major part of the entitlements of the troops was unsurprising, but arrears of pay nevertheless began to mount, with corresponding discontent in the ranks. Equally the growing need for the tax collectors to accept tribute in kind, principally in *dura* (corn) or *damuria* (cloth), encouraged a further malpractice in the discounting of the value of such payments by as much as 75 per cent, another deterrent to trade. Both of Musa Hamdi's visits to the Viceroy – in September 1863 and in November 1864 – involved discussion of the revenue problems of the Sudan. At the 1863 meeting he had received authority to double the incidence of the *werko* tax in addition to funding of 80,000 dollars to purchase cattle for Egypt presently afflicted with cattle disease (Petherick says Musa confiscated Baqqara herds in lieu).

At the end of April 1864, on his return from Kordofan, Musa seems quickly to have aborted a proposed visit to the White Nile and its tributaries to which he had invited Theodor von Heuglin, perhaps in order to deal in Khartoum with the continued opposition of the foreign traders (especially John Petherick), and to take stock of the growing cash deficit. In any case the White Nile rains would already be beginning, though this year they were poor. When Musa eventually reached Cairo in November, it was to seek from the Viceroy no fewer than 30,000 bourses (£E150,000) to pay the mounting arrears of the troops. His application was granted, but the actual availability of the money for distribution to the troops was less swift. A year later, in November 1865, the Sudan's *accumulated* indebtedness to Egypt, despite further subsidies, had grown to 163,000 bourses – £E815,000.

F. B. Garnier, on behalf of the French consul-general in Egypt, M. Tastu, undertook a tour of the northern Sudan from November 1864 to October 1865. In his letter of 5 May 1865 on his return to Khartoum, he castigated the now deceased Governor-General (who had been absent when Garnier first reached Khartoum in November 1864) in these terms:

> Musa Pasha was operating in a vicious circle which, to the extent he expanded it, was enveloping the Sudan in ever growing wretchedness and had ended by ruining it completely. His method seems to have consisted in expanding the Sudan army excessively in order to secure the revenue collection and thereby to augment

indefinitely the revenues to pay his army. This deplorable practice had already produced its consequences in the form of arrears of pay for the army in Khartoum of 8 months, elsewhere of 12 or 15 months; a general impoverishment of the local community and its dispersal; a slowing down of trade; and distant expeditions more costly than productive – and no less damaging to the localities whither they were directed and to those they crossed en route than to the people involved and to those targeted.

Had Musa Hamdi Pasha still been alive, the dragoman would not have so savaged his accomplishments. Admittedly the budget deficit triggered by the enlarged forces was enormous, but there was yet no counterpressure from the Viceroy. Moreover the scale of the subsequent revolt in the summer of 1865 would have been unthinkable under such a ruthless commander-in-chief. His successor Ja'afar Sadiq may have described him as a drunkard, a gambler and a thief, but his reputation for atrocities among the Bisharin, the Selim Baqqara – and indeed the troops of Upper Egypt when he was governor of Keneh (he had allegedly murdered 300 *maghreb* mutineers whom he had promised to pardon) – was intimidatory in the extreme. His record towards slave traffickers and the trade remained bad: von Heuglin was not the only witness of caravans of Black girls belonging to Musa being escorted to Egypt, in this case by the Coptic brother of the United States vice-consul in Khartoum. He administered the quietus to the European slavers but winked at the Turks and Arabs. Improvement of river communications probably owed more to the Viceroy than the *hakimdar*, while agriculture and trade were stunted by penal levels of taxation. Yet at a time of considerable danger to Turkish government in the Sudan, Musa Hamdi had nevertheless successfully deterred the Abyssinian predator and consolidated central control by radical reform of the senior echelons of government and by reinforcing and retraining the armed forces.[24]

Musa Hamdi's death was both sudden and unexpected. He must have been in his early fifties, having fought in Syria and having served, allowing for the nine years' interval between 1853 and 1862, some fifteen years in the Sudan in posts of heavy responsibility. His return from a visit to the Viceroy in Cairo to Khartoum at the end of 1864 coincided with famine caused by the failure of the rains. Within a few weeks he seems to have fallen victim to either, as Garnier, reported, dysentry or to an epidemic of typhus, introduced to Khartoum by a consignment of slaves intercepted by the White Nile patrol and escorted to the capital. Baker, returning from Lake Albert N'yanza on 28 April 1865 (according to his letter to Colquhoun but at sunset on 5 May according to his book *Albert N'yanza*, which is the date, too, of Garnier's report on his return to Khartoum) wrote this description of the epidemic:

> A drought of two years had created a famine throughout the land, attended by a cattle and camel plague that had destroyed so many camels that all commerce was stagnated. No merchandise could be transported from Khartoum; thus no purchases could be made by the traders in the interior; the country always wretched was ruined.
>
> The plague, or a malignant typhus, had run riot in Khartoum; out of 4000 Black troops, only a remnant above 400 remained alive!... [Garnier, however, reported that 2,500 succumbed in an epidemic 'd'un caractère typhoide'].
>
> Two [slave] vessels had been seized and brought to Khartoum containing 850 human beings! [probably the boats of Khalil el Shami, now an Austrian protected person] – packed like anchovies, the living and the dying festering together, and the dead lying beneath them. European eye-witnesses assured me that the disembarking of this frightful cargo could not be adequately described. The slaves were in a state of starvation, having had nothing to eat for several days. They were landed in Khartoum; the dead and many of the dying were tied by the ankles, and dragged along the ground by donkeys through the streets. The most malignant typhus, or plague, had been engendered among this mass of filth and misery, thus closely packed together. Upon landing, the women were divided by the Egyptian authorities among the soldiers. These creatures brought the plague to Khartoum which, like a curse visited upon this country of slavery and abomination, spread like a fire throughout the town, and consumed the regiments that had received this horrible legacy from the dying cargo of slaves.

It may well be that Musa Hamdi's letter, probably sent in early January 1865, advising the Viceroy of the earlier mutiny in October 1864 of a detachment at Kassala, was his last communication to Cairo. Garnier in May 1865 wrote that Musa had 'died of dysentry' a little after his return from Cairo. However, the appointment of his intended successor general-governors was not made until 4 June 1865, suggesting that news of his death was dispatched only towards the end of April, the time of Garnier's return to Khartoum, and that therefore he had been stricken with the disease some months before his demise, weakening the central command of government. He was buried in a domed tomb at Khartoum alongside the body of his guardian and mentor, Ahmed Pasha Widan.

These last years had not gentled his condition:

> For I am long since weary of your storm
> Of carnage, and find, Hermod, in your life
> Something too much of war and broils, which make
> Life one perpetual fight, a bath of blood.
> Matthew Arnold: 'Balder Dead'[25]

3 THE KASSALA REVOLT 1865

On his return from showing the flag on the Abyssinian marches, Musa Pasha had spent the month March-April 1863 in Kassala. The garrison consisted of the Fourth Regiment, largely composed of Nuba other ranks who had been transferred to Kassala from El Obeid five years previously. To these four battalions of regular infantry, each of 600 men, Musa added a fifth from his own force, making a total of 3,000 infantry, 300 *bashi-buzouq* irregulars, 300 Sha'iqi horsemen and 4 guns. While the Nuba preferred the El Obeid station and its proximity to their own rebellious territory, there were precedents in Fung times for garrisoning the Blue Nile capital, Sennar, with Nuba troops. James Bruce had recorded this on his visit ninety years earlier.

Sir Duncan Cumming, in his history of Kassala where he served as district commissioner, underlined inherent dangers:

The recruits brought with them tribal allegiances more binding than those that grew from the indifferent discipline they found in the army... If a soldier had a grievance and dared to express it, he could often count on a support from his comrades which had behind it traditions of extreme self-sacrifice derived from generations of fighting for the survival of the tribe...

A few Sudanese officers of long service and outstanding personality commanded their respect but familiarity with their foreign officers bred a truculence which was restrained only by fear of punishment and the esprit de corps inspired in the primitive mind by military service...

In view of the mutinies that had occurred in the past, the organisation of the Sudanese regiments was also dangerous. Egyptian officers commanded regiments of three battalions but the admixture of Egyptians and Sudanese was carried through all the commissioned and non-commissioned ranks... Complaints of favouritism and dissatisfaction at the choice of men promoted to commissioned ranks were frequent.

The governor of Taka province was Ibrahim Bey Adham el Mahallawi, who had succeeded Elias Bey el Kiridli on the latter's death in 1862. It was he, with Ali Bey Fadli, who had received du Bisson and his party at Kassala in February 1864 and, with the deputy governor, Sulieman Effendi, had put pressure on du Bisson to withdraw from Kufit. Pay was already months in arrears, the Turkish officers taking care to see that they were the last to suffer on this account, and by October 1864 a chronic shortage of grain, compounded by a previous bad harvest, prompted an expedition to be ordered to the Barea country to requisition fresh supplies. The proximity of Ramadan, and the total refusal of a modest request by the newly converted Black Moslem troops for some payment towards the Bairam festival celebration for their families before their departure, triggered a mutiny led by two Sudanese officers who pursued the expedition's advance party of *bashibuzouqs* to Sabderat, killing some, wounding their commander, and capturing their ammunition.

Living in Kassala was a Sudanese religious leader of exceptional standing, Sayyid El Hasan Mohammed Osman el Mirghani, leader of the Khatmi *tariqa*. It may well have been his father, Sayyid Mohammed, who intervened on behalf of Ahmed Pasha Abu Widan as a conciliator with the Hadendoa in April 1840. Sayyid El Hasan, armed with 4,000 dollars to propitiate the mutineers, together with the governor's promise of no adverse report, most successfully negotiated the suppression of the mutiny and the fulfilment of the Barea mission. Contrary to his promise, however, Ibrahim Bey promptly reported the mutiny to the Governor-General on the latter's return to Khartoum from Cairo at New Year 1865. Musa Hamdi in turn reported it to Cairo and himself dispatched Lewa Hasan Ali Pasha Arnaout, commander of infantry, to Kassala to investigate and report.

On 8 February 1865 Khedive Ismail Pasha in Cairo ordered immediate punitive action against the mutineers for an odious crime, 'pour encourager les autres': the ringleaders, officers and men alike, to be shot, likewise one in twenty of the rest – a case of ruthlessness begotten by distance. 400 irregular *bashi-buzouq* cavalry and two guns were to be sent from Egypt as reinforcements. When the order reached Khartoum in early March, Musa Pasha was stricken or dead, leaving his deputy, Omer Bey Fakhri, successor to Ali Bey Fadli, unequal to the crisis. With a typhus epidemic raging among his Khartoum troops, he could only find a largely Dinka battalion for dispatch to Kassala (it would have been after its departure that Baker in early May was to report only 400 surviving Black troops). These men would be sympathetic to the unpunished mutineers of the Fourth Regiment still in arrears with pay. Indeed it is likely that many of the Dinka troops at Kassala and Khartoum had been conscripted by force in the *razzias* against the Dinka in 1862, including those betrayed by the Abu Ruf, who had granted them grazing and cultivation rights. The viceregal order for punitive action against the mutineers returning from Sabderat, if received, was not implemented. They were posted to Beja strong-points.[26]

Gratuitously, the crisis in Kassala was at this moment compounded by an event as remote as the French war in Mexico. The French expeditionary force, within a month of disembarkation at Vera Cruz in March 1862, had suffered ten per cent casualties from yellow fever. Europeans proved unfit for the climate and the French government, finding itself dependent on African and West Indian troops, approached the Viceroy, Mohammed Sa'id, for help in December 1862. Embroiled in discussion over the Suez Canal and anxious to please, in January 1863 the Viceroy embarked a contingent of 447 for Mexico, of whom 386 were officers and other ranks and the balance press-ganged from the streets of Alexandria. They were to acquit themselves with great valour in the Mexican campaign, sustaining a total of 48 killed in battle and 64 dead from disease. Marshal Forey, the commander-in-chief, remarked: 'Ce n'étaient pas des soldats: c'étaient des lions.'

At the end of two years' service by this contingent in a demanding theatre, the new Viceroy, Ismail Pasha, responded positively to French requests in December 1864 for reinforcements (or replacements) by ordering the dispatch of a further battalion of 1,000 Black troops in March 1865.

The following day, 6 March, Omer Bey Fakhri was sent instructions to send such a force to Egypt at once, to be under the command of Miralai Adham Bey el Arifi, a senior Sudanese officer currently stationed on the Blue Nile (whom the late Dr Richard Hill and Peter Hogg, former director of local government, affirm belonged to the 'Arifia section of the Dar Hamid and was not a Nuba). The acting Governor-General, also denuded of troops after having dispatched a battalion already to Kassala, reasonably passed on the viceregal order to Lewa Hasan Pasha, commander of infantry, presently in Kassala. Hasan dispatched a detachment of 500 ex-mutineers to Mektinab in Hadendoa country where the commander of the Fourth Regiment, Miralai Ali Bey Abu Widan, was inspecting other ex-mutineers. Hasan Pasha had concealed from them that their destination was to be Suakin and Mexico, but at Mektinab the two disgruntled forces again mutinied, having guessed the intent. They seized the ammunition and specie, put to flight the commander (presumably now also intended for Mexico) and 150 loyal soldiers, who took refuge with the *nazir* of the Hadendoa, and themselves marched back to Kassala.

It was now 5 July. Lewa Hasan, forewarned of their return, disarmed the remaining Black troops at Kassala. He fortified the government headquarters, the magazine and the residence of du Bisson's remaining force against a siege, and sent off a request for reinforcements from Khartoum. However his order that resistance was not to be offered to the returning mutineers was ignored and fighting broke out. Sixteen officers were killed in the subsequent hostilities. With their comrades set free from prison, a final attack on the government redoubt by the mutineers was only checked by the dramatic intervention of the *khalifa* (delegate) sent by Sayyid El Hasan El Mirghani, just returned from Sabderat, promising pardon and commanding them to lay down their arms. The next day, after the personal intervention of the *sayyid*, the *lewa* and the *mudir* Ibrahim walked to the mutineers' barracks and granted the pardon.[27]

The position was now one of stalemate. The outnumbered government forces had a fortified position and supplies. The mutineers had their arms but due to the stubborn refusal of a commander of the *bashi-buzouqs* guarding the magazine, Sa'id Agha Abu Felga, to give them ammunition, only limited weapon strength and supplies. Outside the town the Dinka, led by one of their chiefs, a fellow captive, were free to pillage townsmen's villages, destroying the inhabitants. The Beja, notably the Hadendoa, were now against the mutineers, massacring those who sought to escape from Kassala. Werner Munzinger, the Swiss-born French consul at Massawa at the time, conjectured why the Beja did not themselves make common cause with the mutineers and slaughter the oppressive Turk. He concluded that notwithstanding their hatred of the regime, their chiefs had a vested interest in it. The Turks protected their enjoyment of the authority and wealth it gave them.Their ideal was for the regime to be weakened rather than broken. Munzinger's admiration was reserved for Sayyid El Hasan El Mirghani, the Sudanese religious leader:

> It is difficult to give an idea of his real power. A word from him would suffice to incite all these discordant elements against the Turks; the Arabs know him alone. The Turks who sought his help in their hour of danger almost fear him because they know he has small liking for them. They are wrong, for Sayyid El Hasan is too intelligent to change the moral and constant power that he now enjoys for the temporal but ephemeral power that was his for the taking. He was the only person who could have made himself master of the situation in those days when everyone had lost his head.

Meanwhile the Egyptian 32-gun frigate *Ibrahimiyya* had arrived at Suakin to embark the relief contingent for Mexico in early July but had left at once on account of a cholera outbreak. Cairo remained ignorant of the Kassala hostilities until 20 August. Despite Ismail's determined efforts notwithstanding to dispatch a relief battalion to Mexico as late as November 1865, it was the French who rescinded their request and ultimately withdrew from Mexico.[28]

Lewa Hasan Ali Arnaout, blessed with the *sayyid*'s uneasy truce, lost no time in summoning help from the nearest military post of Ali Kashef at Gedaref and a major relief force from Khartoum. Seemingly due to contradictory orders from Kassala and Khartoum, Ali Kashef only reached Kassala with 200 cavalry on 27 July. Meanwhile Omer Bey Fakhri in Khartoum took counsel with Abdallah Pasha el Wanli, former governor of Berber and now commander of Sudan irregulars, and decided to mobilise two main columns. The first comprised mounted *bashi-buzouqs* from Berber and Shendi under the Circassian Ismail Bey Ayub. It approached via Abu Deleiq and Qoz Regeb, to be joined en route by Abdallah Pasha from Khartoum. The second column, under Adham Bey, comprised 200 infantry from Khartoum, 200 from Wad Medani, and 343 from the Third Regiment in El Obeid, whither Adham Bey went to muster them. Lewa Hasan at Kassala was anxious that Adham Bey, popular with the Dinka mutineers, should succeed Ali Abu Widan in command of the Fourth Regiment. Despite the greater distance Adham Bey, guided by Sheikh Ahmed Abu Sin, reached Kassala first on 30 August, eight weeks after the battle and ten days after news of it reached Cairo. Since the arrival of Ali Kashef hostilities had been renewed and Sayyid El Hasan the conciliator withdrawn. Nevertheless Adham Bey, through sheer force of personality, was able to negotiate a surrender by the mutineers while instructions were sought from the Viceroy as to punishment. The arrival of the Albanian *bashi-buzouq* column, delayed by rain, a week later and an instruction to imprison the mutineers within the town walls led to a massacre of 600 of the latter, regarding which Adham Bey registered a complaint against Abdallah Pasha. Of the Fourth Regiment's 2,396 mutineers, in all 1,637 were killed and 759 arrested. Government casualties were 31 killed and 83 wounded. By 10 September 1865 the rebels were crushed.[29]

The Governor-General had by then been dead for up to seven months. The successor regime in the Sudan had not been promulgated in Cairo until 4 June, admittedly in ignorance of the further mutiny about to unfold in Taka, but in the certainty that the ports of Suakin and Massawa had now for a second time been transferred by the Sultan, in return for their revenues, into the occupation of the Viceroy – a necessary prerequisite to the ultimate development of his *drang nach Osten*. Perhaps it was on this account that, believing the future rule of the Sudan would be beyond the capacity of a single *hakimdar*, Ismail attempted to revert back to the concept of general-governorates. There were to be three: Taka, Suakin and Massawa - under Ja'afar Pasha Sadiq, president of the Cairo judicial review council; Khartoum with the Blue Nile and eastern White Nile territories under Selim Pasha Sa'ib el Jaza'irli, briefly *hakimdar* 1853–4; and Kordofan, Dongola, Berber and the unoccupied territories west of the White Nile under Ja'afar Pasha Mazhar, governor of Qena in Upper Egypt. Special attention was to be given to customs enforcement on external frontiers, while defence dispositions were to be deferred to a meeting of all generals-governor with troop commanders at Berber after a month's preliminary residence. The immediate withdrawal of Selim Pasha, true to form on medical grounds, and differences between the two Ja'afars led to the whole plan being scrapped within a fortnight and to the appointment of the Circassian Ja'afar Pasha Sadiq as Governor-General with Ja'afar Mazhar as his deputy. Omer Fakhri, the acting Governor-General, would be pensioned off. However Suakin and Massawa would be placed under subordinate governors (*muhafizin*) – Ahmed Mumtaz Bey and Hasan Rifaat Bey respectively. Ja'afar Mazhar would finalise the arrangements for transfer of the ports in person with the *wali* of Jedda en route to the Sudan.

When news of the Kassala rising reached Cairo on 20 August, notwithstanding his appointment as *hakimdar* in mid-June it found Ja'afar Pasha Sadiq still in Egypt. The Sudan had already, effectively at least, been without a Governor-General for six months, yet Ja'afar Sadiq was not to leave for three months after his appointment. The lack of urgency is bewildering. Was he simply waiting for the cooler weather? Certainly at the age of sixty he was handicapped for Sudan extremes of climate. There is another possible explanation which is not offered by Douin. On 19 June 1865, the day of Ja'afar Sadiq's amended appointment as *hakimdar*, the Viceroy precipitately left Alexandria for Constantinople to the embarrassment of his ministers. He was fleeing a cholera epidemic which by the end of the month was inflicting 200 deaths daily in Alexandria, and he did not return until 3 August. In the wake of riots in Alexandria at the end of May, Colquhoun had observed: 'One of Ismail's failings is extreme timidity closely approaching to personal cowardice.' With this example, Ja'afar Sadiq's extended progress becomes perhaps more explicable. His more vigorous and energetic deputy, Ja'afar Mazhar, had by contrast left for the Red Sea by mid-August.

Faced with news of the Kassala latest emergency, but not yet its outcome, the Viceroy the day after his return ordered Ja'afar Sadiq to Kassala direct, together with one Egyptian battalion to be transported from Suez to Suakin; and a further two battalions to be recalled from the Hedjaz where they had been sent to support the Turkish authorities in the suppression of troubles in the Yemen. Once again, however, orders had to be revised in the light of further grimmer news from Kassala at the end of August. Two new regiments, each of three battalions only, were to be sent to the Sudan, one of the regiments now to accompany Ja'afar Sadiq to Khartoum. Still further delays attended its departure because of a shortage of camel transport at Korosko for the passage of the Atmur desert, and it was mid-October when Ja'afar Sadiq left Korosko with four companies only. Having crossed the Atmur he learned of the suppression of the mutiny and, after inspecting the Berber *muderia*, reached Khartoum on 11 November. The remainder of the regiment arrived at the end of that month.

The Second Regiment was sent to Suez in the wake of Ja'afar Mazhar, whose orders to visit Jedda were postponed so that he could now command the regiment personally in the relief of Kassala. Samuel Baker, reaching Suakin from Berber on his return from Albert N'yanza (he was narrowly to miss at Suez David Livingstone en route to his last

African journey), was already there with Ahmed Mumtaz Bey, the governor, to receive Ja'afar Pasha as he arrived on 28 August on the frigate *Ibrahimiyya* with the first contingent of the regiment to be ferried. Ja'afar Pasha Mazhar, like his earlier predecessor as Governor-General, Abdel Latif Pasha, had been a naval officer, 1830–47.

By the time Ja'afar reached Kassala on 12 November 1865 the mutiny had been suppressed for over two months. The conditions were, as Ja'afar reported, dreadful: 'An hour from the town all the soldiers there came out to meet us. All or nearly all of them had fever and an odour of putrefaction arose from the town. At length we proceeded to Kassala and I had the tents pitched at a decent and healthy distance.'

Among those who died from the subsequent outbreak of cholera were Abdallah Pasha el Wanli, Hasan Pasha Arnaout and 150 soldiers. The fate of the governor, Ibrahim el Mahallawi, is less certain. Douin says he died of the disease; Cumming, with the benefit of Kassala service, quotes local tradition that Ibrahim took poison; while Hill quotes a descendant attesting that he survived until the Mahdist siege of Kassala in 1885 – dying of natural causes.[30]

It fell to Ja'afar Pasha Mazhar to conduct court martials of the surviving mutineers and an investigation into the origin of the mutiny. 240 officers, NCOs and other ranks were shot; 531 were condemned to hard labour for life; and the balance, a similar number, set free. A year later, as Governor-General, Ja'afar sought some mitigation of sentences but Ismail Pasha was obdurate. Miralai Adham Bey's protest at the failure of Abdallah Pasha to respect the terms of the surrender he had negotiated with the mutineers was recorded without further comment. Adham Bey was commended for his resolute action by the Viceroy and Sayyid El Hasan El Mirghani's remarkable contribution recognised by a pension.

Ja'afar Mazhar's report was drawn up against a sombre backcloth. Hormuzd Rassam on his way to Abyssinia as an emissary of the British government on 6 November observed:

> We found the town in a most wretched and desolate plight, owing to the late mutiny and a fatal epidemic combined, which had decimated the population. Hundreds of families had fled the place, first to escape the mutineers, and then the Albanians... This town which a few months ago was in a most flourishing condition, is now little better than a heap of ruins... Of the regiments that had mutinied about 800 men had escaped with their lives. These had

been imprisoned with their wives and children; but so badly cared for were they that numbers died during our sojourn in Kassala, and their corpses instead of being decently interred, were cast into ditches outside the town to be devoured by hyenas...

Besides the carnage and anarchy consequent upon the mutiny, cholera and a most fatal fever had carried off their victims by hundreds from July to October. Even while we were there, a tenth of the garrison was laid up with one disease or another.

Once his duty in Kassala was completed, Ja'afar Mazhar was expecting to travel to Jedda to finalise the transfer to Egypt of the Red Sea ports. By November, however, not only was the new Governor-General Ja'afar Pasha Sadiq at Khartoum but the French dragoman Garnier and his travelling companion – under orders of the Viceroy – Miralai Mustapha Bey Sarraj had now returned from their eleven-month reconnaissance of the Sudan. Their report to the Viceroy with its criticisms of the previous *hakimdaria* prompted a further change of viceregal plan. Ja'afar Mazhar's trip to Jedda was cancelled and he was bidden to remain in Taka with the new governor from Massawa, Hasan Bey Rifaat, to exercise a firm hand in ending the perpetual strife among the Beja tribes hitherto indolently ignored by the Kassala *muderia*; and to establish improved intelligence communications in the region.

The Viceroy's concerns did not stop there. He became convinced, not least in the wake of a further attempted mutiny by Dinka troops stationed in Sennar as Ja'afar Sadiq reached Khartoum, that a major overhaul and recasting of the machine of government was essential. On 18 February Ja'afar Mazhar, leaving Ibrahim Bey Lutfi as acting governor (he died soon afterwards, to be succeeded briefly by Hasan Hilmi el Juwaisar, then Hasan Bey Rifaat), left Kassala for Khartoum. When he arrived on 4 March 1866 it was to find that two months earlier the Viceroy had decreed that he should replace Ja'afar Sadiq as Governor-General.[31]

2

Ja'afar Pasha Mazhar:
Brief Years of Promise 1866–69

I A MUDDLED SUCCESSION 1865–66

The military government of the Sudan was the creature of the Viceroy of Egypt from whom emanated all policy directives. Mohammed Ali, his stepson Ibrahim and his grandson Abbas – the first three Viceroys following the Turkish conquest of the Sudan – all had battle experience and the capacity to handle military governors even if, as Mohammed Sabry claimed, the blemished character of Abbas was unrelieved by any single great quality. Mohammed Sa'id, successor to Abbas and the first viceregal recipient of some Western-style education from French tutors, evinced a degree of liberal enlightenment; but an innate timidity, to a lesser extent shared by his successor Ismail who benefited from a far more rounded education in Europe, flawed the capability of each to exercise sound judgement in public appointments and a firm control of reactionary agents.

The important appointment of Musa Hamdi as *hakimdar* of the Sudan in June 1862 and the recentralisation of its government in the face of the Abyssinian threat owed more to Ismail than Mohammed Sa'id. Although content to render appropriate deference to his Viceroy and no harbourer of the dangerous ambitions which had wrought the downfall of his patron and mentor, Ahmed Pasha Widan, Musa Pasha nevertheless, beyond respecting his instructions not to trespass on Abyssinian soil, would interpret his orders to allow himself maximum flexibility. Only after his death did the Viceroy realise how defective had been the supervision of Musa's work.

The confusion over the appointment of Musa's successor in June 1865, the ambivalence as to whether or not to divide the Sudan yet again into general-governorates, betrayed Ismail's indecisiveness. Ja'afar Pasha Sadiq, who finally emerged as Governor-General in June, had left the army in 1849 as a *miralai* in the cavalry to join the Egyptian provincial administration, quitting his post as commissioner of Suez four years later to command an Egyptian brigade of field artillery for the duration of the Crimean War. By 1865, at the age of sixty, he had been president of the Upper Egypt court of appeal and was now effectively too old to restore order and leadership to a demoralised and mutinous army in a country racked by disease and famine.[1]

For all that, in mid-August 1865 following his return from Europe and as yet unaware of the outcome of the further mutiny at Kassala, Ismail Pasha had formally conferred on Ja'afar Sadiq sole authority over the appointment and dismissal of governors and officials in the Sudan, although it was not until 11 November, with only a half battalion of advance reinforcements, that Ja'afar Sadiq reached Khartoum. His limitations may already have occurred to Ismail, who nevertheless ignored the suggestion of his own disaffected uncle, Abdel Halim Pasha, that he would be the man to reorganise the government of the Sudan (he had previously served a brief and inglorious tenure as Governor-General in 1856). Ismail had already in October appointed Shahin Pasha Kinj, an experienced *fariq* recently returned from active service in Crete, to undertake a special mission to Khartoum to work with Ja'afar Sadiq. Shahin Kinj seems to have already served as deputy to Ali Jarkas Pasha the *hakimdar* when *mudir* of Khartoum in 1855–6.

Ja'afar Sadiq acted promptly on his arrival both to relieve the grain shortage in Khartoum and Berber occasioned by a plague of locusts, and to make a number of new dispositions of personnel. The Viceroy had voiced his particular concern about security on the White Nile where the climate at Deinab now necessitated the transfer of the *muhafiz*, Omer Bey, to Berber on grounds of ill health. He was replaced at Deinab by Mohammed Hilmi Bey from Kordofan, who was in turn succeeded, some months later, in El Obeid by Ibrahim Lutfi Bey from Taka. Mohammed Hilmi Bey was encouraged to shift his personal headquarters from Deinab to Lul some twenty miles further south and adjacent to the Reth of the Shilluk's tribal capital of Fashoda. The luckless Omer Bey Fakhri, acting Governor-General during the Kassala revolt following Musa Hamdi's death, was transferred after public censure to Kordofan as deputy governor where he shortly died. Abdel Raziq Haqqi Bey became governor of Taka.

Ja'afar Sadiq seems also to have planned the detachment of Sennar with Fazughli from Khartoum to form a separate province. However by 9 January 1866 the new Governor-General, barely two months in his post and even before Shahin Pasha Kinj had left Korosko, had been deemed inadequate by the Viceroy. Instructions were issued that day that Ja'afar Pasha Mazhar, Deputy Governor-General, should succeed him and proceed at once from Kassala to Khartoum. Within four months of his arrival in the capital, Ja'afar Sadiq was on his way back to Egypt, to take up another judicial appointment.[2]

2 PAYING FOR THE MILITARY

As on Musa Hamdi's arrival three years previously – and indeed off and on over the previous forty years since the Turkish conquest – the essential problem remained to match military security needs with available local revenue resources. This was a vast ill-endowed country with an economy of bare subsistence. *Dura* (sorghum) cultivation provided the staple food for a necessarily limited population, reduced at regular intervals by famine and drought, and there were as yet no cash crops other than gum arabic and some Mahu cotton (for Abyssinia), nor mineral wealth to augment it. Having no prospects of easily enhanced prosperity, even an oppressive government could exact only relatively meagre levels of poll tax and duties as a contribution to the costs of security and administration.

The complement of the occupying armed forces had fluctuated. The Turkish infantry which conquered the Sudan had been relieved in 1824, on the accession as *hakimdar* and *seraskir* (commander-in-chief) of Osman Bey Jarkas el Birinji, by the First Regiment of Mohammed Ali's *nizam el jedid* comprising five battalions each of 800 men. Three battalions had been allocated to Khartoum and the Blue Nile and two to Kordofan. When the successor to Osman Bey Jarkas, Ali Khurshid, faced attack from Abyssinia in 1837–8 he obtained reinforcements from Egypt, in the event to be used for the subsequent suppression of Taka by Ahmed Pasha Widan. These generated in total an army, including cavalry and artillery (but always subject to attrition by disease), numbering on paper some 15,000 men.

So, approximately, it remained for fifteen years but by March 1855 Petherick was writing that, with the recall of 2,200 infantry to Egypt and the disbandment of the *bashi-buzouqs*, the number of effective troops would be reduced to 4,000 spread across the provinces. However, when the Viceroy, Mohammed Sa'id, visited the Sudan in 1857 it was decided both that the provinces should be brought severally under the direct administrative control of Egypt and that the army should be retained under central command in Khartoum. On the death of *seraskir* Osman Pasha Jarkas, commander of the centralised forces, the troops were again posted to the provincial governorates.

That decision had been again amended in 1862. The renewed threat of Abyssinian invasion caused an additional four battalions to be sanctioned for Khartoum, part Egyptian, part Sudanese, enabling Musa Pasha Hamdi, Governor-General of the reunified Sudan, to muster a force of 4,500 regular troops for his expedition to the Abyssinian marches that winter. By June 1863 a standing army of four regular infantry regiments, each of four battalions comprising 600 men, had been authorised, plus cavalry (*bashi-buzouqs* and Sha'iqiya), plus artillery, giving an increased total of under 12,000.

The cost of this army for the Islamic year commencing June 1864, the year preceding Ja'afar Mazhar's arrival, was budgeted at £E366,730 (73,350 bourses), the greater part being that of the cavalry, while total revenue amounted to £E232,500 (46,500 bourses), against which a further £E57,300 (11,460 bourses) of civil expenditure had to be set (see p. 28). Ignoring currency value fluctuation, Sudan revenue back in 1837 had been £E140,000; in 1842 £E200,000 and in 1850 sufficient, Abdel Latif Pasha had boasted, once again to provide a surplus over all Sudan government expenditure of nearly £E100,000, for remission to Cairo. However the economies effected by Mohammed Sa'id Pasha, coupled with the order to desist from military enforcement of tax collection, had by 1862 diminished revenues to £E100,000. A substantial increase in taxation was needed, therefore, if a major contribution to the cost of the expanded army was to be made. Yet despite having more than doubled taxation to £E232,000, Musa Hamdi had, allowing for civil expenditure of £E57,000, still budgeted for a deficit for 1864/5 equivalent to over 50% of total army expenditure. Granted the continuing absence of substantial cash subsidies from Cairo, it is unsurprising that extended arrears of pay had provoked mutinies.

Notwithstanding the cash injection which Musa did indeed obtain from Cairo in November 1864, six months' arrears of army and officials' pay had again accumulated by the time of Ja'afar Sadiq's appointment as Musa's successor. £E100,000 (20,000 bourses) was urgently despatched to the Sudan in July 1865, followed by a further £E30,000 over the next three months. £E55,000 of this £E130,000 was earmarked for the Taka garrisons and officials and the balance for the remainder in the Sudan. That still left outstanding arrears of £E75,000 which the Governor-General requested of Cairo in December 1865.

Total accumulated Sudan debt to Egypt was estimated now at £E815,000.[3]

The Kassala mutiny may eventually have been crushed with exemplary ferocity but Ja'afar Sadiq's arrival in Khartoum in November 1865 had been met with the news of another attempted mutiny in Sennar; while Shahin Pasha Kinj, dispatched by the Viceroy to Khartoum in Ja'afar Sadiq's wake, had scarcely left Berber in early February 1866 when eighty mutineers endeavoured to fire the local ammunition dump. A fundamental reappraisal of garrison strengths and deployment, together with the acceptance of the necessity for Egyptian subsidies, had become mandatory and urgent.

News of the Kassala mutiny had already caused the Viceroy to lose all confidence in the Black First, Second and Third Regiments in the Sudan (the rebellious Fourth Regiment was longer extant). These were now in 1866 to be disbanded, with the exception of one battalion, the men being paid half their dues locally in the Sudan and directed to report to Egyptian barracks to receive the balance. Henceforth, it was agreed, the Sudan regular army would comprise the Ninth and Tenth Regiments, each of four Egyptian infantry battalions, which had been dispatched to deal with the situation on the morrow of the Kassala revolt –two mobile camel-borne battalions each of eight companies; and two batteries of artillery. These troops would be deployed half in Kassala, Suakin and Massawa and half in Khartoum and Kordofan. The one remaining Black battalion would be stationed without artillery in the new White Nile province at Deinab and at Khartoum, all the men to have unblemished records and all Dinka to be excluded. The remaining garrisons, at Sennar and Berber, would for the most part be drawn from the irregular corps, three-quarters of whom were Sha'iqi and *bashi-buzouq* cavalry.

Accordingly the regular army in the Sudan (for the while) would be reduced to a complement of some 7,000. Of Musa Pasha's earlier 10,000 regular Sudanese troops, 4,000 were dispatched for service in Egypt and 2,000 either to the White Nile or to fill the vacant ranks in other province garrisons. The remainder were dispersed through retirement, re-employment in civil roles, or dishonourable discharge. As to the Sudanese irregular corps, they were to be slimmed from 7,000 to something in excess of 4,000.[4]

Ismail Pasha, in his instructions to Ja'afar Pasha Sadiq of August 1865, had already accepted that if the Sudan debt to Egypt were to be contained, the pay of Egyptian regular troops would have to be assumed by Cairo. Following Ja'afar Mazhar's investiture by Shahin Pasha as Governor-General on 4 March 1866, the Sudan military expenditure (Sudanese troops including Sha'iqiya, *bashi-buzouqs* and artillery) shrank dramatically. The Ja'afar Mazhar budget outlined by Douin showed a fall in annual military costs from £E367,000 three years previously to £E86,000. From the names of the governors and the inclusion of a Sudan Council – stemming from Ismail's creation in October 1866 of the Egyptian Assembly of Deputies – it would seem more likely to be for the Moslem year of the *Hijra* 1284 (commencing May 1867) than 1283.

As to revenue, Ismail had already admonished Ja'afar Sadiq to mitigate the additional tax burdens inflicted on the people by Musa Hamdi: to remove them where appropriate if within his authority; and to suspend them pending approval from Cairo if not. The overall financial policy seemed pregnant with the prospects of modest economic recovery. Would it be realised?[5]

3   CIVIL ADMINISTRATION 1866–67

The date of Ja'afar Mazhar's birth is not known but Richard Hill attributes his service as a naval officer to 1830–47, making it probable that he was born 1810/12 and accordingly about fifty-five, some five years younger than Ja'afar Sadiq, on his appointment as Governor-General. Dr Georg Schweinfurth, commissioned by the Royal Academy of Science of Berlin to undertake a botanical exploration of western Equatoria, met this highly literate *hakimdar* for the second time in November 1869, and recalled:

> Ja'afar had been an old captain of a frigate in the stirring times of Mohammed Ali; he was a man of considerable attainments, and had already become known to me on the occasion of my first journey (1863–5) when he acted as Governor of Upper Egypt. In his (Khartoum) house were seen piles of atlases and anatomical plates; he was not wanting in a clear comprehension of, nor indeed an intellectual interest in, my undertaking.

The founder of women's education in the Sudan, Sheikh Babikr Bedri, would describe Ja'afar as a 'cultured man who loved learning and the learned'. Sir Samuel Baker, who encountered Ja'afar Mazhar in 1869, a month after Schweinfurth, had also previously met him – on

Ja'afar's arrival at Suakin in August 1865 in the course of the Kassala revolt, when Baker was returning to Egypt following his discovery of Lake Albert. He had been impressed by Ja'afar Mazhar's extreme courtesy and efforts to accommodate Baker and his wife, but the relationship between Governor-General and the newly appointed general-governor of Equatoria four years later never recaptured its earlier warmth.

Ja'afar Mazhar shared a naval background with Abdel Latif Pasha, Governor-General 1850–2, but the contrast in disposition between the two was striking. Abdel Latif was a man of action, uninhibited in his determination to impose his rule, not brooking dissent – least of all from the expatriate European community. Ja'afar, a devout Moslem, was of a more learned and courteous disposition whose virtues attracted the acclaim of the educated Sudanese. There were now cultural advances – here a little and there a little. Primary schools were founded in Khartoum, Berber and Dongola, and religious *fuqara* recruited to conduct Koranic *khalwas* in all provinces. The Sudanese Sheikh el Amin Mohammed el Darir was appointed president of the Islamic Professors of the Sudan. Literary Arabic was spreading 'through the Azhar-educated *'ulema*. At the same time the introduction of civil law and civil courts from Egypt restricted the area of jurisdiction of Islamic law.' Officers and officials were educated in Sudan geography and ethnology, while examples of animal life and crafts were dispatched to the Paris Exhibition of 1867.

To augment the slim cadres of Egyptian doctors, the Governor-General initiated the training of twenty Sudanese medical assistants, and by 1873 there were hospitals, albeit small, in nearly all provinces. Public health and sanitation remained rudimentary, but in the years 1867–70 Ja'afar embarked on expenditure programmes totalling £E50,000 – especially in Khartoum, Taka, Kordofan, Suakin and Massawa – to erect municipal offices, residences, mosques and forts built of stone, to replace the traditional mud and wattle.[6]

In his first eighteen months of service he displayed firm resolution in handling problems in Kassala, White Nile and Kordofan. The criticism that he was careless of the shortcomings of his subordinates is not made out. The provincial structure had been already put in place by the time of his investiture. In addition to the core provinces of Khartoum, Kordofan, Dongola, Berber and Taka, Musa Hamdi had created that of White Nile at Deinab – the station soon to be renamed, confusingly, Fashoda, the name of the Shilluk *reth*'s capital village sixteen miles to the south. Among the provincial governors, the great Shukriya leader Ahmed Bey Awad el Karim Abu Sin remained *primus inter pares* as governor of Khartoum until his death on a visit to Cairo in 1872. The Turkish heads of the other provinces proved more mutable. Notably, in 1869 the sheikh of the Ababda, Hussein Khalifa was made *mudir* and *bey* of Berber.

In the early years of his administration Ja'afar Mazhar showed himself conciliatory to Sudanese tribal chiefs who had fallen foul of Musa Hamdi, a policy which earned him the approbation of the Sudanese community. The Hadendoa sheikh Ibrahim Musa, whose father had been arrested by Musa Hamdi just before the Kassala rebellion, the Beni Amer sheikh Hamid Musa, and Ahmed Bey Abu Sin's younger brother, the Shukriya sheikh Ali Awad Abdel Karim who had succeeded Ahmed as *nazir*, were among those to be decorated by the Viceroy in 1867, all in aid of the pacification of the eastern Sudan.

By the time of his departure on leave in April 1867 Ja'afar Mazhar had laid sound foundations for political progress. If it was Ja'afar Sadiq who favoured the detachment of Sennar and Fazughli as a seventh separate province, its implementation and the appointment of Ahmed Zanil as the governor was effected by Ja'afar Mazhar in the course of his first year of office. A major part of the new governorate comprised the hill territories of the Dar Fung and Fazughli of which Jebel Gule was a focal point. Their sheikhs, who included Ragab Idris, descendant of the Fung Kingdom *vizirs*, were charged with tribute collection and relied on province troops for enforcement. With mounting arrears, however, and the fresh viceregal requirement to increase revenues, the hill territories in 1869 were made by Ja'afar Mazhar into an administrative district of the province under a *bimbashi,* with a garrison of 800 men, its headquarters at Famaka on the Blue Nile.[7]

In that first year, 1866–7, Ja'afar reacted with energy to two provincial problems. On trek up the White Nile in April 1866, little more than a month after his investiture, news was brought to him at El Ais of *razzias* against the Shilluk and east bank Dinka being planned by a merchant named Ahmed Abu Chiba. Despite Ja'afar's immediate order that the governor White Nile, Mohammed Hilmi Bey, intercept and frustrate the raiders, he took minimum action so that in the event the Shilluk lost 300 women and children and 200 cattle, and rescue was only effected by a successful Dinka attack in which Abu Chiba was killed. A second *razzia* was mounted the following month by a Sennar merchant, Mohammed Isa. This time the deputy governor commanded a larger force, helped the Dinka defeat the new attack, and sent the raiders under arrest to Khartoum – and the captured slaves to Deinab for distribution and auction to the troops in the Musa Hamdi tradition. Ja'afar's immediate replacement of the governor by this deputy, Ali Bey Rida el Kurdi, was followed by the Viceroy's condemnation of the former province governor and the battalion commander to hard labour in Fazughli, and of Mohammed Isa to Bahr el Ghazal in chains. The slaves were released and repatriated or enrolled as recruits.

This was the smack of firm government against slave-raiding which was a feature of Ja'afar Mazhar's *hakimdaria* – sufficient to encourage the Shilluk Reth Kwatker, who came from the southern part of his kingdom, to launch the next year, 1867, an attack on five trading vessels returning from the south laden with ivory if not slaves, killing all their crews except one master and a girl slave, and seizing the cargo and arms. Unwisely, he then slaughtered a government party sent to investigate the killings. Ali Rida's punitive expedition seems to have forced Kwatker back on Tonga opposite the Zeraf river where, in February 1869, Schweinfurth's party found themselves menaced, but it took a further two years before the southern Shilluk were subjugated. Kwatker had meanwhile (in 1867) been deposed as *reth* by Ja'afar Mazhar, and the northern Shilluk Ajiyang installed in his place, so that Schweinfurth was able to report from Fashoda (Deinab, present day Kodok) in 1869 that for three years there had been undisturbed peace in those parts and, within the past two years, the building of a town commenced.[8]

The second intervention arose out of a threat to the Kordofan frontier from the west. In August 1866 the heavy rains which had so severely damaged many Khartoum mud buildings had once again provided the opportunity for the Hamar (Douin says Humr) Arabs, who had quit Kordofan for Southern Darfur, to raid their territory of origin unrestrained by the Sultan of Darfur. Ja'afar Mazhar sent a strong military expedition from El Obeid to harry the invaders and, probably at the urging of the new governor of Kordofan, Hasan Hilmi Bey el Juwaisar, sought authority from the Viceroy to occupy the frontier areas to bring an end to the raids. Ismail Pasha harboured the same predatory ambitions towards Darfur as his grandfather Mohammed Ali a generation before, but with the continuing threat from Emperor Theodore he counselled patience and a conciliatory approach to Darfur, while systematic intelligence gathering would reveal the extent of the Sultan's own defence forces and the logistical problems confronting an invasion force crossing the arid deserts: 'knowledge of

the forces of that country, the exploration of practicable routes, calculation of the number of men and animals which could be watered with
the drinkable water available in that region and of the transport possi-
bilities for troops, artillery and munitions.'

News that Ahmed Shatta, *maqdoum* of south Darfur, was in contact
with Theodore regarding a future joint invasion of the Sudan by
Abyssinia and Darfur seems to have determined Ja'afar, in February
1867, to visit Kordofan himself and to dispatch Mohammed Nadi Bey,
a member of his staff, the following month on an intelligence mission to
El Fasher, ostensibly to cement good relations between Darfur and the
Sudan. After a three-week march and a similar period spent in El
Fasher, including several audiences with the Sultan, Mohammed
Hussein el Mahdi (1839–73), Mohammed Nadi left on 4 May to return
and prepare a detailed report for his Governor-General on the size and
disposition of the Darfur forces and the availability of water supplies
on the route. Ja'afar had himself by then left for Cairo and his personal
reconnaissance of the Red Sea littoral. In the event the implementation
of Mohammed Nadi's recommendations had to wait a further six
years.[9]

On 4 April 1867 Ja'afar Pasha did indeed leave for Cairo, supposedly on three months' leave, unaware that four days previously the
British Government had concluded that only an expeditionary force
could secure the release of Consul Cameron, Hormuzd Rassam and
other hostages from Theodore's bondage. A final ultimatum expiring
on 17 August demanding the release of the hostages was therefore
dispatched to Theodore from London, and already Colonel William
Merewether, British political resident at Aden had been reconnoitring
landing places for a British expeditionary force, with the help of the
Swiss-born Werner Munzinger, now acting British (as well as French)
consul agent at Massawa. Apprised of British intentions by Hasan
Rifaat, the governor at Massawa, and determined that his secret ambitions as regards the western Red Sea littoral as far as the Bab el Mandeb
should not be pre-empted by the British, Ismail Pasha in July interrupted Ja'afar's leave in Egypt and dispatched him in the steamship
Kufit to explore and secure for Egypt the support of the local tribal
chiefs of the coast and to plant the flag. As the British ultimatum
expired on 17 August Ja'afar advised the Viceroy, a shade optimistically, that the coast was indeed now secure against foreign interference.

On his return to Cairo, with British preparations under way to
commission their field force prior to the march on Magdala, Ja'afar's

services were further retained outside his *hakimdaria* by the Viceroy with a view to organising any assistance requested by the British and to exploiting any opportunity for territorial expansion which the campaign against Theodore might offer. It would not be until May 1868, more than a year after his departure, that the Governor-General returned to Khartoum to relieve his deputy (as under Musa Hamdi in 1862–4), Ali Bey Fadli.[10]

4 BACK INTO DEFICIT 1868–69

Potentially far more important for the welfare of the inhabitants of the Sudan as a whole than these administrative dispositions was Ja'afar Mazhar's initial bold handling of the country's expenditure budget. The scale of reduction in the defence costs of 1864/5 to 1867/8 – from £E367,000 to £E76,000 – could not be matched in the civil field, since Cairo was now assuming responsibility for the costs of the regular army. However, major economies in provincial costs were made across the board, so that total budgeted civil expenditure over the same period was reduced by nearly a fifth and the direct expenses of the *hakimdaria* by a third. The survival of any such budgetary figures is rare and these are worth recording in detail (see pp. 52–3).

With regard to revenues, for which, regrettably, outside Musa Hamdi's total budgeted £E232,500 there are no comparable figures, once the Sudan had returned to reasonable stability any concessions made in the Musa Hamdi levels of tax burden were to be quickly reversed. Ja'afar Mazhar had hardly been Governor-General a year when the viceregal requirement was reintroduced in late 1867, probably following Ja'afar's arrival back in Cairo, for the Sudan to make an annual contribution to the viceregal exchequer. This was ostensibly by way of restitution of exceptional payments made to cover the deficit in the previous three years, and as a renewed contribution to the costs of the regular troops whose numbers were to be increased. Indeed by October 1867, with opportunities for territorial expansion opening up in the Abyssinian theatre following the British commitment to hostilities against Theodore, the Viceroy had ordered back to the Sudan the reconstituted First and Second Regiments under the command of the Sudanese hero of the suppression of the Kassala rebellion, Adham el Arifi, now promoted *lewa* and *pasha*.[11]

From this final blow to its prospects of prosperous development

AH 1281 (June 1864–65)
Musa Hamdi

<u>Budgets</u>   (1)   **Civil Expenditure**

	<u>£E</u>	<u>(Bourses)</u>
Khartoum	14,836	(2,967.29)
Sennar & Fazugli	–	
Kordofan	7,887	(1,577.36)
Dongola	5,326	(1,065.20)
Taka	4,337	(867.36)
White Nile	1,544	(308.84)
Berber	<u>5,687</u>	<u>(1,137.48)</u>
Total: Provinces	39,617	(7,923.53)
Hakimdaria	17,692	(3,538.38)
Sudan Council	–	–
Total: Civil	£E <u>57,309</u>	<u>(11,461.91)</u>

(2)   **Military Expenditure**

	£E	Bourses
Army: Regulars	169,325	(33,865)
Bashi-Buzouqs		
Sha'iqiya	197,405	(39,481)
Artillery	–	(–)
Arsenal & Boats	–	(–)
Sudan Posts	–	(–)
Total Military	366,730	(73,346)
Other	2,500	(500)
TOTAL: £E	426,540	(85,308)
Civil and Military		

AH 1284 (May 1867–68)
Ja'afar Mazhar

<u>£E</u>

8,282	} 12,148
3,866	
5,161	
3,899	
4,735	
1,574	
<u>4,561</u>	

32,078
11,666*
<u>3,732</u>

£E   <u>47,476</u>

Hakimdar's salary: £E 2,964

} 72,408

3,455

6,756

<u>3,792</u>

86,411

–
<u>   </u>

£E   133,887

under Turkish rule the Sudan never recovered. Douin is reticent as to its causes, which lay in the profligate financial policies of the Viceroy, compounded by the rapacity of his European creditors and his ambitions for territorial expansion beyond the Sudan. The Sultan's firman of May 1866 granting hereditary rule of succession was rumoured to have cost £E3m in addition to an increase in annual tribute to the Porte from £E400,000 to £E750,000. There followed a second grant by firman in June 1867 of the Perso-Arabic title of *khedive*, involving further disbursements to Constantinople which over sixteen years Vatikiotis estimates amounted to £E10m. The title was bestowed on the eve of Ismail's state visits (expensive in themselves) to Queen Victoria and to the Emperor Napoleon III, coinciding with the Paris Exposition. However Ismail had now gained effective independence in concluding vital arrangements relating to Egyptian finance, economic development and social order including foreign loans, and to administrative and judicial appointments. On the debit side, like his cousin, the late Viceroy Abbas, Ismail had sought unsuccessfully the Islamic title '*Aziz Misr*' (Comforter of Egypt), not least because the Ottoman Sultans themselves were known by the title *Abdel Aziz* – the *slave* of (God) the Comforter – and this was the name of the present Sultan (Abdel Aziz 1861–76). Maliciously the latter could be represented to be a slave to the Khedive.

Further large sums became payable by Egypt in consequence of the mishandling of the Suez Canal project. The cost of paying off the 1864 indemnity award to de Lesseps of £E3,360,000 in time for the ceremonial opening of the Suez Canal in 1869 brought the total sums paid by Egypt to that company up to £E16m. The celebrations themselves involved an expenditure of nearly £E1m. With the coincidental fall in the value of cotton exports at the end of the United States Civil War in 1865 and the burden of a large national army and public works programmes, by 1868 the Egyptian floating debt had already mounted to over £E26m, against revenues of £E7m (for a detailed examination of Egyptian Government borrowing see Douin, *Histoire du Règne*, vol. I, pp. 277–94; vol. II, pp. 37–8).

Although 1868 was a year of increasing financial anxiety, as the British field force in Abyssinia approached Magdala with its strictly limited objective of overthrowing Emperor Theodore (publicly declared), the opportunity for the acquisition of an Egyptian African empire beckoned. In his financial necessity, Khedive Ismail appointed in April 1868 a trusted childhood friend as his new minister of finance,

Ismail Pasha Sadiq, *'el mufettish'*, inspector or steward of the viceregal estates. Of him Carlile McCoan wrote:

> A *fellah* by birth, his mother had been nurse to the future Khedive and the boys therefore became foster brothers... their personal intimacy... was always rather that of near relatives than of Minister and Prince. He was gifted with great natural astuteness and energy and exerted an influence over Ismail that for eight years made him virtually the vice-ruler of Egypt... possessing beyond anyone who preceded or followed him, except perhaps Mohammed Ali himself, a talent for extorting revenue from the *fellahs* and for fencing with creditors of the Government.

Within months the new finance minister had raised a further loan of nearly £E12m but such were the coupon and other exactions that only £E5m was received net of charges. (Indeed of the total loan debt incurred by Ismail as Viceroy, £E90–100m, only half reached Cairo in cash.). Taxation of the *fellahin*, cosmetically assented to by the new consultative Assembly of Deputies, was to be so much increased that by 1876 five million Egyptians were paying £E7m in taxation (the Capitulations continuing to exempt the now 100,000 European residents).

It is against this background of pressure on Egyptian revenues that Ja'afar Mazhar returned from Cairo to Khartoum in May 1868 after a year's absence. He had loyally acceded to the viceregal demand for an annual Sudan contribution to the Cairo Treasury. Georges Thibaut, French vice-consul in Khartoum, claimed that it was to be £E250,000 – necessitating an increase in current local taxation allegedly of up to two thirds - and that without the accompanying burden of the 'commissions' pocketed by the tax gatherers. In 1869 the Khedive claimed that the £E150,000 paid as a subvention to the Sudan by Egypt in 1867 had now effectively become a Sudan contribution to Cairo of £E75,000, Sudan revenues having since doubled. The Sudan was once again economically in thrall to Cairo.[12]

Ja'afar Mazhar can hardly be blamed personally for this volte-face in the financial treatment of the Sudan by his Viceroy. He had exercised himself diligently in pruning civil and military expenditure, and had earned the gratitude of the Sudanese notables in Khartoum. Had he been left free of undue interference from Cairo to govern the Sudan, he gave evidence of possessing wisdom and enlightenment enough to reconcile, albeit reluctantly, the conquered but independent-minded peoples of the Sudan to the potential benefits of alien Turkish rule. But reconciliation and prudent economic development of the Sudan were not Ismail Pasha's prime consideration. Indeed in sixteen years of rule he managed to visit the Sudan not a single time. The interests of the Sudan remained subordinate to the global ambitions of the viceregal dynasty in Cairo. The Sudan was but a springboard for territorial aggrandisement.

Douin, uncritical of the responsibility of the Khedive for the taxation policy which Ja'afar Mazhar had been obliged to adopt, puts the blame for its consequences unequivocally on the Governor-General: 'La politique fiscale de Ja'afar Pasha bouleversait la condition sociale des habitants et rejetait à la vie errante des populations jadis sedentaires; tout comme celle de Moussa Pasha, elle ruinait le pays.' He cites the evidence of three expatriate witnesses in the Sudan of 1869–70: Ferdinand Lafargue, the French merchant based on Berber 1843–71; Dr Georg Schweinfurth, the Prussian scientist who, after a brief visit to the Sudan in 1866, returned two years later to explore the Bahr el Ghazal; and Sir Samuel Baker, an explorer of Sudan and the Nile 1861–5, who arrived to take up the appointment of general-governor of Equatoria in January 1870.

In March 1869 Lafargue complained to Sharif Pasha, minister of the interior in Cairo, that the level of tax imposed by Ja'afar on Berber Province for the year 1868–9 was unacceptable – £E55,000, on top of £E20,000 outstanding from the previous years. As a result of this, if the ruling system of the province did not change, he warned that the number of families who had previously been cultivators of Nile farms and who had now become nomads – 10,000 of them – would increase. Yet the previous year, 1867–8, had been one of moderate taxation countrywide and Lafargue himself, in a report to the French consul-general in July 1867, had volunteered that harsh local Sudan conditions meant that in one year in three there was a scarcity of the staple food-stuff, *dura*, and one year in five a dreadful famine. The price of *dura* in Berber in 1867 was half that in 1866 and in occasional years of overall plenty could even be a tenth of 1866. If in assessing the fairness of taxation, one year needed to be taken with another, Ja'afar was nevertheless under Khedivial instruction to reinstate the Sudan quota.

For Lafargue's animus against Ja'afar Mazhar, one has to consider the former's hostility towards Miralai Ali Bey Uweida, governor of Berber Province, who had been complained against by one of his provincial assistants on the basis of allegations of corruption brought by local sheikhs and merchants in February 1868, while Ja'afar himself was in Cairo. In Ja'afar's absence an inquiry was ordered, but on his return in April 1868 pressure was put on the assistant to retract his allegation. One suspects that Lafargue may himself have been one of the merchant witnesses against the governor: indeed in the previous July he had been complaining about official venality. However, Ja'afar Mazhar pursued the case against Ali Bey. Although acquitting the latter of fraud, he found him negligent in his levying of taxes and the discharge of his duties, dismissed him and appointed Ahmed Rami Bey as governor briefly in his place. Both were to appear before the commission of inquiry investigating *inter alia* a theft from the Khartoum treasury under Ahmed Mumtaz Pasha but were found not guilty of the charges (see below chapter 7, iv).

Schweinfurth also had discrete reasons for criticism of Ja'afar. He had met Lafargue in October 1869 before he too remarked on the depopulation of the riverain lands between Berber and Khartoum since his previous visit in 1866, but he did not distinguish between 1866 and 1869 nor blame Ja'afar personally. In his book published in 1873 he wrote:

> In the course of the last ten years, as a consequence first of increased taxation and secondly, of diminished production, matters have continuously became worse and worse... the fact remains that the culture of the soil is declining, that scarcity is everywhere on the increase, and that distress is consequently more frequent. In the last two months of this year's harvest the market price of the *ruba'a* [8 kilos] of sorghum had risen to a Maria Theresa dollar. Three years before [1866] large villages had been pointed out to me lying completely deserted on account of the emigration of the inhabitants and now again similar evidence of distress was forced upon my notice. In the district between Damer and Shendi the population seemed utterly scared at the increasing emigrations. The unmarried men go to Khartoum in order to be enlisted as so-called soldiers by the merchants of the Upper Nile. The elder people, on the other hand, leave their culture and with a few sheep or goats endeavour to lead a meagre nomad life as shepherds in the steppes and deserts.

Arriving in Khartoum in November 1869 Schweinfurth regarded Ja'afar Mazhar appreciatively: '...who at that time was administering affairs with considerable vigour in all the provinces of the Sudan under the Egyptian dominion above the first cataract'. But when Schweinfurth returned to Khartoum from the Bahr el Ghazal in July 1871 on the eve of Ja'afar's final departure, notwithstanding the latter's cordiality Schweinfurth was vexed because Ja'afar Pasha, very properly, had arrested his servants for the possession of slaves acquired during the exploration. Schweinfurth complained that Ja'afar rather should have been tougher with slave trading in Kordofan – a rather petulant criticism betraying the personal inconvenience caused to Schweinfurth by the charges against his servants.

The third witness cited by Douin is Sir Samuel Baker, newly appointed general-governor of Equatoria, who travelled via Suakin to Berber in New Year 1870 en route to Khartoum and the South. In *Ismailia* (1874), Baker does not say that he too had met Lafargue in Berber, but it is likely. His observations of the Berber-Khartoum Nile are very close to those of Schweinfurth published a year earlier.

> I had observed with dismay a frightful change in the features of the country between Berber and the capital since my former visit (1865). The rich soil on the banks of the river, which had a few years since been highly cultivated, was abandoned. Now and then a tuft of neglected date-palms might be seen, but the river's banks, formerly verdant with heavy crops, had become a wilderness. Villages once crowded had entirely disappeared; the population was gone. Irrigation had ceased.
>
> This terrible desolation was caused by the Governor-General of the Sudan, who, although an honest man, trusted too much to the honesty of others, who preyed upon the inhabitants. As a good and true Mohammedan, he left his territory to the care of God and thus, trusting in Providence, he simply increased the taxes. In one year he sent the Khedive, his master, £100,000 in hard dollars, wrung from the poor peasantry, who must have lost an equal amount in the pillage that accompanies the collection. [Lafargue had in 1867 hypothesised an overall figure of £125,000 (Douin, III, 1, p. 435).]
>
> The population of the richest province of the Sudan fled from oppression and abandoned the country; and the greater portion betook themselves to the slave trade of the White Nile where, in their turn, they might trample upon the rights of others… Thousands had forsaken their homes and commenced a life of brigandage on the White Nile.[13]

The evidence of these three witnesses from the central Nile is insufficiently substantial for Douin successfully to prosecute the charge that it was Ja'afar Mazhar's personal fiscal policy that overturned the economic and social condition of the Sudanese people and ruined the country. There is more than a lingering suspicion that the opinions of Schweinfurth and Baker were coloured in great part by contact with Lafargue, a Berber trader who had quarrelled with the Governor-General, yet even Lafargue had gone on record that the hazardous conditions of subsistence for the riverain peoples north of Khartoum were conditioned by the vagaries of climate and cultivation. In putting the blame uniquely on Ja'afar Mazhar, Douin seems almost wilfully to omit reference to the reimposition by the Khedive in 1868 of substantial annual revenue contributions by the Sudan to the Cairo Treasury, and of a reinflated and disproportionately large and costly military establishment. He prefers to endorse the distorted conclusion: 'The sole objective of the administration is to collect a tax surplus which will swell the Cairo Treasury and provide an endorsement of the fitness of the Governor-General.'

There remains the general charge of corruption which Lafargue propagated in his assault on Ja'afar's *hakimdaria* as if its incidence were an exceptional failure rather than the norm of almost all past Turkish administrations. The quantification of an aggregate in bribes at £E100,000 p.a. is unsubstantiated, but if 'commissions' on tax gathered were an established practice, there is ample evidence that Ja'afar's personal conduct was one of integrity. His budgeted salary of less than £E3,000 p.a. contrasted with the expatriate remuneration of £E10,000 awarded by the Khedive to Ja'afar's junior, Sir Samuel Baker, on his appointment in 1869 as general-governor of Equatoria (Gordon was to refuse to accept more than £E2,000 for this same appointment in 1874). Baker indeed affirmed that Ja'afar was 'an honest man'. Writing ninety years later, Richard Hill remarked: 'There still lingers a story that he [Ja'afar] left Khartoum owing large sums to various creditors, an evident proof in Sudanese eyes of his refusal to live by graft.'[14]

Ja'afar Mazhar was to remain in post as Governor-General for a further two years. They witnessed the first phase of Ismail Pasha's African expansion, in the initial planning of which – notably as to the Red Sea littoral and Bahr el Ghazal – he personally played some part. They were however years of discouragement for himself and for the Sudan. His political responsibilities were progressively to be curtailed, not least by the appointment of independent general-governors. He deeply distrusted both the competence and the ambition of Ahmed Mumtaz Pasha in the East. In August 1871, impatient of Khedivial tergiversation, Ja'afar was voluntarily to relinquish his post. The chronicler of the *Ta'arikh* recorded the universal grief of the Sudanese at his departure notwithstanding the heavier burden of taxation of which he had been the reluctant agent.

5 COMMUNICATIONS AND DEVELOPMENT

Communications   The Viceroy believed emphatically that precedence must be granted to communication needs if his ambitions to develop the strategic and wealth-creating potential of the Sudan were to be fulfilled. This struck a responsive chord with Ja'afar Mazhar on his appointment. Ismail's viceregal predecessor Mohammed Sa'id Pasha had been responsible for introducing a twice-weekly postal service between Cairo and Khartoum taking thirty days. In 1865 the decision was taken to improve contact further by the establishment of a postal line from Qena via Kosseir to the newly reacquired port of Suakin, a development necessitated by continuing delays in the telegraph line project between Cairo and Khartoum of 1863 due to the uncontrollable depredations of white ants. By May 1867 the remaining leg of the latter (via Wadi Halfa and Dongola) across the Bayuda desert to Berber was still unbridged and in consequence the close monitoring of the progress of the Nile annual flood had to be further postponed. The line reached Khartoum North in 1870.

While at Suakin en route to Kassala at the time of the Kassala revolt, Ja'afar Mazhar in his capacity as deputy Governor-General ordered on 8 October 1865 the establishment of a regular postal service between the different *muderias*. Perhaps the most important postal advance however was marked by the viceregal instruction, received by Ja'afar Mazhar shortly after his installation as *hakimdar* in March 1866, to implement a dromedary postal service from Khartoum to Berber to Suakin. Taking eight days only, this was to link with a weekly steamer service, through the agency of the Aziziya Shipping Company (later the Khedivial Mail Line), between Suakin and Suez. Gone now would be the days when a Governor-General could act on his own initiative without reference to Cairo.

The Viceroy was also exercised about the carriage of troops, their equipment, and of merchandise. Aware that the planning, financing and building of railways involved insurmountable delays and recognising the urgency of the need to provide an interim solution, he ordered the preparation of sand tracks suitable for oxen-drawn wooden carts between Suakin and Kassala, along with the provision of ancillary drinking-water resources. This represented a far more economical alternative to the Aswan-Shendi railway which the conclusions of a trace study by Waring Brothers in the winter of 1864–5 had erroneously costed at £E9.6m over six years. Work on the first cataract slipway of the Aswan-Shendi railway was not to start until 1873 and work on the railway from Wadi Halfa to Shendi not until 1875. The trace of an alternative section from Suakin to Shendi had been surveyed in 1867.

The Kassala revolt in 1865 further concentrated minds on rapid facilities for the deployment of troops. While this was best effected by camel, the system was currently blighted, as Munzinger pointed out, by the corvée – the arbitrary requisition of beasts – which prompted their rightful owners to graze them well out of the clutches of the military and government officials. The acquisition of Suakin and the implementation of the Red Sea steamer route to Suez, however, promised a quicker and more reliable line of troop communication with Egypt than the hazardous Atmur desert, as Shahin Pasha had noted. Moreover Ja'afar had the perception to recommend the opening of a Suakin to Berber land route to restore exports from Khartoum, Berber, Sennar and Kordofan.

Development: Suakin and Cotton   Suakin was becoming a strategic point in the Sudan economy. Ja'afar Pasha Mazhar organised bi-monthly merchant caravans connecting the Abyssinian border with Suakin via Taka, and comparable services from Kordofan, the White Nile and Khartoum via Berber. Suakin's trade revenue, in addition to its salt pans, quickly came to exceed that of Massawa where the export of slaves was under European pressure. The enhanced volume of trade by the land routes justified the preparation of economical cart tracks, pending the eventual planning and financing of a railway connection between Suakin and the Nile – the trace Suakin to Shendi proving substantially more viable than that to Berber, although by 1873 well-digging on the route was still incomplete. In all this Ja'afar's efforts won the appreciation of his sovereign.

The potential of Suakin had captured the imagination of the Viceroy. Having installed its governor on 28 August 1865, Ja'afar Pasha was active in Khartoum in preparing the national infrastructure to the newly ceded port. Meanwhile the first Egyptian governor (*muhafiz*), Ahmed Mumtaz Bey, was by 1866 already in direct correspondence with the Khedivial office about the Viceroy's ambitious programme. The coincidence of Mumtaz's tenure of office with the imminent completion of the Suez Canal and the improved land communications with the eastern Sudan, coupled with the initiation of the weekly Aziziya steamer service between Suez and Suakin, gave the new governor the opportunity to by-pass Khartoum in correspondence – an advantage he was quick to exploit. His background – Circassian birth in Egypt, German education, Egyptian military career (corps of engineers) – is not well documented but on his appointment to Suakin he was made *bey* and later *lewa*. He set about pursuing the Khedivial instructions with a will.

These were to develop the Suakin zone for commerce and agriculture. Drinking-water supplies must be assured and permanent buildings, both municipal and residential, constructed with the help of the military, to be aided ultimately by convict labour from the Kassala revolt. The cultivation of wheat and cereals, tree planting and sheep-rearing were to be fostered. Ahmed Mumtaz enthusiastically set about harnessing the rainfall on the Red Sea hills by conduits and establishing near Tokar – transferred to him along with Sinkat from Taka province – an experimental irrigation scheme of fifty acres in the low part of the Khor Baraka delta. For all of this he sought specialist engineers from Egypt.

Ja'afar Pasha left the Sudan in April 1867 for what was to prove a full year's absence. The *hakimdar*, already disquieted by what he deemed Mumtaz's neglect of his basic administrative responsibilities, left the latter free to plan an empire already augmented by the transfer of the territory from Taka.

On his return to Khartoum from Cairo in May 1868 Ja'afar Pasha was no better pleased with Mumtaz's performance. The water plan for Suakin had run into difficulties, one source proving unfit for drinking, another (prodigiously expensive) having to be turned down when the local Beja warned that the supply was not perennial. Tax collection needed to defray the costs was being neglected especially in the tribal areas transferred from Taka. On 13 April 1869 the Governor-General wrote to Cairo requesting Mumtaz's replacement. Instead the Khedive in September complimented the latter on his efforts, and as evidence of ongoing commitment to Suakin ordered plans for a viceregal palace – shades of Mohammed Ali Polis – and proposed a Khedivial inspection of Suakin and Massawa once the opening of the Suez Canal had taken place.[15]

Thus encouraged, Mumtaz developed in a report of 1869 a macro-scheme for cotton growing which he claimed would revolutionise the scale of Sudan revenue for the Khedive. Confessing the water difficulty, he claimed that the costs of the revised plan of 800 bourses (£E4,000) would be soon matched by the proceeds from large-scale cultivation of cotton and the yields from charges, taxation and export dues. In 1869–70 the cultivable area as a start would be increased by 762 acres. He ordered 70 ardebs (say 3 cwt) of cotton seed. With cotton selling at ten dollars per cwt at Suakin, the prosperity of the inhabitants and of the Treasury would be transformed. Mumtaz was invited to Cairo in April 1870 to amplify his plans in person.

With the exuberance of a Kovalevsky, Mumtaz now discoursed on the simplicity of cotton-growing in the Sudan. No crop was so susceptible to successful growth. Unlike Egypt where cultivation required ploughing and frequent irrigation, in the Sudan it would be sufficient to scatter the seed on the ground like *dura*. When it germinated and a small bush started to grow, care must be taken to remove surrounding weeds. Nothing interfered with its growth and production. The basic requirements of fertile soils, rain, population and communications were in place. Nothing could be simpler than cotton cultivation. 2m cwt could be realised after four years: 500,000 cwt would realise £1m. This could be further augmented by the export of sheep's wool and goat's hair.

He claimed, therefore, the current annual revenue being sent to Egypt from the Sudan totalling £E60,000 was derisive. It should be increased to more than £E1m from an anticipated production of 500,000 cwt of cotton. The Khedive was pleasurably persuaded. A month later, on 25 May 1870, he announced the creation – which in the interests *inter alia* of agriculture and commerce, Ja'afar Mazhar had himself proposed in his letter of 16 August 1869 – of a separate general-governorate of the Red Sea littoral. The general-governor to be – Ahmed Pasha Mumtaz. When the news reached Khartoum, Ja'afar Mazhar was wrestling with the problems of the Baker expedition and the White Nile.

Ja'afar Mazhar has been criticised for failing to aid economic development – a charge that has not been argued in detail. Like almost all his *hakimdar* predecessors, his training and experience had been in the armed forces. Internal and external security was the ultimate priority.

Only in respect of agricultural development is there a case to answer. His attention to the communications of this vast country, to the courts, health education and public building, combined with a careful husbandry of public expenditure, was impressive. He had only a period of a little more than a year, March 1866 to April 1867, to plan and implement his improvements before his extended recall to Cairo for the period of the second year in order to contribute his naval experience to a reconnaissance for his Khedive of the Red Sea littoral. On his return to Khartoum in May 1868, after such an interruption, he was burdened once again with a major underwriting of the cost of the regular forces, and of an annual contribution to the viceregal exchequer in all its profligacy. For these the new budget would already require an uplift in the taxation of provinces by as much as two-thirds, enough to halt development hopes for the Sudan of 1866–7.

Of his Turkish predecessors it is Ali Pasha Khurshid (1826–38) who can claim the most impressive record in agricultural development. This was sustained by his ability to withstand viceregal pressure for the transfer of Sudan revenues to Egypt and by the maintenance of government monopolies on cash products. Nevertheless he was responsible for numerous new crop initiatives, including barley, indigo and sugar cane. Cotton growing predated him, at least in Makada between the Blue Nile and Setit rivers, but he was instrumental in securing the services of Egyptians skilled in cultivation techniques.

Mumtaz has had an undeservedly good press over cotton cultivation and his claim for its simplicity and instant profitability. Why, it is asked, did not Ja'afar Mazhar put it to the test? Mumtaz's representations about the crop to Ismail Pasha were to prove facile. The new cost infrastructure in the budget for such development had to be covered, and the switch from *dura* to cotton growing had to be manifestly profitable (taking into account transportation requirements) if the inhabitants were to cooperate. Notwithstanding the province budget deficit he faced, Ja'afar was not persuaded that eastern Sudan cotton with a Kassala ginning factory, requiring as always detailed supervision for productivity and disease prevention, heavy investment and the ability to market the crop successfully, would solve the budget problem. There was competition from Khartoum (two merchant ginning machines were purchased in 1870) and Berber. Ernst Marno's prescient proposal for an irrigation canal in the Gezira was likewise deemed unviable for the time being. Ja'afar's hesitancy not only prejudiced his request for Mumtaz's replacement, but resulted in Mumtaz's appointment to the very general-governorate for which Ja'afar had proposed Fariq Khusraw Pasha. For an informed evaluation of the outcome of Mumtaz's scheme we have to wait until 1873, three years after the formation of the general-governorate, and in the aftermath of Ja'afar Mazhar's resignation and Ahmed Mumtaz's dismissal.[16]

Massawa Hasan Bey Rifaat, governor of Massawa, had a less colourful though necessary role in the modernisation of a port hitherto dependent on slave traffic, of inferior location for Sudan trade and largely deficient of permanent public buildings and fortification. No less ambitious but less in the eye of the Viceroy, he was content to address his needs correctly to Ja'afar Pasha. He was also harbouring ambitions of another kind, stimulated by a démarche of the chiefs of the Tigré province of Abyssinia who, provoked by Theodore's threat to gather arrears of tribute and impressed by the acquisition of Massawa, now sought some link with Egypt. Hasan Rifaat however by August 1866 had his eye on the annexation of the formerly Turkish western Red Sea littoral as far as Tadjoura – near modern Djibouti. The Viceroy, mindful of British warnings not to exacerbate relations with Theodore, dampened his governor's enthusiasm for military expansion, but approved Ja'afar Pasha's action, on the Massawa governor's recommendation, in ordering in January 1867 the occupation of a military post in the agricultural area of Kufit on the route from Massawa to Kassala from which, two years earlier, du Bisson had been ignominiously ejected.

Khartoum Before his departure on his first annual leave in May 1867, Ja'afar Mazhar received from the Khedive acceptance of his proposals for the destruction of purely mud houses and the use of limestone for construction, especially in the case of public buildings, encouraging private householders to follow suit. This policy was a preferable alternative to the rebuilding of the capital on Tuti Island following the damage caused to mud houses by the heavy rains of 1866, a suggestion of the Khedive which Ja'afar firmly and successfully resisted. Ja'afar was also authorised to initiate the formation of police forces in Khartoum and other major towns – an important encouragement for urbanisation. They were to be recruited from the ranks of irregular troops.

On Ja'afar's return from Egypt in May 1868 there is no evidence to refute the statement of the Chronicler that he remained in his capital.

Georg Schweinfurth observed the local consequences of this on his return to Khartoum in July 1871 after an absence in the south of two and a half years, and on the eve of Ja'afar Pasha's final departure to Egypt:

> I found Khartoum itself much altered. A large number of new brick buildings, a spacious quay on the banks of the Blue Nile, and some still more imposing erections on the other side of the river, had given the place the more decided aspect of an established town. The extensive gardens and rows of date-palms, planted out nearly half a century back, had now attained to such a development that they could not be altogether without influence on the climate; in spite of everything, however, the sanitary condition of Khartoum was still very unsatisfactory. This was entirely owing to the defective drainage of that portion of the town that had been built below the high-water level.[17]

3
Interlude: Magdala 1868
The Price of British Misjudgement

I THE UNMERITED ADVERSITY OF CONSUL CAMERON

Eighteen months after the murder in May 1860 of the British consul at Massawa, Walter Plowden, Duncan Cameron was appointed his successor. He would present his letters of credence to the Emperor Theodore II in October 1862 as Musa Pasha Hamdi, the new Governor-General of the Egyptian Sudan, was awaiting the end of the rains before launching a pre-emptive strike against Theodore's threatened invasion of the Sudan. A year later Cameron had been arrested by an Emperor furious with the British government, to be released only by a British Field Force in May 1868. The successful if financially costly campaign of that Field Force in 1867–8 under the command of Lieutenant-General Sir Robert Napier, KCB, RE, a gallant participant in the defence of Lucknow (1857) and commander-in-chief of the Bombay army, had an influence on the Sudan's history well beyond its declared local and limited objective – 'for the recovery of the British prisoners and for that alone'.

Indeed British governments had been unambiguous in their policy of remaining territorially uninvolved in northern Africa, in contrast, as the Egyptian historian Mohammed Sabry observed, with France and other European countries. When Napoleon III had in 1856 proposed to Lord Palmerston, the Liberal prime minister, the division of North Africa whereby France would annex Morocco, Britain Egypt, and Sardinia Tripolitania, Palmerston had expressed his resolute opposition to making Africa a second Poland. Britain and France should jointly oppose unjust aggression, protect the weak against the strong and maintain the balance of power. Now in 1867 the British policy of non-involvement was reiterated. Benjamin Disraeli, the Conservative chancellor of the exchequer told the House of Commons in November: 'We are going to war [against Abyssinia] not to obtain territory, not to secure commercial advantages, but for high moral causes alone.' His

Emperor Theodore II

colleague, the foreign secretary Lord Stanley, son of prime minister the Earl of Derby, was still more explicit: 'It is quite unnecessary to disclaim ideas of conquest. We have as much territory already as we care to hold or can safely hold; and if we had not, Abyssinia is not the part of the world which England would covet to possess. No: this work comes to us as a duty.'

Stanley went on to consider the consequences of not fulfilling that duty to rescue captive government emissaries, and he recalled the earlier impossibility of rescuing the prisoners Colonel Stoddart and Captain Connolly of the Indian Army. Following his participation in the relief of the siege of Herat and the occupation of Kabul in the First Afghan war (1838–40), Stoddart had been dispatched on a mission to the Amir of Bukhara, 1,200 miles from India. After the disastrous evacuation of Kabul in January 1842 the Amir, despite the intervention of the friendly Russian envoy, imprisoned Stoddart, who had been joined by Connolly. It was deemed impossible to mount a rescue and the Amir had them both murdered, with serious harm to British prestige. Even if British opinion would have tolerated leaving Consul Cameron and his companions to be murdered or kept in chains, Stanley affirmed, that was not the whole question.

> We have to consider opinion in India as well as here... Connected with our Indian Empire there is great glory, great responsibility, great danger. You rest your position there on prestige. You hold power not by force but in great measure by the knowledge or belief that, however mildly and justly British authority may be exercised, it is in the last resort backed by force which cannot be resisted. But it follows in consequence from that state of things that you cannot allow that idea to be dispelled, you cannot accept insult from uncivilised tribes and merely say, we are very sorry, it is not in our power to punish them.[1]

The policy of this Conservative government in 1867 with its slim parliamentary majority did not differ markedly from the preceding Liberal administration of Palmerston when, under its foreign secretary, Earl Russell, and under-secretary Sir Austen Layard, Cameron had been appointed in 1861. However the former friendliness of Britain towards the quasi-independent Abyssinia thereafter had quickly cooled with rumours of the Emperor's planned invasion of the Egyptian Sudan, an integral part of the Ottoman empire – to the maintenance of which Britain was committed. Also, in 1862, in the Gulf of Aden

France had with impunity possessed itself of the supposedly Ottoman protected port of Obock and laid claim to the gulf of Tadjura. The status quo and security of the route to India increasingly depended on the buttressing of Turkish frontiers. Symptomatic was the fresh advice of the British consul in Jerusalem to the Abyssinian Church that it must now look to Constantinople for the protection of its buildings.

The policy towards Abyssinia had been spelt out to the new British consul-general in Egypt, Colonel Edward Stanton, who had succeeded Sir Robert Colquhoun in August 1865. In brief, the Treaty of Friendship and Commerce negotiated with Ras Ali Aluba of Begemder by the late Consul Plowden in 1849 had not been recognised by his successor *Negus* Theodore (Tewodros) in 1854, as a result of which, it was now affirmed, Britain had withdrawn its recognition of Abyssinian independence. Britain continued to exercise her influence to restrain Egyptian aggression but would not consent to guarantee the integrity of Abyssinian territory which would be unwise and impracticable. While Britain desired the promotion of trade and intercourse with Abyssinia (the 1849 Treaty provided that reciprocally the British government would receive 'any Ambassador Envoy or Consul whom the Emperor of Abyssinia might appoint') there would be no interference on behalf of the Coptic Christians:

> But considering the short tenure of power of the Abyssinian kings, whatever be their title; the difficulty of reaching with a regular British force their seat of Empire; the little value of a victory gained at Gondar and Shoa; the risk of failure and the certainty of expense: it has seemed to the British Government a preferable course to withdraw as much as possible from Abyssinian engagements, Abyssinian alliances, and British interference in Abyssinia.

Stanton had applauded a policy 'against which so many groundless reproaches and unfounded allegations have been raised'.[2]

If the two British Parliamentary parties did not ostensibly differ on policy, it nevertheless fell to the weak Derby-Disraeli government of June 1866 to reap the consequences of the inept handling by its predecessor of Emperor Theodore's appeal for friendship and support in 1862, necessitating the eventual dispatch of a military expedition to secure the release of British diplomatic representatives.

Since news had reached London in May 1860 of the murder of the British consul, Walter Plowden, near Gondar on 6 March by Garad,

Theodore's brother-in-law and pretender to his throne, there had been a hiatus in communication with Theodore. Raffaello Barroni, the honorary British consular agent in Massawa, was broken in health but Plowden's successor, Duncan Cameron, who had been vice-consul at Poti in the Caucasus, was not appointed until his return to London in December 1860 and was then delayed from embarking for his new post until November 1861. Barroni warned from Massawa both in February and September 1861 of Theodore's intention to send an Abyssinian embassy to the Queen, and requested instructions how to respond, were his anticipated meeting to take place with Theodore at Adowa. Barroni's message reached London on 14 November less than a week before the departure of Cameron, to whom Russell's reply was handed that without further information no instructions could be given as to how to respond to such a mission. Cameron in turn on 18 November promised to 'lose no time, after my arrival in Abyssinia, in obtaining information on the subject'.

Cameron reached Massawa via Cairo and Aden on 9 February 1862, nearly two years after Plowden's murder. He had been appointed, like Plowden, 'H.M. Consul in Abyssinia whose residence will be principally at Massawa', his instructions of February 1861 giving special attention to the suppression of the slave trade, and any de facto frontier changes, but making no mention of the contentious trade treaty with Ras Ali of 1849. After nearly four months in Massawa, Cameron left for the interior, and was finally to meet the Emperor at Gojjam on 7 October 1862 after a protracted halt in Gondar, and to present his letter of introduction from Queen Victoria together with the accompanying presents. Theodore's threat to invade the Sudan had in the meantime precipitated the appointment in June 1862 of Musa Hamdi as Governor-General of the Sudan, whose army of 8,000 men was awaiting the end of the rains to move to the Abyssinian frontier. Theodore was about to learn that his immediate prospect of a successful invasion of the Sudan had already been neutralised and this strengthened his determination to secure the backing of the European Christian powers as the prerequisite to any future onslaught. Accordingly by 31 October the Emperor had written letters canvassing support and proposing embassies to the British Queen, the French Emperor, and the Russian Tsar.[3]

On 1 November Cameron and the Frenchman A. Bardel (the French consul-designate, Guillaume Lejean, did not reach Theodore until 1 January 1863) left Gojjam, Cameron with Theodore's mounted escort. They carried the Emperor's letters for transmission respectively to the

British and French sovereigns. Cameron, forced to take refuge at Axum from a rebellion at Adwa (Adowa), eventually directed his royal letter to Massawa for forwarding to Aden. He sent with it, imprudently as it was to prove, several dispatches to his superiors not only giving an account of his meetings with Theodore but embodying his own suggestion that a reply to Theodore should be expedited (indeed should he return with it to Theodore or accompany the embassy to London?) lest successive rainy seasons postpone the embassy for eighteen months; and that a new draft treaty, amending that of 1849, should be submitted with a new article covering slave trade prohibition. Cameron further advised that he intended to visit Bogos and to write to the governors (*sic*) of Kassala and Metemma (Gallabat).

The British Foreign Office were not pleased to receive on 12 February 1863 either Theodore's letter to Queen Victoria or the news of their consul's 'meddling in the politics of Abyssinia'. Having sidestepped Barroni's original warning about an embassy in 1861, despite 'further information' the Foreign Office were no more disposed now than then to advise the Queen to respond to Theodore's request for support and to receive an embassy from him, while recognising that it was desirable that Cameron should monitor how the French Emperor responded. Otherwise Theodore's request was adroitly kicked into touch, the original being forwarded to the India Office on 5 May 1863. There it remained until returned without comment over a year later, whereupon it was passed to the Treaty Department. To Cameron went a stern rebuke on 22 April 1863: 'It is not desirable for H.M. Agents to meddle in the affairs of Abyssinia and you would have done better if you had returned to your post at Massawa when the King told you to do so. Thus it will be right that you should do at once and you will reside at Massawa until further orders.'

E. Hertslet, a Foreign Office official friendly to Cameron, pointed out in an Abyssinian memorandum a few weeks later that no reply had been sent to Cameron's dispatches on the subject either of the embassy, or revision of the 1849 Treaty, or the transmission of presents. However no action was deemed necessary by the foreign secretary. The errant consul was treated with the same *froideur* as Consul Petherick, shortly to be removed from office in Khartoum – but Cameron was to suffer far more than *froideur*.

The charge of meddling in relations with Abyssinia was to be sustained by the Foreign Office against Cameron over the next five years. But in October 1865, by which time the latter's incarceration had

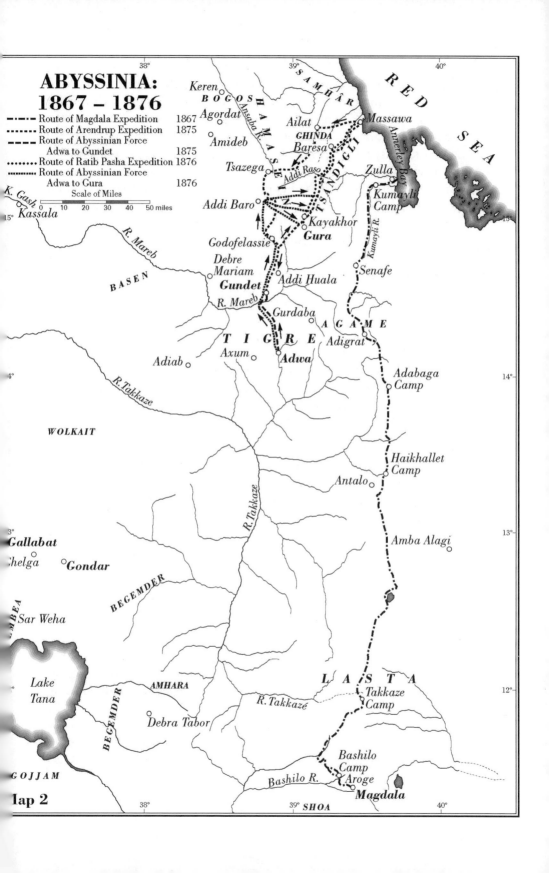

ABYSSINIA: 1867 – 1876

- ·—·—· Route of Magdala Expedition 1867
- ········ Route of Arendrup Expedition 1875
- – – – Route of Abyssinian Force
    Adwa to Gundet 1875
- •••••••• Route of Ratib Pasha Expedition 1876
- ··········· Route of Abyssinian Force
    Adwa to Gura 1876

Scale of Miles

0 10 20 30 40 50 miles

RED SEA

Map 2

been in the public domain well over a year, the sensitive issue of Theodore's request to send an embassy was muted and the criticism of Cameron narrowed to his information-gathering visit to Bogos and the Sudan. Theodore's chief anger was now ascribed to this visit, and to Cameron's suspected intrigue with the Turks, but 'made worse by his return without the Queen's answer': 'There is no reason to suppose Consul Cameron invited the Egyptian forces on the frontier to commit aggressions... But certainly by going to Bogos [he] acted without orders and increased the displeasure of his own government.'

No such rebukes had attended the initiatives of Cameron's predecessor, Plowden, eight years earlier. In November 1855 foreign secretary the Earl of Clarendon had written positively:

> Her Majesty's Government are convinced that the establishment of friendly and intimate relations between Great Britain and Abyssinia would be attended with many advantages to both countries; and you will accordingly inform the King [Theodore] that the Queen will have much pleasure in receiving and treating with due honour the Ambassadors whom the King may send to her Court. This must however depend upon your receiving from the King a distinct assurance that he renounces all idea of conquest in Egypt and Massawa.

Two years later, when Plowden forwarded a letter from Theodore to the Queen expressing his intention shortly of sending an embassy with Plowden to London, Clarendon chose then to send no reply, only a present, perhaps on the grounds that this was still only an expression of intention by the Emperor – a precedent perhaps for the inactivity that was to be the policy adopted on receipt in February 1863 of Theodore's letter of October 1862.

With regard to Bogos (Sennaheit), Plowden's intervention in April 1854 in the wake of the Kassala governor's slave raid had been endorsed, the governor Khusraw Bey being eventually dismissed by Cairo and imprisoned. Believing that Bogos had since been under British protective surveillance and learning that the Shangalla tribe from the Sudan had been rustling Bogos cattle, Cameron believed that he too was justified in intervening. Hence his visit to Bogos and on to Kassala (where he was incapacitated by fever), Gedaref and, en route back to Abyssinia, Gallabat (Metemma). Unconvincingly however, he was later to claim that he was, as instructed, reporting on the comparative merits of Suakin and Massawa as a consulate base. He achieved nothing. As to acting on his own initiative, so did Plowden in 1854.[4]

Between Cameron's departure in November 1862 and return to
Gondar in July 1863 much water had passed under the bridge. Lejean,
the French consul, having arrived with Henry Dufton, presented his
credentials in January 1863. Two months later, on the receipt of a reply
from Russia rejecting Theodore's overtures and on news of Musa
Hamdi's punitive expedition on the Abyssinian frontier, Lejean was
arrested and put in chains though later allowed some local liberty.
Lejean left a perceptive impression of Theodore in 1863:

> Theodore is a man of about 46, medium height for an Abyssinian,
> shrewd, with an open sympathetic countenance... his nose and
> mouth are Semitic supporting his claim to descent from David and
> Solomon... He seems too Black to be of pure Abyssinian blood.
>
> His appearance is imposing, proclaiming that he is really a man
> gifted with agility and tireless energy, gifts of which he is proud...
> Such is the physical man.
>
> The moral man is less easy to identify and I confess I still do not
> grasp it. This is a kind of sly countryman, without scruples, arro-
> gant, once very pious, less so now, although always the mystic and
> respectful of the memory of the king prophet of Judah, his
> supposed ancestor, whom regretfully he copies in two regards:
> massacres and Bathsheba.

At last, in September 1863, the French reply was received at Gondar
by the hand of Bardel, whither Lejean had been summoned to find
Cameron still free, but apprehensively awaiting news from London. The
French missive, without official seal and negative in content, was publicly torn up by the Emperor, who ordered Lejean's immediate expulsion.
Cameron, not without some envy, lunched him and humorously if pre-
sciently inquired about the weight of Theodore's chains. He had not long
to wait for an authoritative answer. On 15 October Cameron's assistant
Kerans arrived from Massawa with a letter from London for Cameron,
the contents of which Theodore demanded to see. It was not the reply
for which the Emperor was waiting but rather Russell's reprimand of
Cameron of 22 April for meddling. Cameron was promptly put under
house arrest. There followed a further written reprimand from Russell
– possibly of 8 September – informing Cameron that the British government approved neither his proceedings in Abyssinia nor his suggestions,
and ordering him to abstain from all interference and remain in Massawa. This, coupled with news from Jerusalem that the British consul
had failed to offer help, in accordance with the 1849 Treaty, to the

Abyssinian convent which was currently under pressure from the Armenians, precipitated the imprisonment on 2 January 1864 of Cameron, his secretary Kerans, three European staff, and seven European Protestant missionaries and their families. Cameron and others were placed in chains. Bardel, the Frenchman, was arrested a month later.[5]

On 15 December 1863 London and Paris newspapers had carried a report of Cameron's arrest, possibly via Lejean now back at Massawa. However the first authoritative news to London may have come via the dismissed British consul in Khartoum, John Petherick. On 31 December 1863 a German named Haussman – belonging to the Society for Promotion of Christianity among the Jews and stationed at Gallabat – had arrived in Khartoum direct from Emperor Theodore and reported that Cameron was under house arrest and two missionaries Stern and Rosenthal were in chains at Gondar. Cameron was unable to write. Theodore had released Haussman. Petherick promptly dispatched Haussman's written report to Colquhoun, the British consul-general in Cairo, and despite his own unfair dismissal as consul placed himself at his government's 'disposal for the execution of any mission to the Court of Abyssinia'. These communications reached Cairo on 19 February 1864 and Colquhoun's comments to Russell were terse: 'I cannot authorise Mr Petherick to take any steps... I shall inform Mr Petherick that he need not proceed into Abyssinia.' Indeed in view of communication delays, if Russell wished to order Cameron's rescue Colquhoun believed it would be quicker for him to inform Aden.

Colquhoun was only just recovering from an attack of pleurisy when Petherick's letters reached him. He was preparing to depart on leave when Petherick's further letter to him of 26 March 1864 confirmed Consul Cameron's imprisonment, and he could only advise London that he now had no means of helping. Petherick was on his way down to Cairo (in fact he left the Khartoum area on 5 July 1864 and Berber in August); Barroni had died; and Baker whom Colquhoun would like to have sent was still uncontactable. The Foreign Office had meanwhile on 9 March 1864 instructed Colquhoun to contact the British Resident in Aden in order to request Theodore to release Cameron, his party and the missionaries immediately and to deport them to Massawa on pain of the British government's serious displeasure.

The Government's error of judgement in ignoring Theodore's missive to the Queen was thus, a year later, becoming public knowledge; but Russell, whose responsibility it was, still refused to accept the mistake. As late as 7 May 1864 he told Lord Shaftesbury, the sponsor of a petition to the Queen by the wife of the captive Protestant missionary, the Revd H. A. Stern (which Russell returned unpresented), that 'he (Russell) ought not to advise the Queen to write to the king of Abyssinia'. On 3 June Austen Henry Layard' MP, the foreign under-secretary, conceded in answer to a Commons question that the government had received 'indirect information' of the confinement of Cameron, the missionaries and also of Lejean, who had been released; but that 'the information might be very incorrect' (so much for the instructions to Aden of 9 March). Russell, however, was giving 'serious consideration' to finding a means of communicating with Theodore. This seems to have been the first official public acknowledgement of what had happened to Cameron, though G. A. Henty, later special correspondent of the *Standard* for the Magdala campaign, notes that relatives of Cameron were now publishing a private letter from Cameron in captivity dated by 4 February 1864 affirming that his release was dependent on the arrival of a civil answer to Theodore's letter to the Queen of 31 October 1862. In a dispatch dated 15 June 1864 Colquhoun, who had already left Egypt, was advised by the Foreign Office that the India Office had now instructed Aden that the assistant agent in Aden, Hormuzd Rassam, was to convey a letter to Theodore from the Queen. Rassam, a Chaldean (Nestorian) Christian from the Kurdish mountains north of Mosul, had assisted Layard in 1846 in the excavations of Assyrian Nineveh. The next day, accompanying the text of that letter, would be an admission that there was 'some reason to suppose' that Cameron had been imprisoned because Theodore had received no letter from the Queen.[6]

In April 1868, nearly four years later, the British Abyssinian Field Force liberated the captives. The cost to the British taxpayer was £9m, to be met by an increase in income tax from fourpence to sixpence in the pound. The finalisation, then the delivery, of the Queen's letter to Theodore were attended by a catalogue of delays. The original letter dated 26 May 1864, signed 'your good friend, Victoria R.I.', was first halted for amendment on the initiative of the Cairo consulate-general and then, with permission still being awaited by Rassam in Massawa for its personal delivery to Theodore, a substitute letter was dispatched to him in February 1865. Whereas the first draft had intimated bluntly that because of the distance involved an embassy to Britain was not required, its successor affirmed that if permission had been granted to Cameron and other Europeans to depart, an embassy would be well received in London; it also referred positively to Cameron's authority to represent the Queen's friendship and goodwill. Russell had nevertheless advised the Queen on 5 February 1865: 'Of course it would be useless to employ force, but continued efforts will probably procure the release of the consul.'

2 THE ABORTIVE MISSION OF HORMUZD RASSAM 1864-66

The letter was not to be delivered by Rassam until 28 January 1866. On arrival at Massawa, Rassam on 24 July 1864 had sent his own official letter by messengers to Gondar requesting the Emperor's permission for him to travel there as well as Cameron's release. He told Theodore of the Queen's willingness to receive an embassy whose travel arrangements he would supervise at Massawa. In the absence of a reply from Gondar, Rassam sent two further letters in October and then in March 1865. Rassam's messengers had in fact been told by Theodore to wait at Magdala and only on 7 July 1865 were they all bidden to return to Massawa, carrying Theodore's unsealed invitation to Rassam to come to him via Gallabat as Tigré province was in rebellion.

It was a year of frustration, and not for Rassam only. Cameron, who had been shackled with twenty-five pound chains since January 1864, secretly sent word to Rassam in April 1865 urging him not to risk coming up to Theodore, with or without a safe-conduct, as 'he will cage you as sure as a gun'. That Rassam was beginning to despair of his prospects may have prompted Russell in July to agree the appointment of Gifford Palgrave, an explorer of the Arabian peninsular, to undertake the mission to Theodore in his place, via the Blue Nile, with Rassam returning to Aden in reserve. Colquhoun in Alexandria meanwhile entered into talks with his French opposite number to engineer, through the presence in Khartoum of Garnier, designated French *élève consul*, escape plans for the captives with the help of the Catholic missionaries in Keren, Bogos. The 500 dollars sent to assist the escape were returned by Garnier to Cairo, untransmitted, in November 1865.[7]

Theodore's invitation to Rassam to join him reached the latter at Massawa on 12 August 1865, the messengers saying they had seen Cameron unshackled on the day of their departure. Rassam told Russell that he could not leave before October on account of the rains and malignant fever on the Kassala-Gallabat road, but he would meanwhile personally seek a viceregal *laissez-passer* in Alexandria, at the same time explaining his plans by letter to Theodore. His sea transport to Egypt brought with it news to Massawa of Palgrave's appointment. Rassam would meet him in Cairo on 1 September on his way to see Colonel Edward Stanton, the new consul-general, in Alexandria. Palgrave was still in Egypt for want of steamers presently requisitioned to suppress the Kassala revolt and, despite Stanton's urging to the contrary, Palgrave's mission was suspended by Russell and Rassam's appointment in his mission reconfirmed. Learning in Aden on his return on 29 September that Cameron, in fact still imprisoned, was positively pressing Rassam's meeting with Theodore – 'If he does not come here now having got leave it may cost us our lives' Cameron had written in a note to Hertslet of the Foreign Office on 14 July – Rassam left Massawa on 15 October 1865 with Lieutenant Prideaux, RE, third assistant resident at Aden, and Dr Henry Blanc for Gallabat via Kassala.

They marched bravely to share, in the event, the same fate of imprisonment that Cameron and his companions had endured already for two years. Following their initial meeting on 28 January 1866 Theodore adopted Pavlovian practices, now treating Rassam as a friend and in February 1866 purporting to release all the captives into his control; then rearresting every European except Bardel and two artisans. In June the captives were transferred to Magdala – whither Theodore, with his army much diminished from desertions, retired from Debra Tabor at the end of 1867.

The psychotic and devious Emperor now imposed a fresh condition for their release, the provision of skilled artisans and arsenal equipment. It was conveyed to London by the German missionary Dr Flad, who was personally received by the Queen. The new minority Conservative government conceded the Emperor's demand, but prudently made it a counter-condition that the physical return to Massawa of the captives must be a prerequisite for the delivery of the British gage. There was no repatriation. By April 1867, with Theodore's bad faith exposed, Abyssinia was – as Disraeli was to put it – 'like the classic cave; there were no signs whatever of returning footsteps'. Lord Stanley dispatched an ultimatum on 16 April requiring the release of the captives by 17 August 1867 and put in hand preparations for the Field Force.[8]

3 RESORT TO A FIELD FORCE 1867–68

Colonel William Merewether, the Aden Resident since 1865, had been on leave in London at the time of Dr Flad's mission and, fortified by

Cameron's urging for strong action, had in September 1866 pressed for the use of Indian troops. While the British government waited for the outcome of Flad's authorised offer to Theodore of artisans and a steam engine Merewether, as 1867 broke, prudently sent the zealous Werner Munzinger, now acting British consul in Massawa, on extended reconnaissances of possible routes from the Red Sea coast through the precipitous mountain barriers to Magdala, territory with which he was familiar from his search for the missing explorer Vögel in 1861. Thus, following Theodore's rejection of the British ultimatum on 13 June 1867 and the consequent resort to force by Great Britain, Merewether was able confidently in October to designate Zulla (ancient Adulis), in Annesley Bay to the east of Massawa, as the landing point for the Field Force; and the route through Tigré and Lasta as the axis for the approach to Magdala. The next month he was to take personal charge of the expedition's advance party's landing arrangements at Zulla and to accompany them to the first camp at Senafé up the Kumayli valley. He was indeed the lynch-pin of its launch.[9]

Lieutenant-General Sir Robert Napier landed at Zulla on 2 January 1868, preceded by his second-in-command, Major-General Charles Staveley, who now assumed command at Zulla, and on 25 January the force set out on its 400-mile trek. The scale of the operations now and the logistical problems especially of transportation from India were formidable, such as to evoke comparison with the Falkland Islands war nearly a hundred years later. Thirteen Indian infantry and cavalry regiments, four British battalions, artillery, supported by forty-four elephants, comprised an army of 14,000 men. 9,000 camels and 7,000 mules – the latter acquired by diligent search as far afield as Spain and Syria – and a local rail track for the landing plateau were mustered to transport the baggage, all in the knowledge that the campaigning season would end by June with the onset of the rains. The Egyptian Viceroy (and the Ottoman Sultan) had not only granted passage through Egyptian territory at Massawa but maximum help to the Field Force by way of waiving customs dues, agreeing the construction of a telegraph line to Suakin, hire of camels and availability of steamers. (Merewether was vehemently mistrustful of the consequences of these favours in alienating Abyssinians, especially with regard to military cooperation.) Ismail Pasha's offer of a letter to Theodore urging the release of the captives was accepted, the British for their part pledging that they had no intention of remaining on Abyssinian soil after the objective was achieved. More crucial however was the cooperation of the Abyssinian chiefs – of

Tigré, Ras Kassai (later Emperor John IV); and of Lasta, Ras Wagshoum Gobazé – through whose territories the 450-mile route to Magdala successively passed. Here the work of Merewether, backed by Munzinger and by Major James Grant of Nile exploration fame, bore ample fruit.[10]

Indeed in the previous months the Foreign and India Offices were recipients of advice and offers of participation from many experienced African hands. Sir Henry Bulwer and Sir Samuel Baker canvassed the benefits of Egyptian government help, the latter advocating a supplementary expedition of 1,000 men to Mek Omer Nimr – 'a great chief whom I know well' and personal friend of Theodore, but unfortunately killed two years earlier. Petherick, his offer spurned three years previously, now advocated blockading the entry of salt from the coast to Abyssinia in order to turn the tribes against Theodore (an idea which caught Gladstone's pacific eye). Napier requested the services of Dr Lewis Krapf, the missionary, who like Henry Dufton (to die) joined the Field Force, and of Mansfield Parkyns who declined on the grounds that he had no wish to fight Abyssinians, so many of whom were his friends. His son John by his Abyssinian wife, arrested seeking to leave for England, was to be released on the capture of Magdala.[11]

The resourceful strategy and its execution by the Field Force in its 400-mile march went closely to plan. Napier met Kassai at Adigrat and Gobazié's uncle after crossing the headwaters of the Takkazé river at the end of March. Supplies were forthcoming though minor chiefs in Lasta attacked the supply line. By 5 April the fastness of Magdala was in sight, at ten miles' marching distance across a valley 4,000 feet deep with the precious drinking water of the Bacillo river at the bottom. Theodore's tents on the plateau in front of Magdala could now be discerned, but it was only at 4 p.m. on Good Friday 10 April 1868 that battle was joined. A British brigade of 2,000 men under Staveley, in great heat and thunderstorms, had that day climbed the five-mile steep escarpment above the Bacillo to the Aroge plain at 10,000 feet, there to receive the onslaught of some 5,000 royal troops backed by the pride of Theodore's ill-directed artillery. Napier had been given time to deploy his riflemen and rockets and the carnage was considerable. By dark the Abyssinians had lost nearly 2,000 in casualties, 700 of them dead. Theodore wrote to Napier that evening:

> Believing myself to be a great lord, I gave you battle, but by reason of the worthlessness of my artillery, all my pains were as nought. I had intended, if God had so decreed, to conquer the whole world;

'The Storming of Magdala', *10 April 1868*; *from Hormuzd Rassam,*
Narrative of the British Mission to Theodore, *vol. 2, 1869*

and it was my desire to die if my purpose could not be fulfilled...
You people who have passed the night in joy, may God do unto
you as he has done unto me. I had hoped, after subduing all my
enemies in Abyssinia, to lead my army against Jerusalem.

Theodore sent word of his defeat at Aroge to Rassam inside
Magdala, seeking his intervention for a 'reconciliation'. Napier offered
'honourable treatment' in return for surrender and safe delivery of the
prisoners. Prevaricating in his reply, Theodore the next day sent for the
prisoners from Magdala and allowed Rassam to leave with them to
Napier's camp. Easter Day passed and Theodore retired for the night
to Magdala. When on the Monday, 13 April, the British carried the two
gates to the fortress it was to find Theodore dead by his own hand. He
was buried in the Coptic Church, his young son at the wish of his
mother taken back to England, to be educated at Rugby School; to die
aged nineteen at the Royal Military College, Sandhurst; and to be
commemorated in St George's Chapel, Windsor.

The Magdala church was the only building reprieved from destruction after the main Field Force retired from the bastion on 16 April.
The British Museum Assistant Keeper of Manuscripts accompanying
the Field Force was able to pack in cases most, but not all, of the royal

treasure, including, nefariously, the sacred ikon, the Kwer'ata Re'esu, recovered from the Fung by ransom c. 1670. Theodore's imperial crown, looted by a British soldier, found its way through the hands of the German missionary Dr Rolfs back to the Prussian vice-consul at Suez and so to Count von Bismarck; but the crown of the Abyssinian Coptic *Abouna* to the Victoria and Albert Museum in London.

Time remained at a premium. The 400-mile return journey had to be accomplished before the heavy rains set in. News of the success reached London via Cairo on 27 April. On 30 May 1868 Rassam and all the captives save Consul Cameron, 'too unwell to leave yet', sailed for England, Rassam to stay with Layard. On 10 June Zulla was evacuated by Napier, the victorious commander, to receive a worthy welcome, promotion, the GCB and a peerage. Captain Cameron, his health broken, left Zulla with other casualties in July, retired in December and died in May 1870 in his mid-forties. Merewether, appointed KCSI, returned to India as Commissioner for Sind, to be succeeded at Aden by Major-General Russell. Rassam was rewarded with £5,000, Prideaux and Blanc with £2,000 each. The Viceroy of Egypt, who had the previous year been appointed GCB in recognition of his help in the promotion of the Suez-Alexandria railway transit route, was now to be invested with the GCSI by General Lord Napier of Magdala.[12]

At substantial cost, the shortcomings of diplomacy had been redeemed by a brilliant exercise in armed intervention in a remote inhospitable land. The axiom of British foreign policy, to remain territorially uninvolved in northern Africa, was publicly confirmed, after a brief interlude in which Britain had belatedly demonstrated that it would brook no insult to its overseas representatives and had the power and the will to enforce civilised conventions on the part of those to whom they were accredited. For the Turkish-Egyptian Sudan however the consequences of Theodore's defeat were to be far-reaching.

4
Khedivial Aggrandisement 1868–73: The East

By some historians Ismail Pasha is credited with the development of a firm plan that under his Viceroyalty Egypt should acquire an African empire. M. Rifaat Bey in his book *The Awakening of Modern Egypt* quotes the prophetic advice of the British ambassador in Vienna in November 1839 to Colonel Hodges, the British consul-general in Cairo, four months after the defeat of the Turkish Sultan's forces at Nezib by Ibrahim Pasha: 'If the object of Mohammed Ali be really the establishment of his family, it is only in Africa that that establishment can be solidly fixed. There he will have all Europe friendly to him; there he may receive from it a guarantee which shall exempt him from all fear of attack.'

Ismail held his father Ibrahim in high esteem, his imagination fired by Ibrahim's Near Eastern military conquests. Their thwarting by the European powers was a lesson which Ismail did not forget. Yet there is little evidence that Ismail's expansionist African initiative had been years in preparation, even if perhaps it had its seeds in the imperial ambitions of Ahmed Pasha Widan, Sudan Governor-General 1838–43.

The rise in the price of cotton during the American Civil War created an economic boom in Egypt that prompted Ismail to embark upon an unprecedented programme of infrastructural development in the early 1860s, the two mega-schemes being the excavation of the Suez Canal and the enlargement of the port of Alexandria. Any immediate plans for African expansion which he might have privately entertained were rendered unviable by the unsettled conditions in the Sudan in 1865–6 and by the continued threat of aggression from the Emperor Theodore. In 1865–6 Ismail did reacquire from the Ottoman Sultan the leases of Suakin and Massawa (see pp. 22–3) previously held by his grandfather, but in the short run this was aimed at controlling lucrative customs charges and removing a convenient haven for tax refugees from Taka, rather than enabling a serious claim to be staked to the Red Sea littoral. However an interesting bargain had been struck in the negotiations whereby, in return for British support of the Viceroy's case with the Porte, Ismail undertook to assist in the abolition of the Red Sea slave trade. The occupation of Massawa in turn prompted the surreptitious reoccupation in January 1867 of Kufit (Agordat) as an Egyptian military station in Barea country between Kassala and Keren, offering local protection to Sudan caravans from raiding by Abyssinian tribes but, if Munzinger is to believed, of limited benefit to the inhabitants. These were but rectifications, in the local context, of Sudan administration. The threat of invasion by Theodore still demanded a low and cautious profile.[1]

It is equally mistaken to identify the appointment of Sir Samuel Baker early in 1869 to lead an expedition south of Gondokoro into the Equatorial lacustrine lands as the first milestone in Khedivial imperial strategy. In so far that such a strategy had been formulated by the end of 1868, it was directed initially to the western Abyssinian march-lands of Tigré-Bogos (Sennaheit), and only possibly Hamasein – and, more urgently, to the southern Red Sea littoral. The quite unpredicted decision of the British government in April 1867 to deliver the ultimatum to Theodore had suddenly presaged the creation of a power vacuum in eastern Africa, which was already scheduled in any case to become a region of enhanced interest to the trading nations of Europe following the opening in 1869 of the Suez Canal and the shortening of the route to the Indies. Preparation of the Magdala Expedition in 1867, accompanied by a British disclaimer of territorial ambition regarded as suspect by the Khedive, was the event which triggered Ismail's positive embarkation on a policy of empire.

If these Khedivial plans, to be gradually activated over some years in the mainland and littoral theatres of Abyssinia (today's Eritrea and Somalia), constituted a proactive strategy of external expansion, the military expeditions led by Baker to the lacustrine kingdoms in 1871–3; by Mohammed el Hilali to the Bahr el Ghazal in 1870–2; and, indeed, of Zubeir Rahma Mansour and of Ismail Ayub to Darfur in 1874 were, by contrast, in part triggered by events within the Sudan. All these military actions were, however, to coincide with a gathering financial crisis in Egypt and so cut short the achievement of Ja'afar Mazhar in consolidating and unifying an economically viable Sudan.

Empress Eugénie's dhahabiya *used for the Suez Canal opening, 1869*

I   THE RED SEA LITTORAL AND THE GULF OF ADEN

Shortly after the Governor-General, Ja'afar Mazhar, returned to Cairo in August 1867 following his successful planting of the Egyptian-Turkish flag at intervals along the African littoral of the Red Sea to the Bab el Mandeb as far as Roheita, he was to learn that his territorial responsibilities as Governor-General (*hakimdar*) were to be seemingly eroded. On 20 October 1867 Ismail appointed Fariq (major-general) Abdel Qadir Pasha, recently returned with the Egyptian troops withdrawn from Crete, as general-governor (*mudir 'umum*) of the Red Sea littoral, with the control of the governorates of Massawa and Suakin, of the Red Sea fleet and of the Second (Sudanese) Regiment of infantry designated for the Sudan under Lewa Adham Pasha el Arifi; and with responsibility to liaise with the British Magdala Field Force. Abdel Qadir and the four battalions of the Second Regiment reached Massawa on 5 November.

Behind the deployment lay the Viceroy's intention to consolidate his claims to the Red Sea littoral staked by Ja'afar Pasha; and his suspicion – notwithstanding British assurances that, once the Magdala prisoners were released, Britain would quit Abyssinia –that in fact Zulla or some other port would be retained. Accordingly small detachments of troops were to be posted at the littoral landing places visited by Ja'afar. In the event only the harbour Edd, which had been visited briefly in May 1866 by the Egyptian governor of Massawa, was garrisoned since, although Ja'afar in January 1868 was himself ordering mini-garrisons to Amphila and Tadjoura, in the confusion of responsibility between the two *pashas* neither place was actually occupied. The arrival of four extra battalions at Massawa however, ostensibly to defend it against Theodore, had really discountenanced the British, despite the fact that two of the battalions were supposedly destined to relieve the Khartoum garrison, and a British démarche to the Viceroy led to the Massawa force being scaled back to one battalion, backed by a second at Suakin to be reinforced by seven companies of the First Sudanese Regiment. Courtesies were exchanged between the British commander and the Egyptian governors, but mutual suspicions remained. Egyptian interference in Zulla was firmly discouraged, but it was recognised by Britain to be Egyptian territory, and an Egyptian official party was indeed stationed at Zulla ostensibly to help – in reality to observe and report. Relations between local commanders reached their nadir when rumours implicating the governor of Massawa, Hasan Bey Rifaat, in an unsuccessful attempt to stir up Tigréan hostility against the Field Force, led Napier to demand of Abdel Qadir Pasha the *bey*'s recall. The latter was replaced by Mohammed Rasikh Bey, ignominiously removed from Khartoum by Musa Pasha in 1862.

Unequivocally the British did hold to their promise to evacuate their Force after the Magdala campaign in June 1868. The admittedly limited facilities including the local railway which had been introduced to Zulla were, moreover, presented to Abdel Qadir with the invitation to buy surplus military equipment, supplies and baggage animals. However despite the Viceroy's encouragement, the latter proposal and the suggestion that Zulla might supersede Massawa were rejected by the general-governor who regarded Zulla as an altogether inferior port. As a further British goodwill gesture, a pair of navigation lanterns were presented to the 'Governor of the Shores of the Red Sea'. If the first, this was not to be the only tacit recognition by Britain of Egyptian authority over the African coast as far as the Bab el Mandeb. No British objection was voiced when two years later, in response to the rumoured claims of French and Italian adventurers, Sharif Pasha the Egyptian foreign

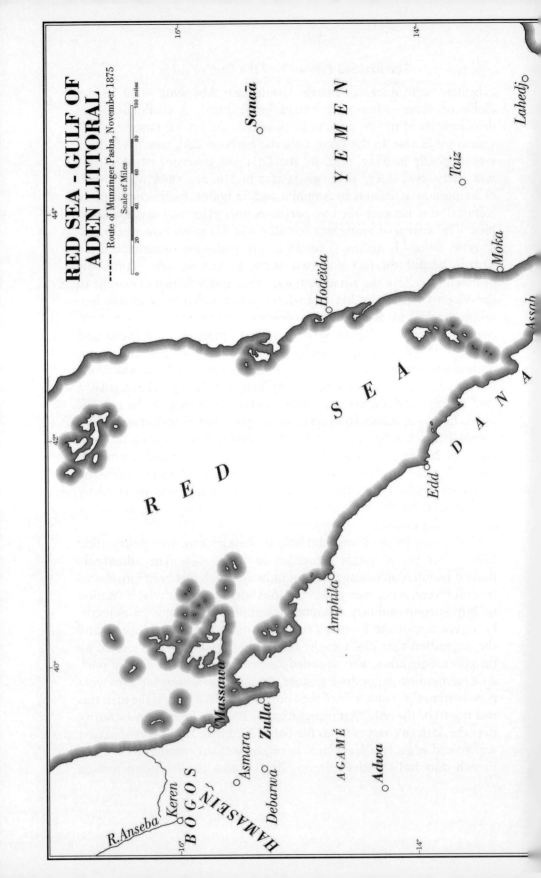

RED SEA – GULF OF
ADEN LITTORAL

--- Route of Munzinger Pasha, November 1875

Scale of Miles

0   20   40   60   80   100 miles

Sanaā

YEMEN

Taiz

Lahedj

Hodeïda

Moka

Assab

RED   SEA

DAN A

Edd

Amphila

Massaua

Zulla

AGAMÉ

Asmara

Debarwa

Adwa

HAMASEIN

BOGOS

Keren

R. Anseba

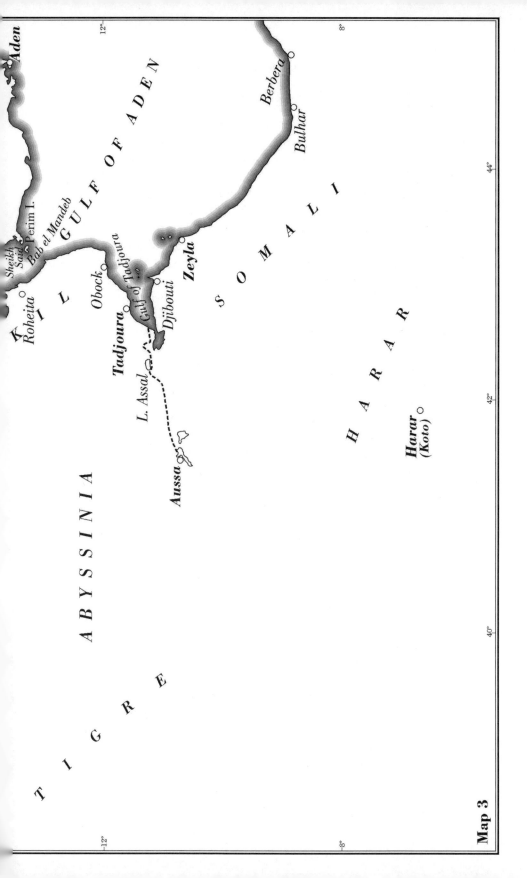

Map 3

minister asserted this coast to be Egyptian territory, even if ungar-
risoned. It included the coast of the future Eritrea.

To put the matter beyond a peradventure, the British government
warned their Swiss-born agent, J. A. Werner Munzinger, in December
1868 that the Massawa British consulate was being suppressed. No
foreseeable level of future trade could compensate Britain for her recent
military expenditure of £9m on the Magdala campaign.[2]

The British decision to close the Massawa consulate was perhaps
more short-sighted than that regarding the Khartoum consulate in
1863, and again in June 1868 when Gifford Palgrave urged the
latter's re-creation, having regard to the events of the past decade.
Admittedly with the return of the Governor-General of the Sudan to
Khartoum in May 1868, Abdel Qadir Pasha appears to have relinquished his general-governorate of the Red Sea littoral, yet within
two years not only was it revived as a separate 'Eastern Sudan' but
the territorial responsibility of the new independent general-governor,
Lewa Ahmed Mumtaz Pasha, based at Massawa, was explicitly
defined to include the Somali port of Berbera, well beyond the Bab
el Mandeb in the Gulf of Aden. British interests in these increasingly
important international waters were protected from Aden, occupied
in 1839. Yet while the northern (Arabian) coastline including the
Yemen was acknowledged Ottoman domain, on the African counterpart only Suakin and Massawa (until 1865) in the Red Sea and
Tadjoura and Zeyla in the Gulf of Aden, by virtue of their allegiance
to the Imam of Sana'a in the Yemen, were internationally recognised
as coming within Ottoman suzerainty. On the shortened route to
India via the Canal, bunkering stations were becoming attractive.
Tadjoura marked the approximate eastern boundary of the Danakil
people of Abyssinia whose coastal lands stretched west to Edd, and
who had already sold the haven of Obock (Djibouti) in the Gulf of
Tadjoura to the French in May 1862 though it still remained
unoccupied. Zeyla was the western limit of the Somali people whose
principal port was Berbera.[3]

To this extended southern littoral, with the exception of Tadjoura
and Zeyla, the Khedive was by 1869 informally laying advance claim to
authority, albeit under the Ottoman flag. To the alarm of Major-
General Russell, now political resident in Aden, the Turkish governor
of Zeyla, in the wake of a visit to Berbera of an Egyptian steamer in
early 1869, sought to transfer his loyalty to Ismail. Fear mounted that
Berbera and Bulhar, both deemed important trading partners with

Aden, would be purchased by Egypt. In January 1870 the Egyptian warship *Khartoum* under Commodore Mohammed Gamali Bey put into Berbera, to be confronted by the British vessel *Sind* and warship *Teazer* on 31 March. The outcome was the abandonment by Cairo of any plan presently to purchase the two ports but, increasingly confident of the support of the Moslem Somalis, Ismail now decided on 25 May 1870 to re-establish the governorate of the Red Sea littoral, as part of the general-governorate of Eastern Sudan, under the current governor of Suakin, Ahmed Mumtaz. However, whether or not the Khedivial flag was left flying over Berbera, when Gamali Bey sailed home to Massawa no garrison was left behind.

For some years to come the British were not minded to confront Egyptian claims. The government of India, under which Aden and Berbera fell, instructed General Russell to avoid exchanges with the Egyptians and vetoed his proposal, perhaps on cost grounds, that Munzinger should be appointed a British consul for the coast. In May 1871, on the rebound, Munzinger was to accept Ismail's appointment as governor of Massawa.

The Sudan *hakimdar* Ja'afar Pasha had himself proposed such an administrative restructuring of the eastern Sudan in a memorandum to the Viceroy of 16 August 1869. He continued to take a keen interest in the affairs of the African littoral, advocating on the very eve of the appointment of the general-governor the purchase of Obock from the French, reminding Cairo that half a century earlier Mohammed Ali's conquest of the Hejaz and of the Yemen had brought a temporary redirection of loyalty by the governors of Tadjoura and Zeyla; and urging prior annexation in order to pre-empt European claims to the coast. When on grounds of work overload Ja'afar had proposed in August 1869 the detachment of a general-governorate, now to include Taka, the Barea country and Barka, from the Khartoum *hakimdaria*, he was influenced by at least four particular considerations.

First, while Ja'afar had already accepted – one suspects with real misgivings – the reinstatement of an annual Sudan revenue contribution to the Egyptian Treasury, further military activity in the eastern Sudan was a cost from which he wished his *hakimdaria* to be spared. Secondly, he had his own hands full with a military expedition to Bahr el Ghazal, nominally to protect it from Fur incursions from the west. Thirdly, he was extremely vexed with the appointment of Sir Samuel Baker as independent general-governor of Equatoria south of Gondokoro, and the duty imposed on Ja'afar in that context. And fourthly, ordered to the Sudan, to coordinate the preparation of Baker's expedition, was now Fariq Khusraw Pasha, armed with powers to remove obstructive provincial governors: who better to become ruler of the eastern general-governorate and perhaps also to relieve Ja'afar of the awkward relationship with Baker? Whether or not Ismail discussed Ja'afar's suggestion with Khusraw, to Ja'afar's regret in April 1870 it would be Ahmed Mumtaz whom the Khedive appointed to the new general-governorate, leaving Baker independent of the control of both Ja'afar and Mumtaz.

Commodore Gamali Bey, accompanied on his naval mission by the *muhafiz* of Massawa, Mohammed Rasikh Bey, had learned when at Zeyla that an Italian shipping company had in November 1869 purchased the port Assab and its hinterland to the west of Roheita. Ja'afar Pasha, advised of this by Rasikh Bey, promptly reported to Cairo and the Italian initiative was neutralised for the while by a diplomatic démarche.

It was an indication to Ahmed Mumtaz of the problems that lay ahead. To hold the Egyptian position on the Danakil sector of the littoral, he had at once increased the remuneration of the chiefs but tribal dissensions compelled him in February 1871, with Mohammed Rasikh Bey and the Sheikh of the Danakil, to beat the maritime bounds of his province as far as Berbera, raising the flag and installing a small garrison at Bulhar, forty miles west of Berbera. In this and with his assurances of help from Massawa, Mumtaz was able to be more self-confident than Gamali Bey a year earlier, for in the interim Khedive Ismail had robustly asserted his sovereignty claims to the British government without direct contradiction, while defeat in the Franco-Prussian War had silenced French, or indeed Italian, protests. Ismail however had warned Mumtaz against tarrying at any Somali port and, secondly (in August 1871), would specifically decree that intervention over Berbera would be sanctioned only in the case of a direct threat. Turkey still controlled Zeyla and Tadjoura, if not for very much longer.[4]

An important new epoch in the affairs of the littoral commences with the appointment in April 1871, following Mumtaz Pasha's return, of the former British and French consular agent Werner Munzinger as *muhafiz* of Massawa. He knew the region exceptionally well. Unfortunately he was to become estranged from the new Abyssinian Emperor John IV. For the first eighteen months Munzinger was to be fully occupied with Bogos and the march-lands of Abyssinia, but in April 1872 he was additionally made responsible for Suakin. Having imposed tribute collection on the Danakil, on 31 October he reiterated Ja'afar's advice of 1869 to the Khedive to pre-empt the acquisitive ambitions of the European Powers and to occupy Roheita, Berbera and Bulhar forthwith as well as the Amphila salt flats. The new Khedivial chief of staff, the former American Civil War general Fariq Charles Stone, set about drawing up plans for the seizure of Berbera; and for the creation of a provincial sub-capital at Roheita with the Gulf of Zeyla between.

Munzinger was summoned to Cairo for discussions in December 1872, following which however Ismail halted the Berbera preparations. He was about to negotiate what was to become the vital firman of 9 June 1873, transferring the hereditary succession of the Egyptian viceroyalty to Ismail's own issue, along with the ports of Suakin and Massawa 'with their dependencies'. This prize, made the more attainable by the death of Ismail's enemy, Grand Vizir Aali Pasha, predicated at this sensitive time the avoidance of hasty territorial initiatives in Africa; and Munzinger, in February 1873 made *pasha* and general-governor of Eastern Sudan and of the Red Sea Littoral, returned to Massawa to await further orders. This time was usefully employed activating a Massawa-Kassala telegraph line project; sailing in March, with the son of the governor of Zeyla, to Roheita; and organising a reconnaissance of the trade route between Assab and Aussa in the interior, the route to Galla country. Shrewdly he instigated an appeal for Egyptian intervention from two Somali chiefs for transmission to Ismail.

The firman meanwhile was signed. The celebrations in Constantinople were extended, but a month before his return to Alexandria on 14 August 1873 after an absence of nearly three months, the Khedive had ordered the dispatch to Berbera of Mohammed Radwan Bey in a corvette, to inform the Somali *sheikhs* that a special commander with military escort was on its way. A fortnight later HMS *Dalhousie* calling at Berbera found the corvette at anchor and a contingent of fifty troops ashore – its commander offering the British captain his government's assistance. A visit in November by an Aden assistant political resident reconfirmed the Egyptian *fait accompli* and the expected arrival of a governor and garrison. The British official simply expressed regret at the consequent reduction in trade with Aden. Munzinger Pasha himself arrived with two infantry companies at the end of December 1873 to establish a local Somali sheikh as stipendiary titular governor of Berbera, with some thirty *bashi-buzouqs* collected from Aden to support him. The Egyptian corvette was to remain patrolling the area until the rains, its commander and officers active in encouraging trade with Harar in the interior, keeping the peace between the tribes and harmony with Bulhar. Munzinger then withdrew his troops to Massawa and reported to Cairo, recommending the absorption of Zeyla and Tadjoura and the eventual occupation of Harar and of Aussa – advice which would be pursued. There remained the question of Obock. No satisfactory exchange of territory could be agreed with the Khedive and it remained French until its independence in 1977.

Thus at the end of 1873 the Egyptian occupation of the southern littoral of the Gulf of Aden (with the exception of French Obock and the Turkish (Yemeni) ports of Zeyla and Tadjoura) at least as far as Berbera was not challenged by Britain but, equally, not formally recognised. The potential challenge of France and Italy to the trade route had yet to be assessed. The administrative responsibility for the littoral now rested with Munzinger, recognised as enlightened – in the words of Hussey Vivian, the acting British consul-general in Cairo: 'a simple earnest, honest and at the same time amiable man whose statements may be thoroughly trusted' – and one who believed Massawa slave exports to be nearly at an end.[5]

2   ABYSSINIA

On their withdrawal from Abyssinia in June 1868 the British had left no *negusa nagast*, no Emperor – only a set of warring provincial chiefs, but it would be mistaken to attribute to the British removal of Theodore the primary cause of this reversion to quasi-anarchy. Scarcely three years previously Tigré had been deemed unsafe for Rassam's journey to Theodore from the coast, while the revolt in Shoa to the south had left the Emperor in control solely of the central region and of Gondar – which he sacked following its seizure by the rebels at the end of 1866.

Leaving aside the Moslem eastern regions of Danakil and Harar, there were now three contestants for the throne of the dead *negus*: Dedjaz Kassai Mercha Abba Bazbaz (Abba Bazbaz was the name of his favourite horse) of Tigré, resident at Adowa (Adwa), a descendant of the Ras Michael Suhul of Bruce's acquaintance, who had signally benefited in arms acquisition from his cooperation with Napier (receiving six mortars, six howitzers and 850 rifles); Wagshoum Gobazé of Lasta, direct descendant of a former line of emperors who, while Napier was at Magdala, had been busy conquering Begemder and Gojjam to consolidate his hold on Amhara in the centre; and Menilek who had himself escaped from Magdala in 1865 and since repossessed as *negus* his kingdom of Shoa (Shawa) to the south, with the help of a Galla queen whose son Theodore had had horribly murdered. Both Menilek and Gobazé were troubled by powerful Galla Moslem minorities. All three coveted the throne. While Wagshoum Gobazé, the strongest, was to act first, having himself proclaimed 'king of kings' in 1868 under the name Hadse Tecla Giyorgis at Amba Tsara, unanointed he drew no recognition from his rivals, nor indeed from Theodore's former retinue.

What opportunity in 1868 did this offer to Khedive Ismail Pasha? He was effectively in undisputed control of the ports and of the arid coastal lowlands as far as the Bab el Mandeb while Dedjaz Kassai Mercha, faced with famine and incipient cholera in his Tigré domain, was presently no threat to Egypt despite the British injection of arms. Yet Kassai was determined to maintain the Coptic Christian independence of his region and he now acted to replace his subordinate, Dedjaz Hailou of Hamasein, who had approached Fariq Abdel Qadir Pasha at Massawa for Egyptian protection on the latter's arrival in November 1867. Kufit and the Barea country had already been reoccupied by Egypt early in 1867, yet between the Barea and Massawa lay Bogos (Sennaheit) which, in Ja'afar Mazhar's view as he returned in August from his Red Sea reconnaissance, had been ripe for annexation. With the arrival of a British Field Force then imminent, the Viceroy wisely had not acted. Now however a year later the British had gone while Kassai was threatened by the larger but less well disciplined army of Tecla Giyorgis (Gobazé). Ismail Pasha could then have moved on Bogos in late 1868, but cautiously he again did not, and neither did he yet instigate the occupation of Gallabat, the key to access from the Sudan to Amhara avoiding Tigré. He was very aware of the prior need at least for French acceptance, granted the latter's concern for the Catholic missions in Bogos. In the event the annexations would be delayed a further four years.

Kassai pursued three objectives: to contrive the installation in Tigré of a new friendly Coptic archbishop, *Abouna,* essential to a valid coronation, to achieve which he was willing to withhold protection from the Catholics in Hamasein; to secure Egyptian military support when Gobazé's anticipated attack materialised; and to seek at least long-term political backing for his ambitions from the British Queen and the French Emperor. In June 1869 the murder of two British missionaries (the Powell brother and sister) and of two Swedes in

Bogos adventitiously put Kassai in renewed contact with Cairo and Europe, and once again the imminence of a strike by Gobazé at the end of the rains prompted him to send a secret request to Ismail Pasha via the governor of Massawa for military reinforcement. The Viceroy confided to Colonel Stanton in Cairo that he was minded to respond if Kassai would open the frontier to travellers and merchandise – the Kufit–Massawa land link through Bogos. Once again however Gobazé's attack was postponed, while the French got wind of Ismail's plans towards Bogos and in October 1869 warned him off intervention. Ismail had nevertheless been consolidating his position in Kufit which commanded the caravan departure routes from Taka both to Massawa and to Adiabo in Tigré, and he continued to await his opportunity towards Bogos.

As for Kassai, not only had an acceptable new *Abouna*, nominated by the Coptic Patriarch Amba Dimitrios in Alexandria, now arrived in Abyssinia who publicly condemned the Catholic missions; but Kassai had secured the services of 'Lieutenant-Colonel' John Kirkham, an instructor in Gordon's ever-victorious army in China and veteran of the Magdala campaign, to train his Tigréan army in their newly acquired weapons. Having safeguarded his flank by dismissing his Abyssinian lieutenant, the recently appointed and ambitious Welde-Mikael Selomon, in Hamasein and Bogos in 1870 for secretly intriguing with the French and the Egyptians, a much-strengthened Kassai could await the inevitable invasion by Gobazé with greater assurance.[6]

Munzinger, still French consular agent at Massawa but no longer accredited to Britain, did his best in March 1870 at a personal meeting to temper Kassai's harshness towards the Catholic missions. Munzinger was recovering from an attempt on his life six months earlier by a Coptic priest and now in late 1870 required surgery in Aden, where he was made a Companion of the Bath for his former consular services to Britain. Returning to Massawa in early 1871 he found the attitude of Kassai, who distrusted him, further hardened against the Catholics and their protectors. Over the next months, until he was appointed to Egyptian government service as *muhafiz* of Massawa by Mumtaz Pasha the general-governor in May 1871, the relations between the two deteriorated into overt hostility, with Munzinger – despite the French defeat in 1870 at the hands of the Prussians at Sedan – spuriously threatening Kassai with a French invasion of Tigré. Kassai, vexed indeed, was all the while watching his southern border.

At last, following the onset of the rains, Gobazé crossed the head-waters of the Tacazzé river in the first week of June 1871 with a strong army and moved on the Tigréan capital of Adwa, where Kassai's troops halted him in a major battle on 21 June. Gobazé's strong cavalry squadrons suffered heavily under the fire of Kassai's guns, 250 horses and 200 soldiers being captured and 1,000 casualties suffered. The more decisive victory fell to Kassai's forces and artillery on 11 July. Gobazé leading the charge had his horse shot from under him, being himself wounded and captured, along with 24,000 men. In Gobazé's camp was found a letter from the Superior of the Catholic Abyssinian mission urging Gobazé to make war on Kassai and promising his support. Their churches on the eastern borders of Hamasein were now burned, the villages pillaged in revenge – a traditional Abyssinian visi-tation of wrath. The Catholic Superior appealed to the Khedive for protection in vain, and by December 1871 Hamasein had been rese-cured by Kassai. On 20 January 1872 Kassai was crowned Emperor John IV of Abyssinia by the *Abouna* in Axum cathedral.[7]

Ismail Pasha had hesitated so long in implementing his plan to seize Keren and Bogos that his adversary had now become nominal ruler of Abyssinia. John however did not yet feel strong enough to move to Gondar to receive the submission of other tribal leaders. Menilek in Shoa remained uncurbed and it was not to be long before his vassal in Amhara, Ras Woronya, was corresponding direct with Ismail. Ismail for his part was encouraged by British inaction on the Red Sea littoral and, being conscious of France's weakness, now felt not only that the time was propitious but that he had in Munzinger a reliable and committed commander to annexe Bogos. A gratuitous *casus belli* was moreover offered by Abyssinian tribal raids on Basen (Kunama) and the Beni Amer in early 1872. Accordingly the Khedive decided to act. Having issued John with an ultimatum in April, he instructed Munzinger to occupy Bogos and to fortify the 600-metre bastion of Keren – but, despite the ultimatum threat, not to invade Hamasein, at least until John's reaction could be gauged. Keren was seized by Munzinger in June while John was returning from a punitive expedi-tion against the Galla.

John's reaction had to be muted. Internally vulnerable, he could not yet afford to commit troops against well-armed Egyptian forces to the north. Fortunately for him, however, the arrival of a British warship bringing letters and presents from Queen Victoria and Lord Granville offered a credible diplomatic channel of response. Colonel Kirkham was in August 1872 dispatched to Europe via Alexandria carrying letters from John complaining against the Egyptian annexation of Bogos and against the Khedive's plans to occupy successively Hamasein up to the Mareb river, the slave market of Gallabat, and the Danakil salt flats near Amphila. John requested protection against such aggression and against Egyptian slaving in Abyssinia, and moral support for his own annexation of Amphila, and the littoral salt plains. In reply to British and French démarches, Ismail forcefully rebutted John's accusations, and in November 1872 ordered Mumtaz Pasha's successor as general-governor in Khartoum, Ismail Pasha Ayub, to instruct the Sudan *seraskir* Adham Pasha el Arifi to occupy Gallabat (it was effected in March 1873) on the grounds that the presently quasi-independent Sheikh Mohammed Jum'a was withholding tribute. He affirmed to the British and French governments that Egypt, not Abyssinia, was the sole opponent of the Red Sea slave trade; that Bogos was historically Turkish territory; and that Hamasein had been threatened by Egypt in order to exact compensation for the Abyssinian raids.

Ismail proceeded to draft an aggressively arrogant second ultimatum to John, to the effect that Bogos had been Egyptian since the time of Governor-General Ahmed Widan (uncorroborated), and Basen and Barea since the Turkish conquest of 1821, but he denied any claim to a Mareb river frontier. Egyptian claims to the Red Sea littoral had been recognised by Great Britain in 1867 and any attempt to occupy any point of it by Abyssinia would be met by an invasion. Meanwhile if captives of the recent Abyssinian raids were not released with an indemnity, Hamasein would be occupied. It was language steeped in hubris. Nemesis would follow three years later.[8]

In December 1872 Colonel Stanton in company with Sir Bartle Frere, a former British governor of Bombay en route to Zanzibar to discuss the east African slave trade, had called on the Khedive for what Stanton rated the most remarkable conversation that he had ever had. Against the background of the exchanges with John IV, Ismail, distancing himself from the expansion plans in the direction of Syria and Arabia cherished by his father Ibrahim and cousin Abbas, declared his ambition to extend his African empire in the interests of civilisation; refuted the charge of seeking to invade Abyssinia; and insisted that his authority in abolishing the slave trade in the Sudan would be undermined if Britain sided with Abyssinia against him. This declamation, which was to be further elaborated in a conversation with the French ambassador in Constantinople following the signing of the firman of 9 June 1873, constitutes the first recorded disclosure of Ismail's ambitions.

Meanwhile the British government's reaction to Kirkham's mission on behalf of the Emperor, when Kirkham reached London in October 1872, had been initially evasive, affirming a historic interest in Christian welfare and suggesting frontier arbitration. Stanton in Cairo remained sympathetic to the Egyptian claim to the whole Red Sea littoral, quoting in aid Plowden's dispatches of eighteen years previously and suggesting duty free passage through Massawa for Abyssinian merchandise. He omitted to probe the Egyptian claim to have ruled Bogos since 1842. Kirkham was not to be put off, delivering separate letters to the French, German and Austrian ambassadors in London and preparing to address the British public on the slave trade via the press. A letter of support from his former commander, General Lord Napier of Magdala, persuaded Granville, with French backing, to censure Egyptian expansionist aims and to urge a third-party conciliator between Ismail and John.

The next six months constituted a stalemate between the two adversaries. Britain was holding back an Egyptian invasion by diplomatic pressure in Cairo and Constantinople but, on account of other Western Power attitudes, could not secure Ottoman intervention against Ismail. John organised major raids on Kufit and Basen. The occupation ordered in November 1872 of Gallabat by the Egyptians was consolidated by May 1873 by Lewa Adham Pasha but, not least in the absence of the Sultan's sanction, Hamasein was not attacked. John at least was gaining precious time and securing his rear to the north while he marched on Gondar to reduce Amhara (without a shot fired) and, later, on Gojjam. Thus by March 1873 only the threat of Menilek in Shoa, once again in strife with the Galla, was undefeated. John had acted in good time, for on the morrow of wresting the firman of 9 June 1873 from the Sultan, Ismail at last felt free to consolidate his hold on the littoral and, so the French ambassador in Constantinople shrewdly deduced, to isolate Abyssinia from the sea and from the Nile and force her into vassalage.[9]

Nubar Pasha however was not to conceal his scorn of the Khedive's Abyssinian aspirations, as voiced to him in May 1873:

He [the Khedive] spoke to me vaguely of Abyssinia, the resources and wealth of this country and I concluded that his gaze was fixed on these regions. I could not but recall my friend's comment: 'You

Egyptians have no brains in your heads; just pulp.' Abyssinia – a wealthy country? Rich in what? In poverty, divided up between turbulent and brutal people to whom freedom and independence are alien. Who had given him this idea? Doubtless Munzinger Bey... whom without doubt he had, with an eye on the future conquest, nominated Governor Massawa.

By now the attitude of the Gladstone government was becoming increasingly ambivalent. Following news of Munzinger's Red Sea expedition of March 1873 and the seizure of Gallabat by May, John had again sought from Earl Granville British arbitration of the frontiers, reaffirming his determination to abolish slavery and the slave trade. To Hussey Vivian, the acting British consul-general in Egypt, on 22 August the Khedive flatly denied any intention to invade Abyssinia and offered to examine John's claims to the coast. This was sufficient, coupled now with a conciliatory response to John's letter of a year previously, to persuade the British government that they should refuse to mediate on the frontier questions. Effectively in October 1873 they were withdrawing their support for John's complaints. Notwithstanding an unfortunate interference by Munzinger with the diplomatic baggage of the French vice-consul at Massawa who was en route to John with gifts from his government, leading to an abject public apology from the Viceroy, the French government were similarly opposed to intervention. Nevertheless when the French President's letter finally did reach him in April 1874, John felt secure enough to threaten his own war on Egyptian occupied territories, having already launched cattle raids on the Khor el Baraka west of Hamasein and on Gallabat in the New Year.

Currently preoccupied with the uncertain absorption of Darfur and aware that he was being watched closely by the European Powers, the Khedive reined back his ambitions towards Hamasein for an indefinite period, maintaining the frontier regions on a war footing but inhibited from yet making a preemptive strike against Abyssinia.[10]

5
Khedivial Aggrandisement 1868–73: The South

I THE SHILLUK CORRIDOR AND THE SLAVE TRADE

Any imperial expansion southwards up the White Nile was strategically conditional not only on the removal of the threat of Abyssinian invasion, but on the security of the White Nile corridor at least as far as the swamps south of Lake No. Ja'afar Mazhar's first principal action after his installation as Governor-General in March 1866 had been to intervene to protect the Shilluk who occupied all this section of the west bank and some of the east bank, especially in the area of the Sobat mouth.

Unfortunately the Governor-General's tough response to the connivance of the then White Nile governor in the Arab *razzias*, and his replacement by the latter's relatively enlightened deputy, Qa'immaqam Ali Bey Rida el Kurdi (see pp. 48–9), had been misinterpreted by the Shilluk *reth* Kwatker Akwot, who came from Ogod in the southern Shilluk province of Luak, opposite modern Malakal. Not only did Kwatker presume to attack five boats of Khartoum traders returning down the Nile from the Bahr el Ghazal with their ivory acquisitions at the end of the 1866–7 dry season, slaughtering their crews, seizing their cargoes and arms and burning their boats (the Coptic trader Ghattas also lost his season's purchases and eighty men). More recklessly, when the new governor sent an officer to investigate the facts, Kwatker received the latter with insolence and had him and two of his escort ambushed and killed on their way back to headquarters.

Mistaking Ali Rida's measured response to his attack on the traders for weakness, Kwatker then raised the southern Shilluk to march on the governor at Lul, whence the *reth* was only repulsed after a major battle involving 1,000 Shilluk casualties. He was pursued to Ogod which was then sacked. To effect his escape Kwatker's relatives buried him ostentatiously in a marked grave, which persuaded the governor he was dead, but Kwatker survived long enough to be disinterred and to flee to the Nuba mountains. He was to come back from the dead, or so it seemed, to seek a pardon from Sir Samuel Baker when the latter was halted by the rains at Sobat mouth in 1870. The Shilluk of Gerr, their northern province, having had serious reservations about Kwatker's rash initiatives, were meanwhile content to acquiesce in the government's installation, as *reth* in his place, of Kwatker's first cousin, the *nyireth* Ajiyang Nyidhok from Fashoda.

From his refuge in the Nuba mountains Kwatker in early 1868 launched an attack on his successor, armed with eighty rifles acquired principally from government deserters. His initial success against Ajiyang, who lost thirty-three killed, was quickly reversed by the governor's regular troops despite government casualties of one officer and twenty-seven men. Kwatker's forces were routed with heavy casualties.[1]

This was the situation to which Ja'afar Pasha returned from Cairo in May 1868, well pleased with the success in his absence of his White Nile governor who was promoted from *qa'immaqam* to *miralai*. A brave soldier, Ali Rida had also earned the respect of the Shilluk, if Schweinfurth's report is to be accepted on his passage to the Bahr el Ghazal in early 1868: 'Ali Rida's lengthy posting with the Shilluk had made him familiar with their customs and practices. He spoke their language fluently, did not socialise excessively with his Turkish officials and this allowed him to develop closer relations with the Shilluk, who constantly brought even their private differences to him for resolution.' However the governor's long-term conciliatory approach to the people earned him the hostility of the local traders, who did not share his sympathy with the Nilotics.

Ali Rida still remained stationed at Lul, as had his predecessor, with 500 troops against 200 garrisoned to the north at Deinab (Fashoda) under his deputy, by whom Schweinfurth had just previously been courteously received.

> The erection of anything like a town had only begun within the last two years [1866–7]. The place was formerly called Deinab, and now consisted of merely a large mass of conical huts of straw, besides the remarkable structure which constituted a fort. The long boundary walls of the fort with their hundreds of waterspouts looked at a distance as though they were mounted with so many cannon, and presented a formidable appearance. In reality the number of cannon which the fort could boast was only four, the rest of the field ordinance being in the camp of the *mudir* [at Lul]...

On account of the shallowness of the water on the side on which the town is built, the boat was moored close by a narrow island which was connected by a kind of jetty composed of faggots. This at the time of high water serves as a mole for any boats that may arrive, which are then able to lie close alongside the doors. Before the walls of the town, on a terrace left dry by the sunken flood, extend fields and vegetable gardens which the governor, following the Egyptian fashion, has caused to be planted.

While the White Nile west bank was peaceful and in the firm control of the government to a point well south of Lul, from Ogod to the Shilluk-Nuer boundary west of Tonga it remained under threat from Kwatker's forces. Ali Rida's sorties proved unsuccessful in bringing him to battle. Thus while river traffic to Gondokoro and the Bahr el Ghazal was ostensibly under the supervision and control of Deinab, the insecurity of the extreme southern part of the territory compelled Ja'afar Pasha to require for 1869 an increase in the garrison of two further battalions, and the consequent imposition of tribute upon the Shilluk and east bank Dinka of 3,000 bourses (£E15,000) – an onerous increase, though thanks to development of grain cultivation in the northerly part of the province it seems that at least in 1869 it was paid. Calculations of the total Shilluk population in the mid-nineteenth century do vary widely. The *razzias* of Mohammed Kheir in the early 1860s took a severe toll and may have reduced the population to some 150,000 by 1869. Allowing for the inclusion of the east bank Dinka – say 200,000 in combined total – the £E15,000 tribute compares with £E8,000 demanded of some 110,000 Shilluk by the author in 1953 (inflation excluded).

With these military dispositions in place, Ja'afar advised his Viceroy: 'When we shall have finished with this region we shall seek to subjugate and civilise the Nuer ... The Khedivial Government will thus extend its influence to the station of Gondokoro, situated at 4.5° latitude north – the navigable limit of the White Nile. Our traders will then be able to press on up the Bahr el Ghazal to the borders of Darfur to deal in ivory and ostrich feathers.'

And so indeed it appeared in the short run. An expedition to occupy the Bahr el Ghazal received Khedivial approval in April 1869, although it did not leave until the November dry season. Likewise in May 1869 Sir Samuel Baker was nominated to command a military expedition the principal, but not the sole, object of which was to join the territories of the upper Nile south of Gondokoro to the Sudan. Baker would not leave Khartoum until early February 1870, within a fortnight to be blocked by floating vegetation at the Zeraf river. The scale of the government forces involved on each account ensured the immunity of the expeditions from Shilluk attack, but the unrestricted availability of local provisions en route was nevertheless a major concern. In the event both expeditions passed through the Shilluk corridor unhindered in the winter of 1869-70 (even though Baker's progress was arrested beyond) and, in the opinion of Ja'afar Mazhar, the Governor-General, this was in main part due to the capability of the White Nile governor, Ali Bey Rida el Kurdi, who had now been in post since 1866.[2]

Unfortunately the relatively tranquil conditions in the Shilluk lands were not long to be maintained. Following two reasonably quiet years (there was at least one attack across the western frontier by Kwatker's exiled Shilluk rebels in 1869–70), the perennial problem of tribute collection, especially in the southern part of the province, once again occupied the governor Ali Rida who was adopting, not altogether untraditionally, rough pressures to ensure that payment in kind was made. Baker had called on him at Fashoda on 15 February 1870, a week after leaving Khartoum for Gondokoro, and had been assured that the Shilluk country was in excellent order, and that Fashoda's strategic position now enabled him, the governor, to intercept slave vessels seeking to pass the station.

The suppression of the slave trade on the White Nile and in the countries to be annexed in Equatoria *south* of Gondokoro was the second, but in Baker's view the principal, objective of his Khedivial appointment. While it survived, the Atlantic slave trade had been the main preoccupation of Western humanitarian opinion, but following slavery emancipation in Europe led by Britain in 1834 and then the conclusion of the American Civil War 1861-5 (on the eve of the Civil War, there had been 4 million slaves – nearly one in seven of the population), attention was increasingly directed to the traffic in the Middle East and Africa. In Egypt Viceregal decrees of Mohammed Ali in 1838 and of Mohammed Sa'id in 1854 had been honoured in the breach rather than the observance but by 1861 when Petherick, now British consul, returned to Khartoum from leave in England, the excesses of slave raiders on the White Nile had become an open scandal, and would be further publicised by Speke and Grant on their arrival in Cairo and London, back from discovering the source of the White Nile, in 1863.

Governors-General in the Sudan could no longer overtly encourage the trade under the guise of ivory expeditions, though the gaps in the ranks of the regiments stationed in the Sudan and depleted by disease had still to be made good by local recruitment.

Slaves were seized from three main regions: Abyssinia, whence they were exported through the ports of Suakin and Massawa to Jedda and also on to Suez; the White Nile from Kawa (El Ais) up to and beyond Gondokoro, whence they were ferried down the river if conditions were propitious – otherwise across Kordofan avoiding Khartoum and, latterly, Fashoda; and the Bahr el Ghazal and the Nuba mountains whence the shortest route led north across Kordofan. Since the discovery of its source, the White Nile was attracting the most European attention, not least on account of the proximity of Khartoum. Coming on top of increasingly heavy trading overheads in size of crews and escorts, the introduction by Musa Pasha of the *werko* tax, unevenly imposed to the deliberate detriment of the European ivory traders and capriciously enforced by river patrols based on the new Fashoda *muderia*, was nevertheless onerous enough to render the ivory expeditions by the Sudanese *jallaba* (merchants) barely viable. When Ja'afar Pasha Mazhar was appointed Governor-General in 1866, the European White Nile traders were on the edge of extinction, and the ivory trade itself deeply depressed. The last Europeans to go, the Poncet brothers sold their stations in early 1868 to Ja'afar Pasha in Cairo acting on behalf of the Khedive, and in return were granted a three-year lease-back for trading. Of the indigenous traders, Ahmed Musa el Aqqad, agent for the Khedive, had now gained a near-monopoly position. Georges Thibaut, French vice-consul in Khartoum, observed of Ahmed el Aqqad's ivory imports of that year: 'Beau produit, s'il n'était pas taché de sang humain.'

It was in 1866 that Ismail Pasha, covertly it seems, had granted a decree in response to a White Nile traders' petition allowing the domestic servants of Arab participants on humanitarian grounds to transport their Black concubines and children – and, *pro tanto*, the latter's 'relatives and friends' – to Khartoum where they could be swiftly sold, giving an overall profit to the ivory trade of ten times the market value of the tusks. In the wake of this dispensation designed to swell the revenues, Ja'afar had levied at Fashoda a charge of 10 dollars per human chattel, yielding 75,000 dollars (£E15,000) per year. This was the levy which Ali Bey Rida had been instructed to collect when he was now to be surprised by Baker *in flagrante*. To

reconcile this new established practice with the high-minded instructions in Baker's firman of 1869 'to suppress the slave trade' was
unreal, even if Baker's personal supreme authority was specifically
conferred in respect of all those countries belonging to the Nile Basin
south of Gondokoro – certainly not including Fashoda.[3]

Having left Khartoum late in the dry season 1869–70, and been
obstructed by clogging river vegetation, Baker was forced to turn back
from the Bahr el Zeraf channel of the main Nile in April 1870 and, on
approaching the Nile mainstream, learned from the southernmost
Shilluk that Ali Bey Rida el Kurdi, whom he had met in February, was
now plundering the neighbourhood with a large military force. On 20
April Baker surprised the governor near the mouth of the Khor Atar
with 155 slaves under guard, only ten of whom were men. The governor claimed that they were hostages, for release against payment of
tribute, and indeed children were released to one of the Shilluk in return
for ten cows. Baker reasonably assumed that otherwise slavery would
be their lot. Although outside his jurisdiction, Baker ordered the release
of the slaves, accused Ali Rida of slave-hunting and undertook to report
the affair to the Khedive. On the question of jurisdiction, Baker was to
write in *Ismailia*:

> I had originally proposed that the districts of the White Nile south
> of the latitude 14°. N [Kawa] should be placed under my com-
> mand; this for some unexplained reason, was reduced to latitude
> 5° N [Gondokoro] thus leaving the whole navigable river free
> from Gondokoro to Khartoum unless I should assume responsi-
> bility of liberating slaves and seizing the slavers wherever I might
> find them. This power I at once assumed and exercised although I
> purposely avoided landing and visiting the slave-hunters' stations
> that were not within my jurisdiction. I regarded the river as we
> regard the high seas.

Not only were the southern Shilluk delighted by his action but,
following Baker's establishment of a camp for the rainy season of 1870
at Tawfiqia, north of Sobat mouth, the news of Baker's intervention
induced the ex-*reth* Kwatker on 1 May to come out of hiding to
Tawfiqia and pose as the aggrieved true king of the Shilluk, victim of
the Ali Rida's excesses in the very recent death of ten of Kwatker's men.
His adrenalin still flowing, Baker imperiously sent his steamer to
summon the governor, still in the vicinity, for a confrontation on 5 May
with Kwatker at Tawfiqia. Although they had never previously met,

Ali Rida claimed Kwatker had died at the hands of his troops three years earlier. The *pasha* now presided over the humiliation of the governor at the hands of the rebel he had vanquished, and told Ali Rida that the Khedivial appointment as *reth* of Ajiyang Nyidhoko in Kwatker's place had been obtained 'under false pretences', namely the governor's false allegation that Kwatker was dead.

As to Kwatker's complaint against Ali Rida's hounding of the former's force, discussion of which Baker's account of the meeting does not mention, Professor Richard Gray quotes Baker's nephew Julian that in fact Reth Ajiyang had been deputed by Ali Rida to arrest the Shilluk responsible for killing two government soldiers and it was in the face of Kwatker's resistance that ten of the latter's force had just been killed.

Baker's conclusion was that Ali Rida 'was a great scoundrel and [Kwatker] a very cunning fellow... shamefully treated'. He explained to Ali Rida that while he (Baker) had no jurisdiction in Shilluk country which was under the governor, nevertheless 'I held the positive and special orders of the Khedive to suppress the slave trade... I also explained that I should send an official dispatch to the Khedive of Egypt, and also to Ja'afar Pasha, describing the state of the Shilluk country and the special case of Kwatker, with a direct report upon the kidnapping of slaves by his government's representative.'

Those dispatches left Tawfiqia by Baker's steamer on 1 July to Khartoum, accompanied by Kwatker's sons who were to plead for their father's resinstatement as *reth* notwithstanding the earlier bloodshed. When Baker followed, arriving on 21 September, he found Ja'afar Pasha embarrassed by his revelation of the 'character and acts of the Fashoda Governor'. On 11 December 1870, resuming his delayed journey to Equatoria from Tawfiqia, Baker recorded:

> I left the Shilluk country at peace. Ja'afar Pasha had paid much attention to the sons of Kwatker at Khartoum, and the Khedive, in reply to my representations, had appointed him chief of the country in place of the pretender Ajiyang. [At his meeting with Reth Ajiyang on 20 April, Baker had described him as 'an extremely blackguard-looking savage, dressed in a long scarlet cloak'.] The Governor of Fashoda had been condemned to disgrace. I left a handsome present for the old king Kwatker and we departed excellent friends.

But at Tawfiqia he had received a letter on 3 December from the Khedive dated 19 September 1870 which included the words: 'From another quarter my attention has been drawn to the dismissal of a chief of the Shilluk tribe', a charge which he countered in a letter to Sharif Pasha written well after his departure en route again to Gondokoro (see p. 126).[4]

Baker was to complain that even on his return to Khartoum in 1873 he had still received no reply to his subsequent letter to the Khedive of 28 December 1870, and indeed the correspondence between the Khedive, Ja'afar Pasha and Ali Bey Rida el Kurdi regarding Baker's accusations was only revealed in the publication of the appendix to part 2 of Douin's volume III *L'Empire Africain* in 1938. Ali Rida's incensed account of his encounters with Baker in April and May 1870 while collecting tribute accuses the latter of attempting to suborn to his own (Baker's) jurisdiction Reth Ajiyang, who had also been present at the Khor Atar. However Ali Rida makes no allusion at all to the women and children made captive, evidence one may conclude of some guilty intent even if many would be ransomed for tribute, and some ground for Baker to report the matter to the Khedive who had charged him with the suppression of the slave trade at least in Equatoria.

Yet in his dispatch of a rather arrogant summons to the governor, whom he had already publicly censured in the tribute context, in order to confront him in front of witnesses with the man whom Ali Rida thought to be dead and whom he had reasonably replaced as *reth*, Baker was exceeding his authority. He was necessarily ignorant of Shilluk history over the past three years and mistaken in accusing Ali Rida of having had Ajiyang (whom Baker took against) proclaimed *reth* and in urging the reinstatement of the rebellious Kwatker.

Ja'afar Pasha supported his governor's protest against both of Baker's accusations in his correspondence with Cairo, but realised the strong international public position Baker held. He was moreover a party to Ali Rida's tax collection/military recruitment practices, and warned the Khedive that Baker's enthusiasm for seizing the occupants of trading boats and inability to distinguish between slaves and military recruits would put an end to commerce on the White Nile. The Khedive in reply approved in principle the need to find a successor to Ali Rida and, while urging the desirability of maintaining the prestige of government, weakly conceded the removal of Reth Ajiyang 'as an accomplished fact'. In fact neither had been replaced by the time Baker left Tawfiqia for Gondokoro in December 1870. Meanwhile Ja'afar Pasha, loyally, had ordered Ali Rida to obey any instructions he should receive from Baker, although outside the latter's defined jurisdiction.[5]

The receipt in Khartoum of the Khedive's rulings did not end matters. Ja'afar Pasha had discussed the question of Kwatker's rein-statement and, he claimed, had convinced Baker that while Kwatker had been pardoned, he could not be reinstated as *reth* but would be allowed back to live in security where he chose. He requested Baker to persuade Kwatker to behave. Whether or not Baker complied, by January 1871 Kwatker had proclaimed himself *reth,* marched against Reth Ajiyang at Fashoda, and ignored the governor's urging to with-draw. Ja'afar Pasha, apprised from Fashoda, ordered Kwatker's com-pliance with an instruction to come and live at Fashoda, or be captured dead or alive. While not complying with the instruction of Ajiyang or of the governor, Kwatker in May 1871 agreed to enter Fashoda and await a boat to Khartoum. Suspiciously he died of sickness or of self-induced hunger four days after taking up temporary residence at Fashoda.

As for Ali Bey Rida el Kurdi, his *muderia* was now relieved at least of the embarrassment of rival *reths*. The southern Shilluk between Zeraf and Sobat mouths shrank to fewer than forty villages. To his credit, and contrary to the anticipation of the Bahr el Ghazal traders who had told Schweinfurth that 'el Kurdi' would quickly revert to a per capita levy on slaves passing through his *muderia* in boats, Ali Rida became most energetic in his exertions against the trade. Schweinfurth chanced in July 1871 to witness him, still in office, with a major force near Tawfiqia confiscating 600 slaves belonging to El 'Aqqād's company from Meshra el Aliab, and commented: 'His measures [against the slave trade] were so summary and executed with such methodical strictness that unless I had known him I could scarcely have believed him to be a Turk.'

Details of all slaves, including soldiers' personal slaves, and their place of capture were recorded, affidavits signed by the traders, and inventories made of the latter's confiscated property, guns, ammunition and ivory.[6]

Ali Rida's *hakimdar* and protector, Ja'afar Pasha, was now however on the point of departing on final leave, the White Nile province with Khartoum and Fazughli to become part of the new general governorate of the South Sudan following the arrival on 5 November 1871 of Ahmed Mumtaz Pasha on transfer from the Eastern Sudan general-governorate. One of the latter's first acts was to dismiss and arrest Ali Rida for his alleged violent and oppressive actions. By this time, Baker being established in Gondokoro and about to march south for the lacustrine kingdoms, Mumtaz decided it was safe to order, probably while on a visit to Fashoda en route to Sennar, the release of the slave dealers and boat captains whom Ali Rida had arrested and held captive in the past fifteen months, and to return to them their confiscated cargoes of ivory, if not slaves, and their sequestrated property. Thus was the trading status quo ante Baker to be restored. White Nile commerce took an upward turn, as did the governorate revenue, while disingenuously Mumtaz wrote off to Baker applauding his courage in 'overcoming all the obstacles to be surmounted'.

A long period of arrest and investigation of Ali Bey Rida in Khartoum under Adham Pasha el Arifi, the *seraskir,* yielded insufficient evidence of wrongdoing for conviction and, late in 1875, he would be reappointed governor of White Nile. Ernst Marno claims, as does Baker, that Mumtaz in November 1871 had appointed one of his headquarter *qa'immaqams,* Ali 'Abu Khamsa Meeya' ('father of 500 [blows]') to succeed Ali Rida.

For the Shilluk the dismissal of Ali Rida in 1871 led to the establishment of a more oppressive regime. His successor was mandated with collecting a major increase in tribute, in respect of which Ali Rida had been accused of undue leniency, and while the former was busy exacting tribute among the southern Shilluk in the winter of 1872–3, the northern Shilluk rose. Provoked to anger, under Reth Ajiyang they overcame the small garrisons south of Kaka, killing seventy soldiers and threatening Fashoda (Deinab) itself. The southern Shilluk would not join Ajiyang, however, and the governor, hastening back from the south, quashed the revolt with reinforcements from Khartoum. Reth Ajiyang took refuge in the bush and for the next two years the government ruled without a *reth.*

Mumtaz had been nevertheless determined to stimulate the revenue producing capability of the Shilluk further by increased agricultural cultivation not only of corn but also of cotton and sugar cane. Ernest Linant de Bellefonds, en route to join Gordon Pasha in the south in October 1874, remarked 800 acres of rain (short-staple) cotton being grown at Fashoda, along with sugar cane and maize.

By then Ahmed Mumtaz Pasha had been deposed, in July 1872. He was succeeded, after a brief interval when Lewa Adham Pasha exercised control, as general-governor by Ismail Pasha Ayub who was responsible for the appointment in early 1873 of the Circassian Yusuf Bey Hasan Khorda (?Kurdi) as governor of White Nile. In December 1873 Ismail Ayub was promoted Governor-General of the Sudan, still however excluding Munzinger's eastern general-governorate and

Equatoria. Reth Ajiyang was eventually captured and in May 1874 brought in chains to Fashoda where, with the sanction of the Khedive, he was to be crucified on the door of the governor's office.

It was Yusuf Bey whom Baker was to meet on his way back to Cairo, at Fashoda on 19 June 1873 – 'an active and highly intelligent Circassian [Richard Hill affirmed he was of Nubian extraction] who held the rank of lieutenant-colonel' – and who declared himself anxious to assist Baker in the total extinction of the slave trade. Of the current condition of the Shilluk or of the fate of his old protégé, former Reth Kwatker, Baker gave no report, nor of the new brick-built and fortified *muderia* and barracks which were erected about this time.[7]

2 EQUATORIA AND THE SLAVE TRADE

Sir Samuel Baker's Appointment 1869   Sir Samuel Baker wrote in *Ismailia* of his appointment to command the viceregal expedition 'to annexe to Egypt all the lands in the Nile Basin and of Central Africa'... 'I had received certain intimations from the Foreign Minister, Nubar Pasha, concerning the Khedive's intentions a short time previous to an invitation... to accompany the Prince and Princess of Wales during their tour of Egypt.'

The suggestion that the initiative originated from the Khedive needs some qualification. On his return from discovering Lake Albert Nyanza in May 1865, Baker had not met the Viceroy in Alexandria; but on his return to England (1866) he had soon published *The Albert N'yanza* in which he extolled the agricultural potential of the region and inveighed against the White Nile slave trade, calling for its suppression by the European Powers as the precondition of civilisation to be effected through commerce and mission. In this Baker was adding weight to the memorandum to Earl Russell by the Royal Geographical Society two years earlier in April 1864 which urged the occupation of the Equatorial Nile by the Viceroy. That proposal did not meet with universal support and its topicality had dwindled, though on his visit to Paris in June 1867 the Khedive had addressed the French and British anti-slavery societies and promised that Egypt would pursue the suppression of the slave trade energetically. Passing on to England, he was to meet Sir Samuel Baker at a dinner given by the Prince of Wales – an encounter, albeit of formality, pregnant with future event.

Baker had previously retired to Hedenham Hall in Norfolk but at the age of forty-six, knighted (seemingly Gladstone's initiative on reading *The Albert N'yanza*) and now a national figure, he was restive and eager to return to Africa. Indeed while he had been away on his voyage of discovery to Lake Albert, Francis Galton, the foreign secretary of the Royal Geographical Society, had on 24 February 1864 written to Baker's brother John to express the Society's wish that the former should lead a new expedition to the Nile source to clear up 'many points left uncertain by Speke's work'. However, probably influenced by John Petherick's opposition, backed by Consul-General Colquhoun, to Egyptian territorial expansion in Equatoria, government enthusiasm for a new British expedition waned. The imminence of the Magdala campaign prompted Baker to propose rather precipitately, in October 1867, that a more economical means of securing the release of Theodore's captives would be a limited expedition which he would lead, via Suakin and Kassala, to his old acquaintance *mek* Omer Nimr, son of the Sudanese rebel exile from Shendi of 1821 (Baker was unaware that *mek* Omer had been killed two years previously). As the *Times* editorial unkindly put it, the result of Baker's proposal would have been more captives to be liberated by next January (1868). Earlier, 8 March 1867, he had responded positively if pessimistically when succour for Dr Livingstone, falsely reported dead, was canvassed by Sir Roderick Murchison, Baker declaring in his letter: 'The hard soil of Africa is a more fitting couch for the last gasp of an African Explorer than the down-pillow of civilised home.'[8]

The meeting with Nubar Pasha, to which Baker referred in *Ismailia*, took place in London on the former's visit to discuss with Lord Stanley in June 1868 the reform of the Capitulations (conventions in virtue of which the subjects of European Powers resident in the Ottoman Empire were placed, in respect of all criminal and civil matters, under the sole jurisdiction of their own consuls). Nubar's recollection was as follows:

We met; necessarily we talked of the Sudan, the Nile, the Lakes region, slavery and the abolition of the trade, and I was led to speak of Ibrahim Pasha's thoughts on the importance of the Sudan, thoughts taken up by the Viceroy at the beginning of his reign and which presently, to my regret, had been relegated to oblivion. Baker seemed to be seeking an opportunity to return to the Sudan, and to return there above all charged with some mission on our behalf.

I told him: 'I think it a good idea to establish stations between Gondokoro and the lakes; to police our savage tribes; to find the means of opening up transport, and thus to begin undermining, along with other measures taken with discretion, the slave trade: that is a dream I trust will be realised one day. But if you were to go for it to-day what would you achieve? The slave traders would erect obstacles to your accomplishing your mission and you could do nothing against them.'

Nubar went on to claim that the mission was only attainable, always granted one wished it to be productive of good, first if the mission *followed* judicial reform of the Capitulations, without which in the eyes of Egyptians it would appear simply as a challenge to their religious authority on the part of European influences which were mistrusted; and, secondly, if the power were there to sweep away the slave traders without having to incur the cost of indemnities. While in Nubar's recollection, Baker seemed enthusiastic ('s'enflammant') to subscribe to this belief that judicial reform and suppression of the slave trade were closely linked, this accord was to be forgotten in the subsequent talks between the Khedive and Baker in Cairo. Nubar went on:

> For the Viceroy it was enough to effect his sovereignty over these countries and to appear preoccupied, in the eyes of Europe, with their well-being and with the slave trade. But as for so directing the men and events to ensure success, that was not his affair. Such was the origin of our occupation of the Lake region.

According to the above, the principal initiative for Baker's return to the Sudan in 1869 is seen to have come from the man himself, with Nubar's acquiescence to the timing conditional on reform of the Capitulations which exempted Europeans from Egyptian courts and taxation and were regarded by the Egyptians as an affront to their religion and status. Later, in 1874, Nubar went on to observe:

> It seemed to me that Egypt was insufficiently stable to undertake [abolition of the slave trade]. She could only prepare for it, and was not this my guiding belief, when I proposed the mission to Baker, in subordinating the timing when the latter could be entrusted to him to the realisation of [judicial] reform? It is a fact that the Viceroy, in his effort to appear liberal and to be agreeable to the Prince of Wales, had not waited on my timescale.

Baker however was to claim that the Khedive was firmly supported by Nubar and Sharif Pasha.[9]

The mission arrangements were not to prove long in gestation. Invited to stay at Dunrobin Castle with the Duke of Sutherland in September 1868 at a house party in honour of the Prince of Wales, Baker and his host were then invited to accompany the Waleses on a Nile cruise in February 1869. Baker arrived in Egypt early in order to superintend the arrangements, introducing a plethora of washbasins into the Esbekiah Palace in Cairo for the royal guests in time for their arrival on 4, and departure to Aswan on 6, February. It seems clear that Ismail Pasha must have received Baker before the Prince reached Egypt, since the initial exchange of royal courtesies on 4–5 February on the Prince's arrival would not have offered an opportunity for substantive talks. William Howard Russell of *The Times* had not accompanied the royal party to Upper Egypt and had met the Khedive at a costumed ball at Ismailia on 17 March 1869 before the latter left for Cairo to greet the royal party, returned from Upper Egypt, the next day (in fact they returned on 16 March). He was to report: 'At the ball, His Highness in the course of conversation communicated his idea of nominating Sir Samuel Baker to take command of a force for the suppression of the slave trade on the White Nile and the establishment of order in the Sudan. He had spoken with Sir Samuel on the subject, but seemed in doubt as to the propriety or likelihood of success of the step.'

Ismail's hesitation was understandable. Not only had Nubar uttered his reservations, but no one of European extraction except Ismail's father Ibrahim's military chief of staff, Sulieman Pasha, the former French officer Colonel Sève, had previously been appointed to high executive rank in the Egyptian government and Sève only after he had embraced Islam. On the Nile cruise Baker, however, had meanwhile had ample opportunity to canvass his ambitions with the Prince of Wales, and on their return to Cairo the latter clearly promoted Baker's appointment and even may have suggested the terms of service. W. H. Russell was later to tell Gordon Pasha that Baker 'was forced on the Khedive by the Prince of Wales who wanted to be rid of Baker's impor-tunities'. Douin is positive: 'During his second stay in Cairo [16–24 March] the Prince…suggested to the Khedive the idea of utilising Sir Samuel Baker to suppress the White Nile trade, militarily occupy and colonise the whole region.' The Khedive was receptive.

To what extent the Prince of Wales had previously consulted Glad-stone's Cabinet on Baker's appointment is uncertain – one suspects not at all. Yet this was a historic decision, in that it represented Britain's first, if vicarious, tentative involvement in the internal government of the Sudan. The Prince of Wales departed to Constantinople and the Crimea on 24 March 1869, and on 27 March the Khedive agreed Baker's written proposal in principle. It was not until 2 April that the British consul-general Stanton informed the Earl of Clarendon, Gladstone's foreign secretary, of the understanding reached leaving Baker, who had already sailed for England, to brief Clarendon on 12 April.

There is a manuscript minute by Clarendon of his meeting which is worth reporting in full:

> I have seen Sir S. Baker who in the same terms as those of Colonel S[tanton]'s dispatch described the nature and objects of the Expedition of which Sir S.B. has been requested to take command. He seemed confident that within a comparatively short time the result would be the total extinction of the S[lave] T[rade] and that by works of irrigation, which would be one of the first objects of the Expedition, tracts of land would be brought into cultivation and large numbers of people attracted (?) to agricultural products, and that when the different Chiefs found honest and profitable means of employing people, the motives for war i.e. kidnapping slaves would cease.
>
> I asked Sir S.B. whether the Viceroy had communicated with the Porte on the subject and whether jealousy on the part of the French in Egypt was to be apprehended – He did not know whether any direct communication had been held with the Porte [highly unlikely granted the current frosty relations] but the Turks in Egypt approved the project and he had no reason to think that a different feeling existed with ... the French authorities in Egypt.
>
> Sir S.B. said that he would not venture to make his preparations until a formal contract between the Viceroy and himself had been signed [S.B. nevertheless did so]. Signed 'C. 12/4.'

Two further minutes follow one upon the other. First: 'I conclude we take no responsibility with regard to this expedition of Sir S. Baker.' Signed (seemingly), 'WEG [Gladstone, the Prime Minister] April 14th.' And the second unsigned: 'I think we might add to the Draft: "You will distinctly understand and make known to all British subjects who may take part in this Expedition, that HMG undertake no responsibility whatever for the consequences of it either as regards themselves or as regards any matters connected with it."' To which Clarendon minuted: 'I will make an addition when I come to the office.'

Four years previously Earl Russell had urged Sir Henry Bulwer, British ambassador to the Porte then visiting Cairo, to press upon the Viceroy the interest felt by Britain in the suppression of the White Nile slave trade, which was now to form one of the major declared objectives of the Baker appointment – though not the only one. Baker, lastly in Stanton's résumé, was 'to establish the Egyptian Government in these regions'. This was contrary to the opinion of Colquhoun, also in 1865 on the eve of his departure from Egypt, who had not only advised strongly against the Khartoum Governor-General Musa Hamdi (with his reputation) having power to extend the Khedive's territory, but had warned that the extension of the frontier to the proximity of the lacustrine kings created doubt whether a fair system of commerce would obtain without the presence of the agents of European governments. Musa however was now dead and Baker, if an Egyptian official, was also a European of public renown. The same Gladstone Cabinet, Earl Granville now having succeeded Clarendon as foreign secretary, was in August 1873 to recommend the Queen to grant Khedive Ismail's request to approve the appointment of another Briton, Colonel Charles Gordon, in the role of Baker's successor.[10]

Douin quotes Baker's plan (in the French text from the Abdin Palace archives) submitted to the Khedive on 27 March as acknowledging that Egypt's prosperity depended on the Nile; affirming the indispensability now of annexing for Egypt the source of the Nile in Lakes Albert Nyanza and Victoria Nyanza; and identifying 'Le premier but de la susmentionée expédition serait d'établir le gouvernement égyptien dans le pays du Nil Blanc.'

Following his April visit to England and Lord Clarendon, Baker arrived back in time to meet the Khedive at Alexandria on 16 May 1869 as the latter embarked for Europe (and Colonel Stanton also left on leave); and to receive the Khedivial firman of his appointment, elaborating Baker's plan of 27 March with some slight modifications.

> An Expedition is organised to subdue to our [Khedivial] authority the countries situated to the south of Gondokoro;
> 'To suppress the Slave Trade;
> 'To introduce a system of regular commerce;
> 'To open to navigation the Great Lakes of the Equator;
> 'And to establish a chain of military stations and commercial

depôts, distant at intervals of three days' march, throughout Central Africa, accepting Gondokoro as a base of operations.'

The Khedive was riding two horses. African territorial aggrandisement in a multiplicity of directions – the Red Sea littoral, Abyssinia, Equatoria, Bahr el Ghazal and Darfur – was the dominant objective, of the full scope of which Baker remained ignorant. However in order to secure European compliance with expansion in such countries the Khedive needed, in Nubar's words, 'to appear preoccupied in the eyes of Europe with their well-being and with the slave trade'. When Sultan Abdel Aziz questioned his Viceroy in June 1869 regarding the declared objective of suppressing the slave trade as it appeared in Baker's firman, the Khedive replied that the goal was the expansion southwards of Ottoman territory.

Baker on the other hand, mindful of the conditions he had experienced at Gondokoro in 1863, had a different priority notwithstanding the wording of his original proposal to the Khedive of 27 March 1869. As he now put it in a letter to Lord Wharncliffe from Cairo of 22 October: 'The main objects of the enterprise are, *after crushing the Slave Trade,* to annex to the Egyptian Empire the Equatorial Nile Basin' etc.

That order of priorities was doubtless also the informal view of the British government but its omission of comment on Baker's draft objectives following the Clarendon meeting on 12 April and its denial of government protection to British national participants, irritating as that was to Baker, is a refutation of the subsequent accusations by Egyptian historians of the twentieth century, that Britain was already 'harbouring secret and ambitious designs on the Sudan'. Henceforward until his return to Khartoum in 1873, communication between Baker and Stanton would be by private letter.[11]

Reverting to the contents of the firman of 16 May 1869 command, extended ultimately from two to four years from 1 April 1869, was conferred on Baker who would possess absolute and supreme power, even (after court martial) of death, over the expedition in all territories south of Gondokoro lat. N.5° (not south of 14° as Baker had originally proposed) 'jusqu'au point le plus sud des sources du Nil'. He would be paid £10,000 sterling p.a. plus expedition expenses. (Ja'afar Mazhar, the Governor-General of the Sudan, currently received about £E3,000.)

The firman designated the status which Baker would enjoy as commander of the expedition. It gave him the rank of *miralai* (colonel) and of *bey,* and named him as *mamur* (commander). These were ranks inferior to the *hakimdar* (Governor-General) Ja'afar Pasha Mazhar in Khartoum and on studying this – Ismail Pasha having left for Europe – Baker appears speedily to have contacted the Prince of Wales. The latter responded by contacting the Turkish ambassador in London, Musurus Pasha, in advance of Ismail's arrival in England at the end of June 1869, representing that Baker's mission would be greatly facilitated if the Ottoman Sultan were to make Baker a *pasha* rather than a *bey*. Without consulting Ismail with whom he was currently vexed, Sultan Abdel Aziz promptly issued his own firman directed to Baker, not to Ismail, which not only granted Baker the rank of *pasha* but advanced him from *miralai* to *lewa* (brigadier-general). Ismail in anger protested to Clarendon on arrival in London in June, but it was a *fait accompli*. Baker however was not, as he claimed to Wharncliffe, to have the rank of Governor-General (*hakimdar 'umum*), that of Ja'afar Mazhar, even if he was to be answerable to the Khedive direct. He was to be a *mudir 'umum*, general-governor, his territorial authority to run south from Gondokoro.[12]

A False Start, 1870 Baker's force was to comprise 800 Egyptian troops, 500 Sudanese and 200 Sha'iqi cavalry, a total of some 1,500 plus 14 cannon. While they would be under Baker's overall command as commandant and administrator of the new territories, the troops would be operationally commanded by a *miralai*, Mohammed Ra'uf Bey, and two *bimbashis*. The ten Equatorial stations, thirty leagues apart, would each be under the command of a *sagh-qol-aghassi* (adjutant-major) but the headquarters, Gondokoro, would have a garrison of 300 men. Baker claims in *Ismailia* that he was authorised to order in England a flotilla for the Equatorial lakes comprising three steel-built steamers fitted with Penn engines and two 10-ton steel lifeboats, all capable of disassembly into components. The Egyptian government were to supply three paddle-steamers and twenty-five barges from Khartoum; together with six steamers, fifteen large sailing barges and fifteen *dhahabiyas* from Cairo – the Cairo fleet with 'the whole of the merchandise' to leave Cairo on 10 June 1869 at the latest, in order to ascend the cataracts during the Nile flood. These latter vessels would join the Khartoum fleet waiting in readiness and they would leave together for Gondokoro on 15 September 1869 in order to arrive at the end of the rains. The plan put by Baker to the Khedive on 27 March 1869, set out in the memorandum in the archives of the Abdin Palace, met with some amendment (cf. Douin).

Baker's camel transport of steamers and machinery, February 1870

In *Ismailia* Baker affirms his awareness that for the White Nile voyage 'all vessels should leave Khartoum early in November' (he could recall Petherick's disastrous late departure in 1862), yet he claims: 'The arrangements that I had made would have insured success if carried out according to the dates specified.' Indeed the Cairo fleet departed not on 10 June but on 29 August 1869 and in consequence of the falling river, was unable to negotiate the second cataract at Wadi Halfa, the passage of the convoy being thus delayed until July 1870. The fifteen sailing barges with the camels meanwhile returned to Cairo. 'Thus twelve months were wasted, and I was at once deprived of the invaluable aid of six steamers.' That however is a shade simplistic.

The delay in the departure of the Cairo fleet was indeed one factor, and certainly ascribable in part to 'the inevitable delay necessitated by the festivities attending the opening of the Suez Canal'. Moreover the Khedive was absent in Europe until 27 July, as had for months been Nubar Pasha, the minister of foreign affairs in Paris – Colquhoun had commented: 'Nubar is the mastermind even when the Viceroy is here [Egypt].' There were, however, many other factors which rendered Baker's departure from Khartoum to Gondokoro by November, let alone 15 September, 1869 impossible. They do not stand out from the pages of *Ismailia*.

After a hectic four weeks in England recruiting the European party of the expedition, purchasing stores for four years, personally selecting every article including 8-pounder and 5-pounder guns and the three Samuda-built steamers and two steel lifeboats dismountable in components, Baker had personally only reached Alexandria to receive the Khedivial firman on 16 May 1869 thereafter to complete his local preparations. His wife Florence joined him in June and they rented a house in Alexandria overlooking the harbour where the fleet of the visitors to the Suez Canal opening began to assemble.

Full particulars of the bills of lading for expedition articles were received by 17 September but the steamer components did not leave England until 28 August by SS *Teesdale*, two only of the Samuda steamers reaching Alexandria on 15 October and in far heavier components than ordered. After its release from customs, forty-one railway wagons took the expedition baggage in November to Cairo, where the personal intervention of the Khedive procured a steamer and eleven barges then to tow this important equipment up the Nile to Korosko. The cataracts being now closed to river convoys, the cargoes were disembarked there and would travel escorted by Sheikh Hussein Khalifa of the Ababda, later governor of Berber, under the skilled supervision of Baker's chief engineer, Edwin Higginbotham, on gun carriages across the 400-mile Atmur desert to the Nile at Berber. They were not to reach Khartoum until early April 1870.

Ja'afar Mazhar in Khartoum had been alerted by the Minister of War, Shahin Pasha, to the formation of the Equatoria expedition only in June 1869. Fariq Khusraw Pasha and Miralai Mohammed Ra'uf Bey, officer commanding Baker's troops, were sent ahead from Cairo on 16 June with artillery and arms, the former to have overall authority for the local preparations for the expedition. Having written off to Baker on 16 July explaining the insurmountable difficulties attaching to mustering his intended large fleet at Khartoum (Baker was in Alexandria), Ja'afar moved to Berber and spent August anxiously and unprofitably awaiting Baker's arrival, uninformed of the setbacks in Egypt. Uncomfortable no doubt with Khusraw's role in Khartoum, though there is no evidence as to what the latter accomplished, Ja'afar also wrote to the Khedive suggesting that Khusraw would make an admirable ruler of a detached Red Sea littoral province. No reply was vouchsafed for eight months when instead Ahmed Mumtaz Bey was appointed. Khusraw had long since disappeared.[13]

Baker, his personal entourage and the remaining baggage did not in the event leave Suez until 5 December 1869, reaching Khartoum via Suakin and Berber on 8 January 1870. Only then was the final obstacle to his original programme revealed to him. Under an urgent order of the Khedive dated 30 September and repeated 6 October 1869, eleven vessels of Baker's planned Khartoum fleet had already sailed with another expedition to occupy the north-west Bahr el Ghazal. Baker had not been made aware either in his preliminary discussion regarding the Equatoria Expedition on 27 March, nor when he received his firman on 16 May, that the Khedive was simultaneously involved in a parallel project on the White Nile for the occupation of the north-western Bahr el Ghazal and of Hufrat el Nahas on the Bahr el Arab – the Dar Fertit – as a future springboard for the invasion of Darfur.

The background was this. After ordering a reconnaissance of Darfur in March 1867 (see p. 50) Ja'afar Pasha had, following his return to Khartoum a year earlier, put to the Khedive a proposal dated 29 January 1869 for an expedition to Dar Fertit, which must have been under study in Cairo by March and was to be approved by the Khedive on 11 April during Baker's absence in England.

If Baker was kept in ignorance of this venture until his arrival in Khartoum in January 1870, so also for the while was Ja'afar of Baker's plans. It was only in June 1869 that Ja'afar received any hint of the impending conflict of priority between the two Khartoum-based expeditions. The Bahr el Ghazal expedition is examined below in chapter 6. Had this latter expedition, as originally envisaged, left by May 1869 before the rains, the competing needs of two simultaneous expeditions six months later for riverain transport would not have arisen. As it was, when the Khedivial order of 30 September 1869 to hasten the arrested departure of the Bahr el Ghazal expedition reached Khartoum and he had still no news of the departure date of Baker from Egypt, Ja'afar can hardly be blamed for allocating the eleven sailing barges to that expedition, which then sailed in November.[14]

Yet, notwithstanding Baker's previous cordial relations with Ja'afar Mazhar when they had met in Suakin in August 1865 (see pp. 38–9), blame Ja'afar he did. Writing to Sharif Pasha on 12 January 1870, four days after his arrival at Khartoum, Baker commended Ja'afar for every possible help rendered not only as *hakimdar* but as a friend but, in his Journal when he left Khartoum hopefully for Gondokoro on 8 February 1870, he attributed that one month's delay to Ja'afar 'who had ignored all the plans I had arranged [for river transport]... The usual Egyptian delays have entirely thwarted my plans... no vessels have arrived from Cairo as they only started on 29 August.'

Such was the animus of his criticism of Turkish-Egyptian colleagues that the relationship with Khartoum, on which he would necessarily have to rely for future communications and reinforcements, was soured from the start. If in Egypt, beyond the Khedivial entourage, 'the expedition was regarded with ill-concealed disgust' in Khartoum, he wrote in *Ismailia,* 'I knew the contentions of the authorities were to procrastinate until the departure of the expedition would become impossible... no personal considerations could palliate the secret hatred to the object of the expedition.' Unable to betray the evident duplicity of his Khedive, Ja'afar could only recommend, but without avail, that Baker postpone his departure until the next season's following wind in perhaps November 1870. Baker did nevertheless acknowledge that 'whenever we differed in opinion upon official matters, we were always cordial in our private capacity'.

Baker was however not now in the role of a gentleman explorer as previously in 1862: he held the appointment of general-governor of Equatoria and *lewa,* a servant of the Khedive like the officials of the Sudan, with whom friendly relations of trust were especially important since they controlled his line of communication. Moreover Baker was not only a foreigner, but a Christian in a Moslem community. Yet his behaviour towards his colleagues was too often insensitive, confident in a superior status marked by his direct access to the Khedive and by his international reputation.

His anger and distrust were, justifiably, to be further inflamed on learning that the Bahr el Ghazal expedition (in fact its *bashi-buzouq* contingent) 'had been placed under the command of one of the most notorious ruffians and slave-hunters of the Upper Nile'. This was Kuchuk Ali, sometimes designated *agha* suggesting military service, who was trading from *zaribas* in the Bahr el Ghazal and from the Zeraf river. Berlioux described him as one of the 'triumvir' of the Ghazal and had been found with 300 slaves on his boats in 1865. Baker equally was contemptuous both of the Egyptian *fellahin and* the 250 irregular cavalry recruited for his own army at Khartoum, this last force being ceremonially paraded and then dismissed from his command.

In a hostile environment, Baker's determination to leave for Gondokoro before his force became further demoralised, notwithstanding the transport obstacles and the lateness of the season, is understandable. That he was able to do so initially by 8 February 1870 reflects his immense energy and tenacity of purpose. Conscious that Higginbotham's collapsible fleet was at least crossing the Atmur desert and dispensing voluntarily with cavalry but necessarily, for want of boats, with the camel train, he sailed with two steamers, four *dhahabiyas* and thirty barges carrying half his planned force – 700 troops and a battery of artillery and supplies for a year. His route took him past Aba Island whither, at about this time, Mohammed Ahmed Abdallah, a *sheikh* of the Sammaniya order, accompanied by his boat-building brothers from Khartoum questing for timber, was establishing himself in spite of the opposition of the local Shilluk. Eleven years later Mohammed Ahmed would be proclaimed the Mahdi.

Baker planned to reach Gondokoro by March but bad luck still dogged him. Fifty-one days later, having been forced to leave the mainstream White Nile even before Lake No on account of floating vegetation (*sudd*), he found a similar impenetrable obstruction south of Kuchuk Ali's station on the Bahr el Zeraf – his departure 'an inconceivable madness had anyone known the character of the river'. On 11 March 1870 he noted: 'So serious is the obstacle to navigation that unless a new open channel can be discovered, the centre of Africa will be shut out from communication'; and, exasperated, on 9 April: 'It is simply ridiculous to suppose that this river can ever be rendered navigable. One or two vessels if alone might be entirely destroyed with their crews by a sudden change breaking up the country and enclosing them in a trap from which they could never escape...' He was thus obliged to return and establish in late April 1870 a separate station north of Sobat mouth, its hinterland depopulated by *razzias*, which he named Tawfiqia after the Khedive's eldest son.[15]

Baker's embroilment with the Deinab *mudir* in the Shilluk corridor during the rains of 1870 has been examined in the previous section. On his return to Khartoum 21 September 1870 in its aftermath, and his arrest of several slaveboats at Tawfiqia belonging principally to Kuchuk Ali but later also to El 'Aqqād, he encountered 'a passive stubborn resistance to the expedition. This is shared by the officials.' Not one of thirty boats ordered for his resumed expedition to Gondokoro was ready and a week later he wrote formally to Ja'afar Pasha to protest. Aware however that protracted delays could prejudice his departure a second time he did concede: 'Some little diplomacy was necessary to smooth the troubled waters of Khartoum. I made every allowance for the passive obstructiveness of the authorities.' Officers over the months of waiting had become intimate with the substantial slave-trading community of Khartoum who sowed disaffection and discouraged crews from volunteering. Only Ismail Bey Ayub, currently president of the council, and Bimbashi Abdel Qadir, since January

A view of the 'cut' between the Bahr el Zeraf and the Bahr el Jebel

1870 captain of Baker's bodyguard – the 'Forty Thieves' – would earn his praise.

Yet he could not depart before he had overcome yet another obstacle while in Khartoum. Ja'afar Pasha unexpectedly explained that the government had assumed legal title to and monopoly rights in all territory to the south of Khartoum and had leased it to indigenous traders (the last Europeans having been forced to sell out: Debono in 1865, the Poncet brothers in 1868), chief among them Sheikh Mohammed Ahmed el 'Aqqād who had acquired, in return for an annual payment of £E3,000, monopoly trading rights to 90,000 square miles. The territory lay in Baker's future Equatorial province where he was committed to establish a *government* monopoly in commerce and to suppress the slave trade. Conscious of the level of hostility, Baker was circumspect. He persuaded Ja'afar to arrange new terms to the lease, whereby the duration of the El 'Aqqād contract should expire at the end of *Moharram* (9 April 1872) three years into Baker's own contract. Until then no ivory would be purchased by the government; and rent would now be payable in kind – forty per cent of the ivory collected – and no longer in cash. Baker commented in his Journal: 'This man [El 'Aqqād] has been unfairly dealt with by the Government. My arrangement will set him on his legs at the same time that it will multiply the Government's profits.'

Unfortunately the arrangements with El 'Aqqād did not end there. Present at these negotiations in Khartoum with Sheikh Mohammed Ahmed el 'Aqqād was his son-in-law, Mohammed Abu Sa'ud. Baker, distrusting Khartoum's ability to meet his supply needs and foreseeing the necessity of an effective chain of local trading posts to provision his expedition in its progress towards the lacustrine kingdoms, struck an agreement whereby Abu Sa'ud would perform the provisioning role and, in case of need, provide armed assistance with his 1,800 irregulars. At one stroke he regretfully lent official recognition to this slave-trader and his private army on whose services he incurred some dependency: a miscalculation Baker would rue.

After signing the new El 'Aqqād contract, Baker sailed for Tawfiqia on 10 October 1870. Ja'afar Pasha 'accompanied by all the big people' came on board to take an official farewell. In his Journal, Baker wrote that he was

> thankful to be free from that hateful spot Khartoum. Nothing can equal the misery of that spot. Mud, no drainage, dense population with exaggerated stench. These enemies to civilisation have at

length vanquished European settlers. Yesterday the arms of the
Austrian Consulate were hauled down as the last European consul
Hansal resigned his post.

The ill-will generated on both sides was to persist with serious consequences, at least until the expedition had entered Bunyoro. Returning
from his botanical exploration of the Bahr el Ghazal in the summer of
1871 after Baker had at last gained Gondokoro, Dr Georg Schweinfurth would report:

> The ill-feeling and smothered rage against Sir Samuel Baker's
> interference, nurtured by the higher authorities, breaks out very
> strongly amongst the less reticent officials. In Fashoda, and even
> in Khartoum I heard complaints that we (the Franks) were the
> prime cause of all the trouble, and if it had not been for our eter-
> nal agitation with the Viceroy, such measures would never have
> been enforced.

At Tawfiqia Baker still had to await the onset of the north wind
which became established in the last week in November, enabling the
advance party to sail on 1 December. Before he followed on 11 December, bound for Gondokoro via the Bahr el Zeraf, he received a letter
from the Khedive dated 19 September 1870 in which he was vexed to
read: 'From another quarter my attention has been drawn to the
dismissal of a chief of the Shilluk tribe.' He wrote on 3 December to
Sharif Pasha to deny the charge, expressing anger that the Khedive
should think him capable of such a breach of etiquette in a territory
over which he had no jurisdiction (see p. 108), rehearsing at length his
achievements in suppressing the slave trade for the Khedive on the Nile
and the benefits from the revised agreement with El 'Aqqād. He delayed
his reply direct to the Khedive until 28 December, reaffirming that he
had never dismissed any Shilluk chief but had simply invited 'le vieux
mek' (Kwatker) to appear before Ja'afar Pasha to explain things.
Baker's name had however been damaged and although a letter from
the Khedive was drafted in February 1872 there is no evidence of any
further personal missive dispatched from Cairo before Baker's return in
July 1873.

Ismailia 1871   Within a week of his departure from Tawfiqia on 11
December 1870 Baker found that a *dhahabiya* in the care of Ra'uf Bey
had sunk at Sobat mouth with sections of a vital Samuda-built steamer

Steamer hauling away severed sudd, *Bahr el Jebel*

and had simply been abandoned, necessitating Baker's return to super-vise its salvage over Christmas, in time to report the incident in his letter to the Khedive. He overhauled Ra'uf on the Zeraf, the latter having taken a leisurely twenty-six days to attain the point reached from Khartoum the previous March in twenty-two days. 'I believe most thoroughly these scoundrels delay purposely in hopes of thwarting the expedition.'

This time they forced a way through the Zeraf *sudd*, joining the Bahr el Jebel at last after five weeks of struggle on 18 March 1871. His steamer reached Gondokoro, near deserted, four weeks later. Denied a following wind, the sailing boats would take a further month to arrive on 12 May. 'I walked up to the old mission station. Not one brick remains upon another', but the avenue of lemon trees still survived to adorn Baker's garden. Two years into his contract, Baker had at last occupied his launching base.

He had passed through an alarming sequence of vicissitudes, irre-spective of their causes. His situation as expedition commander, despite the most energetic and prescient organisation, was sadly different from that confidently planned with the Khedive. The force of 1,300 infantry and 200 Sha'iqi cavalry had already shrunk to 1,200 infantry, but aggravated by a journey through the Bahr el Zeraf *sudd* lasting three months, and by indifferent health, the morale of the troops on arrival at Gondokoro was poor, to be further undermined by a shortage of *dura* and the ill-concealed opinion of their commanding officer, Mohammed Ra'uf, that the expedition should proceed no further.

The local Bari after initial friendliness became overtly hostile – 'I always knew the Baris to be the worst tribe in the Nile Basin.' Alloron (Loro lo Lako of Alibari), their chief with a shared interest in the El 'Aqqād-dominated status quo, coldly recalled Baker's visit of 1863 and now on 9 May denied the new ruler's expedition fresh meat, even grass and wood for the huts. On 26 May the arrival of Baker's river flotilla with Ra'uf now complete, the Ottoman flag was raised in the presence of a group of dissenting Bari chiefs and Baker proclaimed 'Ismailia' to be the new name of his provincial capital. Alloron had been deposed but his elected successor proving equally uncooperative Baker resorted to force, seizing Bari cattle first at Ismailia and then at Belinian, immediately prior to the arrival on 9 June of his 'agent', Abu Sa'ud. The latter was now, following Mohammed Ahmed el 'Aqqād's sudden death in Khartoum, chief local representative of his prestigious company.[16]

This was a critical moment. Baker's own troops (with the notable exception of his loyal bodyguard under Bimbashi Abdel Qadir) were disaffected, the construction of his fortified base was far from completion, and the local community overtly hostile to him and welcoming to Abu Sa'ud and his 500 men. Worse, in pursuance to his contract to provision Baker's expedition, Abu Sa'ud arrived with 1,400 cattle rustled from the neighbours to the Cher, with whose chief Baker had left a small protecting force. Baker accused Abu Sa'ud of 'stealing slaves and cattle from the interior and delivering them here'. He believed the victim owners would hold the Cher and their Egyptian protectors to be in collusion with Abu Sa'ud and seek revenge. Baker tacitly discounted the possibility that the cattle had been rustled by the Cher because, like the Bari, the owners refused to trade. Later it was to be revealed that five of the seven protecting force had been killed in a Cher attack on the victim owners, with or without their officer's sanction, and Douin affirms (without source) that Baker had later 'donné une leçon aux Chers' before departing for Bunyoro – a mystery unresolved.

Thus at their first encounter in Equatoria the new general-governor's agent, monopoly trader of the region, was accused of scouting the law. In March 1863 Baker had been tough on *razzias*, even if he himself was forced to resort to them himself as now with the Bari. If the slave trade with which Abu Sa'ud was notoriously associated were to be suppressed, Baker was on the evidence convinced that there would be no place for such a rogue as agent of the new governorate. Yet the situation was not simple: not only did Abu Sa'ud suborn the Bari and ingratiate himself with Baker's senior officers; he held a signed monopoly trading concession from the government of the Sudan with a year to run; and his trading stations on the route to Bunyoro were critical to Baker's intended annexation, as indeed Abu Sa'ud irregulars might also prove to be.

Though not a man willing to compromise with evil-doing, Baker yet hesitated in his vulnerable and inaccessible location to follow the unbending logic of his conviction and to dispatch Abu Sa'ud in irons to Khartoum – a hesitation which he claimed frankly to regret in his *Ismailia*. Instead he placed a *cordon sanitaire* along the river between his force and that of Abu Sa'ud; accused the latter of collusion against him with the Bari; confiscated the rustled cattle; and ordered Abu Sa'ud to quit the new province on the approaching expiration of the lease agreement, 9 April 1872. Abu Sa'ud, always a dedicated opponent of Baker's Khedivial commission, was now an implacable enemy, well-rooted in the territory and sharing an ethnic and religious sympathy with Baker's force. After three uneasy months, Abu Sa'ud sought Baker's permission to leave on 22 September 1871, ostensibly to return to Khartoum but in fact to Bor in order to take delivery of ivory from his southern outstations without yielding the 40% payment agreed with the government, and to alert them to resist Baker's forthcoming progress.[17]

In Ismailia (Gondokoro) things continued to deteriorate. Since Mohammed Ra'uf will feature regularly in the history of the next ten years, it is well to trace his relationship with Baker whose lieutenant he had been appointed to be by Shahin Pasha. To the Khedive Baker had volunteered on 15 June 1870: 'Jusqu'à présent l'expédition se trouve bien unie les troupes commandées avec soin et énergie par Ra'uf Bey; tous les munitions en bon état; et un bon esprit de corps qui est un guaranti d'un bon résultat.' It was not to last. By 3 December 1870 Baker was requesting of Sharif Pasha the appointment of at least a second *miralai* on account of Ra'uf's persistent ill-health. The episode of the sunken *dhababiya* did not commend him to Baker. At Ismailia matters now came to a head. The expedition's planted harvest had failed for want of rain, necessitating the postponement of the departure to Bunyoro planned for about October 1871 and a distribution of the unpopular rice alternative to *dura*. 'We appeared to have forsaken the known world and having passed the River Styx, to have become secluded for ever in a wild land of our own, where all were enemies like evil spirits and where it was necessary either to procure food at the point of a bayonet or to lie down and die.'

Baker was to be obliged to raid Belinian for grain a second time. The resentment engendered among the Belinian Bari led by Chief Sobek is recorded by A. C. Beaton. Before his departure on this mission on 14 October Baker had drafted a letter to the Khedive dated 8 October reporting his river journey; the vital need for a force to clear the channels of the Bahr el Zeraf and of the Jebel; the hostility of the Bari; the founding of Ismailia; the poor morale of the troops. He went on to lay a direct complaint against Ra'uf Bey who had dared to disobey in front of witnesses Baker's order for the reduction in rank of a *yuzbashi* for major negligence, claiming he had special orders from Shahin Pasha which required the officer to be court-martialled – insolent behaviour by Ra'uf amounting to a gross breach of discipline. Obliquely Baker requested Ra'uf's recall. At 1,400 miles distance Baker insisted on the absolute authority bestowed by the firman of 16 May 1869. Mistakenly perhaps he coupled with the complaint a proposal that his son Lieutenant Julian Baker, RN should be his eventual successor.

Then on 12 October 1871 he was confronted with Ra'uf Bey's conveyance to him of three petitions from his officers (the 'Forty Thieves' bodyguard excepted) for the return of the force to Khartoum due to absence of food. Seven weeks later Baker was to learn from his chief clerk that Ra'uf had himself drafted the petition of the officers to the two *bimbashis;* and of the *bimbashis* to himself, to be enclosed with his own supposedly consequent covering letter. In Fatiko the following March it emerged that Abu Sa'ud with Bari militia had been at Belinian – 'always in league with Ra'uf Bey to ruin the expedition if possible' – when the officers' petition to return to Khartoum was being planned.

Baker resolved to forward the three petitions to the Khedive, and ordered Ra'uf to leave with himself and a force of six companies on 14 October to raid the Rejaf islands of the Bari where they found grain sufficient for two months. Back in Ismailia he added a postscript to his letter to the Khedive on 17 October, enclosing the letters instigated by Ra'uf – the latter full of errors regarding the absence of food as Belinian had shown – assuring the Khedive that Baker would not abandon Ismailia; and requesting a severe response to the conduct displayed by the Egyptian officers.

Douin never found this letter of Baker in Cairo nor seemingly a second letter he wrote, undated, at this time to Sharif Pasha. In it Baker again emphasised the need to clear the *sudd* which had delayed his journey four months and so exacerbated a food shortage, the solution of which depended on *dura* from Khartoum and Fashoda. Communications with the outside world were meanwhile cut. Nevertheless the country was 'superb... a climate ten times better than that of the Sudan'. He awaited his own reinforcements from Khartoum to replace the 700 sick soldiers and sailors he was now sending north. And he repeated his complaint against Ra'uf Bey 'always passively obstructive'.

Yet a third letter, addressed this time to Ja'afar Pasha Mazhar dated 6–19 October 1871 (the latter had in fact quit Khartoum in August), and again not found by Douin, made no reference to Ra'uf's insubordination but emphasised the urgency of the dispatch of *dura* and of 400 Sudanese, rather than Egyptian, reinforcements in the same barges carrying the sick to Khartoum, all to be towed by five steamers.

There is a reply in draft for the Khedive in the Abdin Palace archives, dated February 1872, from which it would appear that Baker had additionally canvassed the desirability of recruiting Abu Sa'ud's irregulars when the El 'Aqqād contract ended, even in replacement of Khedivial troops. Of this there is no evidence in the October letters. The draft reply, and it is no more than that, concedes the immediate replacement of Ra'uf Bey, but the Khedive strongly opposes Baker's plans to recruit El 'Aqqād's 'companions' on account of the wrong message as to behaviour that that would give to the Bari. He instructs Baker to halt at Gondokoro (Ra'uf's preference), fortify the base and commence his given tasks; create a government trade monopoly and respect for the law: 'En un mot, n'avancez-pas; enseignez, colonisez, rendez-vous les habitants amis, et une fois ceci fait, avancez.'

Whether nor not that reply was ever sent, Baker would have left Ismailia for Bunyoro long before its arrival, nor was it or any other Khedivial letter awaiting his return to Ismailia in 1873. His letter to the Khedive and others to the Prince of Wales and, dated 22 October 1871, to Colonel Stanton in Cairo reached the recipients mid-January 1872. Stanton reported to Earl Granville on 21 January 1872 that the Khedive (?influenced by Shahin Pasha) 'though apparently inclined to exonerate the officers for their want of discipline on account of the leadership to which they had been subjected, has assured me that he will show me the letter he sends him [Baker] in reply to his complaint'. Stanton makes no further reference to this in his dispatches – a further indication that the draft reply of February was never sent. This was however the first direct news to arrive back from Baker for over a year, though a message from Ra'uf Pasha had been forwarded to Cairo by Ahmed Mumtaz Pasha in Khartoum in December 1871. The Foreign

Office marked Stanton's report received 29 January 1872 'Extract to President RGS', and the next day *The Times* published letters from Baker addressed to Mr Gustave Oppenheim dated 20 October and to Mr E. T. Rogers, 8 October 1871, the former criticising Baker's officers' attitude to the expedition and emphasising its objective of stopping the slave trade. A vexed Khedive may have found their publication sufficient reason not to reply to Baker.

A week into the local march to Rejaf in mid-October 1871, Baker had ordered Ra'uf back to Gondokoro to expedite the repatriation to Khartoum (on 3 November) of all definitely sick and disabled troops (perhaps 700). In fact Ra'uf dispatched as many as 1,100 persons, including seemingly half the Egyptian battalion in which Baker placed little reliance. At least there were fewer mouths to feed. With them went Baker's requests to Khartoum to send as reinforcements four Sudanese companies and, more important still, for a canal to be opened up through the Bahr el Jebel for communication. The total expedition force was now reduced to 502 troops and 52 sailors.

Ignorant of the Khedive's reaction to his dispatch, Baker resisted the defeat of his plan to advance to Bunyoro. 'If I remained at Gondokoro, my term of office would expire fruitlessly. I should simply have reduced the Baris and have established the station. Abu Sa'ud would remain in the interior among his numerous slave establishments, to ridicule my impotence and to defy my orders that he should quit the country.'

One recalls the words of John Dryden on the Earl of Shaftesbury 200 years earlier: 'A daring Pilot in extremity'. Certainly. 'Pleas'd with the Danger, when the Waves went high, He sought the Storms.' Perhaps. 'But for a calm unfit, would steer too nigh the Sands to boast his Wit'? Baker's preparations for the advance to the Equator had been grievously undermined yet his iron resolve was undiminished; to persevere against all odds, to triumph over incalculable risks; and in that decision his wife, nephew Julian and the officers of the bodyguard and of Mexican war-hardened troops unflinchingly backed him.

Abu Sa'ud had apparently gained his ambition, and the expedition was paralysed...with so small a force I could not reach far from the headquarters... I did not despair but I determined that this reduction of military force should NOT paralyse the activity of the expedition and that in spite of every intrigue I would succeed in the main objects of the enterprise; the slave trade should be suppressed, and the territory should be annexed to the Equator.

On 14 December, with no communication from Khartoum for over a year (Ja'afar Mazhar had retired in August 1871, and been succeeded by a general-governor of the 'Southern Sudan', Lewa Ahmed Mumtaz Pasha), Baker designated Ra'uf Bey commander of the Ismailia base as originally intended, the base now fortified with a garrison of 340 and the 52 sailors. He then set out with six vessels about 22 January 1872 for Bunyoro with a contingent of 212 picked regulars; the smaller steamer no. 3 of 38 tons, dismounted, to be carried on gun carriages for conveyance south of the Rejaf above the Fola rapids to Apuddo/Dufile ('Ibrahimiyya'), there to be reassembled by the English mechanics; and 2,500 cattle. The 108-ton no. 2 steamer *Khedive* remained for assembly at Ismailia with Chief Engineer Edwin Higginbotham – some assurance to Baker of Ra'uf Bey's good behaviour.[18]

Bunyoro 1872–73 It would be mistakenly repetitious to chronicle the progress of the expedition into the lacustrine territories, published by its leader in 1874 in the epic *Ismailia*. How far, however, were the five objectives in the Khedivial firman of 16 May 1869 to be realised? 'I determined that this reduction of military force should *not* paralyse the activity of the expedition, and that in spite of every intrigue, I would succeed in the main objects of the enterprise; the slave trade should be suppressed, and the territory should be annexed to the equator.'

Not even Baker's resolution could overcome the first obstruction which quickly presented itself within a week of departure. The Bari chief of Beddan (?Lugör) who had promised 2,000 porters to carry the baggage including steamer no. 3 above the Fola rapids in exchange for cattle, unilaterally aborted the arrangement on 28 January 1872 and commenced hostilities.

On 27 December Baker had angrily confided to his journal: 'I believe that nothing will ever improve the White Nile tribes... they can only be improved by slavery, horrible as that appears. If left to themselves they will only steal cattle and slaves and fight each other. If made slaves they must work – and they become in some way improved.'

His troops declining the task of porterage obliged Baker immediately to return the English mechanics on two vessels with no. 3 steamer (later to be named *N'yanza*) to Ismailia, there to assist the construction of no. 2, the *Khedive*, for communication with Khartoum. Left now with only one 10-ton steel lifeboat carried by porters from Labore, Baker could no longer achieve the opening 'to navigation the Great Lakes of the Equator'.

Three of the remaining four objectives – the annexation of the lacustrine territories, the introduction of regular commerce and the establishment of the chain of military and commercial stations in the Nile
Basin were inextricably linked; as, less explicitly, was the suppression
of the slave trade. Baker's primary territorial objective was Masindi,
seat of the young king (*mukama*) of Bunyoro, Kabarega, who,
unknown to Baker, had with the help of the traders very recently
outmanoeuvred his brother to succeed his father Kamrasi. El 'Aqqād
had taken over from Andrea Debono his stations of Faloro and Fabbo,
Fatiko and Foweira (the prefix 'fa' or 'pa' = village), but, with the El
'Aqqād trading agreement due to expire on 9 April 1872 and ambitious
to recruit Abu Sa'ud's men to his own force, Baker made his approach
march with 212 men to Masindi via Fatiko – 'le paradis d'Afrique'
Baker extravagantly called it – through a ravaged countryside. Arriving on 6 March 1872, he wrote to Abu Sa'ud's *wakils* (including
Mohammed Wad el Mek currently absent on a *razzia*), warning them
that they had the options to enlist in government service, settle at
Ismailia or return to Khartoum, but that their ivory trade must cease.
However instead of having been previously warned of this by Abu
Sa'ud, the latter had announced that 'the Pasha's firman was ended and
that the whole country was in his [own] hands'.

Leaving half his force in Fatiko under Sagh Abdallah, Baker moved
on to Fuweira by the Karuma Falls where the *wakils* volunteered for
government service, only to find after his departure that on Abu Sa'ud's
orders their militia had bolted with the slaves to Fabbo. Arresting the
wakils, Baker with 112 men finally reached Masindi, 322 miles from
Ismailia, where in Kabarega's presence he ran up the Ottoman flag on
14 May. That day he reported optimistically to the Khedive (it arrived):

I have raised up your Highness's ensign and declared the annexation [of Bunyoro] to Egypt. I have taken prisoner the Aqqad *wakil*
[Sulieman at Fuweira] and I have chased the slavers out of the
country. I have given notice of the confiscation of all ivory in the
different stations. These stations were full of slaves and must be
equated with the boats of slave-traffickers... After a few weeks, it
is my intention to press on to the south of Albert N'yanza and to
raise your Highness's ensign at the source of the great lake...
Before my return I will place your Highness's flag at least at one
degree south of the Equator; thus Egyptian territory will extend
33° south from Alexandria.

The ruins of Fort Fatiko, showing the grain and ammunition store

Ignoring the bold boasts of intent, it was nevertheless a most remarkable achievement to have taken Masindi with such a tiny force.

At the same time he addressed another letter to the departed Ja'afar Pasha, praising the effectiveness of the Snider carbines (400 carabineers were worth 4,000 musketeers) and rejoicing in the abundance of food. He spelt out in detail the treachery of Abu Sa'ud, recording the success of the Madi and the Umiro (east of Fatiko) in resisting the *razzias*. Only now, due to Baker, had legitimate barter of ivory for glass beads and cotton cloth been substituted for Abu Sa'ud's slaves and cattle. Sagh Abdallah at Fatiko had been ordered to arrest Abu Sa'ud and transport him to Cairo, to which Sharif Pasha had been alerted. Zanzibar merchants were well ahead in creating fair-trading stations in Buganda, but the distances were a handicap to them and Baker aimed to reverse this ivory trade to the Khedive's benefit. To achieve this he would need annually *dura* and sixty camels.[19]

However in reality Baker's position was extremely precarious. He had had a tentative discussion with Kabarega on the desirability of trading ivory with the Khedive down the Nile rather than east via M'tesa's Buganda to Zanzibar, but Baker's ambitious plans for agriculture and cotton growing seem not yet to have been touched upon. Kabarega, like his deceased father before him, was primarily interested in defeating his uncle Rionga. He regarded himself as humiliated by Baker's interception of his attempt to steal five rifles, but observed also that Baker's force in Masindi, after the dispatch of troops to Abu Sa'ud's superannuated stations, no longer exceeded 100 regular troops – the remainder being deployed at Fatiko and Foweira.

By 8 June, Baker's fifty-first birthday, open hostilities were provoked by Kabarega in Masindi and by 14 June 1872 Baker was obliged to conduct a withdrawal under constant attack to Fuweira, fifteen miles from Rionga's island headquarters, arriving on 24 June having suffered in all ten killed and eleven wounded, the latter including Bimbashi Abdel Qadir. Four weeks later Rionga, 'a handsome man of about fifty with exceedingly good manners', had in the presence of his Lango supporters been proclaimed by Baker the new Khedivial representative in Bunyoro in place of the deposed Kabarega, and before the end of 1872 Rionga, joined by a force from M'tesa, had defeated and put to flight his nephew – a satisfactory development for Baker who was unwilling to return to confront Kabarega during the rainy season and its long grass. Meanwhile a military post was established by Baker at Magungo on Lake Albert.

Baker was thus enabled, after a dangerous hiccough in Masindi, and notwithstanding his retreat to Fuweira, to claim that Bunyoro remained annexed to Egypt and to call on the cooperative *kabaka* of Buganda to withdraw his troops from the invasion of the southern Bunyoro territory. The country north of Bunyoro and the Victoria Nile in which were located the Abu Sa'ud trading stations, albeit now superannuated, constituted a major threat to Baker on his arrival back in Fuweira. Abu Sa'ud had flinched from actually attacking Baker's *mamur* at Fatiko, Sagh Abdallah, but there and at Fabbo and Faloro Abu Sa'ud still ruled with 870 irregulars, and the slave and ivory trade continued to flourish.

Leaving half his force under Abdel Qadir at Fuweira, Baker pressed on to relieve Fatiko to the north where he came under a severe armed attack from Abu Sa'ud's *wakil*, Mohammed Wad el Mek, an attack which he vigorously repulsed, killing 140 and capturing the latter. Abu Sa'ud and his slave-traders at Fabbo and Faloro were similarly reduced and Abu Sa'ud summoned to Fatiko, but the sheer size of Abu Sa'ud's army of 600 constrained Baker to recruit the maximum number of irregulars possible into his own force (now 146) under Wad el Mek and to accept Abu Sa'ud's feeble self-exculpation. The latter was granted leave to head north to Gondokoro at the end of August with his remaining force, having arranged the safeguarding of his ivory assets at Fabbo and elsewhere. Instead he escaped to Makaraka despite Baker's order to Ra'uf Bey in November to arrest him, proceeding thence to Khartoum.

Thus remarkably by October 1872 the El 'Aqqād trading stations, to the relief of the Acholi and Madi, were garrisoned by mixed government forces and detachments were also stationed with Rionga at Paniadoli, his island base on the Somerset Nile and at Magungo on Lake Albert. Authority lay uniquely with Baker himself, but his contract was due to expire on 1 April 1873 and the 200 reinforcements he now sought in November by the agency of Wad el Mek from Gondokoro were not to reach Fatiko until 8 March (Baker had originally requested them from Khartoum when in Gondokoro in October 1871 – the full force of 400 men were in transit for thirteen months on the Nile).

On 1 January 1873, three months before the expiration of his four-year contract, Baker had rehearsed in his Journal at Fatiko the numerous instances of obstruction to his Khedivial expedition. His principal accusations included the initial failure to prepare the Khartoum fleet; the abandonment of the sunken steamer parts; the contrived delays during the second, in early 1871, passage through the Zeraf river; the conspiracy at Ismailia of Ra'uf Bey and his deputy Bimbashi El Tayib Agha to abort the expedition on grounds of hunger; and their collusion with Abu Sa'ud when he was enlisting Bari tribesmen, putting his stations on a war footing against Baker, and subverting Kabarega to attack him. In 1872 Abu Sa'ud having withdrawn his ivory from Fatiko, had first threatened to attack Baker's garrison and then, on Baker's arrival in August, actually done so, while continuously conducting *razzias* in the countryside.

A few days later, on 6 January 1873, Baker added:

> The true copy of my instructions received from the Viceroy was not [?] sent to Ja'afar Pasha the Governor-General of Sudan but all clauses that referred to the suppression of the slave trade were omitted... The traders have no official notice from the Sudan Government – therefore the entire onus for the suppression of the loved slave trade is thrown upon me alone, and the traders regard it as a personal matter, considering me solely responsible. The want of candour and cowardice of the Government places me in a false position.

Appointing Sagh Abdallah once more to take command at Fatiko, now fortified, and strengthening the other garrisons, Baker marched north with his personal party – including the indomitable Lady Baker, always 'my prime minister, to give good counsel in moments of difficulty and danger' – and his bodyguard, reaching Ismailia on 1 April 1873 – 'filthy'. He was obviously embarrassed, if already aware, that contrary to his request for Ra'uf's replacement to the Khedive of 8 October 1871 (which in the draft reply of February 1872 was being acted upon) Ra'uf Bey had remained in command. No Khedivial letter awaited him from Cairo. Steamer no. 2, the *Khedive*, was assembled and afloat but the architect of the work, Higginbotham, was dead. The Bari, with Alloran back again in office, were friendly.[20]

The absence of further news from Baker since his letters from Ismailia dated 8 and 17 October 1871, received seemingly in Cairo in January 1872, had increased the vexation first betrayed by the Khedive in his draft reply. Ismail progressively revealed his frustration at the seeming outcome of the expedition: the alienation of his officials and the hostility of the equatorial tribes. No compensating territorial annexation, slave trade suppression, nor enhanced White Nile commerce had yet materialised in return for a very costly project. It was the British ambassador in Constantinople, not Stanton, to whom the Khedive unburdened himself on 1 July 1872. The expedition 'had proved very unsatisfactory in its results... having plundered the inhabitants of the country, the effect had been that the people had become so hostile as to render impossible the intercourse which used to be maintained with them'. Baker's replacement must be one, possibly from India, who would 'remedy the evils resulting from the recent mistakes'. Then from Ismail Pasha Ayub, now general-governor in Khartoum – to Baker he was 'my excellent friend' – came a dispatch to Cairo at the end of November 1872. He reported rumours that Baker was at Lake Albert, and in difficulties. Communication via the *sudd* was impossible and Ayub suggested a relief force.

In the aftermath of the American Civil War in early 1870, the Khedive had engaged on contract fifteen United States officers to reorganise the Egyptian army and to replace earlier French appointments. Among them were General Mott, quartermaster general; General Sibley, master gunner; and General C. P. Stone Pasha who in November 1871 had become Chief of Staff. Stone now recommended on 27 November 1872 a force under U.S. Colonel Purdy Bey to approach Lake Victoria – not via Khartoum, but via Mombasa and the

Masai country. The proposal appealed to the Khedive who saw a possibility not only of dampening down local antagonisms but of further territorial expansion. A secret letter of instruction was prepared: 'Enfin le colonel Purdy agira, mais sans le dire, comme s'il formait des établissements de nouvelles provinces pour Son Altesse le Khédive', which, it was suspected, Baker had failed to do. A letter to Baker would terminate his services. It was about this time that the Khedive told Beardsley, the United States consul-general, of his conviction that 'Baker by waging active war against the slave-trade, has defeated the chief object of his mission which was to subject the country to the Egyptian Flag' – a significant indication as to where the Khedive's real priority lay. This relief expedition however was aborted before its much delayed departure from Cairo, following the arrival of news from Khartoum dated 21 April 1873 that Baker was safe and well at Ismailia (Gondokoro).[21]

On 26 May Baker was able to leave Ismailia on a rising Nile drawn by the steamer *Khedive* and benefiting from a stronger current, the consequence of the earlier clearance work of Ismail Pasha Ayub on the channels of the Zeraf river in March and April 1873. Ten days before sailing, Baker recorded that Dr Saleh, the expedition doctor, had revealed that while Baker was away an Egyptian soldier had died under flogging ordered by Ra'uf Bey. Despite threats, Saleh had refused to sign a death certificate attributing death to disease and now feared for his life, and had been prevented from tending the English mechanics. At Fashoda, now garrisoned by 1,000 men, Baker found the new governor, Yusuf Effendi Hasan Khorda (not Ali Bey whom in January, he had learned, had replaced Ali Reda), with two of the six original steamers of 1869 from Cairo, and warned him of the imminent arrival of three El 'Aqqād boats from Bor with 700 slaves which Baker had passed ten days earlier in the Zeraf. The Shilluk now sold their cotton and goods to the government who sold to the merchants.

Unfinished Business, 1873   It was time for Baker to render account to Cairo of the outcome of his mission. Ismail Ayub telegraphed Baker's initial report from Khartoum on 29 June in Arabic addressed to the consul-general of England, with Baker increasingly vexed that there was word neither from the Khedive nor Sharif. Hussey Vivian, now acting in Stanton's absence, initially forwarded to London an incomplete version, sent by the Foreign Office to the newspapers. Vivian corrected the text next day, 1 July, as follows:

We have arrived all well at Khartoum with all the other Europeans who were with us. The country as far as the Equator has been annexed to the Egyptian Government. Revolutions and the intrigues of the Slave Merchants have all been appeased and the Slave Trade annihilated. The soldiers as well as the officers are all well and happy. The natives of the Soudan will pay the demands of the Government willingly. All the country is orderly. The Government is thoroughly well organised and the road practicable as far as Zanzibar. Mathise [M'tesa] Sultan of Aswala [*sic*] has kept his word to the Government. A steamer of the capacity of a ship is on the river.

El Zeraf is navigable, in consequence of the good works which we caused to be executed at the time of our first passage.

A great quantity of elephant tusks in the Stations.

With only 105 of the soldiers of the Government we gained a victory over all the soldiers of the Amioso [*sic*] on the 8th June 1872 – The success of my mission is complete.

Thank God I am well and I report the preceding with respect and homage to His Highness the Khedive.

Vivian as requested by Baker took this to Sharif Pasha who forwarded it to the Khedive in Constantinople. It was to be followed by a lengthy report to the Khedive on the results of the expedition, the problems encountered and overcome, a description of the territory occupied between Ismailia and Fatiko, to be presented on 1 September. Before the Bakers' return to Cairo on 24 August 1873 and their meeting with the Khedive the next day, there had been a further telegram from Baker on 25 July from Khartoum urging the arrest and trial of Abu Sa'ud 'el Ahad, which to Sharif's further vexation was sent through Vivian. Sharif, reluctant to act without proofs, was overruled by Tawfik Pasha, the Prince Regent, who imprisoned Abu Sa'ud pending an inquiry.

While the Khedive and Nubar Pasha had been abroad successfully negotiating (at an estimated cost of £E1m) a new firman consolidating the Khedivial privileges conceded since 1866, Sharif had been acting minister of foreign affairs. In confidence he had shared his fears with Vivian that Baker's original Khartoum telegram report to Vivian of 29 June was 'too highly coloured'; that if a quarter of the contents were true Egypt would be satisfied notwithstanding sacrificial costs. Expressing due reserve until he had met Baker, the Khedive on his return echoed Sharif's misgivings that the expedition's success had been much exaggerated... giving rise to a general feeling of hostility and dislike towards Europeans and his government in Upper Egypt... Baker was brave, energetic and determined, but he doubted his tact and his method of dealing with the natives. He was too prone to fighting and the use of force and neglected conciliation and arbitration between hostile tribes...

A somewhat sweeping conclusion from one who had not set foot in the Sudan, let alone Ismailia.

Nubar likewise was critical, complaining of the publication of Baker's letters in the British press before Baker's report to Cairo and attributing his failure to advance beyond Masindi to the early losses to his force incurred by ignoring Ja'afar Mazhar's advice to postpone his departure in February 1870: 'il ne savait qu'une chose, se battre et aller de l'avant.' Notwithstanding the decorations bestowed on Baker and his nephew Julian (whose qualities of leadership as well as of astronomical observation and cartography were notable), at the meeting with the Khedive on 25 August the atmosphere was cool. Baker believed the authorities had played him false from the beginning and that Abu Sa'ud would be allowed to escape. The latter's case was left for appraisal by a *majlis* formed by Nubar, Sharif and Ismail Ayub.[22]

Much had been accomplished but Baker's claims were exaggerated. The Khedive's flag was not raised on the Equator but at Masindi (latitude 1° 45 N) which was then lost until Kabarega's uncle Rionga regained it. Fatiko at latitude 3° N was the enduring fortified government base and this was well north of Bunyoro. The route had not been opened to Zanzibar nor Lake Albert opened to navigation. The clearing of the *sudd* and the reconciliation of the Bari were respectively the work of Ismail Ayub and of Ra'uf. Above all the slave trade was not suppressed, let alone annihilated, though Abu Sa'ud's henchmen had been latterly driven out of the El 'Aqqād stations. Their colleagues at the stations to the north among the Bor, Dinka, Latuka and Makaraka however remained, exceeding 600 men.

Moreover, as Professor Richard Gray has emphasised, quoting Schweinfurth, the White Nile slave trade, with its maximum movement of 2,000 slaves per year, was dwarfed by the enormously increased overland movement to Darfur and Kordofan in the 1860s, following the discovery of the Bahr el Ghazal access, the creation of the fortified trading *zaribas* and, from 1866, the cooperation of the Rizeiqat Baqqara. The latter movement was estimated to number between 12,000 and 15,000 per year and, based on Hufrat el Nahas and Dar Fertit, was to continue uninterrupted into the 1870s. In April 1873 Stanton had been alerted to impress on the Khedive the need for stringent measures to prevent the arrival of slaves from Darfur and Kordofan.

In the more detached atmosphere of England, Baker was to acknowledge: 'Although the slave hunters were driven out of the territory under my command, there were nevertheless vast tracts of country through which new routes could be opened for slave caravans to avoid the cruising steamers of the White Nile.' For them asylum was offered by the Sultan of Darfur. Baker now summed up his achievement more temperately:

> I had simply achieved the success of a foundation for a radical reform in the so-called commerce of the White Nile. The government had been established throughout the newly acquired territories which were occupied by military positions garrisoned with regular troops, and all the districts were purged from the slave-hunters. In this condition I resigned my command, as the first act was accomplished. The future will depend upon the sincerity of the Khedive and upon the ability and integrity of my successor.

Vivian had been requested by the British Foreign Office to give his opinion on the success of Baker's expedition, especially in the context of the White Nile slave trade, as soon as Baker's initial telegram from Khartoum was received. He waited until he had personally interviewed Nubar and Baker. His report and conclusions, dated 6 September 1873, are remarkably perceptive, fair, even prescient for one who had been acting consul-general in Egypt a bare three months:

> I have come to the conclusion (and I believe the Government think so too) that Baker has rough-hewn the foundation for the establishment of a Civilised Government in the heart of Africa which, if vigorously and skilfully built upon, may lead to great political and moral results. That his work has been roughly and hastily done; that he left it very incomplete, and he made mistakes I have no doubt... Still I believe that... if these foundations are promptly and vigorously built upon by an able man whose heart is in his work, excellent results may follow.

As to the suppression of the White Nile slave trade, Vivian advocated the appointment of Christian governors with Khedivial backing from Khartoum southwards. 'The only chance of success is through the vigorous action of Europeans unhampered by Native prejudices and their passive resistance to any change.'

On Nubar's recommendation, Khedive Ismail Pasha on 30 August 1873 requested the British government's permission to appoint Colonel Charles Gordon, currently Commissioner for the Danube, as successor to Baker, permission granted informally a month later on the eve of the Bakers' departure to England. The latter were to be the honoured guests of numerous public receptions, notably by the Royal Geographical Society and the United Service Institution. In January 1874 at Brighton they would briefly meet Gordon, about to leave for Khartoum.

Public attention in Europe remained concentrated on the White Nile. At (Ismailia) Gondokoro the previous April however, as Baker awaited the rise of the Nile, he had heard 'that the slave traders attacked and defeated the Government troops on the Bahr el Ghazal and killed the commandant, only three months before they had the audacity to attack me. The Bahr el Ghazal is far away from my district.'[23]

6
Khedivial Aggrandisement 1868–73: The West

I DAR FERTIT: THE HILALI EXPEDITION 1869–72

The Egyptian Viceroy had disclosed to Ja'afar Mazhar in August 1866 his long-term ambition to occupy Darfur and incorporate it in the Sudan. Ismail realised however that it was important to proceed cautiously in the face of the aggressive ambition of Emperor Theodore II and of his rumoured association with the Sultan of Darfur's chief minister and general, Ahmed Shatta, in a two-pronged attack on Khartoum and Kordofan in 1867. Magdala had removed the Abyssinian threat by 1868, while the reconnaissance of El Fasher by Mohammed Nadi Bey a year previously provided up-to-date intelligence of the deployment and arms of the Darfur forces under their rival commanders (see p. 50).

Ja'afar Mazhar had been absent for a year in Egypt and the Red Sea littoral but following his return to Khartoum in May 1868, the month of Theodore's defeat at Magdala, the Governor-General's interest turned once again to the occupation of the White Nile basin at least as far as Gondokoro, opening up thereby the additional trading opportunities through the Bahr el Ghazal to the Dar Fertit region. While his ambitions were fully shared by his Viceroy, the coordination of Baker's drive to the Equator and the annexation of the Dar Fertit as an approach route to Darfur were shortly to create a clash of priorities over the allocation of river transport between the two expeditions (see pp. 120–1).

During his visit to Kordofan in February 1867 Ja'afar Mazhar had encountered a Sheikh Mohammed el Hilali (alias el Bulalawi), claiming to be of Baguirmi (Wadai) extraction, who returning from the *haj* (pilgrimage) in about 1850 had journeyed through the Dar Fertit. He had persuaded the local traders (Dongola *jallabas*), vulnerable in their small establishments (*deims*), to put themselves under his protection against the raids of the Darfur Baqqara – notably the Ta'aisha and

Habbaniya – becoming vassals of the Fur Sultan. Hilali's initiative was then accepted by the Sultan in return for a modest annual recompense of 200 slaves, and the arrangement obtained for some fifteen years, to the satisfaction of the *jallabas* and also seemingly of the small pagan Fertit tribes – the Kreish (Kredy), Golo and Sere, resident west of the River Pongo (Dembo), affluent of the Bahr el Ghazal.

In establishing this territorial claim to the Fertit, Hilali had his eye on the important copper deposits of Hufrat el Nahas to the north-west on the headwaters of the Bahr el Arab. However the discovery in 1856 of the Bahr el Ghazal access route from Khartoum via the Bahr el Jebel and the progressive arrival of sizeable trading companies establishing *zaribas* in the region for safeguarding their ammunition, ivory and slaves introduced a presence hostile to Hilali and his pretensions to *own* the territory. In 1867 he sought the protection of the Egyptian Viceroy.

Before this could be achieved, news of Hilali's intentions reached the Sultan. In consequence he was attacked by a Fur government force and obliged to flee with his followers to Kordofan, there in 1867 to entreat the support of Ja'afar Mazhar. The latter seems to have pointed him to Cairo, but by early 1869 procrastination or illness found Hilali still in Khartoum. Conscious perhaps that despite the removal of the Abyssinian threat to the Sudan there remained the predatory interest of Darfur both in Kordofan and the Bahr el Ghazal, Ja'afar decided that the impending danger to Dar Fertit brooked no further delay. Even prior to Hilali's formal submission to the Khedive in Cairo, he should first return with an armed force to the Bahr el Ghazal, there to secure the compliance of its inhabitants to the creation of a new sub-province which would form an integral part of the Sudan. Ja'afar wrote to seek Khedivial approval on 29 January 1869.[1]

Pending the issue of a Khedivial firman, public notice was issued in Khartoum of Hilali's nomination as *nazir*, tribal ruler of the Bahr el Ghazal *qism* (sub-province), the Dar Fertit. Kuchuk Ali, an Osmanli trader, would command the military force comprising a Turkish *bashi-buzouq* company of 400 and a Black *nizam el jedid* company of 200 under Mohammed Mounib. Ja'afar referred to Kuchuk Ali as a former *bashi-buzouq* long resident in the Sudan, and bestowed on him the rank of *sanjak* and the title of *agha*. Since 1862 the latter had managed a *zariba* on the Jur river with an army of 300 irregulars.

The intention was that Hilali and Kuchuk Ali, their expedition arrangements and stores once completed, should leave for Fashoda by the end of February 1869, there to familiarise themselves with the provincial administration of the governor, Ali Bey Reda, pending the arrival of the Khedivial firman from Cairo. However that firman was not to be dispatched before 11 April, reaching Khartoum therefore in May. Baker's expedition plan had been submitted for Khedivial approval on 27 March 1869 (see p. 115). When the firman did arrive, Hilali and his expedition were still in Khartoum, nor had they yet departed when, to complicate matters even more, an envoy arrived there from Sultan Mohammed Hussein, bringing allegedly documentary proof that since 1810 the important copper mines at Hufrat el Nahas had been under Fur military control, and claiming that part at least of the *qism* belonged to Fur notables. Hilali's presence enabled the *hakimdar* to write a rebuttal of the claims and allegations, which was conveyed back to the Darfur Sultan with a covering letter from Ja'afar affirming that the Fur military force now dispatched by the Sultan had in fact been turned back by the local inhabitants before it had even reached Hufrat el Nahas. Meanwhile, by letter dated 20 June, the Governor-General assured the Khedive that the Arabs of Dar Fertit were able to hold their own and that the Sultan would not dare to attack the new *qism*.

Unfortunately the Khedive had quit Egypt for Europe on 17 May 1869, having signed Baker's firman, and was not to return until 27 July. Confronted with two separate expeditions requiring logistical support, and with the start of the rains having now delayed the viability of the Bahr el Ghazal expedition, Ja'afar wrote off to Baker on 16 July explaining the impracticability of meeting all his transport needs. He then left for Berber to await Baker's response or anticipated arrival (see p. 120). Ja'afar Pasha, in the absence of any news of Baker's progess, finally ordered Hilali to set sail for the Dar Fertit via Fashoda and the Bahr el Ghazal only after the Khedive's return to Egypt and the issue in quick succession at the commencement of October 1869 of two Khedivial instructions for the departure of the Hilali expedition. The Khedive added the rider that the *qism* rulers should 'treat the inhabitants with mercy and kindness and not impose upon them onerous taxation'. It was essential to attract the loyalty of the inhabitants and to avoid intimidating them.[2]

For progress reports on the ill-fated expedition we have to rely on the versions of Sheikh Zubeir Rahma Mansour, whom we have already encountered as a young Ja'ali trader in the Bahr el Ghazal region in 1856–62. The *rapporteurs*, both of whom met Zubeir, were Dr Georg Schweinfurth, the German botanist, in January 1871 at Deim Zubeir;

and H. C. Jackson, the British deputy-inspector, in Omdurman in 1911–13. The latter was careful to warn in his preface that while 'the motives assigned by Zubeir for various events are to be received with considerable suspicion', yet they nevertheless 'differed but little from that which he [Zubeir] had recounted to Na'um Bey Shuqair in Ta'arikh el Sudan 1904'. There had however been a great lapse of time between 1870–2 and 1904.

Jackson relates that Zubeir met Hilali and Kuchuk Ali (whom Zubeir would have known from his first entry to the Bahr el Ghazal in the service of the trader Ali Abu Amouri in 1856–8) on their arrival at Meshra el Rek (?end 1869). He had to resolve a quarrel between the two expedition leaders before they moved off through the low-lying Dinka country of the Jur river towards their objective, Dar Fertit. It was at this critical point that the *sanjak* Kuchuk Ali died suddenly of fever (Zubeir claimed that he was poisoned by Hilali). Halted on the Jur at the *zariba* of Ali Amouri, Hilali now appointed Kuchuk Ali's deputy, Ahmed Agha, to the command of the regular troops and summoned the representatives of the surrounding *zaribas* of Biselli (Busaili), El 'Aqqād and Ghattas, together with Schweinfurth's friend Mohammed Abu Sammat, to acquaint them with his firman and to require them to surrender their arms and territory to him.

Ascertaining that Zubeir would be under the same injunction, the traders called for him to appear in order to confirm his submission, only to find that he contested Hilali's authority. This he claimed was limited to the vicinity of Hufrat el Nahas, north of Dar Fertit while, notwithstanding Hilali's firman (so he told Jackson), Zubeir had in a letter learned from Ja'afar Pasha 'that he would not confirm the actions of Hilali unless I approved them'. Thus, Zubeir claimed, the *zaribas* were put effectively under his authority, including that of the late Kuchuk Ali whose property now belonged to the latter's son. Leaving this last issue unresolved, Hilali nevertheless pressed on to Dar Fertit where Zubeir had prepared him a *zariba* near his own, presumably arriving before the May to October rains of 1870.

Before his death, Kuchuk Ali had command of the levy, by compulsory purchase, on the Jur *zaribas* of *dura* supplies for the expedition. This was unpopular enough but now there was Hilali's claim, by virtue of his Khedivial firman, to the lands of the traders' *zaribas*. In such a confrontation he needed the political backing of a Kuchuk Ali, but instead Hilali encountered the public enmity of the strongest slave baron of them all, whose principal *zariba* at N'duggo (Deim Zubeir), where the slave caravan routes from Kordofan and Darfur merged, was now protected by a private army of 1,000 men.[3]

At Deim Zubeir there followed during the rains a period of uneasy stand-off between the two adversaries. That Zubeir's region was now subject to the government requisitioning of the new harvest *dura* was a palpable affront to his dominance, a fact obvious to Hilali who wrote off to Ja'afar Pasha with a request for reinforcement of three companies. Ja'afar was ready to comply on its receipt in January 1871: he had been expressly warned by the Viceroy in April 1869 that he would be held personally responsible to ensure that Hilali's force was sufficient for its objective. Meanwhile at least one major skirmish took place between the forces of the government and Zubeir about the end of December 1870, a few days before Schweinfurth, his further expedition to the Azande aborted, was about to leave the Jur river to visit the Egyptian camp at Deim Zubeir, Nduggo, arriving in company with Mohammed Abu Sammat on 22 January 1871.

From his subsequent meetings there with Ahmed Agha, Ibrahim Effendi, Ahmed's Egyptian chief clerk, and Zubeir himself, Schweinfurth recorded that Hilali's *nizam* troops had begun to raid Zubeir's granaries, only to be then attacked by Zubeir's irregulars; and that in the ensuing battle some twenty were killed on either side. Schweinfurth found Zubeir recovering from a bullet wound in the ankle. In *The Heart of Africa* he goes on to claim that the 'Khartoumers' of the neighbouring *zaribas* rallied to Zubeir's assistance and for several days Hilali's camp was under serious threat. Then at the critical moment Ahmed Agha with his Turkish contingent threw his support behind Zubeir. Hilali's Black troops were disarmed and placed under surveillance and Hilali himself imprisoned and placed under the yoke of the *sheba* of slaves.

This account, hearsay, would have been gathered by Schweinfurth at Deim Zubeir, 11–21 January 1871. He does not claim to have seen Hilali and the story does not tally with Jackson's *Black Ivory and White*, forty years later, from the mouth of Zubeir. The skirmish reported by Jackson allegedly arose from Hilali's order for the release of 6,000 of Zubeir's slaves to him – 'he had been appointed to give them their freedom' (under the firman?) – an order countermanded by Hilali only when Zubeir threatened to kill him. As the slaves returned to Zubeir, Hilali's *nizam* soldiers intervened but were overcome by 'some reinforcements' with ensuing fatalities on both sides.[4]

From the events of the next eighteen months as related by Zubeir to

Jackson it would seem that in his version Schweinfurth was wilfully misled about the truth. By 21 January 1871 Schweinfurth had quit Deim Zubeir, while we learn from Jackson that 'following on these events Hilali and I [Zubeir] made peace one with the other', and that reinforcements – with a cannon – were sent to Hilali by Ja'afar Pasha before the latter left Khartoum in August. They did not arrive however before the end of the 1871 rains. Initially a party of fifty with the mail arrived, the forerunners of the main force of two companies of regular troops from the 1st Sudanese Regiment (Ja'afar refers to one only of 150 men) and an inspector of irregular troops, Ali Agha Jokolmayir, to inquire into the skirmish of December 1870. The firing of the cannon so impressed the Khartoumers that Zubeir was constrained to make a public spectacle of his submission.

However, according to Zubeir, 'as soon as we had come to an agreement one with the other' Hilali announced his intention to reduce the Fertit *zaribas* close at hand in order to appropriate their grain for his troops. He used the advance party of fifty reinforcements to strengthen his force but unaccountably the main force, left behind at Meshra el Rek, never appears to have joined Hilali, an omission which was to have fatal consequences. The first *zaribas* attacked seem to have belonged to El 'Aqqād on the periphery of the Zubeir territory, Hilali then focusing on Zubeir himself. Zubeir's cousin was killed in an attack on a stockade, following which Hilali returned to burn down Deim Zubeir itself. Zubeir claimed that he then defeated Hilali, killing thirty-four of his men and causing him to flee south and west towards the Zande Chief Mopio's district; but he was overtaken twenty miles south of Deim Zubeir and killed by a force under Rabih Fadlallah at Deim Gudyoo, an El 'Aqqād *zariba* – the same day that (imaginative hindsight?) Zubeir was shot in the right foot. It was the news of this outcome to the Hilali expedition which reached Samuel Baker on his return to (Ismailia) Gondokoro in April 1873. He dated it as being three months before the slave traders' attack on Fatiko – and therefore May 1872.

Zubeir told Jackson: 'At this time the Governor at Khartoum was Ja'afar Pasha: and to him I announced my victory over Hilali, the news of my success spreading all over the Sudan.' In fact, as Zubeir was certain to have known, even if it seems to have slipped his memory, Ja'afar quit his post as Governor-General in August 1871, to be succeeded as general-governor of the 'South Sudan' by the ineffectual Ahmed Mumtaz Pasha on 30 September 1871 – knowledge of which doubtless would have encouraged Zubeir to attack Hilali.

Ja'afar's assurance to the Khedive back in June 1869 that the Sultan of Darfur would not dare attack the new *qism* had been confirmed. Nevertheless the Sultan had, according to Schweinfurth, 'prohibited all intercourse between his own frontier and the *zaribas* of the Khartoumers; consequently the traders from Abu Haraz, in Kordofan, found themselves obliged to take a longer and more dangerous route across the steppes of the predatory Baqqara.' The Sultan, Mohammed Hussein el Mahdi (1839–73), was nearly blind and his reign drawing to its end – additionally propitious to Zubeir, now the unchallenged '*mamur*' of the *qism*. Hilali's defeat was to prove only the beginning of his record of conquest but before observing that in detail, the state, prior to the government occupation, of the Bahr el Ghazal region as a whole – and the participation in it of Zubeir Rahma, first as trader then as slaver, finally as *sultan* and *mudir* – need to be examined.[5]

2   THE BAHR EL GHAZAL REGION C. 1830–70

The Bahr el Ghazal region was designated roughly as a box between latitudes 4° and 8° N and longitudes 25° and 30° E, bounded by the watersheds of the Nile and Congo rivers, and comprising an area of some 48,000 square miles. By the mid-nineteenth century the dominant tribe in the area was the Azande. They appear to have come in a second wave of Sudanic invaders from the west having, under their Vungara chief N'gura I, crossed southwards from the Chinko (Shinko) river valley over the M'bomu river, an affluent of the Ubangi, and acquired that territory a hundred years earlier. Seemingly not until c. 1830 did Mabengé, a descendant of N'gura, lead them down to the basin of the Uele (Makua or Welle) and thence over the watershed towards Makaraka. The date explains why the traditional accounts of the emigration of the Luo from Bunyoro in the early sixteenth century, through the Bahr el Ghazal via Atwot on the Rohl river, make no reference to any Zande presence at that time in the area.

Indeed the Bahr el Ghazal west of the Rohl would have been then inhabited predominantly by the Bongo or Dor, and to their east the Mitu and Moru, as far south as the (seasonal) Uele upper river, only to be progressively rolled back northwards following the arrival in the early nineteenth century of the more numerous and aggressive forces of the Azande. The Bongo then became concentrated as cultivators in the sparsely populated heartland, comprising the middle courses of the

Ghazal affluents including the Tonj – some 9,000 square miles of semi-wilderness with a population in 1870 shrunk to about 100,000. Further east the Mitu numbered 30,000. We are indebted to Schweinfurth for his population estimates and for his map of the region, more accurate and informative than that of Petherick of 1858, but even more so to the maps of Junker ten years later.

Immediately to the north of the Bongo, established on the middle reaches of the Jur river, had lived the Jur or Dyoor section of the Luo sixteenth-century migration, numbering in Schweinfurth's contemporary estimate some 10–20,000, with a considerable reputation as black-smiths. (Incidentally the Jur chief whom Schweinfurth visited in May 1870 was called Dino – the name of the Shilluk Nyikango's reputed brother-in-law.) The Jur, a Nilotic people, were sandwiched between the Sudanic-speaking Bongo to the south and the more belligerent but less numerous Rek and Lao sections of the Dinka to the north owning huge herds of cattle. The latter confronted the Humr Baqqara across the Bahr el Arab and the western Jikany Nuer to the east, encompassing in their territory the future trading depot of Meshra el Rek on the Kyt. Petherick was the first organised trader to reach an accommodation with them.

To the north-west the remaining part of the Bahr el Ghazal constituted the Dar Fertit, populated by the pagan peoples of Darfur since they fled there in the fourteenth century. They were now represented principally by the Kreish (Kredy) (20,000), Golo (Gula?) (6,000), and Sere (4,000) tribes, their territory lying east of deserted hill-country of the Dar Banda (also Fertit). The special significance of the Dar Fertit lay in its intermediate position on the line of communication between Darfur, via Hufrat el Nahas to the north-west; Kordofan, via Shakka to the north-east; and the heartland of the Azande to the south.[6]

The (minority) Sudan section of the agriculturalist Azande trace their kingship line to Mabengé who led them down the Uele (Welle) river from the west (c. 1830?). From him were descended (*sons*, according to Wilhelm Junker) Nungé, N'deni and Nyekpati (Yapati) 'the Great', who established themselves initially between 4° and 5° latitude: Nyekpati west, in the vicinity of Tambura north of the M'bomu river; and Nungé east in that of Makaraka. The southern frontier, that of the Kibali–Uele river, separated them from the Mangbattu (Monbuttu), a distinct people probably of lacustrine ethnicity, ruled by two brothers, Tikkibola and Degberra, between 3° and 4° latitude. The former was succeeded by his son Munza, following his murder by Degberra.

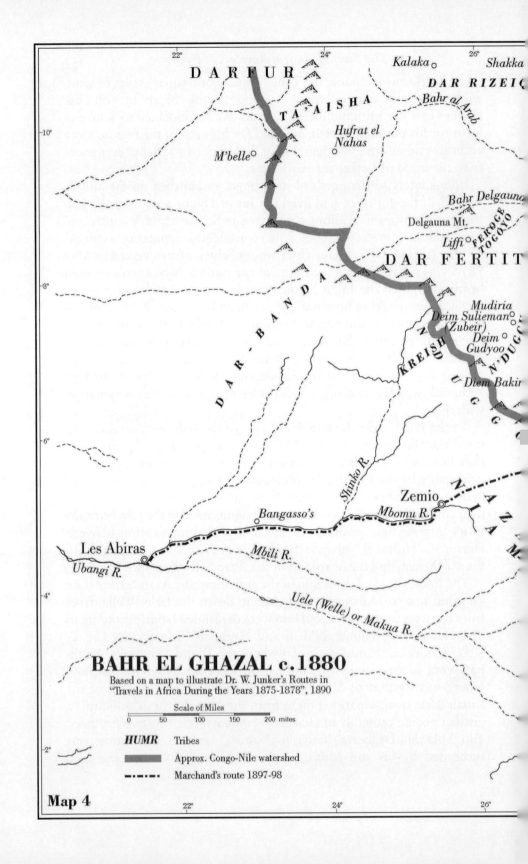

DARFUR

Kalaka ○   Shakka

DAR RIZEIC

TA'AISHA

Bahr al Arab

-10°

Hufrat el
Nahas ○

M'belle ○

Bahr Delgauna

Delgauna Mt.

Liffi ○   FEROGE
TOGOYO

DAR FERTIT

-8°

Mudiria
Deim Sulieman ○
(Zubeir)
Deim ○
Gudyoo

N'DUGG

DAR-BANDA

KREISH

DUGG

Diem Bakir

-6°

N I A M

Shinko R.

Zemio ◎

Mbomu R.

-5°

Bangasso's ○

M.

Les Abiras ◎

Mbili R.

Ubangi R.

-4°

Uele (Welle) or Makua R.

BAHR EL GHAZAL c.1880

Based on a map to illustrate Dr. W. Junker's Routes in
"Travels in Africa During the Years 1875-1878", 1890

Scale of Miles

0   50   100   150   200 miles

-2°

HUMR   Tribes

━━━━   Approx. Congo-Nile watershed

━·━·━·   Marchand's route 1897-98

Map 4

22°   24°   26°

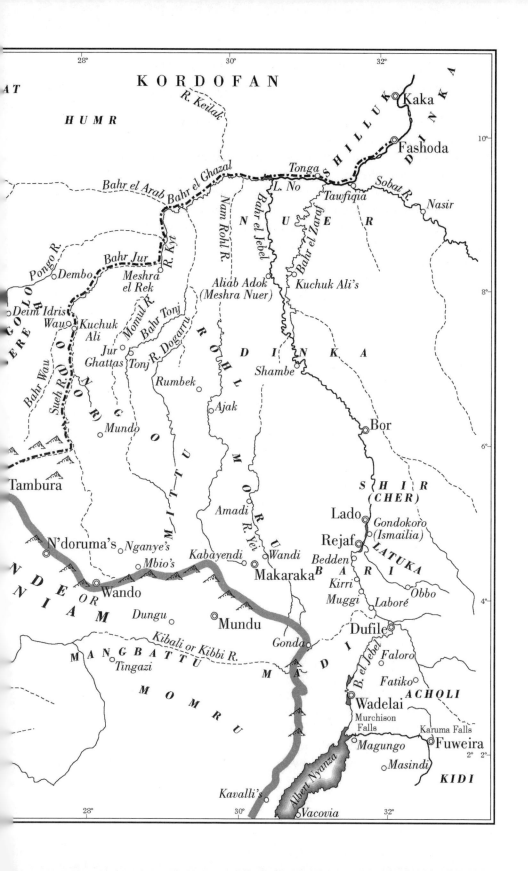

Schweinfurth optimistically gave the Mangbattu 4,000 square miles and a population of a million.

Plotting the northern expansion of these Azande c. 1840–80, numbering perhaps between 100,000 and 200,000, is complicated first by the absence of strict primogeniture, leading to fissiparous dynastic struggles for territory between brothers, sons and grandsons; and secondly by the practice of naming a camp (*zariba*) after its current commander, the latter being succeeded by another on average every decade. By 1870 Schweinfurth calculated that on a north to south crossing of the residual Zande territory he encountered thirty-five independent chiefs.

Thanks to conversations between Junker and Chief Zemio (son of Tikima) at the latter's camp on the M'bomu river on 1 May 1883; to Schweinfurth's genealogical table of 1870; and to Major J. W. G. Wyld, DSO, OBE, MC, District Commissioner Zande District; it is possible to construct a rough family tree of Mabengé's descendants for use in interpreting the several maps of Schweinfurth's (1870) and Junker's explorations (1878–86). The latter show of course no international boundaries, but if the topography is necessarily uncertain, they nevertheless have imposed upon them Mercator's Projection, and the river courses provide an essential aid. From Chief Turabu's recollection to Wyld in 1947, it would seem that following the death of Nyekpati's son Bazingbi, Yambio (Mbio), later known as Gbudue, became the dominant Zande chief. Until his succession the *jallaba* were not a serious threat to the Azande. However, by perhaps 1860 Yambio could no longer repulse the armed slave bands of the Khartoumer raiders. He was captured and, with brothers and sons, imprisoned at Deim Zubeir for three years before purchasing his release and return to his heartland.

The region of Bahr el Ghazal remained until the mid-1850s one of total obscurity to the outside world. European penetration dates from reconnaissance of the infamous Malzac from Shambe on the Bahr el Abiad towards Ronga (Rumbek) in 1854, prior to founding his ivory and slave station there (this was in turn ceded to El 'Aqqād then to Ghattas until destroyed by the Agar Dinka in April 1869); and from the discovery of the navigability of the river from Lake No to Meshra el Rek by John Petherick in 1856. In the preceding decades the Azande had progressively taken control of the lands of the indigenous Bongo and Kreish but not of the Nilotic Dinka and Nuer. Zande Vungara leaders found already established a primitive barter-trading infrastructure in the territory, promoted by individual entrepreneurs, '*jallaba*', from the riverain towns (notably Dongola) of the northern Sudan. The latter used camels, bullocks and donkeys for the transport of their urban wares in exchange for ivory and slaves, deals negotiated with local chiefs especially in the Dar Fertit. There were well-worn caravan routes on a north-south axis to Kordofan and Darfur, and so to the Cairo 'metropolis'. At Hufrat el Nahas on the Darfur route to the north the extraction of copper from the mines had long been pursued for markets as far afield as Kano and Tripoli, and was now to become of special interest to the blacksmiths of Mangbattu and the quartermasters of the Zande militia. The scale of trading however may have remained more domestic than commercial until the late 1850s and, as Professor Richard Gray has observed, quoting von Heuglin:

> The activities of these *jallaba* involved no great large-scale subjugation of peoples, and penetration was not dependent on armed force. As in the Beni Shanqul, the Galla country and East Africa, the Arab trader was forced to pay the local chief a toll for every load of goods which he wished to pass through the territory.[7]

Nevertheless Schweinfurth in 1870 believed (but it was hearsay) that 'long before' the arrival of the Khartoum trading-companies in the late 1850s

> numbers of slave-dealers had already formed settlements in Dar Fertit, then as now streaming into the country from Darfur and Kordofan accompanied by hundreds of armed men, and coming year after year, in the winter months so as to accomplish their business and get back to their homes before the rainy season again set in. Some of them, however did not return, but remained permanently in the land and, under the sanction of the more influential chieftains, founded large settlements (*deims*) to serve as marts or depots for their black merchandise.

Petherick, the first of the ivory traders to establish a *zariba* on the Jur river, found the Jur in 1856 willing to barter a one cwt tusk for a modest quantity of beads, cowry shells and copper bracelets, and over three years was to consign 300 cwt of ivory for sale in Cairo. However, the establishment of *zaribas* by more rapacious Khartoumers was now rapidly to transform the relatively benign trading mores of the independent *jallaba*, and to impose an alien culture of brutality and slavery upon the local inhabitants. The Azande themselves, the dominant force hitherto, assuredly owned slaves but, in Petherick's observation, the

Principal Azande Vungara Descendants of N'Gura in the Bahr el Ghazal c. 1830–80

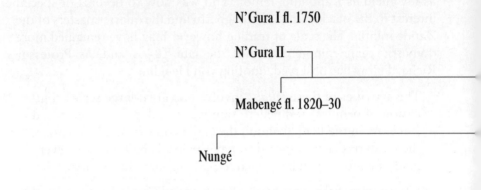

N'Gura I fl. 1750

N'Gura II

Mabengé fl. 1820–30

Nungé

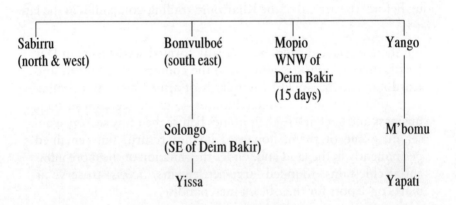

Sabirru
(north & west)

Bomvulboé
(south east)

Mopio
WNW of
Deim Bakir
(15 days)

Yango

Solongo
(SE of Deim Bakir)

M'bomu

Yissa

Yapati

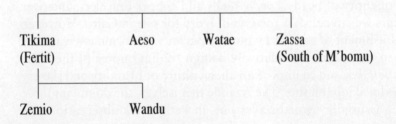

Tikima
(Fertit)

Aeso

Watae

Zassa
(South of M'bomu)

Zemio

Wandu

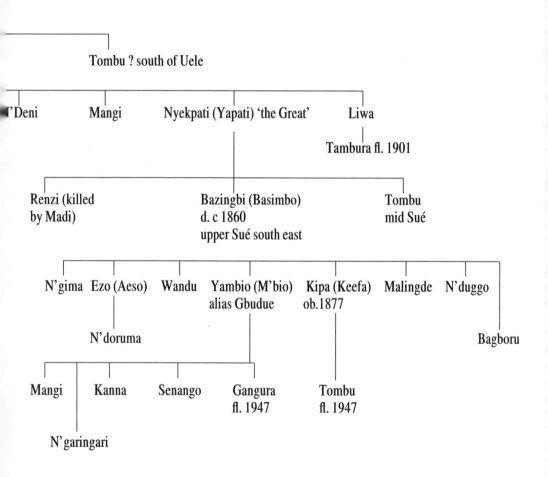

latter were 'treated affectionately and, generally speaking, both master and slave were proud of each other'. The Khartoumers brought with them to the Ghazal over the next fifteen years the contemptible practices they had perpetrated on the Upper Nile – a market now deteriorating thanks to their excesses, to the destruction of the riverain elephant herds, and to the ambivalent intervention of government police patrols to stem any European outcry. Sir Samuel Baker's appointment in 1869 to suppress the Equatorial slave trade enhanced still further the attraction of the more remote hunting grounds of the Bahr el Ghazal over the Bahr el Abiad.

By the late 1850s, then, the principal Arab *zaribas* had become established in the north. They belonged, in multiple stations, notably to the Copt Ghattas based at Tonj who was said to control 3,000 square miles and a local population of 13,000; Ali Amouri on the Pongo affluent of the Bahr el Arab; Kuchuk Ali on the Jur; Mohammed Ahmed el Aqqad at Wau; Biselli (Mahjoub el Busaili) between El 'Aqqād and Ali Amouri; Abu Qurun near the Molmul; Hassaballah on the Wau river; and Mohammed Abu Sammat at Sabby, east of Mundo. Their arrival was especially welcome to the more ambitious *jallaba* of the *deims* with whom mergers were negotiated, offering the additional security of substantial armed bands and a storage location for their merchandise, black and white, and ammunition.

Dr Robert Brown supposed a trader's progress thus:

> The way a beginner went about making his start was something as follows. Borrowing money at 100%, he agreed to pay the lender in ivory at half its value. Then he hired vessels and from 100 to 300 men, chiefly Arabs, half-castes... and runaway scoundrels from all the neighbouring countries.... Each slave-trading potentate had by a convention of the business a district to himself.

For the while the extreme west and south was left in the complaisant hands of the Zande chiefs: Mopio on the borders of the Kreish and Banda west north west of Deim Bakir; Takima around Deim Bakir; Kipa (Keefa) and his sons in the south west; and the descendants of Nyekpati (Yapati) on the upper sources of the Sué river. Relations between the *jallaba* and Azande initially were sufficiently cordial for Mopio at least to be partly rewarded with firearms. Notwithstanding their quasi-vassalage and the requirement that they provision the trader caravans and supply hunters and house builders, the Azande maintained their superior status vis-à-vis less robust tribes like the Bongo, and declined to act as porters to the traders. As the years passed, however, the militia costs of the traders increased and the availability of ivory diminished.

Junker cited a calculation that, such was the destruction of elephants in the years 1856–76, Europe annually received 1.5 million lb of ivory, India 250,000 lb and America 150,000 lb – representing altogether at least 50,000 elephants slaughtered. In Schweinfurth's calculation, '…in 1862 186,000, and in 1866 180,000 kilos of ivory were drawn from the "Upper Nile" region'. He went on to comment that

> …it did not take very long for the traders to discover that the annual produce of ivory was altogether inadequate to defray the expenses of equipping and maintaining their armed force. Finding however that the region offered every facility for the sale of slaves, they began gradually to introduce this unrighteous traffic into their commercial dealings until at length it became, if not absolutely the prime, certainly one of the leading objects of their expeditions… Zubeir Rahma, who had to maintain a fighting force of 1,000 on his territories had as the result of his ivory expedition in the previous year (1870) gained not more than … 120 cwt [Ghattas c. 220 cwt in 1869] raising £2,300 at Khartoum; but at the same time he sent probably as many as 1,800 slaves direct to Kordofan, here to be disposed of on his own account.

Exceptions among the Khartoumers like Khalil, the *wakil* of Kuchuk Ali, who 'emphatically denounced the slave trade', were rare.

Schweinfurth's account of Zubeir's export of slaves to Kordofan omits an important arrangement which enhanced the quality of his troops. The latter were drawn not from Khartoum militia, nor from slaves locally acquired but from slaves escaped from the Dar Ta'aisha Baqqara of Darfur, whom he recruited as volunteers in exchange for a much inflated number of untrained slaves from the Fertit – as opposed to the Azande who were a major element of Zubeir's irregulars. These recruits comprised the 1,000 core of his formidable army under Rabih Fadlallah and among them were El Zaki Tamal and Hamdan Abu Anga, later to be Mahdist generals.

We have no reliable witness of local events and conditions in the Bahr el Ghazal between the calamity of the Tinné expedition of 1863–4 and the visit of Georg Schweinfurth (1869–71), save the suspect recollections (1912–13) of Zubeir Pasha Rahma Mansour in the year before his death. Relationships with the local partners of the Khartoumers, notably the Azande and Mangbattu (Monbutto), who were much alienated by the brutal practices of the *razzias,* deteriorated by 1870 into open conflict. In the meanwhile Zubeir, having carved out for himself in 1865 a strategic territory in the Dar Fertit based at Deim Zubeir at the expense of Tikima and the local Golo chief, now entered into a trading entente with Sheikh Munzal of the Baqqara Rizeiqat at Shakka, opening thence the caravan routes via Abu Haraz in Kordofan to the northern Sudan and Egypt. In 1869 Ghattas and Abu Qurun pressed south-east into the upper reaches of the Sué, provoking puni- tive counter-attacks by Yambio (M'bio) and N'doruma, respectively Zande son and nephew of Nyekpati (Yapti); and in November 1870 an expedition, including 3,000 militia sent by Ghattas, Hasaballah and Kuchuk Ali's *wakil* to avenge the affront, was successfully ambushed, the leaders killed, and the baggage and arms captured. Schweinfurth, compelled in consequence to abort a second visit to King Munza of Mangbattu, observed:

> N'doruma's enmity is not founded only on the exhaustion of ivory but on the repeated *razzias* against the surrounding nations. They [the Khartoumers] have been addicted to the practice of carrying off women and girls and this has aroused the Niam-Niam (Azande), who ever exhibit unbounded affection for their wives, to the last degree of exasperation. It is this diabolical traffic in human beings that acts as the leading incentive to these indiscrim- inating Nubians and has caused so much detriment, by the deci- mation of the Bongo, to their possessions.[8]

Oderint dum metuant: 'let them hate so long as they fear' (Cicero, after Accius, in his *First Philippic*, 14) might have been the maxim of the Khartoumers.

This was not however the kind of hot war with firearms for which the Khartoum militias thought they had signed up. When Schweinfurth had stayed with Zubeir at his *zariba* mid-January 1871, the calibre and morale of the Hilali's 'effeminate Turkish soldiers' excited his contempt – 'the most unsuitable beings imaginable ever to have been sent on an expedition in Central Africa'. The trading fraternity was even more ignoble, though the very presence of government troops had, since the 1870 rainy season (coinciding with Baker's anti-slavery initiatives on the Upper Nile), seen 'upwards of 2,000 small slave-dealers' (to rise to 2,700) arrive at the *zariba*.

King Munza of Mangbattu in full dress c. 1870

The remarkably large contingent of *jallaba* that chanced to be within the place gave the dirty crowds of men, such as are more or less to be invariably found in every *zariba*, a more motley aspect than usual, and altogether the *deim* offered a deplorable contrast to the freshness of the wilderness that we had so long and so recently been traversing. The hawkers of living human flesh and blood unwashed and ragged, squatted in the open places keeping their eye upon their plunder, eager as vultures in the desert around the carcass of a camel. Their harsh voices as they shouted out their blasphemous prayers; the drunken indolence and torpor of the loafing Turks; the idle vicious crowds of men infested with loathsome scabs and syphilitic sores; the reeking filthy exhalations that rose from every quarter – all combined to make the place supremely disgusting. Turn where I would, it was ever the same; there was the recurrence of sights, sounds and smells so revolting that they could not do otherwise than fill the senses with the most sickening abhorrence.

It was to Deim Zubeir that Sheikh Hilali had directed his expedition after the death of Kuchuk Ali near the Jur river at the end of 1869. The Khedive may have charged in the firman that the new *nazir* of the *qism* of Dar Fertit should treat the inhabitants with mercy and kindness, but that was unrealistic. The established practices and interests of the owners of the *zaribas* would no longer allow for such a régime. Slavery had been rife for fifteen years in its most brutal form, and for its suppression the government officials 'did absolutely nothing... Nowhere in the world can more inveterate slave-dealers be found than the commanders of the small detachments of Egyptian troops; as they move about from *zariba* to *zariba*, they may be seen followed by a train of their swarthy property which grows longer and larger after every halt.'

That may have been Schweinfurth's general observation but it does not do justice to Hilali himself (who, mistakenly, the former believed to be imprisoned). On Zubeir's own admission Hilali had already attempted to force him to surrender for liberation 6,000 slaves, leading to a major skirmish. Schweinfurth estimated the total militia forces of the Bahr el Ghazal merchant *zaribas* to number 11,000, the core of which was the quasi-professional force of 1,000 led by the redoubtable Zubeir. Without the major reinforcements which Hilali awaited from Khartoum, and with but 600 undisciplined soldiers, it would have taken a leader of the exceptional qualities of a Samuel Baker to impose his authority. Once reinforced, Hilali did embark on major hostilities to subdue the owners of the *zaribas*. His defeat and death at Zubeir's hands in 1872 was no certainty. Only then could the slave trade be resumed without certain government interference, and the oppression of the Fertit peoples extended. Douin has but speculation for his bold conclusion that, had Hilali conquered, 'il est fort probable que les populations nègres du Bahr el Ghazal auraient continué à gémir sous l'oppression et l'arbitraire comme par le passé'.⁹

3 THE AUTARCHIC PROGRESS OF ZUBEIR RAHMA MANSOUR 1856–73

Zubeir would have been little more than forty years old when Hilali was defeated and killed in N'duggo in May 1872. He proudly claimed descent from the Jamu'ia-Jimiab section of the Ja'aliyin in the vicinity of the old Abdullab capital of Gerri – he was to lend Jackson a copy of his pedigree in 1913 – but had left for the Bahr el Ghazal in 1856 to seek a mercantile fortune.

He earned the trust and appreciation of his employer Ali Abu Amouri within a year of his arrival at the *zariba* in 1856, thanks to his bold and successful resistance to tribal attacks. Having committed his share of the profits to equipping himself independently on a visit to Khartoum in the winter of 1858–9, on his return to the Ghazal he pressed on into Golo, west of the Pango river, and a year later marched south into the homeland of the Zande chief Tikima son of Sabirru, located seemingly south-west of Deim Bakir. Unlike most Khartoum merchants – the notable exception being Mohammed Abu Sammat who married a daughter of King Munza of Mangbattu – Zubeir cemented his alliance with the Zande chief Tikima by marrying the latter's daughter, Ranbu. He traded there until the winter of 1863 when, after a hazardous and nearly fatal journey down the Jur river to Meshra el Rek with Ali Abu Amouri, he would return from Khartoum to a chance meeting with the unhappy Alexine Tinné at Wau in early 1864, while en route to the resumption of his trading activities with Tikima.

In his absence the Zande relationship had apparently soured. Warned by his wife of Tikima's murderous intentions towards him, Zubeir retreated north back to Golo where he defeated the ruling chief Addu Shaku following a series of battles, leaving himself by the end of 1865 the dominant ruler of the Dar Fertit as far north as Jebel Delgauna on the route to Shakka. For his principal *zariba*, however, he selected N'duggo where the trade routes from Shakka and from Hufrat el Nahas converged. Deim Zubeir was now to be the hub of activity in the Bahr el Ghazal, strengthened further in 1866 by Zubeir's strategic

Zubeir Pasha Rahma Mansur

understanding with the Rizeiqat chiefs at Shakka on the Kordofan caravan route which was to underpin seven years of unparalleled prosperity
– until, following the defeat of Hilali, the Shakka chiefs reneged and
Zubeir realised the ambition himself to penetrate Kordofan.

When Schweinfurth met Zubeir in January 1871 he 'had surrounded
himself with a court that was little less than princely in its details' –
divans furnished with tapestries, captive lions shackled with heavy
chains. These reflected the prosperity acquired in the past four years not
only by Zubeir but also by his Khartoumer associates. 'Probably the
overland slave-trade along the roads of Kordofan had never been so
flourishing as in the winter of 1870–1 when I found myself at the very
fountainhead.' The depredations of the past fifteen years had swelled
the numbers of slaves exported, in Schweinfurth's estimate, to between
12,000 and 15,000 per annum, all but some 500 (who went by boat to

Khartoum) marching the overland route to the north. Far in excess of the numbers travelling by the White Nile, totalling perhaps 2,000 until Baker's appointment, the western slave caravans escaped the attention of the European Powers because of the remoteness of the region – to the self-congratulation of the Khartoumers. This could only enhance their collective determination to wreck the Hilali expedition and its threat to their continuing prosperity.

Following the death of Hilali about May 1872, Zubeir confronted a number of further dangers. First – with the exception of the fifty-strong advance party, the *mulazim awwal* (first lieutenant) commander of which had been wounded and captured by Zubeir – Hilali's government reinforcements remained uncommitted under a *yuzbashi*, together with Ali Agha who had been deputed to inquire into the skirmish at Deim Zubeir of the previous December. They were an armed threat to Zubeir and the wounded *mulazim* a witness of his action against Hilali. Zubeir's force was fortunately for him more numerous, while the government commanders were without stomach for hostilities and doubtless compensated for their inactivity. That threat was accordingly removed.

More serious was the hostility of Zubeir's father-in-law, the Zande *sultan* Tikima who, mistakenly believing that Hilali would put paid to Zubeir's hegemony and ambitious to share in the spoils of victory, had sent a force under his uncle to attack Zubeir in the new year of 1872. Battle was waged for thirteen months according to Zubeir until both Tikima and his uncle were killed (the former's son Zemio told Junker his father died of smallpox). By early 1873 the Azande were obliged to capitulate, the multiplicity of their fiefdoms and their incapability of presenting a united front fully exploited by Zubeir in the dismemberment of their empire. Zubeir claims he found time to beat the southern bounds of his sultanate, crossing the River Uele to the territory of the pygmy tribes (*momroo*) south of the Mangbattu. He was now undisputed master not only of the Dar Fertit but of the whole Bahr el Ghazal region.[10]

Zubeir, however, had killed the Khedive's appointed *nazir* of the *qism* of the Dar Fertit. As already observed, he had been fortunate in the Khedive's ill-judged determination to appoint his favourite Ahmed Mumtaz Pasha as general-governor of the South in Khartoum in succession to the popular Ja'afar Mazhar in October 1871; only for Ahmed Mumtaz himself to be arrested and removed in August 1872. The new acting general-governor was a man of exceptional quality and experience, Lewa Adham Pasha el 'Arifi, currently commanding all the armed forces in the Sudan and the first Sudanese national to reach such seniority. Within days of Adham's removal of Mumtaz from office, he was faced with the arrival of two letters from the Dar Fertit: one jointly signed by Ali Agha and the *yuzbashi* commanding one of the reinforcement companies, the other from Zubeir himself – as Zubeir put it to Jackson: 'I announced my victory over Hilali [to Ja'afar Pasha], the news of my success spreading all over the Sudan.' Forwarding these letters to Cairo, Lewa Adham tendered unequivocal advice on 22 August as to how to react to the defeat and killing of Hilali. The responsibility for the costly failure of the expedition to occupy the *qism* of Dar Fertit, and for the defeat of Hilali, stemmed from treachery and the hostility of the *zariba* owners. Zubeir must be arrested but, in view of the remoteness of the Dar Fertit from Khartoum, it should be effected by an expedition mounted by the governor of Kordofan, currently separate from the Khartoum general-governorate. Zubeir should be brought to Khartoum for a public inquiry.

Adham's dispatch reached Cairo to be forwarded by the minister of war to the Khedive on 22 September 1872, perhaps shortly after the departure to Khartoum of the new general-governor, Ismail Pasha Ayub, whom Baker had found helpful as president of Ja'afar Mazhar's Khartoum council in October 1870. The Khedive's reply to Khartoum, notwithstanding the serious military situation revealed in the Fertit, was only dated 13 October, perhaps on account of still more serious matters in Abyssinia following the occupation of Bogos. Nevertheless it was signed barely a week before Ismail Ayub took the oath of office in Khartoum, being promoted *lewa* – the rank of Adham Pasha who had himself clearly been passed over as general-governor, notwithstanding his proven qualifications. Adham had served in the Crimea and played a notable part in the suppression of the Kassala revolt. His knowledge and experience of the Sudan was unrivalled, but perhaps on that account the Khedive feared him. Thus another rare opportunity for the good government of the Sudan was rejected.

Ismail Ayub would on his arrival have discussed the Hilali debacle with Adham, but his report to the Khedive a week later dated 28 October came down quite uncritically on the side of Zubeir. He blamed his former Governor-General, Ja'afar Mazhar, for the mistaken concession of the *qism* to a mendacious Hilali (was Ismail Ayub in post as president of the council in Khartoum in 1869 when Hilali was appointed?). In two years Hilali had failed to create a seat of government, preferring to occupy trading posts; and despite their submission to his authority and Zubeir's active assistance and cooperation, Hilali had attacked and constantly oppressed the law-abiding tax-paying traders. All this was evidence that Hilali's objective was to return to Wadai with his booty. He had become detested. Hilali's fate was justly deserved by reason of his injustice. Zubeir, whose authority was long established in the Ghazal and with the Rizeiqat, and with family relations trading substantially at Khartoum and Dongola, had been provoked to enmity as a direct result of Hilali's attacks on him.

Ismail Ayub therefore dismissed Adham's proposal to send a force to arrest Zubeir as very costly and threatening the destruction of the whole region. Instead he advocated inviting Zubeir to appear before him for an inquiry, especially since to date there was no proof of rebellion on his part. The general-governor would then reorganise the region, appoint a governor, buy out the merchants – as with El 'Aqqād in Upper Nile, the cost to be recovered from taxes.

This prejudiced report betrays something of the ambitions of the new general-governor. His time previously in Khartoum, latterly as Ja'afar's head of council, had brought him into close touch with the trading community who ultimately owned and controlled most of the Fertit *zaribas*. The latter may well have brought their pressure to bear on an old acquaintance evidently sympathetic to their interests, even if committed to support Baker on the Nile. Possibly more significant is Douin's assertion, unsourced, that while still in Cairo in August 1872 after his appointment to Khartoum Ayub was already in talks with the Ministry of War about the occupation of Darfur.

The general-governor's report of 28 October crossed the instruction of the Khedive dated 13 October 1872. The latter rehearsed the contents of the two letters from the Fertit: that of the officers reporting an alleged sequence of events to which they were not themselves witnesses, commencing with the arrival of the advance party at Deim Zubeir under the *mulazim awwal* – the only eyewitness, but himself in jeopardy following Zubeir's arrest; and that of Zubeir, in which the writer claimed to have hugely assisted Hilali but been forced in self-defence to kill him.

In the light of these 'facts', the Khedive provisionally concluded on the hearsay evidence of the two officers that Hilali had been the aggressor against the *zaribas*. Zubeir had had to defend himself. Ismail Ayub was therefore to appoint a trusted investigator to conduct an exacting inquiry in the *qism*. If however he found Hilali the aggressor, he should reassure Zubeir and promise compensation to him and his fellow traders – and this was clearly the outcome which the Khedive expected. Hilali, after all, firman or no firman, was dead, the slave-trading régime in the Ghazal validated by force and the critical European powers unaware of the proceedings. On receipt of the Khedive's direction, Ismail Ayub informed him on 27 November 1872 of the departure of his investigator to the Bahr el Ghazal via Kordofan.[11]

Zubeir's coup d'état was not yet quite legalised. When he had first encountered Hilali at the *zariba* of Ali Abu Amouri on the Jur river, he had obstructed Hilali's claim to become guardian of the late Kuchuk Ali's property. Kuchuk Ali's son Sulieman claimed that Zubeir had retained the part of the property of which he had become custodian and had, along with the government *yuzbashi*, attacked and pillaged the Kuchuk *zariba* and fired his crops. Ali Agha had been party to the treachery. On this evidence of collusion between Zubeir and the Khedivial officers Ismail Ayub in Khartoum felt unable to comment and sent the charge on to Cairo for 'examination'. Kuchuk Ali's relations were not without influence locally.

The heirs and successors of Hilali made similar representations to the general-governor. It is unclear whether they even obtained an audience. They, however, were mindful that the Hilali expedition had been initiated and organised by the former Governor-General Ja'afar Mazhar, now president of the *majlis el 'ahkam* (judicial review council) in Egypt. Sensibly they sought the latter's help as intermediary in their accusations against Zubeir and the Ghazal merchants for the murder of Hilali and his soldiers, and the plundering of the revenues, ivory and copper while the relations were away in Khartoum seeking transport.

Ja'afar did not disappoint them. He wrote to the Khedivial palace, rehearsing the purpose of the expedition to deliver the region from the threats of Darfur and to quell the depredations of the slave traders against the local inhabitants. When Hilali came under attack from Zubeir and his soldiers, Ja'afar had sent reinforcements to Hilali immediately before his own transfer to Cairo. Ja'afar went on effectively to tender the same advice as Adham Pasha, namely that for the security of all the tributaries of the White Nile, and especially the Bahr el Ghazal, and the peace and unity of its inhabitants, vengeance needed to be exacted on the perpetrators of the murder of Hilali and their opposition to this expedition. His letter was dated 18 April 1873.

Meanwhile, tacitly dismissing the relevance of the inquiry being undertaken by the Khedivial investigator, Ismail Ayub concentrated on his reorganisation of the new *muderia* of the Bahr el Ghazal. Zubeir, the intended governor, irrespective of his rebellion, was now in February 1873 invited to Khartoum for discussions, by the hand of a family relation who in the event was denied passage by the Rizeiqat. An arrangement might have had the additional bonus of incorporating in the Khedivial domain these effectively independent Baqqara who, in the vicinity of Shakka, bestrode the road between the Fertit and Kordofan. Whether Zubeir knew of Ismail Ayub's plan, whether he would have agreed to visit Khartoum, is conjectural. In the event he was obliged by early 1873 to respond to a third threat to his sultanate – from the Rizeiqat themselves, his supposed allies since 1866.

The Azande, indeed the Bahr el Ghazal, had been subdued early in 1873 and it seemed evident that Zubeir had little to fear from the intentions of the general-governor in Khartoum. The Rizeiqat had, however, in the latter part of 1872, under two local chiefs of Shakka – Munzal, with whom Zubeir had reached agreement in 1866, and 'Ullayan – raided a number of Zubeir's caravans crossing through Shakka, requisitioned the slaves and killed merchants. Zubeir, his army re-formed and conscious, too, of his dependence on corn supplies from the north, boldly decided to settle matters with the Rizeiqat, taking advantage of a dispute for the head sheikhdom of the Mahria Rizeiqat between Maddibo Ali and 'Uqayl (Egcil). Zubeir unsuccessfully sought the support of Ibrahim Mohammed Hussein (Garad), effective if not yet titular *sultan* of Darfur, claiming these Rizeiqat had 'been outside your control for thirty years'. In his first battle with the Shakka chiefs he sustained 700 killed, but after a seven-week war defeated them near the Bahr el Arab on 28 August 1873. Munzal and 'Ullayan fled to El Fasher and the protection of Ibrahim leaving Zubeir to occupy Abu Sigan, the Shakka headquarters and accept the capitulation of Madibbo Ali.

This was historically Darfur territory, Shakka being a *shartaishia* (district) of the *maqdoumate* of the south currently held by Ahmed Shatta Abdel Aziz, the same who had originally expelled Hilali from the Dar Fertit in c.1867. Again Zubeir wrote to the Sultan-elect Ibrahim on 8 September 1873 requesting his submission to the Khedive, and the surrender of the two chiefs, until which time Zubeir would retain possession of Shakka. Anticipating a repudiation, Zubeir further wrote to acquaint Ismail Ayub of the situation and prepared for a Fur attack.

Douin uncovered no further reference on the part of the general-governor nor of the Khedive to the outcome of the inquiry into the death of Hilali and his troops initiated by the government in November

1872. The inquiry instruction has the appearance of having been window-dressing. Zubeir makes no mention of an investigator whatever. For the Khedive the issue was the same as that which became blurred in the firman delivered to Baker governing his expedition. In short, territorial acquisition, not the suppression of the slave trade, was the real priority. Against the backcloth of the White Nile trade and European concerns it was necessary to dissimulate – and absorb a heavy financial cost. Even his chief minister, Nubar Pasha, believed suppression of the slave trade to be 'a dream I trust will be realised one day'. The brutal conditions obtaining in the Dar Fertit and Ghazal were only to be exposed subsequent to the Hilali debâcle. Hilali had been enjoined to act in his authority with mercy and kindness to his new Sudanic subjects, but the recipient of those instructions had been destroyed, the cost of his expedition fruitlessly expended. A swift affirmative response to Adham Pasha's proposal for a punitive Kordofan expedition offered a practical counter to Zubeir's rebellion but that, at Ismail Ayub's bidding, and with the Khedive's complaisance, had been ignored. 1873 drew on. Ja'afar Pasha Mazhar's intervention in Cairo for Kuchuk Ali's family was received and filed. While Zubeir acted, the Khedive procrastinated. Then came news from Zubeir of his occupation of Shakka in August and his invitation to Ismail Ayub to appoint a governor of the territory which he, Zubeir, now controlled in Bahr el Ghazal and Shakka. That settled the issue of Zubeir's rebellion. He was too powerful

On 22 December 1873 the Khedive issued a firman creating a separate *muderia* of Shakka and the Bahr el Ghazal, and appointing Zubeir governor with the rank of *bey*. Ismail Ayub, now created *hakimdar* of the Sudan, despatched his carefully worked plans for the new *muderia* to the Khedive in early January 1874. The armed forces of the *muderia* would be increased from four to five companies of regular troops (to be brought up to full battalion strength from Kordofan in exchange for young Black recruits); and from 100 to 200 *bashi-buzouqs*. A second gun would be supplied. Tribute would be set at £15,000 worth of ivory, estimated at £25 per cwt. However, added the *hakimdar*, even a contribution of £10,000 would make a helpful contribution to the total Sudan revenue budget.

Thus for the inhabitants of the Bahr el Ghazal, to the oppression of the slave trade was to be added a new burden of taxation – for the most part to be paid in human kind. As Douin observed, nothing had changed. The claim that the Bahr el Ghazal, like Equatoria, was now

Egyptian territory was a chimera. As to Zubeir, Junker reported two years later:

> Thenceforth his influence rose higher and higher, and thanks to the large sums distributed among the ever-venal Sudanese officials of all grades, he became a power in the land. Convoys could be sent under the very eyes of the bribed *mudirs* down the White Nile through Fashoda to the Sudanese capital, and thence to Egypt, or else across the Red Sea to Arabia. This profitable business was thus carried on in perfect security.

At the time of the festivities relating to the opening of the Suez Canal in November 1869 Sir Henry Elliot, representing the British government, had been accompanied to Egypt by the consul-general in Constantinople, Sir Philip Francis, a judge. The Earl of Clarendon had charged him to discuss with Colonel Stanton and local notables the Egyptian attitude to the slave trade and to report. His underlying conclusion was not greatly different from that of Nubar Pasha in his Memoirs (see p. 113).

> Although Egyptian authorities usually simulate the European views on the slave trade, professing to a desire to see the trade, if not the institution itself, suppressed and proffering their concurrence to prevent Egyptian ships carrying on the [export] traffic, yet I totally disbelieve their profession...
>
> I beg to offer the opinion that the will does not exist and that no real effort will be made to prevent or diminish slavery in Egypt...
>
> If I am right in this view it follows that the slave trade cannot be put down in Egypt or Turkey (in both of which slavery flourishes as an approved institution) by any means their governments are likely to employ and that negotiations, representations and moral pressure will prove useless. Hence its suppression must be effected, if at all, from without by pursuing the extreme and objectionable course of European Powers interfering actually, practically and with physical force in Egypt itself.[12]

7

Sudan Fragmentation:
General-Governors 1870–73

1 PARTIAL FRAGMENTATION 1870–71: EXIT JA'AFAR PASHA MAZHAR

Sir Samuel Baker in 1869 had been disappointed that the northern boundary of Equatoria was drawn at latitude 5°N (Gondokoro) and not 14°N (Kawa) as he had sought, the latter parallel intruding well into Ja'afar Pasha Mazhar's *hakimdaria*. The lines of communication and supply of this newly created general-governorate of Equatoria lay nevertheless through Khartoum, and to the consequent blurring of the boundary was added Baker's flexible interpretation of his responsibilities for suppressing the slave trade as far north as the Shilluk corridor.

At the time of Fariq Khusraw Pasha's visit to Khartoum in mid-1869 in preparation for Baker's arrival, Ja'afar, perhaps stimulated by the Equatoria project and sacrificing any personal ambitions, had proposed to the Khedive in August the detachment of Taka, Massawa, Suakin, Basen, the Barea, Kufit and the Red Sea littoral as far as Berbera, to form together a second general-governorate of the Sudan under Khusraw Pasha – such a province had previously been constituted short-term under Fariq Abdel Qadir Pasha in 1867–8 (see p. 86). Whether or not the proposal was put to Khusraw on his return to Cairo, a full nine months later the Khedive eventually responded by approving the re-creation of a governorate of the Red Sea littoral, but placing it under the control of the present *muhafiz* of Suakin, Ahmed Mumtaz Bey, as general-governor. Ja'afar would preside still as *hakimdar* over the residual 'intermediate' territory of the Sudan.

Additionally in October 1870, without apparent reference to Ja'afar, the northern *muderia* of Berber under Hussein Bey Khalifa el Abbadi – sheikh of the Ababda', controller of the Atmur desert caravans since 1869 and protector of Baker's baggage train – would be brought directly under Cairo's administration. Admittedly Berber's revenue collection had remained heavily in arrears. In consequence the residual territories of the *hakimdaria* would now briefly comprise the *muderias* of Khartoum with Sennar under the venerable Sheikh Ahmed Bey Awad el Karim Abu Sin based at Rufa'a; of Kordofan under Hasan Hilmi Bey el Juwaisar; of Fazughli under Ahmed Zanil Bey; of White Nile under Ali Bey Rida el Kurdi; of Dongola under Osman Bey; and the new *qism* of Bahr el Ghazal under Nazir Haji Mohammed el Hilali.

'Can two walk together, except they be agreed?' So it was written in the Book of Amos (3.3) and its truth was evident following the Khedive's appointment, not so much of Baker as of Ahmed Mumtaz to work in harness with Ja'afar Pasha Mazhar, who had sought Mumtaz's replacement for incompetence. Notwithstanding his own seniority, Ja'afar strove loyally to accommodate the forceful and intrusive initiatives in northern White Nile of the new ruler of Equatoria, well aware of the international pressure to which the Khedive had responded in Baker's appointment. Ahmed Mumtaz, however, he regarded as a disloyal subordinate who had forfeited his regard, and the Khedive's decision to appoint him to command a Red Sea governorate of which his, Ja'afar's, own knowledge was second to none seemed both a personal affront and a calamitous mistake. As Richard Hill observed: 'In Khartoum Ja'afar Mazhar fanned in silence the embers of his wrath.'

In the eastern Sudan matters went rapidly from bad to worse. Ahmed Mumtaz, having won his appointment as general-governor from the Khedive following his Cairo visit of April 1870, not only issued orders to his now subordinate governor of Taka, Miralai Abdel Raziq Haqqi Bey, to commence the felling of trees on the banks of the Atbara river for the construction of simple boats in order to float the expected cotton harvest down to Bulak; but he represented to Cairo also that Abdel Raziq endorsed Mumtaz's view that the Gash lands of Taka would prove superior to those of Egypt for cotton cultivation. This prompted an acrimonious exchange between the two, Abdel Raziq advising Cairo that after hewing down 7,000 trees, the experts advised that the boat transport was unviable, and that he had *not* recommended Taka soil for cotton in such optimistic terms. Mumtaz condemned these assertions as fallacious: the wood could be used for floats, while rain and rivers provided abundant water for the Gash lands; and he went on to accuse Abdel Raziq of inciting the opposition of the Halenga people to planting. The acerbity of the exchanges mounted with accusation and counter-accusation. Abdel Raziq wrote to Cairo protesting his good faith but in vain: in January 1871 the Khedive felt obliged to dismiss him after four and a half years in post.[1]

By that time a further dispute was in train, this time originating from the determination of Mumtaz to augment the population of the Gash and of the lower Khor Baraka in order to provide labour for his cotton schemes. A nomad sub-tribe dependent on the Shukriya, who paid tax in Khartoum province, emigrated to the Hadendoa *qism* of Sheikh Musa Ibrahim in Taka, under the jurisdiction of Mumtaz, still owing taxes to Khartoum. The Shukriya Sheikh Awad Abdel Karim Ahmed Abu Sin, who had now succeeded as *sheikh el masheikh,* complained to Taka demanding their return, whereupon Mumtaz took the emigrants under his personal protection and ordered the Taka *mudir* (about to be dismissed) to make them welcome. Notified of this, Ja'afar Pasha in Khartoum wrote a blistering criticism of Mumtaz's behaviour, blaming his lack of experience and demanding the repatriation of the emigrants and the settlement of their Khartoum taxes. When Mumtaz then revealed that he intended to settle the offenders on the Atbara to grow cotton, Ja'afar in June 1871 questioned the whole viability of cotton growing, given its attendant problems; and in any case the Beni Amer under Sheikh Hamed Bey Musa were the proper cultivators of the Atbara region. Compounding his previous error by once again taking Mumtaz's side, the Khedive mistakenly called Ja'afar Pasha to Cairo to explain himself. Ja'afar Pasha's patience was exhausted. Advising Cairo that he would not be returning to Khartoum, he left with his family in August. The chronicler of the *Ta'arikh* observed: 'The catastrophe of his recall befell the Sudan, and universal grief was shown.'

The Khedive, currently examining the feasibility of a Sudan railway project, must have been uneasy about the clashes of opinion and the rifts between Mumtaz and the governor Taka and between Mumtaz and his former Governor-General. In March 1871 he deputed his trusted Privy Council member, Shahin Pasha Kinj, made minister of war the previous year, to inspect and report on Mumtaz's administration of his general-governorate. Shahin had performed a comparable mission for the Khedive in the aftermath of the Kassala revolt in early 1866, whence he had gone on to invest Ja'afar Mazhar as *hakimdar.*

Mumtaz had just returned from a coastal voyage with the current *muhafiz* of Massawa to reinforce the Egyptian presence as far as Berbera (see p. 92) and requested the Khedive to nominate Werner Munzinger, French vice-consul in Massawa, as the new *muhafiz,* personally delivering the firman to the latter on 23 April. Munzinger's opinions had already influenced Mumtaz's optimistic assessment of the cotton-growing potential of his general-governorate and, in advance of

Shahin's visit to Massawa before his return to Cairo, Mumtaz and Munzinger had a further opportunity to concert their views. The purpose of Shahin's visit, judging from the unsigned undated report in the Abdin archives of about June 1871, which Douin attributes to Shahin, was seemingly to reappraise Mumtaz's plan for cotton development in the context of the Suakin railway project and to consider its applicability to other parts of the Sudan. Was the alleged concurrent administrative inspection of the general-governorate a placatory gesture to Ja'afar?

In the space of little over six weeks Shahin appears to have visited Suakin and its hinterland; Tokar in the Khor Baraka; Massawa; and the Gash valley of Taka. Following this brief sojourn, his report was directed almost entirely to cotton growing (but also to cattle-rearing in the Red Sea hills for export on the hoof to Kosseir) and to the consequent requirements for personnel and goods in each of the northern provinces of the Sudan. A report, attributed to Shahin and received in Cairo on 10 June 1871, was plainly influenced by the cotton studies of Mumtaz and Munzinger, and was in large part a tacit and inadequately probed endorsement of their reliability.

The influence of Munzinger, considered something of an authority on the Sudan born of sixteen years' residence and authorship of *Ostafrikanische Studien* (1864), is not to be underrated. Indeed in his own follow-up report to the Khedive dated 31 July 1871, less than two months later, Munzinger affirmed his opinion that 'I in no way exaggerate when I state my firm opinion that the Sudan properly managed will, together with Egypt, produce as much cotton as America' – in particular Taka would contribute 3m cwt, augmented by a further 200,000 from the littoral lands. Munzinger continued:

In résumé we find the Sudan with an immense area capable of feeding thrice its population [1871, over five million] and of growing any kind of grain and especially cotton. It is the natural channel of trade for all Central Africa – *a little America* – promising much but doing little, without any extraordinary export or import; imperfectly developed despite its many navigable rivers. If we look for the reason for this anomaly, there can be not the least doubt that it is because of the lack of a link between Wadi Halfa and Shendi where cataracts interrupt navigation and the Nile makes two enormous turns to the east and to the west [*sic*]... With communications, the Sudan will become in a short time a second

Egypt. The only way of doing this is, I think, to create a wise combination of railroads with Nile steam navigation.[2]

His position thus crucially reinforced, in April 1871 Mumtaz set about his proposal to raise taxes in the new general-governorate for the budget year commencing September 1871. He estimated that currently, of the three divisions of his governorate, the *muhafizat* of Massawa had the largest annual deficit – in 1870 of some £E20,000 beyond revenues of £E13,200 – which he had sought to more than eliminate by an economy in the garrison, effectively of one company of dismounted *bashi-buzouqs*. On Munzinger's appointment as *muhafiz* of Massawa in 1871, Mumtaz seems to have delegated financial authority to him. Suakin, because of its profitable salt pans for export to Jedda, was already in surplus to £E10,000, which Ahmed Mumtaz proposed to augment by a further £E2,500 beyond expenditure of £E34,250.

The third division, Taka, presently in serious deficit, was planned to become a major revenue earner. There revenues of only £E40,000 left a current deficit of £E5,500 but, more seriously, accumulated arrears amounted to £E40,765, the majority owing to government employees. To mitigate that problem, Cairo ordered the Khartoum treasury to send Taka £E25,000. Meanwhile, to transform the financial situation, Mumtaz planned the imposition of a duty per cotton cultivator of two cwt of unginned cotton, to yield an additional net revenue (on the basis of a crop of 100,000 cwt) of £E200,000, thus quintupling Taka revenue. Expenditure would be simultaneously reduced by redeploying one of the two Taka battalions across the whole eastern governorate. Such an ambitious plan, coupled with the optimistic appraisals of Shahin Pasha and Munzinger Bey, must have hugely excited the enthusiasm of the Khedive.

While Ismail Pasha may now have become shot of the hostility between the general-governor of the Red Sea littoral and the Governor-General of the Sudan, nevertheless Ja'afar's peremptory departure from Khartoum in August 1871 left a critical void to be filled.[3]

2 TOTAL FRAGMENTATION 1871–73

Ja'afar Mazhar, sailing down the Nile to Egypt on his final departure in August 1871, shortly to be appointed vice-president of the *majlis el ahkam* (judicial review council) in Cairo, left behind him a still substantial if diminished *hakimdaria*: Khartoum and Sennar, Fazughli, White Nile, Dar Fertit, Dongola and Kordofan. Irrespective of Ja'afar's precipitate departure at the age of sixty, such a formidable appointment was calling for the immediate nomination of a capable successor designate.

Khedive Ismail had now been Viceroy for approaching eight years. He must be credited with the appointments as Governor-General both of Musa Hamdi in the crisis of 1862 – notwithstanding the latter's ruthless reputation – and then of Ja'afar Mazhar who may be regarded as the most enlightened Turkish ruler of the Sudan to date. Ismail had however omitted to inform himself in person of conditions in the Sudan, and that omission was compounded by a weakness in political judgement, already betrayed in his initial hasty and mistaken appointment on the death of Musa Hamdi in 1865 of three autonomous general-governors. This was an edict from which he had been obliged to resile within the space of two weeks, faced with the manifest mutual misgivings of the appointees (see p. 37). Moreover there were other distractions outside the Sudan, not least the truly Byzantine negotiations with the *grand vizir* and first secretary of Sultan Abdel Aziz (1861–76) in pursuit of a firman to restore Ismail's freedom to negotiate foreign loans – now an urgent requirement.

As to the Sudan succession, Ismail had three alternatives: to appoint a new *hakimdar* with or without responsibility for additional Sudan territories; to adopt a policy of indirect rule, to which his predecessor Mohammed Sa'id Pasha had inclined in 1857, and to devolve self-government on local tribal authorities; or to revert to rule by general-governorates, as had happened in the Sudan under Mohammed Sa'id from 1857 to 1862.

The first alternative posited the availability of a man of the right calibre with proven military experience and knowledge of the Sudan. Such candidates were always rare. One man did stand out however: the commander-in-chief of the Sudan armed forces, who had an excellent record in the Crimea and in many crises. This was Lewa Adham Pasha el Arifi. Regrettably he was little known among the higher government echelons in Cairo: above all he was not a Turk, not even an Egyptian, but a Sudanese – of the 'Arifia division of the Dar Hamid tribe of Kordofan with their origins in Darfur and the Bornu border, notwithstanding his nickname 'el Tegali'.

The second alternative, granted that the Khedive was embarked on a multi-directional drive to conquer the African territories to the east and south and west of the Sudan, would be contradictory and hazardous. As to the third, no one was more aware than Ismail of the failure of the régime of general-governorates in the northern Sudan in 1857–62, and indeed of the fiasco of the 1865 appointments, following the death of Musa Pasha Hamdi.

Yet it was this third alternative to which Ismail now resorted, in a still more fragmented form. On 30 September 1871 the *hakimdaria* was abolished. There would be three discrete general-governorates. Ja'afar's former *hakimdaria* would lose Kordofan and Dongola and become the general-governorate of 'South' (Méridional) Sudan under the Khedivial favourite Ahmed Mumtaz Pasha. The latter was thereby detached from responsibility for his grandiose cotton-growing scheme in the east – perhaps so that he could apply his energies similarly to their propagation in the Gezira. His new governorate territory, of which he assumed administration on 15 November 1871, included Khartoum, Sennar, Fazughli, White Nile and the Dar Fertit *qism*.

Baker's Equatoria (which Mumtaz, at least, called 'Central Africa') remained unchanged – there was as yet scant news of his progress, and when Baker finally reached Khartoum in July 1873, it was after leaving Mohammed Ra'uf Bey as locum tenens. The third general-governorate was created under Hussein Pasha Khalifa el Abbadi by the merger of Berber (previously under Cairo) with Dongola.

Kordofan became an independent *muderia* under Abdel Wahhab Bey, promoted to the rank of *mut'amad* first class. The former general-governorate of the Red Sea littoral was, somewhat capriciously, abolished: Taka became an independent *muderia* under Ala el Din Bey Siddiq, previously but briefly *muhafiz* of Massawa; Suakin itself was given to Shakib Bey who proved physically unfit to take up his post and was replaced by one Qa'immaqam Ahmed Bey; and Massawa with its Red Sea territories remained (since his appointment in April 1871) under Werner Munzinger Bey. At the apogee of this governmental mishmash was the Khedivial Privy Council in Cairo, now presided over by Mohammed Tawfiq Pasha, the Khedive's eldest son, aged nineteen. Understandably the Council's first action was to call in all the budgets for the forthcoming year for scrutiny.

The compensating element of central stability lay in the reversion to the precedent in similar circumstances in 1857 of the appointment of a *seraskir* in command of the Sudan military forces and stationed in Khartoum. In 1857 it had been Miralai Osman Pasha Jarkas; now it was to be the *hakimdar* manqué, Lewa Adham Pasha el 'Arifi. He would additionally oversee the Kordofan garrison, to be commanded by a *miralai*; that of Taka under a *qa'immaqam*; and those of Dongola and Berber each under a *sagh qol aghasi*.

The Khedive's latest experiment in governing a fragmented northern Sudan by direct rule from Cairo was to prove comparably as misconceived as that of his predecessor, Mohammed Sa'id, but shorter-lived. The country was already heavily in debt, irrespective of the costs of the Baker and Hilali expeditions and of the Red Sea littoral expansion. The planned engine for new revenue creation, the cotton cultivation schemes of the east, was now to be handed to a relatively inexperienced, if innately able, governor, lately *muhafiz* of Massawa – Ala el Din Bey Siddiq. Sinkat had already a year previously been returned to Suakin. Cairo was left to wrestle with a full spread of financial deficits, augmented by arrears.

It is difficult to keep pace with the velocity of further administrative change over the next two years. In the east, Suakin was reunited with Massawa under Munzinger in April 1872, following which the latter in February 1873 was made general-governor of a refashioned Eastern Sudan, including Taka, and governor of the Red Sea littoral – the status quo ante under Mumtaz of 1870–71. Ahmed Mumtaz, the Khedivial favourite now in Khartoum, fell from grace and was dismissed in July 1872, to be succeeded as general-governor of 'South' Sudan, following a two-month interregnum under Adham Pasha, by Ismail Pasha Ayub, with progressive if nominal responsibility for the whole of Bahr el Ghazal after Ahmed Hilali's murder. The general-governorate of Berber and Dongola seems to have reverted to the status of a *muderia* and, with the independent *muderia* of Kordofan, survived until December 1873 when, under Ismail Pasha Ayub, the *hakimdaria* evacuated by Ja'afar Mazhar little over two years previously was itself once again reconstituted. Equatoria under Gordon Pasha and Eastern Sudan under Munzinger Pasha however were to remain for the following three years, 1874–76, independent general-governorates outside the *hakimdaria*.[4]

3 BERBER AND DONGOLA; AND KORDOFAN

The several experiences of White Nile, Equatoria and Bahr el Ghazal in these two years 1872–3 have already been examined in chapter 5. In Berber and Dongola, Hussein Khalifa el Abbadi, while creating some powerful enemies, seems to have grappled competently with uniting the disparate peoples of his general-governorate, if with limited success in restoring financial equilibrium. As his *wakil* (deputy) in Dongola he appointed another Sudanese, Sheikh Mohammed Abu Hijil, *nazir* of the Rubatab.

In his endeavours to control the deficit and liquidate revenue arrears, Hussein, now a *pasha,* made economies in the number of military units in the governorate, both regulars (four companies) and irregulars (Douin describes the *bashi-buzouqs* as notoriously costly), and sought increased revenue from cotton cultivation with some success. While both the rains and Nile flood of 1871 were poor, and only 4,000 acres planted, that area was more than doubled the next year in improved circumstances, yielding 12,356 cwt after ginning. Like Mumtaz in the eastern general-governorate in 1871, Hussein sought to swell the number of cultivators by attracting back emigrants from his governorate in earlier lean years. This once again led to friction with the Khartoum general-governorate and his own removal at the end of 1873 charged with insolence and corruption. He nevertheless demonstrated for the while the innate ability of Sudanese to govern their own country and was successful in obtaining Khedivial approval for a new appeal tribunal for the governorate at Shendi. It was perhaps significant that the Ottoman Khedive now considered it sensible to limit education in Berber and Dongola schools to the Arabic language.

Kordofan, despite its borders with Bahr el Ghazal and Darfur, which were to become scenes of considerable military activity, remained relatively tranquil. The regular battalion was supplemented by five companies of irregulars, and by 200 *bashi-buzouqs* from Berber and Dongola, but here almost uniquely in the Sudan the annual budget for 1871-2 was in surplus. This enabled Abdel Wahhab Bey to embark upon the building of a new mosque in El Obeid in 1872. We learn also that in early 1873 Sheikh Fadlallah Wad Salem of the camel-owning Kababish, (with supposedly 300,000 followers), while respecting Abdel Wahhab and his officials, saw fit to address himself to the Khedive in person. Like the relatives of the late Ahmed Bey Hilali, he used the good offices of Ja'afar Pasha Mazhar, now returned to Cairo. Sheikh Fadlallah's concerns were the subversion of his people by Fur-based tribesmen seeking their emigration to Darfur; and the usurpation by the general-governors of Khartoum and of Berber and Dongola of the rights, conceded by firman, of the Kababish over the caravan routes to El

Debba, Korti and Khartoum and Kordofan. His concerns were graciously met.[5]

4 'SOUTH' SUDAN GENERAL-GOVERNORATE, KHARTOUM

The fall from grace of Ahmed Mumtaz was Luciferian. Selected by the Khedive as general-governor of 'South' Sudan 'on account of his capability and skills', Mumtaz had received many tokens of his Viceroy's esteem including, it was alleged, 25,000 francs in silver and 600 acres of cotton cultivation in Lower Egypt. Within nine months of his new appointment he had been deposed.

Taking office in November 1871, his first action was to release the commanders of slave boats and *zaribas* arrested over the past year and to restore their confiscated goods, an action which would have enraged both Ja'afar and Baker but which was prompted by the collapse of White Nile trade. Ali Bey Rida el Kurdi at Fashoda (Deinab), active against slave boats as Schweinfurth had noted in July 1871, was deposed, to be acquitted for want of evidence by Adham Pasha el 'Arifi. To restore the financial position, Mumtaz embarked on the policies he had adopted in the east Sudan. Economies were to be effected in the garrison – two battalions of the Khartoum garrison were untrained in weaponry and the whole under strength. Secondly a conference of local leaders from the Khartoum *muderia* was convened and required, within the year, to plant 300,000 acres of cotton. The harvest, aided by the use of Nile steamers for transport and of power gins brought from Egypt, was planned not only to cover the annual tax levy but soon to recoup arrears which, Mumtaz alleged, amounted to £E200,000 and to have been accumulated from the past eight years. This arrears figure was well above the arrears of £E137,500 reported by Ismail Ayub in Cairo in August 1872 and of £E90,270 reported by Adham Pasha in Khartoum the same month in respect of August 1871.

Dismissing redundant *hakimdaria* staff, Mumtaz Pasha moved on at once in January 1872 via Fashoda (Deinab), where the production target of 3,000 cwt of cotton was doubtless ordered, to the *muderia* of Sennar. He was contemplating the creation of a further independent *muderia* comprising Gedaref and the Rahad river, dedicated to agriculture. In Sennar as in Khartoum, the garrison expenditure would be cut, and he envisaged a potential minimum of two million acres of cultivation which would enable the arrears of £E155,000 (Ismail Ayub seems to have reported £E215,000) from the past nine years to be quickly recouped. As a preliminary step, however, a commission was appointed to make a census of the region.

Douin was unable to unearth in the Abdin Palace archives the exact reasons governing the Khedivial decision to dismiss Mumtaz, but there is a suggestion of implication in theft from the Khartoum treasury. We do learn from the report of Adham Pasha el 'Arifi, acting general-governor, following the receipt of his orders to dismiss and (seemingly) to arrest Mumtaz for fraud in July 1872, that Mumtaz's earlier budget proposals had not gained the approval of Cairo, prompting a second submission in which Mumtaz claimed that the military garrisons were no longer required. Not only would such economy in the armed forces have been unacceptable to the *seraskir*, who may well have personally intervened, but Mumtaz's revised and inflated expectations of the numbers and individual tax yields of cultivators lacked all credibility. Actual tax receipts for Khartoum *muderia* in Mumtaz's year of office 1871–2, Adham claimed in late August 1872, amounted to £E20,000 against £E75,000 levied and £E90,000 previous arrears. The inhabitants of the general-governorate were alienated and the chronicler of the *Ta'arikh* was withering in his contempt:

> His character was that of those men of whom God in His precious Book spoke the words: 'Be ye separated this day [from the righteous], O ye evildoers!...' From the day of his arrival he terrorised the people by such wholesale injustice as had never been experienced by them individually or collectively at the hands of any of the rulers who preceded him and as would, if mentioned, blacken the pages of the records and cause the heart of the historian to bleed for pity.

Mumtaz lingered under house arrest in Khartoum, a witness to the building of the new governorate headquarters on which he had embarked, awaiting the appointment in 1874 of a Cairo commission of inquiry into his misdeeds. Meanwhile, curiously, he found himself in June 1873 nominated by the Khedive's council, along with Shahin Pasha Kinj and Ja'afar Pasha Mazhar, as member of another commission to appraise alternative taxation bases for cotton growing in the Sudan. He was to die from typhus in January 1875 before the former commission had reached its conclusion.[6]

Khedive Ismail's appointment of Mumtaz in 1871 had been proved a serious error. In his replacement the Khedive again passed over the claims of the Sudanese Adham Pasha who acted as general-governor for two difficult months following Mumtaz's arrest. Instead the mantle of general-governor fell again on a Circassian, Ismail Bey Ayub, on 8 August 1872. He had been recommended by Mumtaz in February to take command of the First Regiment in Khartoum but another had been appointed and Ismail Ayub had been repatriated to Egypt. He had had many years' service in the Sudan, latterly under Ja'afar Mazhar as president of the Khartoum council but earlier, in tandem with Adham el 'Arifi, as commander of one of the two relief columns sent to Kassala in July 1865 (see p. 36). Ayub had benefited from the presence of Ernst Marno in Khartoum at the end of 1871 to learn German – he was already fluent in French from his time in Marseilles. Evidently he had caught the Khedivial eye.

The fourteen months on which Ismail Ayub was now to embark as general-governor of 'the south', culminating in his appointment in December 1873 as *hakimdar* on the partial reunification of the Sudan (excepting the general-governorates of Eastern Sudan and of Equatoria), were to be demanding. Promoted *lewa*, he gained approval before his departure from Cairo as general-governor for the detachment of Fazughli from Sennar as a *muderia* under an experienced inspector of agriculture, Mohammed Ma'ani Bey, and for the appointment of the elder son, Awad el Karim Ahmed, of the late Sheikh Ahmed Bey Awad el Karim Abu Sin as *mu'awin* of the general-governorate. The more gifted younger son Ali became, until his death in June 1874, *nazir* of the Shukriya in his brother's place. An *amende honorable* was made to Abdel Raziq Haqqi Bey, dismissed from Taka by Mumtaz, with his appointment as governor of the Khartoum *muderia*. Ismail Pasha Ayub was sworn in at Khartoum on 21 October 1872 and pledged the extermination of all old 'traditional' corrupt practices.

Ismail Ayub faced a multiplicity of problems. His reaction to the anarchy in Dar Fertit following Hilali's murder has already been examined (see pp. 166ff). The fragmented Eastern Sudan, and the *muderias* of Kordofan and of Berber and Dongola, remained presently outside his responsibility, although his energies were equal to responding to the belated instructions of the Khedive at least partially to free the Zeraf river from the *sudd* in March–April 1873, much to Baker's delight and benefit on his return from Gondokoro (Ismailia). The most daunting problem confronting Ismail Ayub related to the mounting debt in the *muderias* of the general-governorate. Khartoum, Sennar and Fazughli, and Fashoda, notwithstanding their agricultural potential, were all without funds. Now to the budgetary responsibility of the governorate was to be added the incorporation and fortification of Gallabat, ordered by the Khedive in November 1872 and effected and completed by Adham Pasha el 'Arifi in March–May 1873, Sheikh Mohammed Juma's (Shouma's) duplicitous services being dispensed with on his exile to Cairo.

Like many of his predecessors – Mahu, Ali Khurshid and Ja'afar Mazhar in particular – Ismail Ayub called a conference of the Khartoum *muderia* sheikhs and traders to thrash out a solution to the debt. Agreement was reached that nefarious office holders should be dismissed, their successors to be of proven honesty and experience and to be charged with collection both of the annual tribute and of the arrears, the latter defrayed over eight years at an annual charge equal to a quarter of the levy. The new governor of Fazughli, Ma'ani Effendi, was set to work with military support to collect neglected taxes from the mountain areas, while in Sennar (which Ismail regarded as the most important of all the *muderias*) its inadequate governor was replaced by the experienced Abdel Raziq Haqqi from Khartoum, to be raised to *pasha*. He held with it the joint office of *miralai* of the First Regiment battalion. Adham Pasha would act for Ismail Ayub when the latter was absent from the capital, at least until Ismail Ayub's appointment as *hakimdar* in December 1873.

The accumulated arrears of tax in Sennar to September 1872 amounted to £E215,375, compared with £E137,500 in Khartoum. Ismail Ayub was only saved in December 1872 from seeking a Cairo grant to cover delayed receipts from tax collection in the current year by the unexpected arrival from Gondokoro (Ismailia) of Abu Sa'ud. He brought £E3,250 in cash, being the liquefied assets of his *meshras* in Equatoria which Baker had suppressed at the expiration of the former's contract on 9 April 1872. Ismail Ayub negotiated to borrow this in order to relieve his immediate needs, notably officials' pay arrears.

For longer-term revenue he looked to the harvests of cotton cultivation, though unluckily the poor rains in the past year, 1871–2, had diminished the limited expectations of yield – except by *saqia* irrigation. Fashoda was the exception. Schweinfurth in July 1871 noted no preparations but in October 1874 Ernest Linant was to observe 800 acres of cotton planted out, together with 400 acres of corn and sugar cane. For the future, Ismail Ayub directed his province governors to encourage the acquisition of *saqias,* one per eight acres, for which

cotton cultivation was to be the priority. Inhabitants declining to cooperate in introducing *saqias* would forfeit their land after a year to the
ownership of more complaisant neighbours.

The Cairo Privy Council appointed a commission in 1873 consisting
of Shahin Pasha, Ja'afar Pasha Mazhar, and, apparently, the dismissed
Ahmed Mumtaz, to consider the possibility of reverting to taxation of
cultivated land acreage as under Arakil Bey in 1857, but accepted their
recommendation, as far as Khartoum and Sennar were concerned, to
retain for the present the current system of tax levied on landowners
according to their holdings. Meanwhile 1872–3 proved a better year,
the harvest yielding 3,000 cwt of cotton, though purchasers were few.[7]

It became rapidly clear in the weeks following Ismail Ayub's arrival
in Khartoum to take up his post that he harboured major ambitions
beyond the frontiers of his general-governorate. His handling of the
Zubeir crisis in the context of the planned invasion of Darfur – Ismail
Ayub was evidently involved in discussion with the Ministry of War in
Cairo about it before his departure to Khartoum – was matched on 30
January 1873 by a lengthy submission to Cairo on the fundamental
financial weakness of his limited general-governorate compared with
Kordofan and with Berber and Dongola, all of which had previously
been strong contributors to the budget of Ja'afar's *hakimdaria*. The
latter *muderias* owed their economic profitability to exports – especially of gum and dates – and to the relatively limited costs of their
garrisons, so much so that now both Berber and Dongola collected, or
so Ismail claimed, £E75,000 against costs of £E40,000. Under Ja'afar
all province surpluses had been directed to the Khartoum central treasury and only since 1868–9 had the Khedive once again claimed an
annual contribution of £E75,000. This indeed proved well beyond the
Sudan's capacity and Ismail Ayub pointed out, possibly with satisfaction, that Ja'afar Mazhar had defaulted not least because the well-
found provinces had been detached from the *hakimdaria* and now paid
their contributions direct to Cairo.

That however was not the only reason for the financial weakness of
the general-governorate. Intrinsically the Khartoum and Sennar *muderias* contained the most fertile soil in the Sudan, in extent and in
advantageous location. Yet the benefit drawn by the Gezira from the
White and Blue Niles was squandered. Cultivation was by rainwater
only; agricultural methods were primitive, ploughs disregarded, and
the inhabitants were content with year-to-year subsistence yields.
Imbued with the enthusiasm of his predecessor, Ayub concluded that

once irrigation canals were dug, *saqias* established and cotton cultivation intensified, provincial administration would be simple. While revenues in these *muderias* presently matched those of Dongola and Berber, expenditure was disproportionately high on account of the stationing in the governorate of ten battalions of infantry and seven companies of irregulars, for which the governorate had to pay the wages and provisions; and on account of the central services for the whole Sudan. Military cost economies were an essential prerequisite to the payment of the annual Cairo contribution but now, Ismail Ayub conceded, they could not be addressed while the secret plan to annexe Darfur was in preparation.

At the end of his initial year of general-governorate in September 1873, Ismail Ayub felt able nevertheless to put forward a budget in which revenue exceeded expenditure of £E173,000 by £E7,000. Only further research will reveal whether this budget gained approval and a surplus was realised, for by December a *hakimdaria* had been reconstituted and in April 1874 a new budget accordingly submitted.[8]

5 EASTERN SUDAN 1872–73: AUTONOMOUS *MUDERIAS* MERGED

Prior to taking over the general-governorate of the 'South' Sudan in Khartoum in November 1871, Ahmed Mumtaz had in April-May prepared the budget of two of the three *muderias* of his general-governorate of the Red Sea littoral for the year commencing September 1871. The implementation of budgetary proposals became the responsibility of the now autonomous *mudirs* of the three provinces by the Khedivial decree of 30 September 1871 – Suakin including Sinkat, initially under Shakib Bey, but in April 1872 to be merged with Massawa; Massawa, since April 1871 under Munzinger Bey whose knowledge of agriculture was deemed important to the development of that region; and Taka, likewise since April 1871 under Ala el Din Bey Siddiq, the Circassian former cavalry officer, Munzinger's brief predecessor at Massawa. The general-governorate of the Red Sea littoral was suppressed, and the overall command of troops as in all the Sudan provinces was brought under Lewa Adham Pasha el 'Arifi, though in view of its vulnerability to a hostile Abyssinia, Taka troops were to be placed under a subordinate *miralai*. Such a 'general post' in administrative appointments in the eastern Sudan, and more particularly the transfer to Khartoum of the architect for its local economic development, Ahmed Mumtaz, was scarcely conducive to the realisation of the latter's ambitious agricultural objectives for Taka. Economic development was not however the absolute priority in the eastern Sudan. Territorial expansion on the periphery of Abyssinia came first.

With regard to Massawa, by following Mumtaz's earlier proposal to dispose of the company of *bashi-buzouqs*, Munzinger, in May 1871, had planned to balance the province budget and to initiate cotton cultivation of some 500 acres. However, following his reconnaissance of Tokar on the instructions of the Khedive, he found himself in June made responsible for the cultivation of cotton on an increased scale in Tokar (600–800 acres) as well as in the other environs of Massawa; and for the development of a suitable post, Trinkitat or Aghik (he preferred Aghik), as political and commercial capital of his enlarged territory. The Massawa budget for 1871–2 required recalculation, taking into account not only the transfer of Tokar but the building of an aqueduct for fresh water to supply Massawa, to cost £E8,000. With a central government subsidy of £E1,500, it appears that a revised and approximately balanced budget was struck by March 1872, with expenditure now at about £E20,000. In the same month Munzinger, challenged already by being stationed in Massawa and having to supervise Tokar (a full twelve days' journey distance by land), was now called to Cairo to be informed by the Khedive that his responsibilities had been still further enlarged with the merger of Suakin with Massawa. Within a further twelve months, on 25 February 1873, Taka province proper would in addition be incorporated in a re-created general-governorate of the Eastern (Oriental) Sudan and governorate of the Red Sea littoral, with Ala el Din Bey Siddiq as Munzinger's vice-general-governor.[9]

While his manoeuvring in preparation for ultimate war with Emperor John IV of Abyssinia progressed (see pp. 97–8), Khedive Ismail on 30 April 1873 instructed Munzinger, now general-governor, to report on the acreage and yields of cotton achieved in the Taka, Tokar, Aghik and Suakin regions where, Ahmed Mumtaz had intimated to him in Cairo in April 1870, an annual harvest of 500,000 cwt could shortly be obtained, indicative of a crop area (on the basis of 1 cwt per feddan) of 500,000 feddans (acres) (see p. 63). Three years had now elapsed. Shahin Pasha after discussion with Mumtaz and Munzinger had made his favourable report in 1871, but some considerable water had since flowed down the Gash. And contingent on the cultivation results was to be the Taka railway project.

Munzinger, his mind directed to the impending isolation of Abyssinia, must have been embarrassed to be reminded of his own fulsome *Observations sur la Situation Economique du Soudan*, rated by the Khedive as a seminal authority for his African aggrandisement programme. He was now obliged to confess that the cotton cultivation achievement to date was disappointingly limited. Towards his own affirmed potential for Taka alone of 3m cwt (Mumtaz had anticipated 500,000), in the first year (1871) only 24,000 acres had been planted (the *mamur* in charge claimed 36,000). After part of the yield had been taken in lieu of tax, the remainder was sent to Suakin where, in the continuing absence of gins, a moderate total of 1,200 cwt had been forwarded to Egypt. The cost to the cultivators (principally the Halenga) of transport by camel to Suakin and the continued delay in erecting ginning facilities had thwarted any further expansion in cotton-growing in 1872, while excessive humidity and flash floods spoiled the crop. However Munzinger still hoped for greater things in 1873 with the planned arrival of the gins. Sir Duncan Cumming, then District Commissioner Kassala, and writing in 1940, was critical:

> Let us not be led into believing that there was more than a substratum of truth in the claims of these amateur agricultural economists. Only in the fertile deltas of the Gash and the Baraka will cotton grow and it must, of course, be sown annually and be subject to careful and relatively skilful agricultural methods. The quality of cotton grown is excellent and in fact the cotton schemes of the present government (1940) have been a pronounced success, but only after much experiment and, in the case of the Gash, the expenditure of large sums on irrigation facilities and a railway. Seventy years after Shahin Pasha made his estimate that two million *feddans* (acres) could be grown in the Gash the present government has 100,000 *feddans* under effective cultivation and, of this, only 30,000 feddans can be flooded annually if the fertility of the soil is to be preserved and the growth of weeds kept within manageable limits.

As for ginning facilities, a French engineer arrived in Kassala in 1874 and began to erect the building which now raises an incongruous factory chimney over the town. But no smoke ever came out of it because, although some of the gins and the various other pieces of machinery arrived, the transport of the engine proved to be beyond the skill of the camel contractors of Suakin. One half of the fly-wheel can be seen protruding from the sand behind Berberi's café at Suakin and the other got as far as the outer gate of the town. The gins at Kassala were turned by manual labour for a time and then abandoned altogether.

Cumming's description of the Kassala gins needs to be read with the report of Colonel J. D. H. Stewart who was visiting Kassala en route from Khartoum to Massawa at the end of March 1883. Stewart found Munzinger's cotton factory costing £20,000–£30,000 in 1876 in excellent order, but no cotton being ginned due to official indolence and the practice of travellers and *bashi-buzouqs* grazing their camels on the crops.

So much for the grandiose schemes to yield economic prosperity to the eastern Sudan dreamed up by Mumtaz and Munzinger, and acclaimed by Shahin. Their failure however was not to be allowed to interfere with the principal Khedivial objective: aggressive territorial expansion and the encirclement of Abyssinia.[10]

Of that priority Munzinger had been assured when he was summoned to Cairo in March 1872 to assume the government of the merged *muhafizāt* of Massawa and Suakin. From his many years as French consul in Massawa and adviser to the British Magdala expedition, Munzinger was convinced that Bogos (Sennaheit), and Keren in particular, were the key to access to Tigré and Abyssinia via the passes up to the Hamasein plateau, even if there was no Egyptian historical claim to Hamasein which would justify an immediate occupation. Gordon Pasha believed that Munzinger's Abyssinian wife, a princess, was a prime mover in arriving at this conclusion.

For the while Munzinger was very content to receive Khedivial instructions to lead a limited expedition to occupy Bogos (see p. 97) in compliance with the alleged request of its Bilein tribal inhabitants, thus threatening the Hamasein passes while safeguarding direct communication between Taka and Massawa. The occupation of Keren was effected on 4 June 1872. A garrison of battalion strength was to be based at the strategically fortified post of Keren but Munzinger was strictly denied advance to Hamasein.

To mollify the Emperor John, from whom Bogos had been seized, Munzinger sent his locally experienced official at Keren, Franz Hasan, to Adwa in October 1872 for talks, from which he reported a conciliatory proposal emerged whereby the Emperor agreed to cede Bogos if the Khedive would negotiate a treaty of friendship. The absence of any response by the Khedive or by Munzinger, if that report were correct, would have been indicative of Egyptian intentions.

Following the occupation of Bogos, Kufit (Agordat), evacuated in 1857 and reoccupied 1867 under Taka administration, was transferred to Amideb as a *mamuria*, the better to confront raids from Basen. In 1872 the titular Abyssinian province of Ainseba had been effectively annexed. Now, in February 1873, the reconstituted Eastern general-governorate with the Red Sea littoral was to be re-formed.[11]

8

The Climax of Empire 1874–76: Part 1

By the end of 1873, after five years of preparation, much was in place for the climax of Ismail's expansionist policy in Africa. In the west he had been planning the annexation of Darfur and the eclipse of its ancient sultanate. To the south up the Nile the Egyptian flag had been planted by Samuel Baker in the rich highlands discovered by John Hanning Speke and James Grant, within a few degrees of the Equator. While to the east, following the occupation of Bogos (Sennaheit), a force was being assembled to occupy the Red Sea–Aden–Somalia littoral and to encircle Abyssinia.

At least beyond the frontiers of Egypt proper, all was subordinated to this strategy of aggrandisement. The Sudan, after two years of atypically good government (1866–7) under an able and civilised Circassian Governor-General, reverted to the condition of a neglected colony but with the additional function of a springboard for African expansion. Indeed the then newly appointed Governor-General, Ja'afar Pasha Mazhar, a naval officer, had himself been called away from his Sudan responsibilities in 1867, the second year of his office, to reconnoitre the Red Sea littoral and then to contribute to the strategic plans for annexation. This was a policy with which Ja'afar Pasha appeared to concur; indeed he personally recommended the appropriation of the *qism* Dar Fertit of the Bahr el Ghazal. But his genuine personal concern for the Sudan's well-being was undiminished, even if within months his early efforts to provide for a fair level of taxation and controlled military expenditure as an essential prerequisite of good government – security, justice, agricultural development, even education – were swiftly sacrificed, on Khedivial instruction, to preparations for external conquest. So perhaps the only benefits to the Sudan during these years were an improved infrastructure of communications, especially telegraph and railways, and the geographical and geological surveys under the leadership of American expatriate military engineers. Even these benefits were to prove short-lived in the face of, first, Khedivial bankruptcy and then the Mahdiya.

European interest in the Sudan and East Africa was limited to the security of the route to India and, now increasingly, to the suppression of the slave-trade, being focused on the Upper Nile and Zanzibar. That European interest was more particularly British – France was to suffer from the outcome of the Franco-Prussian War of 1870, while Austrian tentative ambition had long since cooled. To the pressure from British anti-slavery interests Ismail Pasha had been shrewdly responsive, conceding willingly in 1869 the appointment of an expatriate British general-governor for Equatoria. The blurring of primacy as between the two principal objectives in Sir Samuel Baker's firman – to subdue the countries south of Gondokoro and to suppress the slave trade – concealed the priority of the Khedivial purpose: imperial expansion.

The climax to the five years of strategic preparation for conquest was now to be enacted through the agency of a yet further modified administrative structure for the Sudan. With the general-governorate of the 'South' Sudan in Khartoum were now to be merged the independent *muderias* of Kordofan and of Berber and Dongola to form once again a *hakimdaria* under Ismail Pasha Ayub. The two general-governorates – of Eastern Sudan under Werner Munzinger Pasha and of Equatoria under Fariq Charles Gordon Pasha – would however remain separate and responsible direct to Cairo. In effect the separate administrations formed a triarchy.

Ultimate control of policy and of the forces of conquest lay, of course, in Cairo with the Khedive, advised by his second son the Minister of War, Prince Hussein Kamel; by the army chiefs of staff now under the United States former Federal brigadier-general, Fariq Charles Stone Pasha; and by the finance ministry under Ismail Pasha Sadiq, steward of the viceregal properties.

The study of these three years of territorial expansion 1874–76 has been greatly aided by the publication in 1941 of the third part of the third volume of the *Histoire du Règne du Khédive Ismail: L'Empire Africain,* undertaken by the Frenchman Commandant Georges Douin of the Suez Canal Company, under the patronage of the (then) *Societé Royale de Géographie d' Egypte.* Douin died before he was able to complete the fourth part of the third volume planned to cover 1876–79, let alone the projected fourth and fifth volumes. Nevertheless the third part of volume three, together with its preceding parts covering 1863–69 and 1869–73 comprise a monumental total of 2,500 pages of scholarly research, based in great part on translations of original Egyptian government archives. No fewer than 200 pages are devoted to the second disastrous Abyssinian campaign of 1876. In the words of the reviewers of this third part of volume three for *Sudan Notes and Records* (vol. xxv part I, 1942), K. D. D. Henderson and Dr R. L. Hill:

> Monsieur (should one say Commander?) Douin's masterly, yet unobtrusive, editorship has made it possible for the first time to study in detail the working administration of the Sudan during the closing years of Turko-Egyptian rule. All we had before were secondary authorities: chiefly the biographies and autobiographies of foreigners serving in the administration. Now at last, through the initiative of the Royal House of Egypt, we have unfolded for our study the archives of government, the primary authorities which alone enable us to appraise the place in history of an energetic, empirically-minded, well-meaning, if unrealistic Viceroy.

However, the additional financial burdens progressively imposed on Egypt to underpin these external military strikes were so crippling that the policies of the finance ministry under Ismail Pasha Sadiq – '*el mufettish*', 1868–76 – which created them must be examined as essential background.

I THE SLIDE TO KHEDIVIAL BANKRUPTCY 1869–76

By 1867 Khedive Ismail had already borrowed abroad £E11m in order to augment the initial loan of £E3m-odd negotiated by his predecessor (see p. 12) and, additionally, had contracted a floating debt of some £E30m. Confronted with the three-year cost of negotiating the Ottoman firman of 27 May 1866 – enacting the rule of primogeniture to the Viceregal succession (estimated at about £E3m) and the heavy expenditure of the forthcoming festivities for the opening of the Suez Canal in 1869 (£E1.3m), the Khedive in 1868 replaced his finance minister, Ismail Ragheb Pasha, with a trusted friend and confidant Ismail Sadiq, '*el mufettish*'.

Ismail Sadiq was of lowly *fellah* birth, his mother however a nurse to the future Khedive so that, growing up together, they became as foster brothers. In the opinion of McCoan:

> Their personal intimacy... was always rather that of near relatives than of Minister – Prince. He (*el mufettish*) was gifted with great natural astuteness and energy and exerted an influence over Ismail

that made him virtually the vice-ruler of Egypt... possessing beyond anyone who preceded or followed him, except perhaps Mohammed Ali himself, a talent for extorting revenue from the *fellahs* and for fencing with creditors of the government.

The first duty of the *mufettish* in 1868 was to raise a further overseas loan of nearly £E12m which, due to the onerous terms, brought only £E5m in cash to the treasury. The cash was nevertheless urgently needed. To the lavish celebrations planned for the opening of the Suez Canal would be shortly added the cost of the Baker expedition to Equatoria, estimated at £E800,000 spread over four years; but the conspicuous *folie de grandeur* of his Viceroy so vexed Ottoman Sultan Abdel Aziz that he was to veto future Egyptian borrowing which was already spoiling the international market for his own financial requirements. It would cost the Khedive an additional direct gift to the Sultan of £E900,000 to obtain the firmans of September 1872, thus to rescind the veto and, further, to codify the succession firman of May 1866.

The £E12m loan of 1868 was merely a palliative, not a solution, to the growing insolvency of Egypt. While the Khedive lent heavily on his subordinates both in Egypt and the Sudan to enhance local revenues, he shrank from effecting the drastic economies which would bring the mounting deficits under control. The *mufettish* sought meanwhile to raise money internally by the *muqbala* (compensation) law of 1871 which, in return for a six-year advance payment of land tax, granted thereafter a fifty percent reduction on future liability of the subscriber in perpetuity, together with indefeasible title-deeds to the taxpayer's property. Few were wealthy or trusting enough to comply with the terms.

The firmans of September 1872 came none too soon, freeing the Khedive's finance minister again to approach foreign lenders. The £E32m loan now negotiated is believed to have yielded only £E12m in cash and the deficits were already escalating. Hussey Vivian, acting British consul-general in Cairo, in August 1873 advised Earl Granville of Sharif Pasha's opinion that total debt had now reached £E50m, its servicing costing £E5m of an annual revenue of £E7m. 'It is evident that things cannot go on as they are now are, and that if the Viceroy and the Government continue to borrow at the present rate, a crash must inevitably come. The Viceroy's personal expenditure is most extravagant.' Vivian added, two months later, that in reality the Government were 'straining their credit beyond what it will legitimately bear'.

With much difficulty a further £E3m was raised in 1874 but the *ruznamah* loan launched internally the same year – a non-returnable capital levy of £E5m with uncertain interest payments – proved an immediate failure. Yet 1874 was to be the year of the conquest and annexation of Darfur; of the Gordon mission to establish indirect rule in Equatoria; and of early preparations for the encirclement of Abyssinia, all of which constituted additional costs against Khedivial revenues.

> Facilis descensus Averno
> Noctes atque dies patet atri ianua Ditis;
> Sed revocare gradum superasque evadere ad auras
> Hoc opus, hic labor est. [Virgil: *Aeneid* VI, 126]

– a labour that was to prove well beyond the capability of the Khedive and his *mufettish*. Bankruptcy threatened, with no International Monetary Fund to call upon.[1]

Nubar Pasha, the foreign minister, had become increasingly frustrated by the Khedive's refusal to discuss the financial situation in council, while Nubar was kept in equal ignorance about plans for Darfur, if not Abyssinia. Despite French hindrance Nubar was on the threshold of securing European compliance for his great judicial reform, the mixed tribunals, mitigating the privileged status of Europeans under the Capitulations while curbing the unqualified power of the Khedive: in Nubar's view an essential condition to the encouragement of foreign investment and indeed to public acquiescence in the suppression of slavery. On 24 May 1874 Nubar, after a decade of service to his Viceroy, found himself replaced by the more submissive Riaz Pasha.

The *mufettish* imposed increasingly draconian measures, his power awesome. McCoan in *Egypt As It Is* described him as 'the virtual Grand Vizir of Egypt' who 'virtually named every governor and sub-governor and most of even the lower officials throughout the country, levying blackmail from each on his appointment, and exercising nearly absolute authority over the whole up to the day before his fall'. He who once boasted that in one year he had relieved his countrymen of £E15m by taxation continued to enjoy the half-dozen palaces and countryside estates which he had steadily acquired. Nubar described the limited period between his own reinstatement by the Khedive (formally on 9 June but, due to further medical treatment for deafness in Wurzburg, actively in August 1875) and his second dismissal from the joint post of minister of commerce at the end of December 1875:

I only know and can affirm that taxes had ceased for a long while to be other than a name and that they had been replaced by a system of periodic expropriation. There were no tax periods: all was claimed in advance. The *fellah* had only his harvest to settle tax: but the *mufettish* was from time to time making tours, each tour bringing back money for the Treasury which, by direct intimidation or by 'stroking', which always concealed his claws, he extracted from the sheikhs. In the *muderias*, the governors would summon the notables and, at the same time, a money-lender. The notable sold his harvest, not yet sown; the money-lender advanced the cash which, in these conditions, earned him more than 50% interest, the money being paid directly into the government coffers.

Financial difficulties were still not shared by the Khedive in discussion with any member of the Privy Council other than the m*ufettish*. In Nubar's words: 'Les Finances était l'arche sacrée; lui et le *mouffetiche* seules y avaient accès.' The passage of the summer of 1875 saw an acceleration of the crisis, and the decision to seek a British adviser was prompted by a further visit of the Prince of Wales to Egypt en route for India on 30 October. Nubar, ignorant of the full crisis, was surprised by such a formal approach being made but the *mufettish*, in the know, privately warned Nubar not to gainsay that approach which was the sole means of sustaining the Viceroy's position.

In the event it was a British treasury official that the Khedive asked should be attached to the Cairo ministry. Nubar, however, required on the insistence of Colonel Edward Stanton, the British consul-general, to write an official request to London and recognising the grave implication of inviting a British official adviser to the minister, in his letter of 6 November carefully identified the need as being for an economist – not an official. In December, on the appointment of the British judge advocate-general, Stephen Cave, MP, to head the mission, the terms of reference were agreed to embrace all financial matters, with no wish to interfere with Egypt's internal affairs. A confidant of Nubar, the lawyer and journalist Edward Dicey, who was in Cairo at the time, continued to believe it 'more than probable' that the mission was secretly intended by Disraeli to lead up to the establishment of a British protectorate over Egypt but that Disraeli encountered overwhelming hostility to the idea.

As the Khedive's request was submitted to London, there were rumours that the Egyptian government would default on the December

Nubar Pasha Boghos 1825–99

payment of the treasury bills. On 14 November 1875 Nubar sped to the palace to find out the truth, only to be told to address his question to the *mufettish*. It became clear to him, he claimed in his memoirs, that the Khedive and his finance minister were decided on a declaration of insolvency and harboured the facile belief that, by such a default, the interest payment thereby avoided would revert to the treasury to provide credit backing for fresh borrowing.

The treasury were encouraged in this optimism by the issue in Constantinople of a decree in October 1875. The Ottoman national debt accumulated since the Crimean War, mainly loans raised on the London market, now amounted to approaching £E200m. This decree promised speedy payment of only half the interest due and securities for the residue. That promise was quickly to be dishonoured and Sultan Abdel Aziz deposed on 30 May 1876, to be found dead in captivity a week later. A declaration of insolvency followed in July.

For the moment however the Egyptian crash was avoided through the opportunistic purchase on 25 November 1875 by Disraeli's government of Mohammed Sa'id Pasha's original subscription shares in the Suez Canal, for £E4m against an original cost of £E3.5m. Dicey claims Stanton got wind of discussions already taking place in Paris and warned London to act. It was timely, for on 22 November the Khedive had learned of the defeat of the Egyptian army at Gundet on the River Mareb in Abyssinia (see p. 252) and the beheading of its commanders, information which he concealed from Stanton until 25 November. The disaster was followed a week later by news of the defeat of Munzinger's expedition against the Danakil at Aussa (see p. 244). The Khedive was determined on revenge and the re-establishment of his authority in the Sudan, irrespective of financial cost, and by 5 December a second expeditionary force of 12,000 men against Emperor John IV was authorised at a cost of up to £E1m. That was likewise to end in disaster at Gura (see p. 256).

Meanwhile the financial mission led by the Rt. Hon. Stephen Cave, MP arrived in Egypt on 1 December 1875 to report in detail on the Egyptian financial situation. Brought by Colonel Stanton to meet Nubar, whose hackles rose at the prospect of foreign meddling in Egyptian finances, Cave insisted that he was not personally chosen by the British government in response to the Khedive's request but that his report would determine his own government's response. Nubar, claiming that only the Khedive and his *mufettish* were privy to the management of national finances, limited his own briefing strictly to economic affairs. It was immediately clear to Cave however that there was a marked difference of view between the Khedive and Nubar as to his mission, an opinion strengthened by insinuations to Stanton, the British consul-general, by the Khedive (which the former accepted) that Nubar was intriguing with Paris to prevent the success of the mission and the extension of British influence in Egypt.

At the time of Nubar's resignation on 3 January 1876, a French friend returning from an interview with the Khedive believed Nubar's life was threatened and urged him to leave the country. 'Sa [the Khedive's] figure est sinistre; il entre dans la phase de l'assassinat.' When Nubar saw the Khedive a few days later: 'Je n'avais jamais vu le viceroi si sombre de physiognomie; sa figure même me semble épaisse. Ses lèvres et le bas du visage avaient pris un caractère bestial.' Nubar was ordered to quit Egypt for exile in March 1876 following the exposure of evidence that he was seeking, with Russian support, his appointment by the Sultan as governor of Erzerum adjacent to the Turkish-Russian border.[2]

> Turning and turning in the widening gyre
> The falcon cannot hear the falconer;
> Things fall apart, the centre cannot hold.
>   [W. B. Yeats, 'The Second Coming']

'Cannot' or 'will not': the Khedive gave no evidence of any serious intent to arrest the slide to insolvency during the coming months, despite the seemingly frank opening of the books to international inspection and the protracted negotiations over the appointments of three foreign commissioners for the management of a bank. Their role would be to supervise revenues to be specifically allotted to redeem the national debt. Cave's report, completed by mid-March 1876, found that Egypt on the basis of its disclosed resources was basically solvent despite the level of debt. It was the internal administration of the finances which demanded intervention. As the Earl of Cromer (Evelyn Baring) later quoted from the report:

> Two striking features stand out in this balance-sheet [1864-75], namely, that the sum raised by revenue, £94,281,401 is little less than that spent on administration, tribute to the Porte, works of unquestionable utility, and certain expenses of questionable utility or policy, in all amounting to £97,240,966; and that for the present large amount of indebtedness there is absolutely nothing to show but the Suez Canal, the whole proceeds of the loans and floating debt having been otherwise absorbed in payment of interest and sinking funds.

Egyptian debt had grown from £E7m on the death of Viceroy Mohammed Sa'id (1863) to a present £E77.5m but, Cave concluded, on the basis of the figures for revenue and expenditure he had been given, the conversion and consolidation of the debt were manageable in the longer term if the principles of administration he set out were accepted.

The British government was unwilling in advance, and without sight of the Khedive's resultant detailed proposals for the creation of a debt commission, to appoint to it a British member, but had nevertheless encouraged C. Rivers Wilson, controller of the British national debt, to visit Egypt and to make recommendations to the Khedive. En route to Egypt he made confidential contact both with Cave and with

Rothschild's. This carefully measured reaction of the British government was nevertheless too slow, having regard to the gathering pressures on Egypt, for the latter to meet floating debt falling due. The Khedive felt obliged by 14 March 1876 to accept, probably with tougher conditions, immediate loan assistance of £E5m from a French consortium sponsored also by Italy, but coupled it with the appointment of two debt commissioners and of a French counsellor to the ministry of finance. By now he had news of the new Egyptian defeat by the Abyssinians at Gura. The Khedive's arrangement with the French only bought three weeks' respite. In the absence of any sign of serious British intervention, the Khedive was at first prepared to accept the proposals of the French negotiators for the longer term servicing of the debt. When however the terms required proved too onerous, on 8 April 1876 he resorted to the precedent of his Sultan the previous October, and by decree deferred the payments due on the floating debt by three months. His government was in default.

Discussion had nevertheless continued about the publication and adoption of the recommendations of the Cave report and the appointment of a third (British nominated) debt commissioner, following which by 21 April London was encouraged to indicate that, on the basis of the Khedive's intended adoption of the Cave principles and a sound plan of implementation, Britain would in fact nominate a debt commissioner.

Meanwhile the French negotiating group submitted on 26 April their proposals for the consolidation of the Egyptian debt which was now estimated to be in excess of £E90m, allowing for the March short-date loans, as against Cave's original £E77.5m – in the eyes of London 'a growing deficit of menacing proportions'. The French proposals were accepted by the Khedive who, on 2 May 1876, published a decree creating a Commission of the Public Debt – the 'Caisse de la Dette Publique' – with seats for the British, French, Austrian and Italian members, charged to organise the service of a public debt (consolidated five days later at £E91m) and to act as representatives of the bondholders. On 26 May Britain declined responsibility for nominating a commissioner on the grounds that the Khedive had not adopted the Cave recommendations; that the accuracy of the debt assessment presented to Cave had been rapidly disproved; that the Khedivial decree arrangements were unworkable; and that the Khedive was unable to induce European finance houses to work for him.[3]

In the continuing hope that the insensate borrowing might now be halted and the financial system reformed, European pressure led in

October to the appointment as envoys in the specific interest of the British bondholders of G. J. Goschen, a former British Liberal cabinet minister, and of M. Joubert on behalf of the French, to undertake a further investigation into Egypt's finances. On their arrival in Egypt in October 1876 the Egyptian treasury accounts were submitted to a second, more rigorous, examination, in the course of which, contrary to a Khedivial pledge to contract no new debts, subsequent duplicate bonds were discovered in November. The *mufettish*, as the financial minister responsible, was at risk, and the two envoys were referred to him by the Khedive. Already the Khedive had agreed with Vivian, now British consul-general, that a change of finance minister would be well received in Egypt but that the substitution of a European would be impossible. Goschen and Joubert, holding the *mufettish* 'responsible for all the financial malversation', refused to treat with him, instead bringing to the Khedive's personal notice the false accounts, glaring discrepancies and suppression of sources of revenue.

Allegedly the *mufettish* threatened full disclosure if the Khedive himself would not. The deadlock was resolved dramatically on 10 November, the *mufettish* dismissed by the Privy Council for conspiracy against the Viceroy and condemned to exile and confinement in Dongola. Nubar was told by someone seemingly at the Privy Council that, following the dismissal, the Khedive appointed his third son Prince Hasan Kamel, returned from Abyssinia, to take the place of his elder brother, Prince Hussein, as minister of war, and appointed Hussein as minister of finance. Prince Hasan was ordered to take the *mufettish* under military escort to a steamer, ready to depart. The Khedive then displayed to the assembled council documents inciting provincial sheikhs against the Viceroy and Christians bearing the seal of the *mufettish*, and announced his intention to banish the *mufettish* to the Sudan under arrest. He was praised for his clemency. According to Nubar's informant, an officer Ishaq Bey who was then dispatched to seize the seal of the *mufettish*, returned without the seal but with his finger brutally bitten. One Mustapha Bey (?governor of Cairo) was then dispatched to the boat that evening, only to return haggard and half out of his mind, and to remain under medical care for three months – indicative possibly that the *mufettish* had been murdered in a drama to which Mustapha was a party.

Others said that the *mufettish* was transported to Dongola by a *dhahabiya* (Gordon arrived at Korosko on 27 November shortly after it had passed) and that on arrival at Dongola he was strangled by order of the governor. Vivian however was assured by Sharif Pasha that enfeebled by dysentery the *mufettish* died of cerebral congestion, brought on by excessive drinking, on 12 December 1876 three days after reaching Dongola, as was reported by the team of doctors attending the post-mortem.

The respected journalist Sir Valentine Chirol related that the Khedive appeared on that night of 10 November at the opera and that he, Chirol, personally saw him at a formal reception a few days later: 'No one could look more free from black care, let alone from the shadow of black deeds.' Indeed. Dead men tell no tales. And the confiscated property of the *mufettish* enriched the treasury by some £E2m.[4]

If the consequences of foreign intervention proved fatal to the *mufettish*, Ismail Sadiq Pasha, they were shortly to end Khedivial despotism. On 18 November 1876 a Khedivial decree was issued, implementing the Goschen-Joubert conclusion that the funded state 'unified' debt should be fixed at £E59m and secured by general revenue resources; and the balance, including the Khedivial private unfunded debt, made subject to separate arrangement. Egypt's tax revenues and expenditure would be supervised respectively by two controllers-general for revenue and for expenditure, 'the dual mandate'. Captain Evelyn Baring, lately private secretary to the Viceroy of India, on the personal recommendation of Lord Goschen accepted appointment as a commissioner of the bondholders' Caisse de la Dette. The unfunded debt creditors however litigated successfully in the new Mixed Tribunal to establish that no valid distinction could be made between state and Khedivial debt. The outcome in April 1878 was to be the creation of a further International Commission of Enquiry.

This accelerating deterioration in Egypt's financial situation through 1874–76, concealed from ministers and from senior officials both in Egypt and the Sudan, is an essential background to the understanding of the final phase of Khedivial aggrandisement in these years, and of the instructions transmitted by the Khedive to his officials in their respective theatres of activity.

2 THE *HAKIMDARIA* OF ISMAIL PASHA AYUB 1873–77

Civil Administration and Finance   After fourteen months as general-governor Ismail Ayub was on 2 December 1873 appointed Governor-General of the Sudan, excluding the general-governorates of the Eastern Sudan (to which Gallabat was attached in May 1874) and, in

February 1874, of Equatoria. While he served in that capacity until February 1877, Ayub was in fact to be absent from the territory of which he had now been appointed *hakimdar* for all but eleven months, quitting Kordofan for the invasion of Darfur mid-August 1874 and only returning thence to Khartoum for under two months (May–June 1876) before obeying a summons to Cairo from which he never came back. He was of course in constant touch with Khartoum and Cairo during his prolonged absence in Darfur, but meanwhile supervision of the *muderias* of the *hakimdaria* necessarily devolved on his *wakil mamur*. This responsibility had been expressly committed to Ismail Ayub's personal care by the Khedive on his appointment. His own selection of Mohammed Bey Hasan, president of the court of appeal, to deputise on his departure to Darfur was soon to be superseded by the Khedive's appointment in February 1875 of Khalid Bey Nadim, recently heading the commission of enquiry into the charges, *inter alios*, against Ahmed Mumtaz Pasha who had died in January 1875. Khalid also enjoyed the rank of *qa'immaqam,* but he in turn was recalled to Cairo at Ismail Ayub's urging on the return of the *hakimdar* to Khartoum in May 1876, and when Ayub finally left himself in June it was to Abdel Raziq Haqqi Pasha that he handed over as *mamur.*

Until June 1874, when he quit Khartoum for Kordofan en route to Darfur, Ismail Ayub's principal concern was the realisation of a minimum of £E150,000 annual revenue net of expenditure. Kordofan together with Berber and Dongola had been reattached to the *hakimdaria* in December 1873. The superseded general-governor of the latter, Hussein Pasha Khalifa, was accused of failures in revenue collection and of corruption. Along with Ahmed Mumtaz Pasha and others allegedly implicated in theft from the Khartoum treasury, Hussein was investigated by the commission of enquiry headed by Khalid Bey Nadim, with Hasan Bey Rifa'at, a senior Egyptian judge and Hasan Bey Hilmi el Juwaisar, the outgoing *mudir* of Kordofan, as members. The commission a year later had still to complete hearing evidence when Ahmed Mumtaz had died suddenly of typhus, an event leading to its suspension. In mid-1876 Hussein Bey Khalifa was still protesting his innocence and demanding a fresh commission of enquiry. As guardian of the security of the Korosko-Berber route he had meanwhile been succeeded by his brother Sheikh Hamed.

As governors of Kordofan and of Dongola and of Berber, after an interval of several months Ayub Pasha nominated respectively Mohammed Sa'id Bey Wahbi, Almas Bey Mohammed and Ali Bey

Ismail Pasha Ayub

Sharif. Likewise for Khartoum, Ali Bey Fahmi; Sennar, Abdel Raziq Haqqi Bey; Fazughli, Mohammed Fahim; and Fashoda, Yusuf Bey Hasan el Shellali were nominated. The postings were confirmed.[5]

Following Sir Samuel Baker's return to Egypt in July 1873 Equatoria, whose Zeraf river communication Ismail Ayub himself had cleared a few months earlier, became answerable to Khartoum. Ismail Ayub appears to have shared Baker's reservations about Mohammed Ra'uf Bey, now the acting governor in Gondokoro (Ismailia). On his appointment as *hakimdar* in December 1873 he sought to have Mohammed Ra'uf replaced by Ali Bey Rida el Kurdi, formerly governor at Fashoda, and to create an additional *muderia* of Rohl embracing the former *meshras* of Ghattas and the Poncets. Ali Rida had still not been fully exonerated from the accusations of Ahmed Mumtaz and the Khedive did not approve these proposals. Thus it was Mohammed Ra'uf whom Ismail Ayub now charged to produce £E17,500 from ivory sales in Equatoria as a contribution to *hakimdaria* expenditure.

From the respective *muderias*, Ismail Pasha Ayub proposed to raise in his first budget, submitted in April 1874, net revenue of only £E100,000 on account of the additional military costs occasioned by the invasion of Darfur. Of this he hoped some £E45,000 would come from Dongola and Berber; from Equatoria (together with the new *muderia* of Rohl) about £E30,000; and from Bahr el Ghazal £E15–20,000. The re-creation of the independent general-governorate of Equatoria on the arrival of Colonel Charles Gordon in February 1874, however, meant its swift detachment from the *hakimdaria*. The costs of Zubeir's army in conquering Darfur further reduced the revenue contribution of Bahr el Ghazal as did those of Ismail Ayub's force the contribution of Kordofan, while disputes over the land survey in Dongola and Berber adversely affected their tax yields. In short, the surpluses of revenue required to be directed to the Khartoum treasury by each *muderia* fell, in totality at least, well below schedule in the year 1873–4, notwithstanding Khedivial approval of the Governor-General's reduced budget of £E100,000. In 1875 the financial deficit of the *hakimdaria* was to be further increased by the Khedive's order to charge Dongola and Berbera with the costs of the new railway and, subsequently in September, to separate Dongola again from the *hakimdaria* under Shahin Pasha Kinj – the latter having been appointed to control the railway development. When in June 1875 Khalid Bey Nadim, acting for the *hakimdar*, had complained that his Khartoum treasury was already empty, he was warned nevertheless not to appropriate General Gordon's limited Equatoria ivory assets lodged at Khartoum; and generally to threaten with imprisonment any *mudir* deemed negligent in the collection of tax arrears.[6]

Shortly after his eventual return to Khartoum from Darfur in the summer of 1876, Ismail Ayub was summoned to Cairo to explain *inter alia* his failure to submit central budgets and to remit adequate revenues to Egypt. Certainly no budgets for the *hakimdaria* as opposed to the several provinces are extant, with the exception of that of April 1874. Ismail Ayub pointed out his absence for two years in Darfur and in turn requested that the Cairo ministry of finance be in future content with the submission of the individual province budgets – a plea eventually conceded in January 1877 subject to the inclusion of detailed lists of personnel employed, their service arrangements and their specific responsibilities, in addition to province expenses and revenues.

Perhaps more important had been the decision taken by the Khedive in September 1875, in the wake of the exploratory reconnaissances undertaken by Colonels Colston, Prout and Purdy in Kordofan and Darfur, of Mohammed Mukhtar Bey in the Nile-Red Sea region, and of Gordon Pasha in Equatoria, that henceforth all governors and administrative officials should be *military* personnel; and that the Sudan, in its respective regions, would report no longer to the Ministry of Interior but to the Ministry of War in Cairo, in the person of the new Under-Secretary for the Sudan, liaising with the Khedivial office. The Ministry of War was charged to plan the development and prosperity of the Sudan provinces and their peoples, their commerce and agriculture.[7]

Agriculture and Commerce Sudan agriculture was principally directed to *dura* for local food consumption and to cotton, for which Ahmed Mumtaz had distributed ample seed before his dismissal in the late summer of 1872. The Shukriya responded diligently to cultivation of their farms and in 1875 Khartoum bought in 1,000 cwt of raw cotton from Gedaref for ginning and dispatch north to Berber. Rain cotton was dependent upon the variable annual rainfall (1872 and 1875 were bad years), but the irrigated crops were more reliable. Gins were ordered for Berber, Dongola, Sennar and Fashoda and could be harnessed to drive the steam irrigation pumps. 3.5 cwt of raw cotton produced 1 cwt of ginned cotton and Cairo decreed that ginning were best done in the Sudan.

Exports of cotton to Egypt were however negligible, the bulk of exports seemingly being ostrich feathers, gum, ivory and senna which in total value did not in 1875 probably exceed £E600,000. Even that limited commerce was held up by the requisition of river transport for the new railway materials. The tough decree on the abolition of the slave trade by Ismail Ayub in May 1874 and the confiscation not only of the *meshras* and *zaribas* but of the boat cargoes of ivory, now a government monopoly, brought the ivory trade to a virtual halt. Unlike in Equatoria where Gordon granted a dispensation of eight months for the merchants to evacuate their stocks from the *meshras*, by October 1874 437 cwt had been seized by the *hakimdaria* from merchants El 'Aqqād, Hasaballah, Ghattas, Kuchuk Ali, Biselli and Amouri, principally at Fashoda, and a further 344 cwt in November. The merchants petitioned the Khedive in vain. The confiscated ivory sent to Cairo was worth approaching £E2,000 as against the £E140,000 worth reckoned to have been legitimately traded to Egypt in 1875. On the Bahr el Ghazal commerce was paralysed, though Zubeir Pasha insisted that he was too preoccupied with Darfur to comply with the decrees in his private bailiwick. Ismail Ayub was not to be deterred from forbidding the further dispatch of arms and ammunition to that new *muderia*.

As to Darfur, which had in its independence over the centuries conducted a sizeable trade with Egypt and Sudan, conquest and occupation would bring that to a peremptory halt. In the preceding years three or four caravans annually had set out from El Kobbé (El Fasher) by the Darb el Arbain to Assiut with 500–600 cwt of ivory, 1,000–1,500 cwt of rock salt (natron) and over 150 cwt of ostrich feathers and of tamarin. Only individual small caravans left in the summer of 1875 and February 1876. The El Kobbé merchants had taken strongly against the imposition of government monopoly purchases at depressed prices and excessive Egyptian dues, and diverted the export of their produce to Bornu and Wadai. The merchants' leader, Mohammed el Khabir, was a brother-in-law of the late Sultan Ibrahim, third son of Mohammed Hussein.[8]

The Kordofan Survey 1875–76   The expeditions of Purdy Bey and, latterly, Prout Bey in Darfur are considered below (pp. 231–3).

Kordofan Arabs and Chief

Simultaneous with the departure of the Darfur survey expedition in early 1875 was that of Colston Bey, succeeded by Prout Bey, to map Kordofan, its water supplies and cart tracks, approaching via El Safia and Bara. Together they surveyed 1,600 miles, including the town of El Obeid; and Prout himself in December 1875–January 1876, with a substantial escort, completed a 700-mile march including Dilling, Tegali, Jebel Birka, El Rahad, Jebel Dayir, Dueim and back to El Obeid.

Their report published in 1877 (and in the Bulletin de la Société Royale de Géographie 1922) concluded that in the northern part of the province, north of the latitude of El Safia and predominantly Kababish territory, the land was sterile; the 900 wells were not all dependable; and agriculture was unviable. In the southern part, the cultivation of *dukhn,* not *dura*, millet was possible and water supplies reliably adequate only in the depressions of Kagmar, Jebel Abu Haraz, Bara and Melbeis. Of an estimated sedentary population of 165,000, the principal *qisms (aqsam)* included El Obeid 30,000 (the town 4-5,000); Khorsi 42,000; Bara 24,000; Tai'ara 18,000; and Abu Haraz 17,000. The nomadic population totalled 114,000 of whom the Kababish comprised 60,000; the most numerous Baqqara were the Jima'a 25,000, the Hawazma 15,000 and the Habbaniya 8,000. These population totals excluded the Nuba mountains.

Kordofan exports chiefly consisted of ostrich feathers yielding about £E86,000 in Cairo; gum arabic, scarcely profitable, £E55,000; and hides £E2,500: against imports, mainly cotton goods, of about £E50,000. Prout concluded that the possession of Kordofan would never enhance the wealth and glory of Egypt. The incipient bankruptcy of Egypt seemed to lend support to that disappointing and somewhat hasty conclusion.[9]

Public Security: The Shilluk Insurrection, October 1875–April 1876
Against a background of multiple campaigns of aggrandisement undertaken by Egypt beyond the borders of the Sudan and a level of national expenditure so much in excess of revenues, the threat of state bankruptcy was escalating. Repetitive internal reorganisations of the administration of the Sudan; the deaths of experienced, able and uncorrupt governors and officials; an absent Governor-General and Eastern general-governor; and a Khedive preoccupied with gloire: against all these the deterioration of the economy and the progressive disenchantment of the governed were a logical outcome. Yet for the while public

security in the Sudan was maintained, the exceptions being a minor insurrection by the Hawazma Baqqara over taxes at the end of 1874 and a major revolt of the Shilluk of Upper Nile in October 1875. Ismail Pasha Ayub was then involved with the problems of Darfur and Bahr el Ghazal and it fell to his *wakil mamur* in Khartoum, Khalid Bey Nadim – appointed by the Khedive because, although his military experience was limited, he had been advanced to *qa'immaqam* after two years in the Ministry of Interior in Cairo – to deal with the insurrection.

The Shilluk, occupying the White Nile corridor en route from Khartoum both to Gondokoro and the Bahr el Ghazal, had been in a state of unrest since, in 1867, the belligerent Reth Kwatker Akwot had been unseated (supposedly slain) and replaced by his cousin Reth Ajiyang Nyidhok (see p. 106). Ali Bey Rida el Kurdi, appointed governor of White Nile in 1866, had won the commendation of the Governor-General, Ja'afar Pasha Mazhar, and the reluctant respect and acceptance at least of the northern Shilluk. The intervention of Sir Samuel Baker in 1870 had been followed by the somewhat gratuitous dismissal of Ali Reda by Ahmed Mumtaz Pasha, when the latter succeeded Ja'afar in November 1871 as general-governor in Khartoum.

The successor governor at Fashoda (Deinab), Ali 'Abu Khamsa Meeya', soon provoked complaints and the hostility of the Shilluk with his imposition of increased taxation, hostility that culminated in 1872 in an attack on the Kaka area by Reth Ajiyang, killing seventy soldiers and threatening Fashoda. The rebel Shilluk, unsupported by their southern fellows, proved no match for the armed forces of the reinforced governor, and Reth Ajiyang was obliged to flee into the hinterland until captured eventually near Tonga. He was brought to Fashoda and with Khedivial authority publicly crucified in May 1874. The new governor for that past year had been Yusuf Bey Hasan Khorda.

This brutal execution of their *reth* further incensed the Shilluk and at the end of the rains of 1875, the grass still being high, they rose in their wrath and marched on Kaka to exact revenge. It happened that at this time Gordon Pasha in Equatoria was planning to open up a trading outlet on the east African coast and had obtained Khedivial approval for it on the basis that Yusuf Bey should be attached to Equatoria as his deputy. Romolo Gessi, Gordon's agent in Khartoum, was setting out from Khartoum to join Gordon with the steamer *Ismailia* and a contingent of troops when a secret Khedivial package was handed to him for Yusuf Bey, whom he was to take to Lado, Gordon's headquarters.

Gessi had scarcely reached Fashoda at midnight on 15 October

1875, a day or two after Yusuf had narrowly escaped from a local skirmish with the Shilluk in which eighteen soldiers were killed, when news arrived that a major Shilluk force was threatening Kaka. Yusuf sought Gessi's agreement that they should return at once in the *Ismailia* with an armed force to succour Kaka, necessarily delaying their departure to Lado by forty-eight hours. Disembarking early the next morning at Kaka and augmenting his troops with eighty further reinforcements, Yusuf, conspicuous on his horse, advanced at once against an infinitely superior Shilluk force concealed in the long grass. He and all but seven of his men were massacred. Only Gessi's courageous resolve in driving off the attackers persuaded the surrounded garrison to hold out until nightfall when he embarked the remaining troops (the sole gun necessarily abandoned) and 200-odd wives and children, with barely sufficient firewood on board to reach Fashoda.[10]

The governor dead, Kaka abandoned, and approaching half the provincial garrison casualties (in March 1873 it had totalled eleven companies), Gessi was the first to recognise not only the threat to Fashoda but also to Khartoum's communications with Equatoria and Gordon's station at Sobat mouth. Ensuring that the complaisant male population of Fashoda was armed to support the remaining troops, the *Ismailia* sailed to warn Surur Effendi Bhajat, the officer at Sobat mouth who requested Gessi to return at once to Khartoum for reinforcements and arms. Due to recruitment for the Darfur and Abyssinian campaigns, the capital garrison had been reduced to only one regular battalion but no doubt urged on by Gessi, Khalid Bey Nadim, acting for Ismail Ayub, did not hesitate to dispatch at once on the *Ismailia* under the battalion *qa'immaqam* three of the companies and one gun to Fashoda, where they arrived at the end of October. It had been a close run thing. Without the fortuitous intervention of Gessi in the steamer *Ismailia*, Fashoda could have fallen to the Shilluk. With reinforcements, the *qa'immaqam* was able to repulse attacks on Fashoda itself until the arrival of 600 Sha'iqi and riverain Arab irregular reinforcements in the new year.

Meanwhile to restore the status quo Khalid, backed by Ismail Ayub in El Fasher, persuaded the Khedive to reinstate the former governor Ali Bey Rida, still in Khartoum under investigation, in Fashoda. By the time of his arrival at the end of November 1875 the Shilluk, still sensing victory, were gathering a substantial army of many thousands to take Fashoda and were not disposed to offer surrender. Following three unsuccessful attacks alleged to have cost them 1,000 dead, the Shilluk were then themselves attacked in mid-January 1876 by Ali Rida with a force of 700 armed with Remington rifles and four guns. They sustained a further 1,000 casualties before dispersing into the bush. Kaka was quickly reoccupied and the station refortified. Still defiant, the Shilluk bravely moved to battle again in April 1876 just before the rains, only to incur a further defeat and to seek an armistice. From Tonga in the south to Thworokit north of Kaka, the Shilluk were again in submission.

The attempt to rule the Shilluk without a *reth*, even if in the case of Ajiyang Nyidhok he had neither been elected nor indeed gained the acceptance of the southern Shilluk, had proved a failure. Ali Rida, from long experience of the people, now decided to install as *reth* Kwickon (alias Yul), son of Kwatker Akwot who had died in captivity at Fashoda in 1871. Kwickon had been driven into exile by Yusuf Bey Hasan el Khorda, together with 5,000 followers and cattle and had taken refuge under Gordon Pasha south of the Sobat. Romolo Gessi had previously encountered Kwickon at Sobat mouth in June 1874 prior to the expulsion. In May 1877 Gordon as Governor-General was to appoint Kwickon a salaried *bey*.[11]

Dr Wilhelm Junker, the Prussian botanist, passing Fashoda in August 1876, reported that the slave trade was active as ever but that cultivation of millet had been resumed; and a year later the Baqqara were seen purchasing *dura* in Kaka. The observed resurgence of the slave trade may however have been confused with the urgent government recruitment of up to 10,000 Blacks for the regular army, initially and principally from Bahr el Ghazal or Darfur, in return for a gratuity of 500 to 800 *piastres* each, or a tax credit in lieu, to their masters. Following the Shilluk revolt, reward was by way of indemnity.

Since 1874 the Egyptian minister of war, the Khedive's son Prince Hussein Kamel, had been struggling with the personnel demands both of the invading armies of Darfur and the pending military confrontation with Emperor John IV of Abyssinia, in addition to the consolidation of Khedivial territory in Equatoria and the suppression of the Shilluk insurrection. Since Egyptian regular battalions were not only susceptible to the harsh climate of the Sudan but constituted a heavier charge on the *muderia* budgets, the best plan seemed an on-running programme of Black recruitment, to be dispatched for training in Egypt and returned for service in the Sudan (save for the Shilluk who were most liable to desert and would therefore remain in Egypt). Following the reorganisation of Darfur and the suppression of the Shilluk revolt, Ismail Pasha Ayub as well as filling vacancies in the ranks of *hakimdaria* troops would, before leaving for Cairo in June 1876, send 1,400 recruits to Egypt. Others were to follow until the programme was halted in August. By then Egypt had suffered the fresh defeat in Abyssinia and was bankrupt.[12]

The Shilluk revolt was not in the event to prove the only serious military threat with which the *mamur*, Qa'immaqam Khalid Bey Nadim, was faced in the absence of his *hakimdar* in Darfur. The news of the defeat of the Egyptian army under the Dane, Arendrup Bey, at Gundet on 16 November 1875 by the Abyssinians led to an immediate decision by the Khedive to mount a successor campaign under the *sirdar* (commander-in-chief), Mohammed Ratib Pasha, to exact revenge before the onset of the rains of 1876, and this despite the death of Munzinger Pasha on his expedition to Tadjura and Aussa that same November.

Gedaref, part of the Sennar *muderia*, was adjacent to the vulnerable outpost of Gallabat which since 1874 was part of Eastern Sudan, but with a garrison of only 200. Responding swiftly to the likely threat to it from Abyssinia, Khalid in December 1875 ordered two regular companies from Dongola and Berber with a Sha'iqi contingent to reinforce Gedaref, and in January Khartoum was in a position to respond strongly and successfully to any threat to Gallabat and Gadalhi posed by Abyssinian warlords. It was clear that Gallabat would be better defended from Sennar than from Sennaheit or Massawa, and by the end of 1876 the town was again part of the *hakimdaria*.[13]

The Sudan Railway Project 1871–77   In a surge of optimism Munzinger Bey, shortly to succeed Ahmed Mumtaz Pasha as general-governor of the eastern Sudan, had written to the Khedive in July 1871: 'With communications [especially a link between Wadi Halfa and Shendi], the Sudan will become in a short time a second Egypt. The only way of doing this is, I think, to create a wise combination of railroads with Nile steam navigation.' (See p. 176.)

Earlier that year, in February, on the recommendation of the Prince of Wales, the British engineer Sir John Fowler had been recruited on a five-year contract to advise and supervise on the trace, design and ancillary buildings for the construction of railways in Nubia. The priority was to be the linking of Wadi Halfa and Shendi (675 miles) and the by-passing by slipway of the Aswan cataract (navigation above this cataract and as far as Wadi Halfa was not deemed a serious problem),

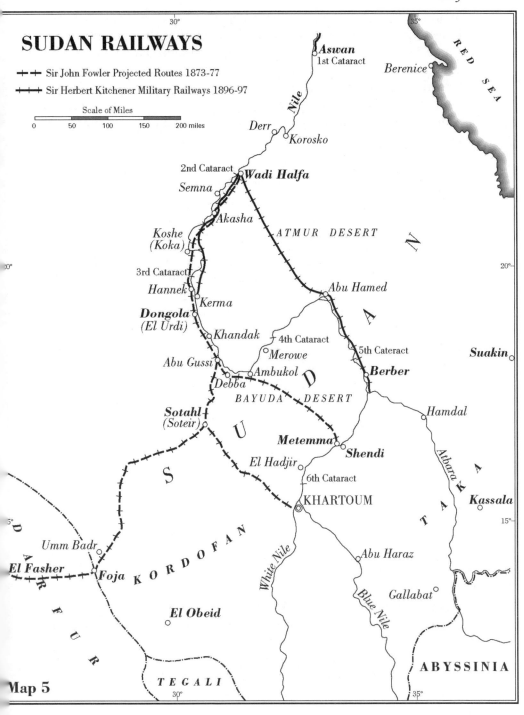

SUDAN RAILWAYS

+—+ Sir John Fowler Projected Routes 1873-77
+—+ Sir Herbert Kitchener Military Railways 1896-97

Scale of Miles

0   50   100   150   200 miles

Aswan
1st Cataract

Berenice

RED SEA

Nile

Derr
Korosko

2nd Cataract
Semna
Wadi Halfa

Akasha
ATMUR DESERT

Koshe (Koka)

3rd Cataract
Hannek
Kerma
Abu Hamed

Dongola (El Urdi)

Khandak
4th Cataract
5th Cateract
Merowe

Abu Gussi
Ambukol
Berber
Debba
BAYUDA DESERT

Suakin

Sotahl (Soteir)
Hamdal

Metemma
Shendi
El Hadjir
6th Cataract

Kassala

KHARTOUM

Umm Badr
Abu Haraz

El Fasher
Foja KORDOFAN

Gallabat

El Obeid

DARFUR

TEGALI

ABYSSINIA

Map 5

S U D A N

TAKA

Atbara
White Nile
Blue Nile

in order to effect continuous river navigation between Wadi Halfa and Lower Egypt. By 10 August 1872, two days after the appointment of Ismail Pasha Ayub to supersede Ahmed Mumtaz Pasha as general-governor in Khartoum, the Khedive felt constrained to go public and brief the *New York Herald* on his plans for the railway link to Shendi, ultimately with the intent also to connect the Nile and Red Sea. Internal commerce in the Sudan would grow and prosper and he put the cost at £E4.5m. He went on:

> All Egyptians have a prejudice against the Sudan [this was in the context of the dismissal of Ahmed Mumtaz]. They imagine that I put them there to rid myself of their presence. Our officers like the capital (Cairo)...A railway will dispel these illusions and once completed the world can be certain that I shall develop the Sudan.

Brave words, not to be realised under Khedivial rule. By February 1873 Fowler was ready with his report. The railway would terminate on the west bank of the Nile at Metemma opposite Shendi, which was both equidistant from Berber and Khartoum and a terminus for caravans from Suakin and Sennar. The construction of the whole line would be a simple undertaking without tunnels or bridges, save across the Nile at Koshe (Koka) from right bank to left. The trace would follow the right bank from Wadi Halfa to Koshe, cross the Nile by bridge and resume along the west bank to Ambukol, traversing the remaining 175 miles of the Bayuda desert to Metemma. The alternative desert crossing of the Atmur, from Korosko to Abu Hamed, would extend 240 miles through deep wadis without sufficient water for locomotives. Fowler estimated a capital cost of £E1m – with Britain bearing two thirds and Egypt one third – to be financed out of traffic revenues. The plan was approved by the Khedive for public tender on 23 February 1873. Appleby Brothers won the tender for track and rolling stock and work commenced at Aswan and Wadi Halfa.[14]

There was an early hiccough in the schedule. Munzinger, now general-governor of a territory including the occupied Bogos, was anxious to extend the railway from Metemma across land (the Atbara being unnavigable) via Qoz Regeb, Barka, and Keren to Massawa – even to Port Annerley – and he secured Fowler's support as to its viability. Originally sympathetic, the Khedive after discussions with Shahin Pasha Kinj, Fariq Stone and Ali Bey Mukhtar, commanding troops in Khartoum, in May 1873 preferred the alternative of a Red Sea link Metemma–Tokar.

Meanwhile, however, having approved Fowler's February 1873 report, the Khedive was having second thoughts about the Wadi Halfa route. A year earlier he had ordered a survey of the fresh water wells on the alternative, shorter overall route via Korosko to Abu Hamed and Berber. Fowler's tenders were put on hold and a government expedition on the alternative Atmur desert trace initiated. The Khedive then left for Constantinople, and on his return in September 1873 ordered yet further reconnaissance of the route from Berber to Berenice on the Red Sea by Purdy Bey. The conclusion from all this exploratory activity was that the fresh water supplies would indeed prove insufficient for locomotives, notwithstanding the promising economies of the Atmur route; and in November 1873, after a delay of nine months, the Fowler Aswan–Metemma route was reinstated.

The imminence of the invasions of Darfur and Abyssinia nevertheless triggered a number of amendments in the original Fowler plan. In place of the Aswan slipway, a ten-mile railtrack would be built round the east bank of the cataracts. A steam ferry, not a bridge, would now carry the railway across the Nile at Koshe; and the railway would terminate above Hannek, transport from New Dongola to Ambukol to be by river. Fowler recalculated the overall railway cost at £E1.4m of which the Egyptian portion, south to Wadi Halfa, would total £674,000; and the Sudan portion, to be levied on the *muderia* of Dongola and Berber, £747,000. The first rails were laid for the Aswan cataract diversion in 1874, but not yet for Wadi Halfa.[15]

At this point Ismail Pasha Ayub, the new Governor-General of the Sudan, who had hitherto been little more than a spectator of the Cairo discussions, found himself actively involved having regard not only to the building plans but to the new financial burden imposed on the *hakimdaria*. His own prior commitment to the Darfur conquest necessitated the appointment of a capable administrator to organise the local logistics of railway building. Once again it was Shahin Pasha Kinj, member of his Privy Council, to whom the Khedive turned in September 1874, the province of Dongola and Berber being transferred back to Egypt under his control. Fowler was authorised to commence works on 1 January 1875 under the chief engineer Mr Kilgour, up to the point of transhipment between Hannek and New Dongola, the work to be spread over five years. On 15 February 1875, in the presence of the newly arrived *mamur*, Shahin Pasha, the ceremonial laying of the first rails was enacted at Wadi Halfa in a sandstorm. It was an ill omen.

The logistical works in the area of railway construction for which

Shahin Pasha assumed responsibility did not extend to the procurement of materials, transportation and technical laying. His principal responsibility, funded by the local *muderia* 'and if necessary, that of Esna' in Upper Egypt, was to supervise the recruitment, deployment, payment and victualling of unskilled labourers. However, the riverain dwellers of the Nile from Wadi Halfa south to El Debba resisted recruitment, insisting that their priority must be the maintenance of their local *saqia* (water-wheel) cultivations, not the laying of railtrack north of and through the *batn el hajar*, the 'belly of stone' above the second cataract. Angered at the news, the Khedive ordered Khalid Bey, the acting *hakimdar* of the Sudan, to conscript 3,500 Dongalawi labourers by force; but by now, mid-May 1875, railway construction had been held up at Abka out of need to order special British equipment to breach the hard rock strata. Not without relief Shahin sought leave to return to Cairo with Kilgour. By July the equipment was arriving at Alexandria only to be halted at Assiut for want of barges. Shahin was given additional responsibility over Aswan district with a view to hastening the consignment of equipment and of wood sleepers to Abka. Perhaps he had now had enough, for in October 1875 he asked to be relieved of his post on health grounds and was replaced by Mustapha Pasha Fahmi of the Ministry of War.

In the period up to December 1876 two further Sudan Railways *mamurs* were to be appointed. Khedivial bankruptcy was now a fact. By December 1875 £E25,000 was owing to Appleby Brothers, by May 1876 £E31,200. The company maintained its obligations but, in the absence of payment, in December 1876 it referred the dispute to arbitration. By now the Khedive had placed the railway in the hands of Ismail Pasha Ayub, presently in Cairo, and optimistically the latter canvassed the possibility of progressing with a military force strengthened with engineers.[16]

The resignation of Shahin Pasha and the impending dispute over the payment of Appleby Brothers did not deter, indeed perhaps prompted, the Khedive to reopen the issue of the Sudan railway trace to the middle Nile in the light of recent events. Since the Bayuda route to Metemma had been reconfirmed in November 1873, not only had Darfur been occupied but the Upper Nile seemed to have been made navigable – with the one critical exception of the Makedo rapids at Dufile – by steamer to Lake Albert Nyanza, facilitating a possible trade route to the Indian Ocean at Zanzibar. Since the somewhat inauspicious inaugural ceremony of commencement at Wadi Halfa in February 1875, few miles of track been laid. The new survey which Fowler was ordered to undertake in November 1875 was to appraise a link by rail between the new province's headquarters at El Fasher and the Nile valley above Old Dongola; and a second direct rail link between Khartoum and the same El Fasher–Old Dongola route. Such a link would supersede the proposed Bayuda desert crossing from Ambukol direct to Metemma. If the El Fasher route were found unviable, then a shorter direct rail route from Ambukol to Khartoum via the Wadi Muqaddam due south across the Bayuda to the Gabra wells was another possibility.

The Anglo-Egyptian team of engineers left Cairo in mid-November 1875. At Wadi Halfa it split into two expeditions: the first would proceed to Abu Gussi between Old Dongola and El Debba on the left bank and, branching south to Sotahl (Soteir, near the Hamadieh wells), would then skirt the western Bayuda desert south east to Omdurman. The second expedition, after taking soundings of the Nile depth at Koshe (the proposed site of the rail crossing east to west south of the *batn el hajar),* would follow the approximate route taken by Purdy Bey in April 1875 via the wells at Umm Badr to Foja. By chance they met Prout Bey at Ergud, arriving from El Obeid in April 1876 en route to El Fasher. The two railway expeditions on their return marches were to rendezvous at Umm Badr in mid-June, the Omdurman expedition having reinforced the survey of the Sotahl–Umm Badr section; and thence they would return to Cairo by the end of August, in the wake of Ismail Pasha Ayub who had inspected the track-laying north of Dongola.

In January 1877 Fowler presented the new findings to the Khedive. The existing Appleby Brothers contract extended to the point of transhipment 250 miles south of Wadi Halfa. For the new Nile–Darfur line, the railway would start once again on the left bank but at the entrance to the Wadi el Melik at Abu Gussi, 75 miles up the Nile. One trace would follow southwards 80 miles to Sotahl, thence another 500 miles south-west to El Fasher via Umm Badr and Foja, of which about 200 miles would be dependent on water reservoirs (*hafirs*). The second line to Khartoum south-east from near the Hamadieh wells would cover 185 miles to Omdurman on the White Nile opposite Khartoum, a total of 265 from Abu Gussi (compared with 305 miles Ambukol to Metemma and 325 miles Abu Gussi to Omdurman via the Wadi Muqaddam).

Fowler accepted that with the conquest of Darfur and the consolidation of Equatoria the Metemma route had lost its priority. Khartoum must now be the prime terminus, whether or not the connection with El

Fasher were additionally undertaken. He calculated that the cost of the Egyptian content of the new Khartoum link would exceed the original Metemma link by no more than 9% (or 7% via the Wadi Muqaddam), and the British content by still less. However the Cairo Dual Mandate was already in place and Fowler recognised the obstacle. Authority was not to be forthcoming from the commissioners of the Caisse who saw no early benefit to the shareholders sufficient to justify such capital expenditure in the foreseeable future. Only the imperative of reconquest eighteen years later brought the authorisation of Anglo-Egyptian funds.[17]

Telegraphic Communications 1864–77   Credit for the development of the early stages of the Sudan telegraphic network must go to the Khedive on his assumption of authority in 1863. After the Abyssinian crisis of 1862 the necessity for accelerated communication between Cairo and the Sudan provincial capitals had been exposed. Even if the Khedive remained unwilling to make personal visits, his ability to supervise the actions of his Sudan lieutenants and to monitor military expeditions would thus be enhanced; critical information relating to the readings of the annual Nile flow would be expedited; and trade development stimulated.

Until 1871 and during the two *hakimdaria* of Musa Hamdi (1862–65) and of Ja'afar Mazhar (1865–71) the administration of the Sudan remained centralised. The priority destination for the telegraph remained Khartoum, even if progress was slow. Commenced at Aswan in Upper Egypt in 1864, the line had reached Korosko by January 1865; Wadi Halfa by February 1866; New Dongola (El Urdi) by January, Abu Dom near Merowe (via Khandak and El Debba) by March 1867 – the last a fine source of uncostly palm trees for the posts across the Bayuda desert to Berber. These posts unfortunately were quickly to fall prey to termites, partly in consequence of which the line was not to reach Khartoum north, on the right bank of the Blue Nile, until January 1870. Indeed rupture of communication for days at a time between Cairo and both Khartoum and Suakin proved not infrequent, whether due to the termites or, as in 1876, atypically violent storms, and despite the establishment of intermediate monitoring repair stations. By 1876 the Khedive had decided to substitute iron for wooden posts across the Bayuda sector from Dongola to Berber.

Perhaps the single most obstructive handicap to telegraphic traffic was the need to tranship messages across the Nile by boat, both at

Khartoum and at Berber. A cable across the Blue Nile from Khartoum north was however introduced in 1874 and at Berber across to Masid in February 1877 before the Dual Mandate was in place.

The parallel development of the telegraphic link envisaged by the Khedive between the port of Suakin and Khartoum took comparably long. The first sector, to Kassala, was only reached in May 1871 after the creation of the general-governorate of the eastern Sudan; while the Kassala to Berber 250-mile extension via Qoz Regeb to join the Aswan–Khartoum line was completed as late as February 1875. Meanwhile Ismail Pasha Ayub had been appointed in October 1872 general-governor of the 'South' at Khartoum and had at once sought Egyptian funds to extend the Aswan–Khartoum line to Sennar and Gallabat, the better to monitor events on the Abyssinian border. Undeterred by Cairo's refusal of funds, he proceeded independently with his objective. By August 1873 the line had reached Wad Medani via Eilafun and by September Mesellimiya, using local palm trees for posts. Ayub secured approval to purchase the necessary 200 miles of wire further to extend the line to Sennar and Gallabat, only to have the project revised in order to connect Sennar instead with Fazughli and Famaka, site of the former Mohammed Ali Polis (Kiri) on the Abyssinian Gojjam border. Gallabat was to look for connection to Doka instead.

The second telegraphic project in which Ismail Pasha Ayub, now in December 1873 promoted *hakimdar*, was personally involved, aided by his new director of telegraphs, Carl Christian Giegler, was the erection of a line with iron posts across the 350-mile desert from Khartoum to El Obeid. This, in October 1875, brought Cairo accelerated communication with Kordofan and, in February 1877, with Foja on the border of the newly conquered Darfur – thence by bull to Zubeir Pasha's heartland of Dar Fertit.[18]

3   THE CONQUEST AND ASSIMILATION OF DARFUR
1873–76

Zubeir the Conqueror, 1874 By the time of Zubeir's defeat of the Rizeiqat and occupation of Shakka in August 1873 (see p. 169), Sultan Mohammed Hussein (1839–73) had died, nominating his third son Ibrahim Garad to succeed. The latter did not however formally succeed to the *sultanate* until 10 April 1874, nor advise the Khedive of his father's death until 17 August 1874, indicating an extended interregnum in El Fasher and even a disputed succession – all at a time of serious danger to the *sultanate*. Yet Zubeir was writing to Ibrahim as *sultan* on 8 September 1873 requesting the return of the Shakka chiefs Munzal and Alyan; and also to Ismail Pasha Ayub as general-governor to offer his conquered territory in Bahr el Ghazal and Shakka to the Khedive. The Khedive, thus apprised and still distrustful in the wake of Hilali's murder, nevertheless on 22 November 1873 conferred on Zubeir the title of *mudir* of Shakka and Bahr el Ghazal, under Ismail Ayub, with rank of *qa'immaqam*, but he declined Ismail Ayub's suggestion that Cairo should formally acquaint the Fur *sultan* with Zubeir's appointment. Zubeir agreed to pay taxes of £E15,000 per annum into the Khartoum treasury.

The new *sultan* of Darfur would not acquiesce in Zubeir's success in Shakka. He ordered Ahmed Shatta, his chief minister and *maqdoum* of Dara, to join with Sa'ad el Nur, *shartai* of Umm Shanga, assemble a large army and march on Zubeir; but his gratification at their initial success at Jebel Zeroug east of Umm Shanga on 14 January 1874, when they put to flight an Egyptian company under El Nur Mohammed Anqara, was to be short-lived. Despite the non-arrival of four companies of reinforcements ordered by Ismail Ayub from Kordofan (but not authorised until 12 February), Zubeir roundly defeated the Fur army at Shakka on 21 January, killing the two Fur leaders and inflicting heavy casualties, at the cost of 200 Egyptians killed.[19]

Only the arrival of news of a second major victory at Shakka, this time against the *sultan*'s army, persuaded the Khedive that at least the plan for an attack on Darfur, initiated originally by Ja'afar Pasha Mazhar in August 1866 (see p. 49), could now be safely implemented. There would however be a price to pay. Granted that Zubeir's victorious troops were now fighting under the Khedivial flag on 21 January 1874, this was not the army which the war ministry in Cairo had been preparing for the invasion, Douin affirms, ever since the appointment of Ismail Ayub to succeed Ahmed Mumtaz in August 1872. For that purpose, an Egyptian army of 10,000 men was now envisaged in order not simply to occupy Darfur but to repulse any consequent attack from Wadai and Bornu.

However, at the moment, on 12 February 1874, that the Khedive announced that Darfur had passed to Egyptian rule, and issued instructions to invade Darfur by a two-pronged attack from Shakka and from Kordofan, Ismail Ayub was still in Khartoum making his dispositions for the administration of his new *hakimdaria*. Recognising the inadequacy of his military preparedness for the Darfur campaign, and the consequent budgetary costs to his *hakimdaria,* Ayub telegraphed the Khedive requesting at once three additional regular battalions armed with Remington rifles, a company of mounted *bashi-buzouqs* and artillery, while seeking an additional Sudanese battalion from Munzinger Pasha. The intention was to create, with his own two Sudanese battalions, a total army of six battalions. Within forty-eight hours of that telegram, the Khedive had countermanded the plan. Instead the reinforcements (now to be limited, in addition to three companies from Kordofan, to the three Sudanese battalions and the irregular cavalry) were to be concentrated on Shakka. The Khedive ordered Ismail Ayub to remain at his post; and committed the invasion command to Zubeir. Dismayed, Ismail Ayub obtained consent, on grounds of cost, to cut the reinforcements to Zubeir further to the single battalion from Gallabat.

The Khedive's pronouncement, that the justification for the occupation of Darfur was the prohibition of the export of slaves to Egypt, was unaffected. On the contrary, praising Zubeir for his administrative zeal and for his attention to the prevention of slave-trafficking, the grateful Viceroy followed up his revised plan of invasion with the conferment of the rank of *bey* second-class on Zubeir. The European consulates-general can scarcely have found the motivation plausible.[20]

The cancellation of the *dual* attack plan on Darfur, and the limitation of the invasion to Zubeir's Shakka-based strike, was the Khedive's personal decision. Privy councillors, even Nubar Pasha, were not consulted. Nubar drew the attention of the Khedive to Mohammed el Tunisi's conclusion that Darfur was not a rich country, indeed predominantly desert sand with water available only 75 ft below the surface, but his intervention and his advocacy, in the alternative, of investment in the development of Taka and Sennar were dismissed. Darfur, with its supposed population of 5 million would yield a revenue of £E2m per annum, while Zubeir's forces lived off the land without cost to the treasury. The Khedive nevertheless conceded that the scheduled progress of the invasion would now be necessarily slowed. Indeed the following three months were marked by relative inaction, enabling the Fur to reorganise their forces. Unhappy with his subordination to Khartoum and with the inadequacy of his delayed reinforcements and conscious of his vulnerability, Zubeir reverted to independent initiative. He personally recruited two mounted companies of Sha'iqiya and a further 1,200 men from his *zaribas* in Bahr el Ghazal, and then peremptorily advised

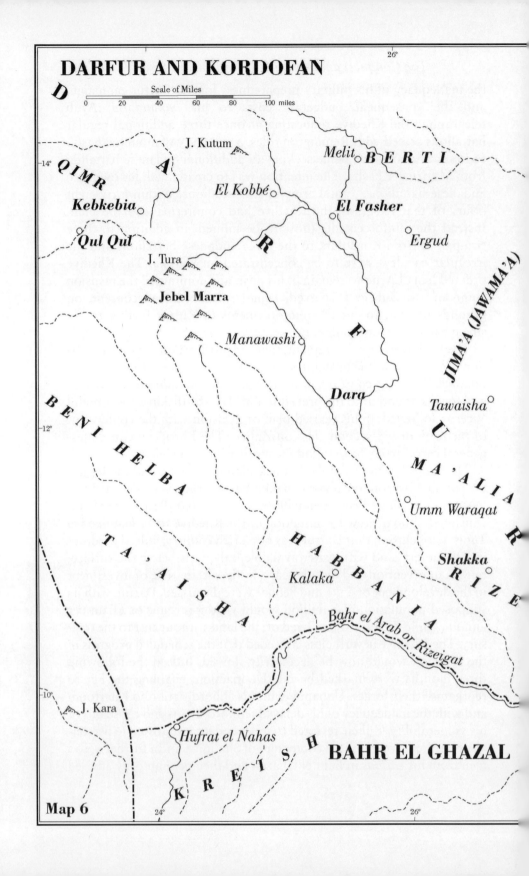

DARFUR AND KORDOFAN

Scale of Miles

0   20   40   60   80   100 miles

D A R F U R

QIMR

Kebkebia

Qul Qul

J. Kutum

El Kobbé

J. Tura

Jebel Marra

Manawashi

Melit   B E R T I

El Fasher

Ergud

Dara

Tawaisha

JIMA'A (JAWAMA'A)

U

MA'ALIA R

Umm Waraqat

BENI HELBA

TA'AISHA

HABBANIA

Kalaka

Shakka

RIZE

Bahr el Arab or Rizeigat

J. Kara

Hufrat el Nahas

K R E I S H

BAHR EL GHAZAL

Map 6

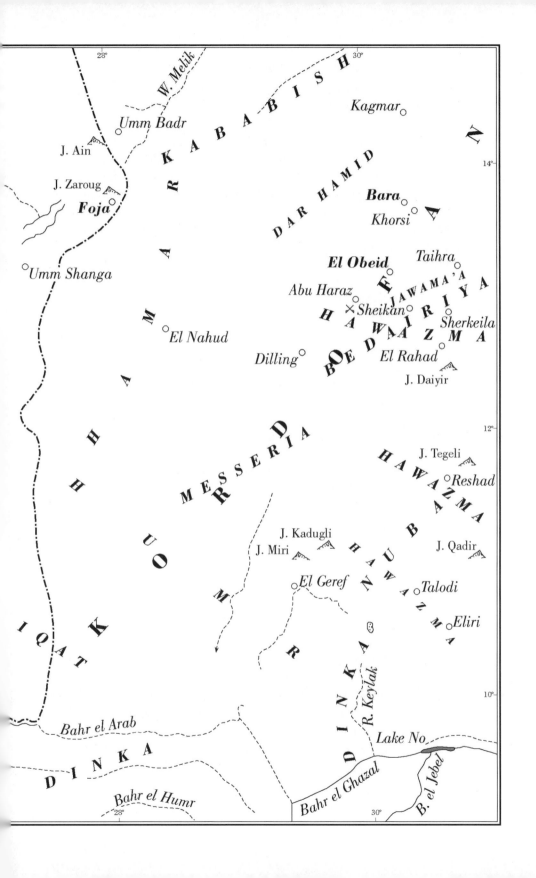

the unhappy Ismail Ayub on 25 May that he was going on the offensive against Sultan Ibrahim's forces.

Four weeks later, on 19 June 1874, Zubeir met an army led by the *sheikh* of the Habbaniya at Kalaka, still within Bahr el Ghazal and west of Shakka and, with his own force of 1,600, roundly defeated them, killing the *sheikh* and 1,200 followers. The earlier news of this impending offensive had provoked Ismail Ayub in his determination to proceed to the scene of action, and he at last successfully obtained from the Khedive permission to leave for Kordofan on 23 June, there to recruit his own force augmented by an Egyptian battalion. A month later at El Obeid news reached him of Zubeir's victory at Kalaka and, without waiting for further Khedivial authority, he personally led his reinforcements west across the desert on 14 August, in time he hoped to take command as Governor-General of the invasion.

The knowledge that Ismail Ayub was en route to Kordofan had already encouraged Zubeir to leave Shakka on 17 July 1874 with an army of 6,000. Marching through the territory of the defeated Habbaniya, he crossed the Darfur frontier to occupy Dara, headquarters of the deceased Ahmed Shatta, on 7 August – which he promptly fortified. This intelligence prompted Ismail Ayub to switch his destination from Shakka to Umm Shanga, a strategic location for both Dara and El Fasher, and he quit El Obeid on 14 August with 3,000 men and four guns, arriving in the Foja area two days east of Umm Shanga and six from Dara on 5 September.

Zubeir had quickly come under siege at Dara, and during the second half of August exhibited to the full his intrepid leadership and military resource to repulse Fur attacks by a new army commanded by the *emir* Hasaballah Mohammed el Fadl, uncle of the *sultan*, supported by the new *maqdoum* of the south, Ahmed Quma'a. Daily skirmishes were punctuated by pitched battles on 31 August and 8 September in both of which Zubeir again proved victorious, inflicting 6,000 dead and capturing 8 Fur guns. Zubeir lost 177 dead and 231 wounded.[21]

Without a clear picture of Zubeir's situation at Dara – he had written to him seeking advice – Ismail Ayub seems to have found discretion the better part of valour, and having beaten off a Hamar (*not* Humr) attack and captured Umm Shanga on 21 September 1874 he decided to stay put, fortify the town and send back to Khartoum for a battalion and a half of reinforcement. On the discovery of a camp of 1,600 slaves from the Bahr el Ghazal, 1,200 of them too weak to move and doubtless a consignment from Zubeir's *meshras*, Ismail Ayub ordered their release and advised the Khedive. Zubeir's evident contempt for Khedivial authority may have sapped Ayub's willingness to run risks for his errant ally. Zubeir had in fact sent Ismail Ayub news of his second defeat of the Fur at Dara on 8 September, but the message had been intercepted by the Hamar and only recaptured by Ismail Ayub in early October, by which time the Khartoum reinforcement, limited to one battalion under Hasan Bey Hilmi, former governor of Kordofan, was only just departing.

When on 23 October, after more than a month's wait, the Governor-General finally quit Umm Shanga for Dara with 3,000 men and 5 guns, leaving behind a garrison of 400, he had received a second message from Zubeir dated 16 October urging his presence, since, following a further encirclement of Dara by the Fur, Zubeir feared a new attack by the *sultan*. In fact the very day of Ismail Ayub's departure from Umm Shanga, 23 October, Zubeir himself quit Dara in pursuit of Sultan Ibrahim Garad. The latter had raised the siege of Dara following a rout of his force earlier by Zubeir on 16 October and retreated to Jebel Marra.

The irresolute tactics of Ismail Ayub accord more with the role of an attendant lord than the commander of an invasion force. Zubeir, in his briefing thirty-five years later of H. C. Jackson, was contemptuous, claiming to have replied to Ayub's message from Umm Shanga: 'If you have come to my assistance, why this delay upon the road when the enemy is surrounding us with innumerable forces?' Ismail Ayub had still not reached Dara nearly a week after leaving Umm Shanga when, about 30 October, news was brought that Zubeir had caught up with Sultan Ibrahim and his host at Manawashi, halfway to Jebel Marra, and that on 25 October 1874, over the space of an hour, had repelled the *sultan*'s brave attack, killing him, two sons and 2,000 Fur, and capturing eight guns, for the loss of 234 government troops. While the Governor-General made his languid dispositions in Dara, Zubeir entered El Fasher unopposed on 3 November. It had been a remarkable feat of generalship – assisted especially by his commanders Rabeh Fadlallah, slayer of Hilali (see p. 149), and El Nur Mohammed Anqara, later to be prominent in the Mahdiyya. Zubeir's campaign extended over almost a year. Although he was ignorant of its outcome at the time, on military grounds there could be no challenging the Khedive's instruction to Ismail Ayub of 5 November 1874 to transfer his own troops to the command of Zubeir, following the occupation of El Fasher, in order for the latter to conquer the rest of Darfur.

The cosmetics of public recognition were otherwise. In reward for their several achievements, Ismail Ayub was promoted *fariq* (general) and awarded the Order of Medjedieh 1st Class; Zubeir made *lewa* and awarded the Order 2nd Class. News of Sultan Ibrahim's death at Manawashi reached Cairo in time for the last Fur caravan of his reign under command of two sons, doubtless a peace-offering, to be seized at Assiut. On 11 November, a week behind Zubeir, the Governor-General himself entered El Fasher in triumph to the salute of a hundred guns, while on 21 November Zubeir's army, augmented by a contingent of Ayub's infantry and 400 cavalry, left again for Jebel Marra to defeat the new elected Fur leader, the *emir* Hasaballah, uncle of Ibrahim. The latter, recognising Zubeir's supremacy, swiftly surrendered.

Although formally excused further campaigning, the Governor-General would have to face costly military attacks from the Fur on his limited detachments sent to collect taxes round El Fasher in late December 1874. It was only Ayub's swift response to intelligence received of an impending onslaught on El Kobbé that enabled him, by sending Hasan Bey Hilmi the new *mudir*, with one of his three battalions, to defeat a serious attack by 6,000 Fur, the rebels losing 600 men. Not until July 1875 were reinforcements from Cairo to reach Darfur, so making a total garrison of three Egyptian and five Sudanese battalions. They were to be based, with *bashi-buzouqs* and Sha'iqi irregulars, at Qulqul and Kabkabiya, west of El Fasher; and at El Fasher and Dara.[22]

There had been a good relationship between Ismail Ayub and Zubeir since the former, briefed by the Ministry of War for the forthcoming invasion of Darfur, had departed from Cairo to Khartoum in October 1872 in the aftermath of the killing of Hilali, *nazir* of the Dar Fertit; but that relationship had deteriorated markedly following Ismail Ayub's appointment as Governor-General in December 1873. Ayub had recognised that Zubeir's military force would prove crucial to his own ability to lead the invasion of Darfur. However the threat both to himself and his corn supplies generated by the revolt of the Rizeiqat at Shakka persuaded Zubeir that he could not rely on Khartoum for help to defend his position nor, when he had shrewdly presented his conquered territory of Bahr el Ghazal to the Khedive, was he ready to wait on Khartoum's authority for military action against Darfur. This was itself a public demonstration of disdain for the *hakimdar* but when, in the face it, the Khedive deferred to Zubeir's independence in February 1874 and then conceded to him the command of the Darfur invasion, the Governor-General sustained a public humiliation while his budget was still burdened with the additional financial cost of military operations. His acquiescence in the reduction of the number of troop reinforcements which he had originally requested of the Khedive was indicative of Ismail Ayub's alienation from the invasion plan now under Zubeir's control, and confirmed Zubeir's conclusion that he must rely on his own forces.

The Governor-General had seized the opportunity presented by Zubeir's inaction, while the latter gathered his force, to secure Khedivial acceptance of his personal intervention in the invasion in June 1874, but at every stage Ayub had lagged behind Zubeir who exacted defeat after defeat – Kalaka, Dara, Manawashi –on the *sultan*'s forces. Zubeir it was who welcomed the unvictorious Governor-General into El Fasher in November. Finally, armed with further Khedivial authority, Zubeir had advanced to inflict a further surrender on the dead *sultan*'s uncle in Jebel Marra.

Zubeir however was essentially a military commander, without Ismail Ayub's qualifications as a civil administrator. It was on the Governor-General that the province reorganisation devolved. He was determined to impose his own authority on the new administration in which Zubeir should have only a subordinate part. But the problem lay in the inadequacy of the Governor-General's army to control a sullen and conquered people – hence his prolonged dependence on Zubeir's irregular army. To and fro between Governor-General and Khedive went successive proposals for Zubeir's definitive role. Since Wadai for forty years had been a protectorate of Darfur and Zubeir was the obvious man to occupy it, should he therefore be nominated its *mudir*? But if so, how could he not also be general-governor of Darfur, in place of the preferred Hasan Hilmi, now himself promoted to *lewa*? By mid-January 1875 Ismail Ayub was minded either to appoint Khalid Pasha Nadir general-governor of Western Sudan or to concede to Zubeir the rule of Darfur and Shakka – but not of Bahr el Ghazal, nor of Wadai which was presently unoccupied.

Then, on 24 January 1875, Zubeir returned to El Fasher from Jebel Marra with a submissive *emir* Hasaballah, recommending that the administration of Darfur should be placed in the hands of the *emir* who would be responsible for annual tribute to the Khedive of £E100,000. Recognising the threat implicit in the proposed alliance, Ismail Ayub would have none of it. He quickly dispatched Hasaballah under escort to Khartoum, followed by his nephew Mohammed Fadl Ibrahim Garad, the non-adult *sultan* nominated by the now deceased Ibrahim, and two brothers. From Khartoum, following a formal reception, they left for Cairo via Suakin on 15 April.

Ismail Ayub Wrests Back Authority, 1875   For a further six months Ismail Ayub felt himself insufficiently strong to impose a definitive new structure of administration. Personal relations with Zubeir deteriorated further with quarrels over the ownership of booty seized at Manawashi. The Khedive sanctioned the appointment of Zubeir as general-governor of Darfur from 1 March 1875 with, as deputy, Hasan Pasha Hilmi and four *mudirs* (replacing the *maqdoums*), but subject to Zubeir relinquishing to the government his *zaribas* in the Bahr el Ghazal and his private bodyguard of Danagla and former slaves – the core sources of Zubeir's power. This was a price too high. Zubeir, critical of his *hakimdar* and opposed to the organisation into four *muderias*, sought leave to decline the appointment and return to the Bahr el Ghazal, intimating his willingness in due course to conquer Wadai and meanwhile, provisionally, to act as *mudir* at Dara. This revised arrangement was sanctioned on the understanding that Zubeir would close the Ghazal *meshras*, but keep some 600 cwt of ivory as his own property; impose, as had Gordon, a central government monopoly in ivory; abolish the slave trade; remit £E25,000 per annum in kind either as ivory or Black army recruits; and retain a personal force of about 4,000 men.

Hasan Pasha Hilmi would take temporary responsibility for the three remaining fortified *muderias* of El Fasher, Qulqul and Kabkabiya; and for Umm Shanga (in March 1876 the headquarters was transferred to Foja). Ismail Ayub by Khedivial order was to remain in El Fasher until the work on the reorganisation was complete.[23]

Privately Zubeir was disgruntled at the arrangement and was determined to prevail on the Khedive to review the decision. On his arrival at Dara, Zubeir now received a telegram from the Khedive ordering him 'not to interfere with administration of the country', a reference to Zubeir's criticism of the *hakimdar*'s proposed 50 *piastre* poll tax level as far too high. Conscious that it was he, Zubeir, who was the real conqueror of Darfur, he made the fatal error of requesting the Khedive to grant him a personal interview in Cairo 'to discuss measures for forming an administration under your auspices' – a request immediately granted. Although in the event he would not reach Cairo until the end of June 1876, Zubeir later confessed to Jackson that on receiving the Khedive's acceptance he thought to himself, 'If I go to Cairo I shall not return to the Sudan.'

The intervening period, up to Zubeir's departure from Dara to El Obeid en route to Cairo in December 1875, was one of considerable activity. Ismail Ayub's army had grown no stronger and in April Bosh, brother of the *emir* Hasaballah (dispatched to Khartoum), proclaimed himself *sultan* and with his brother Seif el Din raised a further revolt in the Jebel Marra, threatening Kabkabiya. The *hakimdar,* while sending Hasan Hilmi to counter the revolt, thought it prudent to call again on Zubeir from Dara. Zubeir meanwhile had become committed to the suppression of a rebellious band of 3,000 men under one El Dabi from his *zaribas*, and until this was complete he could not respond to the Jebel Marra crisis. This however he eventually did, leaving Dara on 20 June 1875 and, although Hasan Hilmi had had some success himself, Zubeir defeated the *emir* Bosh on 19 July near Kabkabiya, killing him, his brother and 2,700 rebels for the loss of 61 men.

Zubeir pressed on immediately, occupying western Darfur and crossing the Terga into Wadai where he received a letter from the Wadai *sultan*, Ali Mohammed Sharif, with a delegation to negotiate his submission to the Khedive. The Khedive, however, pre-empted the discussions by recalling Zubeir to El Fasher, since he intended to negotiate terms with the *sultan*'s *vizir* sent direct to Cairo. At the same time, Zubeir affirmed, the Khedive promoted him to *pasha* and *fariq*. His reception by Ismail Ayub at El Fasher in mid-August was icy. Not only was Ayub incensed by Zubeir's continuous disdain for his authority, criticism of his plans and appeal to the Khedive for appointment to Dara, but his personal position had now become immeasurably strengthened while Zubeir was campaigning in the west. The Cairo military reinforcements had at last arrived. Zubeir had served his turn, and he was peremptorily ordered to quit Dara for Bahr el Ghazal.

Back in Dara Zubeir's remonstration dated 23 August to the Khedive fell on deaf ears. He had found the Khedive's letter of 20 August which congratulated him on his victories in western Darfur and Wadai; confirmed the summons to discussions in Cairo (originally to be accompanied by the commanders of Zubeir's ten armed companies but this was modified); ordered him to return his irregular *bazinqir* troops to Bahr el Ghazal for well-earned leave; and advised Zubeir that Sulieman Bey el Arnaut had been appointed to succeed him as *mudir* of Dara.

Zubeir played for time, reluctant to accede to the order to quit Dara until he had heard again from the Khedive. The reply came dated 22 September 1875, confirming the *hakimdar*'s order to relinquish Dara which could be discussed again when Zubeir came to Cairo. Ismail Ayub was to send Hasan Pasha Hilmi to take over Dara with a sizeable garrison. Vanquished on this issue, Zubeir sent his Black troops to Shakka and left himself for Deim Zubeir on 19 October to make arrangements for his absence; for the exchange of ivory for arms to be sent by the *hakimdar*; and for the hand-over of Bahr el Ghazal and Shakka to his son Sulieman, to be backed by the *miralai* Kenawi Amuri and the irregulars' company commanders. He reached Dara again with an escort of 1,000 men and 165 cwt of his personal ivory, leaving Kordofan via Khartoum for Cairo on 13 December 1875. He was never to return.[24]

After an uncomfortable but active eight months in El Fasher, Ismail Pasha Ayub was at last able, following the arrival of the Cairo reinforcements, to complete his dispositions for the administration of Darfur, previously agreed in principle in March 1875. The four former cantonments had all been refortified under the *hakimdar*'s approving eye – El Fasher, Dara, Kabkabiya (to guard Jebel Marra), and, on the route to El Obeid, initially Umm Shanga and then in March 1876, due to problems of water supply, Foja. The capital had an impressive new *diwan* and barracks. Hasan Pasha Hilmi was definitively appointed general-governor of Darfur at El Fasher in July 1875; Mohammed Sa'id Bey Wahbi became *mudir* of Qulqul and Kabkabiya; Sulieman Bey Fayek of Dara; Zakariya Bey Hilmi of El Fasher; and Ali Bey Lutfi of Umm Shanga and Foja. Tribal administration was in the hands of local *nazirs* and *hukām*.

Each *mudir* was supported by two *qa'immaqams*, one as deputy governor, the other as officer commanding troops. Because of Jebel Marra, where the last of Sultan Ibrahim's lieutenants, the *maqdoum* Rahma Qumu, held out until early 1876, the garrison at Kabkabiya – eventually totalling three and a half battalions, two companies of *bashi-buzouqs*, 400 Sha'iqi and 1,000 Arab dismounted irregulars – was the strongest. Dara and El Fasher each had two battalions, one company of *bashi-buzouqs* and 400 Sha'iqi; Umm Shanga gained only a small force, as dependent on El Fasher.

An Unprofitable Outcome   The quid pro quo for the posting of three battalions of Egyptian infantry to the Sudan was to be the recruitment of young Black former slaves of Zubeir's *zariba* colleagues, whose release was ordered on the imposition of Egyptian rule. These *mourdanes* ('*amrad*: beardless ones) were to be ransomed in return for payment of a price of 500, increased to 800 *piastres* per head, or the tax relief equivalent. The fit were to be dispatched inconspicuously to

Egypt for training, prior to their return for regular service in the Sudan; the unfit for labour settlement in the Sudan. The implementation of the scheme was in the event held up until the rainy season of 1876, by which time Darfur was deemed effectively subjugated and water supply available on the route to Khartoum. Zubeir contributed 1000 *mourdanes*, and Ismail Ayub decided that the four Darfur *muderias* would provide 3,500 to be set off against the tax demands. He personally took with him 1,000 on his return to Khartoum in April 1876.

All this was costly. Leaving aside civil administration, army expenditure totalled £E250,000 per annum and with arrears of pay (already extending to eight months in 1874), the troops took to pillaging the Fur in lieu. On the credit side, into a barter economy based on rolls of cloth Ismail Ayub organised the injection of £E20,000 cash for soldiers' pay. The Khedive's decision to impose a levy of £E30,000 on the richer Sudan provinces of Berber and Dongola for the new railway development shut off a reasonable source of revenue on which the *hakimdar* had looked to draw to meet the costs of Darfur's conquest (Equatoria was a more fortunate beneficiary – from Khartoum, Sennar and Kordofan). Ismail Ayub nevertheless remained adamant that economies in the Darfur garrisons urged by the Khedive were unacceptable. His judgement was to be confirmed by heavy troop casualties from disease, notably typhoid: out of 5,000 Egyptians 1,300 died – in all two thirds of the invading force.[25]

Surveys   Ismail Ayub shared his Khedive's optimism as to the revenue potentials of the new province. Within days of his arrival in El Fasher in December 1874 he had written to Cairo urging exploration for iron and copper mineral deposits. Indeed exploration of the new territory was recognised to have an important strategic dimension also, which had already engaged the attention of Fariq Charles Stone, the American chief of the general staff and himself a mining engineer. Darfur and adjacent Kordofan formed part of his planned survey of the Sudan and, well before the capture of El Fasher, he was organising two major expeditions under his American subordinates assisted by Yuzbashis Mohammed Mahir, Ahmed Hamdi, Mahmoud Sabry and Mahmoud Samy.

The expedition directed to Darfur was under Qa'immaqam Erastus Sparrow Purdy Bey who had previously reconnoitred the route between the Red Sea and Berber. He left Cairo on 5 December 1874, intending to approach Darfur via Selima and the Darb el Arbain. Having failed to arrange guides from Assiut, he took instead the Nile route to Dongola and, re-forming, left for El Debba on 10 March thence to follow south west the watercourse of the Wadi el Melik 130 miles to Ain Hamid; then through the Dar Hamar to Umm Badr; and so, possibly via Umm Shanga, to El Fasher arriving before the rains in early May 1875. He was accompanied by Qa'immaqam Alexander Mason Bey and Yuzbashi Sabry, and the three set out at once to map Jebel Tura west of Fasher, Jebel Marra to its south, and Dara respectively. Jebel Marra, still troublesome, was reserved until the end of the rains in September, Mason then finding samples of coal, lead and iron which he dispatched to Cairo before going to Dara, Shakka and Taweisha. Purdy in February 1876 penetrated the copper mines one kilometre west of Hufrat el Nahas.[26]

The second survey expedition was initially led by Miralai Raleigh Colston Bey. Following an earlier geological exploration of the Atmur desert from south of Kosseir on the Red Sea to Qena in 1874, his objective was Kordofan. After a preliminary reconnaissance from El Debba of the Wadi Mahtoul, the beginning of the Wadi el Melik, he regrouped and set out again for El Obeid following the route taken by the *defterdar* Mohammed Khusraw el Daramali in 1821. He suffered a serious injury, falling from his camel, and having reached El Obeid in a litter he nearly died. Colston's deputy, Horatio Reed Bey, had already been invalided out, and his successor, Bimbashi Henry G. Prout Bey, took over command of the expedition on his arrival in El Obeid via Khartoum on 12 June 1875, as the rains began. Colston was to be invalided back to Khartoum in November.

Covering 1,600 miles in surveying Kordofan, Prout was latterly instructed by the Khedive to join Purdy Bey at El Fasher. Despite delays due to Kababish camels being committed to moving the new telegraph material, Prout on reaching Darfur was most fortunate to encounter the Governor-General at Foja on 3 April 1876, as he was finally leaving Darfur for Khartoum and Cairo. Prout was accompanied by a very energetic Hamburg doctor, Dr Johann Pfund, aged sixty-three, who was much taken with Ismail Ayub:

> The man justifies his reputation for exceptional amiability, very simple amidst the panoply of a court on trek. His conversation is extremely interesting, spontaneous and frank; his remarks to the point and clear; his character generous and impressive; his opinion expressed with tact and discretion.

Yet the *hakimdar* betrayed anxiety and distrust of these undependable 'black dogs', the Beduin Arabs.

Indefatigable Dr Pfund, following their arrival at El Fasher on 24 April 1876, left on 2 June for a six-week reconnaissance of Melit, Anka and Kutum, a round distance of 280 miles, supplementing the earlier sketches made by Mason to Jebel Meidob and by Sabry to Dor, Gaffeila and Qulqul. Prout Bey had already left before Pfund's return to El Fasher with specimen plants in mid-July and instead the doctor was welcomed by Purdy Bey, only to die a month later, leaving a sick wife, two children and no pension. Prout's detailed survey of Jebel Marra completed the first map of the new province. By October 1876 he was in Khartoum promoted to *qa'immaqam* and appointed to succeed Gordon Pasha in Equatoria.

On his arrival in Cairo at the end of August 1876 to meet the Khedive, Ismail Ayub was happy to boast of this new, if vicarious, survey achievement; but funds were unavailable to print the map nor were the reports published. The Caisse de la Dette had now been established and Dual Control was shortly to be instituted. The conclusion of the reports was that, so far as the land of Darfur was concerned, the Jebel Marra soil was rich for cultivation and Dar Kalaka, west of Shakka, of good potential, enjoying reliable rains. As to the north and to the east between El Fasher and Foja, only one sixth of the soil was cultivable during the three-month rainy season.

If this inventory of natural assets was disappointing to Cairo, the aftermath of conquest, compounded by near famine in the winter of 1875–6, had persuaded the El Kobbé merchants to redirect their export outlets to Bornu and Wadai in the west, to escape Egyptian custom dues and the imposition of government monopoly on the purchase of local products at artificially low prices. The commercial consequence to Egypt was soon evident. Up to February 1876, in place of the annual three to four sizeable caravans from El Kobbé to Assiut, only two smaller components had arrived. Had Nubar Pasha been consulted, a serious cost-benefit analysis might have been undertaken years earlier, before the conquest, and on weighing the alternatives, investment in Sennar and Taka might have been preferred.

Douin quotes Prout Bey's opinion that Darfur would add nothing to the power and glory of Egypt. Carl Christian Giegler, visiting as director of telegraphs in November 1876, opined: 'The country is so unhealthy that I have grave doubts as to the wisdom of the Khedive in annexing it.' It was to remain under Egyptian rule for a bare eight years.[27]

By September 1875 Ismail Ayub's administrative dispositions for

Darfur were at last made, an adequate government military force deployed, Zubeir under orders to proceed to Cairo and, but for residual resistance in the Jebel Marra area, the people generally acquiescent. The geographical surveys, the railway trace expedition from El Obeid (which Prout had also encountered at Ergoud on the eastern outskirts of El Fasher on his arrival in April 1876), the erection of the telegraph line from El Debba – all these could be left to the new general-governor, Hasan Pasha Hilmi, to progress. Accordingly, in early November 1875 the Khedive summoned his *hakimdar* to Cairo 'to review Darfur matters and the state of neighbouring governments', but ordered him nevertheless not to quit El Fasher until Zubeir had negotiated the cataracts on his own journey to Cairo.

Exit Zubeir Pasha   Within a fortnight this order had been countermanded, following the news of the first Abyssinian disaster and the death of Soren Adolph Arendrup Bey at Gundet and of Munzinger Pasha in Aussa. Ismail Ayub was ordered to wait, his patience dissipating as the weeks passed so that he was constrained in February to propose himself as general of a second Egyptian army to revenge Arendrup's defeat – scarcely a serious proposal from one presently in Darfur who knew the Abyssinia campaigning season ended in May. Zubeir had, however, now left Darfur and reached Abu Haraz on the outskirts of El Obeid by mid-January 1876. Here a major dispute with the *mudir* who sought to confiscate his ivory, followed by a serious illness in which Zubeir was tended by Dr Pfund, led to the confirmation of the Khedive's order to Ismail Ayub to join him in Cairo. This reached Ayub on 7 March 1876.

Zubeir, accompanied by Yuzbashi Saleh son of Adham Pasha el 'Arifi, had left Khartoum after a further dispute over payment of his expenses three weeks before Ismail Pasha Ayub reached Khartoum on 30 April 1876. Ayub entered in state as the conqueror of Darfur, wearing the cross of the Order of Medjedieh and a gold sword with diamonds presented by the Khedive. Only now seemingly did Zubeir learn that Ismail Ayub was shadowing him and following a further dispute over expenses at Berber, it took Zubeir a full month to cross the Atmur to Korosko, reaching Cairo at the end of June. Any shortcomings in his welcome from the Sudan governors was amply compensated for by the Khedive's reception and his lodging in the Abbasiya palace.

Zubeir's arrival at Korosko on 12 June had triggered the Khedive's further order to his *hakimdar* to leave Khartoum immediately and join him in Cairo with Zubeir. Taking the Bayuda route to Dongola to inspect the railway works, Ismail Ayub arrived on 8 July, nine months after the Khedive's original order to him to leave Darfur for Cairo. The Khedive was preoccupied with the consequences of his reckless financial policies and the humiliation of the further defeat of his new army in Abyssinia. At first serious consideration was given to sending Zubeir to treat with the Emperor John IV, but the limited size of his escort of 300 regular troops from the Sudan seems to have ruled that out. A cat and mouse game followed. On 3 August Zubeir was alerted to return to the Sudan. Then on 19 October he was summoned to the Giza palace to be told by the Khedive: 'It is my wish that you remain in Cairo under the shelter of my roof until I have come to some definite decision about you.' He was sent to participate in the Balkan war against Russia at Varna the next year, and was never to return to the Sudan.

Nor indeed was Ismail Pasha Ayub to return, but of this in the summer of 1876 in Cairo he was unaware. For the time being he was to remain Governor-General of the Sudan, and with regard to Darfur to make the replacement appointments necessitated over the winter of 1876-7. Sulieman Bey Fayek died in September and was succeeded as *mudir* in Dara by Sulieman Bey Arnaout, promoted *miralai*; Miralai Zakariya Bey Hilmi in El Fasher by Yusuf Bey Arnaout; and Ali Bey Lutfi in Foja by Ali Bey Mustapha. In February 1877, Hasan Pasha Hilmi, falling sick after putting down a minor insurrection at Tura north of Jebel Marra, was temporarily replaced by Abdel Raziq Haqqi Pasha, currently Ismail Ayub's deputy in Khartoum. To his vexation the Governor-General then found himself ordered in February 1877 to hand over his responsibilities to his enemy Charles Gordon Pasha, promoted *mushir*, Marshal, and himself become governor of Alexandria. In Khartoum Ayub's sister, out of spite, broke all the windows in the new *hakimdar's* palace.[28]

9
The Climax of Empire 1874–76: Part 2

Eastern Sudan   In response to the plea of Munzinger Werner, now general-governor, in February 1873 for the unification of the military forces on the Abyssinian frontier and in the context of the re-formation of the eastern general-governorate, four military districts were now to be formed on the advice of Fariq Charles Stone in Cairo. Each was to be under a commander with the rank of *bey* and based respectively on Keren, Suakin, Kassala and Roheita (in the Bab el Mandeb). Keren would cover Massawa, Kufit and Zulla; and Suakin, Tokar.

The creation of Roheita district to cover the area from Amphila to Aussa (Zeyla) in the Gulf of Aden was in the event postponed, Munzinger undertaking a preliminary sea reconnaissance in March 1873. For the rest, initially one battalion of the Second Regiment of Sudanese infantry would be stationed in Taka (Kassala); a second divided between the port *muhafizāt* of Suakin and Massawa; a third at Amideb (seemingly superseding Kufit to its north); and the fourth at Keren (Bogos). However, following months of desertions and indiscipline and once again seeking economies, Munzinger suppressed the battalions in Taka and the two port *muhafizāt*, and redeployed them as armed police. Likewise the garrisons at Keren and Amideb (south of Kufit) were amalgamated.

Personally favouring Keren because of its equidistance between Massawa and Kassala, Munzinger originally chose it for his governorate headquarters. In November 1873, now a *miralai*, Ala el Din Bey Siddiq was posted to Suakin to enforce a stricter régime; while Faraj Bey el Zaini, in Keren since October 1872, took Ala el Din's place at Kassala. Important as was Bogos strategically, with its substantial military garrison, the garrison's funding had nevertheless to be generated from the revenues of Taka. On 9 June 1874, with Munzinger himself taking over the administration of the *muderia* personally from Faraj el Zaini who was retired, the capital of the general-governorate was transferred to Kassala. Ala el Din at Suakin became vice-general-governor, and Munzinger appointed a Swiss *mu'awin* assistant at Kassala in charge of exploration and survey, Gustav Haggenmacher. Arakil Bey Nubar had been appointed to Massawa in December 1873 on his own initiative. (He was the energetic blood relation of Nubar Pasha and a former private secretary to the Khedive – disliked by both – and latterly a senior official of the Foreign Affairs ministry.) To each provincial headquarters would be appointed a *mamur* accountant reporting to the Cairo ministry of finance.[1]

The appointment of the politically experienced Arakil Bey was to prove relevant to the preparations for a pending conflict with Abyssinia when that moment should be judged opportune. The general-governorate was approaching a war footing, but notwithstanding Munzinger's exceptional experience of the region going back over twelve years and his close liaison with Fariq Stone Pasha in Cairo, it was not envisaged that he should personally lead any major expedition into Hamasein against Emperor John IV. He remained administratively responsible for the general-governorate, including once again the Red Sea littoral, until August 1875 when, on the eve of his own departure to annexe Aussa via Tadjoura, he nominated his deputy Ala el Din Pasha to act in his place. The Khedive would nominate an experienced naval officer as governor of Suakin – later, in January 1876, in preparation or the second Abyssinian expedition, also to take over Massawa, where naval traffic was necessarily increasing.

Munzinger was determined that the budget of his potentially wealthy general-governorate should be protected. When his accounts for the year from September 1872 showed a deficit of £E77,000, the Khedive decreed that it should be funded by Dongola and Berber. Hussein Bey Khalifa's inability to respond may well have finally triggered his dismissal but eventually, together with a contribution from the *hakimdaria*, the deficit was met in 1874. A similar deficit which emerged the following year would be covered by the imposition of the *werko* tax on non-tax paying merchants of Suakin and Massawa. Conscious however that his ambitious forecasts for cotton cultivation were proving wildly optimistic and the revenue fruits unrealistic, Munzinger, like his predecessor Ahmed Mumtaz, fastened on a policy of economies in the military garrisons, especially now that Bogos had been annexed. The requirements of Gordon Pasha, the new general-governor of Equatoria, accommodated by July 1874 eight companies of regular troops. To this economy Munzinger added the repatriation of three companies from Massawa back to Egypt – a sizeable shedding of expenditure in Eastern Sudan but also of the defence shield.

All these actions drew Khedivial approval but Munzinger was confronted with a new major cost. By May 1873 the tranquil quasi-independence of Sheikh Mohammed Jum'a of Gallabat had been finally terminated with his exile to Cairo, and a well-equipped garrison had been established by Adham Pasha el 'Arifi, to be commanded by a *bimbashi*, as part of Ismail Ayub's general-governorate. Jum'a was succeeded by Sheikh Saleh Idris of the Beni Amer. Now, arising from the transfer of the Abyssinian border *qism* of Gallabat in April 1874 from Ismail Ayub's (now) *hakimdaria* to Munzinger's general-governorate, came the responsibility for a garrison of two battalions and costs of nearly £E19,000 per annum against local tax and customs revenues of £E2,000.

The rationality of the transfer is unclear. The *qism* depended on the tribes of the rivers Rahad and Blue Nile and of the Isle of Meroe, all territories of the *hakimdaria*, for supplies and cash, while Gallabat was as far distant from Kassala as was Massawa. On the other hand Gallabat was a good listening post for Abyssinian territory, and the principal lines of communication for the intended expedition would run through the Red Sea and the Eastern general-governorate. Douin speculated that the balance in favour of transfer to Munzinger may have been tilted by fresh expressions of European concern at reported continuing movements of slaves through Gallabat, and indeed the Khedive was shortly to issue instructions for recruitment of *mourdanes* (*amrad*) – 'volunteer' ex-slaves – from eastern Sudan as well as Darfur. The knowledge that the Gallabat *qism* was under a European governor might be the best palliative for European disquiet.

Munzinger duly received an instruction to recruit 3,000 *mourdanes* in April 1875, tax indemnities to be granted to their domestic well-found employers. He protested that the sheikhs supplying these volunteers would be forbidden from replacing labour on which they were especially dependent after a bad year of cultivation, and he suggested that Gallabat should provide *mourdanes* direct to Khartoum. The Khedive, in a veritable 'blasting of the breath of his displeasure', drafted a reply criticising Munzinger's lax regime as compared with Equatoria and proposing to appoint Ala el Din Bey Siddiq as separate general-governor of Taka and Suakin. The likely consequences of thereby provoking Munzinger's resignation with the Abyssinian expedition imminent ensured that the reply was not sent. No more was

Natives of Doka, near Gallabat

heard about the recruitment of *mourdanes* in the eastern Sudan, but Khedivial displeasure had been incurred.

Burdened with the unsought accretion of Gallabat to his governorate, and already obliged in June 1874 to counter cattle raids from Dembelas (south of Hamasein) on Bogos, Munzinger resolved to see the situation for himself. An outbreak of typhus delayed his visit during the rains of 1874; then an attack on Qadabi in October and on Gallabat in January 1875 by Abyssinian raiders postponed the visit to the *qism*, now incorporated in Taka, until April. Following this, notwithstanding the military threat, Munzinger nevertheless persuaded the Khedive to agree to the reduction of the Gallabat garrison from two battalions to four companies with five guns, the remainder of the force to be transferred to the Khartoum *hakimdaria* for operations in Darfur.[1]

From the time of his appointment as general-governor in February 1873, despite the military ambitions he shared with his Khedive, Munzinger with native Western zeal had continued to seek a balanced governorate budget – (indeed for 1874–5 a surplus of £E5,000) – in which a more equitable basis for levying taxation would yield revenue sufficient to meet prudent development projects. The latter would include the construction of roads, railway, and telegraph communications, and civil buildings and cotton ginning factories for Kassala and

Suakin – all however not exceeding one third of total annual expenditure. Plans were also laid for hospitals, schools and mosques. His energy and ambition were at first rewarded by the realisation of his financial objectives. In 1873–4 a surplus of £2,500 was achieved; in 1874-75 locust famine sapped tax revenues; and in 1875-6, following Munzinger's untimely death, his successor Ala el Din Pasha was compelled to budget for a revised deficit of some £E6,000. Only at Massawa with the growth of Red Sea traffic was a balanced budget attainable.[2]

With regard to justice, it is difficult to appraise whether or not political and economic fragmentation had benefited the northern Sudanese or the reverse. Islamic *sharia* courts under *qadis* had, since the Turkish conquest of 1821, continued to be responsible for matters of personal family life while, increasingly in the towns, civil, criminal, commercial and taxation matters had come before local courts of first instance under paid notables. To augment these twin justice systems there existed the paternal practice of petition to the ruler by the ruled. From the local civil courts appeal lay in the *hakimdaria* while it existed to the *majlis el ahkam* in Khartoum – the Council of the Sudan – and from thence to its counterpart in Cairo, to which Ja'afar Pasha Mazhar had been appointed on his resignation.

Ja'afar had been responsible in 1865 for establishing in Kassala a court for hearing petitions under the local *mamur,* a presidency for which Ahmed Mumtaz as general governor had substituted a tribal leader, Sheikh Hamid Musa, former *nazir* of the Beni Amer, with Sheikh Mohammed Agha el Awad of the Halenga his deputy, plus the *mamur,* and had extended the catchment to Suakin and Massawa. After much correspondence with the Cairo Privy Council, by February 1874 it was agreed that there should be civil tribunals in three towns with appeals from Kassala to Suakin; from Suakin to Massawa; and from Massawa to Taka. Meanwhile comparable courts were set up first in Khartoum and Berber and then, with Privy Council approval, in Kordofan, Dongola, Sennar and Fazughli. These were commendable initiatives, but the extent that the new system was used, at least outside the towns, was very limited.[3]

Red Sea/Gulf of Aden Littoral and Aussa   If the Egyptian occupation of the littoral as far as Berbera was not being actively challenged by the British (p. 93) at the end of 1873, yet there was vigorous debate about its acceptability between the Foreign and India Offices. The former recognised the cost of reversing what was a fait accompli and believed in the Egyptian protestations of anti-slavery support and recognition of British trading interests. The latter was generally distrustful. The discussion simmered on through 1874 until early October when Mohammed Radwan Bey, again dispatched to Berbera by the Khedive, unilaterally closed Bulhar for trade, provoking a request to Bombay by Major-General Schneider, the British Resident in Aden, for a naval task force. Bombay declined, while the new foreign minister, the Earl of Derby, had already instructed his officials: 'Absolutely avoid involving us in these matters in future.' Face was saved with the appointment in February 1875 of a former British naval captain in Khedivial service, Lewa H. F. McKillop Pasha, to make conciliatory explanations in person to Aden. The India Office recognised that subject to an Egyptian undertaking not to cede territory to another power, to the strict regulation of the slave trade, to the maintenance of free trade and of existing tribal treaties, and to the prohibition of port monopolies, an accord with Egypt was possible and would curb other European rivals. Then, in July, Egypt secured the formal cession by firman of Ottoman authority over the ports of Zeyla and Tadjoura with their custom dues, hitherto mandated to the Ottoman *emir* of Yemen, in return for a Khedivial payment of £E150,000 and of £E15,000 per year.[4]

Both Ja'afar Mazhar, in 1869, and Wernher Munzinger, in 1873 and 1874, had successively recommended the acquisition of the ports of Zeyla and Tadjoura. Zeyla not only served the inland route linking the coast with the Wello-Galla and Shoa Abyssinian enemies of Negus John IV, but provided an outlet for the export of Galla slaves by the Shoa to Yemen. From his reconnaissance in March 1873 Munzinger was confident that with the acquisition of Zeyla it would be possible, with a force not exceeding half a battalion, to take the ancient province of Harar, thereby controlling the caravan trade in ivory and coffee; and, with possession of Tadjoura, the capture of Aussa.

Arakil Bey Nubar from Massawa in February 1875 undertook a three-month tour of the western Danakil area, especially of the valuable salt plains of Assalé inland from Amphila from which he calculated a potential export yield of 400,000 cwt and an annual profit from military occupation of £E10,000. He then went on to probe beyond the Bab el Mandeb, learning of French action to assert its rights to the port of Obock. In the course of his expedition Arakil dispatched the *na'ib* of Arkiko with a letter from the Khedive replying to Menilek's of February 1874, addressed to the '*sultan* of Abyssinia', but mistakenly delivered, about May to the Emperor John at Begemder. Apparently not recognising the error, John himself replied to the Khedive in conciliatory terms, favouring a peace treaty between them, an offer however which Arakil now misinterpreted as indicative of John's precarious political situation. In fact at this very time Ras Menilek was reversing his refusal to recognise John as his *Negus*, commencing tribute payment to him, and declaring the abolition of slavery in Shoa.

By early July 1875, doubtless encouraged by the Emperor's apparently peaceful approach, Khedive Ismail became persuaded that the advice of Munzinger could safely be adopted and, with the cession of Zeyla and Tadjoura by the Ottoman Sultan, expeditions should be launched to occupy their respective hinterlands – Harar and Aussa. Nubar Pasha claimed in his *Mémoires* that he opposed the proposed fortification of Zeyla, Tadjoura and probably Harar in 1875, citing a meeting with the Khedive and Fariq Charles Stone at which Nubar warned that forts were like hives which attracted hornets – in this case redcoat troops to enforce the abolition of the maritime slave trade. This was the principal commerce of the ports, and would leave Egypt the choice of allowing the trade to continue and breaching the abolition agreement, or of antagonising the Abyssinian tribes. The counsel was ignored.

Perhaps to the chagrin of Munzinger, however, it was Mohammed Ra'uf Pasha, lately deputy to Gordon in Equatoria, who was ordered on 16 July to leave for Zeyla and ostensibly to reconnoitre the sources of the Sobat river, in reality to occupy Harar. Landing at Zeyla on 9 August to take possession, and appointing the (since 1869) actively pro-Egyptian governor, Abu Bakr Ibrahim, as his *wakil*, Ra'uf marched to Koto, the Harar capital, as had Richard Burton twenty years before. Encountering little resistance, he received the submission of the *emir* on 11 October. He was now about 100 miles from Shoa land. His express instruction from Cairo was to build roads throughout the governorate. For these services Mohammed Ra'uf received the recognition which had previously eluded him, being promoted to *fariq* and made general-governor of Harar with Zeyla and Berbera regions. Abdel Wahhāb Wahbi Bey from Egypt's Beni Suef was made *mudir* of Harar and the *emir*, Mohammed Abdel Shakur, honorary *muhafiz*.[5]

As to the Tadjoura hinterland of Aussa, the Khedive appears initially to have planned in early July for Munzinger to undertake a further reconnaissance with Lewa Radwan Pasha. Late July however found Munzinger in Cairo and Mohammed Radwan shortly to be diverted to accompany H. F. McKillop on the Benadir expedition (see p. 295). By the time of Munzinger's departure on 27 July, he had received instructions to embark an expedition to Tadjoura designed to open up commercial relations with Menilek of Shoa through the development of caravan routes. No opposition was expected from the Moslem population. Menilek's envoy Ras Burou was to carry a letter informing his master of the proposal. However Munzinger, having sailed from Suez and arrived at Massawa on 5 August, was, in view of public press discussion about the imminent occupation of Zeyla by Ra'uf, further warned on no account to cross the Aussa-Abyssinian frontier.

More important than the 'public discussion' was the arrival in Cairo on 8-9 August 1875 of news from Munzinger's newly appointed *wakil*, Ala el Din Bey, that the Abyssinian Negus, alarmed by Egyptian military activity, had moved forward troops into Hamasein (see p. 245). On 10 August Munzinger was instructed to suspend the Tadjoura expedition, leaving Ras Burou to proceed alone to Shoa with an invitation to Menilek to attack the Negus without delay. Munzinger moved at once to Keren to assess and counter the Abyssinian threat to Hamasein.

Only on 26 August 1875, with the Egyptian frontier positions now consolidated, did the Khedive instruct Munzinger finitely to hand over his defence responsibilities and prepare to embark on the suspended expedition to Tadjoura and Aussa, strengthening the contact with Menilek and thereby increasing the pressure on John to withdraw. However Munzinger's force was to be no greater than that agreed a month earlier when, it had been anticipated, the Moslem population of Tadjoura (already occupied) and Aussa would prove compliant. The Khedive appended detailed guidance regarding the clauses of the commercial agreement to be reached with Menilek, leaving the decision to Munzinger as to whether to negotiate it personally in Shoa or through Ras Burou.[6]

Still at Keren requisitioning camels for his expedition, on 15 September Munzinger received a telegram from the Khedive ordering him to leave immediately for Massawa and thence to proceed to Tadjoura and Aussa as a diversion to the coming Egyptian thrust into Hamasein. From a letter he wrote at this time, Munzinger was in deep depression. His young son had just died, he had clashed with the Khedive over the *mourdanes'* recruitment, and he was experiencing intrigues on the part of his ambitious subordinate in Massawa, Arakil Bey Nubar, who was shortly to be appointed political adviser to the Swedish Colonel

Arendrup Bey, commander of the Hamasein expedition. Munzinger wrote: 'Le gouvernement Egyptien m'envoie là-bas pour me faire tuer, et moi-même je ne crois pas que je reviendrai. Si toutefois il m'est possible d' arriver au Shoa, je chercherai à m'y créer une position, mais je ne retournerai jamais en Egypte.'

With a force of four companies totalling 480 men, 4 mountain guns, 2 rocket-launchers and 54 *bashi-buzouqs*, Munzinger arrived with his wife and his Kassala *mu'awin* Hagenmacher at Tadjoura on 5 October, together with the Abyssinian Ras Burou and his military adjutant, Mohammed Ezzat Bey. At once he encountered problems: forty of the *bashi-buzouqs* now refused to serve in protest at their remuneration, and were sent back to Suakin. The Tadjoura merchants, mainly slavers, were hostile, and the only official who had the measure of them, the former Turkish governor Abu Bakr Ibrahim, was at Zeyla. October coincided with *Ramadan* and, with only fifty camels and after designating one company as the garrison of Tadjoura, the depleted expedition now numbering 361 officers and men could only transport, in addition to their weapons, victuals for ten days' march. Conscious of the pressure, Munzinger wrote letters to secure the cooperation of the two Afar chiefs of Aussa, Sheikh Hamad Leheta and Sultan Mohammed Walad Hanfari. He was unaware that, with Hamad Leheta's support, the *sultan* had sworn on the Koran to deny entry to his Aussa territory to all Turks and Egyptians.

Significantly, Munzinger wrote also to Ras Menilek of Shoa advising him of his intention to retire from Khedivial service when the expedition had completed its goal and offering his future services to Menilek. To the Khedive, Munzinger reported by letter his wish to open commercial negotiations with Menilek.

At first all seemed to go well, although when they encountered Hamad Leheta at Aussa lake their food supplies were already exhausted. Hamad purported to submit and received a robe of honour though chose not to wear it. Trusting him, Munzinger mistakenly parted with his guides, sending them back to Tadjoura with mail, requesting reinforcements. Hamad's perfidy became clear when Munzinger and his force set out supposedly to meet Hanfari at his capital (this was probably Furzi near the Awash river which Wilfred Thesiger records visiting in 1933). Hamad vanished. On 14 November, after an ambush, Munzinger's force was attacked near Lake Abhe by Hanfari's small army which was beaten back with 500 Danakil casualties but at a cost of almost half the Egyptians. Munzinger died after hand-to-hand combat with Hamad, dictating his last wishes to Hagen-macher (Munzinger's wife was also dead). Having spiked their guns, the remainder, constantly harried, were obliged to conduct a six-day retreat to Tadjoura during which Hagenmacher and Ras Burou also died. The survivors under Mohammed Ezzat Bey and the *yuzbashi* of the Sudanese company, numbering 4 officers and 146 men, reached Tadjoura on 21 November.

When the report of the rout reached Cairo on 28 November 1875, scarcely a week after the news of the Arendrup disaster, Zeyla and Tadjoura were put on immediate alert against expected further attacks. The Khedive was obliged, following the death of Munzinger Pasha and Ras Burou, to send a new letter to Ras Menilek to be dispatched by the governor of Zeyla, advising the *ras* of the adversities encountered in Aussa and Tigré, and the formation of the further Rateb Pasha expedition of revenge. If Menilek were to establish himself in Adwa (Adowa), the Khedive would recognise him as Negus and negotiate a commercial agreement.[7]

2 THE ABYSSINIAN DEBACLES 1875–76

Miralai Arendrup Bey's Expedition, 1875 The fortuitous détente between Ismail Pasha and the Emperor John IV which followed the erroneous delivery of the former's letter, addressed to Menilek, to the Negus in May 1875 did not last long. Egyptian military activity, perhaps in relation to the departure of Mohammed Ra'uf Pasha to Zeyla, prompted John to order two generals into Hamasein, instigating the flight of 600 tribesmen, more than half of them militia, to seek refuge at Keren in late July. Two intervening mountain passes were simultaneously seized. The action, directed by John from his Adowa headquarters, was interpreted as a threatened invasion of Bogos, and Ala el Din Bey left at once from Kassala to Bogos calling for reinforcements from Cairo. The Khedive responded swiftly, arresting Munzinger's departure for Tadjoura and dispatching six companies to Massawa on 13 August.

Munzinger, presently in Keren, notified Cairo that John at Adwa was building a defensive wall and, having closed the Hamasein frontier with Bogos, had positioned a large army at Tsazega, west of Asmara. Likewise an Abyssinian force from Adiabo now threatened Amideb. Munzinger and Ala el Din urged the issue of an ultimatum to John to withdraw from the frontier and, in the absence of compliance, a strike into Hamasein. This advice however predicated an actual Abyssinian intent to attack Bogos, and hostilities would be triggered only in the event of that attack.

Munzinger at Keren had 1,200 regular troops, 4 guns and 2 machine-guns; Ala el Din at Amideb some 800 and 200 *bashi-buzouqs*; and McKillop, arrived at Massawa, a force comparable to that of Munzinger and Ala el Din combined. Munzinger deployed the army to protect the frontier from Bogos to Massawa and to await any Abyssinian attack which would justify the occupation of Hamasein. Meanwhile on 18 August Cairo ordered Munzinger to write to Emperor John, politely demanding to know his intentions and requiring the withdrawal of his troops to their previous limits. Egypt would still prefer the avoidance of hostilities.[8]

The Khedivial decision on 26 August 1875 to dispatch Munzinger, the politically experienced and responsible general-governor of the Eastern Sudan, to Aussa and to transfer the latter's Sudan authority not only to Ala el Din Bey, his *wakil,* but also to Arakil Bey in tandem with him, was of critical importance. Arakil Bey was politically well located at Massawa, Ala el Din less so at Amideb; and a potential war situation was developing fast.

The affair over the attempted requisition of *mourdanes* in April had already exposed the Khedive's incipient alienation from Munzinger. In the latter days of August 1875 there is evidence that the Khedive was becoming increasingly keen to exploit the legitimate reactions of the Abyssinia Emperor to Egyptian troop movements as an excuse to launch an attack on Hamasein. His ambitious former private secretary, Arakil Bey, seizing the opportunity of his enhanced authority for direct communication with Cairo, captured the ear of his Khedive with the advocacy of a *pre-emptive* strike designed to add to the Egyptian empire.

Arakil had already misled Cairo into thinking that John's friendly message in May betrayed weakness. The Negus now reacted to the arrival of Egyptian reinforcements at Massawa by occupying two strategic passes barring the route between Massawa and Hamasein. Arakil on 2 September insisted that this was not only entirely unprovoked but indicative of the Emperor's aggressive intention to embark on a war of nerves and, intolerably, to hold down a large and expensive Egyptian army indefinitely at enormous cost to the general-governorate. Only 'un acte de vigueur' by Egypt would bring relief. Warming to his task, Arakil recommended forty-eight hours later – exploiting the friendly presence in Massawa of the nephew of the exiled former ruler of Hamasein – the exploitation of the Abyssinian push into that province as an act of aggression and therefore as an excuse to occupy it. To further his case he cited John's appointment of General Kirkham as governor of Ginda and Assalé, the Abyssinian province with the salt pans adjacent to Massawa (all Egyptian territory, Arakil claimed, only to be contradicted by Munzinger). But Munzinger was about to quit the governorate. Abyssinia, Arakil further insisted on the evidence of itinerant merchants, was in complete anarchy. He was to continue in the same vein to Cairo until the end of September, almost daily, proposing that Adwa and all Tigré should be occupied.

His Khedive however had already been persuaded. On 15 September Munzinger, still at Keren, was ordered to leave immediately to establish as a diversion the *mamuriya* of Tadjoura and Aussa. On 17 September the Danish Colonel Arendrup, the newly appointed commander-in-chief of the invasion force for Hamasein, received his written instructions.[9]

Invasion was probably now or never. Ismail Pasha knew that, provided he continued to play the anti-slave trade card and did not penetrate the Abyssinian heartland, Britain and France would remain indisposed to intervene. In February 1875 Consul-General Stanton in Cairo had declined to forward to the Khedive a letter of protest from Kirkham about activities in Massawa, and the Foreign Office did not choose to respond to Stanton's deputy's notification in early August of advice from the Khedive that Emperor John was threatening Massawa. In Darfur Zubeir Pasha had at last been brought to heel and would shortly be called to Cairo out of harm's way. The rapidly approaching financial bankruptcy of the Khedivate would allow of only a further brief interval before its exposure would attract a foreign démarche and a curb on the mounting national debt.

As late as 6 September the Khedive had been still maintaining to Munzinger his intent to remain on the defensive towards Abyssinia. It was in the following ten days that, bombarded with Arakil's belligerent dispatches, he was won over to active preparation for war and the appointment of a commander-in-chief. He acknowledged to Arakil Bey that it was the latter's reports that had persuaded him to abandon the defensive strategy, and that the governor of Massawa should assist the new army commander from his intimate local knowledge and advise the Khedive on the best future form of administration for Hamasein.

According to Franz Hasan Bey, in charge at Keren, Arakil then sent an ultimatum to the Emperor demanding the cession of Hamasein or war.

The commander-in-chief of the Egyptian forces confronting Abyssinia was to be Soren Adolph Arendrup, a Danish artillery lieutenant for four years who, suffering from tuberculosis, had sought convalescence in Egypt and, in 1874, was recruited by the American chief of staff, Stone Pasha, with the rank of *qa'immaqam* to take charge of weaponry. He had not previously seen active service and, until his appointment to command the Abyssinian expedition with promotion to *miralai*, had served in Cairo as a headquarters staff officer. It was an appointment, to the command of a force of 2,500 men with artillery, fraught with risk, for one with no greater experience of the Abyssinian terrain than his battalion commanders. Such was the urgency of the expected advance, however, that there can have been only a limited number of senior officers available.

Arendrup's instructions dated 17 September reflected the arguments of Arakil's reports and Arakil himself was sent a copy. While leaving him discretion whether to call on Ala el Din's force at Amideb (McKillop was ordered to the Indian Ocean), they envisaged the main thrust into Hamasein as comprising two battalions of reinforcements, now augmented by three further companies. Arendrup must first appraise the situation in the light of local intelligence and of any response to Munzinger's letter to the Emperor requiring the withdrawal of the latter's troops. If the latter had complied, Arendrup was not to advance; but if there had been no reply or no compliance, Arendrup was to enter Hamasein without hesitation and to occupy it – but not, except of necessity, to penetrate beyond its borders. Withdrawal would be conditional upon guarantees of compliance from the Emperor. In the case of Kirkham's governorate of Ginda and Assalé, this was Egyptian territory to be re-annexed. That last initiative however was subordinate to the military conquest of Hamasein which, the Khedive alleged, he did not aspire to annexe: simply to put an end to the costly frontier threats of the Negus and the raids on Sudan territory.

The drafting of the instructions was significantly influenced by Nubar Pasha as minister of foreign affairs. On Darfur, an internal matter, he had not been consulted and, in respect of Abyssinia, discussion was solely in the context of John's threat to Massawa, not of Ismail's territorial ambitions. Nubar was not inhibited from warning the Khedive of the historical lack of success of foreign aggressors (except Britain over Magdala, who had quickly withdrawn). Then one morning in October 1875 the Khedive flourished a telegram purporting to state that John was advancing on Massawa after seizing a Catholic mission, and insisted that the foreign consuls must be told that Egypt was moving to defend the mission.

Nubar concluded the telegram had been invented. However the troops were now on stand-by and Arendrup as a foreign commander-in-chief might prove less complaisant with Khedivial instruction than would a Turkish Egyptian. Nevertheless Nubar persuaded Ismail that Arendrup should be instructed that if, on arrival at Massawa, the intelligence about the Abyssinians attack was found unreliable, he was not to advance from Massawa and could even repatriate some of his force. This caveat was reinforced by Nubar in personal talks, but Arendrup was also personally briefed by the Khedive.

News soon reached Cairo of Arendrup's almost immediate advance (conspicuously Nubar in his *Mémoires* never mentions his kinsman, Arakil Nubar) and of Munzinger's earlier departure to Tadjoura. Then a letter arrived from Arendrup addressed to Fariq Stone, communicated to the Khedive and Sharif Pasha but not to Nubar. Nubar would write:

> I know that the letter began thus: 'If I had felt bound to adhere to the instructions, verbal and written, of Nubar Pasha, I would not have moved from Massawa and I would have sent back a part of my force; but having in my mind the conversations with his Highness and the essence of his verbal recommendations, I believed it my duty to conform to them and I am going in a few days to invade Hamasein.'

Accompanied by Qa'immaqam Rustum Nagi Bey, his second-in-command; his adjutant, the American West Point officer Bimbashi James Dennison; and Major Durholz, formerly of the Papal Swiss Guard, Arendrup had left Suez on 20 September 1875 and, in command of the expedition, Massawa on 10 October, by which time the first column had occupied Ginda. In the interim Arendrup familiarised himself with his force and, according to Arakil Bey, after studying the history of the crisis and intelligence reports, decided to move on Hamasein. With only Arakil to brief him, he would have been a strong personality to cross the latter and his ambitions, let alone disappoint the Khedive. On 29 September Arendrup reported to Cairo that he had found the state of affairs 'conformed to the governorate's reports' and that he would proceed to the occupation of Hamasein – doubtless to be marginally encouraged, if misled, by Arakil's report of 3 October that the Abyssinian forces might be dispersing.[10]

On 11 November it was learned in Cairo that the Arendrup expedition of 2,500 men had transited Hamasein after entering the area via Ghinda; had crossed the frontier limits into the River Mareb valley for strategic reasons; had presently established its headquarters at Godofelassie; and had reached Gundet on the river to its south. In reality Arendrup had occupied Tsazega, the chief town of Hamasein, without opposition on 18 October and, after waiting for supplies, dispatched an advance party to cross the southern Hamasein frontier at Debaroa on 29 October, himself occupying Godofelassie, capital of Sarawe, on 1 November – still without an encounter with John who progressively fell back towards Adwa. Meanwhile, concerned about supply difficulties he had met on the Tsazega route, Arendrup switched the garrisons to the alternative camel-friendly trace to the east via Kayakhor in Tsandigle where the Catholic mission felt menaced by Emperor John. John had meanwhile on 23 October 1875 declared war on Egypt.

From Godofelassie Arendrup directed an Austrian Count Zichy, who had been recommended to him in Massawa by Arakil, to reconnoitre Gundet on the edge of the Mareb river crossing, reinforcing him so as to create a force of six companies, and then following in his tracks on 6 November to Adi Huala – two hours' distance away to the north and commanding the route from Adwa.

Arendrup's force at this point had occupied without fighting the provinces of Hamasein, Sarawe and Tsandigle, but he had been enticed a long way from Massawa. The Abyssinian chiefs believed hostile to John had done no more than send sympathetic disloyal messages to Arendrup. The Emperor refused to respond to Arendrup's invitation to talks. Arendrup's force, for all its strong tactical position, remained vulnerable on account of its limited complement and long lines of communication. When the news from Arendrup had reached Cairo on 11 November, the Khedive immediately appraised the necessity of reinforcing Arendrup and a week later promised him four battalions, a cavalry squadron and an artillery battery, half to leave Suez on 26 November. Arendrup was instructed on no account to proceed beyond Adwa.[11]

The French consul in Massawa, de Sarzec, hostile to Egypt, had meanwhile arrived in Adwa with a present of arms for John from the French General MacMahon on 25 October, with advice not to be too

Emperor John IV of Abyssinia

fearful of the Arendrup threat. John determined to march on the Egyptian force, leaving Adwa on 3 November with a force of 1,000 men, to be rapidly augmented to 70,000 five days later following the declaration by the patriarchal *Abouna* of a holy war. News of John's approach does not seem to have reached Arendrup before 14

November. Prudence counselled that his forces presently split between Adi Huala and Gundet should be consolidated. He decided Gundet was the better position for the coming battle and joined Zichy's force of six companies with four of his own from Adi Huala at midday on 15 November.

In the gorge of the Mareb, 2,000 feet below them, the Abyssinians overran the Gundet advance posts that night and Arendrup, calling up the remaining companies from Adi Huala, descended on the morning of 16 November to support Count Zichy at the crossing of the Mareb. He was attacked in a narrow defile, the rifle weaponry of his force overwhelmed by the attackers' spears and he himself killed by a bullet. In this he was more fortunate than Zichy who was found by de Sarzec a week later still alive, grievously wounded and mutilated, yet able to have crawled to the river. De Sarzec's efforts to get him treatment failed and Zichy died en route to Adwa on 4 December. In this battle Abyssinian casualties amounted to 31 dead and 55 wounded. Of the Egyptian force, 150 only survived as prisoners.

Meanwhile, on receipt on Arendrup's order, Rustum Nagi Bey had led the remaining force from Adi Huala in column down to Gundet, only to be attacked by victorious Abyssinians who had climbed the side of the valley thence to fall on the Egyptians from all directions at Guda-Gudi. De Sarzec put the Abyssinian casualties in this encounter at 521 dead and 355 wounded. Just one of these Egyptian companies escaped back to Adi Huala. Rustum Naqi and Arakil were both killed, and the remaining force retreated via Kayakhor to Massawa. Bimbashi Dennison reached Massawa on 20 November 1875 to telegraph Cairo with news of the calamity. In all, of the fifteen companies taking part in the battles, only one had survived.[12]

Sirdar Mohammed Ratib Pasha's Expedition, 1876   The Negus was at first minded to exploit his victory over Arendrup by an immediate attack on Massawa and Bogos and was restrained only by the threat of rebellion by Menilek. The arrival back of the remaining eleven companies garrisoning the – now abandoned – captured Abyssinian provinces reassured the inhabitants of the general-governorate, but stringent efforts were made well into 1876 to conceal from the Cairo community the enormity of the débacle (Stanton was not told of the outcome until 25 November) and the depravity with which the dead, wounded and captured had been treated. Four years later Gordon was to report after visiting the battlefields of 1875–6:

Mountain scenery in the Southern Tigré

The cruelties the King and his people committed were atrocious. Forty Sudan soldiers were mutilated altogether and sent to Bogos with the message that if the Khedive wanted eunuchs, he could have these. Two thousand Egyptians were taken prisoner. They had no food for three days, and then were ordered to march – they objected. They were all naked. The Abyssinians fell on them, and ordering some hundreds to lie on the rocks, shot at them as targets... You know I have seen many peoples, but I never met with a more fierce, savage set than these. The peasantry are good enough.

John's written offer to return the heads of the Christian Arendrup and Arakil for church burial was deflected from Cairo to Massawa. The catastrophe was blamed on the inadequacy of the military force, its lack of preparation and zeal. Discounting advancing bankruptcy, however, the Khedive was now bent on revenge and would brook no alternative response. As he explained it frankly to Stanton, it was impossible for Egypt to retain her position in the Sudan if she submitted to defeat and humiliation and, with Abyssinia, it was only possible to negotiate from strength. Egypt's African territories were worth an expedition costing even £E1m.

As soon as 27 November the first echelons of an army to comprise sixteen infantry battalions, a regiment of cavalry and three batteries were embarked at Suez for Massawa. The instructions to be given to the new commander-in-chief, the Egyptian *sirdar* Mohammed Ratib Pasha (with the American Lewa William Loring Pasha his chief of staff), were finalised by 5 December. At the first council of war the Khedive's son, Prince Hasan, had unsuccessfully asked to take part and accordingly would have necessarily commanded. Nubar for his part had reservations about the project, preferred Loring with American battle experience as commander-in-chief, and had proposed that the expedition should simply stage a mock battle on the Hamasein border and then return to Massawa with a captured cross purporting to come from Axum cathedral. Sharif Pasha and Ismail Pasha Sadiq however backed the Khedive's nomination of the *sirdar* (the most senior officer but once again without experience of active service).

The final instructions read: 'The goal of your expedition is to re-establish our military prestige and therefore that of my government; and secondly to pursue and achieve the goal I set out in sending Arendrup Bey. To attain these two goals you must necessarily invade Abyssinia.' If the Emperor offered battle, having vanquished him Ratib would withdraw to Massawa. But it was likely that John would follow the traditional Abyssinian tactic of luring the attacking force into the highlands. On no account should Ratib advance beyond Adwa in Tigré, but rather seek to detach John's rivals from their loyalties, insisting that the Egyptian aim was not conquest but guarantees of peace. This should force upon the Emperor the choice of battle or negotiation but, if not, Ratib was not to remain in Adwa indefinitely, but to exact reparations and then retire to Massawa, at the same time threatening to return in 1877 if the Emperor had not complied with the Khedive's demand for assurances of peace.

Ratib Pasha, the Egyptian *sirdar*, was – the American *miralai* William Dye was to write (after differences over the conduct of battle) – 'ever small of stature but shrivelled up like a mummy with age'. He arrived in Massawa on 11 December with his headquarters staff, the operational appointments, under Lewa Loring supported by Miralai William Dye, being for the greater part American officers. By now France was seeking to pressurise the Khedive to desist, but Britain was not to be provoked into active intervention. 'Britain had no desire to interfere in the differences between Egypt and Abyssinia' but, if the object of the Ratib expedition was the attempted conquest of Abyssinia, Britain trusted the Khedive would desist since it would further drain Egyptian financial resources and such territory and peoples would prove difficult to govern. Projects like this 'threaten to convert temporary embarrassment into complete financial ruin'. The Khedive for his part believed his declared objective was internationally respectable and long-term financial integrity was no longer the priority. Hence his robust explanation to Stanton on 28 December. The European powers were not yet unduly disturbed.[13]

Early in the new year of 1876 there occurred a development which could have led to negotiations between Ratib and the Negus. On 13 December 1875 John had sent by the hand of General Kirkham a letter urging a cease-fire on the basis of the status quo, to be delivered to Massawa along with 112 Egyptian prisoners. In the event the prisoners were sent in advance, as Kirkham was ill. The Abyssinian situation in Hamasein was uncertain. John had perhaps mistakenly on the eve of the Arendrup expedition restored Dejach Welde-Mikael Selomon, its former governor, in return for a pledge of loyalty. He however was already plotting to switch sides again with his private army of 3,000 men. The arrival of the prisoners, a third of whom had been castrated, provoked fear among Ratib's force. When Kirkham arrived on 5 January 1876 with John's letter to the Khedive, Ratib was instructed to detain him under house-arrest but to treat him with appropriate dignity. The Khedive chose to ignore John's letter.

On 8 January 1876, conscious of the shrinking campaigning season before the rains, Ratib Pasha with an army of 12,000 men finally gave the order to advance to Baresa and to establish a supply depot there. Ratib Pasha, accompanied now by Prince Hasan who had been sent by the Khedive to ensure good relations between Ratib and Loring, arrived at Massawa on 25 January, and reached Gura on 29 January.

Critical to a successful outcome of the campaign would be the ability of the Egyptians to detach the principal Abyssinian *rases* (governors) from their loyalty to the Negus, a strategy anticipated by the Negus when it was clear the second Egyptian expedition was massing at Massawa in mid-December 1875. He warned his *rases* that the forthcoming struggle would be to defend their country and their religion, and again encouraged the *Abouna* to preach a crusade against the Turks. It was clear that by the time Ratib and Prince Hasan arrived at Gura, only Dejach Woronya of Gondar and, uncertainly, Dejach Welde-Mikael of Hamasein who had fought against Arendrup at Gundet were denying the Negus support. The latter did defect to Ratib in return for 500 Remington rifles, but even Ras Menilek of Shoa contributed a modest 500–600 horses to the Negus. On 3 February John felt strong enough to leave Adwa once again to confront an invading army near the Mareb which, when John reached the river on 19 February, numbered at Gura seven infantry battalions, two squadrons of cavalry and twenty mountain guns.[14]

By 3 March John's own army, totalling up to 50,000 men, was deployed east of the Mareb river facing the two positions of Ratib's expedition concentrated respectively at Gura and at Kayakhor – six miles, or two hours, apart. Between the two armies, three hours apart, a river ran northwards through the plain of Gura, dominated by Ratib's force of 7,300 men, and thence past Kayakhor to the plain of Haala. Narrow passes restricted the northern exit from the plain of Gura and the southern entrance to that of Haala by Kayakhor. In between lay a hill, vulnerable to Abyssinian attack by reason of its isolation, where the second Egyptian force of 2,500 infantry, three half-squadrons of cavalry and six guns under the Circassian Lewa Osman Rifqi were stationed to command the defiles. The remainder of the Egyptian force, with supply reinforcements, had already been called up from Fort Baresa through the plain of Haala.

On 6 March a council of war called by Ratib Pasha exposed the differences of opinion which divided Ratib and the Turkish-Egyptian officers on the one hand, who favoured concentration of the army at Gura, and the American staff who counselled concentration at Kayakhor. Language difficulties between Turkish- and English-speaking officers created further misunderstanding of Ratib's decision to concentrate at Gura. The following morning the advance of the Abyssinian army prompted Ratib to lead his force in the direction of Kayakhor, but then to halt it two miles short in extended formation. Loring concluded that Ratib had no intention of unifying the two forces at Kayakhor.

In the early afternoon of 7 March the Abyssinians then attacked the right of Ratib's force and, sustaining heavy casualties, were relieved to see the left of the Egyptian army suddenly retreat, under Ratib's orders and Prince Hasan's command, to Gura. The right flank battalion was destroyed. The commanders and the cavalry on the left reached the security of the Gura fort by 5 pm; not so the infantry following behind who, mistakenly changing direction under threat of attack, marched away from the fort and were also annihilated. Of the 5,200 (seven battalions) who had marched that morning from Gura, Dye estimated that all but 400–500 became casualties, leaving only the Gura garrison of two battalions and the cavalry as a fighting force. In his dispatch,

Ratib roundly blamed Lewa Loring and Miralai Dye, penning a ludicrously exaggerated estimate of 250,000 enemy attackers. His concern for the well-being of the Khedive's son was manifest.

That night Ratib sent an order to the Egyptian commander Osman Rifqi, still at Kayakhor, to join them at once. His troops were now augmented by 2,000 reinforcements from Baresa and numbered some 7,000. They had fired not a shot the previous day. The order was ignored by Osman Rifqi on grounds that the way was barred.

Over the next two days, 8–9 March, Ratib's force, besieged in Fort Gura, repulsed attacks by Abyssinian troops carrying bags of earth with which to fill in the ditches, inflicting on them some 1,800 casualties. Only on the evening of 10 March, under pressure from Prince Hasan and with the Abyssinians having abandoned the siege, would Ratib permit a sortie to rescue the remaining 100 still alive of the original 1,000 Egyptian wounded. Then on 13 March the Negus, after reconnoitring Kayakhor, gave the order for his army to withdraw.

Why did the victor take this decision? Gordon in Khartoum a year later would hear that John, originally doubtful of the battle's outcome, had returned victorious to his camp only to find it had been completely pillaged by his own people. Dye, on the contrary, estimating that the Abyssinian force – despite killed, wounded and deserters – still totalled 25,000 and had now been strengthened by captured Egyptian guns, Remingtons and ammunition, attributed John's decision to the favouring of discretion over valour. Neither of these speculations carries conviction in the light of subsequent disclosures.[15]

One Mohammed Rifaat Bey, Ratib Pasha's dragoman, in his memoirs quoted by Douin relates that having been left out of battle on 7 March at Fort Gura, he had ventured out in the afternoon mistakenly believing the Egyptians to have been victorious. Unable to return to the fort, he was captured by the Abyssinians and the next day, 8 March, interrogated before Dejach Maro, one of John's *rases,* who had previously campaigned against Arendrup. His master having been evidently defeated, he alleges that he took it upon himself to declare that Ratib sought a truce for which he, Rifaat, would be the intermediary. He was then brought before the Negus on 11 March whom he persuaded to write a conciliatory letter to Ratib. By 13 March the victorious Negus was leaving the scene. Prince Hasan, if initially unsuccessfully, was requesting his father's permission to return to Cairo – but nevertheless by 12 April had arrived there. Ratib meanwhile had promptly reopened contact with the beleaguered garrison at Kayakhor, enabling Gura to be reinforced. By 6 April a newly constructed fort south of Kayakhor had been named after the now departing Prince Hasan.[16]

The interval between the departure of John on 13 March and Hasan on 6 April was occupied by secret *pourparlers* between the two. In August Sir Henry Elliot would report to the British Foreign Office, on the credible authority of an Egyptian officer in Constantinople, that an indemnity of 3m dollars (£E600,000) had been paid to the Negus to secure the escape of the Egyptian force and of the Khedive's son. This was at once denied by Sharif Pasha, the Egyptian foreign minister, who nevertheless conceded that the Egyptians had suffered the heavy loss of 15,000 rifles, 70 guns and ammunition in the March battle. Yet certainly by mid-May 1876 many thousand Egyptian troops had already arrived back at Suez, battle participants being forbidden to enter Cairo while the war continued in order that the humiliating loss of six Egyptian battalions should remain concealed. It was remarked that instead of their original Remingtons, which the Negus refused to hand back, the troops carried old muskets or none. Ratib remained on in Kayakhor, having withdrawn from Gura on 23 April, his garrison further denuded by a detachment sent to reinforce Welde-Mikael at Hamasein. John did allow the return to Kayakhor of his surviving Egyptian prisoners: 200 from the Gura battle; just seven from Gundet.

Sharif Pasha's denial of the ransom payment would be undermined by Hussey Vivian's dispatch of 3 November, based on a trustworthy informant then at Jedda affirming that the Khedivial yacht *Mahrousa* 'had gone down in hot haste with the ransom', catching the informant up at Suez with Prince Hasan on board. It was the *Mahrousa* which had carried Hasan from Massawa en route to Cairo on 9 April. Then, years later, Nubar Pasha would testify that he met Ratib at Carlsbad who told him that his expedition, split in two and surrounded by Abyssinians, would have been destroyed but for a 'convention' reached with the Negus (in which Rifaat Bey was the go-between?). Ratib's army had been allowed to withdraw but, Nubar relates, 'I had reason to understand that a heavy sum had been paid to Egypt.'[17]

No sooner it seems had the ransom been paid in late April 1876, and the Egyptian prisoners returned, than Ratib in bad faith refused to sign the truce already sealed by the Negus; whereupon the latter moved his army to Godofellasie, a day's march from Kayakhor. The rainy season approaching and with it the end of the campaigning season, the Khedive was reluctant to make peace and determined to maintain his claim on Hamasein, on account of which Kayakhor, Baresa and

Adiraso must continue to be held – unaware of the local outbreak of typhus at the end of April. The Negus for his part, rejecting the Khedive's claim to Hamasein (and indeed to Massawa), personally took revenge on the Hamasein villages for their disloyalty under Welde Mikael and replaced the latter by Ras Hailou as governor. He demanded the release of General Kirkham who despite some amelioration of his condition, was to die in the house of the Swedish missionary at Massawa on 23 June. At the end of May, John sent a final band of prisoners from the Arendrup campaign and, when the truce remained unsigned, retired to Adwa on 1 June.[17]

Ratib eventually left Kayakhor for Adiraso on 10 September and thence to the frontier at Baresa – where typhus was still rampant – there to await the decision of the Khedive whether he should advance on Asmara and Hamasein. He was ordered to hand over command of Baresa to Osman Rifqi and himself reached Massawa on 27 September. Meanwhile an Abyssinian expedition drove Welde Mikael out of Hamasein back to Sennaheit and threatened Keren, forcing Ratib to fall back from Baresa to protect Massawa. Prince Hasan, after a short spell as *sirdar* with Ratib appointed his ADC-in-chief, was made minister of war on the dismissal of the *mufettish* in November, and Ratib reverted to *sirdar*. By now Sharif Pasha was blaming the expedition's failure on Nubar (in exile); Munzinger (dead); and, surprisingly, Fariq Stone for collectively pressuring the Khedive to undertake it.

No truce would be signed. A personal envoy from the Negus to Cairo, Dr Gabra-Egziabher, authorised to insist simply on the return of occupied Ethiopian territory and Abyssinian access to the Red Sea, returned empty-handed after being detained for three months in Cairo until eventually received by Prince Hasan in December. When, also in that month, the British consul-general suggested sending a European officer to mediate, he was told that Fariq Gordon would be asked to fulfil that role when he returned from England. Meanwhile the last Egyptian armed forces were called back from Massawa, the Baresa station finally evacuated, and Ratib Pasha, sick, left for Cairo with his chief financial officer, Sulieman Pasha Niyazi. He arrived there on 21 January 1877, having handed over to Osman Rifqi Pasha as governor of Massawa and *seraskir*. The second Abyssinian débacle was complete.[18]

10

The Climax of Empire 1874–76 (Concluded): The General-Governorate of Fariq Gordon Pasha

I THE WHITE NILE TERRITORIES OF EQUATORIA

First Contacts: February–March 1874   The decision to look elsewhere for a successor to Sir Samuel Baker in Equatoria probably dates from the arrival of his peremptory letter to the Khedive from Gondokoro in January 1872. Initially, a retired British Indian Army officer was considered the most likely successor to 'remedy the evils resulting from the recent mistakes' and the first sounding of Gordon was to be made at a chance encounter with Nubar Pasha at the British embassy in Constantinople in September 1872. The quest went cold with the planned expedition of Colonel Purdy to Equatoria ostensibly to relieve Baker, which was aborted on the re-establishment of contact between Baker and Khartoum in March 1873. Meanwhile in the previous six months Nubar had briefed himself about Gordon's astonishing success as commander of the Ever-Victorious Army of the Chinese Emperor in 1863–64. After a further visit to the Ottoman Sultan by the Khedive with Nubar, the firm invitation offering Gordon the appointment was handed to the British acting consul-general in Alexandria on 30 August 1873 (five days after Baker's final audience) for transmission to Galatz, where Gordon was becoming increasingly dissatisfied in his role as a Danube Boundary commissioner.

This invitation effectively put an end to the dual plan of Ismail Ayub Pasha, shortly to be promoted Governor-General in December 1873, first to replace Baker's acting successor at Gondokoro, Mohammed Ra'uf Bey, with Ali Bey Rida el Kurdi who had fallen foul of Baker in 1870 and been dismissed by Mumtaz – a proposal vetoed in Cairo; and secondly to create an additional *muderia* covering the trading station between Fashoda and Gondokoro and located on the River Rohl (Rol). Subject to British Army approval, which was forthcoming, Gordon accepted his appointment in principle as an independent general-governor Equatoria in November 1873.

In early October he had paid a brief visit to his dying mother in Southampton and on his return prepared to hand over to his successor in Galatz. His mind being concentrated on the Sudan, he had now formed – whether from England, Cairo or Constantinople – an unfavourable view of his predecessor's conduct of the Equatoria expedition. He had become acquainted with Baker's letters in the English newspapers which in Gordon's view revealed a 'wish to glorify himself' and which had alienated the Viceroyalty. 'I feel quite sure I can do better without Baker; in a month I would know more than he does, whereas if I take him and do not follow his advice he would be vexed.'

A report of a deputation to the British foreign secretary Earl Granville – to make recognition of Khedivial territorial acquisitions in 'Upper Egypt' conditional on the abolition of the slave trade – was attributed by Gordon to Baker's initiative and to the support of the Prince of Wales, the Royal Geographical Society, the Anti-Slavery Society and individuals discountenanced by his, Gordon's, appointment. He was convinced that settlement of the new territories and establishment of communications must precede abolition. 'God has allowed slavery to go on for so many years that it cannot be a vital thing to risk life and success for a few months. ...Born in the people, it needs more than an expedition to eradicate it. My ideas are to open the country by getting the steamers into the Lakes and then, by that time, I would know the promoters of the slave trade and could ask the Khedive to seize them.'

Gordon's views were doubtless strengthened by his first brief visit to the Khedive in Cairo on 19 December 1873. The latter emphasised the need for amicable relations with the tribes and the need to minimise costs. Gordon went to London to meet Earl Granville. Baker had just been enthusiastically received by the Royal Geographical Society and the United Service Institution before proceeding to Brighton to convalesce, and there after Christmas he and his wife met Gordon 'for a few minutes' only. Gordon probably spent longer with Speke's companion, Colonel James Grant. Gordon wrote politely to thank Baker for advice relating to deadlines for the arrival of his stores at Khartoum, but his current antipathy towards Baker deprived him of the opportunity of benefiting from Baker's unique experience of current conditions on the Equatorial Nile and more particularly, one suspects, of learning the valid reasons for Baker's distrust of Mohammed Abu Sa'ud. Baker's *Ismailia* would not be published until September 1874. Meanwhile Gordon had yet to set foot in the Sudan. As he was later, too self-critically, to concede: 'I have a wonderful instinct, but very bad judgement.'

Leaving Dover on 28 January 1874 he was in Cairo on 7 February. Two days later, having been briefed by Stanton, he met Sharif Pasha and then Abu Sa'ud (still under arrest) to whom, with the subsequent assent of a startled Khedive, he offered the post of a deputy at Gondo-koro. Nubar Pasha, who was responsible for Gordon's own selection, seems to have warned Gordon that such imprudence could ruin the expedition and this disagreement, at least in part, provoked a tempo-rary estrangement. Gordon confided to his sister Augusta: 'I think I can see the true motive of the expedition, and believe it to be a sham, to catch the attention of the English people, as Baker said... There has been a mutual disappointment.' Stanton's warning not to make an enemy of Nubar was ill received. Gordon was over-reacting to a surfeit of advice from many quarters.

He was agreeably impressed, however, by his meeting with the Khedive – 'quite innocent (or nearly so) of deception'. From the outset Gordon was determined not to accept the salary paid to Baker – £E10,000 per annum – and settle for £E2,000: 'From whom does all the money come? From poor miserable creatures who are ground down to produce it. ...Pillage the Egyptians is still the cry.' Now he further insisted that if the modest expedition did not prove cost-effective, he would resign after two years.

Already the Khedivate was on the slide to bankruptcy: discounted bond issues were required to cover a mounting deficit, the burden of which lay principally in the Suez Canal venture and the policy of terri-torial aggrandisement. As to the latter the Baker expedition to Equato-ria had already accounted for £E1m net cost. Yet, apart from the suppression of slavery, the fertile lands of Buganda and Bunyoro offered a sizeable reward for the continuing venture and Gordon, exceptionally, was bent on covering his costs. Indeed in the words of Edward Dicey, a frequent visitor to Egypt from 1869 onwards, 'any shrewd man of business' would have tendered advice 'as a man of the world' to a Khedive willing to disclose his liabilities 'to the effect that Ismail's financial position was so desperate it could hardly be made worse than it was, and that his best chance of extricating himself from his financial embarrassments was to keep up appearances... For a time the effort to maintain the semblance of wealth after the reality had vanished proved successful.'[1]

Gordon's instructions from the Khedive were handed to him on 16 February 1874, two days before his departure by special train from Cairo to Suez, and resembled the RGS memorandum of April 1874. His first responsibilities were to put an end to the *'trafic barbare'* in slaves by imposing a government trading monopoly; and to put down brigandage with the force of military law. He should not sequestrate local tribal cultivations to meet his expedition's food needs, as this would forfeit goodwill; and it might prove best to resite the capital away from Gondokoro in an area of more productive soil. He was to give priority to a reliable communications system with Khartoum, and pay particular attention to mitigating its interruption by the Nile rapids south of Rejaf. Finally he was to take care not to alienate local tribal leaders; but where security demanded, to replace their authority with tribal intermediaries rather than with direct rule.

These formal instructions were augmented three days later by an order recognising the independence of the Equatorial province supposedly extending to Fatiko and Dufile from Ismail Ayub's *hakimdaria*. The *hakimdaria* nevertheless was to be the supplier of goods to Gordon's province in return for payment in ivory, ostrich feathers and so on. Gordon would decide the provincial structure, whether in the form of two *muderias* (as previously canvassed by Ismail Ayub) or of a series of districts. Ra'uf Bey and his troops passed under Gordon's command.

Gordon's week in Cairo was also occupied recruiting his entourage. For his civilian deputy he had already approached the Italian interpreter he had met in his Crimean War days, Romolo Gessi, who, after serving Garibaldi, was working near Galatz. Gordon put him in charge of the expedition supplies. As his military chief of staff, the Egyptian government on the advice of Fariq Charles Stone appointed the United States officer Lieutenant-Colonel Charles Chaillé-Long. They also provided Gordon with an Egyptian military ADC. According to Long's (consistently unreliable) account he was approached by Gordon and told: 'You will command the soldiery. I don't want to bother.' Other younger Europeans in the party were over the months to fall victims to the climate – to be succeeded in November 1874 by two Royal Engineer lieutenants, Charles Watson and William Chippindall; and by Ernest Linant de Bellefonds (son of Adolphe, now a pasha and minister in Cairo) whose elder brother Auguste had by then died of fever at Gondokoro.

General Gordon, portrait by Leo Diet

Gessi was left behind in Cairo to bring on the expedition's baggage and staff, while Gordon left with Long and a contingent of 220 troops for Khartoum via Suakin – where he met Ala el Din Bey Siddiq, vice-general-governor of Eastern Sudan – and Berber. He arrived at the Sudan capital on 13 March 1874 to a warm public welcome by the *hakimdar* – 'a first rate man [who] has done much for me by opening the "*sudd*" and putting Gondokoro within 18 Days of [Khartoum] and about 7 weeks from England.' He wrote to the Khedive of his high opinion of the troops, the barracks, hospital and school; met the elders of the community who, as at Berber, were not alone in expressing their opposition to

Abu Sa'ud's appointment; and regarding Equatoria 'issued a stinging decree, declaring the government monopoly of the ivory trade and prohibiting the import of arms and powder, the levying of armed bands by private people, and the entry of anyone without passports: in fact I have put the district under martial law i.e. the will of the General.'

He did not dally long in Khartoum. Learning that Gessi, a month behind schedule, had still to leave Cairo, he sailed for Gondokoro in the small Khartoum-based paddle-steamer 'No. 9' on 22 March.[2]

Four weeks had passed since he had landed at Suakin and the voyage gave him the opportunity to take stock. 'I think the slave trade as far as I have seen is down to a minimum and have witnessed no signs of it at present,' he wrote optimistically to Stanton on 20 March and, to Augusta, undisturbed by criticism of Abu Sa'ud: 'I am going to make two men governors under me – one Abu Sa'ud so he will be a swell; and he is built and made to govern…Now I have taken Abu into the service and I feel sure he will be the most useful man I have got.' As for Long, his stock was falling: 'My American Colonel is not worth anything… and is always going to do something or another and never does it.'

In general Gordon was optimistic:

I have seven steamers, and ought to keep up a monthly communication with Khartoum. It is a fine post, there is no doubt; and I think it will be a profitable one for the government after a time… No one can conceive the utter misery of these lands, heat and mosquitoes day and night all the year round, but I like the work for I believe I can do a great deal to ameliorate the lot of the people. …There is an inestimable comfort in leaning on God to get you out of all difficulties; no one knows the comfort of religion who lacks this. He to whom God gives it is free indeed.

Beating the Bounds: March–August 1874   No. 9 steamer was very slow –

only four miles an hour against the current, which is about two knots. In the moonlight the crocodiles were lying interlaced on the few rocks, with their mouths, garnished with teeth, wide open. The hippopotamuses were very active last night. You could see them walking about, like huge islands, in the shallow water. They are very fat and smooth-looking, and their profile is like a horse. We passed a village of Shilluk who were astonished to see us, and fled when we looked at them with our telescopes.

They reached Fashoda (Deinab), 'a poor place', on 31 March 1874, having two days previously transferred to the *Bordein* steamer which arrived from Gondokoro towing a barge with 80 cwt of ivory seized at the El 'Aqqād station at Bor. Since, under remonstrance from the merchants at Khartoum, Gordon had allowed the stations of El 'Aqqād, Ghattas and Kuchuk Ali eight months in which to dispose of their ivory stocks, his good faith seemed to have been challenged – an urgent problem for resolution. Passing Tawfiqia near Sobat mouth, Baker's camp in 1870 and now Gordon's northern border, the expedition pressed on up the Bahr el Jebel past Zeraf mouth 'like a ditch' and navigated Lake No, leaving the mouth of the Bahr el Ghazal to the north-west. It had become apparent that Ismail Ayub's valuable clearance work on the Zeraf the previous year, to Baker's benefit, had not endured. At that time, in early 1873, after massive cutting of impenetrable vegetation, the current had suddenly and drastically burst the remaining *sudd*, steamers, hippopotamuses, crocodiles being swept four miles down the river. Now the Zeraf was blocked again, but an extremely industrious military engineer, sent with a team from Fashoda, had succeeded in clearing the Bahr el Jebel to Lake No a month before Gordon's arrival at Khartoum.[3]

South from Lake No, up the Bahr el Jebel, they passed the site of Holy Cross, its only remains 'some banana trees which [the missionaries] had planted' and their graves; then by way of Bor, the El 'Aqqād station, they reached Gondokoro on 14 April (according to Gordon's report to Cairo). Ra'uf Bey, the commander, had had no advance warning of Gordon's sudden arrival but duly paraded the garrison of 50 Egyptian and 300 Black regulars – a force which Gordon believed inadequate in the light of the continuing hostility of the Bari chiefs (with the notable exception of the reformed Alloron – Loro lo Lako – at Ilibari). Security did not extend beyond half a mile from the garrison perimeter and Ra'uf, a popular commander, had adopted a tough profile. The only other Egyptian garrisons were at Fatiko, with a garrison of 200, where Baker's loyal lieutenant, Sagh Abdallah, had recently been murdered by a conspiracy of his fellow officers; and at Fuweira. The garrisons were supported by 300 former Abu Sa'ud irregulars under the *wakils* Sulieman and Mohammed Wad el Mek.

Waiting at Gondokoro, fortuitously, were messengers from the *kabaka* M'tesa of Buganda with gifts for the Khedive. Their presence was an excuse for Gordon to get rid of Chaillé-Long, whom he was finding increasingly difficult, by sending him on a goodwill mission to

Mohammed Ra'uf Pasha   *Abu Sa'ud of El 'Aqqād*

M'tesa. Kabarega, *mukama* of Bunyoro, whom Baker had forcibly deposed with the help of M'tesa and replaced by Rionga, had nevertheless survived and now, like his rival Rionga, was also canvassing Khedivial support. Overlooking Kabarega's past hostility, Gordon sent him a letter and gifts in the name of the Khedive, which Sulieman, the former El 'Aqqād *wakil*, delivered.

Mohammed Ra'uf Bey had now served nearly five years with the Equatoria expedition, three of them spent at Gondokoro – where he had clashed with Baker Pasha and survived Ismail Pasha Ayub's attempt to replace him with Ali Bey Rida. Gordon, recognising Ra'uf's likely resentment in being supplanted as general-governor, was to claim that this was a factor in his appointment of Abu Sa'ud with his local slave-trader support as a counterweight. 'If Ra'uf Bey had stayed here and the Dongolawis had not been paralysed, the two would have been too much for me.' Ra'uf knew of Gordon's intentions. In the short run however, the murder of Sagh Abdallah at Fatiko clearly had to be punished and Ra'uf had the necessary authority. His despatch now from Gondokoro to Fatiko enabled Gordon to effect his plan to create two *muderias* in the Equatoria general-governorate by appointing *bimbashis* as 'mudirs' ad interim respectively of Gondokoro (El Tayib Agha Abdallah) and of Rohl (Hasan Bey Ibrahim) pending Ra'uf's return; while establishing a strategic government post at Bor, where Ra'uf had recently raided the El 'Aqqād camp for ivory. Gordon's final action was to exploit the current season by the immediate planting of *dura*, before quitting Gondokoro after a bare week to return to Khartoum, there to seek a confrontation with the Governor-General and to collect his missing baggage.[4]

Gordon's original enthusiasm for Ismail Ayub's helpfulness was thinning. He had already drawn up a sizeable agenda for discussion by the time he arrived at Khartoum on 4 May 1874, only to find that Gessi and the baggage had still not arrived (the baggage had only left Alexandria on 30 March); and the report by Martin Hansal, the Austrian consul at Khartoum, that the troops at Gondokoro were being paid in gin and slave-girls, titillating and reprehensible though that might be, was not his principal source of vexation.

Biographers of Gordon have relied on Gordon's extensive private correspondence with the outside world for this period of his service in Equatoria province. Most important were his letters to his sister Augusta ('my journal'), essentially unrevised. He frequently justified their contradictions: 'My letters are my journal and impressions of the moment. I cannot be bound by them' (10.7.1876); 'They contain my private feelings day by day' (19.10.1876); 'so do not nail me down to anything I may say I "propose to do"' (25.10.1876). The biographers however have not usually benefited from perusal of the interchange of official despatches between Gordon and Khairi Pasha, Privy Seal to the Khedive; and, for the eye of the Khedive in person, the *Maia Sanieh* or Khedivial Cabinet. Many of these were documents made public by Georges Douin in the two sections of part 3 of volume III, *L'Empire Africain*, of his *Histoire du Règne du Khédive Ismail* of 1941 and by M. F. Shukry in his *Equatoria under Egyptian Rule 1874–76* of 1953.

The first major issue on the agenda was that of the Equatorial province frontier which had not been delineated in Gordon's (as it had been in Baker's) Khedivial instructions, but simply described as 'un pays peu connu'. Gordon was very experienced in matters of frontier delimitation. In March, on their first meeting in Khartoum, Ismail Ayub had confirmed his agreement – in a spirit of gracious concession – that the Rohl *muderia* should be Gordon territory. But exchanges between the two men now became sour when Gordon presented Ayub with a map of his proposed province boundaries to include on the east bank of the Nile the Sobat basin (up to Nasir on the upper river) and Fadassi; and, on the west, that substantial part of the Bahr el Ghazal which extended east of the Jur river and into Azande country, where the *jallaba* trading stations abounded for slave raiding. Ayub wrote within the week in protest to Cairo at Gordon's presumptuous claims, which he attributed to the latter's discontent with the size of his governorate, and which were backed allegedly by the threat of Gordon's resignation. Ayub was already simmering with frustration at the Khedive's postponement of his participation in the invasion of Darfur on which Zubeir was independently about to embark (see p. 221) – all this unknown of course to Gordon.

Gordon had himself already written to the Khedive, arguing the need to include a station at Sobat mouth to monitor the passage of slave boats and control the shipment of ivory, arms and ammunition on the White Nile. Camels and mules would be obtainable from its hinterland, which would enable Gordon to dispense with the need for tribal porters and therefore for cattle as hire payment. As to the Jur river region on the west bank, a distance of 150 miles from Gondokoro as against 1,800 miles from Khartoum, Gordon believed there was presently no government control. The respective distances dictated the direction of the export of ivory towards Gondokoro while, without the inclusion of these additional territories and their ivory, Gordon's province could not become self-supporting and would accordingly prove economically unviable as an independent governorate. Gordon however had as yet no detailed knowledge of the Bahr el Ghazal, nor of the scale of garrison needed to stop the slave trade.

Initially the Khedive leaned towards Gordon's frontier adjustments and Ayub was obliged to modify his early intransigence. On the east bank the boundaries of Fashoda and Fazughli were redelineated in Gordon's favour: on the west that of Shakka (Bahr el Ghazal) province would be the subject of accord between the governors, assisted by Abu-Sa'ud.

The quarrel between Ayub and Gordon did not however end there. Gordon's request for 200 Remington rifles was the first issue. His request was denied on the grounds that the rifles had already been sent to Gallabat. This he exposed as a lie: they were in fact still in Khartoum. He next found himself obstructed by a contrived local hike in grain prices for his Equatoria supply needs. He circumvented this stratagem by demanding from Ayub a cash grant of £E10,000 with which he could time his direct purchases tactically. He backed this move with an ultimatum for compliance within eighteen days and requested that meetings between them in person should henceforward be restricted to ceremonial occasions. Furious letters were despatched by the antagonists seeking Khedivial support. There was another confrontation over

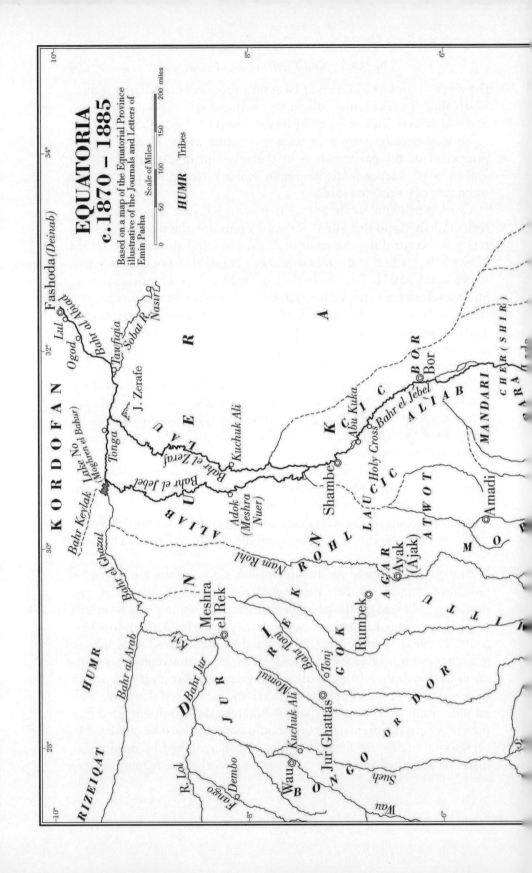

EQUATORIA
c.1870 – 1885

Based on a map of the Equatorial Province
illustrative of the Journals and Letters of
Emin Pasha

Scale of Miles

0   50   100   150   200 miles

HUMR   Tribes

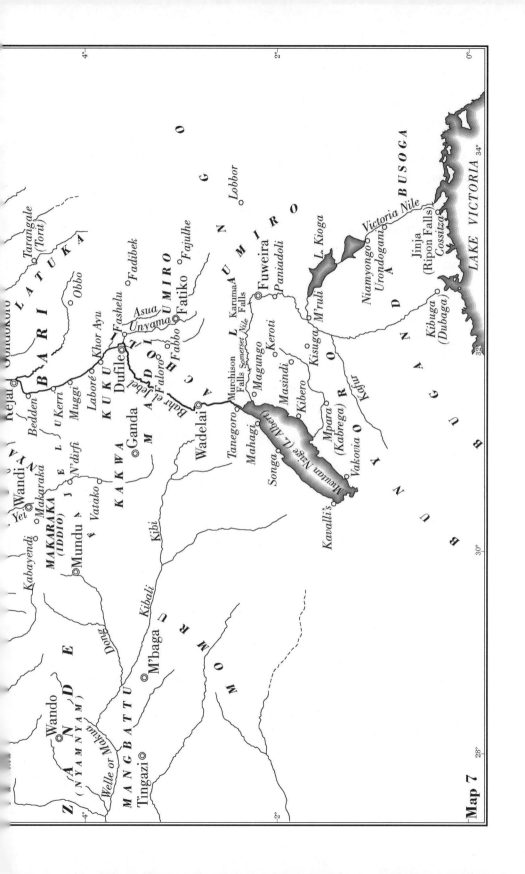

Map 7

the status of 400 cwt of ivory belonging to El 'Aqqād seized as contra-
band at Khartoum by the order of the Governor-General. Gordon
demanded a sight of the proceedings of the court of enquiry, only to be
thwarted by Ayub's subterfuge of suppressing part of the court's findings. Gordon was a formidable man to cross, if not all his manifest rage
was genuine.[5]

This second visit to Khartoum, scarred by further discord, lasted less
than a fortnight. It included a first time meeting with the German Carl
Christian Giegler, just appointed director of Sudan telegraphs, who
gave Gordon the disquieting news that he had observed a dozen slave
caravans between Berber and Khartoum. On 17 May 1874 Gordon
reached Berber to find that Romolo Gessi had recently arrived with
staff and baggage. His principal concern now, reinforced by Giegler's
report, was to strengthen his force at Gondokoro. He had already on 6
May, hearing that Munzinger in Eastern Sudan wished to reduce his
garrison, indented for an additional Sudanese battalion together with
250 Arab troops from Khartoum. Only the intervention of a young
junior Egyptian officer, Ibrahim Fawzi, enthusiastic to serve with
Gordon, had foiled Ayub's attempt to nominate the most disaffected
and least well-armed Arab contingent. Now, having requested Stanton
from Berber to let him have two additional British officers, Lieutenants
C. M. Watson and W. H. Chippendall of the Royal Engineers, Gordon
returned to Khartoum and, disdaining Ayub's friendly approaches
(Ayub attributed the continuing froideur to Gordon's failure to win
control of Bahr el Ghazal), sought a Khedivial instruction that Ayub
should not tamper with the composition of Munzinger's battalion when
it arrived in transit for Gondokoro – which would happen after
Gordon himself had departed.

Ismail Ayub however had remained deeply apprehensive about the
consequences of transferring the Jur river territory from Bahr el Ghazal
to Gordon's Equatoria. Only six months previously the erstwhile slave
dealer and adventurer Zubeir Rahma Mansour had been appointed
governor of Bahr el Ghazal, answerable to Ismail Ayub, now Governor-
General. Zubeir's *muderia* would henceforward be responsible for the
pay and supply of his (government) troops and employees and in addition Zubeir was to make an annual payment of £E15,000 in ivory to
the *hakimdaria* – all this to be derived from his numerous slave-trading
stations.

Critically it was Zubeir's army that had been committed by the

Khedive in February 1874 to the conquest of Darfur. Now on 25 May Zubeir advised Ayub that he was embarking upon his own invasion, Ayub's vexations to be multiplied five days later by the sight of Romolo Gessi – accompanied by the young William Anson, a nephew of Gordon – having been sent up the Nile in advance from Berber by Gordon, leaving Khartoum in the *Safia* for Shakka boundary and Zubeir before Abu Sa'ud had even arrived. Ayub, fearful of the effect of Gessi's boundary mission on Zubeir at this time, telegraphed the Khedive on 2 June, warning him of the threat to Zubeir's principal military supply resource, his Bahr el Ghazal *meshras*. Within hours Gordon had been requested to desist from pressing his claims on Bahr el Ghazal territory and to leave things as they were. Gordon complied. Three weeks later Ismail Ayub himself gained permission to leave for Kordofan and Darfur.

Gessi having already left Khartoum for the Bahr el Ghazal, Gordon's order, carried by J. Kemp, his engineer, and Giegler, to abort the frontier discussions at Shakka only caught up with Gessi at Meshra el Rek on 4 July, where he had been delayed for a week. Gessi put the time before his departure on 10 July to excellent purpose in preparing for Gordon a valuable report on local conditions. In addition to Zubeir's personally-owned *zaribas*, from which Zubeir had now ostensibly distanced himself as governor, there were twelve others: three each of Kuchuk Ali, El 'Aqqād and Abu Amouri; and one each of Ghattas, Hasaballah and Biselli. Zubeir had currently accumulated ivory sufficient to fill a dozen barges. Gessi described the condition of the soldiers, mainly Baqqara tribesmen, paid in merchandise, cattle or slaves, in thrall to the *wakils* of their *meshras* and in consequence perpetrating plunder and brutality on the local peoples to augment their incomes. Looted cattle were then traded with the Azande for ivory or distributed as pay to the soldiers, the *wakils* evincing no concern for the robbed starving villagers who, after all, it was claimed, seldom ate meat. Dead slaves were left for the vultures.

This insight into the conditions of oppression inflicted by the slave brigands of the land between the Rohl and Jur rivers prompted Gordon, when he eventually received this report from Gessi on 16 August 1874, to despatch it to the Khedive as confirmation of the argument behind his original proposal for the transfer of the territory to Equatoria and as a rebuttal of Ayub's claim that there was already an established government administration in Bahr el Ghazal. However he did not challenge the Khedive's decision not to merge Bahr el Ghazal with Equatoria. Not being an Arabic speaker, able to judge the support given to the traders by Zubeir at Shakka, Gordon wrote that he preferred that responsibility for Bahr el Ghazal be placed in hands 'stricter than mine' – for example either Ra'uf Bey from Gondokoro or Yusuf Bey (from Fashoda) – and he could, if the Khedive wished, include also Gordon's new district, under Hasan Ibrahim, of Rohl and with it a garrison of 300. But that new province should be answerable to Cairo, not to Khartoum. The progressive suppression of the Bahr el Ghazal slave traders, which Gordon acknowledged to be the condition of local peace, demanded a stronger army than Gordon possessed. Occupation would now be further postponed until Gordon's appointment as Governor-General three years later. Meanwhile Zubeir remained *mudir* of Bahr el Ghazal and, on his final departure to Cairo in December 1875, handed over to his son Sulieman.

Gordon wrote to Stanton in November 1874: 'My quarrel with the Governor-General was necessary because if I had not shown my teeth he would have baulked my affairs. Now we are all right. I did not care at all about the Bahr el Ghazal territory', meaning evidently that at least he did not feel able yet (in 1874) to take on its problems.[6]

On 8 June Gordon had sailed from Khartoum in the *Bordein* in the wake of his staff who were embarked on the *Khedive* and the *Mansura*. At Fashoda this time he encountered the *mudir* and *qa'immaqam*, Yusuf Bey Hasan Khorda, whose bearing so much impressed Gordon that he recommended his promotion – only to intercept letters from one of the Zeraf station *wakils* advising Yusuf Bey to expect the arrival of slaves. While Gordon's destination was Gondokoro, he planned en route to establish stations at Sobat mouth on the northern frontier of his general-governorate; and, for the *muderia* of Rohl, at Shambe on the west bank of the Bahr el Jebel, Malzac's old *meshra*, where Gessi had now been instructed to build the base on his return from Meshra el Rek. Rohl district would have a second station at Makaraka.

In fact it was nearly three months – in early September 1874 – before Gordon eventually reached Gondokoro from Khartoum. As his first attempt to establish a military camp near Tawfiqia on the right bank of the Sobat proved unsatisfactory, he built a successor on the left bank near the Nile confluence. However deaths from disease still mounted – to forty in July – and he deemed it right to remain personally with the garrison. He found himself involved in July in the interception of slaves crossing the upper Sobat on foot and bound for the north, from the *zaribas* of the Zeraf to whom he had granted an eight-month remission from closure; then in August from the Bahr el Jebel, concealed under cargoes of ivory and ebony, and even on board one of his small steamers. In all he liberated between 500 and 600 slaves but was then confronted with the problem of their future.

Gordon was told that those set at liberty for the most part died of hunger; and he observed both that family ties seemed weak and that many preferred to remain as manual cultivators rather than return to their villages of origin. He pondered the desirability of transporting volunteers to Fayoum in Egypt, for example, to work on the sugar plantations, but to be under strict government supervision headed by a European. He wrote to Nubar Pasha in August 1874 to sound him out, but by October Gordon had concluded that for the next year at least there was ample scope to employ freed slaves in agricultural schemes in his own province.

Abu Sa'ud passed through Sobat mouth en route to Gondokoro on 19 July and by the time Gordon sailed for Shambe on 22 August, leaving in charge a *yuzbashi* with twenty years' Sudan service, Surur Bahjat, he had heard from Ra'uf Bey that all was quiet and that Abu Sa'ud had succeeded in reaching the Garbo cataracts without antagonising the Bari chiefs. Gessi meanwhile, now at Shambe, had overcome many difficulties. Five days after leaving Meshra el Rek and its malignant environment, he had succumbed like Giegler to a severe attack of malaria. Anson nursed him through it, only to fall victim himself and die on the Ghazal on 28 July. Gessi had only reached Shambe on 10 August but, deterred neither by extreme loss of weight nor the rains, he had entered into good relations with the Cic Dinka chiefs and had built the new base by the time Gordon arrived at last en route to Gondokoro on 29 August. Impressed by Gessi's achievement, Gordon decided to take him on to Gondokoro, leaving the new governor of Rohl, Hasan Ibrahim, at Shambe. Hasan Bey had been a former caravan leader of the Poncet brothers, was a fluent Dinka speaker, and familiar with the region extending west into Azande country. Shambe, the *muderia* headquarters, seemed well situated as a wood-station for steamers and, like Bor two days' distance south by river, was endowed with ebony trees for the development of which Gordon was to order 1,500 axes from England.[7]

The New Equatoria Command, September 1874 On his approach to Gondokoro, notwithstanding Ra'uf's assurances that all was well,

Gordon was apprehensive that he would come up against a conflict of authority between Ra'uf and Abu Sa'ud – in which case he was determined to back Abu Sa'ud. On the eve of his arrival, he recalled in a letter to his sister Augusta the experience of comparable rivalries in China: 'They little think I am quite accustomed to this sort of revolt – one speculating on his being my successor, the other on being my *wakil* or second-in-command.' Both men were present to escort him to the military lines on the morning of 3 September 1874 and the good atmosphere, coupled with the submissive behaviour of the Bari, encouraged Gordon to announce Abu Sa'ud's appointment at once as his vice-governor. Ra'uf, remaining impeccably loyal to his Governor but evidently prepared for this development (on his return from Fatiko in July he had already sought and obtained from Cairo six months' leave of absence while Gordon was still at Sobat mouth), now requested nine months' leave. Gordon promptly recommended this on 5 September, along with Ra'uf Bey's immediate promotion to *lewa* and his eligibility for subsequent consideration, in due time, to succeed Gordon as general-governor of Equatoria. The appointment of an Arab to this post was desirable in the long term, and Gordon was personally anxious to explore and open up the little known territories to the east (beyond Buganda). Gordon's glowing report persuaded the Khedive on Ra'uf's arrival in Cairo at the end of October to sanction the leave, to approve the promotion with a pay rise and to bestow on him the Order of Osmania third class. In the event, however, Ra'uf's next external appointment was not to the Sudan *hakimdaria*, nor to Equatoria (as was seriously anticipated in March 1875) but in July 1875 to command the expedition to conquer Harar.

When that last appointment came, it would no doubt have elicited a wry smile from Gordon Pasha. In reality he had no higher opinion of Ra'uf's capability than had Baker Pasha, nor indeed, one suspects, Ismail Pasha Ayub. At this Gondokoro meeting, according to the later recollection of the young Egyptian officer Ibrahim Fawzi, commander of Gordon's bodyguard since May, Gordon had berated Ra'uf for poor administration, for provocation of the Bari over three years, and for the maintenance of an excessively large garrison, which smacked of cowardice: Ra'uf was unfit to govern and should leave for Egypt at once. He did, on 7 September 1874. Tayeb Bey Abdallah would be appointed *mudir* of Gondokoro in his place with a garrison of just fifty men. Gordon confided to his sister: 'This Ra'uf had never conciliated the tribes, never had planted *dura*; and, in fact, only possessed the land he camped on.' But at least Ra'uf had remained loyal to Gordon – which is more than he had to Baker.

To military command, in Ra'uf's absence, Gordon was careful to appoint a regular soldier, Fuad Hasan Effendi. The regular troops under his authority were to be distributed in small forces at the Nile stations above Gondokoro, able to survey any slave-trading activities. On 11 September, in a letter to the Khedive, Gordon praised Abu Saud's achievements (even alluding to him prematurely as *bey*) in conciliating the Bari, especially in effecting the transport of the dismantled small steamer *Nyanza* to Rejaf, which Baker had three years earlier been obliged to abandon at Gondokoro. Despite his past record, Abu Sa'ud was one of a few who knew the country and its people and was acclimatised to local conditions. The Khedive for his part was delighted at Gordon's commendations of Ra'uf and Abu Sa'ud, both of whom Baker had persistently castigated – even recommending that the latter be hanged. Baker's failures, the Khedive claimed, were demonstratively due to his own aggressive actions. (*Ismailia* had just been published.)[8]

Gordon spent less than a fortnight in Gondokoro before sailing south on 15 September to investigate an alternative headquarters – as he had been instructed. These had been hectic days. With the exception of Gordon himself, Gessi (still recovering from malaria) and the engineer J. Kemp, all the Europeans succumbed to tropical fevers, to die or be evacuated north. Gordon's own strict health regime had fortunately carried him through. He had effected his new appointments and, with other officers, the amicable repatriation of Ra'uf, who – commendably – had resisted surprising overtures from Auguste Linant seeking to undermine Gordon's authority and have himself appointed second-in-command. Auguste, now reconciled with Gordon, who tended him in his illness, died on 17 September. On 11 September Gordon had received the submission of twenty-five Bari chiefs and organised for them a trip by steamer to Khartoum. Those of Bedden on the other hand, beyond Rejaf, who had deceived Baker (see p. 133), threatened to kill any messenger of peace. And before he left Gordon had scrupulously addressed the province accounts, even the pay due to departing officers.

When he sailed from Gondokoro on 15 September 1874 there was however a serious piece of unfinished business – his relationship with Abu Sa'ud whom most capriciously and against all advice he had

commended to the Khedive and rehabilitated to become his administrative *wakil*, on the grounds that 'he would at any rate paralyse their
[the slave dealers'] intrigues'. Abu Sa'ud had opposed Ra'uf's departure. He had then exhibited contempt towards the new *mudir* of
Gondokoro and even begun to treat Gordon with arrogance, claiming sole authority in dealing with the Bari and undermining Gordon's
prohibition of bribes. During the voyage to Rejaf he and Gordon
became further estranged and on arrival Gordon served him with
dismissal, despatched him back to Gondokoro with a letter naming
Fuad Hasan in his place, and ordered a public parade recognising
the public status of the new *mudir*. Sensationally humiliated, avoided
by the local chiefs, and with the insubordination of his irregular
troops at Rejaf outfaced by Gordon, Abu Sa'ud confessed his errors
to Gessi and attested his continued loyalty to the Khedive and to
Gordon.

The latter's original appointment of Abu Sa'ud had not been
simply on personal merit. In letters to Colonel Stanton in Cairo
Gordon was later to explain, in the aftermath of attacks on him initiated by Baker in *The Times*, that Abu Sa'ud had been appointed as
part of an astute diplomatic game, first to neutralise the local slave-
dealers and their irregulars prior to Gordon's arrival at Gondokoro;
and, secondly, to utilise their acquiescence to counterbalance Ra'uf's
personal ambitions to be general-governor. These objectives had now
been achieved – 'he [Abu Sa'ud] had done his work.' Moreover
Gordon believed Baker had been badly mistaken in his renegotiation
of the El 'Aqqād contract and in appointing Abu Sa'ud to supply his
expedition without first making him a government-employed direct
subordinate. In tacit recognition of Abu Sa'ud's unconscious useful-
ness to him, Gordon felt it right to mitigate his humiliation – 'I alone
was responsible for his coming up here, which was at my own urgent
suggestion' – and he offered Abu Sa'ud compensation as *mudir* of
Dufile.

The offer was accepted but by the time Abu Sa'ud joined Gordon
at Dufile at the end of September 1874 with an escort of 100 men, the
villages en route from Gondokoro had mysteriously turned hostile
against the government and Gordon's newly created money-exchange
market was shunned. Abu Sa'ud had the effrontery to demand his
reappointment as Gordon's *wakil*, whereupon he was dismissed again
back to Gondokoro and thence, on 20 October, to Khartoum where
he arrived on 28 November 1874. Still evidently harbouring a bad

conscience about his manipulation of Abu Sa'ud, Gordon wrote to the Khedive in October personally accepting the blame for his employment. On 7 February 1875, in a memorandum to Cairo, he added: 'It was the name of Abu Sa'ud that I wanted... His name has achieved the goal which I had intended in taking him on at Cairo.' Indeed in May 1877, at the request of Khalid Pasha Nadim, his deputy, Gordon as *hakimdar* was to give Abu Sa'ud a minor appointment in Khartoum. Nevertheless Abu Sa'ud's extended sojourn in Equatoria had now been terminated, just as the problems presented by Ismail Pasha Ayub and Mohammed Ra'uf Bey had now been resolved.

The Infrasructure Consolidated, January–February 1875   Seven months after his original arrival in Khartoum, Gordon could now concentrate on implementing the Khedivial instructions. In a letter to Stanton in Cairo (18 November 1874) he wrote, prematurely:

> I am now free, thanks to you, of all the geographical business and never need leave this (Gondokoro) which is my proper place to look after <u>my lake</u> i.e. the administration of the Province. ...Now you will kindly tell all scientific folk to address their letters etc. to Watson (arrived four days previously), who will attend to them, for I shall never go to the Lakes if I can help it, I have work enough here and am too old to take these out of the way journeys, besides which my presence should be here.[9]

The instructions had not delineated the 'provinces' confided to Gordon but in the course of the exchanges by telegraph from Khartoum in May, his governorate had been specifically recognised by Cairo to include the Nile east bank, north to Sobat mouth with its hinterland, and east to south of Fadassi near the Galla border; and on the west bank the district of Rohl west to the approximate longitude of Rumbek. '*Mudirs*' had been duly installed at Sobat mouth, Shambe and latterly Bor. Stations at intervals of one-day's march were soon to be established principally on the Bahr el Jebel, south to Bunyoro.

The capital, Gondokoro, was the focus of further rethinking. While Gordon was at Rejaf frustrating the intrigues of Abu Sa'ud, he had initially concluded that a site close to its *jebel* would provide a pleasing, healthy alternative capital (where Abu Sa'ud's writ would no longer run). Not only was Gondokoro encircled by marshland, distant from wood fuel and with poor soil, but it was manifestly unhealthy and with a shallow draft *meshra*; and the government community had over the years become psychologically resistant to the necessity of labouring to develop local resources. On reflection, however, Rejaf's essential merit was limited to its strategic position en route to Dufile – where Kemp had been sent with the small dismantled steamer *Nyanza*, presently destined for Lake Albert. A better alternative capital, perhaps, was Lado, twelve miles north of Gondokoro, which offered other compensating factors – healthy climate, fertile soil and steamer wood in close proximity. Accordingly Gordon ordered the Gondokoro stores to be divided between the *two* new stations, and finally quit Gondokoro on 31 December 1874 to establish his new headquarters at Lado.

Thus the governorate in January 1875 comprised administrative centres at Sobat mouth – with Nasir 140 miles up the river – under a *yuzbashi*, Surur Bahjat, a veteran of the French-Mexican war, with 25 regular and 150 irregular Sudanese troops; at Shambe (Rohl) with 30 regulars and 150 irregulars under Hasan Ibrahim, shortly to be closed down in favour of Rumbek to the west; and posts, under the direct control of Lado, to include Bor; Latuka, which would be linked by telegraph direct to Sobat mouth; Rejaf; Laboré; Dufile; Fatiko; and Fuweira. In all, Gordon's military force numbered 1,800 men, of whom 50 were the surviving Egyptian regulars, 850 Sudanese regulars, and 900 Dongolawi irregulars.[10]

On 14 November 1874 the arrival of Lieutenants C. M. Watson and W. H. Chippendall, and of Ernest Linant de Bellefonds, brother of the recently deceased Auguste, had enabled Gordon to progress his plans for the occupation of Lake Albert. After a fortnight in Lado all three were despatched to Rejaf, the two officers under orders to depart with one of the iron boats to Lake Albert when porters became available; and Linant, an Arabic speaker, with the other boat, to lead a second expedition to the *kabaka* of Buganda, M'tesa, carrying a letter from the Khedive.

Colonel Long had arrived back from his visit to M'tesa after a six-month absence in October 1874. He was sent on by Gordon to Khartoum to recuperate and to bring up the military reinforcements approved by the Khedive when Gordon was in Khartoum in May. The Khedive had earlier intervened to divert Munzinger's four companies from Taka to reinforce Darfur. Now their Egyptian replacements from Gallabat, supplemented from Cairo, after an expedition up the Sobat to Nasir to disperse a Nuer raid, arrived back with Long at Lado on

11 January 1875 unfit, with the majority in early need of repatriation – 'I mourn over the idiocy.' Their commander, Bimbashi Ali el Lutfi, did however remain to supersede the unsatisfactory Egyptian military successor to Ra'uf Bey, Fuad Hasan.

Long was instructed by Gordon to lead an expedition west from Lado, through Niambara tribal country and across the Yei river, to Makaraka on the edge of Azande country. There he was to establish an additional *muderia* and a military garrison drawn from the reinforcements. Ernest Marno, by occupation little more than a trader and someone for whom Gordon developed an increasingly low opinion, attached himself to Long. According to the itinerary in the Abdin Palace archives, Long reached Wandi, the former El 'Aqqād *zariba* on the west bank of the Yei, on 9 February 1875 to be greeted by the former El 'Aqqād *wakil*, Ahmed Atrash Agha, now in government service but retaining his good ivory trading relationship with the Iddio Azande under their principal chief, Ringio of N'gerria.

Elsewhere in the southern Bahr el Ghazal the Dongolawi merchants, especially the Ghattas *zariba wakils*, had exploited the continuing anarchic conditions to their pecuniary advantage. In 1873 King Munza of Mangbattu (Monbuttu) had been assassinated, according to Gessi's subsequent declaration, by the *wakils* Yusuf es Shallali and Fadlallah, now respected *mudirs* at Rumbek and Makaraka. To the west of Makaraka Zubeir Pasha was in control and, in order to impose order and to protect the Nile–Yei route, Long appointed Ahmed Atrash Agha as *mamur* with a strong garrison of 117 Egyptian regulars at Makaraka. Long returned to report to Gordon, now at Rejaf, on 17 March 1875 and then, after five days of discussions, left for Khartoum. In the event he was not to return to Equatoria. Despite the success of his expeditions to Buganda, Nasir and Makaraka, his relationship with Gordon had never been close and regrettably, due to the indiscreet publication of a private letter written by Gordon, it was to turn to open hostility.[11]

By the new year of 1875 Gordon had been committed for four months to Gondokoro and the south of his province. He was anxious to reassure himself about the stability of the administration in the north of the governorate when the leases of the trading stations expired, in anticipation of which the *wakils* were making attempts to export slaves to the north. The dry season was advanced, and Gordon took the opportunity in late January 1875 to escort the repatriation of the now sick Watson and to visit the Sobat *muderia*.

Back in August 1874 at Sobat mouth, finding that an El 'Aqqād cargo of ivory from the Bahr el Jebel concealed ninety-six slaves, Gordon had released the slaves and confiscated the ivory. The day before his departure for Gondokoro he had found another twenty-five slaves on a government steamer, making a total of 500–600 released over two months. The traders of Ghattas and Kuchuk Ali on the Zeraf had deceitfully outmanoeuvred Gordon at Sobat in respect of most of their slaves consigned to the north in August 1874, only to have their cargoes intercepted at Fashoda. Unlike their *wakils*, the traders themselves escaped arrest. A further penalty was however imposed on the Zeraf *wakil* of Ghattas who was arrested for having failed to surrender his balance of ivory to Khartoum by the end of the year, and his stock was confiscated.

The good relations which Gordon had initially forged in June with Yusuf Bey Hasan Khorda, *mudir* at Fashoda since 1873, had deteriorated. In June Gordon had arranged that Fashoda should supply the new Tawfiqia post with *dura* in an emergency. Some four months later, with 3,000 men, Kwickon, alias Yul, son of the deceased Reth Kwatker of the Shilluk, took refuge from Yusuf Bey's oppression at Sobat mouth (he had already complained to Gessi about his ill-treatment in June). Then in December Yusuf Bey roughly refused Surur Agha's request for *dura*. In January 1875 Gordon sent F. J. Russell (son of William Howard Russell) to Fashoda as his liaison officer and to superintend the vital Nile steamers – 'it was the best place for provisions after Khartoum.' Russell had just come to Tawfiqia in search of employment. (Captain Frederic Burnaby was another arrival whom Gordon met there – he had come to cover Gordon's administration for *The Times*.) Within the year Yusuf Bey had been killed in the Shilluk insurrection, which was only narrowly defeated (see p. 210). Kwickon Kwatker would become *reth*.

In the main, however, Gordon was not dissatisfied with the conditions he found in the north of the province. In a letter dated 30 August 1874 the Khedive had stressed the priority of his instruction to suppress the slave trade, to which Gordon rejoined that the Bahr el Ghazal traffic continued unimpaired. For all that, he was confident that in his own governorate progress had been made and that he could relax his vigilance somewhat in the vicinity of the Sobat mouth, hitherto deserted following the *razzias* in the early 1860s against the Shilluk and Dinka.

Punctilious as to his province's revenue commitment to Cairo for the eight months of 1874, Gordon exported 500 cwt of ivory to reach Suez by early February 1875.[12]

2 THE LACUSTRINE KINGDOMS AND THE INDIAN OCEAN 1875–76

An Indian Ocean Outlet?   En route from Gondokoro for the fortnight he would spend on the Sobat, Gordon wrote to Stanton in Cairo on 2 February 1875:

> I am going to Sobat to settle those stations for 8 or 10 months, so as to leave me free to go to Fatiko, so you will not hear much from me for a long time. My great object is to establish safe roads and communication between my stations… I am determined if I live, and if the Khedive does not recall me for any reason, to die here or to make some little improvement in the country.

Fatiko however was not the only objective which Gordon, charged with the opening up of trade and communications with the Lakes, had been pondering. The administration of his Equatoria province predicated not only a geopolitical structure but also a staff to implement the responsibilities. Within the first six months of his service in Equatoria he had lost, through death or illness, his original European team with the exception of Gessi (posted back to Khartoum in November 1874 to ensure reliable river supplies to Gondokoro) and Chaillé-Long (despatched to Buganda in April 1874). Gordon himself had remained fit, increasingly aware that the harsh climate of the Upper Nile was a major hazard to Europeans, as it was to Egyptian troops.

As early as 5 September 1874, with his sick European colleagues at Gondokoro prostrate around him, he had canvassed with Cairo for a second time the reappointment of Mohammed Ra'uf Bey – this time as his direct successor, and had voiced his own interest in exploring the lands to the east between Buganda and the Indian Ocean, a route which had excited the interest of Speke in 1862. In December 1874 he succumbed to an attack of dysentery while alone for a month at Gondokoro, at a time when he was depressed by the calibre of Egyptian officers and by Schweinfurth's revelations of the Bahr el Ghazal slave trade in *The Heart of Africa*. He even began to question his own role in Equatoria: 'Am I a tool to delude the blacks into submission prior to their ruin in perspective? Am I a tool to obtain some favour from our [British] government?... I puzzle my brains as to what the Khedive will do eventually with these countries. He will never get an Arab Government to do anything except with 5000 to 6000 troops and then he will find it hard enough to make it pay.'

By the end of December Gordon was reaching the conclusion that in the establishment of an Egyptian port in the bay of Formosa north of Mombasa, on the Indian Ocean, scarcely 400 miles from Buganda, lay the key to the development of Equatorial Africa. Communications between Khartoum and a remote station like Fatiko could be cut off from the north for six months a year; and between Lado and Khartoum the availability of wood for the steamers was progressively diminishing. He feared that an Equatoria province as at present constituted would not be self-sufficient, whereas a base on the bay of Mombasa would give easier access to the rich countries of central Africa and strengthen the Khedivial province, which was presently dependent on Nile steamers from Khartoum only able to cover the distance three times a year. He wrote to Cairo on 2 and 21 January 1875 advocating an Indian Ocean outlet and also on the 21st to his sister:

> I have proposed to the Khedive to send 150 men in a steamer to Mombasa Bay, 250 miles north of Zanzibar, and there to establish a station, and thence to push towards M'tesa. If I can do that I shall make my base at Mombasa and give up Khartoum and the bother of the steamers etc.... The Centre of Africa would be much more effectually opened out as the only valuable parts of the country are the high lands near M'tesa, while all south of this and Khartoum is wretched marsh. I hope the Khedive will do it.

When Long arrived from Khartoum on 11 January 1875, Gordon must have discussed his plans with him in depth for, before their respective departures to the Sobat and Makaraka, Long wrote to the Chief of Staff, Charles Stone Pasha, in Cairo developing Gordon's plans, urging the despatch of a steamer with 200 troops from Suez to Mombasa Bay and begging the Khedive to appoint him, with Gordon's agreement, to command this mission. Gordon intended to concentrate his attention 'on the territories near the Lakes and to the east towards the sea'. Critical to this plan, however, would be the appointment of a general-governor of the province as successor to Gordon to be based at Lado, and yet again it was the name of Mohammed Ra'uf, now *lewa* and *pasha*, despite his manifest shortcomings, which Gordon urged. The

Khedive's acknowledgement to both Gordon and Long, in cypher dated 15 February, enjoining them to absolute secrecy, simply instructed Long to discuss the plan further with Gordon before coming to Cairo. That doubtless formed the principal agenda of their further meeting at Rejaf on 17–22 March, but in fact Douin says that Long did not receive the message until he arrived back in Khartoum on 7 April. Meanwhile Ra'uf Pasha had been alerted to leave Cairo with Sudanese troop replacements for Long's Egyptian contingent of December 1874.

Without any commitment to Gordon's proposed strategy, Cairo signalled on 28 February 1875 that Ra'uf Pasha would be leaving for Khartoum in ten days' time; and when Long, returning to Khartoum on 7 April, had decyphered the Khedivial message of 15 February, he had indeed been granted authority to proceed to Cairo; and he arrived there on 22 May. No progress was to be made with the Indian Ocean project for a further four months. On 31 May Cairo advised Gordon that Ra'uf would not after all be returning to Equatoria (later Gordon lamented that Ra'uf was to lead the expedition to annexe Harar). Even Gordon in his letter to Cairo of 7 May considered it wise now to halt the Indian Ocean outlet proposal until he had been able to assess the situation when he arrived at Lake Victoria. Meanwhile he urged that Long should remain in Cairo preparing detailed expedition plans. In further letters to Khairi Pasha, the Privy Seal, of 26–27 June and 17 July Gordon continued to refine his plans, speculating that using the land route he might be best advised to make his headquarters no further east than Mount Kenya which could have navigable river access by the Dana river. Cairo fell silent.[13]

While the Indian Ocean venture hung fire, there was only slow progress over the planned string of military stations to Bunyoro and the exploration of Lake Albert. The rigours of the climate had again taken their toll of important personnel – in this case Ernest Linant on the eve of his departure to M'tesa; the engineer Kemp at Dufile; and then of the promising Lieutenants Watson and Chippendall, deputed to lead the expedition to Lake Albert. Succumbing successively to fever by January 1875, Watson and Kemp both had to be repatriated. Chippendall, after a spell of convalescence at Lado, was first to return to Rejaf to head the Lake Albert expeditions and then to leave, with the caravan of porters brought by Wad el Mek from Fuweira with ivory, to explore the navigability of the Upper Nile between Dufile and the Lake. Likewise Linant had recovered sufficiently to leave for Fatiko, Fuweira and

Lake Victoria on 18 January. Gordon however had already concluded in a letter to Cairo of 15 January 1875:

> My experience of the past year has decided me no longer to request [European employees] of the Khedive except engineers to maintain the boats at Khartoum and two masters to command the steamers plying between Khartoum and Lado. As soon as these explorations are complete, I wish to repatriate the English officers and M. Linant who is personally employed by me; it is necessary to govern this country as it will be governed on my departure.

The reality was that at this stage the Khedive, while anxious to afford Gordon all support to annexe the lacustrine kingdoms of Bunyoro and Buganda, was unpersuaded that the best outlet to Egypt for their trade was not down the Nile. The possibility of enlarging his Viceroyalty to include east Africa and Somalia already whetted his ambition – Colonel Purdy, after all, in his planned expedition to seek out the missing Sir Samuel Baker in 1873 (subsequently aborted by the latter's reapappearance), had been instructed to seek a landing on the Indian Ocean. Indeed the Khedive was already cultivating good relations with the Sultan of Zanzibar, but Zanzibar was under British protection and had rival claims to the coastal area. So in the early part of 1875, notwithstanding the proposals of Gordon and Long for the seizure of an Indian Ocean port, the Khedive was not yet willing to commit himself to such a huge territorial acquisition. Gordon's instructions of February 1874 remained unamended: these had simply described the route to the Equator in terms of the opening of communications across the several rapids preventing navigation of some seventy miles of the upper White Nile. Even the Khedivial letter dated 23 July and received apparently on 20 November 1875, while acknowledging Gordon's letters up to May 1875, still made no reference to the Indian Ocean outlet strategy. We shall shortly examine why the Khedive was at last, on 17 September 1875, ready to entertain Gordon's proposal – a year after he had initially canvassed it.[14]

The Lacustrine Kingdoms: a Limited Progress, 1875   With the northern part of the province reasonably tranquil, the slavers' *meshras* disbanded, and progress towards an Indian Ocean outlet stalled, Gordon with his much diminished team set about the geographical exploration of the, as yet, uncharted sections of the White Nile between Dufile and Lake Albert Nyanza; of the Somerset and Victoria Niles between Magungo and Lake Victoria; and the circumnavigation of Lake Albert. All this was finally to be accomplished by September 1876. The accurate location of the many falls and rapids, and the extent of their navigability to steamers and shallow-draft boats was essential knowledge in determining the truth of Baker's untested claim that the locality of Dufile was 'destined to become the capital of Central Africa' and the focus of the region's trade.

Gordon's ultimate political objective was the annexation of the lacustrine kingdoms of the Equatorial region, Buganda being 600 miles from Lado and 3,300 miles from Cairo. Their occupation presently presupposed a chain of military stations to ensure the security of future lines of communication. Gordon had inherited Baker's Fatiko, previously commanded by Sagh Abdallah, now by El Nur Agha Mohammed (with Wad el Mek); and Fuweira under Sagh Bakheit – like the late Abdallah a veteran of the French Mexican war. Both these posts were visited by Chaillé-Long en route to M'tesa at his capital Kibuga (Dubaga), where Long spent a month (20 June to 19 July 1874) discussing the relative merits of trading Buganda ivory with Gondokoro and Zanzibar and listening to M'tesa's urging that the Egyptians should attack the treacherous Kabarega of Bunyoro. Having received a cordial visit from Rionga, Kabarega's hated uncle, on his way up to M'tesa, Long found himself on his return journey by the Somerset Nile through Lake Kioga violently attacked by Kabarega's military. On his safe return to Gondokoro on 18 October after six months' absence, he was promoted at once to *miralai* on his chief's grateful initiative, but Gordon was prudently hesitant to launch any immediate expedition against Kabarega. But, in the face of Baker's experience, Gordon's earlier decision to send him presents from the Khedive had certainly proved mistaken.

Gordon was nevertheless persuaded that additional military posts must be established at Dufile and Laboré and a second reliable envoy despatched to M'tesa. The timely arrival in December 1874 of Lieutenants Watson and Chippendall and of Ernest Linant who, like his deceased brother, became a charge on Gordon's personal funds had provided both the opportunity to garrison Dufile and to appoint an experienced envoy to Buganda.

That envoy, Ernest Linant, left Rejaf on 18 January 1875 across land to Apuddo (Fashali), thence through Acholi and Madi country to Fatiko and to Fuweira on the Somerset Nile bound for M'tesa's capital Kibuga. Douin had access to Linant's pocket diary which, following his subsequent death in August 1875, found its way to the Royal Geographical Society of Cairo and which, together with the Abdin Palace letters from Linant despatched at intervals to Gordon, form the source of our knowledge of Linant's expedition. No formal instructions from Gordon are extant but the diary indicates authority to take control of the frontier district (Fuweira) with Bunyoro and Buganda and command over government troops, conferring on Linant complete discretion regarding the competing claims to Bunyoro of Kabarega and Rionga. The principal task was to forge friendly relations with 'these kings', and further to propagate a money economy of copper coins. Six government soldiers were to be stationed with M'tesa and contact made if possible with the king Ruwanika at Karagwe to the south.

Linant reached Fatiko on 5 February 1875, where he was joined by the new commander for the Laboré post, Ali Agha. Ordering the evacuation of all Dongolawi traders and their militia to Gondokoro, Linant pressed on to Fuweira where on 4 March a similar task awaited him. He found however that Sulieman, the former El 'Aqqād *wakil*, despatched to Kabarega at Masindi on a similar mission, had represented to Kabarega that he came as the representative of Abu Sa'ud, not Gordon, and with his twenty-nine Dongolawiyin had resumed trade in ivory and cattle and in Bunyoro *razzias*. Prohibited by Gordon from direct intervention against Kabarega, Linant was impotent, but by April Sulieman had died from illness. More successful, however, was Linant's meeting with Rionga (aged about fifty) who explained that his grandfather Nyamtoucara had divided Bunyoro between his three sons, Mouguénia being *makama* but that Kamrasi, Rionga's brother, had on his own accession claimed sovereignty over all Bunyoro, encouraged by Abu Sa'ud and his *wakils* on their arrival.

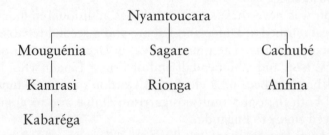

Like Baker and Long before him, Linant was impressed by Rionga's bearing and his cooperative attitude, and he further strengthened the government's hold on the frontier district by entering into friendly relations with Rionga's brother, Anfina, whose headquarters were only twenty miles away but whose territory extended west and to the north of Lake Albert N'yanza.[15]

Two delegations arrived at Fuweira from the *kabaka* M'tesa, the first with letters directed to Gordon, seeking a reader in the Koran and sundry medicaments, the second, when Linant's presence was known, a visit of Moslem missionaries. These expedited Linant's departure from Fuweira for Kibuga and M'tesa on 28 March.

Linant had been pondering Gordon's instructions to establish a frontier communications post at Urondogani between Equatoria and the lacustrine kingdoms – whether it be under government or local control. Now on his march to M'tesa he left behind the ravaged areas of Abu Sa'ud *wakils* and, entering the former Rionga district of M'rouli, he recognised this rich well-populated countryside as the ideal site for a *muderia*. He pressed on to Kibuga where he was received by M'tesa on 11 April and met, fortuitously, Henry Stanley in the course of his circumnavigation of Lake Victoria–N'yanza. Although anxious to extol the merits of the Christian religion, Stanley recognised the prevailing local order and discipline to be due to a poor Moslem teacher of M'tesa. Significantly during their three days together Stanley noted that Linant's somewhat imperious bearing did not excite the respect of the Bugandans.

A serious manifestation of Linant's attitude had already appeared on the day of his arrival at Kibuga when he encountered a Dongolawi, Ba-Baker, who had been M'tesa's emissary to Gondokoro with presents for the Khedive on the arrival of Gordon and Long in April 1874. He had accompanied Long back to Kibuga and now greeted Linant with familiarity, having meanwhile represented to M'tesa that he, Ba-Baker, was the Sultan's representative while Long and Linant were merely Christian officers in the Sultan's army. Warned of this by Sagh Bakheit, Linant had Ba-Baker arrested, beaten, and imprisoned as a public display of his authority and to keep Ba-Baker away from M'tesa.

The meetings with the *kabaka* did not go very smoothly. The latter's first enquiry betrayed his priorities: would Linant join him in war against Kabarega? Linant declined. M'tesa then insisted on offering both slaves and ivory for purchase, to which Linant rejoined that the slave trade was now forbidden. As for trading ivory, M'tesa continued, that was a monopoly in the hands of 1000 Zanzibari miscreants who obtained a better price for his ivory in Zanzibar than they could in Gondokoro, and also had no problem in selling slaves to the coast. In this regard, it was an impertinence of Rumanika of Karagwe currently to close the south route to the coast. Less contentious (in the wake of Stanley) were their discussions on religion and philosophy, following which M'tesa announced on 24 May his willingness to prohibit slave trading in his territories and to trade with Fuweira, Fatiko and Lado in ivory, cattle, coffee and butter.

A week later, on a reconnaissance towards Urondogani, having still failed to gain assent to depart for Lado, Linant encountered an Egyptian officer with a message from Gordon to come back at once. Returning to Kibuga, he advised M'tesa accordingly and said he would be leaving with the militia who had accompanied Ba-Baker from Gondokoro and had deserted on arrival. A new hostile atmosphere was detectable, probably engendered by the escape of Ba-Baker whom Linant had humiliated. A delegation then arrived from Kabarega for talks with the *kabaka*, and when Linant took his leave of M'tesa on 12 June 1875, he was told the presents for the Khedive and Gordon would follow later, while of the deserter militia there was no mention.

On 15 June Linant marched, to be held back eight days from crossing the frontier into Bunyoro while a suspiciously large escort of Bugandans arrived. Convinced of their hostility, he relegated them to the rear. He then embarked on four days of forced marches to M'rouli, sacrificing his baggage and cattle. With his Rionga militia he fought off an attack by Kabarega's brother on 5 July and crossed the River Kafu into the safety of M'rouli. Gordon's order to return denied him his chance to establish a government station. But the shortcomings of the expedition went further than that. On 11 July 1875 he wrote to Gordon from Rionga's capital:

> The intention of M'tesa was to have me assassinated, thinking thus to seize the Khedivial force. He did not dare perpetrate the crime in his own territory in order to preserve friendly relations which he found most profitable. The attack would be held against Kabarega, while he, M'tesa, would have gained the honour and glory for having picked up some of the pieces. In any case if M'tesa is not the author of this attack, he is at least an accomplice.

Despite a Nile in flood he returned safely to meet Gordon at Moogie on 22 August. Two and a half years later Emin would find the initials both of Long and of Linant on a fig tree near Kibuga.[16]

While Linant was approaching M'tesa's capital, Chippendall probing by land the accessibility of Lake Albert by the Nile from Dufile, and

Long arriving at Khartoum en route for Cairo, Gordon quit Rejaf on 30 March 1875. This was his first reconnaissance to determine the navigability of the Nile south through the Makadé rapids to Dufile. As far as Kerri the rapids appeared to present no insuperable problem, strengthening his belief, as he had written to Khairi Pasha on 5 April, that while the overland route to Fatiko might be more direct, the riverside route was preferable in that it afforded protection against hostile attack from both sides. Moreover it provided an assured supply of drinking water; and, with the use of wooden *nuggars*, it avoided the besetting problem of porter recruitment. Thus in addition to a first military station established at Bedden, a second followed at Kerri in early June 1875, a third at Moogie as the rainy season drew to its close in September, and a fourth at Laboré ('the true one at last') fifteen miles from Dufile a few weeks later. The 100-mile stretch between Rejaf and Dufile would be linked by a chain of riverain lightly garrisoned military stations each within a day's walking distance, and requiring a security escort of no more than two men. Moreover once those stations were all established and the Nile torrents over the minor rapids subsided, it should be possible to convey the remaining heavy parts of the steamer *N'yanza* from Rejaf up to Dufile for assembly.

This was a strenuous period for Gordon, working with his men on the rapids manhandling the wooden boats, repulsing attacks from a minority of hostile tribesmen.

'Up at dawn and to bed at eight or nine p.m.; no books but <u>one</u> and that not often read for long for I cannot sit down for a study of those mysteries. All day long worrying about writing orders to be obeyed by others in the degree as they are near or distant from me.' Deliveries were rare, diet poor; companionship sparse. Chippindall had to be repatriated in July suffering from a scrofulous growth on his neck. When Ernest Linant arrived back at Moogie in August, he conceded that Gordon looked ten years older than when they had parted in January. Four days later Linant would be dead. Only El Nur Agha Mohammed, who had arrived from Fatiko in September, 'a truly good officer', proved able to shoulder some of his responsibilities. Yet, Gordon confided to his sister Augusta on 29 June:

I ask God for the following things: – 1. Not to be disturbed if the Khedive sent me away to-morrow. 2. Not to be disturbed if he keeps me. 3. Not to have anything of the world come between Him and me; and not to fear death or to feel regret if it came before I completed what I may think my programme. Thank God, He gives me the most comforting assurance that nothing shall disturb me, or come between Him and me.

In the course of the work linking Rejaf to Dufile, Gordon returned to Lado from 12 June to 7 July. He found a state of complete inactivity – for which Ali Lutfi paid the price of dismissal. The erection of a palisade defence was put in hand but on Gordon's departure the steamers awaited from Khartoum had still to materialise. Worse, when at last mail caught him up at Bedden on 19 July, there was no letter from the Khedive. Not until 20 November did he receive one, written on 23 July. Nevertheless, as Gordon wrote to Watson, 'it is a blessing that a couple of men can go from Lado to Kerri without fear and I have established regular post.'[17]

On 22 August Ernest Linant had found Gordon at Moogie under harassment from bordering tribes and awaiting the arrival of Baker's *Khedive* carrying ninety troops, itself threatened from the right bank. He had had time to brief Gordon on his unfruitful meeting with M'tesa and the overt hostility of Kabarega, and now offered to draw off from the *Khedive* the threat of the same enemy whom he had dealt with so fiercely on his outward journey by attacking their villages. He was ambushed and only four of his inadequate party survived. Many years later Ibrahim Fawzi, Gordon's bodyguard commander, reported that Linant had been found to have suffered a cruel death by crucifixion. Gordon was yet again denied an experienced counsellor and commander.

El Nur Agha now brought 500 men, a force he could ill afford to lose, sufficient to restore Gordon's domination of the river and to establish his last station at Laboré on 23 September 1875. Gordon's revenge on the killers of Linant from the right bank had to await the drying-out and burning of the long grass in December. He was exhausted and, atypically, his morale was suffering, in so much that he was now losing faith in the Ocean outlet plan, having learned from Linant that the overland distance from Lake Victoria to Mount Kenya would be 200, not 70 miles. Without a reference to the outlet, in a letter to Khairi Pasha that day, he scaled down his Equatoria objective from one of civilisation to one of military occupation financed by the export of ivory.

By the month of August [1876] I think that two steamers will be on the Lake (Albert), the stations will be well established, Kabarega will have surrendered and it will be very easy to advance towards Lake Victoria, if the Khedive judges it necessary. That advance will assuredly tumble M'tesa.

Gordon's duty would then be fulfilled. The arrival of an energetic, not a barrack sedentary, successor must precede August 1876, but after that Gordon saw no future benefit from his own presence. With the assembly of the paddle-steamer *Ismailia* completed at Khartoum and of the *Khedive*, having left Lado early July, now approaching Dufile where the 10 h.p. *N'yanza* awaited assembly, Gordon recommended the building at Khartoum of a repair workshop answerable to the Cairo arsenal, not to the *hakimdar*.

The solitude of the summer months had led to further heart-searching. He had written to Augusta on 15 July 1875: 'I think what right have I to coax the nations to be quiet, for them to fall into the hands of a rapacious pasha after my departure?' And to Stanton on 21 September: 'Why should I stay when I see it is hopeless; the civilisers need the civilisation as much as the natives. "We do not want your beads, we do not want your cloth, we are on our land and we want you to go away" is the natives' answer.' His earlier reservations about upsetting Kabarega and M'tesa by going to the Lakes had been dispelled, however, by the verbal report from Ernest Linant demonstrating beyond doubt Kabarega's absolute hostility to Egyptian advance and M'tesa's duplicitous support for Kabarega's stance while affecting friendship for the Khedive. M'tesa's conversion to Islam was a mockery.

At last, on 9 October 1875, Gordon reached Dufile from Laboré to test the navigability of the Makadé (Fola) rapids – seventh cataract of the Nile. 'I have sent for my horses and hope to ride up to Makadé to look at the route.' On 17 October he

> came upon it [the Falls] about 5 [up river] miles from here... there it was, appalling to look at, far less to think of getting anything up or down except in splinters; it was more the rush down a slope of 1 in 6 than a fall... These shoots last for two miles, they are close on the junction of Asua with Nile... of course it is all over – the idea of taking up the screw steamer or the *nuggars* or indeed anything... it is rather sad for it will give a mint of trouble and delay.

Back at Apuddo (Fashelu), east of Dufile and close to Miani's tree (now cut down) on the Unyama river, an affluent of the Nile, he awaited the burning of the long grass before exacting punitive revenge for

Linant's death, and reflected further on his planned approach to Bunyoro via Fatiko. New stations would be needed on the Victoria Nile at Magungo, Anfina, M'ruli and on Lake Victoria. It was a moment of temporary relaxation terminating in a liver complaint. Returning to Dufile, on 15 November, he there received mail including the Khedivial letter of 23 July. In it there was no reference to the Ocean outlet projects, but instead an instruction to explore the source of the Sobat river and to establish telegraphic communication up that river to forestall a threatened Italian expedition. Even more antagonising were the strictures contained in the letter on the financial administration of his province. He at once drafted telegrams announcing his return to Cairo by April and requesting the immediate appointment of a successor. Packing of his baggage was put in hand. Only the discovery of a second letter from the Khedive, dated 17 September, on the next day (16 November) in the same mail bag mollified his anger sufficiently to revoke his decision to resign.

Gordon was determined nevertheless to dispel the criticisms of his financial actions which had touched a sensitive nerve in a man of exceptional probity. He had been denied assistance with his accounts, obliged to send his revenue ivory for sale in Cairo rather than Khartoum and, with his advance southwards, he was inevitably incurring new expenses. He submitted the present computation of his annual military and river transport costs at £E43,000, for which he could find half. While local revenues were unpredictable, he went on to advise Khairi Pasha in January 1876 that he had, over two years, sent to Cairo and Khartoum ivory to a value of £E120,000 against material receipts for his province of £E40,000. £E15,000 worth of that ivory had been recently despatched north.

In that important second Khedivial letter of 17 September there was no further reference to the urgent priority of a Sobat expedition. Gordon had no hesitation in dismissing the idea anyway, reminding Cairo of the station founded at Nasir by Nasir Ali, an agent of Kuchuk Ali under Long's orders late in 1874 (see p. 280), which itself was but a few days' march from Fadassi on the Abyssinian border and, in tandem with Sobat mouth, ideal for monitoring geographical expeditions. Telegraph communication was needed but parallel with a road between Bor and Tawfiqia rather than up the Sobat, and this was budgeted for 1876.[18]

The Indian Ocean Littoral: Failure of an Expedition 1875   The principal content of the Khedivial letter dated 17 September and reaching Gordon at Dufile on 15 November was the belated endorsement of

Gordon's Ocean outlet proposal originally developed in January 1875. It had hung fire for considerations unknown to Gordon, during which time his own enthusiasm had waned.

Warmly acknowledging Gordon's advice to Nubar in a letter of 4 April 1875 that he believed that the slave trade in his province had now been suppressed, the Khedive expressed concern in the letter at Gordon's apparent ultimatum to him that a Sudanese successor would have to be found unless he, the Khedive, sanctioned the establishment of an outlet for trade to the Ocean. He conceded that Gordon had been pressing the idea 'depuis un an' against the Khedive's own belief that down the Nile northwards was the best trade exit, but he affirmed that Gordon's mission to the Lake regions had as its objective the establishment of security, the suppression of the slave trade and, as a necessary consequence, the opening of these vast lands to European trade. 'The first idea which naturally presented itself to my mind is that the commerce should take the Nile route as the most natural and easiest.'

However the Khedive now bowed to Gordon's locally informed judgement, and formally extended Gordon's provincial powers to include all lands between the Lakes and the Ocean littoral with the same objectives, namely to impose security, suppress the slave trade and develop commerce.

As to the location of the outlet, while in his letters to the Khedive Gordon had proposed Formosa Bay 'only 280 miles' (actually 450) from Lake Victoria, he had latterly, to Khairi Pasha, mentioned additionally Juba and Durnford, both north of Formosa Bay, lest Zanzibar had a claim on the last. Juba mouth had the advantage of being the uncontested frontier between Zanzibar and the Somali lands, the north of which were already Egyptian-occupied. A route from Juba would be 100 miles longer to the Lakes but it should avoid any political challenges. Despite having written to James Grant, Speke's companion, in January 1875 'to ask him to get me certain maps of the coast' and enjoining him to secrecy, he had received nothing from Grant and was to blame him on this account for the subsequent débacle.

Juba river, the Khedive now instructed, would indeed be the outlet. Enclosed was a copy of instructions to Lewa H. F. McKillop Pasha, the designated leader of the Egyptian naval expedition, placing him under Gordon's orders. An accompanying letter from Nubar Pasha, now restored to his ministerial post, explained that on Gordon's own recommendation Long Bey would command McKillop's land forces. The supreme objective, it was laboured, remained commerce. As to Gordon, his own land transit force should consist of five companies rather than the single one he had indicated, and the Khedive was sending Yusuf Bey Hasan Khorda from Fashoda to be his deputy. If this were agreeable to Gordon, the former's *muderia* of Fashoda would be transferred to Gordon's government. Already in October Yusuf Bey, however, had perished in the Shilluk rising at Kaka, a month before the Khedive's letter of 17 September 1875 reached Gordon.

The Khedive was wary of the possible claims of the Sultan of Zanzibar to the coast, recognising the Sultan to be under British protection and to have acquiesced in June 1873, following the mission of Sir Bartle Frere, in the prohibition of slave transportation within his boundaries *by sea*. As a reward for his cooperation, the Sultan Bargash bin Said had been invited to Britain on a State visit for a month in June 1875 and, returning via France, he was then received with much honour in Egypt where he spent a further spell (6–24 August) as the Khedive's guest. In the course of private conversation, the Sultan in August let drop to the Khedive his intention of hoisting the Zanzibar flag at the Juba river mouth and at Ras Hafoun on the Horn of Africa just south of Cape Gardafui. A few days after this revelation the Khedive received Gordon's latest outlet proposal mentioning the Juba alternative, that river being the accepted southern boundary of Somalia country.

Faced with the Sultan's challenge to his own claim to Somalia following the recent Egyptian occupation of Zeyla and Berbera, the Khedive, in the wake of Mohammed Ra'uf's successful annexation of Harar, and on the day of Arendrup's appointment to command the expedition into Hamasein (17 September 1875), determined to act. He despatched instructions to McKillop Pasha of the Egyptian Navy, who was currently in the Red Sea, to lead an expedition of four warships and five companies of soldiers under Long Bey; occupy the Juba mouth, install a garrison, and seize a safe mooring in its vicinity. McKillop, placed under Gordon's command, had the overall objective of policing the territory between the littoral and the Lakes; but McKillop was ordered not to march into the interior until his base was secure and the Sultan's aspirations abandoned. En route McKillop, supported by Mohammed Radwan Pasha, was to occupy Guardafui or Ras Hafoun. The prime destination of Juba mouth was to remain strictly secret. The Khedivial letter to Gordon was mailed simultaneously.

Acknowledging the Khedive's letter, Gordon wrote circumspectly on 21 November 1875 to Khairi that he found the Khedive's new instructions 'très claires et très bonnes'; having reached M'ruli, and been supported from the Ocean by the Egyptian occupation of the coast, Gordon would find himself in a strong position vis à vis Zanzibar and must hasten to plant the flag on Lakes Victoria and Albert Nyanza. Stanley's discovery that Lakes Victoria and Baringo were not contiguous would necessarily lengthen the travel distance to the coast; 'mais avec de la persévérance je pense que nous réussirons à temps voulu et il est bon, tout au moins, d'avoir un point sur la côte en vue de l'avenir'.[19]

Nubar, in a covering letter to Gordon also dated 17 September, in which he attributed his own recent silence to absence following dismissal, took the view that when the Khedivial instructions became known in Europe they would gain universal approval. So indeed the Khedive had concluded when, during an unexpected visit of the Prince of Wales to Cairo with Sir Bartle Frere on 23–26 October 1875, the subject being broached, no political difficulty had been seen to arise from the Egyptian occupation.

In the interim, the expedition had made progress. McKillop, having duly raised the Egyptian flag at Ras Hafoun on 7 October, arrived at Juba mouth on 16 October 1875. As the seas were too rough to land, they sailed on that day to Kismayu, Somali populated but in Zanzibar hands, and occupied it by force, Radwan nominated governor. Long returned by land to Juba. McKillop then sailed from Kismayu to take the submission of the Somalis at Brava before returning south again seeking coal, fresh water and provisions. A landing was effected with difficulty eight miles up the Juba river on 30 October but the mooring remained unsafe, and in a letter, drafted if not despatched, McKillop warned Gordon that he was without any means of transport to approach the Lakes. If that problem were overcome, McKillop would best march west south west to Mount Kenya.

Now on 29 October, three days after the departure of the Prince of Wales from Egypt, the Khedive abandoned caution and instructed McKillop (the orders reached him on 16 November) to establish bases in Formosa bay and Durnford – to where the River Uzy or Tana flowed, west-east from the interior, avoiding any existing Zanzibari port. That done he was personally to reconnoitre for safe anchorages and light-beacons along the whole Somali coast between Formosa and Berbera. No suitable moorings could in the event be found south of Kismayu save at Lamu, where a hostile Zanzibari fort forced McKillop's withdrawal to avoid battle. He returned to Kismayu on 29 November.

News of Kismayu's seizure by force had meanwhile reached the Sultan on 7 November, and ten days later protests through the British consul-general at Zanzibar were on their way to the Khedive and to the Earl of Derby, the British foreign minister. On 11 November 1875 Stanton was surprised to learn from the Khedive that he intended to despatch reconnaissances from Harar across Abyssinia to the Blue Nile and Fazughli, and due south to the source of the Juba river.

The protest of Dr John Kirk, British consul-general at Zanzibar, on behalf of the Sultan apparently reached London at the end of November, triggering off instructions to Colonel Stanton to lodge the protest with the Khedive; to express the hope that any Egyptian expedition would be recalled; and to advise him that the action had been impolite and that participation 'in useless and distant wars' would adversely affect Egyptian financial credit over which British help was currently being sought. Another 'distant war', Hamasein, had just ended in the massacre of Arendrup's force at Gondet while at Aussa Munzinger's force had been defeated. Faced with the need both to mount a second expedition to Abyssinia in revenge and to solve the growing debt crisis, the Khedive prudently furled his sails on the Indian Ocean. He ordered McKillop to retire to Berbera, protesting to Britain that such *force majeure* meant the abandonment of his commitment to develop commerce and to suppress the slave trade in the region.[20]

Meanwhile, following a stand-off at the end of November at Brava between the Egyptian military commander and Kirk who, on his own initiative, landed from a British warship in response to a petition from 2,000 Indian British subjects, the Egyptian expedition maintained its positions at Kismayu and Juba mouth, pending fresh orders and the essential acquisition of coal for the steamers. If the Khedivial order to withdraw, dated 14 December 1875, reached McKillop on 22 December, delay in securing coal from Aden postponed his actual departure from Kismayu until 20 January 1876. He reached Suez on 5 February, the Khedivial flag continuing to fly only at Ras Hafoun. The Sultan of Zanzibar had enlarged his empire, but Kirk exacted as a reward a proclamation abolishing slavery in the northern territory and blocking the *land* slave route to Somali country.

Undaunted by yet another reverse to his territorial expansion, the Khedive, still emphasising his objectives of suppressing the slave trade and facilitating commerce with the Lakes, now sought British government help in purchasing Kismayu from the Sultan. However, as Gordon was to comment when on 12 March 1876 he eventually learnt from the newspapers of the McKillop expedition débacle: 'Above all, the Khedive ought first to have got the matter sorted diplomatically as he was recommended to do. He has now missed his chance for ever.' And so it proved.

The bona fides of the Khedivial démarche to Britain was finally undermined by the interception in Lamu, following the order to withdraw from Kismayu, of McKillop's finalised letter to Gordon. This revealed that the Khedive's revised instructions of November 1875 had targeted not only the occupation of the whole 300-mile Somali littoral north of Juba but of a further 200 miles south of Juba; and that McKillop believed Mombasa to be preferable even to Lamu as the Egyptian port for the Lakes. Kirk, invited to give his views on the Khedivial démarche to the British government, now exposed the real Khedivial aims, pointing out that M'tesa had already been approached to prohibit long-standing ivory commerce with Zanzibari merchants, so creating an Egyptian monopoly; and insisting that British influence on the east African slave trade was much more effectively exerted on the Sultan than on the Khedive.

The progenitor of the Ocean outlet plan and military commander designate was not too dismayed when in March 1876 he learned of the outcome. En route to M'ruli on 18 January, Gordon had written:

> I have quite given up the idea of going to the sea with these troops. My proposal was made to the Khedive in January 1875 and answered in November 1875. My proposal was that he took Formosa Bay or rather to the north of it where the Dana or Uzy River debouches… He sent off McKillop and Long to Juba and told them to wait for me. They will wait a long time I expect. I am not going to try this with the undisciplined wretched troops I have here and though he knows it, he does nothing to help me.

Any junction must be effected from the sea to the interior, not vice versa. That conclusion was however academic, for two days later McKillop had withdrawn from Kismayu. Moreover Nubar Pasha had already complacently written to Gordon on 10 November 1875, with news of the fate of Arendrup and Munziger still not known and soon after the fresh instructions issued to McKillop to land in Formosa Bay,

> We have two objectives: the Lakes and the sea… you will not commence your progress, certainly after the occupation of the Lakes and only when you wish and if you wish to. His Highness is in no way hastening on account of a route which sooner or later must be opened and can only be opened by himself.

However when news of McKillop's withdrawal did reach him, Gordon himself wrote to the British foreign minister, the Earl of Derby, claiming full responsibility for having counselled an Egyptian expedition but insisting that the objective of the latter was not territorial conquest such as he was leading to the Lakes at the moment, but simply to open up communications for European trade with the Equatorial region.

When eventually in September 1876 Gordon received a letter from the Khedive dated 23 July, there was no reference in it to the Ocean littoral withdrawal.[21]

The Lakes: a Campaign of Attrition 1876

By September 1875 Gordon had entirely separated his province from any supply dependence on the Sudan *hakimdaria* and had embarked upon a further extension of the chain of stations from Laboré (Laboré and Kerri were the principal stations) southwards not only to Dufile but – en route to Lake Victoria across the desert to Fatiko and Fuweira – to M'ruli, Urondogani and the Ripon Falls on the upper Victoria Nile. Above Dufile there would be the Nile link to Magungo on Lake Albert, thence eastwards by land beyond the Murchison Falls to a new post, Anfina, and so past continuous rapids on the Victoria Nile to Fuweira. Before he could safely establish himself on Lake Victoria (he declined to explore it personally), Gordon was convinced that Kabarega in Bunyoro would have to be quelled by the restoration to their territories of Rionga and Anfina, and by the occupation of Masindi. Similarly M'tesa must be neutralised in Buganda.

As to geographical surveys, Lake Albert would be made the responsibility of Romolo Gessi who arrived in the *Khedive* in November 1875 from Khartoum to oversee the *N'yanza*'s reassembly at Dufile, while Carlo Piaggia, who would leave with Gessi, was to map the Victoria Nile from Magungo to the Ripon Falls (Cossitza), navigable except by canoe only between Fuweira and Urondogani. They would both eventually depart from Dufile on 7 March 1876 in the two iron boats *Dufile* and *Magungo*, each with a capacity of some sixty men.

Having revenged Linant's death at Moogie, Gordon himself marched south across country from Apuddo on 31 December 1875, covering the forty-eight miles to Fatiko in three days ('I have great pain in my back and though I can walk my 14 miles, it makes me feel much fatigued) and the further sixty-five miles to Fuweira by 13 January 1876. On 22 January – to Rionga's delight – he garrisoned and duly ran up the

Khedivial flag at M'ruli, evacuated by Kabarega. As Kabarega had evidently also left Masindi Gordon, himself sick, delegated its occupation to Wad el Mek accompanied by Anfina with a garrison of 100. Gordon would return to Dufile on 8 February 1876, a month before Gessi's departure south to Lake Albert, in order to superintend the replenishment of supplies for the secure stations linking the south with Lado before the onset of the rains in March.[22]

Gordon had now completed two years' service and was anxious to discharge his undertakings in the southern limits of his province before returning to Cairo. He had, too, to reassure himself as to his successor and the stability of his *muderias* at Rohl and Bor, to be amalgamated in March 1876 under Ibrahim Fawzi; at Tawfiqia under Surur Bahjat; and at Lado under El Tayeb Bey Abdallah. The Khedivial flag had still to be raised on Lake Victoria and Lake Albert, and the lacustrine kingdoms of Buganda and Bunyoro brought under Khedivial subjection. Thankful at what had been achieved to consolidate his vulnerable lifeline of communications to the north, Gordon still remained cautious about M'tesa, now ostensibly converted back to Christianity; and by 28 January 1876 he had decided it would be wiser to negotiate M'tesa's compliance before occupying M'tesa's Urondogani between M'ruli and Ripon Falls. Accordingly El Nur Agha, left in charge at M'ruli on Gordon's return to Dufile, had been instructed to approach M'tesa and, if the latter did not agree to Urondogani's occupation, El Nur was to occupy Niamyango instead, nine miles to the north of Urondogani and previously in the possession of Kabarega until Gordon's capture of M'ruli.

Kabarega seemingly presented the lesser problem. M'ruli, Masindi and Anfina were being brought under Egyptian control, but Kabarega had vanished southwards, seeking aid from M'tesa. Not until he reached Wadelai on 14 March did Gessi, en route to Lake Albert, learn that Kabarega was seeking to rally his forces to reinforce Masindi (which, in the event, had not been occupied by Wad el Mek's contingent) in order to wrest back Anfina. Nearing Magungo on 20 March 1876, it was evident to Gessi that hostile Bunyoro forces occupied the eastern borders of Lake Albert to Vacovia and beyond. These forces were now to suffer casualties from Gessi's iron-clads. Only by pressing up the Magungo inlet to the Murchison Falls was Gessi able to effect a landing on 3 April, there to meet Wad el Mek who had just defeated a Bunyoro force.

The Bunyoro militia had taken refuge east of Magungo, and on 13 April they agreed to submit to Anfina and send him their ivory. Gessi, in

Wad el Mek's presence, had meanwhile formally raised the Khedivial flag at Magungo on 9 April, before sailing on to Vacovia and thereafter completing the circumnavigation of the Lake. South-eastern Bunyoro however remained in Kabarega's hands.[23]

Carlo Piaggia took leave of Gessi on 12 April, to negotiate the Murchison Falls and the further rapids east to Fuweira with a collapsible boat; and then south by water to M'ruli without encountering Bunyoro intervention. At M'ruli however on 3 May El Nur Agha was found to be absent: on Gordon's instructions he had already departed with 120 men on 16 April to visit M'tesa at Kibuga (M'tesa's capital), there to secure his goodwill to the establishment of posts at Urondogani and Cossitza (Ripon Falls). Charged with surveying the remaining section of the Victoria Nile, Piaggia set out with an escort direct for Urondogani, but his force being stricken with fever he was obliged to turn back after exploring Lake Kioga – where he formed the mistaken view that a 'hang-tail' branch outlet might connect with the Sobat. On 17 June 1876 he rejoined Gordon at Laboré. Gordon had been by then given to understand – by message from El Nur Agha – that Urondogani had been occupied on 10 May. It had not.

Without reliable news from Kibuga, Gordon continued to harbour his suspicions of M'tesa. A letter from M'tesa dated 6 February 1876 protested friendship, suggesting that they should divide Bunyoro between them: Gordon occupying the north and west, M'tesa the south and east. This was followed by three further letters over the next two months, affirming M'tesa's further religious conversion and requesting gold and rifles. In response Gordon, no bigoted sectarian and distrustful of M'tesa's conversions, sent him a Moslem elder to complement his new-found Christian zeal. At the same time he requested Cairo to despatch suitable gifts to M'tesa (these would come to Gordon's notice back at Khartoum in November). In May he commissioned his new medical officer at Lado, Dr Emin Effendi (Dr Edward Schnitzer, of Prussia), to undertake a further mission to M'tesa. Meanwhile the Khedive, seeking a publicity triumph in the wake of the second Abyssinian defeat, had exaggeratedly announced on 4 May the annexation by Egypt of 'all' the territories situated around the great Lakes Victoria and Albert in the interest of civilisation, agriculture and commerce.[24]

While Gessi, Piaggia and supposedly El Nur Agha were performing their designated tasks, Gordon after a month at Dufile had left on 9 March to visit the vital river stations on the way to Lado where he briefly re-established his personal authority, appointing his bodyguard *yuzbashi*, Ibrahim Fawzi, *mudir* of Bor and Rohl. He still had no time himself to allow a visit to Makaraka.

Following his departure south again on 3 April in the rains, to Dufile to check progress on the assembly of the *Nyanza*, he was to encounter Gessi at Kerri on 29 April returning from Lake Albert. The latter's personal achievement had been outstanding, but his news indicated that Kabarega was far from subdued and that M'tesa's compliance was still at best conjectural. Moreover Gessi's suspected Nile effluent north west from Wadelai suggested a possible tributary to Shambe (Rabat Shambil) which must be probed. Had the news of Bunyoro and Buganda been more sanguine, Gordon was considering leaving for Cairo with the opportunity it gave of further exploring the Sobat source (he had proposed such an expedition to Piaggia in March) and consolidating Tawfiqia against the Shilluk. But now he halted to reappraise the situation. In the absence still of any communication from the Khedive, he advised Khairi Pasha on 16 May that he was sending a member of the El 'Aqqād family to discuss a monopoly arrangement for the commercial development of Equatoria. Gordon would meanwhile return to Lado, but in a private letter to Stanton the next day he wrote:

> I am in rather a quandary as to what to do. The stations are completed to Lake Victoria and the steamer *Nyanza* is nearly finished... The question with me now is, shall I go on? I have the moral conviction that as soon as I leave, there will be a fine trade up here in slaves.

If he terminated his service now, he reckoned that he would have brought in net revenue over two and a half years of £E80,000.

By the end of May 1876 Gordon's mind was made up: he must return south again, boarding the reassembled steamer *N'yanza* above the Makéda rapids and, after probing Gessi's effluent at Wadelai, land at Magungo on Lake Albert, penetrate the southernmost section of the Victoria Nile to the Ripon Falls and there hoist the Khedivial flag at Cossitza. With flags hoisted on the two lakes, backed with military posts, by international law they should be deemed Egyptian domain, although in the case of Lake Victoria the presence of a Zanzibari slave dealer, Sungoro, M'tesa's scribe, with a *nuggar* on the Lake (?at Muanza) made the assent of the Zanzibari government – in the wake of the littoral débacle – diplomatically desirable.[25]

Gordon sailed south from Dufile on 20 July 1876, reaching

Magungo on 28 July, to experience the next day the last shower of the rainy season. On 2 August Wad el Mek and Anfina arrived from Masindi; Gordon had brought them a contingent to be landed at Kibero. However from El Nur Agha at M'ruli advice came by post that it was not at Urondogani that he had in fact built his stockade but, at M'tesa's invitation, at Kibuga. Agreeing to El Nur's proposal of Urondogani, M'tesa had then tricked him into sending back Rionga's porters with an unfulfilled promise to provide them himself, thus making El Nur's contingent virtually prisoners at Kibuga (as indeed had Kabarega previously with Baker's force at Masindi).

Gordon battled on, mapping 'a terrible road' from Magungo to Fuweira and arriving exhausted on 11 August to meet El Nur Agha in person. He was now obliged to telegraph Khairi Pasha, Keeper of the Privy Seal, in Cairo on 13 August about this reverse, with the additional news that M'tesa had hoisted Stanley's British flag and had been buying gunpowder from Zanzibar. The same day he wrote a private letter to Stanton, received about 20 October, confessing that the Ripon Falls would not be reached though he still aimed for Urondogani, and urging Stanton to persuade the Khedive to send up his successor.

El Nur Agha's entrapment in Kibuga had spoiled Gordon's strategy. It had been his shrewd intent to leave a *cordon sanitaire* between his Victoria Nile expedition and M'tesa, and if necessary to occupy Bunyoro's Niamyongo rather than Bugandan Urondogani across the frontier.

> Niamyongo is certainly very near M'tesa, and it is inevitable but that he will fall, for only 40 or 50 miles separate our territory from the Victoria Nyanza; but to my mind the pear is not ripe. We must have a steamer here first to work on the Nile to Urondogani. It will I hope be after I have left.

Indeed it would be, although on his journey through Laboré he had already provisionally planned the dismantling of the *Khedive* (108 tons) for reassembly on Lake Victoria; and by 11 October 1876 the workforce left Lado. He had already in February 1876 ordered seven additional ironclads – four for Lake Victoria, two more for Lake Albert; and one for the Victoria Nile – but their delivery would take a year. As meanwhile a second steamer would be necessary, on the Victoria Nile as well as on the Lake, he suggested to Cairo the despatch of two less bulky steam-launches instead.

His prime task was to extricate his force from Kibuga and for this purpose El Nur left with a substantial escort. They were not however back before 9 September 1876, by which time Gordon had abandoned his plan to establish a second camp at Niamyongo and decided instead to consolidate on M'ruli. The survey to the Ripon Falls would require an alliance with M'tesa's enemies, the Busoga, on the east bank and would take a further two months. Security on Lake Victoria would need a similar arrangement with Sasse island. Accordingly Gordon postponed indefinitely the flag-hoisting at Cossitza and restricted the survey as far as Niamyongo only. Possession of the further stations and of the Lake must be left to his successor, and with a view to reconciling M'tesa meantime to the foundation of M'ruli, he wrote to M'tesa urging him to drop his Zanzibari merchants now that the Sultan had abolished the slave trade, and to direct his commerce north towards Khartoum.[26]

With characteristic frankness, Gordon confided in his sister's letter. 'I dare say the desire to be out of the country is mixed up with my decision.' After two and a half years' unbroken service in tropical conditions he was near exhaustion. As his successor he sought the appointment of the American Henry Prout Bey, with whom he had earlier travelled from Brindisi to Egypt ('God knows if this will be His Will'); and to Khairi Pasha on 19 August he outlined the strategy to be followed. Central to it would be the organisation of the steamers; then the final push to Cossitza and alliances with the Busoga and Sasse Island. Effectively M'tesa would be enclosed on three sides, making an understanding with Karagwe to the east something to be solicited. M'tesa had not replied to Gordon's suggestion of a treaty and of the despatch of an ambassador to accompany him to Cairo.

Having therefore turned back at Niamyongo, Gordon quit M'ruli westwards for Masindi on 19 September 1876 with Dr Emin Effendi, now returned from a month at Kibuga. El Nur Agha was left in charge. With a force of only 100, Gordon was totally unprepared to find that he again had been misled by his subordinates: Wad el Mek's force was established not at Masindi but two days' march to its north at Keroto. Surrounded by dense grass and shadowed by Kabarega's men, he decided he must skirt Masindi, from where, he subsequently discovered, Kabarega himself had departed on his approach. Gordon reached Keroto on 26 September.

Despite amicable exchanges of letters with Gordon, Kabarega clearly remained ruler of at least all southern Bunyoro; indeed Gordon had been prepared to concede that to him. But in a further letter to Khairi

Pasha on 28 September Gordon explained his plan for local forces to defeat Kabarega. Defensive stockades would be erected in support at Masindi and at Kisoga to its east, following a triple advance: from M'ruli on Kisoga; from Keroto on Masindi; and from Vacovia, landed from the *N'yanza* and the ironclads. The advance would commence after the grass had been burned in November. Kibero, on Lake Albert fifteen miles south of Magungo, would be established as an additional lake station. Gordon himself sailed for Dufile on 3 October, marching thence to Kerri where to his extreme discomfiture he learned of the conferment upon him of the Medjedieh First Class for his occupation of Lake Victoria and Kibuga – 'This is dreadful for it is obtained under false pretences' – and he wrote back requesting its suspension until the occupation was a reality.[27]

Remarkable though his achievement had been over two and a half years in establishing firm foundations for his general-governorate almost single-handed, Gordon's departure from Bunyoro signalled only the end of the first phase of his Lakes strategy. The Khedivial flag planted by Gessi flew on Lake Albert but not on Lake Victoria. Kabarega still controlled most of Bunyoro. Only a temporary truce had been effected with M'tesa, Buganda was threatened from two sides. Moreover a relatively inexperienced team was left in charge of the chain of garrisons, led by El Nur Agha (now a *bimbashi*) in M'ruli and by Wad el Mek at Keroto pending the arrival of Gordon's successor. M'tesa and Kabarega remained secretly in touch. Gordon had nevertheless planned the strategy to fulfil his task which, he anticipated, would take a further two years to implement.

In Cairo, Gordon's intended return was greeted with dismay. Not only was the public announcement of the Egyptian annexation of the lacustrine kingdoms manifestly erroneous, but resistance to the Egyptian expansion in that direction was being progressively mounted by Kirk, the British consul-general in Zanzibar; and by Henry Stanley. The latter had, by the hand of Ernest Linant, in April 1875 initiated a successful campaign, through a *Daily Telegraph* letter, for an Anglican mission to be established in Rumanika's Karagwe, with a steamer under a retired British naval officer. That expedition (June–August 1876) had already left Zanzibar. Finally, more ominous, King Leopold II of the Belgians had in September 1876 convened a conference in Brussels of notables from the fields of geographical exploration, anti-slavery and Christian mission which agreed to set up an International African

Association. One of its proposed chain of bases would be Bagamoyo opposite Zanzibar.

On 21 October 1876 Fariq Charles Stone, the Khedive's military chief of staff, issued him a warning memorandum. The situation for Egyptian expansion in the light of Gordon's reports and of intelligence from Europe was pretty serious and any extended delay in Egypt's response could put at risk Egypt's domination of the Equatorial provinces. Egyptian authority must be established in the lacustrine kingdoms without a day's delay if her control of the sources of the Nile were to be consolidated. 'I tremble for Egypt's fortune if she loses the Equatorial provinces, even if she does not push further than to-day.'

Accordingly existing territories (Bunyoro included) must be secured; Buganda conquered; Lake Victoria occupied first by sailing ship, then steamer, under the Egyptian flag; Karagwe occupied without delay; Harar linked by road to Lake Victoria for commercial communication with Zeyla and Berbera; and, finally, the mountainous interior must be occupied between Lake Victoria and Kismayu and Durnford. Gordon would require reinforcements in the persons of senior officers and an additional 1,000 troops. Stone concluded: 'In my belief, the powerful country which possesses the sources of the Nile will always possess the domination of Lower Egypt.'

Stone's recommendations were contingent on certain critical assumptions: the continued sympathy of Great Britain for the Khedive's expansion in the lacustrine kingdoms; the capability of the Egyptian treasury to sustain the military cost in terms of men and materials; and the willingness of a man with Gordon's unique virtues to serve the Khedivial objectives. The current background for the realisation of those requirements was not propitious. Nevertheless a detailed cartographical study of the Upper Nile basin was initiated the following year for the Egyptian general staff.[28]

Gordon's Return to Cairo: October–December 1876 After five days in Lado, where Kukuh Agha was now the *mudir*, Gordon took a steamer northwards to Khartoum, pausing a day at Sobat mouth to inspect Surur Bahjat's impressive station, having ordered Ibrahim Fawzi of Bor (to be promoted to *qa'immaqam*) to join him with Gessi at Khartoum. El Tayeb Abdallah took over Bor, with Yusuf el Shellali at Rohl. Near Fashoda, Gordon encountered Dr Wilhelm Junker, the Russian (of German extraction) naturalist and explorer, en route to Makaraka, before himself reaching the *hakimdaria* capital on 25 October 1876.

There he disembarked his cargo of 750 cwt of ivory, a further instalment of revenue from his province. He was fortunate to miss his 'foe' Ismail Pasha Ayub, but he did not hesitate to address a letter of personal criticism to the Khedive's eldest son, Tawfiq Pasha, regarding the dangerous intention of the *hakimdar* to attack Abyssinia via Gallabat. Gordon sailed for Berbera on 11 November and having crossed the Atmur desert, sailed from Korosko to Aswan, reaching Cairo with Gessi and Ibrahim Fawzi as companions on 2 December, there to enjoy the unwonted comfort of Shepheard's Hotel.

The issue to be confronted with the Khedive related to Gordon's future. Ostensibly his request was to seek local leave in Cairo – it would take ten months to launch the *Khedive* on Lake Victoria. He needed confirmation of the appointment of Henry Prout Bey as his acting successor and advice to be sent to Khartoum accordingly; the earmarking of half the ivory yield to Equatoria province needs; and the transfer to his province of Alexander Mason Bey. In fact he would seek for himself appropriate *final* leave together with a proper level of recognition for the services of his principal subordinate, Romolo Gessi (who was to find the recognition unsatisfactory). The meeting on 3 December 1876 with the Khedive was not entirely harmonious. Gordon's requests were confirmed. Land for an Equatorial Province steamer workshop at Khartoum was approved; and Gordon was invested with the grand cordon of the Order of Medjidieh; and he was granted permission to visit England, but on *short* leave.

At Korosko, however, Gordon had been shocked to hear of the guarded *dhahabiya* with windows nailed up and a guard of two colonels and twenty-five men taking the disgraced Ismail Pasha Sadiq to Wadi Halfa. 'Everyone speaks in bated breath of the affair. I have made up my mind to serve the Khedive no longer.' In Cairo Sharif Pasha succeeded in dissuading him from too impetuous a conclusion, but Gordon had other complaints to unburden against the Khedive. As with Baker, there had been extended periods without letters or instructions from Cairo. Though he had been conspicuously successful in crushing the slave trade and establishing friendly relations with the Nilotic peoples, his achievement was undermined by the corruption and obstruction of the Khartoum *hakimdaria*.

I went in to H.H. with an angry face and heart, determined not to go back... I do not think he cares one jot about me, or the Province and I am quite sure no one else does. Why under these circumstances, H.H. wishes for me to return is one of those mysteries which I cannot solve.

The Khedive made him 'a solemn promise that these irregularities would cease', yet 'He has not the power, even if he has the will, to stop these irregularities, and I doubt him entirely.' Nevertheless when Gordon sailed from Alexandria on 16 December 1876 he had agreed to return. In Paris on 23 December he ran into Nubar Pasha, in exile, who 'talked much against Pharaoh'. Nubar urged Gordon not to return, in accordance with Gordon's obvious clear preference, but Gordon insisted: 'Comment puis-je abandonner ces noirs que je considère comme miens?'[29]

11

Mushir Gordon Pasha:
A Ubiquitous Hakimdar *1877–79*

1 APPOINTMENT

After an absence of nearly three years in the tropical Sudan, scarcely one of Gordon's five weeks' sojourn in England could be called vacation. In January 1877 he was in London, in Cecil Street off the Strand – the erstwhile residence of John Constable (1799) and Charles Dickens (1833) – the better to wrestle with his future plans. He had agreed to return to Cairo, but not to serve further in Equatoria. The Earl of Derby's suggestion of a governorate in the Balkans did not materialise, but Gordon was attracted to William Mackinnon's idea of his leading an expedition, with Zanzibari acquiescence, from the Indian Ocean littoral into the interior, accompanied by Romolo Gessi. The plan was slow to mature. Meanwhile after a démarche from Vivian in Cairo the Khedive telegraphed insisting that Gordon had given his word to return. A second communication, a reminder of his duty to return, was misdirected to the Duke of Cambridge at the Horse Guards. Ismail Pasha wrote on 17 January:

> Mon cher Gordon Pacha… je me refuse à croire qu'un gentil-homme comme Gordon veut sous un prétexte quelquonque reprendre la parole qu'il m'a donné. Je ne puis donc, mon cher Gordon, prendre en considération votre dépêche, et je vous attends, selon votre promesse. Votre affectionné, Ismail.

On 31 January 1877 Gordon sailed for Egypt.

Having discussed his predicament with close friends in London, Gordon decided to present the Khedive with an ultimatum. Only if Ismail's third son, Prince Hasan Pasha, currently minister of war, were appointed *hakimdar* would Gordon return to Equatoria. Otherwise, if he were to continue to serve, it must be as *hakimdar* with responsibility for the whole Sudan including Equatoria, Bahr el Ghazal, Darfur, Eastern Sudan and the Red Sea littoral – an authority without precedent.

His mind was clear. Only thus could his essential objective, the comprehensive suppression of the slave trade in the Sudan, be accomplished.

He engaged the support of the British consul-general, Hussey Vivian, to prepare the way for his successful interview with the Khedive on 14 February 1877. 'He the Khedive gave me the Sudan... I go up alone with an infinite Almighty God to direct and guide me and I am glad to so trust Him as to fear nothing and indeed to feel sure of success.' His predecessor and enemy, Ismail Pasha Ayub, detained in Cairo on Darfur business for the past five months, found himself appointed Egypt's director of education.

The extent of the Egyptian Sudan had reached its apogee when, in March 1875, the slave trader Zubeir Pasha from his independent bailiwick of Bahr el Ghazal had conquered Darfur and been recognised as general-governor; and in January 1876 the slave trade suppressor Gordon Pasha, building on the initial expedition of his predecessor in 1871–3, had run up the Khedivial flag at M'ruli. In the course of 1875 Harar had also been occupied, unopposed. Already, however, the African empire was beginning to crumble. In November 1875 the Arendrup expedition to Abyssinian Hamasein had been massacred, Munzinger simultaneously defeated in Aussa. A fortnight later, on 1 December 1875, the Cave Commission had arrived in Egypt at the Khedive's request to report on the financial situation.

Nevertheless in February 1877, as Gordon observed to his sister, it remained 'an immense command'. The territorial limits of Gordon's *hakimdaria* would be conspicuously greater even than those of Ja'afar Pasha Mazhar. A comparative stranger to most of the Sudan, he still faced the unresolved problems of his predecessors: deficient revenues; inferior and demoralised personnel, both civil and military; endemic corruption, especially in tax collection; and communication systems still inadequate for a dependent country of huge distances. But the Sudan was now to be financially independent as to revenue and expenditure – nothing to be given on either side; outstanding debts were indefinitely waived, annual tribute to Egypt abolished.

Essentially, Gordon enjoyed the trust of and direct access to the absolute ruler of Egypt who appointed him at once to the supreme military rank of *mushir,* marshal. Without that support his foreign extraction, his, albeit enlightened, Christianity ('To me the Moslem worships God as well as I do, and is acceptable, if sincere, as any Christian'), his limited knowledge of Arabic, and the jealousy, whispering hostility and deceit of important subordinates would all soon have wrought his downfall. His experience of irregular warfare in harsh terrain, his uncommonly strong constitution, his exceptional moral and physical courage, above all his inexorable determination to triumph over events – all these invaluable qualities still demanded underpinning by a comparably dedicated team of subordinates if a firm, just and enduring rule over such a country was to be a reality. Lacking robust support, its achievement was impossible. Yet, for all that, the extent of Gordon's accomplishment over the next three years was remarkable.

The reunified and extended administrative structure for which he assumed responsibility fell broadly into five regions: the historic riverain core of the former kingdom of Sennar; the recently independent general-governorate of the eastern Sudan with Bogos, the Red Sea littoral and Harar; the lately conquered western general-governorate of Darfur, adjacent to Kordofan; the, as yet, titular sub-*muderia* of the slave-trading Bahr el Ghazal; and his own formerly independent general-governorate of Equatoria extending into the lacustrine kingdoms. The whole was ethnically, culturally and linguistically diverse, and over the border countries to the south and west the Khedivial flag had flown for very few years. Gordon was enjoined by the Khedive to have three deputies: for the Sudan, properly so-called including Equatoria; for Darfur; and for the Red Sea littoral and the Eastern Sudan.

The consolidation of this vast territory and the improvement of its communications must itself prove a major task, but the supreme priority for the new *hakimdar* would be the definitive suppression of the slave trade on which he had made such an impact in Equatoria. But though the White Nile traffic might now be controlled, he remained under no illusion that progress had been made in the Bahr el Ghazal. All the signs were that while firm action towards suppression could brook no delay, its fulfilment would take years.

It was most unfortunate, given the scale of his task, that at that meeting on 14 February 1877 with the Khedive, when Gordon's conditions for further Khedivial service in the Sudan were unexceptionally conceded, he was additionally invited to seek peace with the Abyssinian *negusa nagast*. The initiative for this may have stemmed from the British consul-general Vivian in a meeting with the Khedive around Christmas 1876, when the former suggested 'sending an European officer, to treat with King John' (p. 259). To this the Khedive replied that he proposed asking Gordon on his return from England to undertake that mission, offering the Negus passage through, but not control of, Egyptian Red Sea ports for Abyssinian goods. Perhaps conscious of his debt to Vivian for intervening on his behalf regarding the *hakimdaria*, Gordon accepted the Khedivial authority to enter into negotiations with the Negus for a settlement.[1]

2 COSTLY DIVERSIONS

Abyssinian Treaty Negotiations Gordon's unwillingness to resist Khedivial pressure to assume this additional responsibility considerably delayed his arrival at his capital. And no sooner was he formally installed at Khartoum on 5 May 1877 than he had to deal with a mounting crisis in Darfur. Added to which, the former *hakimdar* Ismail Ayub, apart from a brief interval in May–June 1876, had himself been absent from Khartoum for two and a half years.

Nor was Gordon well equipped for a complex negotiation with the victorious ruler of an inaccessible hostile country in the wake of two defeated invasions. The languages of the two antagonists were Arabic (in which Gordon's instructions were set out) and Amharic. As a postscript in French, Gordon was simply enjoined: 'The Abyssinian frontier joins the Sudan. Some disputes about the frontier exist. The Khedive authorises you, if you think fit, to settle these questions with the Abyssinian authorities.'

Relations had already been soured when Emperor John's envoy had been detained for weeks in Cairo, and when Gordon reached Bogos via Massawa in March, the dispatch of his offer of 'fair conditions' for peace to John's general Ras Alula Engeda coincided with the departure of the latter to join John in repulsing the attack of Ras Menilek of Shoa on Gondar. Uneasily Gordon was obliged to postpone further exchanges in the hope that the current truce would continue to hold. Meanwhile he concentrated his efforts on persuading Welde-Mikael Selomon, John's former *dejach* of Hamasein, and now resident in Bogos with 3,000 well-armed men, to desist from raiding Hamasein pending Gordon's return later in the year.[2]

Gordon left Keren for Kassala on 3 April 1877, reaching Khartoum on 2 May. Two months had been expended. He was to note in his journal letter from Kordofan of 25 June that he had 'no tidings from Johannes who is engaged with Menilek'. Yet, on the basis of a communication to Kassala from Franz Hasan, in charge at Keren, Gordon had already written to Khairi Pasha in Cairo on 2 June deducing that John had accepted the peace proposals he (Gordon) had set out in a letter to

Sharif. The British Foreign Office congratulated the Khedive. This proved premature. A month later there was no further news but the Khedive, content that the conclusion of the peace treaty must await John's defeat of Menilek and Gordon's return to Bogos for the purpose, felt justified in considering Egypt now at peace with Abyssinia.

Having brought the Darfur revolt under control during the summer months of 1877, Gordon returned to Khartoum to receive on 19 October a reply from John, dated 18 June at Debra Tabor, following Menilek's withdrawal to Shoa. On the critical frontier issue, for which Gordon had stipulated the preservation of ancient frontiers, John, acknowledging British help in securing the return from Cairo of his envoy, condemned the Egyptian attempt to impose their own frontier, insisting that the historical Abyssinian frontier was well known. Undismayed, believing John wished to conclude peace, Gordon left for Bogos via Wadi Halfa, only to learn en route, at Dongola, that Welde-Mikael was threatening the roads between Keren and Kassala and Massawa, and that Sennar and Fazughli were under threat from Ras Araya Demtsu, John's uncle and chief minister.

Unable to ignore these reports but rightly distrusting the truth of the latter – it turned out to have been a frontier tribal raid for food – Gordon returned at once to Khartoum and thence set out on 26 November 1877 for Bogos to meet Welde-Mikael in his encampment of 7,000 men. With a large bribe of £E1,000 a month – the price of peace – he succeeded in dissuading Welde-Mikael from an attack on Adwa and from local raiding; but he was unable to persuade the British government to urge John to pardon him. 'I have Munzinger to thank for all the trouble. The whole of the rows with Abyssinia was brought on by the occupation of the wretched tongue of land Bogos (Sennaheit).' Already aware that John was in Gojjam, Gordon pressed on nevertheless to Keren on 18 December, dispatching a letter to Ras Baryau Gebre, the Tigré frontier-general, urging in vain for John's response. By 10 January 1878 Gordon was back at Suakin after a further month's absence from the Sudan. He had reflected: 'If I could only get rid of Abyssinia, my work would be easier, but as it is now it splits my province into two.' Returning to Khartoum he was to be again diverted from the Sudan, this time to Cairo at the urgent behest of the Khedive to advise him on the Egyptian debt crisis.[3]

There would be little contact between Gordon and the Emperor in early 1878 despite Gordon's visit to Harar. In May he heard from John that Ras Menilek was being allowed to keep his title, but then came news that Welde-Mikael Selomon had attacked and killed Ras Baryau and had left Bogos to occupy Adwa, to be gratuitously congratulated on so doing by Ratib Pasha, now minister of war. A further six months were to elapse until Welde-Mikael, having failed to reach an accord with John, set off for Gondar to offer submission, whereupon Gordon in Khartoum heard on 22 December 1878 that an Abyssinian envoy had now reached Kassala to discuss the frontier question.

Gordon met the envoy, the son of Ras Araya the chief minister, for three days at Gedaref. Confident that John did not actively seek a port, Gordon offered an Abyssinian consulate at Massawa and facilities at Gallabat, and in early January 1879 dispatched his own envoy, Winstanley, back to Gondar in company with the young envoy carrying the Khedive's letter of authority to Gordon. If it were demanded, Gordon would concede Bogos, despite Nubar Pasha's telegram: 'Give up nothing.' Gordon had his authority already from the Khedive in February 1877. If there was as yet no proposal from John, it was at least clear no attack on Egypt was contemplated. 'I look on the Abyssinia trouble, both Welde-Mikael and Johannes, as over.' Cairo offered no comment or appreciation.

Again Gordon's optimism proved excessive. He reduced the Keren garrison to 200 men plus two (in place of twelve) guns, and Ras Alula expelled a mischievous French consular agent in Adwa. Preoccupied with events in Bahr el Ghazal and Darfur, Gordon returned to El Obeid on 8 July 1879 to learn from Tawfiq Pasha Ismail, the new Khedive, that Ras Alula with Welde-Mikael were now threatening Massawa and Bogos, and was calling him to Cairo. Despite sickness and exhaustion, Gordon agreed one last service to Egypt before his departure. In the face of imminent war he telegraphed Aden for gunboats, ordered the doubling of the frontier garrisons and the alerting of the tribes and warned a hostile Privy Council and the debt commissioners of a probable war cost of a third of a million pounds. He wrote off personally to the Emperor urging peace but, under fresh instructions, positively refusing any territorial concession.

Welde-Mikael had finally made his submission to the Negus in August 1878, and on his arrival at Massawa on 6 September Gordon found Bogos virtually under Abyssinian occupation. However at this point Welde-Mikael's son Metfin was murdered by the son of Ras Baryau, Welde-Mikael's earlier victim. Fearing a further revolt, Ras Alula had Welde-Mikael and all his chiefs arrested and taken to Adwa, relieving Bogos of hostile leadership and giving Gordon the opportunity of initiating discussions with Ras Alula and reinforcing the Keren garrison. The discussions, first with Ras Alula at Gura and then with John at Debra Tabor, took place between mid-September and mid-November 1879. After the initially inconclusive encounter at Gura, a truce was nevertheless agreed. Gordon and Ras Alula then travelled 400 miles in six weeks on mule-back through mountainous territory, via Adwa, crossing all the right bank tributaries of the Tacazzi affluent of the River Atbara and arriving at Debra Tabor on 27 October.

In a man to man talk, from which Ras Araya the chief minister but not the Greek consul was excluded, John at last on 8 November set out his demands of the Khedive: the handing over to Abyssinia of Metemma (Gallabat), the Shangallas (Dar Berta), Bogos, Zeyla and Amphila; the consecration of a new *Abuna* by the Alexandria Patriarch; and compensation of between one and two million pounds. Gordon, dressed in the uniform of an Egyptian *mushir*, accompanied only by his trusted multilingual Sudanese secretary, Berzati Bey, and by a tiny military escort of six, faced a serious threat to his official dignity and person to which, despite the pressures of the past years, he proved predictably equal. John, the same age as Gordon, was judged by the latter 'a sour ill-favoured looking being. He never looks you in the face – but when you look away he glares at you like a tiger. He never smiles; his look always changing, is one of thorough suspicion. Hated and hating all, I can imagine no more unhappy man. Avaricious above all his people.' Gordon judged that John was rapidly going mad. He declined to be intimidated, robustly inviting the Emperor to put his demands to the Khedive in writing – demands which he warned him were impossible.

Gordon was kept waiting ten days at Debra Tabor for a letter to the Khedive and when he opened it, having left within the hour of its arrival for Gallabat and Gedaref, he found a refusal to make peace, but a grant of a six-month truce to reply. No sooner had his Abyssinian escort left him on 14 November 1879 at Chelga, than he was rearrested by a military posse from Ras Araya with a further letter from the Emperor. Prudently destroying his diary of events, he was escorted back under constant harassment and redirected to Axum via Gondar. He had fortunately been permitted to send a telegraph to Gallabat for the Khedive, requesting a gunboat and reinforcements to await him at Massawa, but it was HMS *Seagull* from Aden, alerted by Gordon before he left Cairo, not a Khedivial vessel, which was waiting on 8

December to convey him to Suez. The British government were wary of another Cameron-type crisis.

In all, Gordon's inconclusive endeavours for peace with Abyssinia had occupied over seven of his thirty-five months in post as *hakimdar*. With the pacification of Darfur and the suppression of the slave trade as his first priorities, he was to lament how much he was kept away by the 'the Abyssinian trouble, the rows with Cairo, and the finance at Khartoum'.[4]

The Egyptian Debt Crisis The Khedivial decree of 18 November 1876 giving effect to the Goschen-Joubert establishment of the 'Dual Mandate' (p. 202) proved of only limited duration. While both revenue and expenditure were to be monitored, the unofficial British controller-general for revenue incurred criticism for a superficial report. Judgements by the new mixed tribunals against the government and on behalf of the private creditors, asserting that no distinction in payment responsibility could be made between the funded and unfunded debt, were ignored. And by mid-1877 it was apparent that the government revenues had been seriously overestimated. In September 1877 the British consul-general warned his government of an impending crisis, even though since the Khedivial decree of November 1876 the agreed coupon payments on the debt had all been paid. The European countries were agreed that there could be no adjustment of the interest rates until a further commission of enquiry had reported, if only to establish the capacity of the peasantry to bear the taxation. Now the composition and the powers of this new commission were to be the nub of a dispute which was to continue until March 1878.

The Khedive was determined that the expenditure of the Khedivial monies, as opposed to the verification of public revenue receipts, should be excluded from such an enquiry; and that the Caisse representatives of the private bondholders should be excluded from the commission – their public criticism of the head of state being unacceptable. In December 1877, the stalemate being unbroken, the Khedive was evidently preparing to refer the issue to Turkey for decision, in the wake of the Russo-Turkish war to which Egypt had been forced to contribute. There was another alternative however which the Khedive was weighing: to appoint the commission of enquiry over the heads of the Caisse commissioners, and to appoint as its president Mushir Gordon Pasha whom, he was to tell Vivian, the Khedive regarded as 'the greatest person after Him in Egypt'.

On 25 January 1878 Gordon, returning from Bogos then up the Nile from Berber, received a Khedivial telegram requesting his presence in Cairo. 'As there is nothing of very great import in the Sudan just now, I said yes.' A more urgent telegram brought Gordon's departure from Khartoum on 8 February, although on reflection he confided a week later: 'I would have liked better to have gone to Darfur to finish off matters there... I am not up in finance matters and the Khedive has so tied his own hands with his Decrees that I do not see how he will get out of them.' He was received royally by the Khedive on his arrival in Cairo: 'I am dazed and wish for my camel.'⁵

Meanwhile on 30 January 1878 the Khedive had issued a further decree authorising a commission of enquiry to investigate revenues only, leaving the appointment of commissioners for future action and warning the Powers that, if further pressurised, he would refer the issue to the Porte. Two days later the four commissioners of the Caisse indicted the minister of finance (Prince Hussein Kamel) before the mixed tribunals for a serious deficit in the sums paid to defray the current debt. War had been declared. On 23 February the Khedive revealed that on Gordon's arrival he would offer him the presidency of the commission with fullest powers extending to debt and expenditure, but excluding from membership the commissioners of the Caisse on account of their hostility. Vivian represented that the Caisse Convention could not be unilaterally modified; that new commissioners would lack Egyptian experience; that Baring at least was not hostile to the Khedive; and that Gordon lacked financial experience. When Gordon met the European consuls-general on 8 March and made clear that he endorsed the exclusion of the Caisse commissioners, the diplomats insisted that an enquiry without the endorsement of the bondholders would be valueless, and that no arbitrary modification of binding engagements by the Khedive would be recognised.

While Vivian accepted the time-honoured principle that no British government would interfere officially to protect private risk-taking investors, he believed that axiom did not quite apply in the case of Egypt whose credit was impaired by the Khedive's failure to keep engagements under international conventions such as the execution of the sentences of the mixed tribunals. Moreover other governments, such as France and Germany, took a less principled line and Britain could not deny their right of intervention to protect their interests.

Gordon was adamant that it was wrong to impose on a head of state commissioners of enquiry in the person of state representatives of private creditors – some of whom had been showing public hostility to him. To authorise their Caisse representatives to make unrestricted enquiries into Khedivial finance would prejudice the Khedive's prestige and position. Moreover so corrupt was Egyptian administration that no change of Khedive would mend matters. Gordon saw on the one hand avaricious European creditors seeking their pound of flesh and the impoverished *fellahin* of Upper Egypt already mulcted of the fruits even of future harvests. The coupon rates were high and, as Andrew Roberts has pointed out, 'Egyptian bonds were a favoured investment vehicle throughout Europe, vast financial interests were involved. Gladstone himself had 37% of his total personal equity portfolio invested in them.'

Gordon's personal encounter with the British representative on the Caisse, Captain Evelyn Baring, whose signal concern Gordon deemed unfairly was that the creditors were being defrauded, was unfruitful. 'I said: "I will do what the Khedive asked me." He said it was unfair to the creditors, and in a few moments all was over. When oil mixes with water, we will mix together.' Thirty years later, Baring, now the Earl of Cromer, wrote: 'The sole reason the [enquiry] negotiation broke down was that it was evident to everyone concerned, including General Gordon himself, that he was not fitted to conduct any financial enquiry.' They distrusted each other's judgement.

Together Vivian and Baron des Michels, the French consul-general, made a démarche to the Khedive on 10 March urging the acceptance to the commission of the Caisse members en bloc. They were successful to the point that the Khedive (and Gordon) agreed either to accept the delegates for the enquiry commission (sent out by Goschen and Joubert, the original architects of the Caisse), who would represent the bondholders (and the Khedive did not refuse Baring's name); or, the Caisse in any case being the *legal* representatives of the bondholders, to let a discrete enquiry commission work in harmonious tandem with the Caisse. If Goschen and Joubert failed to nominate the delegates, Gordon warned the Earl of Derby, he would urge the Khedive to act unilaterally. The Caisse commissioners for their part insisted that, if excluded, they would sue on behalf of the bondholders in the mixed tribunals.

Seemingly, between 16 and 19 March 1878 the issue hung fire. On 19 March the Khedive gave in and accepted the Caisse representatives en bloc for the commission enquiry. Gordon refused to sit with them, and was replaced as president by Ferdinand de Lesseps, his nominated vice-president. Dicey attributed the Khedive's capitulation to the joint declaration of the British and French 'to cooperate... in any useful measure not inconsistent with the Khedive's independent administration of Egypt', which itself stemmed from the threat of Prince Bismarck to step in to protect German bondholders. The Khedivial decree was published: the commission of enquiry would initially sit from 13 April to 19 August 1878.

As Gordon left Cairo on 30 March 1878, only £E500,000 of the £E2m interest due on the unified debt on 1 May 1878 had been raised. The Caisse commissioners themselves were reluctant to force the collection of the balance within the month but, Lord Salisbury having succeeded Lord Derby as foreign minister on 2 April, the British government was persuaded to espouse the French view that Egypt could afford it despite the impoverished condition of the taxpayers. Baring in 1908 was to ascribe this roughness to the need to conciliate the French at the 1878 Congress of Berlin. 'Egyptian interests had to give way to broader diplomatic considerations.' The money was ruthlessly collected, and on 1 May the coupon was paid.

Gordon was not to be further involved in the accelerating slide to intervention in Cairo. Obliged to concede examinations of his personal finances despite the resistance to it of Riaz Pasha, his minister of commerce and a vice-president of the Commission, Ismail was then faced in the Commission's August 1878 ultimatum with the requirement that the Khedivial private estates (900,000 acres) be restored to the State; or Egypt's administration be placed under international control. Obliged to concede the former, Ismail announced his intention henceforth to rule by a council of ministers of which Nubar Pasha would be chief minister; the British controller of the national debt, Rivers Wilson, further seconded finance minister; and the Frenchman de Blignières minister of public works. The regime was established in November 1878.

It lasted but three months. Following a mutinous demonstration by Egyptian army officers on 18 February 1879 – contrived by Ismail, it was suspected, and unpunished – the Khedive dismissed Nubar, appointing Tawfiq Pasha in his place. When the council's European ministers, who remained loyal to Nubar, appealed to their governments, Ismail replaced them, on 7 April 1879, with Egyptians in a Cabinet now to be headed by Sharif Pasha. With now no prospect that the recommendations of the commission of enquiry for a reformed system of administration would be implemented, the commissioners tendered their resignation. Deeming the Khedive to be in breach of his international engagements regarding the debt and with Prince Bismarck threatening unilateral intervention on behalf of German creditors, rather than themselves embark on a military occupation of Egypt, Britain and France joined Germany in compelling the Ottoman Sultan to dismiss Khedive Ismail. Sultan Abdel Hamid, who had been suffering bouts of extreme paranoia over the previous six months, offered no resistance. Ismail abdicated on 26 June 1879 in favour of his eldest son Tawfiq, sailing for exile and Naples with full honours.

Gordon, leaving Suez, had been away from his *hakimdaria* for four weeks, although he had profited on the way down to Cairo by a visit to the Dongola *muderia*. He had seen first-hand the secondary importance which in Cairo was accorded to the affairs of the Sudan – a repetition indeed of the experience of Gordon's two immediate predecessors, Ja'afar Mazhar and, still more so, Ismail Ayub. Gordon left Egypt disillusioned. 'The Khedive threw me over at the last moment, but far from angry I am very glad for it rescued me from a deal of trouble... I came out a pauper [his personal expenses had totalled over £E1,600] in more or less disgrace.' Reaching Zeyla from Aden on 17 April, he had reflected further: 'I must say that since my visit to Cairo I feel very different about the Sudan and the Khedive... It is only the sense of one's duty that keeps me up to the mark and I do not feel cheerful about the prospects before me...I have no hope whatever in any change for the better.' Declining three invitations to visit Cairo in the winter of 1878–9, Gordon was not again to meet Ismail as the Khedive.

To Julian Baker, Gordon wrote prophetically:

> I have not the very slightest hope of doing anything permanent out here. Absolute as he is, the Khedive is impotent out of Cairo. Things cannot go on long there as they are now... My visit to Cairo opened my eyes to his great weakness. He has no one to guide him in any way... there must come a collapse.

And collapse there duly came. The investments of the European creditors would be buttressed as the first priority; the political rivalries of the Powers accommodated; and Khedive Ismail, his authority publicly undermined, would over the next year be committed to fighting unsuccessfully to wrest back his independence from the Dual Control. In Cairo, the Sudan became a peripheral irrelevance while Gordon declined to respond to invitations to visit again. By June 1879 Ismail

Pasha was obliged to abdicate. The exceptional accomplishments of Gordon, backed by Gessi, during that year of 1878–9 in crushing the slave trade in Darfur and Bahr el Ghazal carried no more than the ephemeral congratulation of a weakened ruler of Egypt, and would not outlive the appointments of their successors. The slave trade would flourish again.[6]

3   EASTERN SUDAN

Taka and the Sudan Ports   The Khedive in his letter of appointment of 17 February 1877 required Gordon to have one of his three deputies charged with 'the shores of the Red Sea and the Eastern Sudan'. The previous independent general-governor, Munzinger Pasha, had in September 1875, on leaving with the ill-fated Aussa expedition, handed over to his deputy Ala el Din Pasha Siddiq who had previously been successively *muhafiz* of Massawa and *mudir* of Taka.

On the return of Ratib Pasha's expedition to Massawa and his recall to Cairo in January 1877, Lewa Osman Rifqi Pasha, who commanded one of the two Egyptian forces at the Guru battle, was appointed not only officer commanding troops in the eastern Sudan but in addition *muhafiz* of Massawa and Suakin. At some time following the recall of Khalid Pasha Nadim as Gordon's vice-Governor-General in Khartoum in the summer of 1877, Osman Rifqi was then appointed in his place. During Gordon's absence from Khartoum in early 1878, seemingly on the order of the *sirdar* Ratib Pasha in Cairo, Osman would send ammunition to Welde-Mikael in Bogos, to be used for the latter's attack on Hamasein.

On Osman Rifqi's departure to Khartoum as *seraskir* Ala el Din succeeded, once again in an acting capacity, to the additional responsibility of the two ports and was responsible for defeating the major attack of the Barea north of Kassala in November 1877, which cost them 300-400 dead. Gordon had met Ala el Din at Suakin on his arrival in the Sudan in February 1874 en route to Berber and Khartoum and regarded him highly, advancing him in 1879 to the rank of *fariq*. In March 1879, by which time Abdel Raziq Pasha had taken over as general-governor Eastern Sudan, Gordon recorded thankfully that the eastern Sudan was free of the slave trade, with no revolts or wars, and was best governed by an Arab.

Gordon's visits to the eastern Sudan were undertaken en route to and

Sheikh Awad el Karim Ahmed Abu Sin, of the Shukriya

from Abyssinia and the littoral. On his return from the initial visit to Bogos in April 1877 he marched rapidly via Kufit through the country of the Barea, Beni Amer and Halenga to Kassala where he made friends with the influential Sheikh Musa Ibrahim of the Hadendoa, although in October, with news of Musa's further participation in inter-tribal fighting, he purposed to arrest him. In 1840, as a young man, Sheikh Musa had been sent in chains to Khartoum with his uncle, the then *nazir*, Sheikh Mohammed Din, by Ahmed Pasha Widan. On his release, he soon succeeded his father as *nazir* and was to rule as *nazir* for over forty years, effectively conceding the responsibility in old age to his son Mohammed.

When Gordon left Kassala with his retinue in April 1877, at his habitual spanking rate, he was unaware until his arrival at Gedaref that the acting *nazir* of the Shukriya, Sheikh Ali Ahmed Abu Sin, was riding with him. On this visit to Kassala, and again in December 1877, Gordon, accompanied by the *mudir* of Kassala, exchanged visits with the religious leader Sharif Sa'id Hashim, who lived on the outskirts of Kassala. As was his wont in all *muderias*, Gordon would inspect the hospital, barracks and prisons, personally dealing as necessary with serious criminal cases. Evenings were spent listening to the military band.[7]

The Red Sea Littoral and the Gulf of Aden   Not only the Red Sea littoral but the Ottoman ports of Zeyla and Tadjoura, Berbera, and the recently conquered Harar were placed under Gordon - 'an immense command'. Not until he had quashed the incipient revolt of Darfur early in 1877 was he able even to contemplate a visit to these territories – Zeyla's semi-independent chief Abu Bakr Ibrahim, now nominally under the Egyptian general-governor of Harar (see p. 242), was a slave exporter strongly entrenched and had provoked the visit of an Italian warship for failing to succour an exploration expedition to Shoa under the Marchese Oratio Antinori.

In low spirits after the rebuff accorded to his proposal for handling the debt enquiry in Cairo, Gordon had sailed from Suez for Aden where, on 10 April 1878, he coincided with Julian, Sir Samuel Baker's nephew and companion on the Equatoria expedition of 1870-3, now (since 1875) first lieutenant of HMS *Undaunted,* Admiral Corbett's flagship. He joined Gordon on the voyage from Aden to Berbera and Zeyla and did much to dissipate the coolness of the relationship between the two former Equatoria general-governors. Gordon learned at first hand of the Bakers' problem with Mohammed Ra'uf Bey at Gondokoro in October 1871. Ra'uf had since become general-governor of Harar and the adjacent ports, having been superseded four years previously by Gordon as *mudir* at Gondokoro. Although he had then been recommended by Gordon in September 1874 as his successor as general-governor Equatoria, Ra'uf had been posted instead to command the Harar expedition.

On arrival at Zeyla, Gordon had become firmly determined to visit Harar, writing to Samuel Baker: 'Ra'uf Pasha is at Harar, out of which I mean to turn him, when I get up there. As your nephew will tell you, I have avenged you.' Persuaded that Ra'uf seemed to be a regular tyrant and mistaken that the *emir*, whom Ra'uf had recently executed, was Burton's acquaintance Ahmed in 1854, Gordon warned Ra'uf that he was being recalled (he also installed Ahmed's son as *emir*). Ra'uf put up no more opposition than he had at Gondokoro. In 'downcast' mode he may even have welcomed repatriation, for Gordon's determination to merge Berbera, Zeyla and Tadjoura (he had previously considered closing the latter two) in order to make them self-sufficient would necessarily reduce the status of Harar. Indeed in Gordon's view 'the most sensible thing would be to evacuate all of them [including Harar]'. Ra'uf left a day in advance of Gordon, but then accompanied him by sea to Suakin, shortly to become *mudir* of Girga in Upper Egypt. He was succeeded in Harar by Mohammed Radwan Pasha from Berbera; in June 1880 by Mohammed Nadi Pasha; and finally in 1882 by Ali Reda el Tubji Pasha.

International interest in the Gulf of Aden had already been building up. Notwithstanding his reverse with the McKillop expedition to the Zanzibar coast in late 1875, the Khedive was anxious to consolidate his position in the Gulf of Aden as far east as Ras Hafoun; and had been persuaded in September 1877 to accept the British terms, establishing free ports and prohibiting slave exports and any cession of territory to another foreign power. The Slave Trade Convention and the Somali Convention were signed respectively in August and September 1877. Under Clause 4 of the former, a British director-general of the Red Sea slave trade courts and maritime police, Captain George Malcolm, RN, was appointed, to be based in Massawa. Unfortunately an over-zealous interpretation of his authority extended to an attempt to remove Gordon's subordinate but powerful and long-established governor of Zeyla, Abu Bakr Pasha, who enjoyed a bad reputation for slave trading. Gordon regarded Abu Bakr as 'too strong to touch unless you have plenty of troops', and Malcolm's imposition on his territory and budget as an obstruction to his own local actions against the trade. Abu Bakr was released and in June 1878 Malcolm resigned.

By December 1878, having failed to draw Gordon to Cairo for talks, and conscious of the latter's lack of enthusiasm for his littoral possessions, Khedive Ismail was planning for Egypt to transfer their control to Cairo. Gordon's swift assent was forthcoming but conditional on Egypt's assuming their administrative costs. Only in 1880 did the possessions become the direct responsibility of Egypt; then, in April 1884, under British supervision, the garrisons were evacuated. The brief Egyptian occupation nevertheless left a favourable legacy of improved road communications, agriculture (coffee and cotton), commerce and primary education. Reverting again to an emirate, Harar was conquered by Emperor Menilek in 1887.[8]

4 KHARTOUM AND THE RIVERAIN NORTH

When Gordon first reached his capital on 2 May 1877 his sojourn lasted little more than a fortnight; then he departed for Darfur to subdue the rebellion of the *emir* Harun which had broken out in

February. Dr Wilhelm Junker, a visitor the previous summer, described the Blue Nile bank of Khartoum with its line, at intervals of about a hundred paces, of *saqia* wheels worked by blindfolded oxen and of *shadufs* which raised water to irrigate the gardens and fields.

> Beyond the gardens is visible the government palace, Khartoum's most imposing edifice. This two-storied solid brick structure with its light-coloured walls and green sun-blinds, presents quite a stately appearance, especially by contrast with the surrounding houses. It fronts the river with its somewhat projecting wings, being enclosed on the three other sides by clumps of trees and the large garden, which is limited on one side by the street leading into the town. All the way from the palace down stream the Blue Nile is embanked by a massive stone wall, while the opposite side of the street is occupied by the *mudiria* or *divan*, which also faces the river, and which contains the public offices and the official residence of the *mudir* of the province of Khartoum.

The population of the town was about 50,000.

With the outbreak of insurrection in Darfur, Gordon set out, leaving in charge at Khartoum as his deputy the newly arrived Khalid Pasha Nadim. Khalid had previously acted in that capacity when in the absence in Darfur of Ismail Pasha Ayub – Gordon's predecessor as Governor-General – he had succeeded Mohammed Bey Hasan in January 1875. Khalid failed to disguise his resentment of the new Governor-General's appearance in what Khalid envisaged as his own bailiwick, a self-esteem bred of his successful handling of the Shilluk revolt and of the Abyssinian threat at the end of 1875. Ismail Ayub on his return from Darfur to Khartoum in May 1876 had encountered the same problem of hubris and had required the recall of Khalid to Cairo. Evidently, on Ismail Ayub's supersession, Khalid had now been reinstated by the Khedive.

Gordon on leaving Khartoum hoped, if not believed, that he had established Khalid's role as one subordinate to himself and additionally he now had a trusted joint British and German consular agent in Khartoum, Charles-Frederic Rosset – 'my factotum, also in my household' and married to Andrea Debono's daughter – to keep him informed. However by the time he had quit Kordofan for Darfur in June 1877, Gordon was telegraphing Cairo for Khalid's removal. Khalid was to be succeeded by Osman Pasha Rifqi from Massawa, who would remain at Khartoum for Gordon's next three brief visits –

for a week in October 1877, and, either side of his journey to Bogos, for four days in November and for ten days, 28 January to 7 February 1878.

However, on the morrow of his departure from Zeyla in May 1878, determined at last to establish his personal control of the finance and administration of a *hakimdaria* stretching 1,640 miles north-south and 660 miles on average east-west, Gordon telegraphed Osman Rifqi to post him to Darfur where the situation was currently tranquil, thus economising the Khartoum post. Having apparently complied and in recognition been recommended for the Medjidieh Order second-class, Osman then reneged on his assent, pleading grounds of health. Cairo gave him notice of instant dismissal as deputy Governor-General and *seraskir* on 28 June 1878, the morning after Gordon's return to Khartoum by night. Until Carl Christian Giegler's appointment on Gordon's departure to Darfur in March 1879, there would be no successor. In Egypt Osman Rifqi was later to be rewarded with the position of minister of war.

As on the occasion of Gordon's first visit to Khartoum, his arrival back in June 1878 coincided with news of a further rebellion in the west, the instigator on this occasion being Sulieman Zubeir. The latter had attacked the headquarters of Bahr el Ghazal at Deim Idris, massacring the garrison and provoking the flight of the *mudir,* Idris Bey Abtar. Gordon was fortunate not only that he was back from Harar but that, despite the disobedience of Osman Rifqi, he was able with the help of Dr Junker to persuade Romolo Gessi to lead the military expedition to quell Sulieman Zubeir's rising. Gessi's own plans for an exploration of the Sobat river had failed in May.

When Gordon took back the reins of central power in June 1878, he faced a far more forbidding responsibility than on his appointment eighteen months previously. An all-powerful autocratic Khedive in Cairo had been humbled by European countries whose interest in and knowledge of the Sudan was minimal, and whose overwhelming concern was to secure the debt, by tightened control of Khedivial expenditure. Gordon wrote to his sister on 20 April 1878:

I have no hope whatever in any change for the better. In headquarters another Khedive would be just the same. Our government lives on a hand-to-mouth policy. They are very ignorant of these lands yet some day or another they, or some other government, will have to know them. For things at Cairo cannot stay as they are. The Khedive will be curbed in, and will no longer be absolute sovereign. Then will come the question of these countries.[9]

Finance   This was Gordon's first opportunity to wrestle with the finances of the *hakimdaria*, the principal item of which was the upkeep of the substantial army, the regular payment of their salaries and wages being his first priority. Until Gessi's arrival in Bahr el Ghazal Gordon's army, numbering over 20,000, was distributed as follows, reflecting not only public security but also local resistance to tax paying.

Dongola and Berber	709
Kordofan	1476
Darfur	4921
Kolkol (Qulqul)	1100
Shakka	1058
Fashoda	910
Khartoum	1922
Sennar and Fazughli	1249
Suakin and Massawa	1151
Berbera and Harar	3400
Equatoria	3563
	21,459 men

In addition to the regular troops, Egyptian and Sudanese, and the artillery, the army continued to be augmented by the *bashi-buzouq* mounted or dismounted irregulars.

One third of the troops were stationed in the conquered Darfur governorate (with Shakka and Qulqul) and another third in the recently occupied lands of Equatoria and the Gulf of Aden littoral. The individual breakdown of the cost of such military containment is unavailable: we can only guess at the calculations of the acting *hakimdars* in the interim years 1875–77, but the cost was substantial. The pay of the troops had been permanently in arrears, making the booty of active service the more attractive, and enhancing the temptation to acquire slaves, despite the abolition of tribute to Egypt and the indefinite waiving of debts on Gordon's appointment.

Gordon was fortunate in having with him in Khartoum until mid-October 1878 the newly promoted inspector-general of Sudan telegraphs, Carl Christian Giegler Bey. The latter worked with Gordon on the compilation of a map showing estimated figures province by province for revenue, expenditure, deficit and debt but, in addition, the geographical distribution of the army. This was submitted to Cairo in October 1878 and resubmitted, with figures for the full year 1878, in March 1879. (See overleaf.)

There had seemingly been no *hakimdaria* budget since that of Ismail Pasha Ayub in April 1874. Thereafter the individual Sudan province budgets had been submitted individually to the Cairo ministry of finance. The decision that all governors and administrative officials should from 1875 be military personnel would have further confused the differentiation between military and civil costs. Gordon's letter journal in July 1878 gives Sudan accounts for 1877 showing a deficit of £E259,000 in expenditure over revenue, which he planned to reduce by economies in 1878 to £E50,000. Three months later he would reckon that *to date* the deficit was £E40,000, due entirely to the Darfur rebellion. In 1878 annual expenditure was budgeted for £E720,000 against revenue of £E579,000, with the accumulated debt standing at £E327,000. Gordon still aimed to contrive a balance between expenditure and revenue and to reduce the debt progressively. The low Nile of 1877 followed in 1878 by a much delayed high Nile had however reduced cultivation and therefore tax yields and led to the high price of *dura* and serious hunger.

Goschen in Cairo had been told that the Sudan contributed £E143,000 annually to Egypt, the requirement placed on Ismail Pasha Ayub when he was made *hakimdar*, later reduced to £E100,000; but, as Gordon observed to his sister, the tribute had not been paid and since Gordon's appointment as Governor-General by agreement 'nothing had been given on either side' (11.7.78). When the Egyptian debt commission of enquiry started to scrutinise Sudan finance in October 1878 and requested payment of a debt of £E30,000, which Gordon calculated to be a credit of £E9,000, he wrote privately to Lord Tenterden in the Foreign Office warning that he, Gordon, did not intend to remain *hakimdar* to be questioned. He received an assurance from Lord Salisbury via the Cairo consulate-general that the commission would not be troubling him further.

Gordon's last dispatch to Cairo on finance, before he left again for Darfur to support Gessi in Bahr el Ghazal in March 1879, advised that the 1878 deficit would be £E109,000 (the tax yields had dropped) and the outstanding debt £E300,000; and 'if you do not believe it, send up and examine the affairs, or else take the finance of the Sudan under you.' He would not take responsibility for ruining the Sudan.

The following is a literal printing of Giegler's handwriting. His financial items are given in pounds sterling and his transliterations of geographical names are his own.

A Soudan and Somalia Provinces
   Troops 24,622
   Receipts   551,103
   Expenditure   656,875
   Deficit   105,772
   Debts   300,379
   Tax by law   444,225
   Tax possible to recover   176,899
   Tax taken   184,634
   Tax impossible to recover   72,692
B Bahr el Gazalle
   In revolt
C Berber
   Troops 430
   Receipts   41,203
   Expenditure   24,795
   Debts   20,213
   Excess of Receipts over
   Expenditure [?16,408]   16,410
   Taxes by law   39,626
   Taxes taken   18,611
   Taxes possible to take   21,015
   Taxes impossible to take   11,015
D Darfur
   Fasher and Dara
      Troops 6,021
      Expenditure   130,000
      Receipts   17,000
      Deficit   113,000
      Debts   99,433
   Shakka
      Troops 1,058
      Receipts   18,994
      Expenditure   26,351
      Deficit   7,357
      Debts   341
E Dongola
   Troops 279
   Receipts   62,699
   Expenditure   10,844
   Debts   1,041
   Excess of Receipts over
   Expenditure   51,855
   Taxes by law   62,271

      Taxes taken
      Taxes possible to take
      Taxes impossible to tak
F Equatorial Provinces
   Expenditure
   Receipts
   Deficit
G Kartum
   Troops 1,922
   Expenditure
   Receipts
   Excess of Expenditure
      over Receipts
   Debts
   Taxes by law
   Taxes taken
   Taxes possible to take
   Taxes impossible to tak
H Kordofan
   Troops 1,476
   Receipts
   Expenditure
   Excess of Receipts over
   Expenditure
   Taxes by law
   Taxes taken
   Taxes possible to take
   Taxes impossible to tak
   Debts
I Sennar
   Troops 1,249
   Receipts
   Expenditure
   Excess of Receipts over
      Expenditure
   Debts
   Taxes by law
   Taxes taken
   Taxes possible to take
   Taxes impossible to ta
J Somali Coast
   Expenditure
      Berberah
      Zeila
      Harrar

31,504	Receipts		
30,777	Berberah	1,757	
8,676	Zeila	4,359	51,280
	Harrar	45,164	
47,000	Deficit		14,241
8,000	Debts		3,761
39,000	K Suakin and Massaoua		
	Troops 1,151		
	Receipts		
136,968	Suakin	18,364	
118,583	Massaoua	18,493	36,857
	Expenditure		
18,385	Suakin	13,578	
128,654	Massaoua	17,978	31,556
79,165	Excess of Receipts over		
294	Expenditure		5,301
49,725	Taxes by law		
24,103	Suakin	15,284	
	Massaoua	17,357	32,641
	Taxes taken		
74,256	Suakin	8,352	
38,998	Massaoua	3,493	11,845
	Taxes possible to be taken		The whole
35,258	Debts		
72,625	Suakin	1,153	
24,032	Massaoua	1,959	3,112
48,594	L Taka		
8,395	Troops 3,163		
13,807	Receipts		63,176
	Expenditure		55,236
	Excess of Receipts over		
52,615	Expenditure		7,940
30,406	Taxes by law		62,333
	Taxes taken		35,899
22,209	Taxes possible to take		26,439
7,434	Taxes impossible to take		9,300
51,321	M Wadi Halfa		
25,513	Railway Expenses		22,258
25,807	Railway Receipts		5,438
11,237	Railway Debts		2,859

17,229	
5,061	65,571
43,281	

Dr Alice Moore-Harell has analysed Gordon's 1879 submission to Cairo of the Sudan's estimated balance sheet for 1878. The map to which the estimates were related is seemingly that attributed to Giegler by Richard Hill. With regard to the deficit, Dr Moore-Harell accepts that there was no substantial gap between the trial submission of October 1878 and that for the whole of 1878 in March 1879. In the light of Gordon's Sudan budget for January–July 1879 forecasting a surplus of some £E55,000, she concludes: 'Gordon's efforts, as well as positive development in trade and agriculture, meant that the Sudan was on its way to financial and economic independence within a few years.'[10]

The Wadi Halfa Railway　A major item of financial contention between Cairo and Khartoum was the contract for the railway to link Aswan with Khartoum. The tender for track and rolling stock, initially to cover the railway to the point of transhipment 250 miles south of Wadi Halfa, had been awarded to Appleby Brothers but they were not being paid punctually. By May 1876 £E31,200 was owing and with the situation deteriorating further Appleby referred the dispute to arbitration in December 1876. Ismail Pasha Ayub in Cairo, about to be replaced as *hakimdar*, was made responsible for the railway project but was soon appointed minister of education. The Sudan portion south of Wadi Halfa had been made chargeable to the *muderia* of Dongola and Berber which, on Gordon's appointment as *hakimdar,* reverted from Egypt to the Sudan, Mohammed Sa'id Pasha Wahbi being appointed *mudir.* Already by April 1877 Gordon was seeking to rid himself of the responsibility, and he reached agreement to contribute only £E50,000 p.a. He did not share the enthusiasm of the British engineers for the project and by November, when he met Fowler's deputy Jansen at Dongola, while he reached an accord about how the work should proceed, he was determined 'to get out of Fowler's fearful contract'. Further discussion was interrupted by the necessity of Gordon's return to Bogos.

Gordon, Jansen and the Appleby director were able to confer further on the financial crisis on the train from Assiut to Cairo on 7 March 1878. The Sudan contribution of £E50,000 was paid, but the failure of Egypt to take more than a quarter of the £E600,000 worth of materials contracted in the period 1873–79 made her liable to a penalty fine of between £E45,000 and £E90,000. Gordon in March 1878 advised the Khedive that he could not in future pay the £E50,000 p.a. and in March 1879 he repeated his refusal, being faced with a current deficit of £E109,000 and debt of £E300,000. The contract, he insisted, had been made by Egypt, not the Sudan, and it was not for the Sudan to be ruined in consequence. Progress on the project was frozen. The railway nevertheless reached Saras, connecting it with Wadi Halfa at top speed within three hours, according to Giegler, in November 1878.[11]

Riverain *muderias*   This railway had been instrumental in bringing Gordon to visit Dongola which had 'not seen a governor for years', unlike its twin headquarters Berber on the link-road from Suakin to Khartoum. Nevertheless Auguste B. Wylde would claim that he had discussed with Gordon in 1877 the possibility of a Suakin-Berber railway, the subject of a favourable commission report in 1883, but not implemented.

Dongola, like Taka, currently enjoyed good public security, and this was reflected in the moderate size of its garrison; and agricultural revenues had been established, even if the enthusiasm for development of Ahmed Mumtaz and Munzinger in Taka was unfulfilled. South of Khartoum, the Blue Nile province remained at risk from a pre-emptive strike by Emperor John, but Gordon's initiatives at least purchased an extension of peace. He visited Abu Haraz en route to Bogos in November 1877, assuring himself of the adequacy of the province's defence capability and at the end of February 1879, at a time when 'forced inaction here kills me', he seems to have made a brief excursion to Sennar for the *eid* festival. In the aftermath of that visit the *mudir*, Mohammed Rasikh, moved apparently to Suakin.

Unusually in his nine-month spell in Khartoum Gordon did not make a visit to Fashoda *muderia* and in May 1877 he had the Reth Kwickon Kwatker appointed *bey*. Here by 1878 El Tayeb Bey Abdallah had succeeded Ali Bey Reda el Kurdi as *mudir*. Gordon would certainly have included Fashoda en route to his intended inspection of Equatoria, had he not been obliged to abandon the whole idea in September 1878 with the arrival of a Lado steamer bringing news that once again 'the grass has closed the route to Gondokoro'. Successive teams were sent to clear the access, but by January 1879 the *sudd* had been only partially cleared. In the Sobat '*mamuria idara*', which previously had been part of his Equatoria general-governorate, Gordon had found it prudent to order the evacuation of the Nasir station up-river in November 1877 while now, in July 1878, Gessi requested El Tayeb Bey at Fashoda to station a *nuggar* permanently at Tawfiqia to aid the garrison of 160 in their wood-cutting duties for White Nile steamers.

Khartoum Life   When Gordon noted in July 1878 'I have for the first time regularly taken up the government', he did not anticipate that a month later, with the challenge of the Province accounts, he would feel depressed, worn, bitter, 'tied by the leg to this place'.

> I get up at 7 am; at 8 am see my chief clerk and go into the night's telegrams, sometimes 25–30 and give any orders. Breakfast 10am. Go down to the Divan and see all letters and any people and then return to write letters till 1p.m. Till 4pm nothing particular. At 4p.m. half an hour of other telegrams: then nothing until 6pm. Perhaps twice a week some Arabs come in or else the Austrian Consul [Martin Hansal] or telegraph superintendent [Carl Giegler] for a couple of hours. [Gordon had promoted the latter director-general of Sudan telegraphs and, additionally, postmaster.] Then I read and go to bed. I never go out beyond my garden for there is nothing to go out for: it is exceedingly dull... Though my official work is all difficulty, I do not see how I could leave the post in which I am placed weary as it is.

He was encountering the consequences, already experienced on the long camel marches, of being unable to converse fluently in Arabic, a continuing major handicap throughout his tenure of office – 'my Arabic is of the most meagre description.' For his work he was necessarily dependent on his private secretary who could speak neither English nor French and to whom Gordon dictated in uncertain Arabic. Latterly this was the Sudanese Berzati Bey, highly intelligent and reliable – 'my most intimate friend for three years'. After the 1898 reconquest a full knowledge of language was wisely made a condition for confirmation of British administrative officers in their appointments.

En route to Cairo in early March 1878, Gordon had at Assiut encountered Daniele Comboni, who twenty years previously had briefly served as a Catholic priest at Holy Cross and had returned to the Sudan in May 1873 as pro-vicar of the vicariate of Central Africa – to found mission stations in Kordofan at El Obeid and Dilling, and an agricultural community at Malbes ten miles from El Obeid. Now, consecrated bishop, he had been received by the Khedive in Cairo. Comboni reached Khartoum in April 1878 in the aftermath of drought, famine and the death of many missionaries from malaria and cholera.

Gordon invited Comboni to accompany him in the coming autumn up the White Nile, but in the event neither could go.

In November, still lacking books (excepting the Bible and Homer's *Iliad*) and social contacts – strangely he does not mention horse-riding for exercise – he spent ten days of his leisure dedicating his cartographical skill to a map of the Sudan, following which he busied himself with the clock repairs.

The cooler weather brought a visit from Frank Lupton, newly appointed in charge of White Nile steamers, to be deputy to Emin Bey (who had replaced Ibrahim Fawzi in Equatoria in July) and ultimately successor also to Gessi Pasha, governor Bahr el Ghazal. The Gedaref meeting in December 1878 with the Abyssinian envoy, and resumed correspondence with the Khedive, further restored Gordon's morale. The critical confrontation at Deim Idris between Gessi and Sulieman Zubeir in January 1879, news of which reached Gordon on 4 March, required his immediate presence in Shakka. Receiving the Khedive's assent to his appointment of Giegler (now *pasha*) as acting Governor-General – rather than Hasan Pasha Hilmi el Juwaisar, general-governor of Darfur and recently arrived from sick leave in Cairo – Gordon left at once for El Obeid and Shakka, riding 26–30 miles a day – 'It is better than the dullness of Khartoum.'[12]

5   HAMMERING THE SLAVE TRADE: DARFUR AND BAHR EL GHAZAL

Gordon had been born in 1833, the year of the emancipation of slavery in the British dominions. Only in 1807 had the slave trade, notably directed across the Atlantic, been prohibited to British subjects and British-flag ships. France, Portugal and Spain had followed suit. Resistance to the progressive amelioration of the conditions of slaves, especially in the British West Indies, was however prolonged and emancipation, which was effected gradually, was accompanied by substantial compensation to the owners. Public opinion was nevertheless falling in behind William Wilberforce and the abolitionists. The concept of the slave as an inferior creature, 'nourishing a vain life within the brain', was being defeated by the moral imperative: 'Am I not a man and a brother?' In 1862, one year into the American Civil War, Abraham Lincoln proclaimed the emancipation of the slaves in the Confederate states, constituting a third of the population. A new momentum towards abolition had been kindled in the western hemisphere. Yet at the African equator Speke and Grant had only just discovered the source of the White Nile, and a further nine years would run before Baker, charged with the suppression of the slave trade, would raise the Khedivial flag at Gondokoro.

Gordon, Baker's successor as general-governor of Equatoria 1874–76, had taken decisive action against the slave trade in his province, proclaiming a government monopoly of the ivory trade, prohibiting the recruitment of private militias, and establishing a string of manned stations from the Sobat river to M'ruli, thus substantially closing the White Nile to the transportation of slaves. Within months of Gordon's appointment to Equatoria, the report of Romolo Gessi from his expedition to Meshra el Rek in July 1874 confirmed what Gordon already believed: that slave trading in the Bahr el Ghazal via Darfur and Kordofan was on a far greater scale than on the Nile. He had been realist enough to recognise that he presently did not have the resources to tackle the armed bands of Zubeir, but the suppression of the slave trade throughout the Sudan became his long-term objective.

Thus the condition of Gordon's acceptance of continued service in 1877 was to be ruler of the whole Sudan, and in this he had British government support, the latter under increasing pressure at home from the British and Foreign Anti-Slavery Society and the Church Missionary Society. In April 1873 the Anti-Slavery Society had presented a memorial address praying that the Khedive should take effective steps for total suppression within his dominions, in response to which Nubar Pasha, accompanying the Khedive on a visit to the Sultan at Constantinople, had on 12 July submitted to Sir Henry Elliot, the British ambassador, a written proposal embodying five articles, envisaging the immediate prohibition of *public* trafficking in Black and Abyssinian slaves and of *private* trafficking after seven years. In return the Khedive looked for a quid pro quo, initially in relation to Abyssinia, then in the acquisition of an Indian Ocean port.

The Khedive would undertake the absolute prohibition on the departure of any Black or Abyssinian from Egypt or its dependencies without a certificate of freedom; and the grant of freedom to Egyptians on birth, irrespective of parenthood. Trafficking in eunuchs would be deemed murder; other slave trading across Egypt's borders would be liable to trial by court martial. All existing slave children in Egypt and the Sudan would be liberated.

Effectively slavery itself would be abolished by gradual measure as in the case of Brazil. The *sale* of slaves would be forbidden within Egypt after seven years, and in the Sudan after twelve years, from the date of signature of the Convention. Captured slaves would be freed 'without exposing the risk of perishing from fatigue or want or falling again into slavery'. Once liberated, male slaves declining domestic or agricultural work would be subject to military conscription, while female slaves would be given domestic work in government or provincial establishments.

The negotiations over four years would be protracted. British reaction was favourable, subject, first, to an absolute prohibition on the importation of slaves into Egypt or her dependencies, under severe penalties; and secondly that enforcement of the prohibition on the export of slaves should be undertaken by British naval vessels with the right to search and detain both Egyptian and Ottoman vessels of all kinds (a reciprocal right would extend to Egyptians in the search of British vessels).

The Khedive, although unbothered by the ownership of some 400 personal slaves in his *da'ira*, and not totally single-minded in his readiness to advance the suppression of the slave trade in his dominions in the face of keen local opposition, was probably genuine in accepting the objective provided he could exact some palpable benefit from his cooperation. On 4 August 1877, conscious of his weakening power, the Khedive assented to signature of the Slave Trade Convention of seven articles. Trafficking in slaves in Egypt would be prohibited in 1884 and in the Sudan in 1889, thereafter to be subject by Khedivial decree to imprisonment for between five months and five years (the Convention equated the offence to robbery with murder). Khedivial sovereignty over the southern littoral to Ras Hafoun in the Gulf of Aden was recognised by a second Convention of 7 September 1877. A British director-general for maritime police was appointed to control the Red Sea and the Gulf of Aden.[13]

The Khedive followed up signature of the Slave Trade Convention with a letter to Gordon who was currently in Darfur quelling the revolt of the *emir*, Mohammed Harun el Rashid Seif el Din, urging him to put an immediate end to the *razzias*. Over the next two years the suppression of the slave traders first of Darfur and then of Bahr el Ghazal was to be Gordon's major concern. In Darfur he already recognised that ending the local *razzias* would be dependent first on the occupation of Shakka, the base of Sulieman Zubeir, with its three to four thousand slaves. Such a number, if a major rebellion were not to be provoked, could only be *liberated* if compensation were paid to the owners and therefore – in the interim – the slaves should be recruited into the army. The scale of the Darfur problem was nothing to that presented by Bahr el Ghazal with its 10,000 hostile slave militia, tackling which was not an immediate option. The whole plan for slave trade suppression troubled Gordon with his limited force, aggravated by the persistent threat of Arab rebellion in Darfur and Kordofan. Emancipation would present incomparably greater difficulties.

On 17 September 1877 he wrote to his sister:

> I tell you plainly that the Treaty by which slaves will be free, after 7 years in Egypt and after 12 years in the Sudan, will never and *can never* be carried out in places away from Cairo, Alexandria, Suez etc, and further that no government either British or Khedivial could enforce it *without militantly occupying the whole country, even Darfur etc.* The edict will be issued but if it is not accompanied by a possible scheme it will be a dead letter. No man in the place of a governor would plunge the whole country into revolt on this question [slavery emancipation]: he would resign or else let things stand. I consider it will be possible to stop slave *razzias* by my people but how, if the border tribes bring slaves to my country, am I to have the expense of cordons along its extent?

Either slave owners must be contemporaneously compensated or else liberation had to be left optimistically for the expiration of the time limits. And again he wrote on 29 September 1877:

> My impression is that there is no solution short of *complete emancipation* either by *an armed force* (in which case great injustice will be done) or by compensation which we have no money to do. Short of this, the best way would be to legalise the transport of slaves and in fact supervise it by the government which idea will shock a great many people.

Indeed Gordon's conclusion after six months' office was not far removed from that of Sir Philip Francis (p. 171). Nor was he blinkered to the tacit earlier acceptance by Britain of West Indies slavery.

> Did not our government once allow slave-trading? Do you know that cargoes of slaves came into Bristol harbour in the time of our fathers?… I must notice to you one thing which is very different

among the society here and that of the planters in the colonies. One never hears of owners of slaves keeping gangs of them for field-labour or for cultivation. They are kept for slave-servants or by the slave dealers as slave troops… I therefore claim for my people a greater kindness of heart than was possessed by the planters with their Christian profession and civilisation.[14]

Darfur 1876–78 The surrender of the Emir Hasaballah to Zubeir Pasha in January 1875, and his dispatch to Cairo by the *hakimdar* with the young nominated Sultan of Darfur, Mohammed el Fadl Ibrahim, had left another uncle of the latter, the *emir* Bosh, as the residual focus of Fur resistance to the Egyptian conquerors – until the latter's death at Kebkebia at the hands of Zubeir in June. Opposition to the conquerors rallied again in Jebel Marra, first under the former *maqdoum* Rahma Gomo and then, in mid-1876, under the *emir* Mohammed Harun el Rashid Seif el Din. Gordon was to hear three years later that initially Harun had been cooperative with the government, until he had been gratuitously flogged by the *mudir* (?Mohammed Sa'id Bey), a precursor to the hanging of the complaisant Fur *vizir*. Zubeir, followed by the *hakimdar,* Ismail Ayub, had already been summoned to Cairo by the Khedive, leaving the general-governor Hasan Pasha Hilmi in control, his substantial army diminishing through disease, with no *hakimdar* in the country for a further year.

Emir Harun saw the opportunity and raised a fresh rebellion, news of which reached Gordon at Massawa in February 1877. Having seized Jebel Si north of Jebel Marra, Harun succeeded in pinning down Hasan Pasha's garrisons in El Fasher, El Kobbé, Kebkebia and Qulqul, Dara, Umm Shanga and Foja; while Shakka in Dar Fertit, now Zubeir was in Cairo, was ruled by Sulieman, his undependable twenty-year-old son. Gordon sought a temporary understanding with Welde-Mikael in Bogos, but he was obliged to curtail his first formal appearance in Khartoum in May to a bare three weeks before leaving via El Obeid for Foja and Umm Shanga on the Darfur borders, reaching the latter on 15 June. He brought with him a very limited contingent of 500 men to augment the more substantial but demoralised garrisons of a territory conquered only two years before.

In this region at least, Gordon shared neither the territorial ambitions nor the commercial hopes of the Khedive and of Ismail Ayub his predecessor. To his sister Gordon wrote on arrival at Umm Shanga, observing the scarcity of fresh water:

You would, I feel sure, feel sickened at this horrid useless-looking country and feel disposed to vacate it and yet I am bound to hold on to it; such a waste of money and all this revolt is caused by the shameful misgovernment of the country – a few months ago you could go from here to Fasher without arms – now 2000 men can scarce go.

He blamed the general-governor Hasan Hilmi el Juwaisar based at El Kobbé for inadequate discipline and fighting spirit, despite a total force of 7,000 strong under his command at El Kobbé and under Abdel Raziq Haqqi Pasha at El Fasher, 'doing nothing'. The *emir* Harun surveyed them from the northern end of Jebel Marra.

With his own force numbering only 500, Gordon decided to advance on El Fasher via El Taweisha and Dara, hoping – by recruitment from the local garrisons – to strengthen it sufficiently to tackle Harun at Jebel Tura. Against his inclination, he sent word to Sulieman, based at Shakka with his own large army, suggesting that the latter accept the appointment as *mudir* of Dara. Gordon arrived at Dara himself on 12 July 1877 to find an Egyptian garrison of 1,800, armed with Remingtons, that had been immobile on Hasan Pasha's orders for the past six months, and to learn that Hasan Pasha in El Kobbé and Abdel Raziq Pasha in El Fasher were themselves cravenly immobile and evidently unwilling to assist Gordon's advance on Harun.

His concern for the religious worship of his troops was roused by the conditions at Dara:

> When the Egyptian [Zubeir Pasha] seized the country, they took the mosque here for a powder magazine. I had it cleared out and restored for worship and endowed the priests [*imams*] and the crier [*muezzin*]… To me it appears that the Mussulman worships God as well as I do, and is acceptable, if sincere, as any Christian.

The first half of August was spent successfully campaigning through Hamar Aulad Nimr country east of Jebel Tura, until Gordon reached El Fasher on 18 August, there at last to meet Hasan Pasha from El Kobbé. Gordon persuaded him to take the initiative – successfully – against Harun, driving the latter back wounded into Jebel Marra.[15]

For Gordon the almost bloodless defeat of Harun's present revolt and the reopening of the road from Umm Shanga to El Fasher ('all the tribes have submitted') – while generously recognised by his Khedive – were by no means the fulfilment of his objective. Professor O'Fahey reports that these years were remembered in Darfur as *a'am kwakwiya* or years of banditry; the province was in a state of chaos with bands of slave troops roaming at will, a bankrupt administration and continual warfare'. Gordon's overriding objective remained the suppression of the slave trade but the full magnitude of the task was only now apparent. That had not featured in the Khedivial instructions to Ismail Ayub for the conquest of Darfur – a task pre-empted in any case by the arch-slave trader Zubeir – even if earlier, in the time of Ja'afar Pasha Mazhar, Hilali's expedition had been enjoined to 'treat the inhabitants with mercy and kindness and not to impose upon them onerous taxation'. Now having instigated the defeat of Harun, Gordon was obliged to grapple with the problem of putting an end to the slave *razzias* and improving the condition of the victims whom day after day he encountered in caravans with their masters.

Reluctantly Gordon concluded that in the short run the solution had to be to recruit the *razzia* bands into the army by buying them, recognising that Shakka, 'the slave nest', had to be captured before the trade could possibly be extinguished. On 30 August 1877 news came that Sulieman Zubeir, who had not replied to Gordon's letters, was now at Dara with supposedly 6,000 armed men. Covering eighty miles by camel in thirty-six hours and outdistancing their escort by about seven miles, Gordon followed by his secretaries rode the next day into an astonished *baharra* (militia) encampment, where the troops were deployed facing the wrong direction. Struggling to reorientate themselves as Gordon reached the fort, they fired a reluctant salute. 'Imagine to yourself the arrival of a single dirty red-faced individual on a camel ornamented with flies arriving in the *divan* all of a sudden: the people were paralysed and could not believe their eyes... Tomorrow I see the troops and the brigands.'

Now dressed in his full uniform as a *mushir*, Gordon had summoned Sulieman and his principal lieutenants to his own *divan*. 'I told them I knew they meant to revolt, that I would break them up... They left me and then wrote to give in. Then came three days of doubts and fears.' Gessi was to learn in December 1878 just how close Gordon came to being murdered at Dara. With the exception of El Nur Mohammed Anqara all Sulieman's lieutenants at a council of war voted to kill Gordon, but El Nur successfully argued that Sulieman should postpone their attack as they were not yet ready for rebellion.

These first few days of September 1877 represented a major victory in Darfur for Gordon, outnumbered though he was by Sulieman. He

Gordon approaching Dara, 1 September 1877

skilfully detached from Sulieman both Sa'id Hussein, brother of a *sanjak* of Sulieman, whom Gordon appointed *mudir* of Shakka and made a *bey*; and El Nur Anqara, whom he appointed *mudir* and *bey* initially of Dara then of the Dar Sula frontier region 150 miles west of Dara. He then ordered Sulieman himself to leave Dara with 1,500 men for Shakka, there to await Gordon's own arrival with Hasan Pasha Hilmi a week later (14 September 1877) accompanied by an escort of four companies only. They encountered no opposition at Shakka. Conscious of the enormous risks he ran, Gordon had nevertheless successfully imposed government rule on this slave base of Dar Fertit. An enormous territory had effectively been brought under the Khedive. Yet if the northern slave route had been interrupted, to the south the Bahr el Ghazal remained unsubdued, with a local militia of some 10,000 men.

Gordon, en route back to El Obeid from Darfur, was reminded that despite his remarkable achievements, 'as I suspected I am convoying down a caravan of slaves. I came on them to-day chained together some 60 women and men... the owner of the caravan had bought them at Shakka; was he to blame?' He sought to reassure himself with the thought that Shakka had fallen only ten days before. 'In six months I hope to have the telegraph line at Shakka and in due course an open road from Fashoda to Shakka.' Would the *razzia* militia disband? As he personally withdrew from the area Gordon was the more convinced that this could be achieved only through the appointment of European officials in Darfur.

On apprehending the situation in Darfur on his arrival earlier in June 1877, Gordon had then written both to the Khedive and to Richard Burton seeking respectively the appointment of Burton as Governor-General of Darfur, and the latter's consent to it – even to consider Harar and the littoral. Burton rebuffed him – and, indeed, a second time in August 1878. Burton wrote:'You and I are too much alike. I could not serve under you nor you under me. I do not look upon the Sudan as a lasting thing. I have nothing to depend upon but my salary, and I have a wife and you have not.'

Burton's refusal was a serious disappointment in the wake of Sulieman's recent departure to Deim Zubeir and Gordon was to express regret in February 1878 that, instead of journeying to Cairo to assist the Khedive in his debt crisis, he had not himself gone to Darfur 'to finish matters there'. Until March 1879 Gordon was personally to be kept away 'by the Abyssinian trouble, the rows with Cairo, and the finance at Khartoum'. For the while, however, until his return to Kassala in July 1878, the experienced Abdel Raziq Haqqi Pasha maintained control of public security in Darfur, if not of the slave caravans. Had Osman Rifqi Pasha not disobeyed Gordon's instructions to take over as general-governor in June 1878 the consequent vacuum in command would not have invited the revolt of Sabahi, the Zubeir *sanjak* of Shakka, at El Odaya and the threat to El Obeid in September. Hasan Pasha Hilmi was not to return as general-governor to El Obeid from convalescence in Cairo until the end of January 1879.

The vulnerability of Darfur despite its sizeable garrison in the latter half of 1878 exercised Gordon's concerns. He had lost confidence in the resolution of the Egyptian officers available. Charles Frederic Rosset of Baden, former trader then consular agent for Germany and Britain in Khartoum, was dispatched as general-governor, only to die of suspected poisoning in November. He in turn was replaced in May 1879 by G. B. Messadaglia, a Venetian soldier in Egyptian service, *mudir* of Dara since August 1878. Rudolf Slatin, aged twenty-two but a veteran of the Bosnian campaign of 1878, would take over Dara at the end of July 1879, having met Gordon en route to Khartoum from Darfur at Tura'a el Khadra on the White Nile. With Romolo Gessi involved in a major campaign across the southern Darfur border against Sulieman Zubeir, it was vital to Gordon that his commanders should not be private sympathisers with the implacably hostile slave traders. Indeed Shukry criticises him for appointing Yusuf Hasan el Shallali (Rohl), El Tayib Abdallah (Fashoda) and Sa'id Juma' (El Fasher) – all ex-traders. Gordon insisted: 'I want in each governor three qualities: courage, honesty and kindness.' Slavery however was not repugnant to Islam; slave-ownership reflected status; and the promotion of expatriate Christian newcomers to the Sudan, in his campaign for the supervision the slave trade, did not endear Gordon to many of their Egyptian subordinates even if the enemy, Zubeir's adherents, would make no discrimination in their resolve to wage war against the government to the death.

Perhaps the argument which weighed most heavily with Gordon was contained in a letter to Sir Samuel Baker: 'No employés [officials], however well disposed, will implicate themselves too much in the ways of a good governor, for fear of hereafter consequences: when a bad one comes, they know they will be spited. This is one of my great difficulties and anxieties, for I fear for my Faithfuls (there are but few of them) if I died, or if I left.'[16]

Bahr el Ghazal 1877–79; Darfur 1879   When Gordon had left his general-governorate of Equatoria at the end of 1876, Bahr el Ghazal – like Lado, Rohl and Makaraka – had been a province district although, because of the proximity of the preponderantly strong Zubeir and, after November 1875, of his son Sulieman, it had been in practice administratively ignored. In Sulieman's elected absence at Shakka, authority effectively lay in the hands of Zubeir's septuagenarian Dongalawi *wakil*, Idris Abtar, formerly a trader with Ghattas and then a participant with Zubeir in the conquest of Darfur. However in May 1877 Gordon, before leaving Khartoum for Darfur, had appointed the loyal Ibrahim Fawzi as *bey* and *mudir* of Bahr el Ghazal under Equatoria. Fawzi, having received the submission of the Ghattas and Abu Amouri *zaribas* in his new territory, was appalled by the corruption pervading Idris Abtar's regime, arrested him, and accompanied him to Khartoum.

Meanwhile Gordon, in September 1877 after the Dara confrontation, had declined to place any government responsibility in Sulieman's hands but, when the latter requested Khedivial agreement to go to Cairo to make his personal submission, Gordon, at Shakka, had relented and sanctioned Sulieman's return to Bahr el Ghazal with the rank of *bey*, but subordinate to Ibrahim Fawzi. That was to prove a costly mistake. In July 1878, when he learned of the consequences, Gordon wrote: 'I regret that I did not take Zubeir's son prisoner when I was at Shakka.' Shortly after Gordon's departure back to El Obeid with Hasan Pasha (who was bound for Cairo) on 17 September 1877, Sulieman, strengthened by a fresh rallying to him of his supporters in Dara, had duly marched for Deim Zubeir, arriving in October. Fawzi had already left with the delinquent Idris Abtar for Khartoum, and Idris's brother, Osman Abtar, had been placed meanwhile in command of the garrison at Deim Idris. Initially Sulieman and his Ja'ali supporters kept their distance.

On arrival at Khartoum in December 1877, where Osman Pasha Rifqi was in charge as deputy *hakimdar* and *seraskir*, Idris persuaded Rosset the German consular agent to telegraph Gordon at Suakin affirming his innocence. After he reached Khartoum at the end of January, Gordon conceded the claim of Idris to be restored to his former authority. Threatened with Fawzi's resignation, Gordon in compensation promoted the latter general-governor at Lado and obtained Fawzi's consent to the appointment of Idris as *mudir* of Bahr el Ghazal and *bey*. On Idris's return in triumph to Deim Zubeir with a government escort of 200 regulars he provocatively ordered Sulieman's dismissal. Encouraged by a letter from his father Zubeir in Cairo of 13 May 1878 urging him to rid the country of this usurper, Sulieman, a proud Ja'ali, rejected Idris's ultimatum and attacked Osman Abtar at Deim Idris, cruelly massacring the whole garrison. Idris fled to Rohl, abandoning his arms in the Ghattas *zariba* whence they were presented to Sulieman, and leaving the *Ismailia* temporarily stranded at Meshra el Rek.

Gordon's return to Khartoum from Harar on the night of 27 June 1878 scarcely preceded by a day the arrival of news from Fashoda of Sulieman's massacre at Deim Idris, though Gordon had heard at Aden of Sulieman's rebellion in May. Fortuitously, Romolo Gessi was in Khartoum following an abortive attempt to explore the Sobat river. Eighteen months later Dr Felkin was to describe him as

> a small wiry man, very impulsive and vivacious. He had grey hair, bright lively eyes and highly nervous hands; he seemed as if he could not sit still for a moment, but was always on the move, and continually occupied in making cigarettes… I think I never met a more entertaining companion.

With the help of Dr Wilhelm Junker, the German botanist researching western Equatoria, who coincidentally had also returned to Khartoum after a nineteen-month absence, Gordon was able to persuade Gessi – rather than Yusuf Bey el Shellali, the less reliable *mudir* of Rohl – to lead the retributive expedition against Sulieman.

Idris Abtar had gone to ground, his Dongolawi support worsted by the rival Ja'aliyin in contingents of Sulieman. Fawzi's report had exposed the iniquities of Idris's rule of Bahr el Ghazal – its cruelty and corruption, the selling of slaves and of the garrison's *dura* to local traders – all to be amply confirmed subsequently by Gessi.[17]

Gessi's plan of campaign was to amass an initial force of 565 regular soldiers, to be partly contributed by Fashoda and Tawfiqia, who – with luck – would be augmented by 2,200 militia at Shambe and by some 4,800 Dongolawis in Bahr el Ghazal. Sailing from Khartoum on 15 July 1878 on the *Bordein*, and thankfully encountering the *Ismailia* returning from Meshra el Rek at El Ais, he sent his second-in-command Yusuf el Shellali to defend Rohl from attack, arriving there himself on 7 September. Heavy rains; the blocking of the Bahr el Ghazal by vegetation; and the non-materialisation of porters delayed his further departure to the Jur Ghattas *zariba* until 17 November and the occupation of Wau, essential to his communications with Meshra el Rek but burned down by Sulieman's forces, until 4 December. Wilfully denied contingents by the Equatoria *mudir* of Makraka , whose arrest was ordered, Gessi felt obliged to await reinforcements to his existing force of 1,500 riflemen before advancing further against Sulieman's forces, reckoned to be at least five times that number. Gessi's known government presence however attracted the important desertions of militia of Abu Amouri and of the *zariba* Biselli whose arrival at Wau on 12–13 December 1878 swelled Gessi's army by some 900 men. They also brought news that Sulieman was currently at Deim Idris, but when Gessi reached there on 21 December, Sulieman had withdrawn.

Gessi learned also that when Zubeir Pasha had finally quit his Deim for Cairo three years earlier, he had called a council of elders including Sulieman and Abu'l Qasim Musa; advised them he would go to seek the *pashalik* of Darfur from the Ottoman Sultan, and if unsuccessful would instruct them to execute the plan of rebellion they had that day sworn to launch 'under the big tree'. Zubeir had met Gordon in Cairo in March 1878, following the former's return sick from Turkey and the Khedive's request to Gordon to allow his return to the Sudan. Gordon had hesitated, believing Zubeir would obey no future Arab *hakimdar*. At their meeting, finding Gordon uncooperative, Zubeir had in May sent the order to start the rebellion.[18]

The initial lines of battle between Gessi and Sulieman were now drawn at Deim Idris, where on 27 December 1878 Sulieman returned to launch a two-day attack on the refortified station. He suffered, in Gessi's computation, 1,087 dead as against Gessi's 20 dead and wounded; his army was now reduced to 7,500 including 1,500 left at Deim Sulieman. Confident of further reinforcements and of desertions to augment his own force, Gessi telegraphed Gordon via Foja for additional Remingtons and ammunition only, to come by river via Fashoda to Meshra el Rek. The attacks on Deim Idris, however, continued throughout January, Sulieman reinforced from the Baqqara to the north, and Gessi from Shambe, Rumbek and Makraka. Again heavy casualties were suffered by Sulieman but Gessi was weakened by dangerously diminishing munition stocks due to lack of porters.

By mid-March 1879 Gessi's force had been built up to 4,000, with the arrival of one company of regulars from Equatoria and with three companies en route from Mustapha Bey Abdallah, the commandant at Shakka. Additionally, two ammunition boats had berthed from Lado. Gessi was now ready on 16 March, having denied the rebels their water sources, to attack and burn Deim Sulieman formerly Deim Zubeir.

Muderia *of Sulieman Zubeir*

Sulieman himself escaped, his cousin Hamid was wounded. Hamid was one of the principal slave trading chiefs, to whom, along with Abu'l Qasim Musa Wad el Haj and Rabih Fadlallah, Gessi believed authority in the Zubeir camp had now passed – men determined to fight to the death for their empire.[19]

Gessi reported to Gordon from Deim Sulieman on 6 May 1879 that on a second capture of the *zariba* the previous day he had found a letter from Zubeir to Sulieman from Cairo urging him to rid Bahr el Ghazal of all Egyptian troops and to attack and occupy Shakka – crucial evidence of complicity in the rebellion, the absence of which Gordon at Shakka on 1 April had been lamenting. Felix Gessi also refers to a second letter to Sulieman from 'El Obeid' found at Deim Sulieman: 'Thy father is still in Cairo in good health. He sent me a thousand *oke* [2,750 lb] of powder which I hold at his disposal. Try however to send for it quickly, so that the government may not get to know of it.' Sir Evelyn Baring subsequently recognised that the first letter, if genuine, would be conclusive proof. Gessi had captured good quantities of ivory, but Sulieman continued to elude capture and, accompanied by Rabih, Abu'l Qasim and a major force was by mid-June reported marching in the direction of Darfur to join Harun.

Gordon, having received news of Gessi's battles at Deim Idris, had left Khartoum in the hands of Carl Giegler in order to reinforce Kordofan and Shakka on 10 March 1879. Covering 26–30 miles per day by camel he reached El Obeid nine days later. Fariq Hasan Pasha Hilmi, returned from Cairo, had been dispatched to El Obeid by Gordon a month earlier to counter the rebellion launched in Kordofan the previous September by Sabahi, the Zubeir *sanjak* for the Humr Baqqara since 1875, though no action had yet been taken. Gordon's principal concern was to guard Gessi's flank against the deployment of reinforcements from Darfur to aid Sulieman, while ensuring that his own communications with the Sudan were not cut. After concerting with Hasan Hilmi in El Obeid on a strategy for the defeat of Sabahi; and for Darfur after Harun had been defeated – namely the appointment of the young *emir* Mohammed El Fadl Ibrahim, exiled in Cairo since 1875, as *sultan* and the withdrawal of the Egyptian garrison – Gordon pressed on first to Shakka (where water was scarce) and then, at the end of April, to Kalaka to expel the slave traders. Approval for Gordon's evacuation plan was not to be forthcoming from Cairo.

It was now that Gordon penned his philosophy as an expatriate ruler with an oriental sovereign:

> As to his *façon d'agir,* I maintain the foreigner should, for the time, entirely abandon his relations with his native land; he should resist his own Government, and those of other powers, and keep intact the sovereignty of the Oriental state whose bread he eats; he should put himself into the place of a native when he has to advise the Sultan, Ameer, or Khedive, or any question which his own, native, or any foreign Government, may wish settled, and his advice should be sealed by – first, what is universally right throughout the world; and, secondly, by what is best for the Oriental state he serves. I do not mean best for the ruler of the Oriental state, but best for the people. Thus, acting as a native of the country, he will take care that the peculiar habits and customs are considered.

In early May 1879, while Gessi was inflicting a further defeat on Sulieman who again eluded capture, Gordon marched boldly via Dara, El Fasher and Kebkebia, reaching Qulqul under attack on 26 May, the first government presence for two years. He would continue to liberate thousands of slaves from the traders, but the proximity of the twenty-one-year-old Harun and his own limited force persuaded him to retire to El Fasher, leaving El Nur Anqara in charge at Qulqul and Kebkebia.

El Nur Bey Anqara, later amir

Here on 5 June a summons to Cairo and news of Gessi's defeat of Sulieman's force limited his stay to a single day before setting out for El
Obeid and Khartoum. Passing through Umm Shanga to Tuwaisha he
was however halted on 24 June by a letter from Gessi with Madibbo
Bey Ali of the Rizeiqat at Shakka, revealing not only that Sulieman was
apparently heading for Jebel Marra to join Harun, but that Gessi had
ordered his deputy Yusuf el Shellali and his force back to Rohl, putting
Darfur at a new level of risk.

Gordon sent instructions to Gessi to meet him at El Tuwaish on 25
June where they had their first encounter since Gessi's departure from
Khartoum the previous July. The two men were not to meet again.
Gordon personally congratulated Gessi on his victorious campaign, his
promotion to *pasha*, the award of the Osmanli Order second class and
the reward of £E2,000. He was also able to agree Gessi's plans for the
Bahr el Ghazal and its unification with Equatoria. But because he was
required urgently in Khartoum, he delegated the responsibility for the
final capture of Sulieman and Harun, together with the future relationship between Bahr el Ghazal and Darfur, to joint action by Gessi and

by Giacomo Messadaglia Bey, general-governor of Darfur. In the event Harun was defeated and killed by El Nur Bey Anqara at Jebel Marra in March 1880, Messadaglia having been recalled at the end of 1879. Mohammed Sa'id Pasha was transferred back from Berber to El Obeid, as general-governor, where he had served under Ismail Ayub from 1873.[20]

Returning to Dara, Gessi set out on 4 July to pursue Sulieman, believed to be three days beyond Kalaka with a force of three columns led by himself, Rabih and Abu'l Qasim and heading for Jebel Marra. Here dissension arose, Rabih correctly distrusting Harun's intentions towards them in the light of Zubeir's previous conquest of Darfur. Rabih with his contingent of 690 militia departed instead for Dar Banda (Lake Chad) to the west, leaving Sulieman with Abu'l Qasim and their forces respectively of 860 and 400 camped at Gara in Qulqul *muderia*, before moving for Jebel Marra, a three-day journey. With a force of no more than 300, and ignoring the rough woodland terrain and the onset of the rains, Gessi reached the vicinity of Gara on the night of 15–16 July 1879. He surprised Sulieman and his force at dawn, delivering an ultimatum to surrender. Misled, he was to aver, by his companion Musa el Haj as to Gessi's greater numbers, Sulieman surrendered, later to be executed by firing squad along with eight lieutenants including Musa el Haj and Sulieman's uncle. Abu'l Qasim, a distance away, escaped.

Slatin, quoted by M. Sabry, who arrived in Dara from Khartoum after the event, affirms that Gessi promised Sulieman a pardon in return for his surrender only to break his word. Slatin does not identify his informant but en passant refers to a *sagh qol aghasi* Mansur Helmi who commanded two Dara companies in Gessi's pursuit force. Slatin would doubtless have met the latter months after Sulieman's death when Slatin arrived to succeed Charles Rigolet as *mudir* of Dara at the end of July. By that time Gessi had crossed the Bahr el Arab en route to Deim Idris, to become his provincial capital, so that Slatin never heard Gessi's version of events which, in respect of facts and timing, is irreconcilable with that told to Slatin. Egyptian dislike of Gessi probably coloured the latter.

Gordon would have opposed a pardon and, on the contrary, took full responsibility for the execution: 'I have no compunction about his death…Gessi only obeyed my orders in shooting him.' Gordon had never forgiven the massacre at Deim Idris the previous year of Osman Abtar and his garrison. In April 1879 he had declined to pardon

Sulieman's emissaries found guilty of rebellion. He was to receive the news of Sulieman's death from Gessi at Berber en route to Cairo on 1 August, having already learned a week earlier at Khartoum that a Cairo council, charged by the new Khedive Tawfiq, had found Zubeir Pasha guilty of sedition and condemned him to death. Gordon himself was to write to the Khedive that, in view of the execution of the ring-leaders of the revolt, Zubeir should be pardoned.

Emir Harun had been killed and his forces dispersed about the time of Sulieman's execution. Likewise Abu'l Qasim was captured at Shakka and executed in accordance with Gordon's orders – by Messadaglia, to Gessi's unconcealed anger, as he deemed Shakka to be Bahr el Ghazal and the knowledge of the whereabouts of an immense quantity of ivory had died with Abu'l Qasim.[21]

6   EQUATORIA 1877–79

On his return to Khartoum from Equatoria in October 1876, Gordon had handed over his general-governorate in an acting capacity to Qa'immaqam Henry Prout Bey, the Khedive Ismail having approved his recommendation. Prout reached Lado in December, to be followed in May 1877, also on Gordon's recommendation, by his fellow American Alexander Mason Bey. The general-governorate presently comprised a number of divisional *muderias*: Lado (Kukuh Agha) extending from Bor (Ibrahim Fawzi) to M'ruli (El Nur Mohammed); Makaraka (Bakhit Agha); Rohl, including Shambe and Rumbek (Yusuf el Shellali); and Bahr el Ghazal, presently closed.

There is scant information about the general-governorate under Prout, who would depart on sick leave leave in May 1877, not to return. Junker reports tribal revolts south of Lado and at Moogie in December 1876, put down by Kukuh and Bakhit. Stationed in Lado was the province *protomedico*, Dr Emin Effendi (the German Eduard Schnitzer), whom Gordon had already employed in a political mission to the *kabaka* M'tesa of Buganda in 1876. Leaving on a second such mission in May 1877, Emin was in July to encounter Mason Bey at Kerri, on the point of returning to Khartoum. He had arrived with Gordon in Khartoum and had just returned from a more detailed circumnavigation of Lake Albert – accomplished in Baker's steamer *Khedive* now transported and reassembled at Dufile. Emin for this second mission was to board the small *N'yanza* at Dufile, sailing to Magungo, marching thence to M'ruli and arriving on 17 August.

His objective was to make peace with Kabarega, *mukana* of Bunyoro, and also to seek a trade understanding with M'tesa, and he was not to return to Lado until 22 May 1878. In the absence at M'ruli of guides and porters for the journey to M'tesa at Kibaga, Emin instead set out for Kabarega's capital at M'para where he spent a successful month from 21 September 1877 gaining Kabarega's consent to the dispatch of an embassy to Khartoum, where it was received by Gordon in late January 1878; this despite an earlier attack on Kabarega's men by the local Egyptian garrison at M'ruli. Returning to M'ruli on 25 October 1877, Emin found that the Lango had in turn attacked that garrison, killing Kukuh, El Nur's replacement – since the latter was now acting general-governor at Lado – 'a worthless mendacious sneak'. Not until April 1878 was Ibrahim Fawzi, since January 1878 substantive general-governor, to lead a force with Bakhit to avenge Kukuh's death.

On 22 November 1877 Emin eventually set out from M'ruli, through torrential rains, to meet M'tesa. His extended sojourn at Kibaga from 18 December to 22 March 1878 was uneasy, although he was to be allowed a brief visit to Murchison Bay on Lake Victoria. Yet, somewhat to his surprise, on his departure he received the assurance of an embassy to Khartoum. He had further cordial meetings with Rionga and Anfina before returning on the *Nyanza* from Magungo. At Lado in May he found El Nur Bey, now demoted to *sub-mudir*; then left for Khartoum to report to Gordon in July 1878. There he found himself unexpectedly made general-governor of Equatoria, on Junker's advice, in place of the disgraced Ibrahim Fawzi.

A year before this latter event Emin had confided in a letter dated 20 August 1877 on arrival at M'ruli from Lado:

> Thanks to Gordon Pasha's eminent talent of organisation, ...the whole immense country from the 9th to the 1st degree (Sobat to M'ruli) is so well organised and so entirely secure that a single traveller can wander through the length and breadth of it... in peace. Arms and ammunition, except for pursuit of the chase, are certainly not required. Only one... who knows what it is to be shut out from all society, and to dispense with the most ordinary comforts of life, can form a true estimate of what Gordon Pasha accomplished here.

Emin had previously journeyed from Khartoum to Lado in mid-1876.

By mid-1878, a year after this letter, in Gordon's absence, slave trans-portation by the Nile was creeping back. Apart from brief visits to Khartoum in May 1877 and January 1878 Gordon himself had been preoccupied with Darfur, Abyssinia, the Gulf of Aden littoral and the Cairo debt crisis. It still however remained his intention to revisit Equa-toria.[22]

Ibrahim Fawzi, for long Gordon's trusted lieutenant, had been promoted from Bor to be *mudir* of Bahr el Ghazal in May 1877. A month later, finding himself threatened with attack by Sulieman Zubeir at Shakka, Fawzi was obliged to call on immediate reinforcements from Makaraka and Rohl, a movement joined by Junker who was able to visit and record many of the slave-trade *zaribas* of the Bahr el Ghazal. In the event the arrival of Gordon at Dara in mid July 1877 caused Sulieman to desist.

The proximity of these *zaribas*, especially of Makaraka under Bakheit and his deputy Ahmed Atrash, and their flagrant persistence in slave-trading somewhat deflected Fawzi from his duties, as surely as the reinstatement of the nefarious Idris Abtar by Gordon in January 1878 whom he had personally arrested. The Bahr el Ghazal remained a hive of slave traders shortly to rebel under Sulieman Zubeir and Ibrahim Fawzi, finding himself in January 1878 appointed general-governor of Equatoria, and with his *hakimdar* presently far away, was unable to resist the temptation to trade in slaves himself. Junker's observation, 'The great slave transports which in former years had been openly carried on the Nile were now rendered all but impossible by the watch-fulness of a few Europeans', needed qualification – if not for too long, for Junker had persuaded Gessi in early July 1878 to accept Gordon's appointment to lead the suppression of Sulieman's rebellion in Bahr el Ghazal, and the aftermath of Gessi's departure would be Fawzi's undoing.

Recently returned from the mission to avenge Kukuh's death at M'ruli, Ibrahim Fawzi had arranged the dispatch of several shiploads of slaves down the Nile. Gessi, having left Khartoum on 15 July 1878, encountered first a *dhahabiya* with 92 slaves off El Ais and then found a *nuggar* unloading 200 slaves at Fashoda. Finally at Shambe he encountered the *Shebbin* steamer arrived from Lado with the general-governor himself. According to the captain of the *Shebbin*, 292 porters carrying ivory and corn from Makaraka had been seized in Lado and embarked. 140 were temporarily disembarked at Bor, half being enrolled into the army and the balance segregated for Fawzi's account, before being re-embarked for Fashoda. The other 133 had been shipped direct to Shambe. El Tayeb Bey Abdallah, the *mudir* at Fashoda, was also clearly implicated. Gessi was told by one of the latter's aides that the garrison were living off the slave trade out of want; and when Gessi handed in his requisition for two companies he could only be given one, comprising mainly sick soldiers, the able-bodied being absent on tax-collection. El Tayeb Bey, destitute of cash, was reliant on Yusuf el Shellali from Rohl for paying the garrison. Fashoda was now a station for exiles and galley slaves.

Both Fawzi and El Tayeb were arrested. Gordon learned of this development in mid-August and, refraining from executing Fawzi, had him imprisoned at Fashoda until dispatched to Cairo. Emin was appointed *mudir* at Lado. Fawzi would be reinstated by Ra'uf Pasha, Gordon's successor; and indeed in 1884, believing Fawzi to have been excessively punished, Gordon would enrol him as commander of the Egyptian troops at the siege of Khartoum: an ordeal and subsequent captivity which he survived to be released and returned to Cairo in 1898.[23]

Gordon's accumulating troubles did not end there. On 23 September 1878 he wrote to his sister that a second Equatoria steamer had arrived with news that 'the grass has closed the route to Gondokoro', as with Baker in 1870, shortly after CMS missionaries to Lake Victoria had passed through. 'I had hoped to go to the Equator again but now I give it up.' Two months later he had news of the expedition he had sent to remove the *sudd*, and dispatched the young Frank Lupton to reinforce the effort. Lupton had been recently recruited to be in charge of steamers and to be *sub-mudir* at M'ruli (in the event he went to Latuka). Meanwhile supplies to Emin Bey, the new *mudir* at Lado, were cut off. In January 1879 Gordon recorded that mail from Lado had got through, overland via Bor to the Sobat and thence by steamer, and on Christmas Day 1879 his hope that after eighteen months' work the *sudd* would soon be cleared. Only in April 1880 did the first steamer get through.

The closing of the Bahr el Jebel was only one factor which decided Gordon that he must evacuate at least the lacustrine extremity of his province. With Carl Christian Giegler he had been working since July on the Sudan accounts and by mid-October had computed a deficit of £E97,000 (revised in March 1879 to £E105,000), to which Equatoria contributed £E39,000 (revenue only £E8,000), second only to Darfur

(£E100,000). He wrote to Baker on 29 October: 'This is a settler! And I mean to evacuate Unyoro [Bunyoro], except Fatiko, and only keep Lake Albert'; and on 20 November 1878:

> Of course I have heard nothing from Equator for several months. I mean to evacuate M'ruli, Latuka, Rohl and Makraka: they are not worth keeping. Rohl and Makraka are slave-traders' nests... I have steamers here to put on Victoria Nile, between Fuweira, M'ruli, Urondogani and the Ripon Falls; but shall use them else-where. In the present state of affairs, I shall do better in concentrating my forces on Lake Albert, south, east and west.[24]

Meanwhile the new inexperienced general-governor at Lado was grievously handicapped in his administration. He was aware that in Makaraka Bakhit Agha was flagrantly participating in the slave trade and disobeying Gessi's orders to reinforce his expedition, while Yusuf Bey el Shellali in Rohl was the appointed second-in-command of Gessi's force. The Latuka were slaved by officials down to Bor, and Gordon's river stations south of Lado deteriorated for lack of mainte-nance. Dr R.W. Falkin, who passed through Equatoria in August 1878, returning the next year, commented on Emin's energetic efforts. 'Stations had been rebuilt, discontent was changed into loyal obedi-ence, corruption had been put down, taxation was equalised and he had already begun the task of clearing his province from the slave-dealers who infested it.' The province hospital was maintained by its *protomedico*, and Emin had applied himself to diversifying agricul-tural crops.

The success of Gessi's campaign in Bahr el Ghazal, culminating in the defeat of Sulieman Zubeir in July 1879, persuaded Gordon to revise his plan of territorial evacuation and he acceded to Gessi's proposal at their meeting at the end of June 1879 at Tuwaisha (see p.350) that Gessi should be made general-governor both of Bahr el Ghazal and of Equa-toria. Emin, doubtless conscious of his own military inexperience, confirmed his subordination by return of post, reaching Gessi on 20 July. At their meeting Gessi may have canvassed a further discussion with Gordon at Lado after the latter's return to Khartoum, but this was not to be. With the Bahr el Ghazal blocked, access to Lado and a meet-ing with Emin (now a *bey*) was no longer an option for either Gessi or Gordon. Meanwhile Gessi instructed Emin, in accordance with Gordon's decision, to close M'ruli, Fuweira, Magungo, Kerota, Fadibek and Masindi, leaving Dufile when the navigability of the White

Nile was interrupted as the furthest outpost. Rehan Agha, deputy to Bakheit, would take over Makaraka.[25]

7 GORDON'S DEPARTURE, 1879

Leaving Darfur in July 1879, receiving the news of the deposition of Khedive Ismail Ibrahim, Gordon reached Khartoum in company with his newly appointed *seraskir*, Hasan Pasha Hilmi, and Yusuf el Shellali. He was a wreck. Exhausted by almost six years' strenuous service in the tropics, he had been suffering *inter alia* from angina pectoris: 'I passed the grave once lately and never thought to see Khartoum.' He was unimpressed by what he gleaned of the new government in Cairo ('I shall give this band my benediction and depart'), although when two months later he met the new twenty-seven-year-old Khedive Tawfiq he was astounded at his talent, energy and honesty. Despite his ill-health Gordon acceded to Tawfiq's request that he should seek an understanding again with Abyssinia. A week later, en route to Massawa, he wrote: 'I am sorry to have this trouble with King John for I had begun to be very tired of the continued wear and tear of the last six years: however under the circumstances I could not think of ratting and leaving Egypt exposed to its enemies.'

Over the months Gordon had been reflecting on his future. The regime in Cairo where unknown civilians ruled the country with the backing of the British and French consuls-general was unacceptable, although 'If Lord Dufferin [British ambassador in Constantinople] was the administrator one could serve under him.' He had successfully discharged a high proportion of his duties, even if the Abyssinia problem remained unresolved. The financial reorganisation of the Sudan had been undertaken and the Equatorial boundaries drawn back although Darfur, its rebellion put down, could not be evacuated; and Gordon had considered whether he should not take personal control of Kordofan and Darfur to crush the slave dealers, but not 'for the moment' – on health grounds.

For it had been his determination to suppress the slave trade in the Sudan that had persuaded him to accept the Khedive's appointment as *hakimdar* in February 1877. His energies as general-governor of Equatoria (1874-76) had been effectively deployed in this aim, not only in that province but on the White Nile. Following his first campaign against Harun and the Dar Fertit slave-traders in the summer of 1877, *razzias* and the trade had been seriously diminished, at least until the departure from Darfur of Abdel Raziq Haqqi Pasha in July 1878. Gordon had appeared to be winning. However on 1 August 1878 he wrote to his sister that the fourteenth caravan in the west with 250 slaves had been apprehended and that three weeks later caravan militia had threatened to fire on the intervening *mudir*. At the same time the complicity of the general-governor of Equatoria and the *mudir* of Fashoda in slave-trading had been revealed; while the *razzias* of the Bahr el Ghazal remained rampant. Following Gessi's campaign and Gordon's personal intervention in Darfur, the Egyptian government had reasserted its ascendancy with the defeat both of Sulieman Zubeir and Emir Harun. The most sensitive regions, Bahr el Ghazal and Darfur, had European military officers as general-governors and Gordon was content to leave the final appointment of the *hakimdar* to the new Khedive. Unhappily, within two years of Gordon's departure the slave trade had been resumed in the vulnerable areas.

Slavery had been an integral part of the domestic economy of the Sudan. Slavery's source of supply, and of commercial profit to the practitioners, was the slave trade. The Anti-Slave Convention of 1877 had allowed for the lapse of years before slavery became illegal, and that the Sudan slave trade would not remain suppressed can be attributed in great part to the deposition of the Khedive Ismail, and the failure to identify a worthy successor to General Gordon as *hakimdar*. Gordon, on his later return to Khartoum to evacuate the garrisons in 1884, has been criticised for his assurance to the people that 'none should interfere with their property, and that henceforth whoever had slaves should enjoy full right to their service and full control over them'. The criticism ignores the distinction between slavery and the slave trade. Under the 1877 Convention, slavery was not to be abolished until 1889. In respect of slave trafficking on the contrary, in the draft contract offered to Zubeir Pasha Mansour to become successor ruler of the Sudan, it was stipulated specifically: 'Trade in slaves shall be stopped, and the lines to be followed herein shall be the Convention of 1877 between England and Egypt.'

At their meeting in Cairo during the last week of August 1879, Gordon immediately confirmed to Tawfiq Pasha that he would be leaving Egypt for good (in fact his resignation took effect on 4 January 1880). His patron, Ismail Pasha, had been forced to abdicate and he faced the rooted hostility of the Egyptian council of ministers and the European officials. Health reasons alone argued against his continuation as *hakimdar*. When he reached Massawa a week after leaving Cairo he was suffering from boils engendered by prickly heat and, back in Cairo after the New Year, he was obliged to consult the British consulate surgeon at Alexandria who diagnosed 'symptoms of nervous exhaustion and alteration of the blood', recommending retirement 'for several months for complete rest and quiet' and wholesome food.

In honourably insisting on accepting the poisoned chalice of Abyssinia again on behalf of Egypt, Gordon was also sacrificing remaining valuable weeks of Sudan service in which to assure the appointment of a reliable successor to conserve his achievements in the Sudan. Only now at the end of August 1879 did the search in Cairo for a successor commence. Khartoum was notified that Gordon would not be returning, but Gordon had few days himself to put forward names. Carl Giegler Pasha, acting deputy in Khartoum, would claim that Gordon recommended him, but that the Khedive's chief minister, Riaz Pasha, insisted on an Egyptian. Giegler however had other handicaps, most of all lack of military experience, even if Gordon preferred him to the *seraskir* Hasan Hilmi.

It would be unfair to claim that Gordon had ignored the importance of the appointment of a capable successor – its absence would greatly influence his refusal to evacuate Khartoum five years later. His overtures to Richard Burton had been twice turned down. He would have favoured a European soldier, but those whom he had appointed as general-governors in the regions of Bahr el Ghazal and Darfur were unsuited to succeed. Captain Charles Watson, RE, whom he had seen daily in London in January 1877 and for whom he had the highest regard, had accepted the appointment as ADC to General Sir Lintorn Simmons.

Of the Turkish-Egyptian officers with Sudan experience, Osman Rifqi was minister of war with intractable problems; Abdel Raziq Haqqi Pasha was sick; Ismail Ayub was governor of Alexandria; Hasan Hilmi el Juwaisar, Sudan *seraskir*, the most experienced of the candidates, had failed in Darfur. The admirable Sudanese general Adham Pasha el Arifi was certainly in retirement.

The appointment of Mohammed Ra'uf Pasha was announced on 21 January 1880. Greeted without enthusiasm, he arrived at the end of May. The first native Egyptian Governor-General, having a Nubian father and Abyssinian mother, he had in his career incurred the wrath of Baker for his association with Mohammed Abu Sa'ud – a relationship which would now be resumed with serious consequences. Ismail Ayub had unsuccessfully sought his removal from the post of acting governor of Equatoria on Baker's departure, while Gordon had encompassed his replacement both in that appointment and, later, as a not unsuccessful governor of Harar. Ra'uf was currently *mudir* of Girga in Upper Egypt.[26]

Stepping Stones to Mahdist Rule
1880–83

I DISSIPATING A LEGACY

A *Hakindar* Found Wanting 1880–82   The newly appointed *hakim-dar*, Mohammed Ra'uf Pasha, would not arrive in Khartoum until the end of May 1880, ten months after Gordon had left for Cairo. The relative tranquillity which attended the passage of these months was a reflection of the reputation Gordon had won for strong but just government, even if for the first five of those months there was no certainty that he would not be returning to Khartoum. Many however remained discountenanced by Gordon's anti-slave trade policies: the commercial houses of the riverain Dongalawi and Ja'ali peoples, along with the Sha'iqiya; and the Baqqara allies of the former *jallaba* proprietors of Bahr el Ghazal *meshras* – the latter now for the most part expelled from their possessions.

When Ra'uf did arrive, his Khedivial firman did not extend to him the absolute executive authority that had been conferred on his predecessor. He was therefore more dependent on instruction from Cairo at a time when Egyptian internal affairs rendered the Sudan an area of decreasing concern. Various Sudan administrative bodies were made directly responsible to the appropriate Cairo ministry and in 1881 the *muhafizāt* of Suakin and Massawa were detached and brought directly under Cairo. Nevertheless Ra'uf's arrival won preliminary acceptance in most regions and he was careful not to revoke Gordon's major appointments.

Carl Christian Giegler as his deputy in Khartoum found Ra'uf easy to work with. Gordon, having left Khartoum, was currently concluding his visit to the Abyssinian Negus when in December 1879 on the advice of Giegler in Khartoum, Ra'uf recalled Messadaglia from Darfur for trial on a charge of humiliating behaviour towards his Egyptian deputy. Ali Bey Sharif, *mudir* of El Obeid, was appointed general-governor of Darfur only to be demoted for corruption by

Romolo Gessi Pasha

Ra'uf in 1881. The charge against Messadaglia would be dismissed in Cairo – Giegler claimed to his friend Blum that the evidence had been blurred by Gordon's contradictory orders – and Messadaglia, returning to Khartoum with Lieutenant-Colonel Stewart, would work hard for Giegler's own recall after Ra'uf's appointment had been terminated. It would meanwhile be the young Rudolf Slatin at Dara, promoted *bey* and *qa'immaqam*, whom Ra'uf appointed to succeed Ali Sharif.

A second, still more intractable, personal difference arose between Giegler and Romolo Gessi Pasha, general-governor of Bahr el Ghazal and Equatoria, a man of strong reputation. Giegler supported, if he did not promote, Ra'uf's effort to impose his authority on Gessi in his remote and dangerous fiefdom, culminating in Ra'uf's demotion of Gessi to *mudir*.

In Khartoum, unfortunately, Ra'uf surrounded himself with officials of questionable standing. His prime confidant, now promoted director of accounts there, was the ill-famed Mohammed Abu Sa'ud, the Equatoria slave-trader with whom Ra'uf had associated at Gondokoro in 1871 (notwithstanding Abu Sa'ud's enmity towards Baker) and who now told Giegler: 'All Ra'uf's friends in Khartoum are my friends too. We have decided to advise him to place his trust in you, for he will not know how he stands with you.' Abu Sa'ud had already become re-established in Khartoum in 1877 as a minor official under Khalid Nadim. Mekki Shibeika describes him as in 1881 assistant Governor-General to Ra'uf.

As his private secretary Ra'uf appointed a Greek named Marcopoli – previously employed, and dismissed, by both Baker and Gordon – and then in 1881 transferred him to take Lupton's place under Emin Bey in Equatoria. Less obtusely, Ra'uf made Mohammed Mukhtar, previously with him in Harar – 'a mixture of rascality and idiocy' in Giegler's view (but a favourite of Fariq Stone in Cairo) – his chief of staff in place of Hasan Pasha Hilmi el Juwaisir.

The tranquillity which had characterised the interregnum between Gordon's departure and Abu Ra'uf's arrival continued for a further twelve months. In Giegler's view:

Life in Khartoum was most pleasant at that time… All was going well. The financial situation was good, for Ra'uf was an excellent manager. The huge amounts of ivory in the warehouses [mainly Gordon's and Gessi's achievement] were now to be sold which was a great event in the world of trade… The first six months of 1881 were the most pleasant months I spent in the Sudan.[1]

Ra'uf was quickly made aware by Cairo that Gordon's independent control of Sudan finance was a thing of the past, despite the presence of Giegler as his deputy (it was Giegler who had collaborated with Gordon in the drafts of the 1878–9 province budgets). Ra'uf initially concentrated on the obvious – the accumulated deficit in revenue collection over the past decade, especially in regard to the cultivable areas of the Sudan. He reasonably concluded that taxation levels were too high and recommended a reduction of up to a quarter to be matched by corresponding economies in administration and the armed forces. Given the current financial stringency in Egypt, however, this recommendation of tax cuts found no favour at the Ministry of Finance, who attributed the revenue collection shortfall to negligence and ordered the appointment of special tax assessment commissioners. Ra'uf's response, to Gessi's rage, was to 'cut off two years' pay that was due to all the servants of the government both civil and military, on the Upper Nile'. The new regime would not last long.

Nevertheless Lieutenant-Colonel J. D. H. Stewart in his Report on the Sudan 1883 would later commend Ra'uf. 'During his rule vigorous efforts were made to limit expenditure and taxes were abated.' In respect of the agriculturally productive Dongola province, the tax on *sagias* had been budgeted at 20% and on *shaduf* in excess of 50% less for 1882, yet still yielding £E30,000 against an overall province expenditure of £E11,000. Granted the deterioration in public security in 1882, however, Stewart concluded that budgeted province deficits would prove 'very far in excess of those stated', and indeed the total deficit had already been set at £E104,000 against £E37,000 in the budget of 1881. Yet when Ra'uf left Khartoum in March 1882 there were, wrote Giegler, a million dollars (£E200,000) in the treasury.

Giegler inspected the province of Sennar – now under Yusuf Pasha el Shellali – in July 1880 and found it quiet with no evidence of the rumoured revival of the slave trade. Following Gessi's return to Khartoum from Bahr el Ghazal at the end of January 1881, Giegler then visited the *mudir* of Fashoda (Salih Bey Hijazi, *muhafiz* White Nile in 1855) to check on Gessi's allegation of slave trading on the White Nile: 'At one of the stations (Fashoda) we found herds of stolen oxen and thousands of slaves; the slave dealers, coming up from all sides like grasshoppers, were buying and driving off the unhappy wretches.' Giegler again found no evidence; it was the same story when with Reth Kwickon he proceeded to the Sobat. Salih was nevertheless replaced by Rashid Bey Ayman. The *hakimdar* for his part undertook in October 1880 an extensive tour of inspection of the eastern territory marching with Abyssinia, including Gedaref and Gallabat (directly claimed by Emperor John IV) to reassure himself that his garrisons were prepared for any Abyssinian attack, following Gordon's brave démarche to the Negus a year previously. In its wake, the Negus remained inactive.

The peoples of the eastern Sudan under Ala el Din Pasha Siddiq, based at Suakin, presently saw no reason to disturb the friendly relations they had established with Gordon and his province officials. Indeed at this time, in the words of Andrew Paul, historian of the Beja, 'there had been little sign of active unrest in the Eastern Sudan, and the Beja, remote and incurious as ever... might never have risen in revolt.' Thus it was also in the provinces of Dongola under the *mudir* Mustapha Yawir; and of Berber, since late 1879, under Mohammed Ma'ni Bey. The former hereditary Ababda *sheikh*, Hussein Pasha Khalifa, unfairly removed from his dual *muderia* on bogus charges of corruption in 1873, would not be reinstated to Berber until 1883 by which time the Mahdist threat had fully developed. Hussein's brother meanwhile remained in control of the lucrative caravan route across the Atmur desert.[2]

Bahr el Ghazal – a Wounded General-Governor   Conditions in the Bahr el Ghazal and Darfur where war and revolt had been pervasive over the past decade were far less predictable, now that an outstanding commander of irregular forces was no longer *hakimdar*. Emin had acknowledged to Gessi his subordination on 20 July 1879 and in the wake of his victory over Sulieman Zubeir and the slave traders, Gessi would ride high in the estimation of the Dinka and other inhabitants. Nearly twenty years later the French leaders of the Marchand expedition to Fashoda found that local tribesmen would compliment them as 'les frères de Gessi' believing, Captain A. E. A. Baratier affirmed, that without Gessi none of them would have survived. Gessi's personal rule however was to last little more than a year, half of which coincided with the rainy seasons.

His first preoccupation was to establish small garrisons of regular troops at Kalaka and Shakka. Then, concluding that Gordon would not make the proposed Lado meeting, he set out on 26 July through glutinous mud across the Bahr el Arab to Bahr el Ghazal. It took him four weeks to reach Deim Sulieman which he had not visited since he had captured it on 5 May. The remaining *jallabas* were surrendering, 600 to be expelled under arrest to Khartoum; 2,000 he estimated had died of hunger in Bahr el Ghazal. Azande chiefs, bearing ivory, progressively made their submission in friendship. Having ordered Emin to close the government stations at M'ruli, Fuweira, Magungo, Kerota, Fadibek and Masindi, Dufile to be the furthest garrison, Gessi's intention was to leave in mid-September 1879 at the end of Ramadan to visit Rohl district and possibly Lado. In the event he was hindered by the urgent need to evacuate 900 *jallabas* and *bazinqirs* to Khartoum, and until his departure in September 1880 he was confined to northern Bahr el Ghazal. Frustrated by Emin's limitations in Equatoria, he would request the *seraskir* Hasan Pasha Hilmi to send someone to establish order in Lado.

Although there was much to recommend Wau with its river connection Meshra el Rek, Deim Sulieman remained Gessi's principal base, under the *mudir* Sati Ali Abu Qasim, his best officer. Here Gessi built a fine mosque. Rehan Agha in Kordofan was due to succeed the mutinous Atrash in Makraka (by 1881 Bakheit Bey had been reinstated); but Rohl, the third *muderia* in Gessi's general-governorate with stations at Rumbek, Shambe and Ajak – previously under Yusuf Pasha el Shellali but now transferred to Sennar after a major clash with Gessi – was losing its value with the continued blocking of the Bahr el Jebel. By December 1879 Gessi had decided that following the disbandment of the *bazinqir* garrison the previous month, Rohl should be evacuated, not least in the interests of economy. Assuming that Shakka and Kalaka would remain his responsibility, he calculated that with the expulsion of the *jallabas*, he would be able to control Bahr el Ghazal with 300 regulars. Then, to Gessi's anger, Gordon from Abyssinia decided that Shakka and Kalaka should be ceded to Dara, in the aftermath of which four *razzias* were staged by Shakka *jallabas* in February 1880 to be firmly quashed by Sati Agha (Slatin was occupied with Harun's activities). The Ngok Dinka north of the Bahr el Arab remained ceded to Dara.

Gessi established the firmest regime to conserve his ascendancy over the slave trade in Bahr el Ghazal. The death penalty was set for slave trading, abduction and premeditated murder, incendiarism and robbery. Maltreatment of local people, forced labour and concealment of wanted persons would incur extradition to Khartoum. The *jallaba zaribas* were destroyed – Gessi reckoned there had been twenty-two. 'It is certain that I have struck a terrible blow at all the slavers without distinction.' He had advised the new *hakimdar* in Khartoum by letter that he would 'continue to proceed with the utmost severity against the slave traders and do all I possibly can'.

Gessi claimed that by March 1880 very many thousand including Rek Dinka were repopulating their lands south of the Bahr el Arab and especially between Meshra and the Jur river. In response to an order from Ra'uf Pash who had arrived in Khartoum in May 1880, requiring Gessi to report on his territory, Gessi addressed the report to Fariq Stone in Cairo (to emphasise the independence of his general-governorate), but it did not arrive until November. In it Gessi recounted his endeavours to create revenue resources to match annual province costs now computed at £E2,500. The Azande had already offered 3,500 cwt of ivory (and 800 rifles, returned to them) in addition to £E100,000 worth of ivory captured from the rebels (and 40,000 dollars); but ivory was a diminishing product. Gessi looked to rubber and tamarind (1,000 cwt of each already collected); cotton (25,000 cwt possible); sugar cane; gum Arabic; honey; hardwood; and horticulture. Agricultural colonies were founded at Wau, Kuchuk Ali *zariba* and Tonj. It was not until Gessi's own arrival in Khartoum in February 1881 that he produced his similar report to Ra'uf Pasha.

Gessi's principal handicap, which confined him for much of his year in the vicinity of Wau and Jur Ghattas, was his dependence on steamers and on the reduced navigability of the Bahr el Ghazal. There were six-month gaps between steamer arrivals. Despite the year-long efforts of Frank Lupton, and latterly of Ernst Marno based at Fashoda, the Bahr el Jebel remained blocked until penetrated by the *Ismailia* coming from Lado. She reached Meshra el Rek early in December 1879 to load ivory for Khartoum and disembark a company of troops from Lado. Dr Wilhelm Junker, returned to the Sudan from Europe for further studies, was able to return on the *Ismailia* and the *Embaba* to Meshra, arriving on 27 February 1880. The *sudd* in the Ghazal had yielded to the steamers, but Junker insisted *sudd* masses could only be broken by a steamer going *against* the current leaving the broken pieces to drift astern. He urged Gessi to have the Ghazal cleared. Gessi in October could not achieve this, with calamitous results. However he had already established a boatyard at Wau to build *nuggars* (barges) of 45–50 tons with which to transport ivory to Meshra. The first of these was completed by May 1880.

Junker accompanied Gessi back to Jur Ghattas (where he found the delinquent Atrash dying of a lung infection), crossing the Jur river to Wau, Deim Idris (Ganda) and so to Deim Sulieman, arriving on 17 April 1880. He left again on 23 April for Zande country, linking Gessi to a region he had yet personally to visit and where dominant chiefs like Zemio wad Takima and N'doruma were trusted as armed agents. M'bio was not in this category. In December 1880, after Gessi's departure, Sati Bey launched an attack against him.

Junker was able to report to Gessi on Zande country conditions of government and trade. In his *Travels* Junker noted: 'Gessi's efforts at improvements... were thwarted by a lack of sympathy and cooperation on the part of his underlings and by the absence of that vigilance which was necessary to control both officials and subjects in the exercise of their rights and the performance of their duties.' The 'officials' covered eight *aqsams*, seven administered by Dongalawis, and one by a Ja'ali. Junker also criticised Gessi for his failure to fortify Meshra el Rek and for the arming of Dinka as well as the loyal Azande. Sections of Dinka were to rise against Lupton three years later.

Increased vigilance however was not an option for Gessi. The onset of the rains would hamper land travel, while there would be no further communication by river for six months. After two unbroken years in Bahr el Ghazal and Dar Fertit he was now, since mid-May 1880, 'nailed to his bed' in Wau with, variously, a bad foot and bilharzia. He was in no mood to respond to Khartoum's demand for governorate reports. Ra'uf, evidently with Giegler's support, reacted vindictively and despite the approaching expiration of Gessi's contract (in March 1881), in September 1880 transferred Lado, Makraka and Monbuttu together with Rohl to Emin's responsibility; demoted Gessi to the rank of *mudir* and to the stipend not of a *lewa* but of *miralai*; and withheld money for staff salaries – a compensation perhaps for the 2,800 dollars which Gessi calculated had been lost to Khartoum by the suppression of the slave trade.

Gessi, though much debilitated, would not buckle. Determined to appeal to Caesar in Cairo, he seized the opportune arrival after five months of the 40 h.p. *Safia* at Meshra to accompany two companies of troops back to Khartoum. Sati Agha was left in command. Delayed in order to nurse a dangerously sick Captain Gaetano Casati, sent to him by Giegler with the Khartoum mail, Gessi only departed on 25 September 1880 on what was to prove a nightmare voyage through dense *sudd* during which the food and medical supplies and wood fuel soon ran out. He blamed the captain for negligence and an inadequate crew. Fortunately Giegler had sent off the *Bordein* to Meshra in late December, collecting Ernst Marno at Fashoda, and arriving up the Bahr el Ghazal in time to succour the survivors on 5 January 1881.

Captain Albert Baratier, who was to reconnoitre the Bahr el Ghazal in January and June 1898, and already had experience of the Jur river, would later question whether Gessi was really a victim of the *sudd*. Had the crew deliberately departed from the main stream? Such cynicism leading to so many deaths seems unthinkable and Gessi never suggested it.

Consul Hansal at Khartoum wrote to Georg Schweinfurth: 'Gessi Pasha arrived here yesterday [25 January 1881] emaciated, a living skeleton. In spite of all the troubles and hardships he had to endure, it is wonderful to see how he has retained his good spirits... To-morrow we expect Ra'uf to return from his three and half month journey on the Abyssinian frontier.'

Gessi remained bent on registering his complaint against Ra'uf to the Khedive. Giegler, regarding Gessi as an arch intriguer and trickster, disgracefully wrote to his friend the financial under-secretary Sir Julius Blum Pasha in Cairo: 'Gessi deserted his post and refused to steam back to Meshra before being engulfed by the *sudd*.'

After spending an unhappy six weeks in Khartoum, Gessi left for Cairo by *dhahabiya*, crossing the desert from Berber to Suakin in a litter slung between two camels, to die of exhaustion in a Suez hospital, after a personal visit from Khedive Mohammed Tawfiq, on 30 April 1881. 'Too opportunely for certain gentlemen,' Schweinfurth would write.[3]

Gessi's Replacements: Emin and Lupton 1880–82   Prior to his reappointment as governor of a separated Equatoria, Emin had been occupied in the latter months of 1879 in obeying Gordon's instructions to withdraw the garrisons from beyond Dufile. By January 1880 he reported that due to the renewed hostility of the Madi, Wadelai could now only be approached by the east bank. Frank Lupton, who had been deputed by Gordon to clear the *sudd* on the Bahr el Jebel in the dry season of 1878–9, had then worked in the Khartoum arsenal during the following Equatorial rains, and at last reached Lado in September 1879. As deputy to Emin, he was stationed at Tarangole in Latuka country, but would leave to succeed Gessi Pasha as *mudir* of Bahr el Ghazal a year later, taking a spell of local leave in Khartoum before reaching Deim Sulieman in December 1881. His local commander of troops was Bimbashi Mahmoud Abdallah.

Emin Bey continued to busy himself inspecting his *muderia* and as a physician taking a daily surgery. He visited Makraka in August 1880 and Laboré, Fatiko, Fuweira, then Anfina's and Wadelai. 'As the result of my journey I have some fresh supplies of ivory ready to be sent off, besides which contracts have been made with the southern chiefs for further supplies, and now I hope the government will be satisfied.' In March 1883 he would tell Schweinfurth that the net revenue for the past year amounted to £E8,000, the greater part being paid to

Khartoum who in return had sent him but one steamer with no supplies for his officials.

Meanwhile Rohl district, which Gessi had already effectively abandoned, had rapidly deteriorated into the former *zariba* culture, bringing the Agar Dinka near Rumbek to Lado in September 1881 to complain to Emin. In response, Emin at once set out to inspect his new district, finding ample confirmation of slave-trading by exiled Danagla from Bahr el Ghazal at Rumbek and Ajak, Rohl stations ruled by one Mula Agha. Having attempted to re-establish his authority by reinforcing the garrison from Lado, he planned to move on to Monbuttu on the Upper Welle river at the end of 1881, an area which had been explored by Junker and his fellow explorer Captain Gaetano Casati, and which offered rich agricultural potential. Ra'uf in Khartoum, however, was unsympathetic to Emin's intention to establish a garrison in Mangbattu (Monbuttu to control the Danagla, and to demarcate the frontier with Bahr el Ghazal, and obliged Emin to withdraw the expedition already dispatched. He would not set out for Mangbattu until the summer of 1883. As for Makaraka, between Rohl and Mangbattu, once again Emin had placed it under Bakhit Bey who had previously been suspended by Gessi.

When Emin did visit Khartoum in March 1882 he found Ra'uf Pasha already relieved and Abdel Qadir Pasha Hilmi in control. Only then did he realise how fast the Mahdi's rebellion was spreading. Leaving again for Lado in June in the *Ismailia*, he was the first to learn at Fashoda of Yusuf el Shellali's defeat at Jebel Qadir, and then to find that Shambe in Rohl had been sacked by the Dinka retaliating against a *razzia*. For the while however Equatoria remained relatively unaffected. Emin would be out of touch with Khartoum again until March 1883.

By contrast Lupton, the new governor of Bahr el Ghazal, was far closer to events. Arriving in December 1881, fifteen months after Gessi's departure, he never had a chance to establish a personal ascendancy over his *muderia*. By now the goodwill generated by Gessi among the Ghazal peoples had diminished with the introduction of tribute payment, coinciding seemingly with an urgent instruction from Khartoum to dispatch Lupton's regular troops to counter Mahdist activities in the region, though leaving in place the military commander, Bimbashi Mahmoud Abdallah, and his irregular *bashi-buzouqs* and *bazinqirs*. Lupton's increased vulnerability was lost neither on the Rizeiqat Baqqara, seeking revenge for the intervention in their independence of Gordon and Gessi, nor on the Togoyo of Liffi (sometimes confused with the Dinka) who, forgetful of their recent liberation, had been pleased to respond to *jallaba* subversion in August 1881 to attack the northernmost outstation of the *muderia* at Liffi near Jebel Telqauna – using Gessi's firearms. Lupton was to defeat a second attack in February 1882, but henceforth at Deim Sulieman he would be on the defensive against Mahdist assaults, with Bimbashi Mahmoud afflicted with ill health and Sati Agha Abu'l Qasim commanding an increasingly threatened Meshra el Req.[4]

Rumblings in the West 1880–81   Notwithstanding the dismissal of the general-governor of Darfur, Messadaglia Bey, by Gordon in December 1879 on the recommendation of Giegler, that governorate remained quiet during the next eighteen months under Ali Bey Sharif, former *mudir* of Berber and general-governor of Kordofan. He was fortunate in having two forceful *mudirs*, Slatin at Dara since August 1879, and the Dongalawi El Nur Bey Anqara at Qulqul, the latter having finally crushed the *emir* Harun in March 1880.

The new *hakimdar*, Ra'uf Pasha, did not think it necessary during his first year of office to visit the western Sudan to establish his presence and in January 1881 Slatin sought permission himself to visit the new *hakimdar* in Khartoum in order to report. Slatin, in addition to attacking Harun, had inspected Toweisha, Kalaka and Shakka and made recommendations for an abatement of taxation levels in El Fasher and Kebkebia. In March he found himself promoted general-governor of Darfur with the rank of *bey* and quit Khartoum to assume his new duties, reinstating Sa'id Bey Guma' as *mudir* of El Fasher. He was accompanied by Bishop Comboni and Fathers Joseph Ohrwalder and Johaan Dichtl as far as El Obeid, whence following a preliminary reconnaissance by Comboni to the Nuba mountains (he died in Khartoum in October) Dichtl left in November 1881 to establish a mission station at Dilling. Ohrwalder had been already apprehensive about security when he met Giegler Pasha in El Obeid in July.

At El Fasher Slatin found himself obliged to retire El Nur Anqara for unseemly behaviour, accompanied on his retirement by Ali Bey Sharif to El Obeid. In his own previous *muderia* at Dara, Slatin appointed the Venetian Emiliani dei Danziger, presently *mamur* to El Kobbé, to take control when he himself left in December 1881 for Kebkebia, now the *muderia* headquarters in place of Qulqul, to meet local sheikhs whose men had been ambushed by Bedayat tribesmen while collecting *natrun* on the Darb el Arbain. It would be here that messengers from

Ra'uf Pasha overtook him with the instruction in cypher: 'A Dervish named Mohammed Ahmed has, without just cause, attacked Rashid Bey near Qadir. Rashid Bey and his troops have been annihilated. This revolt is very serious. Take the necessary steps to prevent malcontents in your province from joining this Dervish.'

Slatin returned to El Fasher, hearing of Emiliani's death at Shakka where recently he had removed Sheikh Madibbo Ali from leadership of the Rizeiqat. He then left for Dara in early 1882 to find the Rizeiqat, Habbaniya and Ma'alia Baqqara already in rebellion, seeking to recover the freedom they had enjoyed before Zubeir's conquest as vassals of the Darfur Sultan. Dara would now be Slatin's headquarters, with Sa'id Guma' his deputy in El Fasher and Mohammed Bey Khalid (Zuqal), a cousin of Mohammed Ahmed the Mahdi, deputy *mudir* of Dara.

In Kordofan likewise there remained a considerable disaffected element of *jallaba* traders who had previously either profited from the lucrative supply trade to the Dar Fertit and Bahr el Ghazal *zaribas*, or had been expelled by Gordon from those areas to supervised residence in government stations. In 1877 Gordon had made a rich but co-operative El Obeid Ja'ali trader, Ilyas Ahmed Umm Birair, *mudir* of Shakka following Sulieman Zubeir's departure to Bahr el Ghazal and then, in 1878, transferred him to El Obeid as ruler and *pasha*. Possibly on account of his inaction against Zubeir's rebel *bazinqir* officer, Sabahi, who had been defeated only in May 1879, and certainly because of hostility engendered among his merchant peers culminating in a minor revolt, Gordon had replaced Ilyas, on Hasan Pasha Hilmi's promotion to *seraskir* in Khartoum, with the Turkish Lewa Mohammed Sa'id Pasha Wahbi – *mudir* of Taka and previously of Kordofan. Relationships at El Obeid between the *lewa* and Ilyas deteriorated.

Thus it was to investigate local complaints against Mohammed Sa'id that, at the end of June 1881, more than a year after Ra'uf's arrival, Giegler departed to El Obeid via Bara where he stayed with the 'chairman of the merchants in Kordofan' (?Ilyas). The complaints at El Obeid were preponderantly by a Baqqara chief against a merchant rival of Ilyas, Ahmed Dafa'allah el Awadi. Intimidating Baqqara besieged the *muderia* during the protracted proceedings on which Giegler was still engaged when, on 12 August, he received by cypher an instruction from Ra'uf Pasha in the light of an incident at Kawa (El Ais) to mobilise the El Obeid garrison and dispatch it under the command of Mohammed Sa'id to the White Nile to capture one Mohammed Ahmed. The expedition of four companies left on 15 August 1881.

Kordofan bull riders

A month later, his work complete and with no further news, Giegler returned to Khartoum via the telegraph station of Abu Qarad. Only on meeting Mohammed Abu Sa'ud aboard a steamer at Tura el Khadra did Giegler learn of Mohammed Ahmed's escape to Jebel Qadir in advance of Mohammed Sa'id's arrival.

Giegler betrays no awareness that Mohammed Ahmed had recently paid two visits to Kordofan: the first seemingly in late 1879 after the dismissal of Ilyas as governor; the second in about April 1881 when he stayed with El Sayyid Mohammed el Mekki, head of the Ismaili sect, secretly seeking local support before making a similar approach to Mek Adham Dabbalu, *mek* of Tegali since 1860, who had however ignored Ilyas when *mudir* of El Obeid.

It would be to Tegali that Mohammed Ahmed would first seek to withdraw after quitting his home at Aba in September 1881 but, being urged by Mek Adham to retire further into the Dar Nuba, on 31 October he moved to Jebel Qadir instead. Father Ohrwalder left El Obeid four weeks later, aware of the happenings at Aba Island, and reached Dilling, his new mission post, on 5 December. Despite the first battle of Qadir four days later, 'at Dilling the news of this Dervish was very meagre'. So ended 1881.[5]

Mohammed Ahmed, the Mahdi

2 MOHAMMED AHMED THE MAHDI: *EL ZUHUR*, *EL HIJRA* AND *EL JIHAD* 1881–82

The Vocation   Mohammed Ahmed was born on an island in the Nile near Dongola on 27 Rajab 1260 (12 August 1844), the son of Abdallah, a boat-builder claiming descent of the Prophet Mohammed, and having three brothers and a sister. Uniquely among them he felt a deep spiritual vocation to Islamic studies and to the asceticism of the Sammaniya, a Sufi order, to which he was licensed in 1868. Since his childhood he had been living at Kerreri north of Khartoum, studying under Sheikh Mohammed el Kheir Abdallah Khojali near Berber but in 1870 he joined his boat-building brothers when they moved to the Shilluk Aba Island south of Kawa (El Ais). The *sheikh* of the

Sammaniya order, Mohammed Sharif Nur el Da'im, established a residence on the mainland near Aba, but in about 1878 Mohammed
Ahmed's extreme piety obliged him to censure some lax behaviour on
the part of his leader. This brought about his expulsion from the order
and no self-humbling achieved its reversal; so Mohammed Ahmed and
his followers transferred their allegiance to an equally senior *sheikh* of
the order, El Quraishi wad el Zein, at Mesellimiya on the Blue Nile.
Granted permission by the *sheikh* to return to Aba to pursue a religious
life, Mohammed Ahmed soon thereafter embarked on his first visit to
Kordofan.

Mohammed Sharif, who in early September 1884 would make his
submission to the Mahdi on the latter's arrival at Shatt en route to
Omdurman, would later claim that he had expelled the Mahdi from his
tariqa in 1878 because the Mahdi had revealed to him his divine
mission and asked Mohammed Sharif to become his *wazir*.

Shortly after his return to Aba, Mohammed Ahmed visited El
Obeid in 1879, meeting among others the deposed Ilyas Pasha.
Sheikh el Quraishi died in the latter part of 1880 whereupon
Mohammed Ahmed left for Mesellimiya to superintend the building
of a fine *qubba* (domed tomb) over his grave. While engaged on this
task, he was approached by Abdallahi Mohammed Turshain, of the
Ta'aisha Baqqara of southern Darfur but now residing in eastern
Kordofan, begging acceptance as his disciple. Abdallahi, after joining
as a divine the resistance of the Rizeiqat to Zubeir Rahma's attack on
them in 1873, had narrowly escaped execution, but that had not
inhibited him from seeking verification from Zubeir as to whether he,
Zubeir, might not indeed be the expected Mahdi – to which there was
a negative rejoinder. Abdallahi would not encounter the same denial
from his new master. Within a month he would be one of
Mohammed Ahmed's flag-bearers and within a year the first of his
Khalifas.

Prince El Hassan bin Talal of Jordan describes the Prophet
Mohammed's idealised concept of the state – which the Mahdi was
seeking to emulate:

> The Islamic concept of the state is that of a perfect and righteous
> society – a community in which the Divine Laws of God will
> prevail.
>   Islam, as such, knows no distinction between a religious and a
> temporal realm. There can be no differentiation between state and

church, since there is no church in Islam. The state is, in theory at least, an integral part of the religious law.[6]

El Zuhur The flowering or revelation, *el zuhur*, of Mohammed Ahmed Abdallah is identified by Professor P. M. Holt, an acknowledged international authority on the Mahdiya, with multiple occasions spread over the period March to June 1881, straddling his second journey through Kordofan to Tegali and back to Aba culminating on 29 June. Now successor to Sheikh el Quraishi in the Sammaniya order, he had already begun on his original return to Aba from Mesellemiya to study the traditional prophecies of the Islamic Mahdi as applicable to his own person and, finding them confirmed by divine voices and prophetic messages, he first privately communicated this revelation to close friends and Islamic leaders in the Sudan, notably to Sheikh Quraishi wad el Zein and Sheikh Mohammed el Kheir, a while before his encounter with the future Khalifa, Abdallahi Mohammed Turshain, and a widening circle of disciples in March 1881. Leaving then for El Obeid, where he stayed with the head of the Ismailiya order, Mohammed el Mekki Ismail, he declared his divine election to his religious companions there, administering an oath of allegiance in secret to them and to the notables he then met en route to Tegali before returning in June to Aba.

The Oath was in these words:

> We swear allegiance to God, His Prophet, and to you, by God's unity, we will not associate anything with Him, nor steal, nor commit adultery, nor accuse anyone falsely, nor disobey you in rightful things. We swear that we will renounce this world, being content with what God has decreed, desiring God's mercies in this world and the next and that we will not flee from the *jihad* (holy war).

This Oath was in addition to the extended *shehada* (credo):

> I bear witness that Mohammed is the Prophet of Allah, and that Mohammed Ahmed ibn Abd Allah is the Mahdi of Allah and the representative of his Prophet.

The *haj* (pilgrimage to the holy places) would be held in abeyance pending the forthcoming time of *jihad*. The patched *jibba* was adopted as the dress of the *Ansar*, his companions, signifying equality.

It was again at Aba that the third stage of the *zuhur* was accomplished: by the personal self-revelation of the Prophet. It took the form of letters (*indharat*) dispatched to a wider circle of leaders, signed by Mohammed Ahmed el Mahdi, urging them to emulate the Prophet's *hijra* (flight or migration) and rally to him in the Faith to be with him within Ramadan – mid-July to mid-August in 1881 coinciding, as Holt notes, with the rains and the necessary deceleration in the potential speed of government response.

A hostile Sheikh Mohammed Sharif had warned Khartoum of developments. It is likely now that one of these *indharat* fell into the hands of the Khartoum government and it is certain that a telegram sent by the Mahdi from Aba to Mohammed Ra'uf Pasha was received in Khartoum at the beginning of August 1881, halfway through Ramadan. According to Colonel Stewart's subsequent account, Ra'uf Pasha at once dispatched the military commander and the *qadi* of Kawa (El Ais) with some notables to Aba where, on 3 August, they met the Mahdi and urged him to remain quiet. The advice being rejected, Ra'uf then sent his ADC Mohammed Abu Sa'ud to interview the Mahdi on 7 August. On his own initiative, Abu Sa'ud advised him to come to Khartoum for talks before resorting to force. Abu Sa'ud told Giegler later that the Mahdi – an essentially godly man but of puritanical views – was not entirely averse to debating his vocation, but that then, overborne by his followers, he had reaffirmed his divine appointment as the *Mahdi el Muntasir* (victorious) and threatened hostilities against all infidels. One detects the influence of Abdallahi, a man motivated by the wisdom of this world as well as his Moslem beliefs. The deputation retreated to Khartoum on 11 August empty-handed.

El Hijra   The shortcomings of the Governor-General, especially his dependence on ill-chosen associates, were now further exposed. Having been publicly rebuffed, he was obliged to restore his authority but his plan was risible if indeed Abu Sa'ud, a participant, is to be believed. Command of the 200-strong expedition on the *Ismailia* was given to Abu Sa'ud, but command of the troops to two *saghs qol aghasi* (adjutant-majors), one of them a friend of Ra'uf's family. These latter two disagreed on tactics and, on arrival at Aba on 12 August at 3 a.m., one officer, ignoring Abu Sa'ud's wish to try persuasion through the *qadi* of Kawa, landed with half the contingent, mistook a visiting Arab for the Mahdi and shot at him, only to be ambushed by the Mahdi's men with spears who drove back the soldiers to the steamer at a cost of twelve dead. Next morning a single artillery round was fired from the gun on the steamer's barge, along with some desultory rifle shots, one of which wounded the Mahdi in the shoulder. The defeated force then withdrew to Kawa and to Khartoum.

The Nile being in flood and much of Aba inundated, Abu Sa'ud was blamed for not relying on the gun. Humiliated, Ra'uf sent the order to El Obeid for Mohammed Sa'id to march to Kawa with 400 regulars and 100 irregulars, there to meet his own similar force plus a contingent from Fashoda. This they would do three weeks later. They were then to advance on Aba and there capture the Mahdi. To no avail – the Mahdi, with the swelling ranks of followers elated by their defeat of a government force, had already crossed to the west bank of the Nile the very next evening and advanced, under divine guidance in accordance with Koranic precedents, to Jebel Qadir, or to 'Jebel Masa' as it was renamed (a Moroccan *jebel* conforming with Mahdist tradition). All the time he was gathering support on his progress, especially from the neighbouring Kenana and Dighaym and from the Gawama'a Baqqara of south-eastern Kordofan, where Abdallahi's family had previously resided. Mohammed Sa'id, following in the Mahdi's tracks towards Tegali, concluded that it would be reckless to penetrate the Nuba hills with his small force and so returned.

Some time after the *zuhur*, conceivably during the *hijra* to Aba but traditionally at Jebel Qadir, the Mahdi appointed three *Khalifas*, not so much deputies of himself but as successors of the Prophet's closest family. Abdallahi Mohammed Turshain, the senior, became *Khalifat el Siddiq*, the successor of the Prophet's Abu Bakr el Siddiq. Ali Mohammed Hilu of the Dighaym became *Khalifat el Faruq*, the successor of Omer el Khattab; and Mohammed Sharif bin Hamid, a young relative of the Mahdi, became the successor of Ali, *Khalifat el Karrar*. A *Khalifa* successor of the Prophet's Osman Affan was not yet to be appointed. The Mahdi's companions became known as the *Ansar*, the Prophet's 'helpers'.[7]

If Ra'uf Pasha meanwhile was left the unwelcome task of reporting to Cairo the failure of this mission, worse was to come. Ossa would be piled upon Pelion. Within six weeks of the Mahdi's arrival at Jebel Qadir on 31 October 1881, a far larger government force, of allegedly some 400 soldiers with 1,000 Shilluk tribesmen under the Reth Kwickon, had left to engage his forces. The expedition was led in person by the *mudir* at Fashoda, Rashid Bey Ayman, who had only been in office a few months. He had learned of the Aba defeat and of the arrival of the Mahdi at Jebel Qadir. Ignoring instructions from Khartoum not to proceed, and advancing by forced marches, the expedition was detected and ambushed on 9 December 1881 as the men broke ranks at some wells on their way to attack the Mahdi at Jebel Qadir, believing him to have been driven out of Tegali by Mek Adham. Both Rashid and Reth Kwickon were killed – scarcely 100 survived. The Mahdist companions, the *ansar*, lost about thirty dead. Worse, the government force had been defeated by a Mahdist force without rifles, and their arms now fell into Mahdist hands. Giegler left Khartoum for Fashoda with two companies on 19 December, ten days after the disaster, to reinforce and fortify Fashoda against a Mahdist attack that did not in the event materialise.

El Jihad The *jihad*, holy war, was now joined, and repeated victories increased tribal commitment to the Mahdist camp, especially of the Baqqara, and also of disaffected *jallaba*. Letters were sent to all parts of the country challenging the tribal leaders to forsake the government and join the Mahdi, and to each part was appointed an *amir El Mahdi* as his deputy. These initiatives would be followed by the outbreak of a number of disturbances in areas sympathetic to the Mahdi.

Meanwhile Cairo had received Ra'uf's reports and endorsed Giegler's private conclusions that 'Ra'uf was largely responsible for the troubles' and was paralysed in inaction; and that Abu Sa'ud was completely unsuitable for his missions. Despite their preoccupations with the struggle for control of Egypt, on 23 February 1882 the new militant ministry announced that the office of *hakimdar* had been abolished, and that an Egyptian ministry of the Sudan had been established of which a Syrian military engineer, Fariq Abdel Qadir Pasha Hilmi, aged forty-five, would be the minister. Ra'uf Pasha left Khartoum with full honours on 4 March 1882, handing over to Giegler. Within a fortnight his discredited assistant, Abu Sa'ud, had died suddenly. Abdel Qadir would not arrive on his first visit to Khartoum for a further two critical months, during which Giegler discharged his responsibilities energetically but took it upon himself to telegraph Cairo that reinforcements were unnecessary.

Asked by the new minister on his appointment what action should be taken, Giegler recommended a massed attack by over 3,000 men on Jebel Qadir to be launched from Kaka. This was approved by Cairo and Giegler ordered this army, drawn from Khartoum, El Obeid and Sennar, to be under the overall command of Yusuf Pasha el Shallali, Gessi's former campaign deputy, now governor of Sennar but still under investigation for corruption. Miralai Mohammed Sulieman Bey, a

Sha'iqi veteran of the Mexican war with the Légion d' Honneur deco-
ration, would command the twelve companies of regular troops. The
El Obeid contingent was led by Mahmoud Bey Abdel Aziz, the irregulars by Abdallah Mohammed Dafa'allah. Giegler had previously gained
some logistical experience in mustering the initial force against Aba in
August 1881. The Khartoum force sailed in two parts on 20 and 30
March 1882 to Kaka.[8]

Scarcely had the Jebel Qadir expedition left Khartoum than news
arrived that an *amir El Mahdi*, Ahmed el Mekashfi, exploiting the
departure from Sennar of Yusuf Pasha and an important part of the
garrison, had rebelled against the new governor, Hussein Bey,
temporarily occupying much of the town. Giegler acted promptly in
recalling the Sha'iqi commander of Yusuf Pasha's irregulars, Salih Bey
el Mek, presently halted at Kawa, who then marched swiftly across
the Gezira to relieve Sennar at heavy cost to the Mahdist rebels and
none to himself.

Giegler on 15 April had himself left Khartoum for Sennar by steamer
with reinforcements, to be joined by a battalion summoned from
Kassala, and he was able to accomplish the defeat of a second rising
near Abu Haraz instigated by another Mahdist claimant. Giegler was
most fortunate to be accompanied in this second operation by Sheikh
Awad el Karim Ahmed Abu Sin of the loyal Shukriya and 130 cavalry
and on 18 May they arrived in Sennar to a formal welcome.

The town was repossessed, but not the southern Gezira of the
Kenana Baqqara to which the rebel remnants withdrew following a
further rising fifteen miles to the south of Sennar. Indeed only a limited
control had been reasserted in the Gezira, Hasan Sadiq Bey being now
appointed governor of Sennar. Dueim and Kawa, but not Jebelein and
Shatt, on the White Nile would resist Mahdist capture on 28 August
and again under Giegler in November, but by December 1882 the *amir*
Ahmed el Makashfi was again threatening Sennar, the first Egyptian
reinforcements proving irresolute.

The new minister for the Sudan, Fariq Abdel Qadir Hilmi, with
whom Giegler had been in regular contact since the former's arrival at
Berber, had reached Khartoum on 11 May 1882 to take charge in an
incipient civil war. Khartoum was at once fortified. Though with much
administrative experience from the Sudan railway project and the Suez
Canal zone, Abdel Qadir had not yet seen military action.
Nevertheless he was held in high regard and proved a most sound
appointment.

By contrast the choice of Yusuf el Shellali to lead the south Kordofan expedition was to prove a disaster. His force had been mustered at Kaka since 22 April and was already diminished by the diversion to Sennar of Salih Agha el Mek, when in a hot early May he advanced on Jebel Qadir before the full contingent from Kordofan had arrived, then halting at Jebel Funqur for eighteen days to regroup. Overweeningly confident that the Mahdi could be no match for his Remingtons and cannons, with provocative brutality Yusuf had had two captured Mahdist scouts publicly hacked to death before marching a further seven days through now muddy terrain to the village of Qadir, in the vicinity of which a large protective *zariba* with gun emplacements was built.

It was an inadequate defence. A surprise Mahdist attack was launched at dawn on 29 May 1882, penetrating the *zariba* and annihilating a well-armed but exhausted Egyptian force, 2,000 strong, in close hand-to-hand fighting and in subsequent hot pursuit. Among the limited Mahdist casualties was Hamid Abdallah, the Mahdi's brother. The Turkish killed included Yusuf Pasha Hasan el Shallali; Mahmoud Bey Abdel Aziz; and Abdallah Mohammed Dafa'allah el Awadi, brother of Ahmed, the enemy and merchant rival of Ilyas Ahmed Umm Bireir at El Obeid. An abundant haul of weaponry and booty fell into the Mahdi's hands.[9]

The defeat of this well-organised government expedition had a devastating effect on the respect in which the Egyptian government was regarded by the Sudanese and offset the successes achieved recently against the Mahdist rebellions in Sennar province. Further supporters flocked to Jebel Qadir. Sheikh Madibbo Ali, until recently *sheikh* of the Rizeiqat and Gessi's ally against Sulieman Zubeir, came in person to be sent back by the Mahdi as an *amir* to lead Darfur to the Mahdist cause. Ilyas Pasha, whom the Mahdi had already met in El Obeid, remained there to co-ordinate the Kordofan revolt, while Abdallahi el Nur would complement their efforts in the Hamar–Bideiriya–Hawazma region. Dilling, where Father Ohrwalder was stationed, had successfully fought off a Baqqara threat in April, but would be obliged to capitulate in September 1882.

Neither side was inactive in the aftermath of the second Jebel Qadir massacre. To reinforce the White Nile, the *hakimdar* called up three battalions of regulars with *bashi-buzouqs* from Gallabat and Bogos and *bazinqirs* from Bahr el Ghazal and Lado. Mohammed Sa'id,

according to Ohrwalder, sent a successful small expedition in July
against a Mahdist gathering at El Birka [Birket], but was soon forced
to retire to El Obeid, where the garrison of 4,000 was set to fortify the
government quarter with a trench and parapet. Bara however resisted
rebel attack. Despite an early intent to proceed first against Dar Fertit
Ilyas, through his son Omer, persuaded the Mahdi that El Obeid, the
second most important town in the Sudan, was ripe for occupation,
and half way through Ramadan, on 28 July 1882, the latter personally
left Jebel Qadir with the secret destination of El Obeid, the rains still
heavy but water correspondingly ample. By the end of August when
the Mahdi camped three hours from El Obeid, government resistance
in Kordofan was limited to El Obeid and to Bara. Abu Haraz had
fallen in April; Ashaf three hours north of Bara, in May; Shatt
(between Dueim and Kawa) and El Tayyara (east of El Obeid) in
August.

Still rejecting firearm weaponry on religious grounds and encouraged by the desertion of many of the undefended civil population led
by Ilyas, the Mahdist army on 8 September assaulted the garrison of El
Obeid across open ground from the south west and from the east. They
attacked with outstanding bravery but at enormous cost, being forced
to withdraw five hours later having suffered many thousand dead,
among them two brothers, Mohammed and Abdallah Fahil, and a
nephew of the Mahdi and a brother of Khalifa Abdallahi. It was a
major defeat but the governor, Mohammed Sa'id Pasha Wahbi, against
the advice of his now assistant Ali Bey Sharif and of Ahmed Dafa'allah
was, reasonably enough, reluctant to follow it up with a pursuit by his
own very limited force lest El Obeid be left exposed. The Mahdi
ordered a siege of El Obeid and took the decision to send for the many
firearms stored at Jebel Qadir to arm a new contingent of captured
government troops. Slatin and Lupton were to be harried.

Notwithstanding the major setback to the Mahdi's September plans
to capture El Obeid, spurred on by the actions of the Rizeiqat *sheikhs*
Madibbo Ali and Ujail el Jangawi all the southern Fur tribes were
nevertheless committed to revolt. In October 1882 Slatin, after an inde-
cisive skirmish with Madibbo, set out in an attempt to recover Shakka
with an army of 8,000 men, only to be ambushed at Umm Waraqat and
his force literally decimated. Madibbo had been joined by the Dinka
chief Yanqu (Jango) of Telgauna who, in August, had massacred
Lupton's garrison at Liffi on the Bahr el Arab. Slatin was forced to
retire to Dara, sending to Lupton in Deim Sulieman a request to attack

Abdel Qadir Pasha Hilmi

the Rizeiqat and Habbaniya – a request with which Lupton was in no position to comply. In January 1883 Slatin learned of El Obeid's capitulation, exposing himself at increased risk in Dara and El Fasher. Umm Shanga was evacuated.

Lewa Mohammed Sa'id Pasha in El Obeid, dependent on the materialisation of a substantial relief force, had immediately in September 1882 petitioned Abdel Qadir Pasha for assistance. The latter's request of Cairo on 24 October for the dispatch of reinforcements, unlike that of Ra'uf Pasha the previous December 1881, was given urgent attention by the Egyptian government on the morrow of the suppression of the Arabi rebellion and the disbandment of the defeated Egyptian army (as indeed was the question of Abdel Qadir's replacement by Ismail Ayub). However the formation of a relief force for the Sudan would in any case take weeks. Meanwhile Abdel Qadir set about mustering in Khartoum a new sizeable army from Eastern Sudan, Gallabat, Dar Fertit and Lado, part of which he intended to send as a limited local relief force to Kordofan. Giegler claimed that Abdel Qadir originally intended that Giegler would command the local relief force and, on arrival at El Obeid, would supersede Mohammed Sa'id as general-governor of

Kordofan. To contemplate sending a Christian with little military experience in such circumstances seems most improbable.

In the event the relief force, led by Ali Bey Lutfi, of two battalions of
regulars and 750 *bashi-buzouqs* was unable to reach El Obeid. It was
intercepted and the surviving half forced to make for Bara, which itself
now came under siege. On 28 December 1882, with no relief in sight,
the commander at Bara, El Nur Bey Anqara, was obliged to enter negotiations to capitulate. The event demoralised El Obeid's famished garrison. To quote Father Josef Ohrwalder, prisoner in the Mahdi's siege
headquarters, in his account of conditions at the end in the siege of El
Obeid:

> Deaths by starvation had reached an appalling figure. The dead
> and dying filled the streets; the space within the fortifications
> being so limited, there was not room for all people, and in conse-
> quence many lay about in the streets and in the open spaces. The
> air was poisoned by the number of dead bodies lying unburied,
> while the ditch was half full of mortifying corpses... They (the
> soldiers) became desperate, all discipline was at an end and they
> often broke into the houses by night in search of food.

El Obeid was surrendered on 19 January 1883. The Mahdi entered
in triumph to lead the Friday prayers in the mosque. Arms and ammunition were seized and all valuables sequestrated by Ahmed Sulieman
who was appointed in charge of the treasury (the *beit al mal*). The
valuables were to be augmented by the enforced surrender of loot
seized previously by local tribesmen. Mohammed Sa'id and his principal lieutenants dispatched a secret report to Khartoum justifying the
surrender, only for it to be betrayed by one of the signatories, leading
to the execution of his companions.

Thus by the end of 1882, within the space of little more than a single
year, despite some rebuffs – notably in Sennar and the first battle for El
Obeid – the Mahdi was established as the *de facto* conqueror of
Kordofan. The camel-owning Kababish of northern Kordofan – historically controllers of the Bayuda desert routes from Debba and Korti
towards Khartoum – whose *nazir* El Tom Fadlallah Salim had opposed
the Mahdi and forfeited his life following the fall of El Obeid, uniquely
remained suspect in their loyalties to the new ruler. Darfur and Bahr el
Ghazal were isolated and themselves immediately threatened, while the
future of the Gezira between the Blue and White Niles was still actively
contested. All these events had unrolled without evidence of any

Egyptian government determination to reverse the tide. It is time to identify the reasons for this inaction.[10]

3 THE QUIETUS TO KHEDIVIAL RULE 1879–82

Mutiny   Khedive Ismail had, on the order of the Ottoman Sultan, abdicated in favour of his eldest son Mohammed Tawfiq (not Mohammed Abdel Halim Pasha, his uncle, as the Sultan preferred) on 26 June 1879. Dicey attributed the ill-concealed long-term hostility of Ismail to his eldest son and heir-apparent to Ismail's having had no more than a fleeting relationship with the boy's lowly-born mother. She had been soon supplanted by new favourites whose offspring, younger half-brothers of Tawfiq, were accorded a superior status, education and paternal affection conspicuously denied to the eldest son. In Dicey's words Tawfiq was 'a man of twenty-seven, spare of figure, with a plain but not unkindly face, gifted with good intentions, but with narrow views; a devout believer in Islam; a Turk of the Turks... a good husband; a man according to Oriental ideas of moral domestic life; a frugal administrator.' His good constitutional intentions had been previously rewarded for the brief period 22 March to 9 April 1879 with his appointment as president of the Egyptian Council, set up immediately following Nubar's dismissal to assist his father Ismail's endeavours to claw back power. In June Tawfiq would assume the Viceregal throne on the condition that he acceded to Anglo-French insistence on the re-establishment of the Dual Control to direct Egypt's finances. The Controllers-General would be Major Evelyn Baring and M. de Blignières. Riaz Pasha succeeded Sharif Pasha in September 1879.

The Khedivial estates having been restored to the public domain, the work of the former Commission of Enquiry which had reported a year earlier, would, on 2 April 1880, be supplanted by an International Commission of Liquidation whose duty would be to take over the servicing of the public debt under the presidency of Sir Rivers Wilson, formerly minister of finance. The unified debt was now set at £E58m, the privileged debt at £E2.2m. Baring, on his appointment as financial member of the Viceroy of India's council, was succeeded as Controller-General by Auckland Colvin in June 1880. Following a clash between Lord Vivian and Sir Rivers Wilson regarding Ismail's determined stand to maintain his authority, Vivian had already in March 1879 been succeeded as British consul-general briefly by Sir Frank Lascelles, then in October by Sir Edward Malet.

For the while Egypt seemed to have become reconciled to foreign financial control. To Baring visiting Cairo en route to India in December 1880 (he had opined to Malet on the latter's arrival a year earlier that 'on the whole the start has been favourable'), it appeared that Egypt had at last entered the path of reform, and that all that was required was time to complete the superstructure of which the foundations had been so laboriously laid. Baring did however warn the chief minister, Riaz Pasha, regarding army indiscipline in the wake of the earlier mutiny of February 1879, a warning that Riaz mistakenly dismissed as unnecessary. Notwithstanding his absence in India, Baring (Cromer) in *Modern Egypt* was to leave a blow by blow account of subsequent events.

By February 1881 a second far more serious mutiny had broken out engendered by the same underlying cause – the latent Egyptian officers' distrust of Turkish leaders and commanders, and this time in their inequitable treatment of Egyptian officer counterparts placed on half-pay by the Ottoman decree reducing the army strength by two-thirds. Egyptian officers led by Colonels Ahmed Arabi, Ali Fahmi and Abdel Al petitioned the chief minister on 15 January against unjust actions of the minister of war, Osman Pasha Rifqi, as regards promotions and dismissals of Egyptian officers, and demanded his replacement by a fellow conspirator, Mahmoud Pasha Sami (Baroudi), serving in the ministry of Riaz. When the Khedive responded on 1 February 1881 by arresting the colonels, their regiments marched on the Khedivial palace, to be dispersed only with the announcement that Tawfiq, capitulating, had duly made Mahmoud Sami minister of war. The government then increased the pay of unemployed officers and promised equal treatment irrespective of race. For the second time within two years the army had successfully mutinied and government authority had again been humiliated.

Rebellion   There followed an uneasy summer, the Egyptian officers deeply suspicious of a counter-strike and plotting, with French encouragement, the downfall of Riaz Pasha. Arabi Bey was made a member of a commission enquiring into army grievances and preparing a military law. In September 1881 the replacement of Mahmoud Sami by the Khedive's brother-in-law, followed by orders to the mutinous regiments of February to leave Cairo for the provinces, provoked on 9 September another march led by Arabi Bey with 2,500 men and 18 guns on the Abdin Palace. His weakening resolve stiffened by the advice of Sir Auckland Colvin, Stone Pasha, ministers and other senior officers, the Khedive Mohammed Tawfiq was persuaded to confront Arabi in person in the Abdin Square and then to leave Colvin and the British and French consuls-general to negotiate the rebels' demands for the dismissal of all ministers, the convocation of a parliament and the raising of army numbers to the Porte's limit of 18,000. Arabi Bey had already assumed the authority of one 'representing the Egyptian army' and believed he enjoyed the sympathy of the Porte, but he and his associates remained evidently fearful of meeting the fate of the '*mufettish*' (see p. 201), a principal motivation in this third mutinous confrontation with the Khedive.

An armistice was eventually arranged with the additional help of the members of the Chamber of Notables (established in 1866) under Mohammed Sultan Pasha, its president, in consequence of which Sharif Pasha was accepted as chief minister on 14 September 1881 in place of Riaz and the European controllers-general reappointed, as was Mahmoud Sami in his former office to supervise the new military law. No commitment was made to increase the army size, but Dual Control of financial authority was confirmed in name. After a triumphal march round the streets of Cairo, Arabi was content to withdraw his regiment to Suez. The Sultan however endeavoured to re-establish formal Turkish advisers to the Khedive, only to be deterred by the visit of British and French warships to Alexandria.

The army meanwhile displayed frequent insubordination to the civil power and the separation of the military party, led by Arabi – the real ruler of Egypt since September and, in January 1882, made under-secretary for war as a formal member of government – from the populist national party to be represented by the Chamber of Notables became increasingly difficult, yet this was critical to the political balance whereby the armistice could be transformed into peace. Europeans became a target in the press on political, racial and religious grounds. In this unsettled situation, contingency planning for military occupation of Egypt, by Turkey as much as by Britain and France, became a necessity. Already in October 1881 the Turkish dispatch of envoys had only been halted by a naval demonstration, even if basically such Turkish intervention was anathema to the French rather than to the British.

Foreign Intervention   In the wake of the French annexation in 1881 of the protectorate of Tunis with its Ottoman connections, Leon Gambetta, French *président du conseil*, in mid-December 1881 urged an Anglo-French démarche, ostensibly to lend authority to the Khedive against the interference of Turkey, in fact to strengthen Anglo-French dual influence at a time of Egyptian nationalist pressure. A joint note delivered on 8 January 1882 to the Khedive affirmed their 'resolve to guard by their united efforts against all cause of complication, internal or external, which might menace the order of things established in Egypt'. Action in support however was, critically, not agreed between the Powers. Earl Granville, Gladstone's foreign minister since April 1881, favoured Turkish, Gambetta Anglo-French armed intervention. This note, in the words of Sir Edward Malet on 9 January,

> at all events temporarily alienated us from all confidence... for the moment it has had the effect to cause a more complete union of the national party, the military and the Chamber, to unite these three in a common bond of opposition to England and France... Arabi Bey is said to be foremost in protesting against what he is represented to consider an unjust interference.

Within hours a major confrontation was generated. The Chamber of Notables claimed independent control of revenues not assigned to debt payments, excluding the controllers from voting *inter alia* on the army budget. French intransigence precluded compromise. A deputation of the Chamber to the Khedive forced the resignation of Sharif's ministry and the appointment on 5 February 1882 of Mahmoud Pasha Sami as chief minister, Arabi Bey as minister of war, Mustapha Pasha Fahmi as foreign minister and a ministry drawn totally from the national and military parties. By then (on 31 January) Gambetta had resigned to be succeeded as French prime minister by de Freycinet, but too late for the consequences of the former's intransigence to be undone.

The new Egyptian ministry was soon under the military domination of Arabi, the Khedivate effectively in abeyance, and Dual Control eliminated. The controllers-general were ostracised. The *mudirs*, bereft of authority, had no control over undisciplined, overpaid and overpromoted soldiery; and interest rates soared as public confidence waned. The Sultan, who had protested at the joint note, was nevertheless warned that the status quo could only be modified by the Great Powers acting with Turkey, and these for the while simply watched the deterioration. Arabi embarked on the court-martial of forty Turkish officers, including Fariq Osman Pasha Rifqi, as a pre-emptive strike against their hostility, sentencing them to deportation to the Sudan. This the Khedive insisted on commuting in part, leading on 18 May 1882 to a deeper rupture of relations between the Khedive and the ministry.

None would now accept the Khedive's nomination as chief minister, fearful of the military party which – in the face of the proposed dispatch of an Anglo-French squadron to Alexandria, accompanied by a request to the Porte to abstain from action – had now strengthened its own relations with the Sultan. An Anglo-French ultimatum on 25 May requiring the resignation of the Egyptian ministry, the exile of Arabi, and the retirement from the capital of the colonels Ali Pasha Fahmi and Abdel Al Pasha was only productive as to the first. Arabi and the military leaders, confident of the Porte's collusion with them, rejected 'exile' out of hand and on 28 May the Khedive, effectively a prisoner in his palace, was predictably forced to yield to the reinstatement of Arabi as minister of war and to call on the Sultan for an imperial commissioner to Egypt.

Occupation On 19 May 1882 the small Anglo-French squadron, commanded by the British Admiral Sir Beauchamp Seymour, reached Alexandria to support the Khedive and on 29 May Seymour would report: 'Alexandria is apparently controlled this morning by the military party', as indeed already was Cairo. Within a fortnight of Alexandria's takeover by Arabi, as correctly prophesied by Sir Edward Malet, Moslem rioters attacked the Christian population on Sunday 11 June, massacring some fifty Europeans and seriously wounding the British consul. The intercession of the two Sultan's commissioners prompted Arabi in Cairo to order troops to restore order in Alexandria. Arabi would now receive the *grand cordon* of Medjedieh from the Sultan, but he would not be deflected from henceforth ignoring the Sultan's commissioners. Meanwhile 20,000 Christians sought to quit the country.

Having dismissed from his mind the reality of any Turkish intervention, in early July Arabi set about fortifying the sea batteries in defence of Alexandria. He ignored a British ultimatum to desist, whereupon his batteries were bombarded throughout 11 July 1882 by the British fleet, the French Admiral Conrad declining to cooperate. It included HMS *Inflexible* commanded by Captain John (later Admiral of the Fleet) Fisher, who observed that half of the British shells from the muzzle-loading guns failed to explode. Arabi ordered the withdrawal of troops on 12 July, and the setting fire to the city, provoking a reluctant British government to sanction its occupation, claiming that Turkish refusal to intervene had left no option. The planned French naval cooperation having evaporated on the eve of the bombardment, the French admiral was ordered by the de Freycinet government in Paris to steam instead to Port Said, reflecting perhaps the pressure from Ferdinand de Lesseps, anxious on account of his Suez Canal to propitiate nationalist opinion; but, more probably, French suspicion of German intentions to dissipate French armed strength. On 12 July Gladstone invited Musurus Pasha, the Turkish ambassador in London, to get Turkish troops sent to Egypt, but the Sultan declined to act.

Massacres of Europeans in other Egyptian towns continued, and already on 22 July 1882 a British expeditionary force under General Sir Garnet Wolseley, 'in support of the authority of His Highness the Khedive', was approved despite the continued absence of French moral backing. Arabi was formally dismissed by the Khedive the same day but anarchy would obtain until the British force of 13,000 men and 40 guns, having first seized Port Said, landed at Ismailia under Wolseley on 22 August and, marching west across the desert to El Qassassin, attacked Arabi's prepared defensive position at Tel el Kebir at 4.30 a.m. on 13 September. Within twenty minutes the position was carried. The cost to the British was 52 killed and 380 wounded, against Egyptian losses of 1,500 and 40 guns. Mohammed Sultan Pasha, president of the Chamber of Notables, was present as the Khedive's civil commissioner. Lieutenant-Colonel Charles Watson led the entry to Cairo through the *bab el wazir* next to the Citadel. The next day Arabi was arrested and within a week all resistance was at an end. On 24 September 1882 the Khedive, accompanied by Wolseley and Malet, entered Cairo in state.

The Ottoman Sultan Abdel Hamid II, who had declined to proclaim Arabi a rebel, was at once assured that, Arabi's insurrection having been defeated, the British government contemplated the early with-drawal of British troops. Indeed Britain on 23 June 1882 had with the other Powers signed a protocol not to seek, following action in Egypt, 'any territorial advantage nor any concession of any exclusive privilege, nor any commercial advantages other than those which any other nation might equally obtain'. The Earl of Dufferin, formerly Governor-General of Canada and ambassador to Russia, now to the Porte, was instructed by Earl Granville to advise the government of the Khedive (an Ottoman Viceroy) in the arrangements which would have to be made for re-establishing His Highness's authority – effectively the reconstruction of Egyptian administration and a replacement for Dual

Control. Granville assured Malet that Dufferin's appointment was simply because 'the settlement of Egyptian affairs involves matters so complicated and connected closely with the Eastern Question, that undivided responsibility can hardly with fairness rest on one individual'. The relationship of ambassador and consul-general would prove entirely harmonious, with Malet continuing to conduct current political business.

Lord Dufferin arrived on 7 November 1882 to find already under way the preliminary commission of enquiry under Ismail Pasha Ayub regarding the court martial of Ahmed Arabi, Mahmoud Samir and three others. British legal counsel appointed for the defence claimed that the mutiny was in reality a patriotic movement. In the event of conviction by the court for military rebellion Khedivial authority would require the death penalty but the British government whose forces had overthrown the conspirators, having ascertained that Arabi was not implicated in the Alexandria massacres, were against it. It was a case of a successful mutiny backed by the whole army with the sympathy of the civil population and quelled by foreign intervention. Dufferin, who had already advised the release of the mass of military prisoners and a general amnesty for all officers up to the rank of captain, arranged guilty pleas by the main conspirators to rebellion, whereupon a sentence of death was at once commuted to one of exile – in Ceylon. Dufferin would write:

> With regard to Arabi, I am by no means prejudiced against him. I imagine he was quite honest and sincere; but the grievances of which he complained were not of a nature to justify him in plunging his country into a war which has certainly been very disastrous to the population at large... Never has a rebellion been so tenderly dealt with.

Riaz Pasha, now minister of the interior, resigned rather than sanction the reprieves. Tawfiq Pasha had been dead eight years when, in 1900, the rebels were released, with Khedivial authority meanwhile manifestly dependent on a prolonged British occupation which, Arabi would confess to Sir Valentine Chirol in Ceylon, was doing in Egypt most of the things Arabi had wished to do.

Dufferin's report would be submitted on 6 February 1883. Despite French objections, Dual Control was abolished and Sir Auckland Colvin, with marginally less authority than a controller, made financial adviser. A new Egyptian army was to be formed under a British *sirdar*

(Sir Evelyn Wood) aided by British staff officers and a new constabulary (under Inspector-General Valentine Baker Pasha). A constitutional structure was created with provincial and legislative councils, a general assembly and a council of state.

Dufferin acknowledged: 'Before a guarantee of Egypt's independence can be said to exist, the administrative system of which it is the leading characteristic must have time to consolidate.' Implicit in Dufferin's advice was the conclusion that the British occupation must be indefinitely prolonged. Had he been commissioned to exercise 'the masterful hand of a Resident' he would have bent matters largely to his will, but this he recognised would be unacceptable to Gladstone's government. In September 1883, however, Sir Evelyn Baring, KCSI, returning from India to succeed Sir Edward Malet as consul-general, would effectually fulfil that role.

The Sudan Question If Dufferin's expertise as the senior Near Eastern diplomat had been enlisted to advise his government on Egypt's future in the wide international context, Egypt's boundary was nevertheless implicitly assumed to lie at the first cataract of the Nile at Aswan. Events in the Sudan would be relevant solely in the military context, the implications for the new Egyptian army of the future threat of a Mahdist conquest to Egypt proper as yet underestimated. Already on 30 October 1882 Malet had been instructed that the British government was not prepared to undertake any expedition into the Sudan and that his concern should be directed to ascertaining the condition of affairs in the Sudan which could bear on the strength and deployment of the Egyptian army. Dufferin's report included only four paragraphs devoted to the Sudan, and he acknowledged privately to Granville: 'I have carefully avoided having anything to do with the Sudan business except keeping myself informed of what was happening.'[11]

Such proper restraint on the part of Dufferin had not however inhibited the views of the military adviser seconded to the Cairo consulate-general, Lieutenant-Colonel Sir Charles Wilson, Royal Engineers – Fellow of the Royal Society, cartographer and presently consul-general for Anatolia. A month before Dufferin's instructions had been issued, Wilson had prepared a memorandum for Sir Edward Malet on 2 October 1882 as to Sudan policy. Deprecating the useless conquests of Ismail Pasha which had made the Sudan always a source of weakness and expense, and claiming that the conquest of Darfur had 'failed to exert any influence on the suppression of slavery', Wilson predicated the creation of the Sudan as 'a paying province' on, first, peace with Abyssinia through the restoration of Bogos and Gallabat, the establishment of Massawa as a free port, and facilitation of the appointment of Abyssinian *abunas* by the Coptic Patriarch; secondly, the evacuation of Darfur and perhaps part of Kordofan; and thirdly the opening of the 'natural' trade route to Egypt via Berber to Suakin instead of down the Nile. Wilson recommended the appointment of an English Governor-General and *seraskir* and an army of 5,000 men, and foresaw the need to fight the Mahdi either with Egyptian troops under English officers or with English troops. The first need, and this Malet agreed, was the dispatch of two English officers to report on the Sudan situation and the steps necessary for its pacification.

On the basis of an imprecise account of a telegram of the *hakimdar*, Abdel Qadir Pasha Hilmi, dated 24 October, which was misinterpreted to envisage the imminent fall of Khartoum if British assistance were not rendered speedily, and notwithstanding the declared Egyptian intention to appoint Ismail Pasha Ayub *hakimdar* and Stone Pasha chief of staff to Khartoum and to raise a requisite relief force for soonest dispatch thither, on 28 October Wilson now urged the dispatch of British officers to fortify Khartoum, and as material assistance, the diversion to Aden of Indian troops returning to India. 5,000 troops were needed. Wilson even canvassed possible military help from Abyssinia. In case of Khartoum's fall, Korosko and Aswan should be prepared for a possible attack. Betraying pardonable ignorance of senior Egyptian generals – such as Abdel Qadir, Ala el Din and Osman Rifqi – Wilson proposed General Gordon's reappointment.

The reply of the Foreign Office on 30 October 1882 was brusque: no Indian, or indeed British troops would operate in the Sudan; and if Gordon, in what capacity? The new officer commanding British troops in Egypt, Lieutenant-General Sir Archibald Alison, of like mind with London, was planning to halt the Mahdist threat at the first cataract for which British, or preferably Indian, reinforcements would be required. So far as the Sudan itself was concerned however, that was quintessentially an Egyptian government responsibility. British intervention should be limited to the dispatch of Lieutenant-Colonel J. D. H. Stewart to the Sudan in November to report. As to Gordon, Malet advised his only role could be that of Governor-General but unless that was demanded by the British government, it would certainly not be suggested by the Egyptian government. At a meeting with Granville on

17 November, Gordon for his part recommended Sir Charles Wilson. Wilson remained in Egypt as adviser until 24 February 1883.

These proposals for British military intervention in the Sudan were indeed the personal initiative from Sir Charles Wilson, and unendorsed by Malet who, on 4 November, submitted that Egypt should treat the Sudan question 'as best it can without our aid and advice'. Britain, resolved to withdraw from Egypt, should incur no responsibility lest, if measures failed, she could be drawn into military operations in the Sudan. That same day a telegram from Khartoum recorded the arrival of the denuded relief force at Bara, Kordofan signalling that the Sudan was safe pending the arrival of reinforcements from Egypt.

The Khedive and his ministers were seemingly content to act alone on the Sudan, enjoined only to consult the British government on the appointment of the *sirdar* of the new Egyptian army and gendarmerie. The request, made in the light of Abdel Qadir Pasha's telegram of 24 October, for a British chief of staff for the Egyptian force to accompany the Egyptian reinforcements of seven to eight thousand men was turned down and Ala el Din Pasha Siddiq, general-governor of Red Sea Provinces at Massawa, was selected to be the *seraskir*. The names of Ismail Ayub and Stone were dropped from consideration – indeed Stone was being 'got rid of on liberal terms' by the British. The mustering of the new force recruited from the disbanded troops of the old Egyptian army would necessarily take time, but by 20 December the British military attaché was commending Egyptian logistical efforts to transport troops and weaponry via Suakin and Berber to Khartoum.

Meanwhile the British cavalryman Lieutenant-Colonel Stewart, recently vice-consul in Konya, Anatolia, had left Egypt on 24 November 1882 with the former Italian general-governor of Darfur, G. B. Messadaglia, instructed under no circumstances to presume to act in any military capacity. Stewart was to report rapidly on the route from the Red Sea to Khartoum; to ascertain the current situation in the Sudan and to telegraph this from Khartoum; and to sketch and report on the defensive capability of Khartoum. Dr Mekki Shibeika affirms that the general-governor, Fariq Ala el Din Pasha Siddiq, at Massawa knew nothing of Stewart's mission until the latter's arrival at Suakin, the governor there to be cross-questioned about locations and numbers of the garrisons on the Red Sea littoral. Stewart then presumed to recommend the dismissal of the governor Suakin; the dispatch of his deputy with the Sudanese troops to the interior; and their replacement by Egyptian reinforcements from Cairo. Abdel

Qadir Pasha Hilmi in Khartoum, on receipt of similar enquiries from Stewart, now at Berber, about the Beja tribes, their sheikhs and taxes, was prompted to telegraph Cairo for instructions. He was ordered to offer information but to keep Stewart and his companion under surveillance and to report in cypher on their activities, while the Egyptian government sought enlightenment on the purposes of Stewart's mission. Egyptian suspicions were dispelled, but Stewart's request that his advice should be listened to was withdrawn. Giegler stated that 'we were at loggerheads because of his [Stewart's] brutal behaviour in Khartoum, but later we got on better... I told him about everything that had happened.'

Stewart's first dispatch to Malet dated 10 December 1882 from Berber, en route to Khartoum where he would arrive on 16 December, was optimistic. Abdel Qadir had telegraphed him that the siege of El Obeid had been raised, Khartoum was quite safe, the other provinces quiet, and the first contingent of 800 Egyptian reinforcements had already arrived. On 18 December the Kordofan picture was less good. The latest El Obeid news, six weeks earlier, was that the besieged garrison of 3,500, too weak to make a sortie, was calling for relief; while communication with Bara, also surrounded, had been severed and fourteen days earlier Bara food supplies were failing. Six months previously, Slatin Bey in Darfur had advised that he could not control his province unless reinforced. The subsequent silence was ominous – he was in fact now confined to El Fasher and Dara.

The encouraging factor for Stewart was the strength of character, ability and energy exhibited by Abdel Qadir Pasha, busy drilling his troops. The latter needed seven battalions before marching to relieve Bara, and was hoping to be ready in one month. Stewart had good reason to expect his success. 'He will take the field in person.' Abdel Qadir had indeed called up Sudanese troops from East Sudan, as he had previously from Bahr el Ghazal and Lado but he recognised the need for Arabic-speaking officers. Khartoum had been fortified and a four-kilometre section of the protective ditch completed.

The new year of 1883 however would bring bad news.[12]

4 KORDOFAN AND DARFUR FALL TO THE *ANSAR*

Colonel Stewart's Report   Stewart arrived at Khartoum from Suakin on 16 December 1882 – a principal British witness of the death throes

of Egyptian Empire. The previous eighteen months had seen an astonishing political transformation both in Egypt and the Sudan. In Egypt,
internal rebellion had precipitated foreign occupation with the belated
and reluctant assent of a sovereign Porte – political control passing to
Britain's, albeit unwilling, hands save in respect of the dependent
Sudan. And in the Sudan itself a state of civil war prevailed, effective
Egyptian rule now limited to territories little more extensive than those
of the Fung Kingdom of Sennar which the Turkish Viceroy had
conquered in 1821–2. The outcome of this struggle was far from
certain.

News reaching Cairo of the first stirring of the Mahdist rebellion in
August 1881 coincided with the second mutiny led by Ahmed Arabi; of
the first Mahdist triumph at Jebel Qadir in December 1881 with the
bêtise of the Anglo-French Joint Note; and of the second triumph in
May 1882 with the Alexandria massacres. There had been a firm if
qualified response by the newly appointed Egyptian ministry of
Mahmoud Pasha Sami with Arabi as minister of war. In February 1882
Mohammed Pasha Ra'uf had been removed from the Governor-
Generalship and Abdel Qadir Pasha Hilmi appointed Minister of the
Sudan but, to meet the latter's request in June 1882 for reinforcements,
only arms could be immediately spared.

The repulse of the first Mahdist attack on El Obeid in September
1882 followed by the failure of Abdel Qadir's own relief force to
deliver assistance to the governor of Kordofan prompted Abdel Qadir
in late October, now aware of the outcome of Tel el Kebir, to threaten
to evacuate Khartoum and the Sudan unless 10,000 men were
dispatched as reinforcements. Initially the Khedive planned to react
positively but also to send Ismail Pasha Ayub to replace Abdel Qadir,
but this proposal was cancelled when the threat to Khartoum was
deemed less immediate. Ismail Ayub remained in Egypt as minister of
the interior. There then followed the news that approaching half the
Kordofan reinforcements had successfully fought their way through
to Bara.

As the Mahdi administered successive coups de grâce to the besieged
garrisons of Bara and El Obeid over the following two months, ever-
increasing sections of the Sudanese people acknowledged their allegiance to him, leaving Darfur and Bahr el Ghazal ripe for the picking.
Abdel Qadir strove to gather 2,000 camels and to instil some discipline
into his Egyptian reinforcements in preparation for his own advance
against the Mahdi in Kordofan, as well as personally in January 1883

countering further insurrections in the Gezira region of the Blue and White Niles. Lieutenant-Colonel Stewart in Khartoum was now compiling his report on the Sudan for the British government, which Giegler was to rate 'an exemplary achievement... the most exhaustive report which has ever been published on the Sudan'.

Stewart's preliminary draft of his Report dated 29 December 1882 – within a fortnight of his arrival in Khartoum but after Abdel Qadir's reservations about him had been laid to rest – consisted of a history of the Sudan to date; a biography of the Mahdi; road reports; and valuable maps. This intelligence report was founded on documents placed in his hands by Abdel Qadir prior to the latter's departure to campaign in Sennar, having left Giegler in charge in Khartoum, now reappointed deputy governor-general and minister. Thereafter, no doubt relying on Giegler's information, Stewart was able to dispatch his *Report on the Soudan* to Sir Edward Malet in Cairo on 9 February 1883, whence it was forwarded to London on 6 March shortly before Stewart's departure from Khartoum to Massawa and Cairo on 8 March. Duly revised for publication it would appear as British Parliamentary Blue Book, Egypt, No 11. The map of the Sudan was by Messadaglia.[13]

The 11° N latitude was identified by Stewart as dividing the north – to the west, mostly Baqqara; to the east of the White Nile, Arabs – from the south, 'where the negro race begins' (section 3). Roads were camel tracks and with Giegler's help a comprehensive list of eight telegraph lines was compiled (sections 4, 5). Abdel Qadir's previous experience as chief engineer of the Sudan railway project was incorporated (section 11). Perhaps the most interesting contribution related to the revised administrative structure of the Sudan (section 7), and details of the (otiose) budget for 1882 (section 10).

The Sudan had now been divided by Minister Abdel Qadir Pasha into three *hakimdarias*: of west, central and east Sudan, each consisting of several *muderias* subdivided into administrative districts, *mamuriyat idara*, and tribal districts, *aqsam*. The *hakimdars* corresponded direct with the minister, ostensibly in Cairo but compelled by circumstances to reside in Khartoum. West Sudan comprised the *muderias* of Darfur, Kordofan, Bahr el Ghazal and Dongola. Its capital was El Fasher with, paradoxically, its *hakimdar*, Mohammed Sa'id Pasha Wahbi, in El Obeid. Darfur and Bahr el Ghazal *muderias* were under general-governors (Slatin Bey and Lupton Bey); Dongola under a *mudir* Mustapha Yawar Bey. Under Slatin there were two administrative districts, at Qulqul and Dara; otherwise the *aqsam* were under *nazirs* of tribes. Under Lupton, tribal chiefs were responsible locally. Under the *hakimdar* in El Obeid was Ali Bey Sharif as deputy.

Eastern Sudan comprised the *muderias* of Taka (Kassala); and of Suakin and Massawa with the Red Sea littoral. The capital was Massawa, the *hakimdar* Ala el Din Pasha Siddiq. Taka *muderia* was under a general-governor, seemingly Rashid Kamil Bey, with Gallabat an administrative district. The *mudir* of Massawa and Suakin, who did not impress Stewart, may have been Firhad Muhhib.

Central Sudan, capital Khartoum, embodied the riverain *muderias* of Khartoum, Sennar, Berber, Fashoda and Equatoria. Two of these, Equatoria and Sennar, were general-governorates. Equatoria under Emin Bey had six districts – Latuka, Bor, Makraka, Monbuttu, Wadelai and Fuweira; Sennar had Fazughli under Marno until his death August 1883.

Sui generis was Harar, reporting direct to the minister (but not a *hakimdaria)* under Ali Rida el Tubji Pasha, comprising the *muderias* of Harar; Berbera, under Abdel Rahman Bey Fa'iz; and Zeyla, under Abu Bakr Pasha.

At the ministry itself were the Minister, his ADC, an inspector-general for the suppression of slavery, and five *saghs-qol-aghasi*. Stewart assessed an overall need for eighteen battalions of irregular troops in the Sudan, infantry to be recruited from Black peoples. That however assumed that the territories west of the White Nile and south of the eleventh parallel would be given up in accordance with his recommendation below.

Stewart's 1882 budget, which doubtless owed much to Giegler, who had worked with Gordon on the 1878 Budget, had been overtaken by events – 'there can be no doubt that the deficits of many provinces are very far in excess of those stated. Probably no revenue whatever has been collected in the province of Kordofan. Much the same can be said of Dara and Fashoda. Sennar with, perhaps, Darfur must also be pretty much in the same plight' (section 10). Comparison between the 1878 and 1882 budgets does not appear to indicate that the 'vigorous efforts... made to limit expenditure' (section 1) during the rule of Mohammed Ra'uf Pasha were very effective.

In his recommendations as to suppression of the slave trade Stewart noted that the inspector-general and some inspectors already in place could do a great deal but that, additionally, on the Darb el Arbain the westernmost wells should be policed. British consuls should be appointed at Suakin to watch the coast and at Khartoum to travel the interior. A railway should be built between Khartoum and the Red Sea to open up commerce. Tax collection should be committed to village sheikhs with a call on regular troops, not on the *bashi-bazouks*; and an auditor-general be brought in to reorganise the accounting system. As to justice, the Khartoum and provincial appeal courts should be presided over by qualified lawyers with no local ties, sitting each with four paid court members.

Most far-reaching was the recommended reform of political administration. The new organisation of a minister and three *hakimdars* should be abolished, with a consequent annual economy of £E20,000. The system would revert to that of a single Governor-General appointed for five years, with provincial *mudirs*. Stewart went on: 'I am firmly convinced that the Egyptians are quite unfit in every way to undertake such a trust as the government of so vast a country with a view to its welfare, and that both for their own sake and that of the people they try to rule, it would be advisable to abandon large portions of it.'

He therefore proposed, echoing Lieutenant-Colonel Sir Charles Wilson's memorandum of 2 October 1882, that some territories west of the White Nile – Darfur, Fashoda and the southern part of Kordofan – should be handed over: Darfur to its former ruling family; Fashoda and southern Kordofan to their tribes and sheikhs. 'I am not altogether sure if it would not in the end be better for all parties if the Mahdi or some other leader were successful, and the Egyptians compelled to restrict their territory to the east bank of the White Nile.' A slave trade policing post should be retained at Sobat mouth but government establishments in Bahr el Ghazal and Equatoria provinces 'might be restricted to mere commercial agencies. To each province a European agent might be appointed and in his duties, strictly limited to trade and the prevention of slave-dealing', be backed by a small force. For some years yet the White Nile should be closed to private trading.

Stewart's expectation that such recommendations, if implemented, would still prevent a recrudescence of the slave trade was optimistic in the extreme. In the event, of course, they would not. Not only the territory to the west bank of the White Nile would fall under the Mahdi.

Stewart left Khartoum on 8 March 1883 via Sennar, Gedaref, Kassala, Sennaheit to Massawa which he reached on 15 April. In the month between the dispatch of his report to Cairo on 9 February and his departure from Khartoum he had, as directed, been keeping Malet in Cairo informed of events in the Sudan and of the mistaken preparation for the supersession of Abdel Qadir Hilmi by Ala el Din Siddiq.

1882: SUDAN ADMINISTRATIVE STRUCTURE AND BUDGET

Hakimdar	Provinces	Capital
West Sudan	Dongola	Dongola
Mohammed Sa'id Pasha Wahbi	Kordofan	El Obeid
El Fasher (El Obeid)	Darfur	El Fasher
	Bahr el Ghazal	Deim Idris
East Sudan	Taka	Kassala
Ala el Din Pasha Siddiq	⎧ Suakin	Suakin
Massawa	⎩ Massawa	Massawa
Central Sudan	Sennar	Sennar
Abdel Qadir Pasha Hilmi		
Minister for Sudan	Berber	Berber
	Khartoum	Khartoum
Khartoum	Fashoda	Fashoda
	Equatoria	Lado

Sudan Rly Charg

TOTAL DEFICIT   **SUDAN (EXCLUDING SOMALIA)**

Based on *Report on the Soudan* by Lieutenant-Colonel Stewart, Egypt No
    11, 1883 (c. 3670)

[Figures rounded to nearest £E100]

Revenue £E	Expenditure £E	Surplus / *Deficit*
1882	1882	1882
54,600	10,600	44,000
74,500	70,400	4,100
56,100	70,600	*14,500*
14,700	18,500	*3,800*
53,600	121,400	*67,800*
26,000	20,500	5,400
26,100	42,600	*16,500*
40,900	42,700	*1,800*
42,500	18,600	23,900
75,800	123,400	*47,600*
7,600	25,700	*18,100*
31,400	35,500	*4,100*
3,000	9,800	*6,800*
506,800	610,300	*103,500*

When news arrived of the fall of Bara and El Obeid, Stewart followed up his report by advising that there was now a very great risk in dispatching a Kordofan expedition; and that instead Berber and Dongola, the latter increasingly threatened by the part defection of the Kababish to the Mahdi, be reinforced. Slatin Pasha in Darfur should be ordered to destroy stores and to retire on Bahr el Ghazal if he was hard pressed. Stewart could not conceal his forebodings about the inadequacy of the Egyptian troops being prepared for the Kordofan field force.

> It is impossible for me to criticise too severely the conduct of the Egyptian troops, both officers and men, towards the natives. Their general conduct and overbearing manner is almost sufficient to cause a rebellion. When to this conduct cowardice is added, it is impossible for me to avoid expressing my contempt and disgust.

Stewart's journey through Sennar and Taka did little to redress his pessimism. In Sennar he met the *mudir* Busati Bey Madani who believed his posting constituted exile on account of his having served Gordon Pasha as secretary. Rashid Kamil Pasha, now general-governor of Eastern Sudan in place of Ala el Din, was unfit for the post, and the *mudir* at Massawa needed to be changed. In Sennar no revenue had been collected for two years, and arrears were comparably large in Kassala. The outlook was bleak, except perhaps in Sennaheit (Keren) where the garrison was substantial but communications with Gallabat insecure. Before quitting Khartoum Stewart had handed over, as instructed, his diplomatic cipher books to Colonel William Hicks just arrived from Cairo, so that the latter could forward Sudan news.[14]

Abdel Qadir Pasha's Gezira Campaign, January–March 1883

Abdel Qadir in December 1882 was still awaiting the arrival of Egyptian reinforcements for the garrisoning of Khartoum after the departure of the new expedition to relieve the besieged towns of El Obeid and Bara – that expedition being in turn dependent on the massing of 2,000 camels as transport – when the uneasy control of the Gezira reasserted by Giegler and Salih Agha el Mek came again under threat. Ahmed el Makashif, brother of Omer the Mahdist *amir* who had primed the Blue Nile revolt of April, had arrived from the Mahdi with orders to take Sennar. Abdel Qadir determined to utilise the interval before the Kordofan relief expedition was ready and indeed thus to protect its rear, by himself defeating El Makashif in person with a force of three battalions, later to be augmented by the Shukriya cavalry of Sheikh Awad el Karim Pasha Ahmed Abu Sin.

Following Abdel Qadir's departure from Khartoum on 2 January 1883, the Egyptian acting military commander, Hussein Sirri Pasha, was faced with a rebellion of the Hassaniya on the White Nile to which a cowardly response was made by the Egyptian garrison at El Qarrasseh. Hussein Sirri took it upon himself to by-pass Giegler, now deputy *hakimdar*, and to report a victory to the Khedive Tawfiq who, congratulating Hussein Sirri, instructed him to order Abdel Qadir to suspend his campaign in Sennar and concentrate in Khartoum. The Governor-General was enraged by news of such meddling with his military responsibilities, the more so as he was poised to defeat a rebel force on 27 January at Ma'tuq. He replied to the Khedive that the consequence of such a defensive tactic would be to encourage rebellion in the East Sudan and the forfeiture of Kordofan and Darfur. Abdel Qadir reinforced his remonstration with a request to Colonel Stewart to secure British intervention through Sir Edward Malet with the chief minister, Sharif Pasha, in Cairo.

Having defeated the Mahdist force at Ma'tuq, Abdel Qadir continued south-west to Kawa (under the command of Saleh Bey Hijazi), whither he rallied the garrison of El Qarrasseh, ordering his own force of three battalions to march east to Wad Medani. Leaving himself by steamer to Khartoum on 3 February with 500 Black recruits sent by Lupton from Bahr el Ghazal, Abdel Qadir intended thence to proceed up the Blue Nile to Wad Medani. However in Khartoum to his vexation he found the continuing instruction from the Khedive to remain there, and a week was spent securing its cancellation and permission to proceed first to defeat El Makashif at Sennar, leaving on 13 February, before turning to the relief of Kordofan. Aided by Shukriya cavalry, Abdel Qadir was eventually able to lead his force from Wad Medani on 22 February and two days later to defeat El Makashif's force with a loss to the latter of 2,000 killed, before moving on to relieve Sennar. The redoubtable Salih el Mek was sent in pursuit and on 4 March the Mahdists were again defeated with 550 killed, including Ahmed el Makashif. A triumphant Governor-General, after marching to Karkoj up the Blue Nile and clearing the east bank of Sharif el Hindi's rebels, returned to Khartoum at the end of March – to find himself to have already been replaced on 26 March by Ala el Din Siddiq and recalled to Cairo. Hussein Sirri Pasha became deputy *hakimdar*.

In fact no sooner had Abdel Qadir Pasha left Khartoum early in

February 1883 to resume his Blue Nile campaign than Khedive Tawfiq secretly issued a *firman* making Fariq Ala el Din *hakimdar* of the Sudan in his place. Indeed Abdel Qadir had told Giegler that he suspected he would be replaced. Ala el Din arrived in Khartoum with Sulieman Pasha Niyazi, a sixty-one-year-old *lewa* who was designated to take Abdel Qadir's place as *seraskir* and commander of the Kordofan relief expedition (and whom Giegler deemed 'an old wreck'), on 21 February 1883 – two days after news of the surrender of El Obeid to the Mahdi of 17 January reached Khartoum. Pending the publication of the firman, Giegler refused to acknowledge their authority, while Colonel William Hicks, the intended chief of staff, telegraphed Sir Edward Malet on 13 March complaining of the administrative confusion, distrust and intrigue – 'I can get no active cooperation and no full information' – pending a decision as to who should be *hakimdar*. When the firman was at last published on 26 March 1883, with Abdel Qadir still on the Blue Nile, Giegler was ordered back to Cairo and left on 31 March. He would encounter Abdel Qadir Pasha again in Cairo in January 1884 when Abdel Qadir, then invited by the Egyptian government to organise the withdrawal for the Sudan, requested Giegler to be his deputy. In the event, as will transpire, Abdel Qadir declined to go. Giegler's loyalty to his friend was unswerving. He would not have left his Khartoum post as deputy in 1883 had not Abdel Qadir been recalled.

Dr Shibeika appends a note to his book reflecting on the continuing mystery surrounding Abdel Qadir's recall, suggesting that his cooperation with Colonel Stewart, who was personally supportive of him, aroused the suspicion of the Khedive and his ministers. The recall was certainly to prove a major mistake, and Abdel Qadir's request to Stewart for British intervention to enable him to save the Gezira situation in late January 1883 may well have vexed Cairo. But behind this clash lay deeper hostility and distrust. Abdel Qadir's appointment as Minister for the Sudan had followed after the resignation of the Sharif Pasha ministry in February 1882 in the aftermath of the Anglo-French joint note – its replacement by the Mahmoud Sami ministry dominated by Arabi Bey as minister of war; and the humiliation of the Khedive.

The victory at Tel el Kebir on 13 September 1882 led to the settling of scores. On his dismissal by the Khedive with the Sultan's approval, Arabi had sent a letter to Khartoum on 26 July 1882, for forwarding to all provinces, ordering the Sudan not to recognise the Khedive. A copy of this letter addressed to Firhad Bey, *mudir* of Berbera, was intercepted in Aden and following the Battle of Tel el Kabir Firhad Bey, anxious to exculpate himself, had telegraphed Cairo saying he had refused to publish it in Berbera and placed it on file. Khedivial suspicion of Abdel Qadir was further heightened. On 26 October Malet was told in Cairo of the intention to reappoint Ismail Pasha Ayub as *hakimdar* and Fariq Stone as *seraskir* in Khartoum though neither posting would in the event be implemented. Abdel Qadir however now wanted for friends in Cairo and the Khedive was evidently biding his time. When the axe fell at the end of March 1883, there was no propitiatory new appointment in Egypt such as the governorship of Alexandria now held by Ra'uf Pasha. Abdel Qadir Pasha retired to his estate.[15]

Darfur and Bahr el Ghazal Isolated, 1883   The months of 1883 which followed the capitulation of El Obeid to the Mahdi on 19 January reflected the isolation and increased privations of the Egyptian government's surviving western provinces of Darfur and Bahr el Ghazal. Slatin and Lupton, the respective general-governors and commanders, bravely maintained the loyalty of their garrisons in deteriorating circumstances; cut off from Khartoum and, in the case of Lupton, also from Emin in Lado. They were unaware that even before news of the fall of El Obeid had reached Khartoum, Colonel Stewart in his report to the British ambassador in Cairo, and Giegler Pasha acting Governor-General in Abdel Qadir's absence in the Gezira, had recommended the abandonment of both provinces. Giegler says that he wrote long letters in German, one of which at least Slatin 'mentions in his Book', but Slatin refers only to one letter received over the year to 25 December 1883, the surrender of Dara: 'a little slip of paper from Ala el Din Pasha' advising Slatin of his appointment as commandant of troops in Darfur, although other letters had been intercepted. To Ala el Din Slatin latterly sent from Dara a small situation report sewn into the shoulder of a donkey which reached the former on 28 September 1883 just before the departure of the Hicks expedition from Shatt for Rahad. Slatin had previously been concentrating the garrison of Foja in defence of Umm Shanga.

Since the end of 1882 Slatin had remained based in Dara with Mohammed Khalid –alias Zuqal Bey, a relative and later to be *amir* of the Mahdi – *mudir* at Dara; Sa'id Bey Guma' at El Fasher; and Adam Amer at Kebkebia – but without mutual inter-communication. According to Giegler in Khartoum following news in mid-February 1883 of the fall of El Obeid, Slatin was ordered by the Khedive to withdraw from Darfur and join Lupton in Bahr el Ghazal (Wingate says retire to

Inspector-General Slatin Pasha on trek, 1902

Khartoum), but there is no evidence of Slatin receiving such an order. Indeed Slatin after the disaster at Umm Waraqat in late 1882 had requested an attack on the Shakka area from Lupton which the latter was in no position to undertake.

With his dispatch of 20 March 1883, Malet enclosed a letter from Lupton at Meshra el Rek in Bahr el Ghazal to Khartoum (?Giegler) dated 28 January 1883, reporting that in early December 1882 things had looked bad, but were now better, despite his being ordered to send recruits to reinforce Khartoum yet being otherwise ignored. Lupton had dealt with some local risings and was confident presently that the slave trade, but not domestic slavery, had ceased to exist in Bahr el Ghazal. Within weeks of this message, Lupton would have sustained a further attack on Liffi by the Dinka chief Yanqu (Jango), previously armed by Gessi and now supported by the Mahdist *amir* Madibbo Ali at Shakka. This move was to be successfully defeated by Rafa'i Agha and Liffi then successfully held by Lupton for the next six months.

Lupton must have felt reasonably confident of holding his vulnerable province in these months. The Zande chief Zemio in the south, whom Junker was visiting, would prove a tower of strength to Lupton. When in July 1883 the Agar Dinka sacked Rumbek, Lupton was willing to respond to an urgent request for help from Emin Bey and dispatch 400 men and 17,000 cartridges to help the Lado expedition quell the rising, notwithstanding that it was outside Lupton's eastern boundary.

Sati Bey, Lupton's *mudir* at Meshra el Rek, remained nevertheless under threat from the north and in September 1883, since Emin at Lado had not responded to Lupton's requests for food and reinforcements, Lupton sent Satti Bey by the steamer *Ismailia* to seek them in Khartoum while he himself, anticipating an attack on Deim Sulieman after the rains, retired there to re-form – only to learn that Rafa'i at Liffi had that very month been overrun and killed. The Dutch explorer J. M. Schuver, previously arrived on the *Ismailia*, had been murdered by the Rek Dinka en route by land to Deim Sulieman. Nothing daunted, Lupton in December 1883 himself returned with 1,600 men to repossess the Liffi *zariba* but then, prudently, leaving the *nazir* in charge, returned to Deim Sulieman and prepared for a siege.

Meanwhile Slatin in Dara was a helpless witness to the progressive subversion of the loyalties of his Moslem garrisons. On the morrow of the fall of El Obeid, with his Dara garrison threatening mutiny and being personally unwilling to entertain the thought of withdrawal to Bahr el Ghazal, Slatin announced that he was embracing Islam in solidarity with his companions. He then dispatched Zuqal Bey to the Mahdi in El Obeid to restrain the latter from attacking Darfur. Within weeks the news of the supersession of Abdel Qadir Pasha by Ala el Din Siddiq and the preparation of an Egyptian counter offensive against him persuaded the Mahdi to prepare to do battle in conquered Kordofan, rather than expand his lines of communication further to the Nile.

For Slatin the focus of his future hopes of relief lay in a successful Egyptian outcome to the coming contest. The weary months crawled by as Slatin manufactured optimistic messages of the Egyptian preparations to sustain his troops' dwindling morale. Dara's fortifications were strengthened and a rising of the Beni Helba to the west was successfully crushed, but Slatin's burden was increased by a painful attack of guinea-worm. Recovering, he was able to defeat a Madibbo Ali raiding party. However his proposal to evacuate Dara and concentrate at El Fasher was unpopular with his colleagues. By October, with the Hicks expedition now en route for El Obeid, Slatin felt constrained, this time with the assent of his Moslem lieutenants, to buy the last essential weeks of time by offering to negotiate with the Mahdi the surrender of Darfur, and so relieving the immediate pressure on his besieged garrisons. As he had previously indicated to Zuqal Bey, when he had sent him off to the Mahdi in February, 'if the Mahdi is successful – which God forbid – then we shall be entirely cut off from all hope of relief and will probably be forced to submit, in which case it will be an advantage to him to have the country handed over in fairly good condition.'

On 20 December 1883 definitive news of the defeat of the Hicks expedition was brought to Slatin at Dara, with a letter from his former deputy Zuqal, now the *amir* Mohammed Khalid, calling on him to surrender. His lieutenants had previously refused even to concentrate at El Fasher. Bahr el Ghazal as an ultimate resort therefore was out of the question. On 25 December Slatin surrendered and on 15 January 1884 El Fasher fell. An order from Cairo to fall back on Dongola was irrelevant.

Mohammed Khalid would continue to rule Darfur from El Fasher until after the fall of Khartoum, followed by the death of the Mahdi in June 1885. Madibbo Ali however continued presently as *amir* and *sheikh* of the Rizeiqat, based on Shakka, and exercised quasi-independent authority.[16]

Preparations for an Egyptian Counter Offensive   Egyptian ex-Arabi reinforcements for the planned advance to defeat the Mahdi in Kordofan, even if untouched by local commitment to a Sudanese Mahdi and stiffened by the disciplined drill enforced by Abdel Qadir Pasha in Khartoum, soon proved devoid of the stamina required to match the religious zeal and high morale of the enemy. Moreover the enemy had now overcome their inhibitions towards the use of firearms and had since Jebel Qadir, both at Bara and El Obeid, taken possession of substantial financial booty and armaments. Colonel Stewart on 16 February 1883, pondering the likelihood of desertions in battle of recruits from Arabi's former army, reported their loud imprecations uttered in minor skirmishes: 'Oh, Effendina Arabi! If you only knew the position Tawfiq has placed us in!'

The Khedive Tawfiq, restored by British arms to power, was unbending in his determination to hold on to the former Khedivial empire,

Khedive Tawfiq Pasha Ismail

notwithstanding the unequivocal opposition of the Gladstone government 'to any military expedition to the Sudan being undertaken by the
English Commander-in-Chief Egypt'. Britain affirmed that she had no
desire to interfere in any way in the choice of officers for employment in
military operations in the Sudan. Negatively, for unrelated reasons,
Britain was nevertheless responsible for easing out the last of the United
States cadre of officers, Fariq Charles Stone, chief of Tawfiq's general
staff, leaving a virtual void of experienced military commanders.
Osman Rifqi Pasha, returned from Arabi exile in Constantinople, was
seemingly passed over for command and would die in 1886, yet for

reasons already examined the Khedive was determined to retire the present successful incumbent in Khartoum, Abdel Qadir Hilmi.

Ill-informed about the land they sought to reconquer and lacking judgement in military matters, the Khedivial Council had originally chosen Ala el Din Siddiq to command the army and Colonel William Hicks to be his chief of staff. The Council, which until May 1883 still numbered Ismail Pasha Ayub as minister of the interior, had then appointed a sixty-one-year-old *lewa*, Sulieman Pasha Niyazi (who had seen action thirty years previously in the Crimea), to be *seraskir* and Kordofan expedition commander. Colonel Stewart appraised him as 'a miserable-looking old man of 70 or 75'. Ala el Din was instead to succeed Abdel Qadir as *hakimdar*.

Colonel William Hicks, now to be Niyazi's chief of staff, had served in the Bombay army from 1849 and had participated with distinction in the Magdala campaign of 1868. He was fifty-three years old, having retired in 1880, devoid of experience of the Sudan or knowledge of Arabic. He had arrived on Egyptian government appointment in Cairo at the end of January 1883 with a number of other European officers, there to be joined by Colonel Arthur Farquhar of the Egyptian army.

This was no strategy to encompass the defeat of an outstandingly successful rebel army. The only Sudan veteran, Ala el Din, had thirteen years' service with promotion to the ranks of *fariq* and general-governor, but that service was entirely limited to the eastern Sudan – where Sulieman Niyazi had himself served as chief financial officer in Massawa for the Abyssinian campaign of 1875–6. Neither of these Circassians could converse in English with the chief of staff. The leadership plan was inept. Giegler, on his return to Cairo in April, met Sharif Pasha, the chief minister, one of the progenitors of the appointments, and formed the opinion that the latter

> was very little interested in the Sudan question... The whole Mahdi movement was still not considered especially important in leading circles, as I soon noticed. Hicks had been sent to the Sudan to do what he thought fit. Troops and weapons had also been sent to the Sudan. There was therefore no point in worrying unduly about what might happen in a distant land which most people only knew by name.

Even the Khedive 'did not seem to share that feeling of anxiety which so occupied my mind'.

Giegler advised Lord Dufferin 'very strongly to try – at least for the present – to prevent anything from being undertaken against the Mahdi', but was doubtless ignorant of British determination to keep well clear of the problem. However, notwithstanding London's instruction, Dufferin had already in vain warned the new Cairo head of the Sudan department, Ibrahim Bey Tawfiq, on 2 April 1883 that 'if it were wise, it would confine its present efforts to the re-establishment of its authority in Sennar'. As Cromer would observe, returning to Egypt from India on 5 September 1883: 'Lord Granville appears to have thought that he effectually threw off all responsibility by declaring that he was not responsible. He could have been in no greater error.'

Hicks Pasha arrived in Khartoum on 4 March, accompanied by Qa'immaqam Henry de Coëtlogon Bey, his staff officer, to join his superior, but Abdel Qadir Pasha was still officially unacquainted with his own recall. A fortnight later both officers were complaining about the lack of local co-operation, information and military supplies. Despite the frustrations, Hicks had planned to launch the expedition as soon as possible, but by April 1883 felt obliged first to reinforce Dueim, under local threat, which would be the Kordofan expedition's departure point from the Nile. On arrival there, he then concluded that a rebel force at Jebelein to the south would first have to be reduced. This he accomplished successfully at Marabia on 29 April against an enemy force of 5,000 armed with spears, then occupying Aba island, the Mahdi's former home. Omer el Makashif, brother of Ahmed and instigator of the Sennar revolt of April 1882, was killed in this action.[17]

Only now, with the rains imminent, could Hicks appraise on the spot the best route for his army to take to Kordofan, which he concluded would be the Bara road. There had already been friction between the Moslem commander, Niyazi Pasha, and his European chief of staff. The latter, ignorant of the depth of sensitivities of largely Egyptian Moslem troops when faced with a Moslem adversary, pressed Cairo on military grounds for recognition of his personal 'indisputable command' of the field force, before returning with his White Nile force to Khartoum by late May. There then followed a summer of dispute between Hicks and Niyazi while Ala el Din in conformity with Abdel Qadir's plan left for Shukriya country to secure expedition camels, others seeking them in Dongola, Berber and Sennar. Initially Hicks was assured by Malet that Sharif Pasha had ordered that no military movement be undertaken 'without your advice and consent' but Sharif believed the appointment of a Christian as expedition commander 'would fan fanaticism'. Initially Hicks professed to understand Sharif's reluctance on this account, but by August he no longer considered there would be 'any danger in appointing me commander-in-chief'. His self-confidence had been strengthened by his White Nile success.

A major complication in these extended acrimonious exchanges over the command was a lack of clarity regarding Hicks's relationship with the British agent and consul-general in Cairo. Like Stewart, Hicks had been charged to keep the British informed of events by cipher, which Malet was wont to pass on to the chief minister Sharif Pasha, while dissociating himself from responsibility for the events or, more specifically, for Hicks's insistence on undisputed command of the field force. This flow of information Malet would also report to London.

Controversy over the field force was to be further exacerbated when, at the beginning of June 1883, Hicks claimed that his force must be increased by 6,000 men over the 5,000 (excluding *bashi-buzouqs*) already assembled, 2,000 of whom would need to be detached to guard communications on the Kordofan route. Already on 24 May Malet had forwarded a copy of Ala el Din's request for an enlarged monthly instalment to cover the emergency military costs, Malet commenting that it was 'more than ever desirable to satisfy the demands of the troops already in the country for the payment of arrears', while acknowledging that the Egyptian Treasury would be quite unable to meet the need. Now on 5 June Malet, enclosing Hicks's telegram for more troops, commented by his telegram no. 37, 'Money is wanting and risk of failure considerable unless the expedition is on large scale and well found in every aspect.' Malet, like Lord Dufferin, questioned whether Hicks should not be instructed to confine his operation to the Gezira.

Recognising the threat to the expedition for want of finance Granville circulated the papers to H. C. E. Childers, Chancellor of the Exchequer, whose irritation was acute:

> I do not at all like the look of these papers. Our opinion I think generally was that we had no interest in keeping up the dependency of the Sudan on Egypt... we have recognised apparently this heavy drain for the Sudan operation on Egyptian finance... The tone of Sir E. Malet's telegram no. 37 of 5th June is very dangerous... clearly implies that directly or indirectly we are to give General Hicks instructions based on his representations to Sir E. Malet.

Granville sought to mollify Childers, conceding that the British government had not committed themselves further and that Malet would be reined back by Granville's telegram of 11 June. Childers continued to urge that direct communication between Hicks and Malet should be stopped but the Foreign Office was unwilling to cut off its principal source of intelligence on Sudan affairs.

In the event, on 12 June the Egyptian Council of Ministers decided to send 600 infantry, 600 *bashi-buzouqs*, a second mountain battery, and 1,800 'old soldiers now unemployed', having been rejected by Fariq Valentine Baker Pasha, for recruitment as reinforcements; these the price of maintaining the field force. The sanctioned cost of maintenance for emergency troops to the end of 1883 would be £E107,000 plus £E80,000 for arrears of pay but Hicks pointed out that these sums would cover pay only, and Cairo's assumption that there was £E40,000 in the Khartoum treasury was fallacious. Nevertheless he was ready to undertake the campaign.

Hicks continued to write to Malet as well as Baker, head of the Egyptian gendarmerie, on recognising that Lord Dufferin's return to Constantinople 'has been a calamity to me'. Having at one point advised that the Kordofan expedition should be abandoned, on 16 July he named Niyazi Pasha as the stumbling block, and on 23 July informed both Baker and Malet of his resignation as chief of staff of the Kordofan field force. This did prompt the early transfer of Niyazi Pasha to East Sudan to relieve Rashid Kamil but four weeks later, despite a further caution from London to Malet not to become involved, Hicks learned that he was appointed supreme commander of the Sudan forces, rather than Ala el Din Pasha, as Cairo had intended. The latter was both *hakimdar* and a Moslem but Hicks, to his peril, too readily discounted the cogent arguments for a Moslem Arabic-speaking commander, asserting that in his opinion there was 'no fear of any increase in fanaticism'. He nevertheless welcomed Ala el Din Pasha's help and presence with the expedition: 'Ala el Din and I will get on very well.'[18]

Sheikan, the Climactic Battle; and the Beja Insurrection Detailed news of the preparations at Khartoum for the shipment of troops, stores and equipment for the expedition to Dueim reached the Mahdi in Ramadan in July 1883, if not before. Sheikh Ali Jula, a Mahdist cavalryman and *sheikh* of the Messiriya, recorded 'much artillery, long Krupp guns and machine guns, not with one barrel but with five; and there were many horses for the cavalry and thousands of camels for the water and provisions' – all monitored by the Mahdi's spies. By mid-September an army of 8,000, principally Egyptian but also Ja'aliyin,

Sha'iqiya and Black Sudanese troops, with 5,500 camels, was assembled at Dueim. De Coëtlogan, under Hussein Pasha Wasif Sirri, was left commanding the depot in Khartoum and commenced digging a mile-long defence ditch and parapet.

Ala el Din Pasha now differed with Hicks over the Bara route, which was then changed to the more southerly route via El Rahad on account of better water supplies. A more serious altercation arose at Shatt between Hicks the vice-*hakimdar*, and his Egyptian chief of staff, Lewa Hussein Pasha Mazhar, on the first day of the expedition's departure – 27 September 1883. Thereafter march orders became a very frequent matter of dispute at the senior commanders' conferences.

For all that, a reasonable level of morale was sustained on the march for the first ten days to Nurabi, with water supplies sufficient. Hicks, mindful perhaps of Isaiah's account (XLVIII) of the Israelite departure from Babylon – 'they thirsted not when (God) led them through the deserts' – remained optimistic. Already however on 29 September, hearing of the Hicks's departure from Dueim, the Mahdi moved his camp to the eastern outskirts of El Obeid.

An ex-government official, Hasan Habashi, had been captured at El Obeid and impressed into the position of chief clerk to the Mahdist *amir* Abdel Halim Musa'id. The latter, together with *amir* Mohammed Osman Abu Qarja (Abu Girgeh), was sent to shadow Hicks's field force en route to El Rahad, closing up the wells after the force had passed. Their instructions were to avoid major contact with Hicks, thus allowing his expedition to suffer the extended privations of the march to El Obeid as long as possible.

Moving on from Aigella (where a first skirmish with Ansar took place) after the feast of Korban Bairam on 14 October, the poor discipline of Hicks's troops began to take its toll. Water consumption was inadequately controlled, the Krupps guns failed to work, camels were neglected. Distrust of local guides led to compass-bearing marches through impenetrable bush. El Rahad watering-place was reached on 24 October. On 23 June Hicks had received a messenger from Mek Adham of Tegali saying that he or his *wakil* would join the field force on the march near his mekdom, ostensibly as camp followers. Hicks, reluctant to make such a diversion, had attempted to meet the *wakil* up the White Nile but without success. His somewhat ingenuous belief nevertheless persisted that Mek Adham would bring succour, and at El Rahad four valuable days were now wasted while the enemy massed for battle.

According to Hasan Habashi's later report to Cairo, it appears that the *amir* Abdel Halim continued to shadow Hicks when he left El Rahad for Alluba. Here Hicks would spend another four days awaiting news from an informant sent to El Obeid to report on Mahdist strength. Abdel Halim himself meanwhile retired ahead with his force and joined up with the main Mahdist army together with the Black *jihadiya* led by the senior *amir* Hamdan Abu Anja, a former lieutenant of Zubeir Pasha. Together they numbered 40,000 men.

Hicks reached Alluba on 1 November. His water supply had become increasingly critical and his plan to advance on El Obeid via El Birka, a major watering place, was frustrated by its prior occupation by the Mahdi. Instead, on 3 November Hicks marched ten miles towards the Khor Kashgil, his troops suffering from excessive thirst, to halt the next day two miles from Sheikan. He was still some thirty miles from El Obeid, and virtually surrounded by Abu Anja's force in thick woods. Having camped the night under fire without sleep, the Hicks expedition was annihilated the next morning soon after it had moved off in three battle squares. Fewer than 300 escaped with their lives.

Ala el Din Siddiq, Hicks, Hussein Mazhar and all senior officers were among the dead, together with Gordon's secretary, Berzati Bey. Sheikh Ali Julla, the Mahdist cavalryman, paid tribute to Hicks's valour: 'Verily he was a brave man, the bravest of all the brave men.' Ismail Abdel Qadir el Kordofani relates that 200 of the Mahdi's *Ansar* were martyred in the battle. The Mahdi and the victorious *Ansar* again entered El Obeid in triumph a week later. Among the Sudanese notables anxiously awaiting the outcome had been Mek Adham of Tegali, who now came with his followers to make their submission.[19]

The most reliable European eyewitness description of the Mahdi is perhaps that of Rudolf Slatin, his captive:

> He was a tall broad-shouldered man of light-brown colour and powerfully built; he had a large head and sparkling black eyes; he wore a black beard, and had the usual three slits on each cheek; his nose and mouth were well-shaped and he had the habit of always smiling, showing his white teeth and exposing the V-shaped aperture between the two front ones which is always considered a sign of good luck in the Sudan, and is known as '*falja*'.

The Mahdi's commitment to the life of an ascetic Moslem dated back to 1868. Over the following ten years his piety had drawn him to a fundamentalist interpretation of Islam, the aspiration to a community in which the divine laws would prevail. His succession to leadership of the Sammaniya order of Sheikh el Quraishi wad el Zein at Mesellimiya, on the death of the latter late in 1880, had been preceded by the personal revelation that he was the awaited Mahdi appointed to over-throw the unbelievers who denied the truth and rejected his vocation.

Mid-1881 had coincided with the presence of a weak Egyptian Governor-General in Khartoum, while the threatened internal collapse of Khedivial government under international pressure culminated the next year in military rebellion and in the reluctant occupation of Egypt by a British government rigorously opposed to any British intervention in the province of the Sudan. No circumstances could have been more propitious for the overthrow of sixty years of Turco-Egyptian rule and the establishment of a separated Sudan. Moreover the leader of the theocratic rebellion persuasively claimed the high moral ground. And as Napoleon, scarcely a religious leader, had recognised, 'A la guerre, les trois quarts sont des affaires morales; la balance des forces réelles n'est que un autre quart.'

Thus two years after arriving at Jebel Qadir and after numerous victorious battles commanded by his principal lieutenants, the Mahdi ruled the western Sudan. Ismail Abdel Qadir, author of *The Life of the Sudanese Mahdi (The Sira of the Mahdi)*, who acknowledged his alle-giance to the Mahdi when the latter was laying siege to El Obeid in September 1882 and was personally present at Sheikan, volunteers that:

> despite painstaking enquiries, [he, the author] could not establish that the Mahdi himself had actually fought in any of the campaigns. Although the Mahdi was with the Companions during the fighting, it was his habit to pray and to immerse himself in the state of beholding. No sooner had he done so than God destroyed the enemy.

In the initial skirmish at Aba the Mahdi had indeed been wounded, but Ismail was uncertain whether the Mahdi was an active participant.

The prescience of Colonel Stewart (and of Sir Charles Wilson before him) in recommending the abandonment of Darfur and at least of southern Kordofan had been confirmed. Kordofan had fallen in Janu-ary 1883; by mid-January 1884 Darfur would have surrendered. Had both been conceded to Mahdist occupation in early 1883 without further military contest, an Egyptian army of some 8,000 men with its armaments would have been retained in the field to defend at least the original boundaries of the Fung Kingdom of Sennar. The Mahdi, on the contrary, who had been content to prepare his defence positions in conquered territory against a field force that had to march continuously under harassment across the sparsely watered desert of eastern Kordofan, would then himself have been forced to confront the dilemma: to settle for a western kingdom; or to launch a campaign against a well-equipped army holding the upper Nile basin.

Admittedly there is no evidence that, short of a serious military defeat, the Mahdi would have acquiesced in the former course. His *amirs* had been defeated on the Blue and White Niles, but his supporters there bided their time under cover. Nor was he idle as he awaited the arrival of the Egyptian expedition against Kordofan, already planning the conversion of the ancient Beja tribes of the eastern Sudan to his cause. On 8 May 1883 he had dispatched Osman Abu Bakr Digna (who, following the fall of El Obeid, had come from Berber to swear allegiance) as his *amir*. *Prima facie* Taka was not fertile ground for the Mahdist cause, the Beja being Anaj people, possessors of the Nile valley long before the coming of the Arabs to the Sudan. Andrew Paul believed they dated back at least to 2500 BC. 'Wanting nothing of the world, they ask nothing better than that it should ask nothing of them.'

As long as the experienced Ala el Din Siddiq had been general-governor, later *hakimdar*, of East Sudan, the Beja country had been tranquil. However Rashid Kamil, Ala el Din's *mudir* at Taka, had then become commander of troops East Sudan before being appointed general-governor and *pasha* Eastern Sudan and Red Sea coast in early 1883 on Ala el Din's promotion to *hakimdar* of the Sudan. Colonel Stewart quickly assessed Rashid as being unfit for the responsibility as well as a threat to peace with Abyssinia. It was a judgement confirmed to Gordon by Ali Bey Tuhaini (who had also served as Gordon's secretary) when they met at Ismailia at the end of January 1884. Ali Bey attributed the insurrection of the Hadendoa in response to subversion by Osman Digna ' to the passage of Egyptian troops [via Suakin to Berber for Hicks] under Rashid Pasha and Ibrahim Bey. The Arabs had been promised seven dollars for the hire of each camel, and they only got one dollar.' This would prove the costliest fraudulence: the Egyptian government had paid the full amount to Rashid, and he had eaten six of every seven dollars. In consequence despite a smaller section of the

Hadendoa remaining loyal to the government under the 'regent' son Mohammed of Sheikh Musa Ibrahim (Gordon's friend), the majority supported Osman Digna.

The perfidy of Rashid Pasha was not however the sole reason for the success of the Mahdi's *amir*, Osman Digna. Dr Mekki Shibeika has analysed the development of events in the Red Sea local area in the months July–November 1883, beginning with Osman's return to Berber where, prior to his earlier visit to the Mahdi and following his expulsion from Suakin, Osman had become established as a trader. He was of Kurdish extraction, his mother of the Hadendoa, his family influential as traders in Suakin; and he was a personal friend of Sheikh el Tahir el Tayib Majdhub, local Suakin head of that religious fraternity which was based among the Ja'aliyin at Damer. To him the Hadendoa inclined in their spiritual loyalty – in preference to the more recently founded Khatmiya of the Mirghani family, established in 1840 in Kassala and other towns and committedly friendly to the Turkish-Egyptian government.

Osman Digna, armed with his letter of commission as a Mahdist *amir*, had been immediately successful in June 1883 in securing the allegiance of Sheikh el Tahir, but his approach to Sheikh Mohammed Osman el Mirghani's local adherents was rejected and betrayed to the government. Armed additionally with letters to the tribes, Osman then concentrated on subverting the Bisharin and Amarar on the Berber-Suakin route, and having recruited a force of some 1,500, he joined Sheikh El Tahir in attacking the government post of Sinkat on 5 August.

Due to the energy of the Suakin governor, Mohammed Tawfiq Bey, Osman was decisively defeated at Sinkat and, having withdrawn wounded to Erkowit, defeated a second time on 14 September. More determined action and a better calibre of reinforcements for Tawfiq Bey might well have put an end to the revolt, but the new sexagenarian general-governor, Sulieman Pasha Niyazi – belatedly removed as *seraskir* from the Khartoum *hakimdaria*, where he had obstructed Colonel Hicks and been replaced by Ala el Din Pasha – chose instead to reprimand Tawfiq Bey and to appease Osman Digna. Thus by November 1883 Osman had been given time to gather a larger force and to lay siege to Tokar, the granary town to the south of Suakin, as well as to Sinkat.

The Suakin-Kassala telegraph line had already been cut and a small force of gendarmerie sent to the relief of Sinkat was annihilated in mid-October. The news reached Cairo on 29 October. A fortnight later further news reached Cairo that a relief force, led by the new Egyptian military commander at Suakin, Mohammed Pasha Tahir, and accompanied by the British consul at Jedda, had been defeated at El Teb (El Ta'ib) and put to flight the very day of the Battle of Sheikan, although the latter catastrophe would only be authenticated in Cairo on 21 November. The Egyptian military commander was recalled to be court martialled for cowardice; the British consul had been killed in action.

For Sulieman Pasha Niyazi there was no prospect of meaningful reinforcements from Cairo nor from Hussein Sirri, acting *hakimdar*, in Khartoum; and Sulieman left for Massawa seeking to bring four reliable Black companies to the aid of Sinkat and Tokar. With the arrival of Fariq Valentine Baker Pasha with his force of gendarmerie at Suakin on 23 December 1883, Sulieman Niyazi having himself been recalled to Cairo, Baker became for a short spell general-governor of the Eastern Sudan. Egyptian authority however, notwithstanding the military and naval reinforcements, no longer extended east of Suakin much beyond the littoral.[20]

The Structural Collapse of Egyptian Rule
1884–85

1 THE POLITICS OF ABANDONMENT:
NOVEMBER 1883–MARCH 1884

Egyptian Opposition As late as the autumn of 1883, discussions had been taking place in London on the initiative of Sharif Pasha, the Egyptian chief minister, regarding the timing of the withdrawal of the British occupation force from Egypt. The *sirdar* of the new Egyptian army, Sir Evelyn Wood, and Baring were agreed that as a first stage the force could be reduced from 6,700 to 3,000, all to be concentrated in Alexandria. No reference was made to the Sudan. Indeed Sharif was optimistic about the impending Kordofan expedition. When Baring had canvassed the abandonment of the Sudan Sharif had replied: 'Nous en causerons plus tard: d'abord nous allons donner une bonne raclée [hiding] à ce monsieur [the Mahdi].' As Baring would later observe in *Modern Egypt*, the British government had been blind to its acceptance of vicarious responsibility in that direction when it acknowledged, if it did not sanction, the appointment of British officers to the Hicks field force. By 29 October Baring was privately voicing his fear to Granville that 'the Sudan will give a great deal of trouble. It is impossible wholly to disconnect the Sudan from the rest of the Egyptian question. The financial question presents itself in the most unpleasant way to the front.'

On the morrow of the confirmation of the Sheikan disaster, Baring was instructed by Granville on 22 November 1883 to discuss with Lieutenant-General Sir Frederick Stephenson, general officer in command of the British troops in Egypt, and with the new *sirdar,* whether the defeat constituted a threat to Egypt proper. Granville received their emphatic reply on 24 November that the Mahdi did indeed constitute a danger to Egypt; that withdrawal of the British garrison from Cairo should be postponed; and that the army should be maintained at its present strength – an opinion backed by the Khedive and by Sharif. A further Cairo meeting of the British triumvirate was influenced seemingly by the Khartoum telegram of 25 November of Miralai Henry de Coëtlogon, the retired British officer now commanding the Khartoum garrison, who insisted to Wood that, for want of provisions, Khartoum and Sennar would have to be abandoned within two months. Baring telegraphed their unanimous view that Khartoum should be held only until the outstations had been withdrawn, whereafter administration should be based on Suakin. Pending further information, London concurred.

Meanwhile Granville's dispatches of 22 and 25 November 1883 advised Baring that Vice-Admiral Sir William Hewett, VC, commander East India station, Aden, had been ordered to maintain Egyptian authority at Suakin, Massawa and the Red Sea, but that

> we can take no steps which will throw upon us the responsibility of operations in the Sudan, which must rest with the Egyptian Government relying on their own resources. We think that restricting the operations as proposed by the Egypt government to defensive operations [Gladstone deleted 'at Khartoum, Suakin and Berber'] seems reasonable.

The loan of English or Indian troops remained specifically ruled out, nor should British officers be encouraged to volunteer. If consulted, Baring should recommend 'the abandonment of the Sudan within certain limits'. This was contrary to the advice to the secretary of state for war, the Marquess of Hartington, by the adjutant-general in London, lately victor of Tel el Kebir, that Khartoum, Berber and Suakin be immediately reinforced under British officers, and the Sudan east of the Nile be defended.

Already on 23 November the Khedivial government had resolved to try to hold Khartoum and Sennar; to reopen the Suakin–Berber route with a task force of 2,000 gendarmerie and 6,000 Bedouin; and to withdraw from Darfur, thereby, it was hoped, augmenting the Nile army by 5,000. The Equatoria (Gondokoro was named) and Bahr el Ghazal governors were ordered to retire to Khartoum. That the Sudan remained the sole responsibility of Egypt was not contested by the Khedivial Council, but Britain was asked to support any approach to Constantinople for Turkish troops, a proposal backed by Baring. Britain acquiesced in not opposing it.[1]

The next six weeks were marked by increasing political and diplomatic exchanges between Cairo and London as the British government sought to reconcile the consequences of Sheikan with their role as an occupying power of Egypt determined not to be embroiled in the Sudan. If by mid-December 1883 both British and Egyptian attitudes had become further crystallised, both parties were nevertheless inattentive to the velocity at which support for the Mahdist mission was spreading in the Sudan, notwithstanding urgent military advice as to the consequences of inaction.

On 2 December an Egyptian force sent to relieve Sinkat was annihilated at El Teb, its commander Mahmoud Taha Pasha being court-martialled for cowardice. With the decision of the Egyptian government to retain Sennar for the while, no active preparations had yet been taken for the evacuation of Khartoum and Sennar provinces – the former under Hussein Sirri Pasha with Ibrahim Haidar Pasha commanding troops; the latter under Hussein Bey Sadiq, with Saleh Bey el Mek. Indeed the Berber–Suakin route was presently closed, thus precluding an uncontested withdrawal from Khartoum down the Nile. However Fashoda was duly evacuated, the garrison of 1,300 reaching Khartoum on 26 December while the lower White Nile forces from Kawa (El Ais), Dueim and Shatt appear to have arrived about the same time.

When these White Nile withdrawals had been effected, the Khartoum garrison should be increased from 2,500 to 6,000. Sennar would number 3,900; Gallabat 600; Amideb 900; Sennaheit 1600; Massawa 2,500; Kassala 1,300; Suakin 1,800; Dongola 900; Berber 600; Equatoria 2,100; Harar 3,600; Berbera 300. In the wake of Baring's lengthy appraisal of the current Egyptian military position in the Sudan; of the agreed conclusion of Generals Wood and Baker that Khartoum could not be held; and of his own endorsement of Colonel Stewart's opinion that Egyptians were quite unfit for the government of so vast a country, Baring at midnight on 10 December sent off a private letter to Granville insisting that it was essential that he be given instructions. Should he advise the Egyptian government to hold Khartoum, the Nile valley to its north and east Sudan, as Cairo wished: or to retire to Wadi Halfa or the frontier? Britain could hardly insist on the latter. Of the three effective options to implement the former, the sending of either British or of Indian troops was the worst; and forbidding Egypt from seeking Turkish help must invite the rebellion to spread. The least of the three evils was to sanction Turkish help. Gladstone reckoned 'that wretch the Sultan' as much a danger to Britain, yet sanctioned that option. On 13 December the instruction came from Granville (the

Sultan Abdel Hamid II

preceding telegram is missing):'HMG have no intention of employing British or Indian troops in the Sudan. HMG have no objection to the employment of Turkish troops provided they are paid by the Turkish government and restricted exclusively to the Sudan.' Except for securing the safe retreat of garrisons still holding positions in the Sudan, HMG could not agreed to increase Egyptian financial expenditure which was of doubtful advantage to Egypt. 'HMG recommend the Ministers of the Khedive to come to an urgent decision to abandon all territory south of Aswan or at least Wadi Halfa.' Britain would assist in maintaining order and defending Egypt proper 'as well as posts in the Red Sea'. Fariq Valentine Baker, head of the Egyptian gendarmerie, would under Egyptian orders proceed with his men to reinforce Suakin, but the employment of Zubeir Pasha as their experienced immediate commander was vetoed by London under pressure from the Anglo-Slavery Society – '[it] appears to HMG inexpedient both politically and as regards the Slave Trade.'[2]

For the next week Sharif's government was agonising how to resist the British recommendation to abandon the Sudan, regardless of their incapacity to maintain government. On 22 December, sheltering in part behind the Sultan's firman of 7 August 1879 which forbade the Khedive to alienate territory, and emphasising the threat to Egypt proper by Mahdist forces consequent upon abandonment of the Nile valley, the Bayuda desert, Berber, Dongola and the east (the loss of Kordofan could be conceded), Sharif replied that Egypt could not therefore abandon territory necessary for the safety, perhaps for the existence of Egypt. He indicated, too, some awareness of the consequences of abandonment to the tribes hitherto loyal to Egypt – the Shukriya, Sha'iqiya, Bisharin, Ababda – even the Kababish.

Forwarding the reply to Granville that same day, Baring did not shrink from urging that Egypt must now be forced on financial grounds to abandon the Sudan, if necessary by the appointment of compliant Egyptian (or British) ministers and by the dispatch of a senior British officer to Khartoum to withdraw the garrison and make the best practicable arrangements for the future. Faced with such a crucial decision, London was evidently unpersuaded that the passage of the coming days was critical to Khartoum and Suakin. The English Christmas was as always extended. Baring for his part was reconciled that his new instructions should wait upon the discussion in London with the undersecretary for India, who would be returning from a two-month spell in Cairo, fully briefed. This took place on 29 December.

Admittedly Frank Power, the *Times* correspondent in Khartoum, had telegraphed on 20 December that Khartoum now had provisions for its civil population and its six British subjects sufficient for a year, while a good harvest was expected in Sennar; but on 30 December 1883 Power described the situation, forty days after the news of Sheikan, as 'very desperate' – the Mahdi's army in El Obeid only eleven days' march away, and no suggestion from Cairo of reinforcements. Baring telegraphed London on 1 January 1884 not to delay answering his telegram of 22 December. Sharif similarly urged Baring the next day for a response to his note, advising him that he would be requesting the Porte for 10,000 men if the state of uncertainty was not ended.

A British Ultimatum Accepted It took three days over the 1884 New Year for Earl Granville to secure Cabinet approval for the mandatory advice eventually tendered by Baring to Sharif Pasha on 6 January – advice which not only confirmed the recommendation for abandonment of the Sudan but invoked British responsibility, as the provisional occupying power, to insist on the implementation of British policy or to exact the resignations of recalcitrant ministers. The Khedive acquiesced, perhaps influenced by C. F. Moberly Bell, the *Times* correspondent in Cairo, whom the Khedive had earlier assured that 'no minister would accept office and surrender Khartoum, not even Nubar'. Sharif Pasha and his ministers declined and resigned. Riaz Pasha refused but on 8 January 1884 the veteran Nubar Pasha accepted to form a new government. On 11 January the new cabinet was announced. Abdel Qadir Pasha Hilmi had been named the new minister of war and marine on 9 January.[3]

With the acceptance by the Khedive of British instructions to abandon the Sudan and the formation of an Egyptian ministry under Nubar Pasha willing to carry them out, responsibility for evacuation remained with Nubar. Authority moved back from London to Cairo: the focus from the political to the military. On 4 January 1884 General Lord Wolseley, adjutant general in London, had urged on his minister, the Marquess of Hartington, that Miralai de Coëtlogon be instructed immediately to undertake the withdrawal, once the White Nile, and perhaps the Sennar, garrisons had assembled at Khartoum, and to withdraw preferably down the Nile. The Kassala and Sennaheit garrisons should seek Abyssinian acquiescence in their march to the coast. De Coëtlogon however was under Khedivial, not British, command. Nevertheless on 9 January, recognising that no reinforcements from

Egypt could reach Khartoum in under two months, he telegraphed the Khedive, backed by Hussein Sirri, acting *hakimdar*, and Ibrahim Haidar, *seraskir,* and requested immediate leave to withdraw.

Nubar's ministry now contained Abdel Qadir Pasha Hilmi as minister of war who would arrive in Cairo 'tomorrow (10 January) to finalise orders'. Nubar himself, Abdel Qadir, Baring and Sir Evelyn Wood, *sirdar* of the Egyptian army, attended by Gordon's former lieutenant, now Miralai Charles Watson Bey, Egyptian surveyor-general – and sometimes by Qa'immaqam F. Reginald Wingate Bey, back from typhoid sick leave and made ADC and assistant military secretary to Wood – convened to plan the withdrawal requirements over the next four days. On 11 January Baring advised London that Khartoum had been authorised to prepare measures to evacuate 'women, children and all civilian population wishing to leave to Berber', but the option for Fariq Valentine Baker Pasha to open the Suakin–Berber route west of Sinkat by force, as opposed to negotiation, was cancelled in the hope that withdrawal from Khartoum would itself facilitate the peaceful passage of the Khartoum refugees.

Also on 11 January Abdel Qadir Pasha, according to Bernard M. Allen, reported that, having regard to a total of 21,000 Egyptian troops and 11,000 civilians wishing to withdraw, thousands of camels would be needed to cross the Atmur desert to Korosko and the operation would take seven months. Allen appears to rely for these details on Watson Bey's confidential minutes of the planners, which Baring did not communicate to London nor reveal in *Modern Egypt*.

Abdel Qadir Hilmi – A Solution Forfeited   Baring described Abdel Qadir Pasha, former minister for the Sudan and successful military commander in 1882–3, as ' a good man and plucky', who 'knows the country and is a brave and competent officer'. This was the man whom the Khedive Tawfiq had churlishly and mistakenly dismissed and replaced as *hakimdar*, in March 1883, by Ala el Din Pasha. Abdel Qadir supported the new policy of abandonment; he had previous military and ministerial experience and in Khartoum his reputation was high. Above all, he was an Arabic-speaking Syrian-born Turkish Egyptian and a Moslem. Now it was he, on 14 January 1884, who was designated by the planners, with the agreement of Baring and Wood, to be sent personally to superintend withdrawal of the garrisons from Khartoum and Sennar; and to undertake the very difficult task of evacuating the civilians down the Nile, notwithstanding the limited navigability for steamers at the time of year, the great distance through unpredictably hostile tribes and terrain, and the absence of local provisions. Baring, undaunted, optimistically wrote privately to Granville on 14 January that the crisis was over and Nubar was in the seat of authority. The next day the London *Times* editorial concluded that Abel Qadir's mission to Khartoum via Korosko and the Nile valley indicated an intention to withdraw via Berber and across the Atmur desert, with only the Murrat (Chiggré) Wells for drinking water. Indeed within the week Abdel Qadir could have reached Khartoum to take command of operations.[4]

If both the British and the Egyptian governments were now of one accord in regarding the immediate abandonment of the Sudan (with the exception of the Red Sea littoral) as imperative, in London public opinion, fanned by the media, was equivocal. On 8 January W. T. Stead, editor of the *Pall Mall Gazette,* seized on the presence of Major-General Charles Gordon, the esteemed former Khedivial (though British-born) Governor-General of the Sudan, to prevail upon him to give his opinion on the Sudan crisis. Gordon had just accepted appointment in the Congo under King Leopold II and was ignorant of Granville's direct instruction to Baring of 3 January 1884 that the Sudan must be abandoned. Gordon gave his own negative view to Stead, which was published at length on 9 January in the *Gazette.* 'Whatever you may decide about evacuation, you cannot evacuate, because your army cannot be moved. You must either surrender absolutely to the Mahdi or defend Khartoum at all hazards.' To which Stead commented editorially: 'Why not send Chinese Gordon with full powers to Khartoum?'

The Times and other national and provincial newspapers reproduced the interview on 10 January and, on 14 January, despite Gordon's employment commitment to King Leopold the *Times* commented: 'It is not impossible that General Gordon's capacity and experience may be made available for the defence of Egypt, if not for the restoration of the Khedive's authority over a part of the Sudan.' Yet the following day, Abdel Qadir's mission to Khartoum having now been announced in Cairo, *The Times* agreed that the British government policy of evacuation was almost the only possible course, and that the withdrawal of the Khartoum garrison must be accomplished 'after an inexplicable delay'.

Press speculation had however disturbed both the British public and the government. As long as Sharif Pasha was in office, as on 2 December 1883, the Egyptian government with Baring's backing had resisted suggestions for the re-employment of Gordon ostensibly on the grounds that he was a Christian, and Baring's advice to Granville had been not to press the subject. Even when Nubar Pasha had succeeded, on 11 January 1884, the services neither of Gordon nor of Colonel Sir Charles Wilson 'could be utilised at present'. Conscious of growing public enthusiasm for the recall of the former Governor-General of the Sudan, albeit again in Egyptian employment, the British cabinet decided, notwithstanding Cairo's objection, to sound Gordon, arrived in England and about to leave via West Africa for the Congo, whether he would be willing to go to the Sudan. General Lord Wolseley therefore saw Gordon on 15 January at the War Office and, ignorant of Abdel Qadir's appointment by the Cairo government to evacuate Khartoum, asked whether Gordon was prepared 'to go to Suakin to inquire into the condition of affairs in the Sudan'. Gordon was prevailed on to agree, if requested by the British government, 'to report on the military situation of Sudan and return' (his words); and not being privy to Wolseley's subsequent meeting on 15 January with Granville and Hartington, left the next morning, 16 January, for Brussels. As Allen points out, there was as yet no necessary conflict between Abdel Qadir's executive appointment by Egypt to evacuate Khartoum and Sennar and Gordon's intelligence-gathering diplomatic mission to test the viability of the Berber–Suakin escape route through the Beja tribal lands.[5]

On the night of 15 January Granville telegraphed Baring that Gordon was willing to go straight to Suakin, omitting Cairo, to report on the military situation in the Sudan and to return, after which his engagement would cease. Gordon's report to London would be telegraphed via Baring, but Granville enquired privately of Baring whether Gordon 'might be of use in informing you and us of the situation' – still, implicitly, in an advisory capacity. However, Granville was unaware of the collapse over the past thirty-six hours of Abdel Qadir's executive mission to Khartoum. Only on the morning of 16 January did the Foreign Office learn from Baring that there were now serious difficulties in effecting the withdrawal from Khartoum because Abdel Qadir, who had accepted the task, 'now declines to go. The Egyptian government would feel greatly obliged if Britain would select a well qualified British officer to go to Khartoum instead of the war minister. He would be given full powers, both civil and military, to conduct the retreat.'

A detailed account of Abdel Qadir Pasha's volte-face is hard to find. He himself appears to have left no written explanation. Baring's dispatches throw no light: *Modern Egypt*, published in 1908, merely repeated his 16 January dispatch. Sir Henry Gordon in 1886 observed the omission of an explanation, and commented:

> The true facts are these: Abdel Qadir agreed to go, but with the understanding that the abandonment of the Sudan was not to be proclaimed, since if it were he would be powerless, and could do no good. The Government not only would not agree to this but, in his instructions, actually made the abandonment a leading feature and he, consequently, very properly declined to go, since he knew his undertaking would be a failure. Colonel Watson says that Abdel Qadir always remained of the same opinion, that to proclaim the abandonment of the Sudan was to make the removal of the garrisons impossible.

Allen wrote that this statement 'is based on a minute made in Cairo at the time by Colonel C. M. Watson and communicated subsequently to Sir Henry Gordon'. Its location has not yielded to research, though Watson in his biography of Sir Charles Wilson, a year after *Modern Egypt*, wrote regarding Nubar's first rejection on 10 January of the services of Gordon and Wilson:

> It was then proposed that Abdel Qadir Pasha... should be sent to withdraw the garrisons. He agreed to do this on the understanding that he was given a free hand; but when he found that he was to be hampered by instructions that, in his opinion, were impossible to carry out, he declined the mission, as he believed it would not succeed; and it is to be regretted that, while the fact of his declining to go was stated in the papers presented to Parliament, the reason for his decision was not also given.

Curiously, Sir Evelyn Wood, although a major participant in drawing the instructions, makes seemingly no reference to January discussions in his autobiography – except that he writes: 'In the summer of 1883 [*sic*] I was directed to ask the Turkish Pasha [unnamed] who had been serving at Khartoum if he would return there as Governor; and his observations in refusing – on Englishmen putting Turks in posts of danger – were so unpleasant that I offered Nubar Pasha to go up myself. This he declined.' The Turkish Pasha sounds like the former Minister for the Sudan, Abdel Qadir. But why return in *summer 1883* when Ala el Din Pasha had just succeeded him? Nubar Pasha was not prime minister until January 1884 and Wood must have meant that occasion. At the least it suggests some animus was generated between Wood and

Abdel Qadir. F. R. Wingate, Wood's assistant military secretary, is similarly puzzling in his assertion in 1891 that when Abdel Qadir was proposed by the government successor to Sharif 'to proceed to Khartoum and bring away the troops. That officer declined without hesitation.'

Shibeika who researched the Egyptian official archives at Cairo Citadel – and probably the Arabic biographies listed in Richard Hill's *Biographical Dictionary* – did not evidently discover any account by Abdel Qadir himself of his rejection of the instructions. Professor Roger Owen's new biography *Lord Cromer* sheds no additional light on Baring's insistence on the proclamation of abandonment. Perhaps we must await the publication of the contemporary private letters of Nubar Pasha for further light. According to Dicey (see source notes), Nubar strongly disapproved of compulsory evacuation and only accepted the premiership because it was futile to resist the will of the occupying power, and because he believed that he could direct the evacuation with more regard for Egyptian interests and with least detriment to Egyptian independence. Notwithstanding, could the Khedive, who distrusted Abdel Qadir, have withheld from him his personal support?

Nevertheless the persistence of the evacuation planners in including in the instructions the proviso that the abandonment objective should be publicly proclaimed was gravely mistaken. Abdel Qadir Pasha was the only capable Egyptian general with battle experience and first-hand knowledge of the Sudan. To cast around for a British alternative meant the loss of precious weeks needed to effect the withdrawal before the Mahdists threatened the escape route from Khartoum; while the appointment of a Christian general in an intrinsically Moslem civil war and in the wake of the Hicks precedent was dangerous. And contrary to determined British and indeed Egyptian policy hitherto, responsibility for the Sudan would now be thrust into the hands of a council dominated by the British consul-general on whose instruction, after General Gordon's departure to Khartoum, charge of the Sudan bureau was transferred from Abdel Qadir to Sir Evelyn Wood.

Why then the insistence on publicity for abandonment? Was it the belief that it was the only way of ensuring that the tribes of the Berber–Suakin route would allow safe passage to the Khartoum refugees? Or the belief that the loyalty of peoples like the Shukriya, Ababda, Bisharin, even the ambivalent Kababish, would thus be retained until the withdrawal was complete and 'some sort of rough government under tribal chiefs' – to use Baring's words – organised the more quickly? Or to pacify French suspicions? Or, perhaps most importantly, to assure the Mahdi that the mission had a peaceful objective? In the event second thoughts would after all prevail, and the mission commander on 26 January 1884 was granted absolute discretion on publication. But by then Abdel Qadir, albeit evidently judged right, was no longer a contender for the task.[6]

The Recall of Gordon Pasha The fortuitous arrival of Granville's telegram no. 28A of 14 January not only offered a timely solution to the void occasioned by Abdel Qadir's rejection of his instructions, coinciding as it did with Baring's formal request to London for a replacement, but also a pretext not to tender further explanation as to Abdel Qadir's change of mind. Baring's request on behalf of Egypt stipulated a head of mission in an executive, not advisory, role. To Granville's naming of Gordon to carry out the withdrawal policy, Baring conditionally assented at once on 16 January: 'I would have him rather than anyone else provided that there is a perfectly clear understanding with him as to what his position is to be and what general line of policy he is to carry out; otherwise not' – in which case Baring would prefer Colonel Sir Charles Wilson, then Lieutenant-Colonel J. D. H. Stewart.

In response to an instruction by Wolseley on 17 January to return from Brussels to London by the evening train, Gordon took leave of King Leopold and on 18 January, after a morning meeting with Wolseley, saw Granville, Hartington, Sir Charles Dilke (former Foreign Office under-secretary) and the Earl of Northbrook (Admiralty) at 3 p.m. On his acceptance to evacuate the Sudan, Gordon left Charing Cross for Paris that evening accompanied by Colonel Stewart, and seen off by the Duke of Cambridge and General Lord Wolseley. His instructions in Earl Granville's hand, written in haste that evening, were a touch ambiguous, ordering Gordon to Suakin to report and advise on steps to be taken (including arresting any recrudescence in the slave trade), but making reference to executive power 'to conduct the retreat' obliquely only in the final words: 'perform such other duties as may be entrusted to him by the Egyptian government through Sir Evelyn Baring'. Worse, Hartington's report to Gladstone currently at Hawarden indicated that, initially at least, Gordon was simply going out to report. Thus the reconcilability of Gordon's dual roles of advice to the British government and executive action on behalf of the Egyptian government was tenuously still preserved, but at the cost of future public confusion and ministerial recrimination.[7]

A week would elapse between Gordon's departure from London and his arrival – not in Suakin, but in Cairo. Granville, as Gordon was leaving, had suggested that Baring met him at Ismailia to decide whether Gordon should stop at Suakin and send Stewart to Khartoum, or Gordon himself go to Khartoum by the Nile. In the event Gordon was intercepted on arrival at Port Said by the *sirdar*, Wood, with Watson Bey and brought to Cairo via Ismailia on Baring's insistence, who nevertheless wrote a note to say how exceedingly glad he was over Gordon's and Stewart's involvement. Daily military conferences had been held meanwhile; in attendance were Abdel Qadir Pasha, still minister of war and now with the Sudan bureau transferred to him by Nubar on 17 January; General Sir Frederick Stephenson, commanding British troops; the *sirdar* Sir Evelyn Wood; and Sir Evelyn Baring, with Watson Bey and Wingate Bey. Decisions needed to be taken whether to hold Khartoum until the Sennar garrison and civilians elected to retire on Khartoum or, alternatively, on Kassala; whether to withdraw from all Sennaheit (Bogos) or only from Gallabat; whether the Khartoum forces should withdraw either via Shendi or Berber down the Nile, or via the Blue Nile, Abu Haraz and Kassala to Suakin (accepting the Atmur desert to Korosko to be impassable to an army). Lupton in Bahr el Ghazal and Emin in Equatoria were left full discretion over withdrawal, but Emin was warned against approaching Kassala and south Sennaheit.[8]

The arrival of Gordon and Stewart in Cairo on the evening of 24 January 1884, followed by an amicable call on Khedive Tawfiq with Nubar, Baring and Wood, effectively marked the transfer of authority for the Sudan – if unacknowledged or even recognised in London – from Egypt to Britain. Already on 19 January Nubar Pasha had told Watson Bey: 'I am to be congratulated: the weight of the Sudan is off my shoulders. If anyone can manage it Gordon can.' The Khedive agreed to appoint an exiled son of the late Sultan of Darfur to succeed his father and to accompany Gordon to the Sudan, but it would be Baring, Nubar, Wood, Gordon and Stewart who returned to Baring's house on the afternoon of the 25th to draw up definitive plans for Gordon's departure to Khartoum. Abdel Qadir Pasha was no longer a participant, despite his ministerial responsibility and close acquaintance with Stewart in Khartoum two years previously. Abdel Qadir did attend with Nubar Pasha the large farewell dinner to Gordon and Stewart on the 26th, the evening of their departure to Assiut by train, hosted by Sir Evelyn Wood, but thereafter on Baring's request Wood took charge of the Sudan bureau.

Under the 22-point plan drawn up on 25 January the most crucial decisions were: that the Khedive would no longer telegraph on his own authority; that Gordon would communicate only with Baring and Nubar, who had sole authority to instruct him; that the evacuation of the Sudan would be gradual; that Wadi Halfa would mark the new frontier; that Gordon would be armed with two alternative firmans: the one appointing him Governor-General, the other 'our (Khedivial) representative, with full authority to agree with in [*sic*] establishing a peaceful and amicable way of withdrawing from those parts; that the Khedive would select a new sultan of Darfur to accompany Gordon; and that Fariq Valentine Baker Pasha was confirmed general-governor of East Sudan and the littoral. A meeting was planned for the next day at which Zubeir Pasha would meet Gordon, Nubar and Baring, before which Baring handed Gordon his written instructions embodying the 22-point executive plan for evacuation.

Gordon, mindful of the failure to appoint a strong successor on his own departure in 1879 (with disastrous consequences), was keen to take Zubeir Pasha with him: as a proven Sudanese general and a ruler he should be able to trump the charisma of the Mahdi. Zubeir however, bitter at his criminal conviction for instigating his son Sulieman to rebellion and at the latter's execution, displayed considerable animus against Gordon. Despite Gordon's willingness to run the risk of working in harness, Watson's belief (endorsed seemingly by Ibrahim Fawzi) that one of them would not then come back alive, led to a veto on Zubeir's return, at least presently, to the Sudan. In old age Zubeir would nevertheless comment: ' In fact I only once came across a man whose life was absolutely pure and unselfish, and that man was Gordon.'

Understandably perhaps, no effort was made to approach Abdel Qadir, the Turkish-Egyptian general, as an alternative to Zubeir, but nor was Abdel Qadir examined over his continuing refusal to undertake the withdrawal himself. A crucial element in Gordon's instructions, however, unlike those rejected by Abdel Qadir, was that he was given not an order but 'the widest discretion' as to whether or not to publish the firman (and, if appropriate, on the timing) which publicly announced to the Sudanese the intended evacuation of the Sudan. Nubar's advice was to delay publication, at least until they reached Khartoum.[9]

Sudan Abandonment Proclaimed   With Major-General Sir Gerald Graham, VC, bound for Suakin, Gordon and Stewart left Cairo on 26

January, electing with some misgiving to wear in identification the Turkish-Egyptian *tarbush* and accompanied by Ibrahim Fawzi as Gordon's personal assistant (he had been released from prison having been sentenced for supporting Arabi's rebellion). 'A dark cold evening saw [Gordon] at Bulak station and the dim light of the carriage showed the cheerful faces of Gordon, Stewart and Graham as the train rolled away into the night.'

News of the submission of the Bisharin to Hussein Pasha Khalifa at Berber encouraged the Gordon party's strenuous crossing of the Atmur desert from Korosko to Abu Hamed by camel in fifty-two hours, no longer encumbered by the entourage of the Darfur sultan-designate who had timorously disembarked at Aswan. However Gordon, impetuously, had then weakened Hussein's authority when, having left the steamer at Korosko with Stewart, he had dismissed the Ababda irregular forces gathered by Hussein to buttress Gordon's prestige. After meeting Mohammed Abu Hijil, *sheikh* of the Rubatab, at Abu Hamed, they joined Hussein Pasha to reach Berber by steamer on 11 February. Armed with public proclamation, Gordon in turn addressed the Berber *ulema'a* (religious elders), merchants, and the Egyptian garrison of 1,200 men, affirming that he came in peace and had no quarrel with the Mahdi, and promising the halving of taxes. Unhappily news arrived of the defeat of Baker Pasha at El Teb en route to relieve Tokar.

Perhaps it was these ill tidings, which were certain to spread quickly to Khartoum, that persuaded Gordon to send for Stewart at 5 a.m. the next morning. Gordon had decided that he must exercise his discretion and proclaim the divorce of the Sudan from Egypt and the appointment of a Sudanese administration and local militias. Accordingly three hours later Hussein Pasha Khalifa and the *qadi*, Sheikh Mohammed El Tahir, were summoned and shown the Khedive's *firman* which authorised the evacuation of the Sudan. A public proclamation was fixed to the gate of the *muderia* proclaiming the formation of a provisional council of six chief notables, Berber henceforth being independent of Egypt but subject to Gordon as *hakimdar* and commissioner of the British. Gordon further announced the dismissal and recall of Hussein Pasha Wasif Sirri in Khartoum and his replacement by de Coëtlogon as Gordon's *wakil*. Questioned as to the continued validity of the November 1877 treaty providing for the abolition of slave owning (as opposed to slave-hunting and trafficking) he affirmed it to be cancelled. Existing slaves would thus remain the property of their masters and no payment of compensation would be required. The next afternoon, by which time the Mahdist occupation of Sinkat was known, a second council of notables was shown the *firman*. Gordon had enacted the policy against which Abdel Qadir Pasha had remonstrated. 'Profound astonishment' and 'great delight' greeted the revelation of the *firman*.

Hussein Khalifa however was not slow in private to condemn publication as a mistake, and to express his consternation. He was already critical of Gordon's order to him to dispatch in Arabic a letter to the Mahdi offering to recognise him as *sultan* of Kordofan, together with a robe of honour (an offer which would be summarily rejected).

Now aware of the future vulnerability of his position as *mudir*, on parting with Gordon Hussein sent a neighbouring *feki*, Sheikh Mohammed el Kheir Abdallah Khojali, of whom the Mahdi had in youth been a former pupil, to El Obeid to investigate the Mahdi's claims, honourably agreeing between themselves that Berber's surrender must in any case be contingent on the fall of Khartoum, The *feki* would return in April, appointed *amir* by the Mahdi, and despite Hussein's resolute opposition to the *amir's* intention to breach their understanding, would attack and, after a siege, capture Berber on 19 May 1884.

Granville had meanwhile anxiously enquired of Baring on 4 February whether Gordon had accepted any appointment from the Khedive, to be told that 'Gordon has at his own request received a firman appointing him Governor-General of the Sudan with full powers civil and military. It was very necessary that this should be done.' Gordon and Stewart had agreed by the time they reached Abu Hamed that if the Nile Valley retreat route were closed, they would withdraw by way of Equatoria to Zanzibar; and Gordon had already, via Baring, written at Korosko to King Leopold urging him to occupy Bahr el Ghazal and Equatoria and to appoint Gordon their governor. The plan was unattractive on political grounds to Baring who telegraphed London that Gordon 'for the present at all events' should not be allowed south of Khartoum. Gordon at Berber affirmed that he would not go south without permission.[10]

On 18 February, one month after their departure from London, Gordon and Stewart reached Khartoum via El Damer and Shendi, having swapped steamers, on account of the Nile level, in the Sabluka gorge with Hussein Sirri, en route as ordered to Cairo. Gordon, the former *hakimdar*, had returned after an absence of four years in vastly different circumstances. Frank Power, the courageous British consular agent and correspondent of *The Times*, bore witness to the warmth of the reception of the local populace. Only one further European, the French consular agent Herbin, would reach Khartoum from Berber, on 3 March, before the route was closed.

At once Gordon's firman was read and a Council of Notables appointed. President would be Awad el Karim Pasha Abu Sin, Sheikh of the Shukriya; minister of finance would be the chief Egyptian merchant, Mohammed Pasha Hasan. Lewa Sa'id Pasha Hasan, commander of the Khartoum *bashi-buzouqs*; and Sheikh El Amin Mohammed el Darir, *sheikh el Islam*, were also members. Lewa Ibrahim Pasha Fawzi was initially placed in command of Omdurman and Miralai Faraj Bey Mohammed el Zaini, a veteran of the Mexican war and commander at Keren, of Sudanese battalions. Finding a new mosque begun under Mohammed Ra'uf Pasha, his old bête noir, which the latter had named after himself, Gordon renamed it '*El Sudan*'.

Ibrahim Pasha Haidar, the *seraskir,* was appointed on 23 February to precede the main body of Egyptian troops withdrawing north in order to make the arrangements for their reception and ongoing travel, accompanied by de Coëtlogon in a *dhahabiya*. First went the few senior officials, then the wounded and sick Egyptian soldiers with their families, followed by the *bashi-buzouqs* and the main contingent of Egyptian troops. The first detachments had left Berber by the end of the month, six officers and 411 troops and civilians on 27 February, while fast dromedary-borne messengers were sent to Korosko to give advance warning of the detailed numbers arriving. Miralai Francis Duncan had on 28 February left Cairo for Aswan and Korosko with two Egyptian battalions, aided by Giegler Pasha and his wife, to prepare reception areas. On 30 July Gordon would advise Cairo that a total of some 600 soldiers and 2,000 other refugees had passed safely down the Nile to Berber before an *Ansar* force cut the escape route on 12 March near Halfaya. Gordon's plans to evacuate the Egyptian junior officials and their families with the fit Egyptian troops were then frustrated, and Gordon would resolve that, without the arrival of a successor as governor, 'I will not leave these people after all they have been through.'

A Khartoum Successor Rejected and Relief Refused   Who was to have been Gordon's successor when the evacuation of the Egyptian population was complete? At Abu Hamed Gordon had mentioned to the *sheikh* of the Rubatab the names of Hussein Pasha Khalifa or Zubeir

Pasha Rahma Mansur. The successor must be Sudanese. On the day of his arrival in Khartoum, Gordon was adamant. 'Zubeir alone has the ability to rule the Sudan and would be universally accepted by the Sudan.' This dispatch urging Zubeir's appointment by Gordon to Baring in cypher on 18 February, along with others sent from Khartoum between 18 February and 10 March 1884, still appears in cypher (FO 78/3744) despite Sir Henry Gordon's request in 1885 that it be decyphered. On 19 February 1884 Baring endorsed Gordon's proposal, 'I believe Zubeir to be the only possible man', but the two men should not be in Khartoum simultaneously: Zubeir should leave Cairo only after Gordon had quit Khartoum. The proclamation of Zubeir as ruler should be made with British approbation but his exercise of authority should be denied British moral support.

Granville's initial response of 22 February was 'that the greatest objections exist to the appointment by British authority of a successor to General Gordon'. Gordon, interpreting the reply as an inflexible refusal, spelled out the alternative for the protection of Egypt proper in an unfortunate phrase, which Gordon's enemies in London claimed betrayed a belligerent intent. That must be 'the smashing up of the Mahdi', requiring British troops to Wadi Halfa and Indian Moslem troops for the Berber–Suakin route. Baring, with Nubar supporting Gordon's plea for Zubeir, warned the British government: 'Whatever may be said to the contrary they must, in reality, be responsible for any arrangements which are now desired for the Sudan, and I do not think it possible to shake off that responsibility.'

On 1 March Granville requested further justification for the immediate appointment of a successor to Gordon 'whom they [the Cabinet] trust will remain for some time longer in Khartoum', conceding that 'it could be necessary to make an arrangement on the subject eventually.' Gordon insisted: 'My weakness is that of being foreign and Christian and it is only by sending Zubeir that this prejudice can be removed'; and Baring on 4 March affirmed: 'I have carefully reconsidered the whole question and am still of the opinion that Zubeir Pasha should be allowed to succeed Gordon.' Zubeir should, subject only to Baring seeing him again, depart at once since delay would be injurious. Colonel Stewart advocated that Zubeir accompany a small British force to Berber on his way to Khartoum.

The British Cabinet met under public pressure on 11 March 1884. Despite Gladstone's personal support for Gordon's plea, critically he was absent sick and his colleagues concluded: 'They do not consider the arguments against the employment of Zubeir Pasha have been satisfactorily answered.' Baring remonstrated that, the consequences of this instruction being so serious, he needed clarification. Prolonging Gordon's duty as Governor-General was the reversal of the abandonment policy. The government instruction of 12 March was nevertheless repeated on 16 March. Baring then recorded his regret, looking forward 'with considerable apprehension to the results of the policy.' On 12 March, *Ansar* troops had already daringly occupied Halfaya, two hours north of Khartoum, and cut the telegraph to Berber.

Still unaware of the outcome of his plea, Gordon wrote to his sister on 15 March: 'We are all right. The enemy has established himself some 6000 strong nine miles from here [north of Omdurman] and we hear his drums from the palace. We are well off for food.' And in another, undated:

> I have asked the government [telegrams of 9 and 10 March] to give me categorical orders what to do. If they do not mean to relieve us, then there is no use waiting and we had better evacuate at once. I have proposed to take all the Black troops in the steamers up to Equator and to send Stewart to Berber with the White (Egyptian) troops. I should then go to Congo via Bahr el Ghazal but I fear that as the telegraph is just cut I shall not get an answer to this telegram.

Pending London's reply Baring had instructed him to hold on.

Such a withdrawal strategy without Egyptian or British military assistance was however contingent on the Mahdi's acquiescence in Gordon's peaceful intentions and in the unobstructed evacuation of the Egyptian officials and their families. The Mahdi's reply to Gordon's letter from Berber would not have been received until 22 March, but Zubeir's appointment being unlikely to materialise, preparations for the progressive departure of remaining Egyptian troops and officials had presently to be aborted and the defences of Khartoum and Omdurman comprehensively manned.

Gordon now had few illusions. On the day before the *Ansar* cut his communications north at Halfaya, he wrote to Lord Dufferin:

> The tribes around here, owing to our weakness have gone over to the Mahdi; and are about to hem us in… [They] see by our sending down the sick that we do not mean to keep the country. Of course one cannot expect them to be faithful to me, when they

know I only want to get the Cairo employés and white [Egyptian] troops down... They laugh at my proclamations. I do not blame them for they know we are retreating.

On 1 March Stewart had written privately to Baring, received 22 March, urging that General Graham should push on from Suakin to Berber to make withdrawal from Sennar possible. Since that was written, the Zubeir plea had been refused, the Khartoum–Berber route cut and war effectively joined since the Mahdi demanded unconditional surrender. To Granville's enquiry whether Egyptian troops to Wadi Halfa or some English officers posted to Berber would lend moral support to Gordon, Baring replied that two officers to Berber would help (approval was given) but he warned Granville that Gordon might still not have received the instructions of 12/15 March, and that Gordon and Stewart would not quit their post alone. Accordingly on 24 March Baring urged that either Gordon must be trusted to last until the autumn when the rising Nile would make possible the Berber–Suakin exit; or Graham's troops should be sent at once to open up the Berber–Khartoum communication. Generals Stephenson and Wood concurred that, compared with Suakin, the retreat across the Atmur desert to Korosko was impracticable, even if the military and health risks of the Suakin–Berber route were extraordinary. Baring advocated that route.

Advised by return that the Cabinet did not think it justifiable to send a British expedition to Berber on 26 March, for the second time within a fortnight Baring questioned his instruction which might not reach Gordon anyway. 'In any case I cannot reconcile myself to making the attempt to forward such a message to him without laying the case before your Lordship.' The Zubeir mission proposal had been rejected which, if acted upon, would have altered the situation. The new instruction would mean to Gordon and Stewart that they were being abandoned. It was impossible with both Nile banks in enemy hands presently to pass boats down the Nile; and the land route was equally unviable. Nor would Gordon and Stewart quit alone. Having sent Gordon out it was 'our bounden duty both as a matter of humanity and policy not to abandon him'. Again Baring was turned down. In short London was willing to give Gordon full discretion to remain or if necessary to retire by the south or any other route, but in the autumn no more than now would a relief expedition be agreed. Without further news of Gordon's actual situation and security, London would not add to the instructions. Baring on 27 March was admonished by his cousin, the Earl of Northbrook, formerly (1872–6) Viceroy of India (to whom Baring had been private secretary) and presently First Lord of the Admiralty:

> It is quite true that in three of your recommendations we have not been able to agree, but pray recollect that the responsibility rests upon us, not upon you... Lastly comes your telegram of 26th... one thing appears to me to be clear, that upon this question the Government at home must be better able to judge than you can possibly be. We are much better able than you to balance the general interests of this country against the obvious considerations of the Sudan difficulty.

To which Baring bravely rejoined on 4 April: 'I view with great misgiving and mistrust the policy of waiting upon events in the Sudan.'

Following the closure of the Berber–Nile route Gordon would never receive the British government's decision not to send Zubeir to Khartoum. As to the refusal of a relief expedition via Suakin to Berber, only on 9 April 1884 did Gordon receive a message from Berber conveying Baring's belief that no British force would be sent to Berber. From this Gordon correctly guessed that he was refused both Zubeir and a relief force and accordingly considered himself free to act according to circumstance. Granville's definitive instructions of 28 March never reached Gordon.

The British Cabinet was much taken up with the international conference on the Egyptian financial situation about to open in London, judging it essential to have Baring's presence there for advice. He left Cairo on 21 April, not to return until September 1884.[11]

2 THE MAHDIST OCCUPATION OF THE SUDAN

The defeat of Hicks's expedition at Sheikan on 5 November 1883 and the conquest of Kordofan had coincided with another important Mahdist success in the east. Osman Digna had defeated a small Suakin expeditionary force under Mahmoud Pasha Tahir at El Teb (El Ta'ib) on 2 December, leaving Sinkat and Tokar still besieged and Egyptian authority limited to the coast. The Mahdi had demonstrated the wide extent of his appeal across the Sudan as an ascetic religious leader with the military strength to wrest the control of the remaining centres still

SUDAN c.1894

▪▪▪▪▪ Approximate boundary of Mahdist rule, 1894

Scale of Miles

| 0 | 100 | 200 | 300 | 400 miles |

EGYPT

RED SEA

Aswan

Toski
Korosko
Balaja
Saras   Wadi Halfa
Akasha
ATMUR   Murrat Wells
Firkat
Qinnis   Suarda
Kerma
Hafir
R. Kirbekan
Dongola
Khandak
Debba
Korti   Merowe
Jaqdul
BAYUDA
Abu T'laih
Metemma
Sabaluqa Gorge
Omdurman   Khartoum
Umm Dubban

Abu Hamed

Handub   Suakin
Sinkat   Trinkitat
El Teb
Tokar

Berber
Atbara Fort
El Damer
Aliab   Adarama
Shendi
R. Atbara
Keren
Massawa

Jedda

Rufa'a   Kassala
Mesellimiya
Abu Haraz
Agordat
Amadeib   Asmara

Gura   R. Mareb   Adwa

DARFUR
KORDOFAN

El Fasher   Foja
J. Marra   Umm
Dara   Shanga
Taweisha
Dilling

Bara
El   El Dueim
Obeid
Umm
Debeikerat
Jebelein
Teqali
Nuba
Mountains
J. Qadir

Wad Medani
Kawa
Aba I.
Karkoj
Renk
Roseires

Sennar
Gallabat

Kaka

L. Tana

ABYSSINIA

Gondar

MASALIT   *TAMA*

Kalaka   Shakka
Bahr el Arab

Fashoda
Bahr el Ghazal   Malakal

Deim
Zubair   Wau
Meshra
er Rek
Bahr el Zeraf

R. Sobat   Nasir

Shambe
Rumbek
R. Sueh

Bahr el Jebel
Blue Nile
R. Dinder

E Q U A T O R I A

Tambura   Amadi
Bor
Lado
Rejaf   Gondokoro

Dufile
L. Turkana

C O N G O

L. Albert

Map 8

Blue Nile   *White Nile*   *R. Nile*

under Egyptian administration and to establish a theocratic independent Sudan.

To the west, Darfur fell to him immediately after Sheikan. Bahr el
Ghazal and Equatoria might not command the same priority of
importance, but nevertheless his newly appointed *amir* Karamallah
Mohammed Kurqusawi, with some Dinka backing quickly threw
Lupton Pasha back on the defensive, his province to fall in April 1884.
The outbreak of further disturbances in Bahr el Ghazal would spare
Lado and Equatoria from Mahdist occupation in the summer of 1884.

After Sheikan, the essential target of the Mahdi was the conquest of
the Nile Valley and of the Blue Nile Gezira. The capital however was
too strongly defended at the end of 1883 for the Mahdi and his
Companions presently to entertain the launch of an expeditionary force
across the 250-mile desert which divided El Obeid and Khartoum. Nor
could victories any longer be achieved by patiently awaiting the
dispatch of further Egyptian expeditionary forces against his prepared
positions, granted his proven superiority in morale and now in arms.
The *Ansar* were mindful however of the efficacy of siege in a land still
relatively undeveloped as regards communications and sparsely
endowed with rainfall and cultivable terrain. Accordingly the strategic
isolation of the heavily populated capital from its supply lines, whether
local to the Gezira and the Isle of Meroe, or long-distance to Egypt via
Dongola, Berber and Suakin, became the first objective.

The Mahdi's reply to Gordon's letter, translated and forwarded by
Hussein Pasha Khalifa from Berber on 16 February 1884, was self-
confident and inflexible:

> Your letter has been received and its contents have been read and
> understood... Be it known to you that I am without pride, the
> promised Mahdi and the successor of the Prophet. There is no
> need for me to be sultan or king of Kordofan... The Prophet has
> informed me that those who declare enmity against me shall fail,
> and be conquered by the power of God... Take heed, therefore,
> and give yourself up to us that you may be saved... Otherwise you
> shall perish with [all those under you] and your sins and theirs
> shall be on your head.

This letter had been written from El Obeid dated 5 March 1884 and
was delivered to Gordon at Khartoum by three *Ansar* on 22 March,
bringing with them a patched 'jibba' for Gordon to wear as a token of
submission, which was returned to them. Gordon signalled in his reply

Sabaluqa cataract: Mahdist fort

that the Mahdi's letter had been likewise understood 'but I cannot have any more communication with you.' The truce had been rejected: war declared. The Sudan would take a further ten months to conquer, notwithstanding the inaction of London.

Already, before the Mahdi's letter was sent, his father-in-law Mohammed el Taiyib el Basir had again arrived in March to incite the Blue Nile tribes to revolt against the troops of Salih Bey el Mek at Mesellimiya, forcing him to surrender. Now Sheikh El Ubeyd Badr sent a force of 4,000 down the right bank of the Nile to cut the Khartoum–Berber telegraph line at the Sabaluqa gorge, causing Gordon to withdraw the 800 Sha'iqi force at Halfaya on the opposite bank to Khartoum on 13 March. Three days later an Egyptian force under Lewas Hasan Pasha Ibrahim el Shellali and Sa'id Pasha Hussein, sent to dislodge the Mahdist force, was driven back. It was alleged the commanders had betrayed their men into offering no resistance to the Mahdist attack, and they were court-martialled and shot. Six months later Gordon had conscientious reservations about the reliability of the evidence. Meanwhile until August the Sabaluqa gorge passage would remain in Mahdist control, Berber and Shendi then having already fallen to the *amir* Mohammed el Kheir.

The Mahdi remained in El Obeid, mustering a large army in preparation for his advance on Khartoum, placing an increasingly heavy strain on the local supplies of food and water. Colonel Stewart on two reconnaissances up the White Nile at the end of February 1884 found that the left bank villages had been seized by Mahdist forces gathering *dura* for El Obeid and in April the Mahdi moved his headquarters to El Rahad, where Hicks had paused on his advance, and where sufficient water was now available for the dry season. Only in August 1884, after a campaign against the determined Nuba people of Jebel Dayir, would the *Ansar* army move off from El Rahad via Shatt on Khartoum. As the months of preparation passed, the Mahdi remained in regular touch with his appointed *amirs* in the ever-expanding occupied areas of the independent Sudan.[12]

Darfur, 1884   Orders to Slatin Pasha to retire on to the Nile valley would not have been feasible even if received. Within days of the news of the outcome of Sheikan he surrendered Dara. El Fasher, and therefore Darfur, fell three weeks later on 15 January 1884, as Cairo wrestled with implementing the decision to evacuate Khartoum. Slatin, now a prisoner of the Mahdi, remained in El Fasher from February to May, when he left to join the Mahdi at El Rahad and would accompany the latter in his advance to Omdurman. Until the Mahdi's death Mohammed Khalid Zuqal, a relative, would remain ruler of Darfur with Sultan Yusuf, son of the late Sultan Ibrahim, his chief *amir*, to the anger of Sheikh Madibbo Ali, *amir* of the Rizeiqat.

Bahr el Ghazal, 1884   Lupton most bravely held out at Deim Sulieman with his force of 1,200 regular infantry and four companies of *bashi-buzouqs*, augmented by irregulars and artillery. When in January 1884 news reached Lupton of Hicks's defeat he passed the ill-tidings to Emin at Lado (the letters arriving 26 March and 23 May 1884).

To strike down Lupton's resistance, the Mahdi selected Karamallah Mohammed Kurqusawi, a Shambe merchant, participant in an unsuccessful Dongalawi anti-government conspiracy at Deim Idris the previous June. With an army of 8,000 Baqqara, *jallaba* and four Black rifle companies, Karamallah in April 1884, having secured the inevitable defection of Lupton's outpost at Liffi (Lefi), dispatched an ultimatum to Lupton to surrender Deim Sulieman. It was accompanied by a short note from Slatin. Despite his impossible situation – and, like Slatin, embracing Islam as '*amir* Abdallah', to retain the loyalty of his troops – Lupton resolved to fight to the last; but in vain. His message to Emin on 26 April reported that 'everyone has joined the Mahdi'.

Lupton surrendered two days later and on 2 May wrote again, under duress, advising Emin to surrender and Junker to come to Wau to collect his belongings. These letters reached Lado on 27 May.

Lupton's impossible predicament had not been ignored in Cairo. Nubar Pasha, the new chief minister, in ordering the evacuation of the Sudan, had on 16 January 1884 recognised his plight and advised Lupton that only he could judge the best course to adopt. Events of April 1884 had overtaken that advice.

Karamallah would serve another two years as *amir* in Bahr el Ghazal and later Equatoria, nominally under the command of the Khalifa Mohammed Sharif. Karamallah's brother Mohammed was the Mahdist agent in neighbouring Shakka. As for Lupton, he with his Abyssinian wife and child were marched in September 1884 via Sheikan, where he viewed the carnage of the battlefield, to El Obeid; thence to captivity in Omdurman in November, where his youth and intransigence denied him the relative creature comforts allowed to his fellow *mudir*, Slatin – who would do his best to mitigate the privations and suffering which attended the years until Lupton's death in 1888.[13]

Equatoria, and Withdrawal 1882–5   Under the *hakimdaria* of Ra'uf Pasha in 1880, Equatoria had been expanded as a general-governorate but on account of the *sudd* increasingly isolated. Following his visit to Khartoum in March–June 1882, Emin Bey at Lado would receive a call from only one steamer, the *Telhawin*, in March 1883, bringing but few supplies from Khartoum. Having hitherto remained at Lado, Emin spent the summer of 1883 first in Monbuttu, then Makaraka following the sacking of Rumbek.

When Dr Wilhelm Junker reached Lado from Monbutto via Makaraka in mid-January 1884 he found Emin's general-governorate now directly controlling Lado, Amadi (fortified), Gondokoro and Rejaf. The provincial garrisons were concentrated there and in (now only) six districts: Rohl (Ajak), once again separate from Makaraka, under Sulieman Agha; Mangbattu (Tingasi) under Rihan Agha, formerly at Makaraka; Makaraka (Wandi) under Ibrahim Gurguru Agha; Kirri (Labore); Dufile (including Wadelai and Fatiko under Hawash Agha); and Bor under Abdel Wahab Agha. Latuka, Fuweira and Fadibek (the last in Acholi country, east of Dufile) were abandoned to the full local control of the Bunyoro chiefs, Anfina and Rionga's son Kamisoa. Thus Dufile district, including Wadelai where the steamers *Khedive* (20 h.p.) and *N'yanza* (10 h.p.) were based for use on Lake

Albert, was the most southerly part of Khedivial territory. The total Equatorial garrison included 2,000 regulars armed with Remingtons.

Emin had returned from Khartoum in June 1882. In mid-1883 he was visiting Wandi and Mangbattu when news reached him of a rising of the Agar Dinka in Rohl. These tribesmen, spread over some 200 square miles (their tribal shrine lies just east of Rumbek) and disillusioned over the prospects of effective support from Lado, had turned on the Dongalawi *razzia* practitioners of Rumbek and Ayak. On 27 July 1883, led by Wol Athiang with Dok and Jagei Nuer support, they massacred the Rumbek garrison of seventy and its commander, Abdallah Agha el Sudani, before marching on Shambe where they killed some 150. Emin now returned from Wandi via Makaraka whence he dispatched its *mamur*, Ibrahim Mohammed Agha, to collect reinforcements from Amadi, restore security to Rohl and recover Rumbek. This was achieved by 15 December 1883 with the assistance of reinforcements sent by Lupton. Emin had meanwhile himself retired to Lado, arriving on 23 August seriously ill.

Lado itself, however, remained generally tranquil, if now totally devoid of basic supplies like cloth, soap and coffee, until the arrival of Lupton's letters – the first towards the end of May 1884 telling of Lupton's surrender. Junker was still with Emin at Lado to help him assess the consequences. On 27 May 1884, with Lupton's second letter, came a general missive of admonition from the Mahdi to the inhabitants of Equatoria, dated 5 January 1884, claiming their universal allegiance; and also a letter from Karamallah Mohammed el Kurqusawi, the Mahdi's appointee as *amir* of the south following Sheikan. Karamallah had conspired in June 1883 to seize 800 government *jihadiya* (slave soldier) recruits at Deim Idris (Gonda) destined for the Hicks expedition. Foiled, he had fled with his companions to join the Mahdi in time to take part in the Sheikan battle. Karamallah now required of Emin his personal oath of allegiance to the Mahdi and the surrender of the Equatoria province and his presence with his troops at Aswan. There was no concealing the turn of events and Emin, summoning his officials to a conference, read them Karamallah's ultimatum. In the aftermath of Sheikan and the surrender of Bahr el Ghazal, Junker wrote: 'It was unanimously resolved to surrender the province and to avoid any further useless bloodshed. Emin Bey on his side was ready at once to set out for Bahr el Ghazal' and asked for followers to accompany him.

Junker, less compliant, declined and admitted: 'I could only concur with the resolution of the conference but I acknowledge that I thought Emin Bey's journey a mistake and considered that a written declaration of the surrender of the province would be quite enough for the present… only the road to the south, and eventually to Zanzibar was open to me.'

Within forty-eight hours Emin too had thought better of his plan. Instead he dispatched the deputation without himself on 3 June. It would disintegrate through divided loyalties by the time it had reached Ajak, the leaders thwarted from their secret plan to return with troops and to seize Emin and Lado. Karamallah would not in 1884 advance to the Bahr el Jebel, delayed by insurrections in Bahr el Ghazal and rains, returning probably to Shakka to organise his province. Meanwhile Emin ordered Rihan Agha, accompanied by the explorer of the Upper Uele river, Captain Gaetano Casati, to abandon Monbuttu and to close on Makaraka, and had discussed with Junker alternative routes of retreat from Lado in the event of Karamallah's approach. Makaraka in fact had already been abandoned by its *mudir*, Ibrahim Agha who, having pillaged neighbouring bases, would be killed en route to join Karamallah at Tonj.[14]

Assuming correctly the Mahdist threat to Khartoum had not been lifted and the northern route via Bor was still unsafe, Emin in Lado further decided by mid-June 1884 to abandon Rohl (Rumbek and Ajak), as well as Fuweira, Fadibek and Latuka and to concentrate his forces in the fortified stations of Lado, Amadi and Makaraka – the last no longer threatened. The state of insurrection to the north should prove another major obstruction to Karamallah's return from Shakka, while from Bor in August came news that all was presently well there. The lull was not to last. Meanwhile Junker, who had in June withdrawn to Dufile, hoping in vain for a steamer up the Bahr el Jebel, had returned to Lado in September 1884, still with his diaries and Monbuttu specimens, but having earlier abandoned his natural history collections at Wau.

Abdallah el Samad Abu Safiya, a Tonj trader deputed by Karamallah to command his invading force with 1,600 Remingtons, attacked Amadi three times with Agar Dinka support in November–December 1884. Unsuccessful, he was obliged then to lay siege to the undefeated garrison (strengthened by the government militia withdrawn from south of Dufile) who five times refused to surrender. Eventually, delayed by the August rising of the southern militia on the Wau-Rumbek road against the Mahdist invader – Emin would write in January 1885: 'The greatest anarchy seems to have prevailed in the Bahr el Ghazal province

ever since the retirement of poor Lupton Bey' – Karamallah himself
arrived at Amadi with 2,000 *Ansar* in mid-February 1885. Whereupon,
after a further month's resistance, their supplies exhausted, the Amadi
troops successfully broke out through the lines of the besiegers, some
260 fighting their way to Wandi, eastern Makraka where they at last
found the garrison withdrawn from Monbuttu. By 19 April, the consolidated force had withdrawn successfully to Bedden and to Rejaf.

Further letters soon arrived to Emin at Lado from Karamallah,
ordering him to surrender and, on 18 April 1885, came news that
Khartoum had fallen. Enemy forces were scarcely three days from
Lado. Its food supply was threatened. The Bor–Khartoum route was
impassable (the Bor garrison remained determined to stay put, until it
was overwhelmed by Dinka in September 1885). Emin resolved to
delay no longer. On 24 April, having convened a council of all the officers, he created a military post of three companies at Lado under Rihan
Agha, and himself withdrew south towards Dufile and Wadelai in the
wake of Junker. Junker had already departed in January 1885 for the
lacustrine region, abandoned since 1879, and by March he had arrived
at Anfina's. Emin now asked Junker on his return from Bunyoro to
await his own arrival at Wadelai which Emin reached on 10 July there
to join Casati. Junker was not to meet them until 11 December 1885.

The anticipated attack on Lado by Karamallah Kurqusawi never
materialised, despite that further ultimatum of 18 April 1885 demanding Emin's surrender. The subsequent death of the Mahdi, Karamallah's
relative, and the succession of the Khalifa Abdallahi provoked disturbances in Bahr el Ghazal among Dongolawi *amirs* who declined to
recognise the legitimacy of the Khalifa's election. Diminishing ammunition supplies, another *zariba* mutiny and the onset of the rains obliged
Karamallah about June 1885 to fall back from Wandi towards the west.

On the orders of the Khalifa, he would cross the Bahr el Arab reach-
ing Shakka in October 1886 with 3,000 troops and a host of slaves.
Troubles had developed further following the departure of Mohammed
Khalid (Zuqal) to Omdurman in December 1885, leaving Emir Yusuf
Ibrahim at Jebel Marra as senior *amir* in Darfur, the west being under
Karamallah's brother and *wakil* Mohammed in Shakka, and Madibbo
Ali, *amir* of the Rizeiqat. The last, exploiting the hiatus in El Fasher,
prepared to capture Shakka, requiring Karamallah's urgent return with
his army to Shakka in October 1886 to defeat an angry Madibbo.
Karamallah then mistakenly assumed himself to be the heir to
Mohammed Khalid as ruler of Darfur, only to be driven back to Shakka

by Emir Yusuf. This was the background to Emin's inaccurate reference on 2 October 1886 to 'the retreat of Karamallah and the destruction of himself and all his people on the border of Kordofan'.

The withdrawal of the Mahdist threat encouraged Emin's designated commanders at Lado and Rejaf to resume their cattle *razzias* against the Bari. Karamallah's retirement and the successful risings of the Dinka against Rumbek and then Bor encouraged the Bari in turn to retaliate against Emin's outposts. Alloron, their former chief at Gondokoro and Baker's old enemy, had been murdered in May 1884 planning an attack on Lado, to be succeeded seemingly by Chief Kenyi; but the sieges now directed by the Bari against Lado, Gondokoro and Rejaf in October 1885 ultimately failed notwithstanding Dinka and Shir support.

Nevertheless Emin would insist in a letter to Dr Felkin in July 1886, while still holding out in Wadelai and hoping for instructions from Cairo, that contrary to the beliefs expressed by H. M. Stanley and Georg Schweinfurth, the former slave-dealers put down by Gessi were not 'over-running this country'; that on the contrary Bahr el Ghazal district had by Karamallah's 'retreat been totally freed from the slave-dealers' and that 'in my province I have but 62 Danagla left'. The erstwhile slaves repossessed by the *jallaba* on the departure of Lupton would however have since gone north with their former masters.

At Wadelai since July 1885 Emin would keep contact by steamer via Dufile with his remaining outposts, sustained by a caravan of supplies from Bunyoro paid for by Junker.

Having failed to establish relations with Kabarega on his Bunyoro visit in 1885, Junker resolved to try a second time on 2 January 1886, intending to move thence to Buganda and so to Zanzibar. Sailing on the *Khedive* to Lake Albert, he marched to Mpara, Kabarega's present capital, armed with letters from Emin to Sir John Kirk, British consul-general, which Junker would send on via Buganda to Zanzibar, despite hostilities breaking out between Bunyoro and Buganda. By 26 February 1886 Junker's escort and courier had returned from Zanzibar with a letter from Kirk with news of Gordon's death and a telegram from Nubar Pasha dated 16 January 1884 advising Emin of the evacuation of the Sudan and authorising him to retire on Zanzibar.

Bunyoro would emerge victorious in the war against the new Buganda *kabaka*, M'wanga son of M'tesa (who had in October 1884 been responsible for the murder in Busoga of Bishop Hannington), so enabling Junker to escape via Lake Victoria to join a caravan reaching

Zanzibar in September 1886. His recommendation of a British expedition to relieve Emin and consolidate Equatoria fell on deaf ears in London. Emin, after many years' isolation, was conscious that collectively his Lado militia were split between withdrawal north and south. Meanwhile he sent Casati to his friend Kabarega as a communication link with the outside world. In April 1887 Emin would write to Felkin:

> I have been obliged to evacuate Lado, as it was impossible for me to supply the garrison there with corn; but, as a set-off to the loss of this station, I have been able to reoccupy the district of Makaraka. At present therefore we occupy the whole of my former stations in Makaraka: Rejaf, Bedden, Kirri, Muggi, Labore, Khor Ayu, Dufile, Fatiko, Fadibek, Wadelai, Songa and Mahagi, nearly all the stations which were originally entrusted to me by General Gordon; and I intend and expect to keep them all. I should like here again to mention that if a relief expedition comes to us, I will on no account leave my people... All we want England to do is to bring about a better understanding with Uganda and to provide us with a free and safe way to the coast.[15]

In 1887 Emin would be promoted *lewa* and *pasha* for his services to Egypt.

Eastern Sudan   Fariq Valentine Baker's instructions in assuming command at Suakin included the pacification of the region between Suakin and Berber and maintenance of the telegraph: primarily through diplomacy; only if resisted, by force. His arrival in Suakin on 23 December 1883 was followed by a column of reinforcements of Black troops but not, as intended, under Zubeir Pasha, for British public objection led to its cancellation on 14 January 1884. Sinkat and Tokar remained besieged, Massawa, Kassala and Sennaheit quiet. By the time Baker had reconnoitred his governorate Nubar Pasha was chief minister, necessitating fresh instructions on 11 January 1884 in the context of the abandonment of the Sudan. The directive to open the Suakin–Berber road westwards of Sinkat must now be executed by diplomatic means not by force, following advice from a Khartoum governorate anxious to facilitate the safe evacuation of their civilians.

Indeed the cancellation of Zubeir's command of the gendarmerie and of his reinforcements left Baker little immediate alternative. He had been planning to commit the latter at once to the relief of the Tokar garrison which was running out of ammunition. The calibre and morale of the existing Suakin troops in Suakin was decidedly low, and the prospects of successfully relieving the courageous Tawfiq Bey in Sinkat – besieged now for over six months, desperately short of provisions, and accessible only through vulnerable mountainous country – were even more pessimistic (see pp. 418–19). Tawfiq was therefore sent authority to negotiate terms with the besieging force at his discretion and Baker, on 18 January 1884, set out by sea to Trinkitat himself to relieve Tokar with 3,500 men. On 4 February they were attacked by the Beja Mahdist force near the wells at El Teb once again under the *amir* Abdallah Hamid, where Mahmoud Tahir's force had been massacred previously. The Egyptian battalions panicked, broke the square, and ran. C. F. Moberly Bell, the *Times* special correspondent in Cairo, would write: 'Baker refused for a long time to leave the field and was apparently indifferent of his life. At last Colonel Hay forced him to go, and he, Hay, Burnaby and Harvey, without drawing their swords, charged through the rebels who were surrounding them and who made way for them.' 2,000 government troops were killed; 300 *Ansar*.

Four days later, faced with starvation and resigned to the fact that no relief would reach Sinkat, the heroic Cretan *qa'immaqam* Mohammed Tawfiq Bey held a council which determined to risk death in a breakout to Suakin thirty miles distant, having spiked their guns and destroyed all immovable equipment. The 500-strong garrison were caught one mile away, formed a defensive square surrounding their families, and only thirty women and six men survived. Osman Digna paid tribute to Tawfiq: 'One of the ablest of the accursed 'Ala el Din's men, renowned for his bravery and good administration.' As for the Tokar garrison, hearing of the defeat of the Baker relief force, they promptly negotiated a surrender.

News of the Sinkat massacre reached London on 12 February 1884 (but of Tokar not until 24 February) as the government faced a vote of censure in the House of Commons on its Egyptian policy in the wake of Baker's defeat at El Teb, a censure they were nevertheless able to escape on the last day of the debate when Gordon had successfully reached Khartoum, emboldening Lord Hartington's winding-up to dismiss any responsibility for the evacuation of the Sudan. 'I contend that we are not responsible for the rescue or relief of the garrisons either in the Western or the Southern or the Eastern Sudan': here was a reinterpretation of Granville's hand-written instructions to Gordon a month before. Nevertheless, to placate public opinion Major-General Sir Gerald Graham, VC, was ordered by Cairo to Suakin with 4,000

British-Egyptian reinforcements to arrive mid-February and strengthen the resistance to Osman Digna's, largely Hadendoa, encircling force of 20,000.

As already related, the arrival of Gordon and Stewart on 11 February 1884 at Berber unhappily coincided with news of Baker's defeat at El Teb, prompting Gordon's proclamation of the 'abandonment' firman the next day as news of the loss of Sinkat was received. Graham was one who believed he was aided by Gordon's proclamation, but the submission of the Bisharin to Hussein Khalifa was quite undone. General Graham was successfully able to restore the local situation at Suakin itself with two consecutive victories. The first – the 'Third Battle of the Coast' in Mahdist history – took place again at El Teb on 29 February 1884, the advance having been originally intended to relieve Tokar; and resulted in the death of the *amir* Abdallah Hamid and 3,000 *Ansar* casualties of whom half were killed. Graham lost 34 killed. Brigadier-General Herbert Stewart commanded the cavalry. The second victory, at Tamai (El Tamaynab) in scrub eight miles from Suakin on 13 March, was achieved at the cost of heavy casualties on both sides (Rudyard Kipling paid tribute to the breaking of a British square – the Beja armed only with spears and swords fighting with great ferocity). Osman Digna's forces then retired to the hills.

If the craven British government were content that Baker's defeat had been publicly avenged, their leading backbenchers of what Cromer would call 'the party of bellicose philanthropy', backed nevertheless by the Conservative opposition, used the occasion to condemn the slaughter of Arabs by General Graham, while an erroneous *Times* newspaper report that Lieutenant-Colonel J. D. H. Stewart was advancing on the White Nile with a hostile party of *bashi-buzouqs* was deemed to constitute Gordon's guilt by association with Graham's initiative. The outcome was that the 10 March Parliamentary debate on the Graham expedition estimates became a political vehicle to criticise Zubeir's proposed appointment. Public opinion became further exacerbated and the recommendation of General Graham, backed by Vice-Admiral William Hewett, VC, and by Baring, that the military successes should be followed up by an advance to Sinkat in order to purchase local tribal acquiescence in the opening of the Suakin–Berber route, was met by Government prevarication. At last on 26 March, now nearing the hot season, Graham was pusillanimously instructed that 'the operations in which you are now engaged must be limited to the pacification of the district around Suakin and restoring communication with Berber, if possible by other means and influence of friendly tribes... and preparations made for the immediate embarkation of the bulk of your force.'

Moberly Bell would later write to Baring:

Those government telegrams of 5 [opposing Zubeir's succession to Gordon] and 26 March 1884 would have given me such a feeling of contempt for their inability to grasp the whole situation that I should have been tempted to throw them over and have acted on my own judgement. In that case is it not possible that they might have recognised the fait accompli and followed you – I mean if you had sent Zubeir in spite of them?

Baring, to his considerable credit, had on 24 March 1884 telegraphed Granville recommending that an effort be made to help Gordon from Suakin, while conceding that Stephenson and Wood identified great risk to health and 'extraordinary military risks'. When on 26 the Cabinet directed that the dispatch of a British force to Berber was unjustifiable Baring wrote in expostulation (see pp. 439–40). In *Modern Egypt* he would affirm not only that Stephenson and Wood, despite the risks, had thought the undertaking possible but that 'the operation should be undertaken'. Baring was rebuffed, and three weeks later called to London for the international conference on Egyptian finance, which Gladstone regarded as far more important than the Sudan and indeed its positive outcome to be a prerequisite for the evacuation of British troops from Egypt. In the event the London Convention of March 1885 would be signed a year later but on terms too onerous for the creation of a successor Egyptian government. Baring meanwhile would be absent from Cairo in the crucial months April–October 1884.

As for General Graham at Suakin, obediently he embarked for Suez on 3 April 1884, followed by his troops. Vice-Admiral Hewett remained in command of Suakin and the littoral. Osman Digna's Beja forces would continue to control the hinterland of Suakin – Sinkat, Tokar and the Berber route – though increasingly troubled by the hostility of the Amarar supplied from Suakin.[16]

Suakin was a beleaguered port. With its five forts, gun emplacements and warship protection it was however too strong for subjugation. Meanwhile the south of the province remained quiet with the American Mason Bey, formerly of Equatoria, made governor of Massawa by Baker. Gordon, on arrival at Khartoum on 18 February 1884, had at once expressed concern about the evacuation of Kassala, which could not be effected westwards via Khartoum, but equally could still afford an alternative escape route from Sennar to the Red Sea. Indeed on 11 February an attack by the Mahdist-appointed *amir* for Kassala, Mustapha Ali Hadal, had been successfully repulsed by the *mudir*, Ahmed Pasha Iffat, who a year later, despite authority after the fall of Khartoum to evacuate the garrison to Abyssinia, would steadfastly defend Kassala town against a siege which would last until 29 July 1885. In this Ahmed Pasha was initially much aided by El Sayyid Mohammed Osman el Mirghani who, despite his earlier failure with the Hadendoa, continued to express staunch support from neighbouring Khatmiya for the besieged force until, in May 1885, he felt obliged to withdraw to Egypt. Iffat, having allegedly refused to surrender in July, is reported by an eyewitness, Yuzbashi Abdallah Adlan, a survivor of Khartoum's capture, to have been executed by the Mahdist commander, (Mohammed) Osman Abu Qarja. Holt however states that Iffat's life was spared and that he subsequently conspired to take Kassala after Osman Digna had been defeated by the Abyssinian ruler of Bogos, Ras Alula Engeda, in September 1885. Only then was Iffat executed, by Osman Digna on the latter's return to Kassala.

The Egyptian littoral extended east of Aden nominally to Ras Hafoun, incorporating Berbera and Harar. With abandonment of the Sudan now the adopted policy, Baring had been requested on 19 January 1884 to send a British officer to report on the viability of reductions in the garrisons of Harar with Zeyla, and of Berbera. Major Hunter (Indian Army) from Aden was ordered at the Cairo meeting on 25 January 1884 to make a personal reconnaissance.

The administration at least of Harar being found seriously defective, Mohammed Radwan Pasha (previously sent by the former Khedive in 1873 to occupy Berbera) was deputed in co-operation with Hunter to organise the evacuation of both the Somali coast and Harar. Radwan sailed from Suez on 13 September 1884, collecting Hunter from Aden, and sailing to Berbera where the Khedivial proclamation of evacuation was publicly read. While Radwan and Lieutenant Peyton proceeded to Harar, there to publish the Khedivial firman and withdraw part of the garrison to Zeyla, Hunter at the instigation of the British India Office went on to Zeyla to hand over occupation of both Berbera and Zeyla to the British consul. He then joined Radwan in Harar for the handover of rule to the son of the deposed former ruler Abdallah Mohammed Abdel Shakur. Together they evacuated the remaining 6,500 Egyptian troops in April 1885.

Earlier, following his arrival as general-governor in Suakin at the end of 1883, Baker Pasha had recommended negotiations with Emperor John's minister Ras Alula in order to ensure the security of the Kassala–Massawa road via Keren in Bogos, while in return prepared formally to cede Gallabat and southern Bogos into Abyssinian hands. By May 1884 these negotiations had had the approval in principle of London, and Vice-Admiral Hewett led a mission to Adwa in Tigré. Notification was given to Abyssinia of Egypt's intention to withdraw from Kassala (still besieged); Gedaref (already captured in April 1884 by the Mahdists through the agency of the Shukriya Sheikh Abdallah, brother of the loyalist Sheikh Awad el Karim Pasha Abu Sin); and Gallabat, eventually evacuated with the help of Abyssinian soldiers in February 1885, via Massawa. Under this Adwa (Adowa) Peace Treaty of 3 June 1884 Bogos was surrendered by its Egyptian garrison to Ras Alula, and Abyssinia was granted the right of free importation of goods, including arms and ammunition, through Massawa. In the event the Negus would have gained little from the withdrawal of his former Egyptian enemy, for he would now confront the more formidable and independent Mahdist rulers across the uncertain frontier. Indeed to his rage, Britain, citing the Treaty clause that Massawa was to remain 'under British protection' proceeded, on the evacuation of Egyptian troops, to hand over the port to Italy on 5 February 1885. From there, even before the death of Emperor John IV in 1889, the Italians would commence their advance to occupy Bogos and Hamasein, despite a massacre of their first garrison by Ras Alula Engeda of Asmara in 1887.[17]

Berber and Dongola   Gordon's February 1884 proclamation in Berber of the intention to withdraw from the Sudan, coupled with the multiple successes of the Mahdi's *amir* Osman Digna in the Suakin hinterland, had rendered impossible the position of Hussein Pasha Khalifa, reinstated in December 1883 as general-governor both of Berber and Dongola. As already chronicled, the Mahdi was emboldened to appoint his former mentor Sheikh Mohammed el Kheir Abdallah Khojali an *amir*, and, in April 1884, to proceed to claim Shendi, El Damer and Berber for the Mahdist cause. In vain Hussein Khalifa petitioned Cairo for troops to save Berber. When, after a seven-day siege, Berber was conquered on 19 May and Hussein Khalifa sent captive to the Mahdi at El Rahad, £E60,000, deposited by Gordon at Berber on his way south to facilitate the evacuation, tumbled as a windfall into Mahdist hands. Already the Suakin–Berber route had been cut in

February 1884 and the Berber–Khartoum route in March so that Gordon, denied assistance by the Gladstone government, was trapped but remained equally determined not to abandon those whose safety had been formally committed to his charge.

On the reinstatement in December 1883 of Hussein Pasha Khalifa as general-governor (see p. 203) after his unjust detention ten years earlier, the *mudir* of Dongola since 1879, Mustapha Bey Jawar, had been retired. Mustapha however would be himself reinstated to Dongola by Cairo on the arrival of Gordon and Stewart, and to him was sent from Berber a copy of Gordon's proclamation of abandonment. Ohrwalder claimed that like Hussein Khalifa, Mustapha Bey now wrote to a friend in El Obeid to enquire further into the credentials of the Mahdi. A Circassian by birth and a former slave of Viceroy Abbas, Mustapha was himself shrewdly exploring the respective strengths of the two combatants. The Mahdi decided to send two trusted *amirs*, Mahmoud Mohammed and Ahmed el Hudai, to take over the Dongola *muderia* and to call Mustapha Jawar to meet the Mahdi in person at El Rahad.

Amir Ahmed el Hudai seems to have set off from El Rahad in May 1884, striking north probably along the Wadi el Melik and arriving at Merowe soon after the suppression by Mustapha at the end of May of a Sha'iqi rebellion at Korti and Merowe. Retracing his steps west down the Nile, Ahmed el Hudai was defeated by Mustapha in late July at Debba, returning to Merowe to await reinforcements from Mahdist Berber. On 2 July the Mahdi had already dispatched a further force of 800 from El Rahad under Amir Mahmoud, who was to be appointed senior *amir* of Dongola over a supposedly compliant Mustapha and Ahmed el Hudai. Major Herbert Kitchener also arrived at Dongola in July to investigate on the part of the Egyptian army Mustapha Bey's leanings, and would accompany the latter to Debba and Ambukol. Meanwhile Mahmoud and Ahmed el Hudai, who had joined forces at Merowe in early September 1884, would both be defeated and killed by Mustapha at Korti – the Mahdi's letter to Mustapha Bey being recovered from Mahmoud's body.

This was a serious, if temporary, reverse for the Mahdi and sustained in spite of his own family antecedents in Dongola. With the Atmur desert crossing from Korosko to Abu Hamed already threatened by the occupation of Berber by the *Ansar*, the only alternative land access from Egypt to Khartoum was via the Nile and then across the Bayuda desert from Korti to Metemma and Shendi. The possession of Dongola was thus crucial to any relief force sent to assist the evacuation of Khartoum, granted the government had already set its face against the recapture of Berber. Cairo's suspicions of Mustapha Bey's real intentions had now been allayed. His powerful ascetic personality coupled with his monopoly of local intelligence sources persuaded the government to identify him as the future Governor-General of the Sudan after Gordon had evacuated Khartoum. Kitchener was meanwhile encouraged to enter discussions with Sheikh Saleh Fadlallah of the Kababish.

No one was more conscious of the importance of Dongola and the Bayuda route than Gordon besieged in Khartoum. On 7 April 1884 he had at last received a messenger from Berber carrying Baring's message of 10 March warning Gordon of his understanding that 'there is no intention on the part of the (British) government to send an English face to Berber', a decision confirmed by London to Baring on 28 March. On 19 May Berber fell to the Mahdists and on 23 June, the Nile now rising, Gordon successfully sent a tiny piece of paper to Mustapha Bey at Dongola asking for news of an expedition from Cairo, a message which safely reached its destination four weeks later, before Mustapha Bey's victory at Debba.

When Gordon's enquiry was transmitted to London, there was no news to be had of any expedition because, having at the end of March turned down Baring's plea, the British Cabinet at the end of July remained still deeply divided about its need. Several members were quite unsympathetic on the grounds that Gordon's absence of reply to their telegrams of 23 April and 17 May was deliberate – neither in fact reached him until respectively 29 July and August 1884. They affirmed that he was disobeying his instructions in seeking to set up a successor administration and in embarking upon aggressive strikes against Mahdist forces in the vicinity – a view which the Marquess of Hartington (War Office) and the Earl of Selborne (Lord Chancellor) quite rejected. Gladstone remained opposed to an expedition for it would invite conflict – 'a war of conquest against a people struggling to be free'. Nevertheless Hartington was determined that before the summer recess there should a Cabinet policy on the relief of Khartoum. On 15 July 1884 Hartington, the Earl of Northbrook (Admiralty), General Lord Wolseley (presently Adjutant General) and Sir Evelyn Baring (in London since April to wrestle with the report of the International Conference on Egyptian Finance) had unanimously recommended that, while Dongola's protection was contingent on the question of the Khartoum relief expedition, 'the Cabinet must decide on whether Gordon is to be left to his fate or to be rescued by force'. Again the Cabinet was divided but while avoiding a commitment to relief operations agreed that a contingent grant of £300,000 should be approved in case of its need.

Further valuable time was lost due to a disagreement between General Stephenson, who reasonably if belatedly favoured the shorter Suakin–Berber relief route, and General Wolseley who, influenced by his 1870 Canadian river campaigns, advocated the Nile route. Moreover Stephenson was also insisting on passing the expedition steamers over the second cataract at once. The issue was to be resolved only by the former's replacement by Wolseley on 22 August. By 9 September Wolseley had arrived in Cairo, the expedition now formally sanctioned. Baring as well as Northbrook (ostensibly to deal with unresolved Egyptian financial problems) accompanied him. By 21 September 1884 the three of them had drafted Wolseley's instructions, whereby Wolseley as well as commander-in-chief would, by Khedivial firman, assume full civil and political powers in the Sudan as far south as Khartoum. By early October Wolseley was at Wadi Halfa planning for Mustapha Jawar to succeed as the future independent Governor-General of Khartoum, Berber, Abu Hamed and Dongola under nominal suzerainty of the Khedive; and on 3 November Mustapha Jawar received his firman from Wolseley and was made *pasha* and KCMG.

Gordon, who knew of none of these developments nor of Mustapha Jawar's victories over the *Ansar* at Debba and Korti, had himself, after successful military sorties in the vicinity of Khartoum, suffered on 5 September a disastrous reverse at Umm Dubban on the Blue Nile in which his commander and 1,000 men were killed, gravely restricting his freedom of movement thereafter and undermining morale. With the Nile flood now at its peak, concluding that he could forseeably do nothing himself to recapture Berber nor anticipate a relief force, he gambled on Colonel Stewart in the steamer *Abbas* forcing a passage through the Sabaluqa gorge and past Berber, in order to represent in person in Egypt the extreme urgency of the Khartoum and Sennar situation. With the British consul, Power; the French consul Herbin and Levantine merchants, Stewart left in an armed convoy on 9 September. The gorge and Berber were successfully negotiated but the *Abbas*, now mistakenly unescorted and having ridden the fifth cataract to pass Abu Hamed, would 200 miles beyond, on 18 September, unhappily strike a rock following the wrong channel. Lured from pursuing their descent of the Nile in their small boat by Manasir elders with the bait of camels for hire, the three Europeans were then murdered. They were only a hundred miles from Merowe, where Major Kitchener was present. With them were lost the journals of Gordon's chief of staff Colonel Stewart since early March and, importantly too, the cipher books.

Wolseley's main relief force reached Korti on 16 December. He planned to send one column to advance up the Nile via Abu Hamed on Berber, and the main force under Major-General Sir Herbert Stewart across the Bayuda desert to Metemma. Wolseley intended to accompany the latter in person but, with unpredictable consequences, was dissuaded from doing so by Lord Hartington in London. Stewart eventually left Korti on 8 January 1885, but because of the necessity for the force to carry its own supplies of food and water across the Bayuda desert and the non-availability of sufficient baggage carriages it was necessary to halt halfway at Jaqdul pending the camels' return from Korti having collected the additional supplies – a delay of nine days and the forfeiture of the element of surprise.

On 30 December 1884 a message dated 14 December had arrived from Gordon urging Wolseley to hasten on via Metemma or Berber, but not to leave the latter unsubjugated in his rear. Near Metemma Gordon's armoured steamers had been awaiting the relief force since October. To his sister Gordon insisted on 5 November: 'I decline to agree that the expedition comes for my relief; it comes for the relief of the garrisons, which I failed to accomplish. I expect Her Majesty's Government are in a precious rage with me for holding out and forcing their hand.'

Wolseley meanwhile felt obliged to send immediately a separate force under Major-General William Earle by the Nile to take Berber. In the event Earle would be killed in February before Berber had been reached. Meanwhile on 16 January 1885, across the Bayuda desert at Abu Klea (Abu Tulaih), General Stewart's desert column found its route barred by 10,000 *Ansar*. Major Kitchener, who had effected the transportation baggage to the halfway point, had himself been obliged to return to Korti.

This Mahdist force comprised one contingent, largely Ja'aliyin, raised by Amir Mohammed el Kheir and commanded by Abdel Magid Ahmed; and a second under Musa Mohammed, brother of Khalifa wad Hilu, dispatched in haste to counter this threat by the Mahdi, now at Omdurman. Stewart roundly defeated them the next day, killing 1,000 including Musa wad Hilu, only to be ambushed two days later, on 19

January 1885, four miles from the Nile by further reinforcements from Omdurman under El Nur Mohammed Anqara, formerly government commander at Bara and now a Mahdist *amir*. In this second brief but again victorious encounter Stewart himself was mortally wounded and his deputy, Colonel Frederick Burnaby, killed. General Stewart's last action was to hand over command of the expedition to his column intelligence officer, Colonel Sir Charles Wilson, previously designated to leave immediately when Gordon's steamers reached Metemma in order to contact Gordon at Khartoum. The steamers arrived at 10 a.m. following which Wilson was to attack Metemma on the west bank on 21 January 1885.[18]

Khartoum and Sennar   The British Cabinet had declined to heed the firm, unequivocal advice of Baring in late March 1884. They had sent Gordon and Stewart to Khartoum to evacuate the Egyptian resident population of Khartoum and Sennar (much of which, in the former case, had been accomplished before the closing of the Berber route and the effective declaration of war by the Mahdi) and to create a successor administration. They were in honour obligated to send succour to withdraw their besieged servants. Gladstone's government, adherents to a British policy of non-involvement, despite having been temporarily drawn in to the occupation of Egypt, were unwilling to recognise that, as had been the case with Consul Cameron twenty years earlier, Gordon and Stewart were acting under British orders, in this case exercised by the British consul-general in Cairo. Unlike Cameron and his companions, Gordon and Stewart were not under arrest by a foreign power but, in implementing an authorised humanitarian mission, they had been interrupted by the *force majeure* of advancing Mahdist conquest. As the British foreign minister at the time of Magdala, Lord Stanley, had put it, even if British public opinion would have tolerated leaving Cameron to his fate (the matter was not put to the test), 'You hold power not by force but in great measure by the knowledge and belief that, however mildly and justly British authority may be exercised, it is in the last resort backed by force which cannot be resisted.' (See p. 69.) As yet there was no recognition of such reality.

The British government had chosen instead to eschew Baring's advice both that a relief column be dispatched to reopen the Berber–Korosko or Berber–Suakin routes for evacuation, and that Zubeir Pasha be sent to bolster the successor Khartoum administration. On 21 April 1884 Baring had been temporarily withdrawn from Cairo to attend allegedly more demanding problems in London relating to European financial interests in Egypt. The fact also that their servants, Gordon and Stewart, were cut off from communication with Cairo was not recognised by the British government. Four months of summer and inaction would pass before, on the approach of the August Parliamentary recess, belated reconsiderations of honour and the pressure of British public opinion brought about a reversal of that policy of military non-intervention. Its dramatic failure, due to earlier ministerial divisions and procrastination, would nevertheless eventually have its influence on the future direction of British Nile policy under the pressure of other European interests.

Meanwhile the military strategy of the Mahdi, his Khalifas, his *amirs* (now named *a'amils*) and his Ashraf (circle of relations) had been attended by successive triumphs in the wake of the victory of Sheikan. Amir Osman Abu Bakr Digna had by March occupied the eastern Sudan except for Suakin, Massawa and Kassala. Amir Mohammed el Kheir Abdallah Khojali would by May possess the Ja'ali and Ababda towns of the Nile from Shendi northwards to Abu Hamed. Amir Hamdan Abu Anja with Amir Abdel Rahman el Nejumi in February and again in May had crushed rebellions by the Nuba of Jebel el Dayir.

The *Ansar* tactics adopted towards Khartoum and the Gezira were less clear cut, in the light of Egypt's implementation of the policy of abandonment. The Mahdi's father-in-law Amir Mohammed el Tayyib el Basir had by February 1884 arrived in the Gezira to claim the adherence of the tribes, prompting the Egyptian commander at Mesellimiya, Lewa Salih Pasha el Mek el Sha'iqi, to call on Gordon for military assistance. Sheikh Awad el Karim Abu Sin of the Shukriya, whose brother at Gedaref had already defected to the *Ansar*, felt similarly vulnerable and although he was Gordon's appointed leader of the Council of Notables, threatened to lead his tribe to join the Mahdi. The Council of Notables felt forced to send troops both to the Blue and White Niles to strengthen the garrisons and Gordon, publicly committed to peace, could not gainsay them. It was without avail. Two months later his supplies exhausted, Salih would surrender with his steamer *Mohammed Ali*.

Sheikh el Ubayd Bakr, despite Gordon's personal plea not to resort to force, had meanwhile marched his rebel contingent from Umm Dubban northwards avoiding Khartoum and on 12 March seized the Egyptian strong-point at Halfaya nine miles to its north – even as the Mahdi was dispatching from El Obeid his reply to Gordon's letter from Berber which had affirmed Gordon's peaceful intentions. Whether or not it was in accordance with Mahdist strategy, the trap had been sprung, evacuation halted and communication with Berber and Cairo interrupted. Learning of Gordon's subsequent refusal to surrender on 18 March, the Mahdi dispatched Mohammed Osman Abu Qarja to enforce the surrender of Salih Pasha besieged on an island near Mesellimiya.

In the summer months until the Nile commenced to rise Gordon, his officials, his garrison and Sudanese adherents were besieged, able to make only the occasional foray such as that, unsuccessfully, of Sati Bey, Lupton's lieutenant, up the White Nile in early July. A victim of the tergiversations of the London government, Gordon was helpless to pursue the abandonment policy, 'obliged to trust to God alone'. He might write to his sister of the great advantages he possessed with the fleet of steamers, but their mobility and the power of his position were dependent on the rise of the Nile not due before June. At the end of July, with the Nile now risen, his commander Lewa Mohammed Ali Pasha Hussein cleared the *Ansar* from their position near Khartoum commanding the Blue Nile, and then three weeks later swept Amir Abu Qarja out of Gereif and Abu Haraz. Halfaya was recaptured on 24 August, Sheikh El Ubayd driven back to Umm Dubban, thus enabling Gordon to plan the capture of Berber by a steamer force under Colonel Stewart. Then, on 9 September, came disaster, with the annihilation of Mohammed Ali Pasha at Umm Dubban, imprudently separated from his three steamers and tricked into an ambush in thick woods.

Meanwhile, with his army, massed at El Obeid, having proved too heavy a burden upon the supplies of the neighbourhood, the Mahdi had moved on in April 1884 to El Rahad to prepare for the encirclement of Gordon in Khartoum but, equally, to await the end of the rains. Mahmoud Abdel Qadir, his uncle, veteran of the annihilation of Yusuf el Shallali's force at El Qadīr two years earlier, was left in charge at El Obeid. The advance guard of the planned siege of Khartoum led by Amir Abdel Rahman el Nejumi, back from a minor war with the Nuba of Jebel Dayir, moved off on 25 June 1884 towards the left bank of the White Nile, reaching it in September and moving on to the vicinity of Khartoum and Omdurman. There they redeployed with the forces of Osman Abu Qarja, recently expelled from Gereif, and El Ubayd Bakr from Halfaya, in order to encompass Khartoum and Omdurman.

The Mahdi quit El Rahad on 22 August with an army numbering perhaps 60,000, seemingly retracing the route taken by Hicks through Shatt, reaching the White Nile at Dueim, and moving by the east bank to Tur'a el Khadra. He encamped an hour's march south of Omdurman on 23 October, at once commencing preparations for an assault on the fortifications of the town which was under the command of the Sudanese Lewa Faraj Allah Pasha Raghib. The strong walls defending Omdurman town against enemy infiltration between it and the river were fronted by a deep trench, and this was attacked by the *Ansar* troops led by Hamdan Abu Anja under the orders of the Khalifa Abdullahi on 12 November. The defenders were aided by Gordon's two remaining armed steamers, the *Ismailia* and the new small *Hussainiya* (which was sunk in the shallows), and by sorties from Khartoum against the besiegers.

For two months, although latterly cut off from the river, the Omdurman garrison would tenaciously hold out until, its food and munitions exhausted, Gordon signalled leave to surrender on 5 (or perhaps 15) January 1885. Heavy casualties had been incurred and great courage displayed on both sides. The noose around Khartoum had been drawn tighter and the morale of its inhabitants further sapped. Only the swift arrival of the Relief Force could save Khartoum and its Governor-General, his troops commanded by Ibrahim Pasha Fawzi. Food supplies were now so much diminished – Gordon originally believed rations could not be extended beyond the end of December – that some ten days into January 1885 he ordered, perhaps belatedly, that civilians should be permitted to cross the two Niles by boats and appealed to the Mahdi to succour them, a request the Mahdi heeded.

To the north, the consequences of the succession of Sir Charles Wilson to command the relief force near Metemma on the mortal wounding of Sir Herbert Stewart would prove critical. Bernard Allen, whose account of Gordon's achievements in the Sudan 1874-79 and 1884-85 remains, seventy years after its publication, unrivalled, investigated the responsibilities for the delay in Wilson's departure from Metemma for Khartoum in the light of his instructions from Lord Wolseley – received when he was intelligence officer, not expedition commander – on the expedition reaching the Nile. These instructions ordered Wilson to leave to Khartoum 'as soon as Lord Charles Beresford [head of the Naval Brigade] reports he is ready to proceed with one or more steamers to Khartoum', there to deliver Wolseley's letter to Gordon. Three of the four steamers of the flotilla, dispatched by Gordon to Shendi under Miralai Mohammed Nushi (Nutzi) Pasha to patrol the Nile in the vicinity of Metemma (which they had reached originally on 5 October

1884), arrived at El Qubba (Qubat) two miles south of Metemma at 10 a.m. on 21 January 1885 even before Wilson's successful attack on the town. Nushi not only brought six volumes of Gordon's *Journals* but three letters, recently fetched from Gordon and dated 14 December, urging haste lest Khartoum be lost. Wilson however, now force commander, delayed three days until 24 January before setting off with the Sha'iqi flotilla commander, Mohammed Khashm el Mus Bey, for Khartoum with two steamers – the *Bordein* and the *Tel Hawain* and an escort of 220 troops including twenty British redcoats.

In this decision Wilson was influenced by his responsibilities for the safety of the force he was leaving at Metemma; by the temporary incapacity of Beresford who further contributed to the delay by urging the interim use of the steamers to reconnoitre to the north; and by the understanding that he, Wilson, would be delivering Wolseley's letter and conferring with Gordon before leaving three officers with Gordon at Khartoum and returning to Metemma. On a falling Nile, the *Bordein* on 25 January, the day after the delayed departure for Khartoum, first struck a rock and then ran aground on a sandbank. The two steamers would eventually reach Khartoum on 28 January, two days after the *Ansar* captured Khartoum.

Other final messages from Gordon may well have been intercepted. His clerk kept an Arabic copy of one dated 29 December 1884, given to a messenger to take to Dongola, but never delivered. The copy was concealed in a rifle cartridge and survived the clerk's captivity under the *Ansar* and his subsequent escape. It read:

> I would at once, calling to mind what I have gone through, inform their Majesties of the action of Great Britain and the Ottoman Empire who appointed me as Governor-General of the Sudan for the purpose of appeasing the rebellion in that country.
>
> During the twelve months that I have been here these two Powers, the one remarkable for her wealth, the other for her military force, have remained unaffected by my situation. Although I am personally too insignificant to be taken into account the Powers were bound, nevertheless, to fulfil the engagement upon which my engagement was based, so as to shield the honour of their Governments.
>
> What I have gone through I cannot describe. The Almighty God will help me.

News of the defeat of the *Ansar* on 17 January at Abu Klea arrived at

Omdurman on 20 January and an urgent conference of religious and military leaders was convened to discuss the wisdom of a retreat to El Obeid in anticipation of the arrival of the Relief Force – a course initially favoured by the majority together with the Mahdi. The *feki* Medawi would later comment that if the British 'had come at once... the Mahdi might have carried out his intention of making a *hijra* south, but the delay strengthened Abdel Karim'. Mohammed Abdel Karim, the Mahdi's uncle, resolutely opposed the concept of retreat. By 25 January, in the absence of fresh news of the British advance, having crossed the White Nile by boat to Kalaka south of Khartoum, the Mahdi convened a second conference of all his followers and commanders and ordered the attack on Khartoum for that night. The troops, crossing by a sandbank exposed by the falling White Nile, rapidly overcame the resistance.

The young Sheikh Babikr Bedri, an *Ansar* participant in the battle, affirmed in his autobiography that in the very early morning of 26 January 'the Mahdi insisted to us: "Gordon is not to be killed, nor Sheikh Hussein el Majdi [Yousef Bedri suggests Hussein el Mohamedi], nor *feki* El Amin el Darir" nor another head of the Sudan *'ulema*, Sheikh Mohammed el Saqqa.' Babikr relates that he arrived at the Khartoum Palace at '4 o'clock' to find Gordon struck down and covered with blood, and Sheikh Hussein also dead – both of whose lives two hours earlier the Mahdi had ordered to be spared. Sheikh el Amin El Darir was not harmed.

The exact circumstances of Gordon's death are uncertain. He may, as related by Father Ohrwalder (at El Obeid until April 1886), have been speared on the staircase of the palace; or – as attested by a Turkish sergeant, who escaped to Suakin in November 1887 and claimed to have been an eyewitness and one of Gordon's four orderlies on that morning – after he had descended the staircase. According to the sergeant's recollection, a Baqqara *sheikh* and escort galloped up and told Gordon that the Mahdi had ordered him to bring Gordon to him alive. The *sheikh* repeated the order three times, and Gordon three times refused to go, insisting that he would die where he was. The *sheikh* then drew his sword and struck Gordon, who was looking him straight in the face unflinching, over the left shoulder. Gordon's head was taken to the captured Slatin in Omdurman for identification, his body buried close to the palace, and a tomb built over it.

Felix in opportunitate mortis. Perhaps the words of Stephen Spender are an apt valediction (Poems XXVIII, 1933):

I think continually of those who were truly great.
Who, from the womb, remembered the soul's history.
Through corridors of light where the hours are suns
Endless and singing…
The names of those who in their lives fought for Life,
Who wore at their hearts the fire's centre.
Born of the sun they travelled a short while towards the sun,
And left the vivid air signed with their honour.

Gordon had never contemplated surrender. In November 1884 he had written in his Journal: 'I will stay here and fall with the town and run all the risks.' Previously in August he had written to a naval friend at Massawa: 'There is one bond of union between us and our troops – they know if the town is taken they will be sold as slaves; and we must deny our Lord if we would save our lives. I think we hate the latter more than they hate the former.' Clearly the Mahdi would not have sought of Gordon an abjuration of his faith, but for the latter himself to escape the fate of his companions was unthinkable. The bloody massacre of the inhabitants, especially of the Egyptians and Sha'iqiya of Khartoum, would continue until the afternoon of 26 January. Among the dead were Martin Hansal, the Austrian consul, and many remaining Levantines. Lewa Ibrahim Pasha Fawzi, wounded, survived a prisoner.

The Mahdi, as was his wont, entered the conquered town to pray the Friday prayer on 30 January – two days after Wilson had gallantly run the gauntlet of *Ansar* river bank artillery until, reaching the junction of the Niles, he took in the reality that the town had fallen and had to turn back. Captive in Omdurman remained Rudolf Slatin Pasha, Salih Pasha el Mek the Sha'iqi general, Ibrahim Pasha Fawzi and the British governor Lupton Pasha, recently arrived from El Obeid. There is no evidence that Gordon knew Lupton's whereabouts after Shakka fell, and both Gordon and Wilson would have been helpless to secure his release. The Mahdi, having entertained the possibility of making Khartoum his residence, would move from his encampment outside Omdurman to the proximity of its fort a few weeks later, obliging the Khalifa Abdullahi, who had himself taken residence in the palace at Khartoum, to quit the town for Omdurman.

Miralai Charles Watson Bey, formerly with Gordon in Equatoria and at this time surveyor-general at the Egyptian War Office, would in the preface to his biography of Colonel Sir Charles Wilson summarise the reasons for the failure of the Gordon Relief Expedition under five headings. First, the refusal of authority to General Graham at Suakin in March 1884 to force open the Suakin–Berber road. Secondly, the delay in authorising the expedition by the British governorate. Thirdly, the loss of time occasioned, on a falling Nile, by Lord Wolseley's insistence on delaying the passage of expedition steamers over the second cataract, pending the delivery of 800 whalers being built in Britain. Fourthly, the policy adopted with regard to the *mudir* of Dongola, Mustapha Jawar – whom Wilson cordially disliked but whom Major-General Sir Herbert Stewart correctly recognised to be the key authority at Dongola. And fifthly, the halting of the expedition at Jaqdul, the staging post and wells in the Bayuda desert. Watson believed that the want of sufficient camels preventing the expedition from an uninterrupted crossing of the Bayuda desert, causing a delay of twelve days and time enough for news of the expedition to alert the Mahdi so as to dispatch reinforcements, could have been avoided if the task had been taken in hand in good time.

In all, Watson estimated that the aggregate consequence of these errors to be a delay in the arrival of the relief expedition of nine months.[19]

News of the fall of Khartoum reached London on 4 February 1885, by which time Wilson had returned to El Qubba outside Metemma and Wolseley, still at Korti, had requested instructions of London, sending Major-General Redvers Buller, his chief of staff, to take command on 11 February of 1,600 men who were withdrawn twenty miles to Abu Klea wells, now under enhanced threat from Khartoum.

Such was public anger at the news that the British government now irrationally reversed its policy towards the Sudan. A new expedition was commissioned on 20 February 1885 under General Graham to muster at Suakin, totalling four brigades, including the Guards Brigade and artillery. It left Suakin on 20 March 1885 to attack Osman Digna – Tamai was occupied after two battles – and to supervise the first stage of the building of a new railroad to Berber.

'To my extreme astonishment, the Cabinet there have determined to fight it out with El Mahdi,' Wolseley would write. Allowed to exercise his own discretion as to when to attack, what objectives to target and what reinforcements to summon, Wolseley's initial plan was to attack in the autumn and meanwhile to seize Berber and Abu Hamed. The slow advance of his river column, and on 10 February 1885 the death of General Earle at Kirbekan, led him to delay the latter objectives and to re-concentrate his force at Dongola. By mid-March public anger in

London having abated and a Russian threat to Afghanistan looming, the British Cabinet had had still fresher thoughts. They recognised that even Wolseley doubted the value of a revenge, if temporary, occupation of Khartoum, and wished only to defeat the Mahdi. Meanwhile the Desert Column had been withdrawn across the Bayuda to Korti en route to Dongola. Baring wrote to London on 15 April counselling the avoidance of a fresh war in the Sudan and on 2 May the new Khartoum campaign was cancelled.

General Graham withdrew. His oversight of the new Khartoum project, the Suakin–Berber railway which at a cost of £E850,000 had advanced eighteen miles inland and been accompanied by some ineffectual raids, was similarly abandoned. The Beja army, despite an accumulated total of 10,000 killed in battle, remained unvanquished, possessing fighting qualities deeply respected by the British and immortalised in Kipling's soldier's epitaph:

> We've fought with many men acrost the seas,
> An' some of 'em was brave an' some was not:
> The Paythan an' the Zulu a' Burmese,
> But the Fuzzy was the finest o' the lot…
> Then 'ere's *to* you, Fuzzy-Wuzzy, an' the missis and the kid;
> Our orders was to break you, an' of course we went an' did.
> We sloshed you with Martinis, an' it wasn't t'ardly fair;
> But for all the odds agin' you, Fuzzy Wuz, you broke the square…
> 'E's the on'y thing that doesn't give a damn
> For a Regiment o' British Infantree!

Britain's declared objectives for recapturing Khartoum of February 1885 were to succour the surviving inhabitants of Khartoum; to create a government friendly to Egypt; to curtail the slave trade; and to assist the garrisons of Sennar and Kassala. These were now seen to be unrealistic, while Afghanistan ruled out a second Khartoum expedition. The definitive abandonment of that expedition needed to be executed without publicity, Dongola province continuing to be held until the Cabinet could agree its evacuation. Dongola's incorporation in Egypt under the governorship of none other than Abdel Qadir Pasha Hilmi was being canvassed by Baring – as in early October 1884 Gordon had canvassed Abdel Qadir's name as his own successor. The decision-making was overtaken by the defeat of Gladstone's government (on Irish Home Rule) on 8 June 1885, to be followed a fortnight later by the epoch-making sudden death of the Mahdi. On 1 July the new Conservative government of the Marquess of Salisbury concluded that the Sudan (and Dongola) must indeed be abandoned.

Before his death, the Mahdi had ordered his *amir* Mohammed el Kheir Abdallah to advance on Dongola in the wake of the British departure north across the Bayuda desert, and it was he who would occupy Dongola after its evacuation. At the point of time of the Mahdi's death, 22 June, except for Dongola, Suakin and distant Harar and Berbera, and southern Equatoria, only Kassala – to surrender on 29 July 1885 – and Sennar, in August 1885, were unconquered. The governor of Sennar, El Nur Bey Mohammed, appointed by Gordon in 1884, offered a nigh indomitable resistance in the ancient fortress town although cut off from Khartoum, which it had supplied with *dura* up to September 1884. Ismail Abdel Qadir el Kordofani relates at length the number of defeats inflicted on the *Ansar* during the siege, following the arrival of their new commander, the Mahdi's cousin, Mohammed Abdel Karim, two months after Khartoum had fallen. The garrison of 3,000 were determined to maintain resistance. The 700 famine-stricken survivors only surrendered following the dispatch to Sennar of the veteran general Abdel Rahman el Nejumi. The governor, El Nur Bey, who had served Gordon in Equatoria as commander at Fatiko in 1874 and M'ruli in 1876, and who lost both legs in battle, survived to be decorated by Khedive Abbas II in 1901.

Notwithstanding the fall of Khartoum and the ultimate withdrawal from the Sudan of the British Relief Force, the Sudan in 1885 did not remain uniformly quiet. The aged Mek Adham of the Tegali Nuba mountains who had committed his people to the Mahdi following the Hicks disaster of November 1883, had died accompanying the Mahdi to Khartoum after the rains of 1884. The Nuba peoples rebelled until suppressed by the rough hand of Amir Hamdan Abu Anja in the early part of 1885. Likewise the *jihadiya*, captured Black troops of the Egyptian army drawn from the Nuba and Southern Sudanese tribes, of whom Abu Anja was supreme commander, rebelled in El Obeid in August, exploiting the absence of Mahmoud Abdel Qadir following the death of his nephew, the Mahdi. They withdrew with their arms to the mountains and there defeated and killed the returned Mahmoud, their rebellion once again to be put down by Abu Anja. Omer, son of Mek Adham, would become *a'amil* of the Khalifa in succession to his father.

The death of the Mahdi however would excite further cases of disaffection and revolt in the new independent Sudan.[20]

14

The Mahdiya: Independence Recovered
1885–96

I TRANSPOSITION TO A THEOCRATIC STRUCTURE

As he entered the Mosque El Sudan in Khartoum on Friday 12 Karama
el Tania 1302 AH (30 January 1885), Mohammed Ahmed Abdallah
the Mahdi, aged forty, had by his religious leadership and military
achievement restored independence to a Sudan greater in extent than
the Fung Kingdom of Sennar, extinguished by the abdication of its king
to the Egyptian conqueror on 11 Ramadan 1236 AH (13 June 1821).
Moreover the new government was theocratic in its character.
Religious zeal was its driving force. There would be no secular allegiance to an Egyptian Viceroy of an Ottoman Sultan, who nevertheless
claimed the hereditary office of *khalifa* (Caliph), successor of God's
Prophet. The Mahdi's claim was none other than himself to be the
direct descendant of the family of the Prophet Mohammed, both the
Mahdi's grandparents claiming descent from El Hussein son of Ali, the
fourth successor (*khalifa*), son-in-law and cousin to Mohammed. The
Mahdi's God-given duty was the subjection not simply of the Sudan
but of the Islamic centres of Cairo, Mecca, Jerusalem, Baghdad and of
Kufa (Kerbela).

Yet if he was only occasionally an active participant in battle, the
Mahdi, as P. M. Holt points out in his influential study *The Mahdist
State in the Sudan 1881–98*, was no figurehead – neither in regard to
proclamations and letters by reason of his prerogative, nor as ultimate
authority for the acts, military and administrative, of his subordinates.
Professor Holt, formerly archivist to the Sudan government, was personally responsible for examining and cataloguing the surviving correspondence, both of the Mahdi and of the Khalifa Abdallahi, with their
generals and provincial and civic officials, together with statistical and
financial records and with documents relating to the judicial system of
the Mahdiya. Originally accumulated by the British military intelligence department in Cairo, these documents had been all transferred to

the civil secretariat in Khartoum in 1915 and, until Holt's work began in 1951, left virtually undisturbed, at risk to progressive deterioration.

In his 1954 paper on 'The Archives of the Mahdiya' Holt relates that, notwithstanding the quality of the paper on which the original manuscripts were written, microfilming and photostatting were then in train in the interests of posterity. This author regretfully has not had the opportunity to access this collection, nor the subsequent theses and publications based on them by Sudanese scholars, in regard to which the bibliography of Fergus Nicoll's *The Sword of the Prophet* will be found helpful.

Two copies at least of *The History of the Mahdi* by Abdel Rahman Ibn Hussein el Jabri, written in 1926 with the permission of El Sayyid Sir Abdel Rahman el Mahdi, the sole surviving son of the Mahdi, and using information offered by the family and the *Ansar* would later, following the grant of the Sudan's independence, find their way into the University of Khartoum Library. The book was initially confiscated in 1926 by the Sudan government in the aftermath of the assassination of the Governor-General and mutiny of the Egyptian troops in Khartoum of 1924. It relies for sources on proclamations and letters of the Mahdi which had escaped destruction on the Battle of Omdurman, and background information relating to the Mahdi's armies and the Khalifa's campaigns. Mohammed Omer Beshir, in an article in *Sudan Notes and Records* 1963, quotes extensively from a summary and interpretation of El Jabri's history prepared by the British former acting director of intelligence, S. Hillelson, but difficult to trace.

Chief among the Mahdi's subordinates were the three *Khalifas* appointed by the Mahdi at Aba (see p. 378); beneath them the senior *amirs* (*umarā*), and the *Ashraf*, kinsmen of the Mahdi. As the months wore on and military victories were recorded, initially in great part attributable to the Baqqara of the western Sudan from whom was descended the Khalifa Abdallahi Mohammed of the Ta'isha of southern Darfur, the latter achieved the additional rank of military supremo, 'amir of the armies of the Mahdiya', in addition to commanding the Black Flag Baqqara division. The pious Khalifa, Ali Mohammed Hilu, likewise commanded (according to Slatin) the Green Flag, the less numerous division of the southern Gezira and Kordofan; while the Khalifa Mohammed Sharif bin Hamid commanded the Red Flag division recruited from the *Ashraf* and the riverain Arabs. Subordinate to the *Khalifas*, the comparative rank and standing of the *amirs* progressively emerged from the fields of battle. Chief among them were

Mohammed Khalid (Zuqal), cousin of the Mahdi;; Abdel Rahman el Nejumi – Ja'ali; Hamdan Abu Anja – Ta'aishi (originally recruited by Zubeir Pasha – see p. 159); Osman Digna – Hadareb Beja; Mohammed el Kheir Abdallah, Ja'ali; Mahmoud Abdel Qadir, uncle of the Mahdi; Mohammed Osman Abu Qarja, Dongalawi; Karamallah Mohammed Kurqusawi, Dongalawi; recognition initially being given to the most senior by the rank *'amir el umarā'*.

Beneath the *amirs*, formally styled *a'amils* or agents from mid 1884, came the *muqqadams* or *maqdums*, an office derived from Darfur. However as territory was reconquered from the Egyptian government, responsibility for civil administration was assumed by the military in a system not far different from the existing Turkish organisation based on the *muderia* (province) and the *qism* (district). These authorities were appointed as being *Ansar*, companions of the Mahdi, as previously of the Prophet Mohammed. All wore the patched *jibba* and white turban (*'ama*).

A new system of regional government had come into being by the time of the fall of Khartoum and the British withdrawal from the Nile. The corrupt Turkish-Egyptian system of tax collection had disintegrated, and the payment of the vast rebel armies while the civil war was in progress required new sources of finance and new regulation of expenditure. For the Baqqara troops especially, booty and the spoils of war had historically provided both the incentive and the reward for armed combat – something they had been conspicuously denied in Gordon's anti-slave raiding campaigns. The Mahdi however sought to impose the Moslem *shari'a* rule that booty belonged not to the individual but to the community, claiming, to quote Holt: 'You have preferred earthly life to the world to come and loved to gather booty and wealth and deserted with it… I have warned you in this my letter out of mercy towards you… so that you may restore the booty you have taken.'

Accordingly, at least from the time of the occupation of El Obeid in January 1883, revenues would be lodged in a provincial treasury under a trusted commissioner *amir,* who would have responsibility for their safe-keeping and for their equitable distribution: one fifth to the Mahdi and the rest to the *Ansar* warriors, to the weak and to the poor. 'Let relief for all the *Ansar* be from the treasury. Let him who has relatives and family, whether many or few, disclose this; also he who has but little, and he shall be allotted sufficient from the treasury.' The annihilation of the Hicks expedition in November 1883, to be followed by the capture of Berber, Gedaref and Khartoum, yielded quantities of booty, but the funds of the treasuries would be further augmented by the imposition, again according to *shari'a* law, of the *zakah* tax on grain and on cattle and of the tithe. Authority for the levying of these taxes as for the collection booty was made the personal responsibility of the Khalifa Abdallahi.

The Mahdi himself by the actions of Providence had been charged to revive the Islamic faith incorporated in the Koran, together with the *Sunna* (traditional teaching) which at the time of his death he was revising. Decisions on matters of law, as on the matter of pardon of repentant rebels, lay therefore within his unique prerogative. 'Information came from the Apostle of God that the angel of inspiration is with me from God to direct me and He has appointed me', but he felt no inhibition in delegating authority to subordinate rulers. Most significant in this sphere was the appointment of a *Qadi el Islam* (supreme Islamic judge): the first Mahdist holder, Ahmed Jubara, was a Turkish graduate of El Azhar in Cairo. On his early death in the first battle of El Obeid he was succeeded by Sheikh Ahmed Ali, hitherto judge at Shakka, in 1882. By 1894 political intervention in the strict application of the *sharia* law would have led to a succession of arrests of holders of that increasingly vulnerable office (see p. 496).[1]

2 THE SUCCESSION OF THE KHALIFA ABDALLAHI

This new theocratic structure was in place by June 1884, the whole of the Egyptian Sudan conquered with the exception of Suakin; Massawa and the littoral; eastern Equatoria; Kassala, Sennar and Dongola Provinces – the latter three to be occupied within months. As the Mahdi and his immediate family took up residence in his new capital of Omdurman there was no presentiment that within weeks he would have died, smallpox suspected.

Holt has analysed three elements in the Mahdist state: first, the ascetic religious committed to reform, among whom were the Mahdi's early converts and adherents – the Khalifa Ali wad Mohammed Hilu, Mohammed el Mekki Ismail, and Ahmed Sharfi, his father-in-law; secondly, merchant malcontents, especially the Dongolawi and Ja'ali *jallaba*, from the riverain and western towns but including the *Ashraf*, the Mahdi's family relations; and, thirdly, the Baqqara, also the Gezira and other campaigning irregulars, into which category fell perhaps the better trained *jihadiya* – Black former Egyptian troops who had been captured and pressed into service with the victors.

Despite the sudden collapse of Egyptian rule there were however murmurings of discontent among victorious groups who regarded themselves as cheated of their just expectations. On Friday 12 June 1885 the Mahdi felt compelled to deliver a sharp rebuke at the midday prayers: 'O ye people, I am weary of advice and discourse with my kinsmen, the *Ashraf*, who have persisted in foolishness and error, and think that the Mahdiya is for them alone. I am innocent of them, so be my witnesses between the hands of God Most High.' Ten days later the Mahdi was dead, and the *Ansar* obligated to choose a successor.

Islamic precedent required that the *Ansar* have regard to the Mahdi's strict adherence to the precedents which followed upon the equally unexpected death of the Prophet Mohammed in Medina in 11 AH (AD 632). The Prophet had in his lifetime appointed no successors, *khalifas*, but on his death the Prophet's 'helpers', the *Ansar*, elected Abu Bakr el Siddiq, father of the Prophet's second wife Aisha, as the first *Khalifat 'el Siddiq'*. Abu Bakr would then be succeeded by Omer, *Khalifat 'el Faruq'*; by Osman; and by Ali Abi Talib, *Khalifat 'el Karrar'*.

While leaving the post of current successor to Osman vacant (it had been offered to, and declined by, the *imam* Mohammed El Mahdi of the Sanusi of Kufra, Cyrenaica), the Mahdi had already some four years previously appointed Abdallahi Mohammed *Khalifat el Siddiq*; Ali Mohammed Hilu *Khalifat el Faruq*; and Mohammed Sharif bin Hamid *Khalifat el Karrar*. Khalifa Abdallahi, always *primus inter pares*, had commanded the strongest fighting division, comprising mainly Baqqara, to successive victories under the Black Flag at Jebel Qadir and El Obeid. On the fall of El Obeid the Mahdi, on 26 January 1883, had issued a lengthy proclamation which left no dubiety about the primacy of Abdallahi among the Mahdi's *khalifas*.

> Know that the Khalifa Abdallahi, *Khalifat el Siddiq*, the Commander of the Army of the Mahdiya, was designated in the prophetic vision… All that he does is by command of the Prophet or by permission from Us, not by his mere independent judgement… He is now in Abu Bakr el Siddiq's place… He whom we have mentioned is Our *Khalifa* and his *khilaf* is by a command from the Prophet… The *Khalifa* is the leader of the Moslems and Our *Khalifa*, Our representative in all matters of the Faith.

And to the Mahdi's uncle Mahmoud Abdel Qadir, governing Kordofan, the Mahdi wrote from Omdurman shortly before his death: 'He who does not love the Khalifa Abdallahi will not be benefited or revived by converse with the Mahdi as the rain does not revive the dry, cut herb.' However, as already observed, ten days before the Mahdi's sudden death and burial discontent was already affecting the *Ashraf*.

No sooner had the burial taken place, beneath the room of the death bed as with the Prophet himself, than open dissension broke out between the *Ashraf* – who were agreed that their kinsman, Mohammed Sharif bin Hamid, *Khalifat el Karrar*, should be the successor to the Mahdi – and the unanimous opinion to the contrary of the other notables gathered there. The contest was rapidly resolved in favour of Khalifa Abdallahi – the senior member of the *Ashraf*, Ahmed Sharfi, himself pledging allegiance and presenting Abdallahi with the sword of the Mahdi and the turban. With evident reluctance, the generality of the kinsmen then pledged their allegiance, last being Khalifa Mohammed Sharif. The other junior *Khalifa*, Ali Mohammed Hilu, would prove loyal to Abdallahi to the death. Abdallahi was careful to follow the strict precedent established by the Khalifa Abu Bakr el Siddiq when he succeeded the Prophet, sensitive in insisting that his accession would be only through the mediation of his dead master, the Mahdi, and of the Koran-attested eminent saint El Khidr, Abdallahi's guardian.[2]

3 THE *ASHRAF* RIVALRIES AND SUSPICIONS 1885–86

Abdallahi's accession to the role of *Khalifat el Mahdi*, in accordance with the expressed wish of the Mahdi, had been achieved in the face of some powerful opposition – not so much the young inexperienced *Khalifa,* Mohammed Sharif, as from the senior *amirs* drawn from the *Ashraf*: Mahmoud Abdel Qadir in El Obeid: Mohammed Khalid (Zuqal) in El Fasher; Mohammed el Kheir Abdallah Khojali in Berber with Dongola; and Karamallah el Kurqusawi in Shakka, Bahr el Ghazal and Equatoria west of the White Nile. Fortuitously Abdallahi's doubts about Mahmoud were quickly resolved when, contrary to Abdallahi's orders, he led an expedition in person to revenge the earlier mutiny of the El Obeid *jihadiya* who had retired to Jebel Dayir and was killed in the action in December 1885. He would be replaced as overall commander in Kordofan by Abdallahi's most trusted general, Hamdan Abu Anja, a fellow Ta'aishi, whose first task would be the subjection of the Nuba. The west was in secure hands.

The Black Flag Baqqara army was now placed under the command of the Khalifa's brother Yaqub Mohammed; able, unpopular, ruthless. The subjection of Kassala in July 1885 had already been wrought by Osman Digna, and of Sennar the following month by the general Abdel Rahman el Nejumi and these successes, coupled with the sudden abandonment of Dongola province by the British, allowed the new ruler of the Sudan precious months in which to establish his authority and to redeploy his forces in anticipation of a further bid for power by the *Ashraf*. By the end of 1885 however the Khalifa found himself under direct threat: in the north once again from Egypt; from the west, especially Darfur; and from Omdurman. Here the antipathy of the *Ashraf* had not been dispelled and moreover the commissioner (*amin*) in charge of the central treasury (*beit el mal*), Ahmed Sulieman of Rufa'a, had been personally appointed by the Mahdi, having originally discharged that responsibility in El Obeid following its capture in January 1883. His first loyalty and affection lay with the *Ashraf*.

The threat from Egypt if pressed would have revealed Abdallahi's vulnerability, notwithstanding the published objective of the Mahdi to launch the *jihad* against Egypt. The reoccupation of Dongola province by Mohammed el Kheir Abdallah Khojali had been cautious, attended by probing attacks on the retiring Anglo-Egyptian force, while Abdel Rahman el Nejumi was being sent from Sennar to Berber to prepare for a future Egyptian expedition. In late December 1885 an attack was launched by Generals Sir Frederick Stephenson and Sir Francis Grenfell, the latter successor as *sirdar* to Sir Evelyn Wood, at the village of Qinnis near Khusha (Maqraq) which had the effect of halting the Mahdist advance. Stephenson however had no intent to pursue and Wadi Halfa became the southernmost Egyptian held town. Indeed the threat from Darfur would prove altogether more serious than that from the north. Nevertheless the minor reverse at Qinnis offered Abdallahi in the summer of 1886 the opportunity to cast blame on Mohammed el Kheir who was successively replaced first as *amir* of Dongola where he was initially succeeded by El Nejumi, and then as *mudir* of Berber by a Ta'ishi cousin of the Khalifa, Osman el Dikaim, brother of Yunus who had been an early adherent of the Mahdi at Jebel Qadir. But El Nejumi also attracted the suspicions of the Khalifa on account of his Ja'ali origins, and for the next three years would have inflicted on him as *wakil* and minder the Baqqara Habbaniya Musa'id Qaydum, until, as El Nejumi set out to invade Egypt, Yunus el Dikaim arrived to succeed him in 1889.

In Darfur, Mohammed Khalid (Zuqal) possessed a large army estimated by Holt at 30,000 infantry, 1,000 cavalry and 3,000 *jihadiya* Black conscripts. Belatedly, and in collusion with the *Ashraf* in Omdurman, Mohammed Khalid announced in December 1885 that he was setting out with his forces for Omdurman, ostensibly to swear allegiance to the Khalifa, in reality to occupy the Gezira. Hamdan Abu Anja, presently in the Nuba mountains, was ordered to invite Khalid in March 1886 to divert his march to join him in Jebel Dayir, enabling the Khalifa to preempt the secret move by Mohammed Khalid on the Gezira by ordering Yunus el Dikaim to take command there, pending Abu Anja's return from Jebel Dayir. In Omdurman the Khalifa required the two junior *Khalifas* to hand over their forces, *jihadiya*, arms and flags to his brother Yaqub under the Black Flag, while to Kordofan he dispatched his Ta'aishi young cousin Osman Adam as governor under Abu Anja.

The Khalifa's pre-emptive strike was successful. Mohammed Khalid was intercepted in Bara in April 1886 and the majority of his followers joined Abu Anja. His command was abolished, his treasury absorbed and he himself held captive in El Obeid. The central treasurer (*amin*), Ahmed Sulieman of Rufa'a , found himself in chains, his commission in Omdurman bestowed upon Ibrahim Mohammed Adlan, a former El Obeid merchant and then a deputy of Ahmed Sulieman, who had proved his loyalty to Abdallahi in impounding the treasury of Berber. He was secretly kind to the captive Slatin.[3]

4 JIHAD 1886–89

Thus by the end of the first year following the Mahdi's death the aspirations of the *Ashraf* had been dealt a crushing blow even if already, in Ohrwalder's words, 'the glow and fervour of religious enthusiasm was gone'. Ohrwalder was now brought from El Obeid to Omdurman to join Slatin and Lupton. His companion and former fellow captive Father Alois Bonomi, erstwhile head of the Dilling Austrian Catholic Mission, had escaped with British assistance to Cairo in June 1885. The resistance movement against the new leader of Mahdism however was not suppressed. That first year was the harbinger of further outbreaks of militant hostility which the Khalifa would seek to quash as part of his own inherited commitment to *jihad*.

He was fortunate in inheriting an army of war veterans led by a handful of successful generals, notably Hamdan Abu Anja, Osman Abu Bakr Digna, Abdel Rahman el Nejumi and to be joined by Osman Adam. Instinctively aware of Napoleon's dictum that you can do anything with bayonets except sit on them, Abdallahi wholeheartedly endorsed the Mahdi's previous ultimata to neighbouring Moslem as well as Christian countries, that they must accept Mohammed Ahmed as the Mahdi of Allah and the *Khalifa* of the Prophet. Doubt on the issue would be ranked as apostasy: the Mahdi had affirmed 'The Prophet informed me saying "He who doubts your Mahdiship is a disbeliever in God and his Apostle"'; while non-compliance would invoke *jihad*. Thus by early 1886 new ultimata calling for submission would be dispatched to Egypt, and to both the Hejaz and Nejd in Arabia, to be followed by personal letters to Queen Victoria, the Ottoman Sultan Abdel Hamid II, the Khedive Mohammed Tawfiq and the Emperor John IV.

Western Sudan 1886–89   For Hamdan Abu Anja, returned from his Nuba expedition and now based in Kordofan with Osman Adam his subordinate, Darfur was far from tranquil. When Mohammed Khalid had quit Darfur on his ill-fated march on Omdurman in December 1885 he had left Yusuf, son and successor to his father the Fur Sultan Ibrahim who had been vanquished by Zubeir Pasha in October 1874, as chief *amir*, and an uneasy understanding between his subordinates, Sheikh Madibbo Ali, *amir* of the Rizeiqat, and the *amir* Karamallah Mohammed Kurqusawi, ruler of Shakka, Bahr el Ghazal and part of Equatoria. This Karamallah was also a member of the *Ashraf*, albeit currently absent in Makraka threatening Emin Bey before the rains, and Abdallahi thought it prudent on his own accession to recall him to Shakka, obliging him to abandon his plans for an assault on Lado. On Karamallah's arrival back at Shakka in October 1886 he was vexed to find that his *wakil*, his brother Mohammed, was menaced by Madibbo's Rizeiqat. Karamallah's substantial army did however enable him to offer timely reinforcement to his brother's resistance to Madibbo and, after a successful skirmish, to pursue the latter northwards to Jebel Marra where he was captured by Yusuf Ibrahim. Karamallah correctly ordered Madibbo's removal to Abdallahi in Omdurman but Abu Anja, with a score to settle, intercepted him in El Obeid in December and, mindful of his personal ill-treatment by Madibbo in the war between Zubeir and the Rizeiqat in 1873, had him executed. Darfur settled down to an uneasy truce veiling a relationship of mutual suspicion between '*sultan*' Yusuf Ibrahim in El Fasher and Karamallah in Dara. It would not endure, and Abdallahi would confide to Slatin his personal regret at Madibbo's death.

Darfur was not the only sector of hostility in the western Sudan during 1886. At least the ruling Nurab section of the proud camel-owning Kababish of northern Kordofan, commanding the strategic access to Dongola across the Bayuda desert, had not forgotten the insult inflicted on them when, after an unsatisfactory meeting during the siege of El Obeid, the Mahdi in May 1883 had seized and executed their permanent Sheikh El Tom Fadlallah Salim, leaving the latter's successor and brother Saleh a sworn enemy. Saleh had already entered negotiations with Major Herbert Kitchener in preparation for the Desert Column of the Gordon relief expedition in August 1884. Notwithstanding the British withdrawal from Dongola in September 1885 Sheikh Saleh, with his southern base at Umm Badr at the southern end of the Wadi el Melik, had maintained the rapport with Egypt and, aware of his vulnerability, successfully sought from Egypt in late 1886 the dispatch of Remington rifles and other armaments. The departure of a camel caravan from Wadi Halfa laden with supplies to protect him from Abdallahi's increasing hostility was ambushed at Selima on the Darb el Arbain in February 1887, the cargo captured and Sheikh Saleh thereafter hounded to his death in May by Amir Osman Adam with the aid of the Dar Hamid. El Nejumi had meanwhile left Berber with his troops for New Dongola in October 1886 in preparation for the invasion of Egypt.[4]

By January 1887, following Madibbo Ali's execution, Abu Anja was reporting to the Khalifa that Yusuf Ibrahim had restored the administrative structure of his region to that of the former Sultanate, claiming that hereditary title for himself and provoking the wrath of the Kurqusawi brothers at Shakka. For the while the Khalifa preferred to confirm Hamdan Abu Anja's decision that Yusuf should continue to be supported as governor in El Fasher, but then in April 1887 Abu Anja was needed to transfer his military prowess to growing problems on the Abyssinian frontier, while Yusuf continued to ignore the Khalifa's official *hijra* (directive) to pay his respects to Omdurman.

Left in command in El Obeid on the departure of Abu Anja in April was the very young Ta'ishi Osman Adam, who had superintended successfully the subjection of the Kababish. To him was now committed the responsibility to muster all the Kordofan troops (17,000) excepting the El Obeid garrison, and in October to march first to

Shakka, where Karamallah Kurqusawi was experiencing further trouble with the Rizeiqat, and thence to confront the offending Yusuf Ibrahim at Dara. After three battles he captured Dara at the end of December 1887 and El Fasher a month later. Osman, scarcely twenty years old, having won his spurs was appointed *'amil 'umumi,* effectively general-governor, of the western territories of Kordofan and Darfur with his headquarters now to be at El Fasher and having a deputy at El Obeid.

Following the capture of Dara and El Fasher, Osman Adam pursued Yusuf relentlessly to his fastness at Jebel Marra and defeated him in March 1888. Yusuf's head, like those of Amir Madibbo and of Sheikh Salih of the Kababish a year earlier, was dispatched to Omdurman for public exhibition and his robe to adorn the new *beit el antikat* in the *beit el mal* (treasury). Surviving males of the blood of the Fur sultanate were executed or sent captive to Omdurman. (The practice of publicly exhibiting the severed heads of political losers, public proof of death, was not of course limited to the Arab world. In England Henry Percy, Earl of Northumberland, and his son Hotspur suffered that fate under Henry IV; Thomas More under Henry VIII.)

The brutality with which Osman Adam treated the Darfur adherents of the defeated Yusuf Ibrahim led their surviving *sheikhs* to concentrate in the extreme western lands of the Dar Masalit and Dar Tama. The approach of Osman's marauding troops under the Mahdist *amir* Abdel Qadir wad Delil provoked a defensive insurrection inspired by a young *feki* styled Ahmed Abu Jummaiza, who first claimed to be a *Khalifa* of Mohammed El Mahdi el Sanusi. Jummaiza's followers successively defeated the *Ansar* forces three times in the region of Kebkebia during September–November 1888, forcing Osman Adam to fall back on El Fasher and encouraging the rebellion of the Rizeiqat and other Baqqara.

Abu Jummaiza however had contracted smallpox at Kebkebia, and the respite from pressure enabled Osman Adam to be reinforced. By the end of February 1889 the army besieging Osman Adam at El Fasher had been defeated; Abu Jummaiza had died; and the Khalifa had been relieved of anxiety regarding his personal homeland exit route. By June Dara, El Tuwaisha and Jebel Meidob 140 miles north-east of El Fasher were under control. Innately distrustful of the undisciplined disposition of the Baqqara, Abdallahi could congratulate himself that earlier, at the beginning of 1888, he had instructed his new *amir* to implement a *hijra,* effectively exile, to Omdurman of tribesmen especially of the

Rizeiqat, Ta'aisha and Habbaniya in order to damp down the smouldering embers of revolt. Only when threatened with a punitive expedition in May 1888 did the Ta'aisha, numbering perhaps 11,000, yield and obey.[5]

Blue Nile and Abyssinia 1887–89 When Osman Adam had set out from El Obeid in October 1887 to subjugate Darfur, his superior, Abu Anja, had already been recalled to Omdurman in April in the face of deteriorating relations with Abyssinia.

Following the Egyptian evacuation of Gallabat with Abyssinian support two years earlier at the end of February 1885, and of the neighbouring garrison of El Jira in July, the two towns had been successively occupied by the *Ansar* with Mohammed wad Arab being made governor of Gallabat. Ras Adal Tasamma of Gojjam, provoked by *Ansar* raids and spurred on by Hamran Arab refugees and by the previous Egyptian governor of Gallabat – the Takruri Saleh Idris – in January 1887 launched a major incursion. Gallabat was captured, its governor killed, and Ras Adal advanced down the Atbara river towards Gedaref, before withdrawing with the loot to Dembea west of Lake Tana.

Uncertain how serious this Abyssinian threat would prove, the Khalifa had ordered the Ta'aishi Yunus el Dikaim to counter the invasion. The now undefended Gallabat was reoccupied, under orders evidently to prosecute retaliatory raids into Abyssinia. Meanwhile a letter was sent threatening the Negus John IV with war unless he returned all Moslem captives, but the Khalifa was not pressing a *jihad* during 1887.

The presence of Abu Anja's considerable force in Omdurman during the summer of 1887 offered the Khalifa the opportunity to deal with a problem on the Blue Nile. Despite the surrender in 1884 of Gedaref by Abdallah, brother of the Shukriya Sheikh Awad el Karim Ahmed Abu Sin, the Shukriya had omitted to renew their allegiance following the Mahdi's death, leading to Sheikh Awad el Karim's arrest and imprisonment in Omdurman, where he died in December 1886. Awad el Karim's estrangement from the Khalifa was shared by Sheikh Yusuf el Mardi Abu Ruf of the neighbouring Rufa'a el Hui people – like the Shukriya major grain producers but on the west bank of the Blue Nile. Yusuf's increasing hostility towards him and refusal to come to Omdurman now persuaded Khalifa Abdallahi to dispatch a detachment of Abu Anja's army to suppress the Rufa'a el Hui with brutality, *pour encourager les autres*. Shortly afterwards the news that Emperor John was preparing an expeditionary force against Yunus el Dikaim at Gallabat provided the occasion for Abu Anja's main army to be sent further in support in October 1887.

Meanwhile the claim of a local Takruri, the dominant trading community of Gallabat originating from western Darfur, to have the recognition of the Khalifa that he was the awaited Prophet Isa (Jesus) had drawn the allegiance of Mahdist officers of Yunus's force, leading to their execution with that of the pretender in December 1887 and the return of Yunus to Omdurman. Abu Anja, effectively taking over command of the frontier, launched a major raid on Dembea. On 18 January 1888 he defeated a major Abyssinian force at Sar Weha (Debra Sin) thirty miles to the north, then went on to sack Gondar and to seize as hostages the wife and children of Ras Adal Tasamma before withdrawing again to Gallabat. The Khalifa followed up this success with a further minatory letter to John that a *jihad* was in the offing. However notwithstanding Abu Anja's victory, his awareness of John's preoccupation with Ras Menilek of Shoa and the threat to Tigré by the Italians in occupation of Massawa, the Khalifa still retained a healthy respect for the Abyssinian combatants and the defeats they had inflicted on the Egyptian expedition at Gundet in November 1875 and at Gura in 1876.

Abu Anja endeavoured to follow up his success with a second campaign in June 1888, penetrating east of Lake Tana but underestimating the effect of the rains on the health of his troops and indeed perhaps of himself. He did not succeed in bringing the Abyssinians to a serious contest, but nevertheless was called back to Omdurman by the Khalifa in November to be received with honour. By December Abu Anja was back in Gallabat, his return coinciding with the dispatch on 25 December of a conciliatory letter from Emperor John to the Khalifa via Abu Anja, urging their common interest to agree to fight and conquer the encroaching Europeans. In January 1889 Abu Anja suddenly died – Ohrwalder relates from typhoid.

News of Abu Anja's sudden death may well not yet have reached Omdurman when the Khedive replied to John's conciliatory note. The document is missing but may be presumed hostile since notwithstanding the current threat to El Fasher Abu Anja's successor, El Zaki Tamal, penned a peremptory reply to a similar note from the Emperor: 'There is nothing but the sword between the two countries until you become a Moslem and follow the Mahdi's creed.' Yet El Zaki had been enjoined in his orders to maintain a defensive stance with his army, for the very good reason that the whole of Darfur was at risk.

Whether this was known to John, or whether he saw a window of opportunity to settle with the Mahdist threat before addressing his problems with his Shoa rival Ras Menilek and with the Italians, John decided on war. On 9 March 1889 he attacked Gallabat with an overwhelming force. In the moment of victory however, with the Mahdists in flight, John was mortally wounded by a chance bullet – a catastrophe for his followers for he had only an illegitimate heir. Even *in extremis* he refused to designate Menilek his successor, in consequence of which the Abyssinian troops broke off the engagement having now a more important preoccupation. Abyssinia was veering to Menilek. El Zaki had snatched success out of the jaws of defeat. Two days later the dead body of the Emperor was captured, in a long box sealed with wax. El Zaki's dispatch to the Khalifa announcing the outcome was accompanied by the head of the late *negus nagest*. The news reached Omdurman in the wake of the report of Osman Adam's victory at El Fasher.

Abdallahi found himself at the apogee of his power. Ohrwalder described the scene in Omdurman:

> Here the wildest excitement prevailed; the Khalifa Abdallahi ordered the great war drums and the *onbeia* (an ivory wind instrument) to be sounded. A large review took place... The Abyssinian heads were put upon the gallows and left no doubt that a great victory had been won; then three days afterwards came the news that the King had been killed. Fixed high up on a camel's back, John's head was paraded up and down through the marketplace... The Khalifa was quite intoxicated by his success... On the same day of its arrival, the Khalifa ordered the King's head to be sewn in a piece of leather and sent it on to Dongola, from whence it was to be sent on to Wadi Halfa as a warning to the Khedive and the English that a like fate would await them if they did not at once submit.

The other severed Abyssinian heads joined those of the Takruri prophet Isa from Gallabat, and of the vanquished rebel leaders of Darfur, in a pit by the Omdurman marketplace.

Menilek would quickly gain the recognition of the whole of Abyssinia as *negus nagest* with the exception of John's homeland, Tigré. Here, obliged to wage war against Ras Mangasha – John's illegitimate son named *negus* on his father's deathbed – Menilek bought off potential intervention by the Italians through tacit assent in May 1889 to Italy's progressive occupation of Bogos – first Keren, then Asmara –

until ending Tigréan resistance in May 1893. For Abyssinia the *Ansar*, his African neighbours, would at least until 1895 remain the principal threat, even if there were no actual hostilities. Following the annihilation of the Italian invasion at Adwa on 1 March 1895 and, more significantly, Kitchener's first major victory over the *Ansar* at Firket in June 1896, en route to Dongola, both the Khalifa and the Negus were then persuaded of the mutual benefit to them of a defensive entente.[6]

Egypt 1889   Despite this providential delivery from the Abyssinian threat, the prosecution of that *jihad* against a country held in the highest respect on account of the fighting reputation of its army and its forbidding mountainous terrain was not a priority, no more to the Khalifa than it had been to the Mahdi. Egypt was the important target, even if the Omdurman victory celebrations of 1889 offered a timely circus to distract the attention of a population already suffering from the consequences of the onset of a serious famine, engendered by the failure of the harvest of late 1888.

Dongola and Berber were especially burdened by the food demands of the invasion army still being steadily amassed by Abdel Rahman el Nejumi, in preparation for the *jihad* against Egypt which had been the subject of a threatening ultimatum from the Khalifa as long ago as early 1886 and repeated in April 1887. El Nejumi had moved his force northwards from Berber to New Dongola, arriving in November 1886.

Himself a Ja'ali of great popularity, El Nejumi had enjoyed the exceptional approval of the Mahdi. One of the first to join the Mahdi at Aba Island, he had fought with distinction at El Obeid, Sheikan and Khartoum and earned the designation *amir el umara'*. Having been sent in pursuit of the British Relief expedition retiring to Dongola (which would be evacuated in June 1885), El Nejumi had received from the Mahdi the following proclamation dated 26 May: 'In truth I tell you, the war in the province of Dongola is of the greatest import, for the enemies of God are there in multitudes... You are my beloved, wise and sagacious, who know that this enterprise of ours is with God and for God, from beginning to end.' On the Mahdi's death, however, he was recalled by the Khalifa. He fulfilled his instructions to reinforce the subjugation of Sennar in August, eventually reaching New Dongola in November 1886. Here he would be spied on by a Baqqara Habbaniya *wakil*, Mus'aid Qaydum, a young protégé of the Khalifa Abdallahi, who was charged to report on El Nejumi's relationship as military commander with the major contingent of his army, drawn from riverain tribes and originally under the command of the Khalifa Mohammed Sharif.

In January 1888 El Nejumi sought to reinforce his second-in-command Abdel Halim Musa'id's advance headquarters on the Egyptian frontier south of Saras (only twenty-five miles from Wadi Halfa) with a force under Musa'id Qaydum. Whereupon, doubtless tipped off by the latter, the Khalifa peremptorily overrode El Nejumi's orders, forbidding such dispositions without his personal approval. In March 1888, when El Nejumi visited Omdurman, he was, according to Babikr Bedri, publicly berated by the Khalifa: 'Wad el Nejumi, you are a thing of scorn. Those who were your companions have all achieved martyrdom; and you, how long will you remain in terror of death?'

For the remainder of 1888 El Nejumi's relationship with Musa'id Qaydum would fester, further aggravated by the dispatch by the Khalifa of commissioners to New Dongola to investigate. While El Nejumi devoted his energies to recruiting local tribesmen, and wrestled with the problems of famine and supplies for his expedition, his position as commander was being systematically undermined. At the end of the year came news that Yunus el Dikaim, cousin of the Khalifa but displaced as leader in Gallabat at the end of 1887 by Hamdan Abu Anja, had been appointed as ruler of Dongola province with Musa'id his deputy. El Nejumi, still lacking the authority to launch his invasion of Egypt, had been publicly slighted. He made no protest.

In January 1889 a council of war was convened at last by El Nejumi on Abdallahi's orders, to plan the attack on Egypt pending Yunus el Dikaim's arrival as a senior-ranking 'amil 'umumi. Reinforcements for El Nejumi from Omdurman were however diverted to the defence of Gallabat and only following the victories of Osman Adam at El Fasher and of El Zaki el Tumal at Gallabat did the Khalifa feel confident in April 1889 to authorise El Nejumi's advance to join the forward positions at Saras. El Nejumi's orders may not have envisaged an occupation of Egyptian territory in 1889 much beyond Aswan, but he was confronting a well-trained, well-led, well-armed and reorganised Egyptian army under experienced British commanders, following the withdrawal of the last British detachment in February 1888. In April, the Khalifa's final ultimatum to Queen Victoria, the Sultan, the Khedive and Sir Evelyn Baring was issued.

The conditions for the invading force were not propitious. The reliability of some of the troops was in question – especially of the Batahin of the Isle of Meroe who had resisted taxation the previous year and in retaliation had had sixty-seven of their number seized and publicly hanged in Omdurman. Undernourished before they left New Dongola on 3 May 1889, the troops had still received no fresh rations up to the time they crossed the contemporary Egyptian frontier on 2 July, heading for a pro-Mahdist trading district north of Aswan. The army numbered a pitiful 5,000, encumbered by 8,000 family camp-followers whom the Khalifa calculated would inhibit troop desertions but who enormously increased the demand for provisions. The hope that sympathetic Egyptian *fellahin* would contribute to the invaders' rations was quickly confounded.

El Nejumi chose a route northwards on the high ground west of the Nile in order to avoid government military posts and patrolling gunboats, a precaution ignored by Abdel Halim Musa'id. The latter sought water from the Nile after crossing the frontier, leading to defeat in a pitched battle at Arqin and the loss of 900 killed and 500 prisoners. It was mid-summer. Horses died, men deserted, including almost all the artillerymen. It is alleged that after Arqin Abdel Halim, El Nejumi's military second-in-command and friend, sought to abort the expedition – despite El Nejumi's determination to advance – he was only able to maintain the loyalty of his army at the cost of allowing 500 voluntarily to retire.

In the face of daunting odds, El Nejumi pressed on twenty-five miles to Balaja south-west of Abu Simbel, there to halt two weeks in order to rally his depleted forces, acquainting Abdallahi and Yunus el Dikaim by letter of his seriously diminished resources.

The day after his arrival he received a call to surrender from the Egyptian *sirdar*, Fariq Sir Francis Grenfell Pasha, who had reached Aswan to take command about 10 July. Reinforcements of 500 Ja'aliyin would shortly reach El Nejumi, but his invading force would still number no more than 3,300, with 4,000 followers. Undismayed, he replied to Grenfell, who claimed that the Khalifa by appointing Yunus was wishing to rid himself of El Nejumi: 'Our object itself is to come to all the country and to cause its people to enter the Faith... Be not deceived by your soldiers and guns and rockets and the quantity of your powder which is devoid of God's help.' But the Mahdists had still found no sympathetic response in Upper Egypt, no provisions, no help. Babikr Bedri, present with the expeditionary force at Balaja, claimed that twenty-seven days had passed without his tasting bread and, with others, he would be lured into capture by the bait of bunches of dates. He personally witnessed El Nejumi overcome by dizziness due to hunger when leading the evening prayer. Having written a last dispatch to the Khalifa, Abdel Rahman el Nejumi bravely advanced again with Abdel Halim against two Egyptian brigades of 3,000 men, to perish in battle at Toski (Tushki) five days later on 3 August. 1,200 of his troops were killed, and only 800 escaped south to assist in the evacuation of Saras. The Egyptian victors, the cavalry commanded by Miralai Kitchener, sustained 25 killed and 140 wounded.

Slatin related that the Khalifa was shattered by the destruction and death of El Nejumi, at once dispatching reinforcements to Dongola where Yunus was authorised, in the event of an Egyptian advance, to retire to Merowe in Sha'iqi country. Once again the awaited Egyptian counter-invasion did not come. Yunus el Dikaim would be replaced by a pardoned Mohammed Khalid Zuqal in April 1890, only to return a year later. But within the space of seven months Khalifa had lost the services of two most successful generals: Hamdan Abu Anja and Abdel Rahman el Nejumi.[7]

Eastern Sudan 1885–91   The withdrawal of General Graham's railway building escort force in May 1885 had left Osman Digna still in command of a military force which except for Suakin, and for a little while longer Kassala and Bogos, continued to rule the eastern marches unchallenged in the Khalifa's name. Massawa, beyond Osman Digna's grasp, had been created a free port, then ceded by the British in late 1885 to the Italians; Bogos similarly to Emperor John, until wrested by the Italians along with Asmara in 1890 following John's death the previous year. But the Suakin–Berber route remained under Mahdist control.

Osman's troops had nevertheless taken a battering, and his difficulties were accumulating. Andrew Paul appraised his situation:

> His main strength was drawn from the Hadendoa, some of the Atbara Bisharin, several sections of the Otman Amarar, and some of the Tokar tribes such as the Hassanab, Ashraf, and Kimmeilab. From now on, however, all but a few of the most devoted were to desert him, and he was forced to rely more and more on reinforcements of Baqqara and riverain tribes, who were very far from popular and, as the Beja began to fail him, Osman's full ferocity was unleashed.

The Amarar would be severely punished for their equivocation by the execution of their *nazir* and a deputy *sheikh* in 1886, but the Gemilab

Amir Osman Digna after the Battle of Omdurman, 1898

section of Hadendoa now withdrew their support, causing Osman to visit Omdurman to seek reinforcements. The Khalifa responded by authorising the dispatch of a force of some 4,000 men, mainly Baqqara, under the Dongolawi *amir* Abu Qarja (Girgeh) to Kassala, which Osman visited on his return to Tokar, his headquarters. These reinforcements arrived in March 1887.

Before Osman's visit to Omdurman, where his reputation for brutality had preceded him, a new *hakimdar* of the East Sudan and the Red Sea littoral (to succeed Miralai Watson Pasha, appointed in May) had reached Suakin on 1 September 1886 – Miralai Herbert Kitchener, who had organised the supply caravans for the Gordon relief expedition. The arrival of the Baqqara reinforcements at Kassala, notwithstanding the bad relations quickly engendered between them and the Beja, was shortly followed by Kitchener's decision that he could dispense with two battalions from the Suakin garrison.

Profiting by this over-optimistic assessment by his adversary, Osman occupied Handub, fifteen miles north of Suakin, in the autumn of 1887, strengthening the siege of the port and joining in a major battle with the Amarar who declared against him. Kitchener obtained permission to reconnoitre Handub, in fact personally conducting another unsuccessful attempt to capture Osman on 17 January 1888. During this operation he was severely wounded in the jaw, but he successfully brought his force back within the Suakin fortifications, having inflicted 300 casualties on the *Ansar*. Evacuated to Cairo, Kitchener was back in early March to complete the fortifications but, quickly repatriated to England for further treatment before returning again in September 1888, he was now made Adjutant-General of the Egyptian Army and would join Lewa Charles Holled Smith Pasha, his successor as *hakimdar*, at Suakin. In December 1888, each leading a brigade at the Battle of El Jummayza (the Suakin garrison had been increased to 5,000 including 750 British), the two successfully broke the siege trench of Suakin built by Osman, inflicting 500 Mahdist casualties. Osman was then ordered by the Khalifa to retire from Handub to his former headquarters at Tokar in January 1889, effectively raising the siege of Suakin. Kitchener returned to his Cairo duties.

So far had the uneasy relationship between Osman Digna and Mohammed Osman Abu Qarja deteriorated that a commission of enquiry was sent by the Khalifa in February 1889 under the former ruler of Darfur, Mohammed Khalid (Zuqal), imprisoned for a year in

Kordofan in connection with the *Ashraf* rebellion but now rehabilitated to conduct the hearings. These culminated at the end of April in a Khedivial edict confirming Osman's senior position with Abu Qarja as his *wakil*, to be endorsed by a public act of reconciliation in Tokar. This was not a time for public altercation. Mohammed Khalid was sent on to Abu Hamed to report on the loyalties of the Ababda, then to Dongola.

Abu Qarja however was not mollified. On the morrow of El Nejumi's 1889 defeat at Toski he was writing to the British Suakin *hakimdar* encouraging an Anglo-Egyptian advance. By mid-1890 he had been transferred to Berber, but in January 1891 was back at Kassala where he resumed his duplicitous discussions with the enemy, this time the Italians at Massawa. By the end of that year he had been 'exiled' to Rejaf.

Osman's Tokar was indeed the granary of the north coastal areas but its inhabitants, who included troops, were not totally insulated from the hunger which beset less fortunate peoples of the Sudan following the failure of the 1888 harvest. Osman Digna, a trader by upbringing, was given leave by the Khalifa to augment, with the connivance of Suakin traders, the maritime trading links which he had already established with their counterparts across the Red Sea in the Hejaz, utilising safe anchorages north of Suakin. Ohrwalder from Omdurman related that Osman relieved the local famine in his territory by imports through the port of Trinkitat. The British authorities had been relaxing trade restrictions with the hinterland tribes with a view to encouraging their desertions, notably the Amarar and Hadendoa. The British military however were opposed to a policy of feeding the enemy and the presence now of a powerful ally in Cairo, the new Adjutant-General, wrought the closing of Suakin and Trinkitat to grain exports. By September 1890 Osman's trading post at Handub was breaking up, to be captured in January 1891.

Osman Digna had been thrust on to the defensive but he was still undefeated. Baring, now an ally of Kitchener, joined the latter in a successful démarche to Lord Salisbury, who authorised in February 1891 the capture of Osman's headquarters at Afafit, Tokar. It was no walkover, the battle hard fought on 19 February 1891, but this time with the participation of well-trained, well-led troops – Egyptian as well as Sudanese (among them, now commissioned, the Shilluk Yuzbashi Ali Jafoun). Osman, alerted by the earlier attack on Handub, fought tenaciously but having lost 700 dead out of his 7,000 force yielded the camp to Lewa Holled Smith and retired to high ground at Adarama on the Atbara river south of Berber before reporting to the Khalifa. The defeats at Tushki and Tokar, albeit mitigated by the death of Emperor John and the stabilisation of Darfur by Osman Adam before his sudden death in 1890, signalled the termination of the Khalifa's *jihad* strategy. The Suakin routes to Berber and Kassala were no longer blocked.[8]

The South 1885-93 No further *jihad* was directed towards the south in the years immediately following the death of the Mahdi. The forces of the *Ashraf amir* Karamallah had already occupied the Equatorial east bank of the Nile opposite Lado, leading to Emin's withdrawal to Wadelai where he arrived at the end of April 1885 (see p. 448). However it was the Egyptian government's remaining outposts under Rihan Agha between Lado and Dufile which were unexpectedly to be relieved from Mahdist pressure by the outbreak of disturbances in the western Bahr el Ghazal, necessitating Karamallah Kurqasawi's withdrawal from Equatoria and, in October 1886, his reinforcement of his brother and *wakil*, Mohammed, at Shakka under threat from Madibbo Ali.

The Khalifa, necessarily absorbed with the priority of stabilising an intermittently rebellious northern Sudan, displayed no immediate commitment either to the occupation or Islamisation of territory south of Fashoda and Shakka. When Omer Salih was eventually dispatched to Equatoria in July 1888 to demand Emin's surrender, Omer would report back that in the interim all efforts at conversion to Islam had proved quite unsuccessful, and thereafter proselytisation in the south did not seriously figure. Indeed to Ohrwalder in Omdurman, the 1888 expedition under Omer, a Ja'ali *amir* from Shakka – consisting of 1,500 men in three steamers and *dhahabiyas* – had the dual purpose first of securing Emin's submission; and secondly, of bringing back supplies of ivory and slaves from the former hunting grounds of Equatoria. (In fact Emin had by now jettisoned some 578 tons of ivory into the Bahr el Jebel.) Reaching Lado on 11 October 1888, Omer pressed on to capture Rejaf a week later.

Meanwhile Emin, created a *Pasha* in 1887, still at Wadelai, had by now learned of the proximity of H. M. Stanley's relief expedition, financed in Britain by private subscription. The arrival of Dr Junker via Zanzibar in Egypt with letters from Emin had persuaded Stanley in January 1887 to offer to lead the expedition, with the authority of the Khedive. In April 1888 Emin sailed in the *Khedive* to meet him at

Tunguru at the north-western end of Lake Albert. It was tentatively and secretly decided between them that Emin should withdraw from Equatoria to Zanzibar. Stanley then left back to Yambuya on the Aruwimi river to seek his rearguard.

Stanley had handed Emin the Khedive's invitation to Cairo, promotion to *lewa*, with authority to stay in Equatoria if he so decided but to expect no government assistance. Back at Wadelai, Emin found that suspicions had been awakened among his garrison that he was intending to abandon them and the province. Mutiny was in the air. Seeking to reassure the various outposts, and to make a final appraisal as to his withdrawal, Emin embarked on a tour of the province down the White Nile to Rejaf, but on reaching Kirri north of Dufile he learned that Rejaf was hostile and accordingly turned back to regain Wadelai. This time in Dufile, however, on 18 August 1888 Emin and Stanley's officer Mounteney Jephson were seized by a Sudanese officer, Fadl el Mula Mohammed, now in control of the Egyptian battalion at Dufile, who after due enquiry proceeded to depose Emin as governor of Equatoria on 25 September.

On capturing Rejaf in October 1888 and unaware of these developments, Omer Salih in October dispatched three envoys to Emin to require his submission, only for the envoys to be seized at Dufile and after many days of torture, bravely borne, to be thrown to the crocodiles. The Dufile rebels having failed to capture Rejaf and being under threat of retaliation, their new commander Salim Bey released Emin and his companions on 17 November, enabling the latter to return to Wadelai by steamer, before repulsing Omer Salih's attack ten days later and forcing him back to Rejaf.

Emin would meet with Stanley again on Lake Albert in January 1889 and on 17 February, joined by Salim Bey from Wadelai, the three in council agreed to evacuate Equatoria on 10 April, Salim returning to Wadelai to prepare the evacuation. Fadl el Mula and his contingent, now at Wadelai, determined however to stay in Equatoria, seized the arsenal and withdrew to the hinterland, leaving Salim with his followers to return again to Lake Albert, but too late. Stanley and Emin with 1,500 men, including 600 Egyptian soldiers, had already left on 10 April for Zanzibar which they reached in December. Emin would be murdered exploring in the Congo Free State in October 1892. Here on the steep slope of Kavalli south of Lake Albert, Frederick Lugard would himself encounter Salim in September 1891 – six feet tall, fifty years old: 'He is no fool... I had met a man who was shrewd and suspicious and strong-willed' – and was impressed by Salim's continuing devoted loyalty to the Khedive. Of such loyalty Lugard would himself become the beneficiary (see p. 552).

Only in mid-1889 had the return of one of Omer's steamers to Omdurman, laden with residual ivory from Emin's storehouses and the fruits of slave *razzias*, brought news of Omer's arrival at Rejaf. Of his reversal at Dufile the Khalifa was not told. The successor steamer rapidly sent back to Omer with reinforcements would not arrive again at Omdurman for many further months and its news being no better, two *amirs* were dispatched to acquaint Omer that Equatoria was to be regarded solely as a place for exiles, peripheral to the Mahdist Sudan.

Omer Salih had been careful to establish good relations with the Bari and other local peoples, but they would not acquiesce to military occupation. With the help of his Omdurman reinforcements, bringing his garrison up to 2,300 men, Omer nevertheless pressed south to occupy Muggi, Kirri, Bedden and Dufile by mid-1890 and also captured Makaraka. Fadl el Mula at Wadelai sent in his submission, to be made an *amir* by Omer, but this was not to the liking of his troops who repulsed Omer's approach in March 1891 with 700 casualties, before joining Salim at Lake Albert. Fadl el Mula himself escaped south by steamer, while Omer in December 1891 found himself with a mutiny at Rejaf on his hands. News of these reverses reaching Omdurman, an irate Khalifa in March 1893 ordered Omer to withdraw to Rejaf.

The Dongolawi *amir*, Mohammed Osman Abu Qarja, recalled from Kassala at the end of 1891 and investigated regarding his governorship there, had already been nominated months later to succeed Omer at Rejaf, sailing in late 1892. Unamenable to his intended exile, on reaching Fashoda Abu Qarja feared assassination by his Baqqara companions. He decided to jump ship and retreat to the Nuba mountains, eventually reaching Rejaf with 141 followers to succeed Omer in June 1893 where, like the latter, he found himself under strict surveillance by the Ta'aishi second-in-command. Already the Khalifa had appointed as Abu Qarja's successor his own cousin, Arabi Dafa'allah – formerly a lieutenant of Mohammed Khalid during the latter's brief succession to Yunus Dukaim at Dongola. Departing Khartoum in August with two steamers, 300 men and the now exiled Mohammed Khalid (see p. 499), Arabi skirted Bor, which was possibly in Dinka control, to reach Rejaf in October 1893.

By the end of 1893 Arabi had put Abu Qarja on trial for peculation, convicted him and imprisoned him on an island at Rejaf. Having quashed the simmering rivalries between the Ta'aisha and Danagla, in November Arabi led an expedition against the Latuka, defeating them in a major battle and convincing the hostile Bari, probably led by Mödi Adong Lado, that they should make their submission. Arabi was now able to turn to confront a new enemy – the Congolese from beyond the Nile-Congo watershed.[9]

The Equatoria expedition of July 1888 commanded by the *amir* Omer Salih had had an uninterrupted journey through the Shilluk corridor to the Bahr el Jebel. Since the disastrous attack on the Mahdi at Jebel Qadir by Rashid Bey Ayman, *mudir* of Fashoda, in December 1881, with Shilluk backing, in which both he and the Shilluk Reth Kwickon were killed, relationships between the Mahdi and the Shilluk had been non-hostile. Yor, son of Reth Akoc Awot, ignoring his brother Jok who had been left acting *reth*, successfully sought the Mahdi's approval of his own claim as 'Reth Omer' and, at least until the famine of 1888–9, the Shilluk seem to have been exempt from *razzias* in return for a willingness to fight on the Mahdist side.

In that year, in order to feed immigrant Ta'aishi vigilantes in Omdurman, Ta'aisha were arbitrarily sent up the White Nile to the Shilluk territory, accompanied by a military force in two steamers to levy the *sharia* tax on grain and cattle. Yor (Omer) objected to the invasion, and responded to the Mahdist demand by sending 2,000 sacks of grain to Omdurman as a free will offering. Ohrwalder affirmed that it was these supplies that saved Omdurman from absolute starvation.

This response was deemed unacceptable behaviour by the Khalifa who instructed Amir El Zaki Tamal, the fortunate victor of Gallabat, to lead a punitive expedition to the Shilluk territory in 1891. El Zaki appears to have marched to Kawa (El Ais) at the end of the rains, embarked his force on steamers to land at Fashoda, surprising Reth Yor who was captured and executed, his head exhibited in Omdurman, just as Father Ohrwalder escaped to Egypt at the end of November 1891. When El Zaki returned to Omdurman, leaving a garrison of 500 armed men at Fashoda, he took with him Kur son of Reth Nyidhok (1845–63) whose candidature to succeed Yor was then approved. He became 'Abdel Fadil' and would rule the Shilluk until deposed in 1903.

El Zaki's brutal onslaught was staunchly resisted by the Shilluk – in Slatin's opinion the finest and bravest of the Sudanese Black tribes. Notwithstanding that it was spears against Remingtons, they even captured a Mahdist flag in a successful encounter on the east bank near the Sobat with the help of the Nuer and Anuak. By March 1892 however the whole country had been pillaged, the survivors dispersed, male captives put to the sword, and women and children shipped as slaves to Omdurman. An attempt to preempt Kur's installation by Akol, son of Reth Kwatker of the southern Shilluk, was defeated in two battles, Kwom and Dettim, seemingly with the assistance of Amir Arabi Dafa'allah, then en route to Rejaf in September 1893. Akol would join the other exiles. Douglas H. Johnson found the atrocities perpetrated by El Zaki's *Ansar* still unforgotten by the Nuer and Dinka south of the Sobat river in the 1980s.[10]

5 THE TURN OF THE TIDE 1889–92: CIVIC APPOINTMENTS AND THE *ASHRAF* REBELLION

The decisive defeat of the *amir el umara'*, Abdel Rahman el Nejumi, at Toski in August 1889 did not mark the end of the *jihad*, but would signal the point of time whence Mahdist policy of territorial expansion in the cause of religious conversion was progressively forced on the defensive. Northwards the road was now blocked. To the east, the Khalifa had accepted that Suakin was unassailable and had ordered his *amir* to retire on Tokar, while an increasingly ambitious Italian colonial intrusion, based on Massawa, was now wresting Bogos from an acquiescent Menilek, an as yet unapprehended threat to Kassala. In Equatoria the Mahdist attack had spent itself in 1886 and was only now being revived by Omer Salih's riverain expedition and the capture of Rejaf.

In the far west, after a series of hard fought battles and some defeats, the young and courageous Amir Osman Adam had suppressed the uprising of Ahmed Abu Jummaiza, the Masalit *feki*, by early 1889 but that had not totally curbed the aggression of the vengeful divisions of the non-Arab tribes of the Wadai border of western Darfur – notably the Dars Masalit, Tama and Qimr joined by the survivors of the Beni Helba and Beni Hussein. With the support of the Sultan of Wadai and, less enthusiastically perhaps, of Rabih Fadlallah, Sulieman Zubeir's former general (see p. 351), these frontier peoples kept up the pressure on Osman, effectively holding him to the frontier of Kebkebia and Qulqul. In 1890 Osman, retiring from a further expedition against them, seemingly contracted typhoid fever from his troops and died on arrival at El Fasher – to be succeeded as *amir* by another young, but less gifted, nephew of the Khalifa, Mahmoud Ahmed.

The years 1886–89, which followed the defeat of the pre-emptive bid for the succession by the Mahdi's *Ashraf,* had been marked by a series of military victories. While the Khalifa himself must be credited with the strong leadership and strategy, there were certainly remarkable displays of generalship, notably by Hamdan Abu Anja, Osman Digna and Osman Adam. To their names should have been added that of the Mahdi's *amir el umara'* Abdel Rahman el Nejumi but, despite his help in the defeat of the Sennar garrison in 1885, he was innately distrusted by the Ta'ishi Khalifa on account of his Ja'ali origins. These armies however constituted a formidable cost burden on the central and provincial treasuries, to which from 1888 onwards had to be added the heavily subsidised living of the Ta'aishi and other immigrants to Omdurman, contrasting sharply with the penurious conditions in which the *Ashraf* had been forced to live after 1886.

Civic Appointments   Internally, the Khalifa Abdallahi had been the legatee of able occupants of two major civic appointments. The *Qadi el Islam,* Sheikh Ahmed Ali, had been the choice of the Mahdi back in 1882. Father Ohrwalder rated him 'a particularly good man' if 'of rather a vacillating, timorous disposition' leading to miscarriages of justice, but nevertheless a judge who gave protection to Europeans from abuse. Presiding over the supreme court, Sheikh Ahmed was used also by the Khalifa as a conciliator and would serve his master faithfully for many years. Holt has analysed the contemporary reorganisation of the judiciary of the Khalifa's succession. Sheikh Ahmed Ali did however over the years, according to Slatin, continue progressively to amass considerable wealth – 'immense estates, … immense herds of cattle and quantities of camels and magnificent horses; but his most coveted possession was his harem.' These would progressively arouse the cupidity of the Khalifa's brother, Yaqub, and son, Osman Sheikh el Din, culminating later in 1894 with Sheikh Ahmed Ali's arrest and death with the confiscation of the assets, a fate suffered a year later by his successor, Hussein Ibrahim el Zahra.

Since the abortive *Ashraf* conspiracy of 1886 Yaqub's power base had been his command, as *wakil,* of the Khalifa's Black Flag division, at least until the manhood of Abdallahi's son, the putative heir apparent (even if traditionally the other *Khalifas* had the first claim). The arrival of the Ta'aishi militia in Omdurman in 1888 lent further strength to Yaqub's authority and all the while he had daily access to his brother.

Sheikh Ahmed Ali would not be the only member of the ruling oligarchy to fall foul of Yaqub in the later years.

The *Qadi el Islam* necessarily worked in close liaison with the *wakil mahkamāt el Islam* who, as deputy of the Omdurman law court, had the responsibility in association with the regional *amirs* for, *inter alia*, supervising the courts and recommending the appointments of provincial judges. Such a *wakil*, Sulieman el Hajjaz, held office at least during the period 1886–92 and would, in Omdurman, sometimes sit on trials with the *Qadi el Islam*.

A second major civic appointment, that as commissioner (*amin*) of the central Treasury (*beit el mal*) of Ahmed Sulieman, had been originally made in April 1883 following the fall of El Obeid. A trusted friend of the Mahdi, he had not troubled to disguise his support of the *Ashraf* conspiracy and in April 1886 had been thrown into prison. His subordinate at Berber, Ibrahim Adlan, became the Khalifa's commissioner in his place.

Ibrahim Adlan soon proved a most able servant of the Khalifa. Born in Wad Medani, a merchant in El Obeid, the Mahdi had originally appointed him to his financial cadre. He was now about thirty-five, exercising unique authority, comparable perhaps with that of the *mufettish* under Khedive Ismail, but in a less corrupt, far more scrupulous manner. Reporting daily to the Khalifa, Adlan was responsible for intra-departmental reforms and many innovative revenue-enhancing policies. Ivory (from Equatoria) and gum (from Kordofan) reverted to being government monopolies, with huge profits forthcoming from the mark-up of the auction sale over the *beit el mal* purchase price. Ohrwalder reports Adlan's facility, based on his personal prestige, in raising loans from subscribing merchant partnerships. Grain supplies were controlled from a government store. Camels, sheep and goats were sold by government auction. Trade channels with Egypt and with Suakin were sanctioned by the Khalifa. A new, but depreciated, currency was issued. Taxes continued to provide the principal source of revenue, the 2.5% *zakah* yielding good returns because deemed tolerable in its incidence.

Ibrahim Adlan's regime was altogether a success story until he appears to have overreached himself in arguing with Abdallahi, leading to a cautionary two weeks in the notorious El Saier prison; and then, a few months later, having been sent to the Gezira to appropriate without payment *dura* for the Omdurman battalions, he was deemed to have treated his fellow countrymen with too much leniency in the aftermath of the famine. Conspired against in his absence by the Ta'aisha, Adlan was recalled in January 1890 and berated by the Khalifa for infidelity. Slatin claims that Adlan responded:

> You reproach me now, I who have served you all these years; and now I do not fear to speak my mind to you. Through preference for your own tribe, and your love of evil-doing, you have estranged the hearts of all those who have hitherto been faithful to you. I have ever been mindful of your interests but as you now listen to my enemies, and to your brother Yaqub who is ill disposed towards me, I cannot serve you any longer.

Yaqub seized the opportunity to urge his public execution, superintending the event in February 1890 in person. Adlan submitted to hanging with dignity and courage.

Adlan was succeeded by his subordinate at Berber, El Nur Ibrahim from Gereif, Khartoum – under Egyptian rule a Khartoum local court member – who would introduce the *ushur* tax, ostensibly of one tenth the value of crops and the goods of merchants. In 1894, now in charge of the mint, he would effect the further debasement of the Mahdist silver coinage.[11]

The *Ashraf* Rebellion   Adlan, unlike his predecessor Ahmed Sulieman, had not benefited from the protection which stemmed from close association with the Mahdi. Ahmed Sulieman, following the confiscation of his goods, had gained release from prison. Mohammed Khalid (Zuqal), the Mahdist relative and *amir* deeply implicated in the *Ashraf* conspiracy of 1886, had also regained his liberty. In January 1889 the Khalifa sent him as a personal emissary first to Amir Osman Digna, charged with reining back the latter from his hostility to the Beja; and secondly to Abu Hamed to report on current attitudes of the Ababda frontier people. Following El Nejumi's defeat in August 1889 at Toski and the subsequent oppressive excesses of Yunus el Dikaim in Dongola province, Khalid found himself for the while appointed governor on Yunus's recall.

Khalid busied himself in liaison with El Nur at Wadi Halfa, but was subjected to the military supervision of two *amirs* – his deputy the Habbani Musa'id Qaydum, El Nejumi's old enemy; and the Ta'aishi Arabi Dafa'allah – respectively commanding Baqqara and Black *jihadiya* contingents. These Baqqara commanders quickly clashed with the *aulad el balad*, the major riverain Arab troops, notably the Ja'aliyin

Amir Yunus el Dukaim at Umm Debeikerat

and Danagla. Khalid in March 1891 found his authority successfully flouted and although his Baqqara 'minders' were summoned by the Khalifa and replaced by Yunus el Dukaim, they were able, with the ready connivance of Yaqub, to bring accusations of treachery against Khalid. On recall to Omdurman in late summer 1891 Khalid was found guilty and this time imprisoned for life (prior to the impending *Ashraf* rebellion). Two years later in 1893 he would be sent under Arabi Dafa'allah to exile in Dufile.

Ever since the undoing of the original conspiracy of the *Ashraf* in 1885–6, the indignities subsequently visited upon them, and in particular upon the Khalifa Mohammed Sharif, had left festering wounds. Their subordination in status and public respect to the Ta'aishi compatriots of the Khalifa was now, with the partisan humiliation and imprisonment of Mohammed Khalid, cousin of the Mahdi, instrumental in provoking a second more determined effort to overthrow one whom the *Ashraf* deemed the usurper of the Mahdist succession.

The Khalifa Abdallahi for his part felt substantially confident, subject to the propitiation of the Western tribes, in embarking upon a further trial of strength with the Mahdi's relations. It was now six years since the Mahdi's death and the charisma and the religious devotion he had commanded had been steadily fading, as increasingly the country moved from theocracy to military dictatorship. The reverses at the hands of the new Egyptian army at Tushki in 1889 and at Tokar in 1891 had not, in the event, precipitated any planned Egyptian invasion to threaten the Khalifa's supremacy. Despite the untimely death of Osman Adam, east Darfur at least for the while remained compliant. Moreover the pervasive grimness of family life in the wake of the harvest failure of 1888 had by 1890 been substantially relieved.

Ample warning of the coming storm was given to the Khalifa Abdallahi at a meeting convened in the house in Omdurman of Ahmed Sharfi, whose daughter was mother to the Mahdi. It took place, according to Father Ohrwalder, early in October 1891, but to Father C. Rosignoli on the 24th. Abdallahi, Mohammed Sharif and Ali Wad Hilu, the three *Khalifas*, were all present, together with the *Qadi el Islam*, Sheikh Ahmed Ali. Khalifa Mohammed Sharif, with all the rashness of impatient youth, roundly accused Abdallahi (according to Ohrwalder who escaped from Omdurman during the stand-off) of excluding his fellow *Khalifas* from his counsels, their place usurped by Yaqub; of directing the revenues to the exclusive benefit of his family and the Baqqara; and of neglecting the religious precepts of Mahdism. Only the intervention of Sheikh Ahmed and Ahmed Sharfi prevented violence – that and the arrival of Yaqub and a military posse whereupon, on Abdallahi's promise to share his counsels, the meeting broke up.

If not before that gathering, Abdallahi had soon become aware of Mohammed Sharif's plans to stage a coup d'état with the backing of *aulad el balad* supporters from the Danagla and Ja'aliyin. By 23 November 1891 the rebel force under Khalifa Mohammed Sharif had gathered in the vicinity of the Mahdi's tomb in Omdurman but with no more than 100 Remington rifles. The Khalifa was ready. 1,000 rifles were issued to the Baqqara and the rebels surrounded. Shrewdly, to allow passions to subside and to restrain his undisciplined Ta'aisha, Abdallahi sent Sheikh Ahmed Ali to seek a reconciliation, but initially without avail. Sporadic firing commenced during which five *Ansar* were killed. Khalifa Ali wad Hilu was then sent to negotiate with Mohammed Sharif, eventually with success on 25 November. The *Ashraf* were conceded a general pardon for the rebellion and a seat on the council. The Red Flag standards inherited by El Nejumi were to be returned to Khalifa Mohammed Sharif, and proper financial provision made for the Mahdi's relatives. In return the rebels surrendered their arms and submitted unconditionally to Abdallahi.

The Khalifa Abdallahi had no intention that this should be the end of the matter. A commission of investigation was appointed. By the beginning of 1892 seven notables, including two uncles of the Mahdi and Ahmed Sulieman, the former treasury commissioner, had been accused as ringleaders of the rebellion. They were to be transported to Fashoda but, intercepted en route, were summarily executed by El Zaki Tumal, currently wasting the Dinka. The general pardon, it was claimed, had been cancelled on the authority of a prophetic vision vouchsafed to Abdallahi by the departed Mahdi. Khalifa Mohammed Sharif's *jihadiya* were seized in the Gezira by the end of January and Mohammed Sharif himself arrested, tried by a special court under Sheikh Ahmed Ali, and imprisoned indefinitely for disobedience. Two young sons of the Mahdi were committed to the supervision of Ahmed Sharfi. Thus was this apology for a rebellion quashed.

Yaqub, Abdallahi's brother, had yet another score to settle. Notwithstanding the complicity at Fashoda of El Zaki Tumal in the beating to death of the seven exiled *Ashraf*, and his unswerving loyalty to Abdallahi over the years, the scale of the booty brought back to Omdurman after suppressing the Shilluk antagonised Yaqub. El Zaki was posted back to his command of the Abyssinian marches, now to be based at Gedaref, but despite being initially supported by the Khalifa the Ta'aisha were bent on El Zaki's downfall. Failing to surrender his loot he was recalled to Omdurman in March 1893, arrested and immured in a stone hut. To the horror of the populace, he starved to death twenty-four days later. Only Arabi Dafa'allah is said to have had the courage to plead for Zaki's release. He would be dispatched to Dufile.[12]

6 HOLDING ON 1892–96

If the *jihad* had been discontinued by 1892, the frontiers of the Mahdist Sudan being now somewhat contracted, internally the defeat of the *Ashraf* conspiracy had persuaded the Arab *aulad el balad* of the riverain territories that a further trial of strength with Abdallahi was futile, however unpopular his Ta'aishi *amirs* might be in their respective province commands. Dr A. B. Theobald published the important intelligence report of Mustapha el Amin, the Ja'ali cousin of the *Qadi el*

Islam Sheikh Ahmed Ali, to Major Reginald Wingate, director of military intelligence in Cairo, dated 12 December 1892:

> When the Khalifa first began to rule, he exercised the greatest tyranny and oppression over the people, but now that the authority of his own tribe, the Baqqara, is undisputed and that internal dissensions have been suppressed, he is profiting by former experience and is doing his utmost to establish a more lenient and popular system of government; and his efforts are not altogether unsuccessful... Thus a slow but gradual consolidation is being effected and it is not unlikely that when the [Egyptian] government does eventually decide to re-enter the Sudan, it will meet with opposition on the part of those very tribes who have been most clamorous for its return... The Baqqara have become nationalised in their homes, the other tribes are accepting the situation, and now there is a more or less general feeling that an advance on the part of the Egyptian Government must be considered as an attempt to interfere with their independence. This feeling is strongest in Omdurman and its vicinity, and weakest amongst the population immediately in contact with outside influences.

Eastern Sudan   From 1892 for the next four years there would be no further significant loss of territory by the Khalifa save in respect of Eastern Sudan. Indeed a number of daring raids were launched north from Suarda, the frontier post on the borders of Mahas and Sukkot, in 1892 and 1893, the impetus of which carried the *Ansar* beyond Saras and Wadi Halfa into Egypt and the Kharja Oasis west of Esna; and also east to the Murrat Wells of the Atmur desert, causing concern in Cairo. Osman Digna maintained his command at Adarama on the left bank of the Atbara river, with first Abu Qarja, then Musa'id Qaydum, governor in Kassala.

Ahmed Ali Ahmed, a former lieutenant of Hamdan Abu Anja, had been appointed to succeed El Zaki Tumal still at Gallabat, becoming complicit in the latter's arrest in March 1893. He would soon perish with 2,000 men in an abortive expedition to recover Bogos that December in a clash with Italian troops at Agordat. Under El Zaki's orders, the military headquarters of the province had been shifted from Gallabat to Gedaref and it was here that Ahmed Fadil, who had fought under Osman Adam against Abu Jummaiza and had assisted Yaqub

Mohammed in the suppression of the *Ashraf*, came to take up command. Within months the Italians, encouraged by their success against Ahmed Ali Ahmed and exploiting Ahmed Fadil's withdrawal of reinforcements, had moved on Kassala town, left under the command of Musa'id Qaydum. The remaining *Ansar* garrison, angered by the oppressive regime of their commander, offered no resistance and in July 1894 retreated north to Qoz Regeb there to be joined by Osman Digna. Such a withdrawal would have been unthinkable by *Ansar* inspired by the personal charisma of the Mahdi. From now on the eastern frontier of the Khalifa would be the left bank of the Atbara river from Adarama in the north (east of Damer) through Qoz Regeb, El Fasher (Atbara) and Asubri to Gallabat (a much diminished garrison), with the mounted camel corps at Gedaref in reserve.[13]

Equatoria The troops of a second European country had thus established themselves in the Sudan. Nor would these prove the only European occupations, although the Equatorial Sudan could scarcely be claimed as *Ansar* territory of comparable significance and tradition with the lands north of the eleventh parallel. Since the withdrawal by Karamallah Kurqusawi from the environs of Lado in 1886, two years would elapse before the conquest of Rejaf by Omer Salih in October 1888 and, following his subsequent unsuccessful attack on Dufile the next year, the Khalifa had resolved that Rejaf should be considered the furthest *Ansar* garrison, a penal settlement for disloyal exiles and a source of ivory and slaves.

Father Ohrwalder, before his escape in late 1891, had in his restricted surroundings reviewed the recrudescence of slave-trading from the early days of Mahdism, especially following the conquest of Bahr el Ghazal and Darfur, and Hamdan Abu Anja's suppression of the Nuba rebellion of 1886. He concluded that at least by 1891 'slave-hunting is not carried on in the same way that it used to be'. The description 'slaves' encompassed the forcible recruitment of Black *jihadiya* recruits, such as Arabi Dafa'allah would be seeking in his *razzia* on the Latuka in November 1893. The commercial profit motive of the Dongolawi traders of the Egyptian occupation was much diminished.

During his brief exercise of authority as *amir* of Equatoria Abu Qarja had, in August 1893, sent a force of 480 to inspect Makaraka, only to find that a Congolese army with the support of the Zande *sultan* Zemio had conquered the territory and, with Fadl el Mula Mohammed's *jihadiya,* established three well-defended *zaribas* on the Congo–Nile Divide. Abu Qarja's ultimatum to surrender would be ignored. This Congolese invasion by some 800 trained soldiers, led by Belgian officers and financed and directed by King Leopold II of Belgium in his private capacity, had left Leopoldville on the Atlantic seaboard in February 1891 believing it had, through a draft agreement of 1890 with the Imperial British East Africa Company, a licence to occupy the west bank of the Nile north to Lado. On arrival near Wadelai in October 1892 the Belgians had persuaded Fadl el Mula at Dufile to join them and to establish a *zariba* at Ganda, and had then occupied Labore, Moogie (Muggi) and Kerri for a short period in the summer of 1893, until the belligerence of Mahdist Rejaf persuaded them to evacuate.

This was the unexpected threat encountered by Arabi on arrival at Rejaf in October 1893. Having refortified his base and subdued local tribes he marched on Fadl el Mula, catching him on 10 January 1894 en route from Ganda to Dufile, encircling and annihilating him and his force. The survivors fled to Wadelai, thence to Lake Albert. 300 rifles, two brass guns and 150 *jihadiya* were captured but, more significantly, also the treaty correspondence between the Belgian King's Congo Free State and Fadl el Mula which recognised the former's claim to the west bank of the Nile, including Azande land. These documents were dispatched at once to the Khalifa, while Arabi – unaware that for a brief twenty-four hours a British officer from Uganda had planted a Union Jack at Wadelai in January – relentlessly pursued the inland Congolese garrisons westwards to Dungu on the Uele (Welle) river border of the Congo Free State. As late as 2 September 1894 Arabi defeated the Congolese but, still awaiting further reinforcements from Omdurman, was himself defeated east of Dungu in December, only to revenge the reverse by successfully ambushing the Congolese on 11 February 1895. The Belgian Congolese would not be free to advance from Dungu on the 'Lado enclave' until December 1896.

His vulnerability exposed by this defeat east of Dungu in December 1894, Arabi at once dispatched Omer Salih (evidently re-posted to Rejaf) back to Omdurman to seek further help, unaware that already eleven barges carrying Baqqara and *jihadiya* had left on 23 November 1894. Neither Omdurman nor Arabi knew that once again the White Nile had been blocked by *sudd* – this time at Shambe, so that Omer with two boats would not gain Omdurman until July 1895. He returned at once with three steamers – the *Ismailia, El Fasher,* and *Mohammed Ali* – and apparently, after a further delay at Fashoda, regained Shambe at last in January 1896 to find the *sudd* again impenetrable. Arabi having inexplicably received neither news nor reinforcements had called in the Makaraka garrison to Rejaf and now dispatched a land force via Tonj to seek help from Omdurman, presumably via Meshra el Rek, only for his force to be crushed by a Nuer attack, the survivors bringing news back to Rejaf from Fashoda of Omer Salih's isolation at Shambe.

Arabi decided to split his force again between Rejaf and the more navigable Bor, at last to be met at Bor by the *Mohammed Ali* which uniquely had cut through the *sudd*. Returning with it to Shambe, he discovered Omer Salih's reinforcements reduced to 300, half of whom he brought back to Bor. The *Ismailia* north of the *sudd* would reach Omdurman in September 1896: the *El Fasher*, inextricably trapped, had to be sunk. Arabi's total complement was now 1,400 men, short of food, with whom in February 1897 to confront the new Congolese arrival at Bedden.[14]

Bahr el Ghazal   Arabi at Rejaf was not the only Mahdist *amir* to find himself threatened by the Congolese invasion plan of what was loosely described as the Bahr el Ghazal. Until late 1893 the Mahdists, occupied with the attacks of the Western frontier tribes, had been content to accept the Bahr el Arab as their de facto border with Bahr el Ghazal. The news from Abu Qarja of the Congolese presence in Makaraka prompted the Khalifa to instruct Mahmoud Ahmed, the new *amir* of the Western Sudan, to divert El Khatim Musa, a former senior commander of Osman Adam, from an intended attack on the Dar Masalit on the Wadai border and to reoccupy the Feroje (Faruqi) lands around Liffi, compelling their chief Hamad el Abbas Musa to seek Zemio's protection. The latter's advance north under Congolese direction obliged El Khatim to retire to Shakka, while two Congolese expeditions from the Uele basin established themselves respectively on the Adda, south of Hufrat el Nahas, with Fur support and at M'belle 120 miles to the west in March 1894; and finally at Liffi, by the end of June, with Feroje assent.

The Khalifa had meanwhile ordered reinforcements to Shakka for El Khatim, in order as he told Slatin 'to drive out the Christians'. The rains delayed the departure of El Khatim's impressive force of 3,800, including 1,800 rifles, but when news reached the Belgian Congolese commander that he had crossed the Bahr el Arab by September 1894, orders were given to abandon Liffi and fall back on Morjan on the

Congo–Nile divide. El Khatim did not pursue the Congolese, whose own plans to resume the offensive were aborted by instructions at the end of November that, under the Franco-Congolese agreement of August 1894, they must evacuate the Bahr el Ghazal and keep behind the 'divide'. By February 1895 these Congolese had gone. El Khatim Musa was however instructed not to occupy the abandoned territory which reverted to a further interlude of anarchic independence.

Thus if, territorially, the Khalifa's position was for the moment relatively undiminished, French acquisition of the Nile–Congo headwaters was already planned (see pp. 561–2). Meanwhile, as Slatin escaped from Khartoum early in 1895, permission had been granted to reinstate El Khatim's punitive expedition against the rebellious non-Arab tribes west of Kebkebia and Qulqul. Only 800 men would return to Shakka.[15]

Central Government   Through these four fairly stable years 1892–96, the Mahdi's Khalifa continued to hold the country together by the indefatigable exercise of autocratic authority. In this latter regard he matched the Turkish Governor-General Ahmed Pasha Widan (1838–45) – and that was well before the conquest of Darfur in the 1870s – and Gordon. Unlike Ahmed Widan however, the extent of whose inspection tours and campaigns rivalled those of General Gordon, Abdallahi was reluctant to absent himself from his capital where he was well protected against enemies. The frontiers of the Khalifa's military commands presently varied with contemporary need, the *amirs*, aided by their subordinate *maqdoums*, reporting personally to the Khalifa at irregular intervals and maintaining regular communication with Omdurman, in the absence of telegraph lines, by dromedary couriers. In the event of error, *amirs* would be required to submit to investigative enquiry by commissioners who would report their findings. If this administrative structure did not differ substantially from that of the Turkish-Egyptian provinces, under the Khalifa's rule it was nevertheless indivisibly military, there being no necessary distinction between governor and military commander.

Following the escape of Slatin to Cairo in February 1895, a General Report on the Egyptian Sudan was compiled by Major F. R. Wingate which, taken with Slatin's comprehensive plan of the distribution of the Khalifa's military forces, gave a reasonably accurate picture at least of the deployment obtaining in 1895; and with minor revisions it has been reproduced here (see table opposite). Slatin pointed out that, of the whole complement of rifles/smooth bores, not more than 22,000 were

Distribution of Mahdist Forces by Military Command 1895

Position and Garrison	Amirs	Armed Strength			Guns	Rifles and Smooth Bores
		Jehadia	Cavalry	Swords Spearmen		
Omdurman (*Mulazimiya*)*	Osman Sheikh el Din	11,000	–	–	–	11,000
,,	Yaqub Mohammed	4,000	3,500	45,000	46	4,000
,, (in store)		–	–	–	–	6,000
Rejaf	Arabi Dafa'allah	1,800	–	4,500	3	1,800
Western Sudan						
El Fasher	Mahmoud Ahmed					
El Obeid	,, ,,	6,000	350	2,500	4	6,000
Shakka	,, ,,					
Berber	El Zaki Osman	1,600	500	1,300	6	1,600
Abu Hamed	El Nur Mohammed Anqara	400	100	700	4	400
Eastern Sudan						
Adarama (Qoz Regeb)	Osman Digna	450	350	1,000	–	450
Asubri	Hamid Ali	900	400	1,400	–	900
El Fasher (Atbara)		1,000	200	500	–	1,000
Gedaref	Ahmed Fadil	4,500	600	1,000	4	4,500
Gallabat		50	–	200	–	50
Dongola	Yunus el Dikaim	2,400	500	5,000	8	2,400
Suarda	Hammuda Idris	250	100	1,000	–	250
Total		34,350	6,600	64,000	75	40,350

*Khalifa's bodyguard

Source: Based on Slatin, Rudolf, *Fire and Sword in the Sudan*, 1896, p. 536

sound Remingtons. Of the 64,000 sword/spearmen, a quarter were unfit for combat, either too young or too old. And of 75 guns, six were large-calibre Krupps, eight machine guns, and the remainder brass muzzle-loaders for which the ammunition was inferior – it was also most limited for the Krupps guns.

On his recall once again from Dongola in June 1895, Yunus el Dukaim was succeeded by Mohammed Bushara, another Ta'aishi who despite his youthful years had been a veteran of Sheikan and Khartoum and then second-in-command to Osman Adam. The inner core of military rulers outside Omdurman (all Ta'aishi except for Osman Digna) was thus, as 1896 broke: Osman Digna (Suakin Frontier); Ahmed Fadil (Gedaref); Mahmoud Ahmed (Western Sudan); Arabi Dafa'allah (Rejaf); El Zaki Osman (Berber); El Nur Anqara (Abu Hamed); and now, Mohammed Bushara (Dongola). Arabi Dafa'allah (Rejaf) was out of communication.

Omdurman – the residence of the Khalifa, his brother Yaqub and eldest son, Osman Sheikh el Din – was the command centre for the Blue and White Niles, divided into a multiplicity of predominantly fiscal districts extending to Karkoj and Fashoda respectively. Professor Holt writes that: 'Before the Reconquest the whole extent of Mahdist territory on the Blue Nile from El Aylafun (Eilafun) southwards had been joined with the Gezira in a single province under Ahmed el Sunni' – tax-collector and administrator for the Gezira and a native of Wad Medani who, like other provincial commissioners, was responsible also to the central *beit el mal*. Within this large territory, divided into twenty districts each under a *wakil*, Ahmed el Sunni would be assisted, uniquely, by four confidential clerks and a Ta'aishi commandant of the *jihadiya*.

Omdurman also constituted the base both for the permanent garrison of 11,000 trained *jihadiya*, now called the *mulazimiya* or bodyguard, armed with Remingtons (with a further 6,000 in store), under the personal command of Osman; and for the Black Flag division including 30,000 sword and spearmen of the Baqqara under Yaqub – together with perhaps 8,000 of the Gezira tribesmen in the Green Flag division of the Khalifa Ali wad Hilu. The cavalry central reserve was also stationed in the capital. If the security forces in Omdurman were predominantly Baqqara and especially Ta'aisha, the latter were ill-equipped to staff the important civil service of the *beit el mal* and of the judiciary, where those not drawn from the riverain tribes, notably the Ja'aliyin, were for the most part former Egyptian, frequently Copt, officials. Daily the *qadis* and the most senior officials would meet with the Khalifa at the mosque enclosure adjacent to the Mahdi's tomb to report and receive his commands.

In the Khalifa's inner council until 1896 had been the occupants of the two principal civil offices – *Qadi el Islam*, head of the judiciary; and *amin, beit el mal*, commissioner of the treasury. The imprisonment and death of Sheikh Ahmed Ali in 1894, and likewise of his immediate successor in 1895, seem then to have brought an end to the office of *Qadi el Islam,* with its duties towards the interpretation of the *shari'a* as well as the supervision of the courts. Nevertheless the reorganised judicial system survived in its essentials.

The successor to the *amin* Ibrahim Mohammed Adlan, executed in 1890, had been more astute in the discharge of his central treasury responsibilities. El Nur Ibrahim el Gereifawi, after four years in office – during which his most notable achievements perhaps were the *ushur* tax, and (despite the contempt of the Khalifa for commerce) some development of external trade, especially through Suakin – had in 1894 been made commissioner of the mint. Further demonetisations of the currency facilitated the issue of 'new money' which was, however, quickly recognised as still less acceptable in an ostensibly cash economy. Revenues nevertheless continued to sustain in real terms both the central treasury, from which the military and other salaries and pensions were paid, and the Khalifa's private treasury which looked after the needs of himself, his household and his kinsmen.

If the regular payment of an inflated army was an essential condition of its discipline and contentment, and therefore of public security, that was not the only one. The army had also to be fed from internal resources and the Khalifa was fortunate that, during his reign, there was no repetition on a countrywide scale of the failure of the harvest of late 1888. The population of the state had undoubtedly shrunk substantially during the Mahdiya from the effects of the *jihad* and of famine – how far is unsubstantiated: some have opined that it was by more than half from an original 8 million – but the satisfaction of food demands was basically dependent on the output of agriculture in the riverain areas and, as under the Turkish-Egyptian occupation, the brutal incidence of tax gathering was a discouragement to the maximisation of productivity. Nevertheless the Gezira harvest of 1896 was abundant enough for the *'amil 'umumi*, Ahmed el Sunni, to export sufficient grain to Omdurman to sustain the critical interim redeployment of the *amir* Mahmoud Ahmed's garrisons, from Darfur and Kordofan, shortly to swell the forces confronting the Anglo-Egyptian invasion of Dongola.

As long as external invasion threats remained in abeyance and internal hostilities were contained, an uneasy quiescence on the part of the civilian population endured. Already, however, the consequence of major military operations, as in the case of the El Nejumi campaign against Egypt in 1889, had been experienced in the predatory raids on cultivators by undisciplined *Ansar* soldiery. Now external military threats would lead to the defensive concentration of troops and a repetition of the oppression to which the civil population had earlier been subjected. Nor would it be only in the northern frontier areas. Already by mid-1896 Arabi Dafa'allah, hemmed in by the impassable *sudd* at Shambe, had been forced to concentrate his military forces at Bor and then at Rejaf and, in quest of food supplies, had by December embarked on *razzias* against the Azande of the interior.[16]

15
The Mahdist State Crumbles 1896–98

1 ADWA (ADOWA) 1896

Long after the death of the Mahdi in June 1885 his mission under divine inspiration would still be prosecuted. His fundamentalist Islamic beliefs must progressively extend outwards to achieve the redemption of the lapsed Islamic and infidel worlds. Beyond the Sudan, the conquest of which against such odds had been the manifestation of the truth of his faith, all was *dar el harb* (war zone), lands designated in the fullness of time for further conquest, with whose peoples communication would meanwhile be limited to occasional ultimata, *indharat,* warning them of the fate that awaited them if they did not submit to the new enlightenment.

Abdallahi derived his authority and mission as the *Khalifat el Mahdi* by direct published appointment by the Mahdi, in his lifetime, as his designated successor; and, in confirmation of that prophetic vision, by Abdallahi's own subsequent *Proclamation of the Hair*, which made public his instructions from the Prophet Mohammed mediated through the Mahdi and El Khidr. The *jihad* was thus actively pursued until eventually blocked at the second cataract of the Nile by the Anglo-Egyptians; and by them and by the Italians along the Red Sea littoral. To these obstacles would be added the intractable opposition of the most westerly peoples of Darfur backed by Wadai; and, most recently, by the determined ambitions of King Leopold II towards the reaches of the Upper Nile.

Granted that he had been checked in his expansionist aims by 1890, the Khalifa did not for the while anticipate any serious external military threat to the Mahdist state of which he remained the relatively untroubled ruler. If he did not match the spiritual charisma of the Mahdi, he nevertheless ruled by a divine right complemented by the temporal experience of a rude tribal upbringing. Professor Holt summed him up: 'In Abdallahi, religious enthusiasm, administrative talent, and personal ambition competed for mastery.' As the outlook darkened, he would need all his resources.

The non-existence of serious intelligence of the outside world – the *dar el harb* - was evident in the Khalifa's council decision of 13 January 1896 that a campaign to recapture Kassala, lost to the Italians in July 1894, should now be launched. 'Come the three corners of the world in arms and we shall shock them' might have been the justifiably self-confident attitude of a generally victorious Khalifa towards the indigenous immediate neighbours of the Mahdist state. Kassala had however been possessed by a European power, a member (with Austro-Hungary and Germany) of the Triple Alliance, and its possession at least temporarily by Italy had been recognised by Britain in 1891. This decision of the Khalifa to attack was seriously provocative, though the British prime minister, the Marquess of Salisbury, deemed it presently of no great interest to Britain.

The degree of self-confidence which lay behind the Khalifa's decision became further apparent in the cool, if not actually hostile, tone of Abdallahi's response to Emperor Menilek's suggestion for an indefinite truce on their common frontier. Abdallahi was aware that the Italian invasion of Abyssinian Tigré, initially successful with the capture of Adwa and Axum in April 1895, had been thwarted by the Negus at Amba Alagi in December, but he did not of course know in January 1896 that its resumption would lead to the serious defeat of the Italians at Adwa on 1 March. That last development might, *prima facie*, have ensured a successful Mahdist reoccupation of Kassala, but the full repercussions of Adwa would be far from local and well beyond the strategic concepts of the Khalifa. British realpolitik of the time required the preservation of the Triple Alliance and therefore, it was concluded, an urgent purposeful gesture of solidarity by the British on Italy's behalf.

In the European great power context, contrary to the view of Baring (Lord Cromer since 1892) in Cairo, the Mahdist threat to Kassala was reckoned of little immediate importance. It was the catastrophe of Adwa, and the request by the Italian ambassador for a military diversion, that triggered the issue of instructions on 13 March 1896 by the British prime minister to Lord Cromer to make a feint up the Nile to Dongola. Thus it came about that the mobilisation of *Ansar* troops would in due time be directed not to an attack on Kassala – which would be retroceded to Egypt by the Italians under Kitchener's supervision in December 1897 – but to the defence of the northern Sudan where Akasha, thirty miles south of Saras, the Egyptian frontier post, would be occupied on 20 March 1896 by an Anglo-Egyptian force.

Menilek too was not immediately aware of the alarm in European chancelleries created by his victory at Adwa. The tone of his correspondence with Abdallahi, following the latter's haughty dismissal of his earlier overture, remained for the while comparably frigid but by 17 July 1896 Menilek had realised the dangerous implications of the advance on Dongola, and now regarded Abdallahi as an essential ally. He wrote to Abdallahi that in the light of the Anglo-Egyptian advance it was his wish 'to establish friendly relations with you [the Khalifa] and to cease friendly relations with the Whites, the enemies of God... Your enemy is our enemy and our enemy is your enemy, and we should stand together as firm allies.' Menilek had concluded that his African victory could incite fears among Europeans of further *Ansar* attacks and inspire counter-measures.

If the initiative towards an entente came again from the Negus, this time it was to be reciprocated by the Khalifa. The latter's personal envoy would return to Omdurman from Addis Ababa in early 1897 with a provisional peace agreement, thus safeguarding the Mahdist eastern frontier – it had become increasingly apparent that Dongola was not the limit of British objectives. And the Khalifa had also to consider his western and southern flanks. In the Bahr el Ghazal, the retreat of the Belgians in early 1895 on French insistence had enabled the Khalifa to send his much delayed punitive expedition against the western Darfur rebels, holding that front for the while. As for the Upper Nile there was little that could be done. Arabi Dafa'allah remained quite cut off by the obstruction of the *sudd* but with, for 1896 at least, his forces concentrated at Rejaf. His territory was not yet under serious threat.[1]

2 DONGOLA AND MEROWE 1896

The consequences of Adwa for the northern front of the Mahdist state developed by irregular stages, leaving the Khalifa guessing as to Cairo's as yet unformulated objective. Initially the British Cabinet to help the Italians had sanctioned an advance up the Nile 'as far – and no farther – than we can [go] without any undue effort on the part of Egypt'; but, to intimidate the Khalifa, an advance to Dongola was publicly canvassed. This however would be no second Sudan Gordon relief expedition even if, in the words Hilaire Belloc would attribute to his fictional Captain Blood, 'Whatever happens we have got/The Maxim gun and they have not' (*The Modern Traveller*).

By the latter part of March 1896 Abdallahi would have learned of the Anglo-Egyptian troops' advance from Saras, south of Wadi Halfa, to Akasha and perhaps also of the mobilisation by Cairo of the Egyptian reserves. He ordered his young relative *amir* Mohammed Bushara at Dongola to reinforce his advance post at Suarda, 130 miles to the north, and summoned the officers of the mobilised Kassala expedition from the White Nile and Gezira for new instructions. The Khalifa nevertheless still remained in ignorance of the strategic intentions of the invaders, which by May 1896 had yet to crystallise, although it was apparent that a new railway was being built from Akasha south through the *batn el hajjar* east of the Nile. The *Ansar* meanwhile under the Dongolawi *amir* Osman Azraq had marched as a precaution further from Suarda to Firket (Farka), thirteen miles south of Akasha, the Egyptian advance position and, some distance still further north of Firket, they met Sir Herbert Kitchener's advance guard and were worsted in a skirmish on 1 May. Five weeks later, on 7 June, the *Ansar* were surprised, outnumbered and defeated by an Egyptian army of 9,000 at their camp at Firket, suffering heavy casualties.

Suarda being no longer defensible, the Khalifa sanctioned the *Ansar* withdrawal to the new defensive line at Hafir and Dongola (El Urdi). He was still uncertain of the ultimate Anglo-Egyptian objective which, following the outcome of the Firket battle, had now been confirmed by London as the occupation of Dongola province including the Sha'iqi stretch of the Nile, east to Merowe only.

As the full summer of 1896 wore on, the Anglo-Egyptian force waited for the Nile to rise and the railway to progress. Kitchener's proverbial 'luck' faded. Throughout July the gunboats and supply steamers waiting below the second cataract remained halted because the Blue Nile surge was late and, for forty consecutive days, in Winston Churchill's words, 'the wind blew hot and adverse from the south'. To an impatient message from Kitchener as to the delay in the river convoy, the fabled reply was sent: 'Colonel (Archibald) Hunter can make wind, but not a north wind. Colonel Hunter can make water, but not a Nile flood.' Meanwhile a cholera epidemic from Cairo, spreading up the Nile beyond Aswan, forced the abandonment of Firket in favour of Kosheh (Maqraq) ten miles to the south and exacted 800 casualties.

At last on 23 August 1896 Kitchener was ready to resume his advance, with an army of 15,000 men including a British battalion, to Dongola itself. Mohammed Bushara's force was established at Hafir. Tricked into believing that the Egyptian steamers were by-passing him en route to

Dongola itself, so rendering his fortified positions at Hafir untenable, on 19 September Mohammed Bushara ordered their evacuation, and those at Dongola and Merowe within the following week. His correspondence with the Khalifa, as at Firket, fell into Kitchener's hands. Kitchener regarded Merowe as essential, being protected by the fourth cataract from up-river attack. Dongola fell to him on 23 September.

The Khalifa would perhaps have been relieved had he learned Cromer's immediate opinion that 'the Sudan campaign is virtually over', and was contemplating a stop 'for two or three years at Dongola before making any further advance'. The victorious Kitchener, however, now KCB and a major-general, was able to persuade the British government by the end of November 1896 that he should advance on Berber, even if the financial responsibility for the further campaign costs and the route to be followed were unresolved. In the event, Britain would advance the money.

If the Khalifa was evidently facing a far better trained, officered and equipped Egyptian army, to which he had been obliged to concede important territory, there was presently no threat from that quarter to the western Sudan; while the Suakin and Tokar Egyptian garrisons were in defensive attitude towards Osman Digna (no resumption of railway building to Berber there). Overall the recent *Ansar* casualties sustained had been serious but not crippling. The Sudan's natural defences – the Bayuda desert between Korti and Metemma, and the Atmur desert between Korosko and Abu Hamed – posed the same historical problems of logistics, water and climate to invaders. In the wake of Amir Mohammed Bushara's evacuation of Dongola province in September 1896, Abdallahi prudently dispatched the experienced ruler Yunus el Dukaim to command the strategic frontier province of Berber, bringing back the remaining *Ansar* of the Dongola campaign to Metemma, there to reinforce what must be the principal bulwark against a predictable advance across the Bayuda desert.[2]

3   ABU HAMED AND BERBER 1897

No one knew the problems of the Bayuda route better than Kitchener, veteran of the Gordon Relief Expedition. The 1885 railway from Wadi Halfa via Saras and Akasha had admittedly been reinstated and extended up the east bank of the Nile to Kosheh before the last stage of the advance on Dongola; and in October 1896 work on the final stretch to Kerma had commenced, to be completed in May 1897. By this time Berber, but no further than Berber, had been sanctioned as Kitchener's target for 1897. How was it to be approached?

The hardships encountered in the camel-borne crossing of the Bayuda desert from Korti to Abu Klea (Abu T'laih) in 1885; the crossing's continuing vulnerability to raiding groups; and the subsequent delays experienced by Major-General William Earle's Nile river passage east from Merowe towards Abu Hamed: all these now persuaded the *sirdar* that notwithstanding the water problems, the solution to the successful advance to Berber lay in a *second* railway extending from the same technical workshops at Wadi Halfa (not Korosko) across the Atmur Desert via Abu Hamed. Finance was approved in London by December 1896 and work on this second railway commenced in January, to be greatly accelerated on the completion of the Kosheh–Kerma section along the Nile from May 1897.

By mid-July 1897 Kitchener at Merowe had learned of the arrival of Amir Mahmoud Ahmed at Metemma from Omdurman, while the trans-Atmur railway had only progressed half way. Recognising the now even more crucial importance of Abu Hamed to the completion of his railway, Kitchener, despite the heat, dispatched a flying column of 3,600 men by night marches covering 133 miles to capture Abu Hamed nine days later on 7 August 1897. They were assisted by an Ababda force led by a son of the late Hussein Pasha Khalifa, three weeks later to be reinforced by five Egyptian gunboats hauled up over the fourth cataract.

The Khalifa had accepted the need for reinforcements against Egypt following Mohammed Bushara's cession of Dongola the previous September. He needed a battle-seasoned Abu Anja or an El Nejumi to take command in the north, but in his necessity he had ordered his thirty-year-old nephew Mahmoud Ahmed, hitherto *amir el umara'* of the west, to quit that station in September 1896 with his army – excluding certain tactical garrison dispositions – and to march to Kerreri, Omdurman where from early 1897 he would form the strategic reserve against the northern invader. Due to the efforts of loyal representatives like Ahmed el Sunni, principal agent in the Gezira, sufficient stores of grain were obtained to victual the new troops for the few months until their movement north to Metemma in June 1897. Mahmoud was appointed overall commander of the northern Sudan including Abu Hamed and Berber.

The movement to Metemma was precipitated by the Khalifa's conclusion, following their *sheikh*'s summons to Omdurman, that the loyalty of the Ja'aliyin at Metemma could not be assumed and that Sheikh Abdallah Sa'ad Farah should at once evacuate Metemma on the west bank and cross the river. The Khalifa and Mahmoud believed that would be the objective of Kitchener's thrust. Refusing to comply, Sheikh Abdallah sought Kitchener's help at Merowe, but before the relief could reach Metemma Mahmoud had attacked, on 1 July 1897, massacred Sheikh Abdallah, his force and the inhabitants, and sacked the town. This action and the ensuing undisciplined behaviour of the Baqqara troops excited the enduring hatred of the Ja'aliyin. Nor was that the full extent of Mahmoud's misjudgement. Three weeks later he was still ignorant of the increasing importance to Kitchener of Abu Hamed, seeking guidance from the Khalifa as to whether Berber should or should not be held in the event of the anticipated Anglo-Egyptian crossing of the Bayuda from Korti.

By July perhaps himself aware of the progress of the Wadi Halfa–Abu Hamed railway, if not of the flying column from Merowe, the Khalifa counselled the immediate fortification of Berber as the key to the navigable main Nile and to the Atbara river defence line. However when, by 11 August 1897, news came from Mohammed el Zaki Osman, Yunus el Dukaim's successor governor of Berber, that Abu Hamed had fallen, Mahmoud, perhaps still fearful of attack from the Bayuda, had still not moved his main force to Berber. Nor, contrary to his assurance to the Khalifa, had he done so by 31 August, by which time, faced with a mutinous garrison, Mohammed el Zaki had evacuated the town, which on 6 September fell to the Anglo-Egyptian force without a contest.

Within weeks Metemma was being raided by enemy steamers while the arrival of the retreating Berber garrison would add to the serious shortage of corn. In February 1898 Osman Digna, ordered by Omdurman five months previously to vacate Adarama on the edge of the Butana grain districts and subsequently operating on the lower Atbara, would himself arrive at Shendi from Qoz Regeb with his force, to aggravate the food situation even more.[3]

4 THE ATBARA 1898

The months of September 1897 to January 1898 were expended in the exchange of opposing plans between the Khalifa with his advisers in Omdurman, and Mahmoud with his military council in Metemma.

Faced with the loss of Berber, the Khalifa initially urged Mahmoud's withdrawal to the Sabaluqa gorge, a position by the sixth cataract which had the advantage of closer proximity to the Gezira food supplies. Mahmoud countered with a proposal to attempt the recovery of Berber, thereby also relieving the grain shortage on Metemma; but, while they backed the policy, Mahmoud's officers had no stomach for its implementation. It is extraordinary that neither the Khalifa nor his brother took personal command (there was disagreement between Yaqub and Osman Sheikh el Din). The Khalifa enjoyed the luxury of extended procrastination only because the Anglo-Egyptians, for their part, were reasonably apprehensive of their ability to defend Berber, only lightly reinforced from Merowe, against attack from Metemma which, it was confidently predicted by Wingate, would be led by the Khalifa in person. Considerations of good maintenance for his steamer fleet on a falling Nile persuaded Kitchener to establish a fortified dockyard just north of the junction of the Nile and Atbara, but he was reluctant to advance further south, preferring the location of any decisive battle to be as close to the railroad at Abu Hamed (established on 31

Wingate questioning Amir Mahmoud Ahmed after the Battle of Atbara

Sir Herbert (later Earl) Kitchener

August 1897) as practicable. The Berber–Suakin route had now been opened.

In mid-January 1898 Mahmoud for a second time rejected the Khalifa's proposal (it was not an order) to withdraw to a defence line at Sabaluqa where corn supplies were now accumulating, safe from steamer raids. The die was finally cast. In the wake of the fall of Berber Osman Digna marched with his 2,000-strong contingent from Qoz Regeb consisting mainly of Beja and *aulād el balad* to Metemma, there to form with Mahmoud's contingents a single group consisting of 10,000, men but with two commanders. Following Osman Digna's plan, they would now cross to the east bank in the last week in February 1898 at Aliab, halfway between Metemma and Kitchener's Fort Atbara and, striking across the northern isthmus of the Isle of Meroe, construct a *zariba* in thick bush on the east bank of the almost dry bed of the River Atbara. Here after a stand-off lasting a fortnight Kitchener, having advanced from the north with 12,000 men, attacked on 8 April, driving the *Ansar* back into the river bed with 3,000 dead and 4,000 wounded. Osman Digna and Ahmed Fadil with the cavalry rode off to the protection of Gedaref, leaving Mahmoud a prisoner, to die in 1906 in Rosetta. The Anglo-Egyptians suffered 560 casualties including 5 British officers killed and 13 wounded. It was a decisive victory. Kitchener regarded that battle, not Omdurman, as the turning-point of his career. Now, with the onset of summer, both sides prepared for the final struggle.

5   THE ABYSSINIAN FLANK 1897–98

At least since early 1897 Kitchener had insisted that the taking and holding of Berber predicated 'our flank, being secured by Kassala, being held'. He had in November 1897 personally arranged the retrocession of Kassala to Egypt by the Italians on Christmas Day. Meanwhile, with his agreement with Emperor Menilek concluded in early 1897, the Khalifa, anxious to avoid the possibility of a pincer movement from Tigré as well as Berber, continued to exchange cordial missions. Mohammed Bushara, erstwhile defeated *amir* of Dongola, led the exchange of December 1897 to Addis Ababa and, as a further earnest of goodwill, proffered the Beni Shanqul territory to Menilek which the latter duly occupied, with its gold-bearing potential, in February 1898. Menilek reciprocated with the somewhat unrealistic offer, granted the terrain difficulties, of arms and ammunition for Abdallahi. Menilek had already insisted a year earlier that the religious difference between them was irrelevant in the face of European invasion.

Nevertheless, uncertain of the eventual outcome of the Sudan war, Menilek was simultaneously in negotiation with both Britain and France. The Rennell Rodd mission of May 1897 exposed the current lack of muscle of the British negotiating position, pending the defeat of the Khalifa, in settling the mutual frontier; but nevertheless led to the appointment of a resident British agent to improve communications. In March 1897 Menilek had already concluded a superficially substantial accord with the French, partitioning between the two countries, on paper at least, the territory south of the fourteenth parallel (Dueim) along the line of the White Nile and Bahr el Jebel.

This negotiation was diplomatic reinsurance on the part of Menilek. He had no intention of implementing the accord and was far more concerned with the lands of the Blue Nile tributaries. Even here, following the Khalifa's defeat at the Atbara in April 1898, Menilek desisted from their occupation lest he weaken the Khalifa in his necessity. This would not dissuade the *sheikh* of Gallabat, following the summons of Ahmed Fadil and his Gedaref garrison to the defence of Omdurman, from preferring the protection of the ruler of Tigré, John IV's declared successor and now liegeman of Menilek, to running the implicit risk of a return to Egyptian rule.[4]

6 REJAF 1897–98

The southern outpost of Rejaf, of which the last news to reach Omdurman with the Bahr el Jebel blocked may have been by the *Ismailia* in September 1896 (see p. 505), can hardly have figured as a concern of priority for the Khalifa in the face of the Anglo-Egyptian advance to Dongola, Abu Hamed and Berber. Cairo would only receive intelligence of the occupation of Rejaf by Leopold's new Congolese mission in October 1897. In such circumstance the reaches of the Upper Nile had to be considered by the Khalifa as expendable, their general value narrowed to the proximate supply of grain for Omdurman. Grain however was also a necessity for the shrunken garrison of Amir Arabi Dafa'allah at Rejaf, entailing the dispatch of a major *razzia* into Zande country in December 1896, which precipitated a battle with Chief M'bio's forces on 5 January 1897 in which the *Ansar* lost 120 men. On their return to Rejaf, Arabi heard the alarming news that a new Congolese force was now occupying Bedden.

This mission to take possession of the Lado Enclave on behalf of King Leopold's Congolese State, totalling initially 3,000 men, had left Leopoldville under Baron Dhanis in October 1896. On 13 December Dhanis sent a 700-strong advance guard under Louis Chaltin, commandant at Dungu, to seize Bedden. Arabi reacted by sending all his garrison bar himself and forty men from Rejaf where they attacked a force of similar size augmented by Zande irregulars at Bedden on 17 February 1897, suffering a heavy defeat in which Omer Salih was among the dead. The survivors were hotly pursued over the seventeen miles to Rejaf which Arabi abandoned in the night, sailing by steamer and boats to Bor. The former *amirs* Mohammed Khalid and Osman Abu Qarja were released by the Belgian force.

Three days before the Bedden battle, Dhanis's main Congolese force had mutinied against their conditions and their treatment by Belgian officers at N'dirfi. Thereafter the expedition dissolved, not only precluding Chaltin from marching from Lado on Bor but defeating Leopold's ambition to press north to Fashoda. A year later Chaltin was still at Lado awaiting orders. Arabi would launch a number of attacks in an attempt to recapture Rejaf, notably in June 1898. Still cut off by the *sudd* from news of Omdurman and learning in November that an Anglo-Congolese force was approaching Bor, Arabi eventually decided to evacuate Bor; burned the small steamer *Mohammed Ali* and other boats; sent off his report to Omdurman – where its interception benefited British intelligence; and headed off with his garrison across country via Rumbek and Wau for the Bahr el Arab. Only in March 1899, nearing Wau, did he learn of the Khalifa's defeat at Omdurman. The news decided him to press on to join Sheikh Musa Madibbo at Shakka. Obliged to retreat thence to Ta'aishi country, he successfully fought off a British expedition in December 1899, and would continue to offer resistance until, under threat from Sultan Ali Dinar of Darfur, his force mutinied and he surrendered in 1902. He lived a free man in El Fasher before being arrested and executed by Ali Dinar in 1916.

7 OMDURMAN 1898

Any doubt in the Khalifa's mind as to the ultimate objective of Kitchener's expedition had been progressively removed. Following the Atbara defeat, the Khalifa built forts to guard the Sabaluqa gorge against gunboats for when the Nile rose in 1898, and the summer months were spent preparing for the final confrontation. The Khalifa had soon decided that the northern outskirts of Omdurman, Kerreri, would provide the most advantageous field of battle, with short lines of communication. Thus it was at Omdurman that his force of 60,000 would be concentrated, his weapons and supplies deployed.

Kitchener for his part halted around Berber pending the completion of the critical Abu Hamed desert railway line which, by July, had at last reached Fort Atbara, approaching 1,000 miles from Cairo and 400 from Wadi Halfa – much of it laid in summer months. With reinforcements and supplies now unloaded, Kitchener's army of nearly 26,000 men, of whom nearly a third were British, was ready to move forward on the west bank of the Nile escorted by their ten gunboats to the northern end of the sixth cataract, sixty miles from Omdurman. On a rising Nile, a gunboat attack on 26 August caused the Sabaluqa gorge forts to be evacuated and the skeleton *Ansar* garrisons retired to Omdurman. On 1 September Kitchener reached Kerreri, his infantry digging in within *zaribas* backing the Nile. On the east bank a force of 2,500 Ja'aliyin, keeping pace with Kitchener's gunboats, had reached a point opposite Omdurman where a howitzer battery was landed to bombard the city.

That evening the Khalifa's army occupied Jebel Surgham under cover of darkness. The Battle of Omdurman was fought in the hours between dawn and noon the next day, 2 September 1898, between the Kerreri Hills and Jebel Surgham, and has been amply described in detail. The

The Mahdi's tomb, immediately after the capture of Omdurman

principal Mahdist commanders – Yaqub commanding the Black Flag Baqqara, Osman Sheikh el Din the *jihadiya*, and Khalifa Ali wad Hilu the White Nile contingent – all lacked battle experience. Not so the lesser commanders: Osman Digna; Osman Azraq' Mohammed Isa of El Nejumi's and Mohammed Bushara's armies; and Ibrahim el Khalil Ahmed, commanding *jihadiya*, brother of Mahmoud now a prisoner of the Egyptians. By 11.30 a.m. Kitchener's force had won the battle by steadiness under attack and dominant firepower. Mahdist casualties were estimated at 10,800 killed and 16,000 wounded; Yaqub had fallen under the Black Flag, Osman Azraq and Ibrahim el Khalil were also among the dead. Kitchener's dead were 48 and wounded 382 – 25 and 50 of them respectively in the famous charge of the 21st Lancers. Theobald quotes the British *Daily Mail* war correspondent, George W. Steevens, present at the battle: 'The honour of the fight must still go with the men who died. Our men were perfect but the Dervishes (*Ansar*) were superb beyond perfection. It was their largest, best and bravest army that ever fought against us for Mahdism, and it died worthily of the huge empire that Mahdism won and kept so long.'

The pillaging of Omdurman lasted several days. The Mahdi's fine tomb was demolished.[5]

8 FASHODA 1898

The erstwhile Egyptian Sudan, of uneven duration in its occupation, was thus reoccupied by the successor authority save for Equatoria, Bahr el Ghazal and western Darfur – the last claimed by Ali Dinar as a grandson of Sultan Mohammed Fadl. Archival correspondence of the Mahdiya fell into Anglo-Egyptian hands after the battle.

There would be however a dramatic international confrontation following Omdurman, at Fashoda on the Upper Nile (examined on pp. 559–71). Its immediate antecedents must be recorded here. In about January 1898 news had reached Omdurman of the presence of a French invading force in Bahr el Ghazal, although it is unclear whether rumours that the Khalifa then sent a counter-force, possibly from Shakka, were ever confirmed. At this time the main French expedition under Commandant Marchand would have been halted north of Tambura (Fort Hossinger) and the Nile-Congo divide on the upper reaches of the Sueh river, unable to navigate on a falling river until the arrival of the May rains. The advance party on foot would meanwhile

Fashoda, the Governor's House

establish a camp at the confluence of the Sueh and Wau, Fort Desaix, before reconnoitring and occupying Meshra el Rek on 24 May 1898.

As to the second French expedition of exploration across Abyssinia now under Christian de Bonchamps and accompanied by guides reluctantly provided by Menilek, it had been halted at Goré on the Baro affluent of the upper Sobat in July 1897. The expedition would gain the confluence of the Baro and Pibor rivers above Nasir at the end of December, only to be forced to return a few miles to Goré. Eventually a mere reconnaissance would reach the Nile-Sobat junction on 22 June 1898, spending but a few hours to plant the French and Abyssinian flags before its immediate recall by Menilek (see p. 566).

When soon after dawn on 8 July 1898, in heavy intermittent rain, Commandant Marchand's expedition, having quit the Sueh for the Wau and Bahr el Ghazal rivers on 4 June, eventually passed Sobat mouth, many floating islands of *sudd* were remarked but no flags. After a brief stop at Lul, enabling a delegation of French officers to visit Reth Kur (Abdel Fadil) of the Shilluk at his royal village of Fa Shoda and then Marchand to receive a cordial visit in return and to present the Reth with a rifle, the expedition sailed for the Mahdist headquarters at Fashoda. They arrived at 5 p.m. the next day, 10 July, to find 'a heap of bricks and mud', and to raise the French flag. The last local sighting of the Mahdists had apparently been a steamer visit within the past month.

It would not however be the last. As the rains continued, two steamers with ten barges attached, dispatched by the Khalifa on 29 July to bring grain for the army at Omdurman, appeared at Kaka on 22

August and at dawn on the 25th these two steamers, *Tawfiqia* and *Safia*, captured in 1884 and now flying Mahdist flags, opened fire on the French. After passing and re-passing the French positions, the vessels made off again to the north. The *Ansar* casualties from French rifles exceeded 100. The French suffered two wounded, but expended nearly a third of their ammunition. The *Safia*, damaged, halted at Renk on the east bank downstream, while the *Tawfiqia* found her way back to Omdurman to seek reinforcements.

Four days after the river battle, the small French steam-driven launch *Faidherbe*, carried across Africa and reassembled on the Sueh, at last rejoined Marchand at Fashoda, to leave again on 1 September in order to reconnoitre the Sobat under Captain Albert Baratier and, it was hoped, to dispatch mail to Paris in Abyssinia. Having reached the Baro river beyond Nasir the party returned a fortnight later to confirm that in June the small Abyssinian party including two Frenchmen had reached Sobat mouth, having signed a treaty with a Nuer chief near Nasir acknowledging Menilek's protection, and returned at once to Abyssinia via the Baro. Meanwhile on 3 September a treaty in French and Arabic had been signed by Marchand and Reth Kur Nyidhok recognising the French protectorate over the Shilluk from Tonga to Kaka and on 7 September another with a Dinka chief Ayang on the east bank. The *Faidherbe*, carrying duplicate news of Marchand's occupation of Fashoda and the treaties with the Reth and the Dinka, left for Meshra el Rek on 14 September; the on-going passage of these dispatches to Paris via Ubangi and Brazzaville was expected to take in excess of six months. The *Faidherbe* was instructed to return from Meshra with reinforcements and munitions.[6]

On 29 October 1897 Salisbury had telegraphed Cromer regarding a French threat to Fashoda: 'It is, of course, as difficult to judge what is going on in the upper Nile valley as it is to judge what is going on on the other side of the moon... but... if we ever get to Fashoda, the diplomatic crisis will be something to remember, and the "what next" will be a very interesting question.' Thus it was that early in August 1898 as he commenced his final march on Omdurman Kitchener received sealed orders from London which he was ordered to open immediately following the fall of Omdurman. Finalised by the British Cabinet on 25 July in the presence of Cromer, and signed by the Queen in person on 2 August, Kitchener's instructions from Salisbury in his twin capacity as prime minister and foreign minister were personally to take command of an armed flotilla in order to reconnoitre the White Nile for foreign intruders. Should they be Abyssinian, he would avoid a collision by all possible means, but should he encounter a French force not only would he advise them that their presence 'on the Nile valley is an infringement of the rights both of Great Britain and of the Khedive'; but thereafter 'the course of action to be pursued must depend so much on local circumstances that it is neither necessary nor desirable to furnish Sir Herbert Kitchener with detailed instructions.'

Kitchener's armed expedition was to be borne in the steamer *Dal* and four gunboats towing twelve barges and would consist of two Sudanese battalions, an Egyptian battery, Maxim guns and a British company of Cameron Highlanders. Preparations were approaching completion when, on 7 September, the *Tawfiqia* arrived from the south and was arrested. Its captain, interrogated about the clash at Fashoda, was able to draw the invaders' disposition in the sand and to describe a coloured flag over the fort. Significantly the vessel's hull was pockmarked with sophisticated bullets.

The French arrival thus confirmed, Kitchener handed military command to Lewa Sir Archibald Hunter and accompanied by Wingate sailed on 8 September; on the 15th, at Renk, they engaged the *Safia* (which was further damaged by an accidental boiler explosion) and the post at Renk was duly reduced. Three days later the *Dal* moored at a landing place a short distance north of Fashoda, and two Shilluk NCOs were dispatched by night to deliver Kitchener's message in French early on 19 September, addressed to 'Le Chef de l'Expedition Européenne à Fashoda'. Marchand's reply, conveyed by a delegation of two French sergeants in a whaler flying the French Tricolore, was signed by the 'Commissaire du Gouvernment Français sur le Haut Nil'. Wearing only the Turkish flag, except for the barge carrying the company of Cameron Highlanders, the *Dal* and its escorts anchored at Fashoda for courteous, correct but inconclusive discussions led by Kitchener and Marchand. That same evening, having delivered a formal letter of protest, Kitchener would sail on to establish a post at Sobat mouth, leaving at Fashoda one largely Shilluk Sudanese battalion under Qa'immaqam Herbert Jackson, now appointed commandant of the garrison and supported by one gunboat, barges and four pieces of artillery. Wingate had selected the old bastion to the south of the French position to hoist the Turkish, but not the British, flag. By 24 September Kitchener and Wingate were back in Omdurman to dispatch their report on Fashoda to London.

At Fashoda the relationship between Jackson and Marchand was

Kitchener and Wingate watching the arrival of Marchand's messengers
19 September 1898

well-mannered but correct until the sudden departure of Marchand in an Egyptian steamer for Cairo in mid-October, in the wake of Baratier having been called to Paris. Thereafter Capitaine Joseph Germain took command of the French expedition, to be reproved on Marchand's return for his aggressive conduct towards the British garrison. Already the protracted and increasingly acerbic diplomatic exchanges between London and Paris were under way against a threatening canvas of war, the origins and climax of which will be explored in the next chapter; but currently this news had not reached Fashoda. However no sooner had Germain taken command than, contrary to all Marchand's assurances to Jackson about his successor observing their agreement, he flagrantly broke it when the *Faidherbe,* which was not to leave Fashoda without Jackson's authority nor to carry arms other than rifles, was secretly dispatched on patrol with a mounted gun. In the last resort failure to comply with the agreement was to be met by Jackson with the use of force, but this Jackson now skilfully avoided. A French messenger was nevertheless intercepted with a letter to the French mission in Abyssinia to invite an Abyssinian advance to the White Nile. The situation was only defused by the return of Marchand who confirmed his instructions had been ignored and apologised.

On 11 December 1898, some five months after the French arrival at Fashoda, their flag was lowered and the French party evacuated their station with full honours, having been granted an official dispensation which enabled them, avoiding Cairo, to leave the Upper Nile via the Sobat with the *Faidherbe,* thence across Abyssinia via Addis Ababa and Harar to the French coaling port of Djibouti (Obock), where they arrived on 16 May 1899.

The Anglo-Egyptian Condominium Agreement on the Sudan had been signed in Cairo on 19 January 1899 without public challenge by any of the European powers. The new rulers reverted to the Turkish organisation of administrative government. British officers were seconded to take the responsibilities of *mudirs* (governors) and of *mufettishin* (inspectors) and would be supported by Egyptian *mamurs.* Thus Khartoum *muderia* came under Miralai John Maxwell, with the *merkaz* (district) of Khartoum under Bimbashi Brian Mahon and of Omdurman under Bimbashi Seymour Vandeleur. The other *muderias* were Dongola, Kassala, Sennar, Berber and Fashoda; and, by 1901, El Obeid and Wadi Halfa.

The final implementation of Salisbury's policy 'not to share with France political rights over any position of the valley of the Nile' came with the Anglo-French Declaration of 21 March 1899 delimiting the western frontier of the Sudan so as to run northwards from the Nile-Congo watershed at the M'bomu river source (south of which was the Congo Free State), and ensuring that all Darfur, including the Dars Tama, Qimr and Masalit, was incorporated in the Sudan; but leaving Wadai as part of the French Central African sphere of influence. The challenge to the British occupation of the Sudan had been faced down.

Returning to Cairo from leave overland to Marseilles in 1901, Henry Boyle, oriental secretary at Cromer's residency, was detained at the Paris Gare de Lyons to enable the Governor-General of the French Soudan to join him for urgent talks on the train. The Governor-General wished to discuss the 'irritation' excited in France by the retention of the place-name 'Fashoda' as the British *muderia* for the southern region of the Sudan. Boyle's wife claims that her husband on his return to Cairo suggested that Kodok, a Shilluk village near Jackson's original fort, should be substituted. Fashoda (literally, the village of the horn-less cattle) is the historic name of the Reth's capital (Fa Shoda) sixteen miles further south. In December 1903 the maps were duly altered and Kodok substituted for Fashoda as the place name of the new *muderia* of Upper Nile.

Nor was this the only British gesture towards French sensitivities at a time of blossoming entente. On the outside wall of the old government office at Kodok (later to be the district office of the author in 1952–4) would be affixed a small rectangular copper plaque simply inscribed: 'Marchand 1898' – a worthy tribute to the feat of an exceptionally intrepid French officer who successfully led an expedition 2,500 miles across Africa.[7]

9 AFTERGLOW 1898–99

Even when by midday on 2 September 1898 the battle for Omdurman had been manifestly lost, the Khalifa Abdallahi still endeavoured to rally his surviving troops to defend the city itself; and regaining the Khalifa's house, he set out to seek divine guidance by prayer offered once again at the Mahdi's now battle-torn tomb. With his troops no longer able to respond to his command, the *Khalifat el Mahdi* then reluctantly withdrew from Omdurman with his family and son Osman Sheikh el Din, accompanied by the Khalifas Ali Mohammed Hilu, wounded in the thigh, and Mohammed Sharif, and by the *amir* Osman Digna. With the exception of Osman Digna, who returned to the Red Sea hills to be arrested in 1900, the group retreated south and then westwards, with such élan that the pursuing force of Egyptian cavalry and camel corps, with two gunboats shadowing them from the White Nile, were unable to intercept their progress. Mohammed Sharif surrendered a month later and was sent under house arrest to Shukaba near Wad Medani, the Mahdi's two elder surviving sons, El Fadil and El Bushra apparently in his care.

Abdallahi, his son and Ali Wad Hilu, having thrown off their pursuers, retreated to the Baqqara heartland of south Kordofan. Deter-mined not to yield, Abdallahi set about rallying the core of his military strength, his followers proclaiming to have seen the 'Khalifa of the Mahdi (on whom be peace) turn his face towards the east and with him the Flags and the army, until he entered Omdurman without the least hindrance', and to have learned that 'the unbelievers are all dead and the land is clear of them'.

Initially Abdallahi, having probably called at Aba Island before turning west, would make his headquarters in the well-watered basin of Sherkeila in eastern Kordofan. Here, at the end of January 1899, after a forced desert march of 125 miles from Aba, a first British expeditionary force of 1,600 predominantly camel corps, under (the newly created) Lord Kitchener's brother Walter, was obliged to abort its intended attack when its commander found himself confronted by a well-armed Baqqara force of 7,000. Prudently, and mindful no doubt of the dénouement of the Hicks expedition, the expedition was withdrawn, fortunate not to be harried back to the Nile.

Abdallahi's new Kordofan contingent was not the only Mahdist force to have survived Omdurman. Ahmed Fadil, Ta'aishi *amir* at Gedaref, had been summoned with his army to reinforce Omdurman but arrived too late for the battle. He returned three weeks later to find the now Egyptian Kassala garrison had crossed the river Atbara in flood and was on the point of occupying Gedaref. When his determined efforts to retake the town proved unsuccessful, a month later he withdrew his besieging force before Egyptian reinforcements arrived, and set out to join Abdallahi in Kordofan.

Marching south, Ahmed Fadil was thwarted by an Egyptian brigade under Miralai D. F. Lewis Bey, a veteran of the Dongola and Atbara campaigns and of Omdurman, from crossing the Blue Nile at Karkoj. The *amir* tried again south of Roseires, only to be brought to battle by Lewis in the act of crossing at Dakhila on Christmas Day 1898. 2,000 of his force were killed or taken prisoner. The remainder withdrew to Renk where they were forced to surrender to a British gunboat, Ahmed Fadil himself escaping. With a small contingent he crossed the White Nile to bring much diminished succour to Abdallahi, who had just, in January 1899, successfully rebuffed Walter Kitchener's force at Sherkeila.

Before the rains of 1899 Abdallahi moved his camp to Jebel Qadir, scene of two memorable Mahdist victories, where he was located by Sir Reginald Wingate's intelligence agents at the end of August. A new force was sent to Kaka to threaten him from the Jebel Fungor road, a destination disastrously pursued nearly twenty years earlier by the

Colonel (later General) Sir Reginald Wingate, 1899

Fashoda *mudir*. By the end of the rains in October however, Abdallahi had moved north in the direction of Aba Island, rendering nugatory the now misdirected efforts of the government force to Kordofan led by Lord Kitchener himself. News of Abdallahi's approach to Aba reached Khartoum in mid-November 1899, where Wingate, returned from four months' sick leave in Britain, was appointed to command the new counter-operation.

Wingate's flying column, landing on the west bank opposite Aba, surprised and defeated a Mahdist advance force gathering grain for Abdallahi under Ahmed Fadil. They killed 400 before moving on by two night marches south to where Abdallahi's force was encamped at Umm Debeikerat, seven miles south of the Gedid wells near the town of Kosti today. There Wingate deployed his well-armed column in a strong tactical position to await the final Mahdist attack at dawn of 24 November 1899. The Mahdist losses were some 600 killed, the Mahdi's fourth son Siddiq among them, and 3,000 prisoners. The Khalifa Abdallahi was found dead on his prayer rug: Khalifa Ali Mohammed Hilu to his right; Ahmed Fadil to his left. His entourage met death with comparable dignity. Osman Sheikh el Din would die of his wounds as a prisoner. By the end of 1899 Kordofan had surrendered. Darfur, recognised as an autonomous but tributary *sultanate* under Sultan Ali Dinar, chose to support Turkey in the First World War, and was occupied by force in 1916.

Since their surrender in November 1898 Khalifa Mohammed Sharif, the two late teenage sons of the Mahdi and other prisoners had been held under house arrest at Shukaba on the west bank of the Blue Nile near its confluence with the River Dinder. In August 1899, about the time that Abdallahi's new camp was identified at Jebel Qadir, Mohammed Sharif was reported to be preaching Mahdism and, in company with the Mahdi's sons, to be intending to escape aided by a force of Kenana, the Gezira people of Ali wad Hilu, to join Abdallahi. On the orders of Lewis Bey, now military governor Sennar, the three captives were seized in a raid on their quarters. In the incident in which their followers joined, three soldiers were wounded and 17 Mahdists killed. The governor ordered a court martial of the three dignitaries, who were summarily executed by firing squad. Khartoum, if consulted, did not question the justice of the sentences, but the Mahdi's family, whose subsequent loyalty to the conquerors proved unremitting, must have found the executions at least of the two young sons hard to accept. The only son now surviving was El Sayyid El Imam (Sir) Abdel Rahman el Mahdi.

Winston Churchill, a young participant in the charge of the 21st Lancers at Kerreri, Omdurman, would write of their father, Mohammed Ahmed El Mahdi who had died in June 1885:

> Whatever misfortunes the life of Mohammed Ahmed may have caused, he was a man of considerable nobility of character, a priest, a soldier, a patriot. He won great battles: he stimulated and revived religion. He founded an empire...
>
> When the Christian priests, having refused to accept the Koran, were assailed by the soldiers and the mob and threatened with immediate death, it was the Mahdi who 'seeing them in danger turned back and ordered them to walk in front of his camel for protection' [Father J. Ohrwalder].

Two senior *amirs* survived. Mahmoud Ahmed, captured at the Atbara, died a prisoner at Rosetta, Egypt, in 1906. Osman Abu Bakr Digna evaded arrest until 1900, and would die in honourable confinement in Wadi Halfa in 1926. El Nur Mohammed Anqara – formerly *amir*, and once chief of staff to Zubeir Pasha and then Gordon's former *mudir* – had surrendered Gedaref to the Egyptian army in 1898 and died in Omdurman, in retirement, twenty years later.

As to the victors, Lord Kitchener, *sirdar* and first Governor-General of the Anglo Egyptian Sudan in 1899, left for the South African war a month after the Khalifa Abdallahi's death. He was succeeded by General Sir Reginald Wingate, his long-serving director of intelligence, who ruled until 1916.[8]

16
Imperial Predators on the Upper Nile
1869–99

Sultan Selim I (1512–20) had conquered Egypt and occupied Cairo in the name of the Ottoman Empire in 1517, his new annexation later being extended south to include the third cataract of the Nile and the province of Habesh encompassing Suakin (1527); Massawa (1557); Zulla and Debarwa near Asmara (1575). The conquest of the Yemen, also in 1517 by Selim I, may have led to the further Ottoman annexation of Zeyla and Tadjura, or alternatively they may have been captured subsequently from the Portuguese. These latter ports were crucial to Yemeni cross-sea and indeed Indian trade with Shoa and Harar.

Ottoman interest in the Abyssinian Nile region then faded until the accession to the Viceroyalty of Egypt by Mohammed Ali, an Albanian native of the Macedonian port of Kavalla, in 1805. He would fifteen years later embark upon the conquest of the Fung Kingdom of Sennar and, in 1840, be awarded the *hereditary* Viceroyalty of Egypt and of the Sudan provinces by a Sultan in Constantinople who cared little for the Upper Nile. By now, in a population of Egypt exceeding two million, the Osmanli Turkish ruling minority had dwindled to some 20,000, yet its ascendancy was still complete. The Turkish ruling house would in 1873 under Mohammed Ali's grandson, now Khedive, Ismail Ibrahim, purchase a hereditary succession restricted to his own issue.

For a period of three years from July 1798 Egypt had by conquest been effectively created a French protectorate. 'The ultimate aim was the colonisation of Egypt for the benefit of France,' to quote Professor P. J. Vatikiotis. The French would however be driven from Egypt by British naval intervention. By September 1801 the French army had been expelled. The victors were an Anglo-Indian, supplemented by a Turkish, army. No effort would be made by the British to administer Egypt and, by the Treaty of Amiens, her garrison was withdrawn in 1803 and Egypt returned to Ottoman rule.

France would not again be allowed to threaten India as had

Napoleon from Egypt in 1798. British naval power would see to that. But, having defeated Napoleon's threat, British governments would set their face against European territorial involvement in North and East Africa (see p. 67) and, indeed, in the Levant. British interests focused on the twin objectives of safeguarding Constantinople and the Bosphorus against Russian control; and of the maintenance of secure and speedy communications with India – whether that route to India best lay via Syria to the Euphrates or, as became evident after the opening in 1835 of the improved 'overland route' across Egypt from Alexandria to Suez, via the Red Sea and the Gulf of Aden. Palmerston's conclusion in 1833 had been clear: 'Turkey is as good an occupier of the road to India as an active Arab sovereign would be.' The Ottoman empire must be maintained. Nevertheless in 1839 Aden would be captured, to become a coaling station victualled from Berbera and Bulhar.[1]

Determined to maintain France's dominant commercial interest in Egypt, the Emperor Napoleon III articulated a new territorial vision for North Africa in 1856. Morocco should become French; Egypt, British; and Tripolitania, Sardinian. The ideas received a blunt rejection from Palmerston as being inimical to the maintenance of the Mediterranean status quo. A new development in global maritime trade was however to be launched that year, albeit without British support. Following the report of an International Commission, the Ottoman Porte approved in principle the project of Ferdinand de Lesseps to excavate a canal through the Isthmus of Suez linking the Mediterranean and Red Seas – a project for which the Egyptian Viceroy had granted the concession. To the benefits stemming from the lately originated construction of turbine-driven steamers would now be added the bypassing of the trans-shipment delays inherent in the overland route across Egypt. The excavation of the Suez Canal would also kindle external interest in the potential of the Upper Nile region.

1   OTTOMAN EGYPT 1869–79

The Suez Canal was opened in November 1869, not by the Sultan but by the Empress Eugénie, only months before the French defeat at Sedan by Germany. The Khedive Ismail had long been alive to the potential of the Canal in enhancing Egypt's commercially strategic position as a land-bridge between Europe and Asia; and to the opportunity for territorial expansion both along the Red Sea littoral and, following the discovery of its source by Speke, up the equatorial Nile. Through the early years of his reign the omens grew increasingly propitious for Ismail to launch his ambitious bid for an East African empire.

Well before the completion of the Suez Canal, Khedive Ismail was quietly preparing his plans. Half a century previously, under the guidance of French officers, Egypt had built a naval fleet well before her participation, on behalf of Ottoman Turkey, in the Greek war of independence, which culminated in the destruction by the British of both Turkish and Egyptian fleets at Navarino in 1827. Ismail Pasha shared the maritime interest of his grandfather, Mohammed Ali, and as a preliminary move in 1865, ostensibly to prohibit the export of slaves to Jedda, Ismail had successfully enlisted British pressure on the Ottoman Porte to cede the ports of Suakin and Massawa to the Khedivate. These were ports whose occupation Mohammed Ali had secured in 1846, only for the leases to be relinquished on his death by Abbas I in 1849.

Next, in June 1867, Ismail secretly dispatched Ja'afar Pasha Mazhar, a former naval officer and currently *hakimdar* of the Sudan, on a reconnaissance south along the Red Sea littoral as far as the Bab el Mandeb to plant the Turkish flag, allegedly with the consent of the Danakil people. Only Edd, the western extremity of the Danakil, was to be presently garrisoned, but, indicative of the Khedive's lingering apprehension of British intentions, Ismail followed up the reconnaissance with the appointment in October 1867 of a general-governor of the Red Sea Littoral. Britain however was not predatory, reassuring Mohammed Ali in November in the context of the forthcoming Magdala expedition: 'We are going to war, not to obtain territory, not to secure commercial advantages but for high moral causes alone.' Abyssinia was duly evacuated by June 1868, the British Foreign Office, if not the India Office, content with the naval bunkering port at Aden and unconcerned about the French acquisition of Obock in 1862.

The Khedivial acquisition of the Red Sea littoral being uncontested, in August 1869 Ja'afar Pasha was advocating further expansion beyond the Bab along the southern littoral of the Gulf of Aden. Tadjura, which marked the eastern boundary of the Danakil, and Zeyla (Somali) remained in Ottoman hands by virtue of their allegiance to the Yemen. These ports, along with Obock (still unoccupied by the French), invited Egyptian occupation but so did the Somali ports of Berbera and Bulhar (see pp. 90–1).

The British Viceroy of India harboured increasing misgivings about the latter, on which Aden was dependent for supplies, confronting

Khedivial naval approaches to Berbera in 1870 and 1871. London however would tacitly acquiesce in the Egyptian occupation of Berbera in December 1873, following the appointment of its own erstwhile and well-regarded honorary British consul at Massawa, Munzinger Pasha, as general-governor of the Eastern Sudan; and, in 1874, the undertakings given by the Khedive especially regarding the slave trade and freedom of commerce. The next year, 1875, Egypt negotiated the lease by Constantinople of the ports of Zeyla and Tadjura, leading swiftly to the Egyptian capture of Harar, but not of Aussa.

Thus the Khedivial encroachments along the maritime littoral of eastern Africa provoked no challenge. Ismail however also harboured inland territorial objectives on a major scale. Harar was seized in 1875 but that was peripheral and short-lived. Far more substantial were the Nile headwaters and western Sudan goals. When he had succeeded to the Viceroyalty in 1863 the White Nile Sudan boundary did not extend beyond Kaka, south of the eleventh parallel where river patrols would now be introduced. But beyond the *sudd* beckoned the ivory wealth of the equatorial Nile and the prosperous lands of the lacustrine kingdoms of Bunyoro and Buganda, which again attracted no interest from the European powers.

When therefore, immediately prior to the Canal opening in 1869, Sir Samuel Baker was appointed by Ismail to lead the Equatoria expedition, the British prime minister would comment, though supporting the intended suppression of the slave trade: 'I conclude we take no responsibility with regard to this expedition.' Likewise France, in the aftermath of defeat in the Franco-Prussian war of 1870, was content to limit her national interests to Egypt proper, but with a watching brief on Ismail's further territorial objective, the Abyssinian province of Hamasein beyond Bogos.

Neither East African enterprise would prosper. Hamasein was to be the scene of successive Egyptian military débacles in 1875 and 1876 while the endeavour, prompted by Gordon's suggestion, to seize an Indian Ocean port as alternative access to the lacustrine territorial gains fell foul of the Sultan of Zanzibar by January 1876. Egyptian military stations established in Bunyoro would be finally evacuated on the orders of Romolo Gessi shortly after Gordon's departure as Governor-General to Cairo in July 1879, three years after the Khedive's erroneous public proclamation that the lacustrine kingdoms had been annexed in the interests of civilisation, agriculture and commerce. Of the imperial dream, only the ethnically alien territories of the

White Nile and Darfur would remain under Turkish-Egyptian rule and they not for long.

First off the mark perhaps, but the Khedivial bid for an expanded African empire had foundered, and the Viceroyalty was bankrupt. European interest had meanwhile been awakened in the region. In September 1876 King Leopold II of Belgium had convened the non-governmental International African Association 'pour exprimer la traite [slave trade] et ouvrir l'Afrique centrale', nominally for scientific and humanitarian purposes, actually as a cloak for independent royal Belgian colonisation. The writing was on the wall for Ottoman Egypt. In October 1876, recognising that Egypt's aspirations to hitherto unchallenged hegemony on the Upper Nile were under threat, Ismail Pasha's American chief-of-staff delivered an anxious memorandum: 'I tremble for Egypt's future if she loses the Equatorial provinces, even if she does not push further than to-day... In my belief, the powerful country which possesses the sources of the Nile will always possess the domination of Lower Egypt.'

Fariq Stone urged the immediate occupation of Lake Victoria; of Buganda and Karagwe; the establishment of communications between Lake Victoria and Harar, Zeyla and Berbera; and later, the occupation of the mountains between Lake Victoria and Kismayu and Durnford on the Indian Ocean. The advice was unavailing. By 1879 the garrisons south of Rejaf had been withdrawn, Khedive Ismail had been forced to abdicate. By 1882 Britain had occupied Egypt in support of his successor, but by 1885 the Mahdi had wrested the Sudan from Egyptian occupation.

The dependence of Egypt on the sources of the Nile was understood in general but still not in detail. Until 1821, with the discovery of long-staple irrigated cotton and the technique for its large-scale cultivation, Egyptian agricultural needs had been satisfied by the annual Nile flood (monitored at the Nilometers), generated by the Blue Nile and Atbara rivers. The contribution of the White Nile to the flood was small, but in the low season dominant since determining the area which could be irrigated all the year round. The rainfall which governed the flow volumes of the constituent affluents of the Nile was God-given. The flood spate from Abyssinia was of a volume unmanageable by man, but unlikely to fail more than once in a hundred years. That was not so with the White Nile, where the net volume of flow after dispersal in the *sudd* was critical to growth in the perennial cultivated area of Egypt. Could the White

Nile flow be so diverted or stored as to threaten Egypt with dearth? In 1876 there had been as yet no storage barrage constructed on the Nile. The first would be opened at Aswan only in December 1902.[2]

The British landings of 1882 purposed to defeat the Arabi rebellion against the Khedive Tawfiq; to re-establish public security; to train a new Egyptian army; and then to evacuate. In the Egyptian Sudan the successful Mahdist rising to gain independence forced a reappraisal, but not presently an abandonment, of the British evacuation objective. The massacre of Hicks's expedition however, the siege of Khartoum and the failure of the Gordon relief expedition brought British occupied Egypt under threat of invasion. The Sudan, Harar and Berbera were abandoned. Britain's residual national interest in the security of the Red Sea route to India would be covered by the fortification of Suakin.

The French government were originally to be joint participants in the 1882 intervention on behalf of the Khedive but having voluntarily withdrawn while applauding the British victory at Tel el Kebir, found themselves victim of a public outcry over what extremists saw as a humiliation comparable with defeat at Sedan. The International Financial Agreement on Egyptian finance, for the negotiation of which Baring had been detached from Cairo during the critical months of deterioration in the Sudan, was concluded in March 1885 and had gained the consent of Ottoman Turkey and the participating powers. Britain, as recognised occupying power, reasonably refused the restoration of the Anglo-French dual control, but insisted that she still adhered to her evacuation policy from Egypt. French determination however strengthened, under pressure from their bondholders, so as to hamstring British financial controls. This froideur between the two most interested powers would extend over many years.

Nothing better demonstrated the commitment to evacuation of Egypt by the British government, whether led by Gladstone or Salisbury, than the British initiative of the Drummond-Wolff mission. Its purpose was a Convention under which Turkish troops would, at an appropriate moment, take over from British troops withdrawn from Egypt. After two years' negotiations in Cairo, on 22 May 1887 Sir Henry Drummond-Wolff and the Sultan's representative, Ghazi-Mukhtar Pasha, agreed that, subject to peace prevailing, British troops would be withdrawn three years after the Convention was signed; British officers of the Egyptian army would resign two years later; and thereafter, in case of invasion or insurrection, Turkish troops, *with or without British participation*, would be sent to defend Khedivial authority. Quixotically the militant French government, acting in tandem with the Russian government, at once leaned diplomatically upon the Sultan to prevent him signing the Convention, thereby gratuitously forgoing the desired British evacuation on the ground that French interest in Egypt had not been recognised by French participation in the negotiations. The Ottoman suzerain for his part implicitly forfeited a legitimate claim to occupation.

The Khedivial government was relieved. With the defeat of the Mahdists at the Battle of Toski in August 1889, the economic rehabilitation of Ottoman Egypt could be resumed within the much diminished frontiers. The British for their part now had second thoughts. Already in June 1889 Sir Evelyn Baring had written privately to Lord Salisbury, identifying

the real reason why the evacuation policy is well-nigh impossible of execution. The main argument – which it is difficult to use – is based on the utter incapacity of the ruling classes of this country… Really the more I look at it, the more does the evacuation policy appear to me to be impossible under any conditions.[3]

2 KING LEOPOLD AND THE CONGO 1876–97

Having in September 1876 convened his International Africa Association, Leopold was quick to establish his first 'independent' territorial base at Bagamoyo opposite Zanzibar – the launch pad first for Burton and Speke, then Speke and Grant in their searches for the source of the White Nile. No fewer than four Belgian-led expeditions would within a few years converge on the south-east shore of Lake Tanganyika, there to found a fortified station at Karema. Meanwhile a Belgian consulate was established in Zanzibar.

The as yet unproven benefit of this eastern route of entry into central Africa was fortuitously overtaken by the rival benefit yielded by H. M. Stanley's remarkable expedition which left Zanzibar on 11 November 1874. He had circumnavigated Lakes Victoria and Tanganyika, and thence by canoe voyaged down the Lualaba-Congo river to the Atlantic Ocean, arriving in August 1877. In the face of British lack of interest in what he saw as these new opportunities, Stanley accepted King Leopold's prompt offer of employment to explore the commercial potential of the Upper Congo in 1879, abandoning his present interest in the Bagamoyo' hinterland. It would take Stanley over two years, after leaving Boma at the Congo mouth, to establish a wagon route, bypassing the cataracts which rendered the lower Congo unnavigable, so to reach Stanley Pool – the point at which the 5,000-mile navigable Congo debouches. He had been beaten in attaining this goal by the young naturalised French Count Savorgnan de Brazza, explorer of Gabon and now financed secretly by the French national committee of Leopold's International African Association, who had disembarked at the mouth of the Ogowe river, to avoid the Congo cataracts, and had reached the Pool in August 1880. With his disassembled steamers *Royal* and *En Avant*, Stanley only arrived in November 1881. Six months later he left on the *En Avant* intending to create a new Belgian trading empire up to the Stanley Falls at the junction with the Lualaba river, just as Brazza's last lieutenant was withdrawn from the Pool.

Meanwhile Brazza had found his way back to Paris, arriving in June 1882 and in August reporting to the French government the chronicle of his expedition, his treaty with the Congolese chief at the Pool and the raising of the French flag at stations on his entry route. Against a backcloth of governmental timidity towards the Ahmed Arabi rebellion in Egypt, French nationalist sentiment rallied to Brazza's support, culminating in the affirmation of French sovereignty over Brazza's Congo and a commission for him as governor to extend the boundaries of the new French colony.

Leopold's purported plan for the non-political establishment of African commerce, civilisation and progress, even if it had been always a cover for an intended Belgian colony, was no longer credible. Neither Leopold nor the French seriously intended free trade. Protectionism for national exports was the policy, albeit covert. To pre-empt Brazza's new French mission, Stanley, who had returned briefly to Europe in the summer of 1882 incapacitated by malaria, was dispatched back to the Congo mouth in December 1882, four months ahead of Brazza, thence to establish further stations on the Upper Congo in the name of the International Association of the Congo. Privately Stanley still wished for a British protectorate.

The rival ambitions of France and Belgium for the Congo territories would be settled, not by British, but by German influence in the negotiations which took place at the West Africa conference of November 1884 convened by Chancellor Prince von Bismarck. Already, as a shrewd gambit, Leopold had offered France in April the right of pre-emption on his royal Free State, which now replaced the Association, should he decide to sell. Subject to protection for German trading rights and agreement on territorial boundaries between the French and Leopold, Bismarck, backed by Britain, now recommended the recognition of Leopold's Congo Free State. The French colony would be limited to territory north of the lower Congo and, by the Franco-Congolese Agreement of 1887, to the right bank of the Ubangi river. The twin capitals of Brazzaville and Leopoldville would be established at the southern outlet of the Pool. Britain's African 'Monroe doctrine' was thus ostensibly at an end. Only the African coasts, excluding European (mainly British) protectorates which constituted much of the vast littoral, would be subject to new rules of administrative occupation. The interior of the Continent was open to all comers.[4]

Back in March 1880, following his resignation as Governor-General of the Egyptian Sudan, General Gordon reiterated his commitment to spur the end of the slave trade in the Nile region. At William Mackinnon's suggestion Gordon – in person – had , en route to stay with Hussey Vivian now stationed in Berne, offered his services in the Congo to King Leopold in that context, whenever the current slow progress of Stanley's expedition from the Congo mouth should merit it. A royal response came initially in the summer of 1882 when Stanley returned on leave and Gordon was in South Africa, and then in October 1884 when Gordon was in Palestine – an invitation which on return to Brussels he accepted in January 1884, only to be diverted to Khartoum at the request of the British government. Gordon would otherwise have been charged with taking possession of the principal source of the Arab slave trade in the Upper Congo basin east of the Stanley Falls and Yambuyo, extending 400 miles west of Lake Albert and 600 miles down the Lualuba river from Mweru. A major destination of that trade was the Sudan via the Bahr el Ghazal.

In September 1886 news arrived in London from Dr Wilhelm Junker who had left Emin a second time for Bunyoro in January 1886 thence to withdraw from what had become a war zone to Zanzibar. Junker reported that Emin, now at Wadelai, still held out but needed ammunition and supplies. Britain declined the advice of Sir John Kirk who, mindful of the wealth potential of Buganda, supported Junker's recommendation for a British relief expedition. Lord Salisbury commented dismissively: 'It is really [the Germans'] business if Emin is German.' Baring however, in Cairo, approved an Egyptian financial contribution to augment the private sponsorship of the expedition by Mackinnon's Imperial British East Africa Company while Leopold, his eye on the upper Nile, sanctioned its leadership by Stanley on condition that it approached Wadelai from the Congo, not from Zanzibar. Stanley was privately charged by Leopold to persuade Emin to transfer his Equatoria province to the Congo Free State, a proposal which Gordon had himself addressed to Leopold, via Baring, when en route to Khartoum in February 1884. Stanley however was also beholden to Mackinnon, whose intention was to counsel Emin to withdraw from Wadelai to Lake Victoria.

Stanley, having returned via Zanzibar to Congo mouth, left Yambuyo with the first part of his expedition on 28 June 1887, alerted to the scant progress made so far in the Free State in ivory and palm oil trade and facing a six-month battle through unexplored forest to Equatoria. He emerged in December 1887 west of Lake Albert, demoralised by hunger and disease, more than half of his porters dead or deserted. Stanley's steamers had meanwhile returned from Yambuyo to bring up the rear column and its supplies from the coast, before that column followed in Stanley's wake to Lake Albert. This in fact they never attempted. In April 1888 Emin, with the steamships *Khedive* and *N'yanza*, finally met Stanley at Tunguru on Lake Albert and was invited to choose – between the Leopold proposal that he become Congo governor of Equatoria and the Mackinnon alternative that he move his garrison and headquarters to the north-east of Lake Victoria under a British protectorate. Stanley, needing to locate and bring up his own Congo rear supply column, left Emin to determine which of his garrisons would support his decision to leave Wadelai – for Emin rejected the Leopold option. On Stanley's return from Yambuyo a year later, Emin was still vacillating after having been made captive by his own troops. Stanley forced their departure to Zanzibar in May 1889 – the relief expedition a multiple failure. They reached Bagamoyo in December to find it transformed into a German town and to be welcomed by the German Commissioner for East Africa.

What if – one conjectures; what if Gordon had not been intercepted by General Lord Wolseley in Brussels in January 1884 and diverted to Khartoum, but had taken the steamer on 5 February from Lisbon to 'serve willingly with or under' Stanley in the Upper Congo? 'No such efficacious means of cutting at root of slave trade ever was presented as that which God has I trust, opened out to us through the kind disinterestedness of [King Leopold].' Had it been Gordon who encountered his former lieutenant Emin Pasha at Lake Albert in 1888, not only might Equatoria have joined the Congo, despite the barrier of the Nile-Congo divide, but the brutality of the military rule by Belgian officials, exposed progressively after 1890, might never have developed. 'Kind disinterestedness' was not to be the mark of the Free State regime. On 20 May 1903 the British House of Commons would intervene to pass unanimously a resolution that Congo natives should be governed with humanity.

Leopold was not discountenanced by the failure of his Equatoria bid of 1888. Stanley had led the Congolese expedition to Lake Albert, one of the sources of the White Nile. The route through the forests of the Upper Congo valley had now been blazed. And even while Stanley had been forcing that passage, Leopold had been invited by the British prime minister, Lord Salisbury, to convene an international conference in Brussels of seventeen nations to agree the anti-slave trade Brussels Convention of 1890. Increasingly confident, the Nile still his objective, Leopold had actually ordered Stanley on 30 December 1888 to occupy a few suitable places in the Bahr el Ghazal.⁵

Within weeks of Stanley's arrival with Emin at Bagamoyo opposite Zanzibar in December 1889, Stanley had been briefed by Leopold to negotiate a treaty with Sir William Mackinnon's, now chartered, Imperial British East Africa Company whereby the Congo Free State gained access to Lake Albert; and reciprocally, the Company access to a corridor linking Buganda with Lake Tanganyika. This 1890 document, its international validity always questionable but made known to the British prime minister, provided Leopold with ample pretext to dispatch a Belgian-led Congolese expedition which by August 1892, its left flank guarded by Congolese posts north of the Uele (Welle), had crossed the Nile watershed from the Free State. Its objective was the west bank of the Bahr el Jebel stretching north to Emin's old provincial headquarters of Lado. By October of that year the expedition had reached Wadelai and contacted Fadl el Mula and his mutineers, but when no close understanding was concluded, the Free State regulars were withdrawn back to Ganda near the watershed. In July 1893 the Congolese were back to occupy Laboré and Muggi but by now the Mahdist garrison at Rejaf was on the alert and the Congolese retired again to Ganda, to find their Azande allies now actively hostile. Within weeks of the arrival of the new Mahdist *amir* Arabi Dafa'allah at Rejaf, the Azande had joined the attack on the Congolese who were in 1894 progressively bundled back by Arabi's

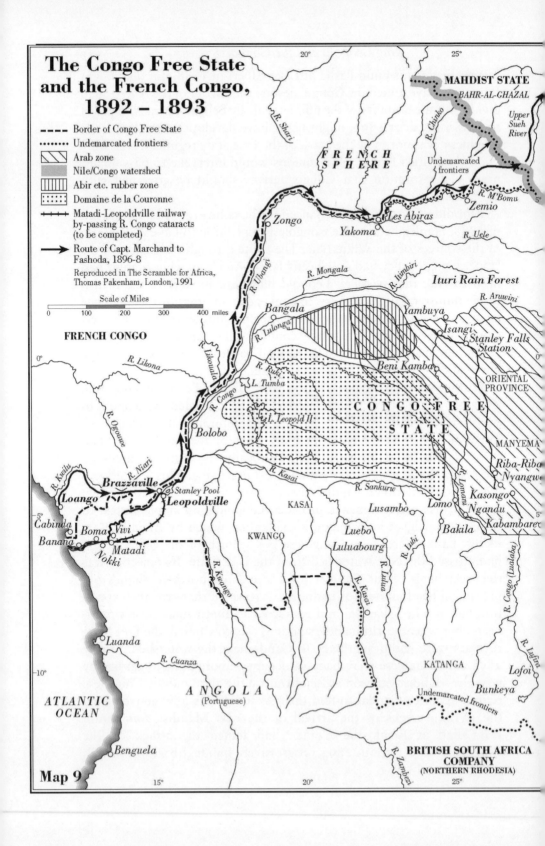

The Congo Free State
and the French Congo,
1892 – 1893

- - - - Border of Congo Free State
.... Undemarcated frontiers
Arab zone
Nile/Congo watershed
Abir etc. rubber zone
Domaine de la Couronne
Matadi-Leopoldville railway by-passing R. Congo cataracts (to be completed)
Route of Capt. Marchand to Fashoda, 1896-8

Reproduced in The Scramble for Africa, Thomas Pakenham, London, 1991

Scale of Miles

| 0 | 100 | 200 | 300 | 400 miles |

FRENCH CONGO

MAHDIST STATE
BAHR-AL-GHAZAL
Upper Sueh River

Undemarcated frontiers

R. Shari

R. Chinko

R. M'Bomu
Zemio

FRENCH SPHERE

Les Abiras
Zongo
Yakoma

R. Uele

R. Ubangi

R. Mongala

R. Iumbiri

Ituri Rain Forest

R. Aruwini

Bangala

R. Lulonga

Yambuya

Isangi
Stanley Falls Station

R. Likona

R. Likouala

R. Ruki
L. Tumba

Beni Kamba

ORIENTAL PROVINCE

0°

R. Ogowwe

R. Congo

Bolobo

L. Leopold II

**C O N G O   F R E E
S T A T E**

MANYEMA

Riba-Riba
Nyangwe

R. Niari

Brazzaville

Stanley Pool

Leopoldville

R. Kasai

R. Sankuru

Lomo

R. Lomani

Kasongo
Ngandu
Kabambare

R. Kwilu

Loango

KASAI

Lusambo

Bakila

5°

Cabinda
Banana
Boma Vivi
Matadi
Nokki

KWANGO

Luebo
Luluabourg

R. Lubi

R. Lulua

R. Congo (Lualaba)

R. Kwango

R. Kasai

Luanda

R. Cuanza

A N G O L A
(Portuguese)

-10°

KATANGA

Lofoi

Undemarcated frontiers

Bunkeya

R. Lufira

**ATLANTIC
OCEAN**

Benguela

R. Zambezi

**BRITISH SOUTH AFRICA
COMPANY**
(NORTHERN RHODESIA)

Map 9

wakil westwards over the Nile-Congo watershed via Mundu to Dungu on the Uele river. By 1893, however, both the British and the French were becoming active competitors for influence in the Upper Nile valley and Leopold would need increasingly to rely on diplomacy to attain his objective, secretly advantaged by mendacious reports in the Belgian press of the Congolese reoccupation of Wadelai and by continuing European ignorance of the defeats suffered by that Congolese expedition.

Two further probes were nevertheless undertaken by Congolese expeditions northwards through Bahr el Ghazal: the first in December 1893 towards Hufrat el Nahas; the second in March 1894 to Liffi in Dar Fertit, augmented by Azande reinforcements to meet the Mahdist threat. Both would be withdrawn finally to Zemio and had been reinforced when news of the Franco-Congolese agreement of September 1894 arrived. A final Congolese sortie towards Meshra el Rek was ambushed in February 1895 and obliged to retreat.[6]

Following his agreement with Mackinnon's IBEAC in 1890, so unguardedly if tacitly endorsed by Lord Salisbury, for the next three years Leopold exploited his superior intelligence and communications with the Upper Nile zone in seeking territorial expansion, both there and on the north bank of the Uele river. Too late, when the advance guard of Leopold's expedition had already left in August 1890, did Salisbury discover his error, an error compounded by his government's refusal to fund adequately the railway project from Mombasa to Uganda – the *sine qua non* of IBEAC's extended occupation. This last Uganda reverse would only be retrieved at the eleventh hour following the belated resignation of Gladstone as Liberal prime minister in March 1894 and the succession of the Earl of Rosebery. As to the Congolese annexation of the Equatoria Nile which Britain was powerless to oppose, it would be the Mahdist offensive of Arabi Dafa'allah, unbeknown to London or Paris, which would drive Leopold's expedition back to the Free State in early 1894.

Benefiting from British ignorance of local conditions, Leopold was shrewdly representing to Britain that he was the best means of resisting a French drive to the Nile; and to France that British friendship was the sanction for Congolese expansion north of the Uele and M'bomu rivers. So long as the Liberal government was divided, Britain was in no position to counter the threat to the Nile either from France or Leopold. Moreover if Egypt could be made militarily self-sufficient against Mahdist invasion, the withdrawal of British troops could still be on the agenda. Britain, insufficiently alert to the growing influence of the French colonialist lobby and its determination to use the occupation of the Nile basin as a lever to restore French authority in Egypt, nevertheless regarded Leopold as a preferable neighbour for Uganda – a situation of which Leopold was well aware.

Leopold, having suppressed news of Congolese reverses at the hands of the Mahdists and exaggerating the imminence of a French Nile expedition under Commandant P. L. Monteil which he was himself obstructing, had by 12 April 1894 negotiated with the British an Anglo-Congolese Agreement granting Leopold a life-long lease of territory west of the Bahr el Jebel stretching north to Fashoda (shutting out the French) – and this while Franco-Congolese negotiations were simultaneously in train. Unfortunately for the British the draft Agreement included a 'corridor lease' clause for purposes of communication along the German East African boundary between Lake Tanganyika and Lake Albert Edward above Lake Albert. Leopold for his part relinquished claims under the IBEAC Agreement and recognised the British position in Uganda, now a Protectorate. However the French and Germans had signed a Protocol in March wilfully inimicable to British claims on the Niger, achieving a rapport which the French, in their anger at the new Anglo-Congolese Agreement, were pleased to develop, granted matching German anger at the 'alteration' of the German-Congolese border of 1884. Britain was obliged to withdraw the 'corridor' article – but ending thus the brief Franco-German détente.

The French, bereft now of German help and unable to pressurise London into abandoning the Nile leases to Leopold, nevertheless set about forcing Leopold, unsupported by his Belgian government, to surrender these lifelong leases save for that covering what would become the 'Lado Enclave' south of latitude 5° 30′ N; this in return for French recognition of the M'bomu river as the frontier between the two Congos. Agreement was reached in August 1894. Britain conceded; Rosebery was unable to carry his Cabinet faced with possible war. Britain's claim to a monopoly sphere of influence on the Nile had been successfully challenged by France. *L'appétit vient en mangeant.*

Only in early 1897 would Leopold take possession of the Lado Enclave, having defeated the Mahdist *amir* Arabi Dafa'allah. It would revert to the Anglo-Egyptian Sudan on Leopold's death in 1910, following which the Sudan-Uganda Protectorate frontier was rectified in 1914.[7]

3 THE FIRST GERMAN REICH: EAST AFRICA AND UGANDA
1884–94

The transient détente between Britain and France, which in 1882 might have instigated a joint Anglo-French military intervention in Egypt, had by 1884 dissolved. Bismarck, conscious of Continental Germany's political and new industrial strength, supported by the secret Triple Alliance with Austro-Hungary and Italy of 1882 (itself preceded by the revival of the *Dreikaiserbund* in 1881 with Austro-Hungary and Russia) was interested in assuaging French bitterness over defeat at Sedan. Bismarck was riled by British disdainfulness towards countries who challenged her 'Monroe doctrine' in Africa. Despite his assertion as late as 1881 that, while he was Chancellor, Germany would pursue no colonial policies, between May and July 1884 South West Africa, Cameroon and Togoland had become German-occupied and new markets for German exports. The Berlin Conference, convened by Bismarck in November, had by February 1885 further decided that, barring the occupied littorals, contiguous to existing British protectorates, there would be free access to the African interior.

An immediate effect of this Berlin Act was to establish Germany as a power in East Africa with a protectionist trade policy. Six months previously Dr Carl Peters had created a private Society for German Colonisation. He had left with three colleagues and, disowned by his government, crossed from Zanzibar to the mainland. Within five weeks he had acquired the signatures of twelve chiefs of the Usagara territory to documents handing over their domains to Peters's Society. By the end of the Berlin Conference in February 1885 he was back in Berlin. His 'protectorates' however were concealed from the members of the Conference until ratified by the Kaiser in person in early March. The Sultan of Zanzibar learned of this annexation of Usagara in April, and that was only the beginning of his adversities.

The protests to the British government by Sir John Kirk, British consul in Zanzibar who had so effectively sabotaged the Khedive Ismail's expedition to Kismayu in 1875, no longer gained protection for the Sultan from invasion. Had the threat come from Leopold, it would have been otherwise. In June two German cruisers anchored off Lamu by the mouth of the Tana river and on 7 August 1885 a squadron of five warships steamed into Zanzibar harbour, its commodore bringing an ultimatum to the Sultan to recognise immediately German claims to Usagara, to Chaggaland (Kilimanjaro), and to Witu near the island of

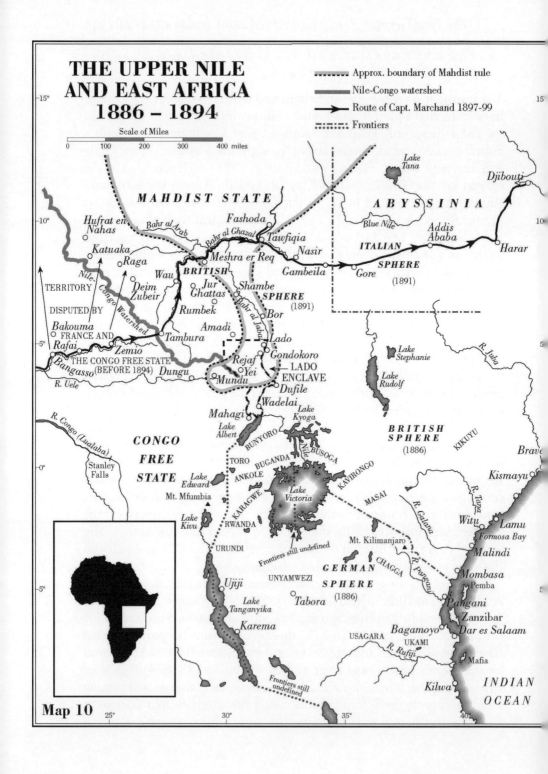

THE UPPER NILE
AND EAST AFRICA
1886 – 1894

-15°

Approx. boundary of Mahdist rule
Nile-Congo watershed
Route of Capt. Marchand 1897-99
Frontiers

Scale of Miles

0   100   200   300   400 miles

MAHDIST STATE

Lake Tana

Djibouti

15

ABYSSINIA

-10°

Hufrat en Nahas
Bahr al Arab
Fashoda
Blue Nile
Addis Ababa
Harar

10

Katuaka   Raga
Bahr al Ghazal
Tawfiqia
Nasir
Meshra er Req
ITALIAN

Nile-Congo Watershed
TERRITORY
Wau
Deim Zubeir
BRITISH
Jur Ghattas
Shambe
Gambeila
Gore
SPHERE
(1891)

DISPUTED BY
Rumbek
SPHERE
(1891)

Bakouma
FRANCE AND
Amadi
Bor
Lake Stephanie
R. Juba

-5°
Rafai
Zemio
Tambura
Lado
Lake Rudolf
5

Bangasso
THE CONGO FREE STATE
(BEFORE 1894)
Dungu
Rejaf
Yei
Gondokoro
LADO
ENCLAVE

R. Uele
Mundu
Dufile
Wadelai
Lake Kyoga

Mahagi
Lake Albert
BRITISH
SPHERE
(1886)
KIKUYU
Brava

CONGO
R. Congo (Lualaba)
BUNYORO
Nile
BUSOGA
Kismayu

FREE
Stanley Falls
TORO
BUGANDA
KAVIRONGO

0°

STATE
Lake Edward
ANKOLE
Lake Victoria
MASAI
R. Galana
Witu
Lamu

Mt. Mfumbia
KARAGWE
Formosa Bay
Malindi

Lake Kivu
RWANDA
Frontiers still undefined
Mt. Kilimanjaro
R. Pangani
Mombasa
Pemba

-5°
URUNDI
CHAGGA
Pangani

Ujiji
UNYAMWEZI
GERMAN
Zanzibar

Lake Tanganyika
Tabora
SPHERE
(1886)
Bagamoyo
Dar es Salaam

Karema
USAGARA
UKAMI
R. Rufiji
Mafia

Frontiers still undefined
Kilwa
INDIAN
OCEAN

Map 10

25°   30°   35°   40°

Lamu. Britain's prime ministers, facing a Russian invasion of Afghanistan in the wake of rebuff to her belated expedition to Khartoum, were not minded to add German hostility to their problems. Gladstone on 12 March 1885 had told Parliament: 'If Germany becomes a colonising power, all I can say is: "God speed her."' Salisbury later was more guarded: 'The German proceedings are not creditable. But, if we had no motive for standing well [with Germany], I do not quite see our interest in this Zanzibar quarrel.' By August he believed British credit built up with Germany in rejecting the Sultan's overtures had been matched by German help in Russia, Turkey and Egypt.

The subsequent Delimitation Commission, in which Britain, France and Germany were participants, would in December 1886 confine the Sultan's future jurisdiction to the islands of Zanzibar, Pemba, Mafia and Lamu, together with the littoral territory to a depth of only 10 miles and south for 700 miles from the Tana river. The 'unoccupied' interior would be divided: between Germany, which acquired Dar el Salaam (ceded as the one port) and a 'sphere of influence' stretching from Rovuma north to the contemporary Tanzania-Kenya border and west to Lake Victoria; and Britain to whom was ceded Mombasa and an adjacent 'sphere of influence' corresponding with modern Kenya, to be administered by the Imperial British East Africa Company led by Sir William Mackinnon. Thus it was that Stanley and Emin arriving back at Bagamoyo in December 1889 would be welcomed by the German Commissioner for East Africa. By the end of March 1890 Emin had elected to join the German colonial service. After leading an abortive German expedition towards Buganda, while exploring alone towards the hinterland of the Cameroons, he was murdered near the Lualuba river.[8]

The Anglo-German partition of 1886 led swiftly to the German occupation of her sphere, to which would be added Witu and then, in October 1889, the Benadir coast to its north; and to a British occupation by the 1888 IBEAC. Despite Bismarck's assurance in 1889 that 'Uganda, Wadelai and other places to the east and north of Lake Victoria' were outside the German sphere, Dr Peters did not see himself bound by such agreements and in July 1889, with homeland but no governmental backing, launched his expedition from Witu, ostensibly to relieve Emin but really to occupy Buganda as he had successfully occupied Usagara in 1884 – this time in the name of his German East Africa Company. In September 1888 the *kabaka*, M'wanga, had been forced into exile by Christians and Moslems alike, but with Christian support was back by February 1890. By now, across the Nile in Busoga, Frederick Jackson with an IBEAC caravan had arrived in November 1889, but was forbidden by his instructions to enter Buganda despite M'wanga's plea for help. Returning from an ivory sortie, he learned in March that Peters had passed through his camp on 4 December 1889, opened his correspondence, and with the backing of the head of the White Fathers mission ('the Franca') in Rubaga, concluded a German protectorate treaty with M'wanga on 2 March 1890. Jackson set off for Rubaga to find a seeming *fait accompli.*

That was however a chimera. Peters returned to Bagamoyo, triumphant, to learn that in the interim the Kaiser had dispensed with the services of his Chancellor, Bismarck; and had agreed, in exchange for the cession by Britain of Heligoland in the North Sea, a British sphere of influence extending north from latitude 1° south to the Egyptian border; a British protectorate over Zanzibar; and the cession to Britain of Witu and all territory north of the Tana river. Peters had to be content with the governorship of the Kilimanjaro district. Emin's German expedition to Equatoria and Buganda was recalled. The Anglo-German Treaty was signed on 1 July 1890. On 26 December Captain Frederick Lugard by sheer determination faced down M'wanga and compelled him to sign a treaty with the IBEAC, so implementing the Anglo-German Agreement by accepting Company protectorate status.[9]

During 1891 Lugard would consolidate and extend his Company's position. Thwarted by the rains from subjugating Bunyoro, he marched in April with his Baganda militia to possess Ankole and Toro to the west before reaching his objective, Kavalli's south of Wadelai, in September, there to recruit the remnants of Emin's Khedivial militia under Salim Bey. Returning to Buganda in December 1891 Lugard was astonished to learn that IBEAC, faced with bankruptcy, were instructing him to abandon Buganda and return to Zanzibar – by the end of 1892. Skilfully reconciling the insurrectionist Baganda Moslems with the *kabaka* M'wanga and leaving his deputy Captain Williams in control, Lugard departed in June for Zanzibar and London, there on his arrival in October to benefit from a further extension of the IBEAC lease of three months, bought by the threat of Lord Rosebery's resignation.

In November 1892 Sir Gerald Portal, consul at Zanzibar, was sent as commissioner to recommend guidelines for British Uganda policy. In Kampala by March 1893, he had coaxed M'wanga into signing a

THE WHITE ELEPHANT.

Present Proprietor (*log.*). "SEE HERE, GOVERNOR! HE'S A LIKELY-LOOKING ANIMAL,—BUT *I* CAN'T MANAGE HIM! IF *YOU* WON'T TAKE HIM, I MUST LET HIM GO!!"

new treaty on 29 May accepting a provisional British Protectorate. Portal arrived back in England in November there to revise his final report. Its consideration by the Cabinet seems to have been slowed by Rosebery until Gladstone's resignation was tendered in March, by which time Portal had died of fever from Uganda, there to be succeeded by Colonel H. Colvile. Presented to Parliament in April, and debated on 1 June 1894, the report recognised Uganda to be 'the natural key to the Nile Valley' and recommended that it become a British Protectorate. The report further recommended the abolition of the IBEAC, and the building of Mombasa–Kampala railway. The first two recommendations were approved, but not the last. That last consent to the railway would only follow with the successor British government in August 1895.

After 1890 British policy in the Nile region would remain unchallenged by Germany, save that the mistaken inclusion in the Anglo-Congolese Agreement of April 1894 of the 'corridor clause' affecting the German East Africa boundary not unreasonably provoked a hostile reaction. British policy in Europe meanwhile continued to lean towards a continuing amicable accord with the Triple Alliance countries.[10]

4 THE KINGDOM OF ITALY: MASSAWA, BOGOS, HAMASEIN AND KASSALA 1885–96

On the determined initiative of Piedmont, with its capital Turin, the unification of Italy as a kingdom was accomplished by 1861. Piedmont had been united with Savoy east of the Rhone since 1034, becoming part of the Kingdom of Sardinia in 1718. Its king, Victor Emmanuel II, with his chief minister Count Cavour achieved the political unification largely at the expense of Austro-Hungary, but at the cost of now ceding to France, their ally, the province of Savoy and Nice. Lombardy in 1859; Naples, Tuscany and its northern neighbours in 1860; Venice in 1866; and finally Rome in 1870 became additional constituent members of the kingdom. Italian maritime influence thus had its roots long in the past. On the Nile, the presence of a Sardinian consul-general in Cairo and of the vice-consul, Antoine Brun-Rollet, in Khartoum, where he resided from 1834 to 1858, has already been observed in volume I (1504–1862).

Following unification, the first Italian move in the Nile-Red Sea region anticipated the opening of the Suez Canal in 1869. By November that year the Rubattino Shipping Company completed the purchase from the Danakil people of the port of Assab on the Abyssinian coast west of Roheita. Khedive Ismail was having none of it and forced the back-pedalling of the project until 1882 when it became an Italian colony. Meanwhile Italy increasingly looked to Britain and her navy to safeguard her against French encroachment and, in 1882, had joined with Germany and Austro-Hungary in the Triple Alliance to which Britain, anxious always about Russian ambitions in the eastern Mediterranean, found herself diplomatically drawn.

With the evacuation of the Sudan decided upon, the 'Hewett' Adwa (Adowa) Peace Treaty of June 1884 had granted Abyssinia limited rights to Massawa as a free port; but nine months later, notwithstanding the port's British protection, it had been evacuated and handed over in February 1885, not to Abyssinia, but to Italy (see p. 455) who ignored the free transit concession. By 1887 Lord Salisbury was reckoning that handover to be a mistake, by which time the Italians had extended their territory outside Massawa. Unlike France at Zeyla and Obock, Italy was of a more territorially acquisitive bent in this area. She was fortunate that Emperor John's viceroy in Shoa, Menilek, was not only hostile towards the Emperor, thus weakening John's negotiating position, but would in October 1887 make a local trade agreement with Italy. When John was killed fighting the Mahdists at Gallabat in

March 1889, Menilek II would succeed him and on 2 May sign the Treaty of Wechale (Uccialli) with the Italians, granting Italy possession of Bogos and Hamasein (Eritrea, the northern part of Tigré). A month later Keren was occupied and on 3 August Asmara; thence but *ultra vires*, the River Mareb. The Italian, but *not* the Abyssinian, treaty version granted Italy the whole of Abyssinia as a protectorate, a claim duly notified to and accepted by the international powers with the notable exceptions of Russia, France and Turkey. When Menilek protested at this trickery and at the Italian incursion south to the River Mareb, and no *amende* was forthcoming, in February 1893 he proclaimed the 1889 treaty void and imported arms from France and Russia via Obock and Zeyla in preparation for hostilities.[11]

Francesco Crispi, promoter of the Sicilian rebellion in 1860 against the King of Naples in collaboration with Giuseppe Garibaldi, had become prime minister of Italy in 1887. An advocate of the Triple Alliance, he was also a principal protagonist of the Italian colonialist lobby, and had been the initiator of the Treaty of Wechale in 1889 signed by Emperor Menilek, a further boost for *irredentismo*. However Crispi's ambitions were still far from satisfied.

Following the defeat of the Mahdist invasion of Egypt at Toski in August 1889, with uncertainty as to whether the Sudan régime could suddenly crumble, Sir Evelyn Baring in Cairo as representative of the protecting power focused his mind on Italian activities on the Bogos-Kassala border. On 15 December 1889 he warned London that the capture of Kassala from the Mahdists would lead not only to Italian control of the waters of the Atbara river if not of the Blue Nile but, backed by European engineering technology, would constitute a threat to Egyptian agriculture. 'Whatever Power holds the Upper Nile Valley must, by the mere force of its geographical situation, dominate Egypt.' Although the Sudan had been evacuated by Egypt de facto, de jure it remained an Ottoman possession, but doubtless the Italians would if they captured it claim Kassala as a protectorate under the Berlin Agreement of 1885.

Nor was it Kassala only that might be swallowed. Baring was anxious that Tokar, under Mahdist control, should be recaptured, constituting as it did a strategic position in the event of a future reoccupation of the Sudan via Suakin and Berber, and proximate to any Italian encroachments on the littoral. London however in the current wider context did not wish to antagonise Crispi, Salisbury insisting that 'Tokar has nothing to do with the Nile Valley'. Kassala by contrast did and clearly was an Italian ambition which Crispi was not willing to renounce. Salisbury resorted to procrastination. Talks in London, Naples and Rome commencing March 1890 had reached no agreement when, at the end of January 1891, Crispi was obliged to resign, having steadfastly declined to recognise the Egyptian de jure claim to former territory. Salisbury under fresh urging from Baring and the army now agreed to the – successful – attack on Tokar in February.

Crispi's successor (until the former's return to office in December 1893), the Marchese di Rudini, was of a less inflexible disposition. In March the frontiers of Italian colonial territories east to and south from the Horn of Africa were delimited, and in April 1891 a further Protocol was signed under which Italy recognised Egyptian de jure claims to the Sudan. While the *temporary* military occupation of Kassala was conceded, it was subject to Italian recognition of the obligation to retrocede it as soon as 'the Egyptian Government shall be in a position to reoccupy the district in question… and there to maintain order and tranquillity'. Eritrea would revert to Egypt were Italy to withdraw, but Britain had no present plans to extend Egyptian rule in that direction in return 'for a consideration' in the Mediterranean. Di Rudini would nevertheless persist in his request for an Anglo-Italian naval agreement which would protect Italy against France with the consequence, pointed out by Professor G. N. Sanderson, that by July 1891 it had led to the Franco-Russian entente, naval building programmes, and, in 1894, a military convention. The enhanced Franco-Russian naval threat to the eastern Mediterranean made a third naval base, Alexandria, in addition to Gibraltar and Malta, a mandatory strategic requirement for Britain.[12]

Following Crispi's return to power, the merits were again canvassed in February 1894 of an Italian move on Kassala in concert with Britain. After weeks of unsuccessful advocacy of this plan, Italy decided to attack Kassala alone, while assuring Britain that no breach of the 1891 Protocol was planned, and that Massawa and Suakin would both be safeguarded thereby. An ill-organised Mahdist incursion against Agordat had been roundly defeated the previous November (see p. 502) and now in July 1894 Kassala was occupied without a fight.

The acquisition of Kassala was not the only Italian success in the region during 1894. The Treaty of Wechale might have been unilaterally abrogated by Menilek to whom the Tigréan chieftains, who had previously been in friendly relations with the Italian governor of Eritrea, had since transferred their allegiance; but in December 1894 a rising against the Italians, in which Ras Mangasha, John IV's son, was a participant, was quickly crushed, much of Tigré east of the Takazzé river falling into Italian hands, including Adwa, Axum and Makale. Menilek was preparing for battle nevertheless, and the Italians opted to pre-empt the attack – by advancing into southern Tigré. However they lost Amba Alagi on 7 December 1895 and the three captured Tigréan towns and in an attempt to recover Adwa were put to flight on 1 March 1896 with heavy casualties. Only exhaustion and the absence of food supplies persuaded the victors to march back to Addis Ababa. Peace would be signed in October. Menilek secured Italian agreement to the abrogation of the Treaty of Wechale and the unqualified recognition of Abyssinia's independence. Menilek for his part even conceded the revised southern frontier of Hamasein on the River Mareb – creating Eritrea.[13]

Despite the humiliating reverse at Adwa, Italy was substantially established on the north-east African littoral including Assab, now incorporated in Eritrea; the Somali sultanates of the Horn of Africa; also the, formerly Zanzibari, Benadir coast, acquired with British backing in 1889. The effect of Adwa in Italy however was serious. For a day or two demonstrators possessed the streets, Crispi was forced to resign, and Italy's membership of the Triple Alliance threatened. Not until 10 March 1896 had a new government been installed once again under di Rudini. Two days later, the British government was urgently requested to create a diversion to draw off Mahdist troops attacking Kassala, 'du côté du Nil'.

This Kassala rumour had surfaced in London originally in January, and after discussion Salisbury had decided that if such action were authorised it should be for political and military considerations by way of advance to the recapture of Dongola, rather than the dispatch of a relief force from Suakin. Now on 12 March 1896 the occupation of Dongola was approved, principally to succour the Italians, but thereby also to restore lost territory to Egypt and to deter any possible Abyssinian collusion with the Mahdists. It would not just be a feint: Dongola would be retained, the foot of Egypt planted rather further up the Nile.

The French Marquise du Deffand had once remarked: 'La distance n'y fait rien: il n'y a que le premier pas qui coûte.' How would the French react? As Baring, now Lord Cromer, warned, there might be a diplomatic crisis: 'If once Dongola is occupied the whole Sudan question will possibly be raised.' Meanwhile the Triple Alliance had been saved.[14]

5 THE FRENCH THIRD REPUBLIC: 'UN COUP DE PISTOLET SUR LE NIL' 1893–98

Criticising the failure of the French Chamber of Deputies to accord their government authority – even for a limited intervention in Egypt to safeguard the Suez Canal – at the time of the British invasion of 1882 to put down the Arabi insurrection, Gabriel Charmes wrote in *Revue des Deux Mondes* of 15 August 1883 of 'ceux dont l'ignorance a causé des grands malheurs, ont infligé à la France dans la Méditerranée une défaite presque aussi désastreuse et plus humiliante que celle nous avons subie sur le continent'.

Tel el Kebir became equated in level of tragedy with Sedan, but perhaps still more discreditable since palpably avoidable. The Dual Control arrangements had been invalidated. Britain had become the accepted international protector of Ottoman Egypt and its European financial interests. For France the objective of evacuation proclaimed in good faith by successive British governments needed to be achieved with the maximum dispatch. However the subsequent success of the Mahdist rebellion in the Sudan, coinciding with the progressive awakening of European powers to the mercantile advantages of territorial acquisitions in East Africa, particularly in the contiguous Upper Nile basin, made the policy of evacuation increasingly hazardous for Britain. The last bona fides attempt by Britain to implement evacuation, the Drummond-Wolff mission proposal of 1887, would be gratuitously undone by a hostile French government with Russian support.

Apart from the French governorate established at Obock with its handy access to Abyssinia's ruler, French interests in this region remained centred *par excellence* on Egypt, and on King Leopold's threat to the French Congo. For the while French pressure on British rule in the former could not be effectively exerted but Count de Brazza, acclaimed a national hero, had been recommissioned in 1882 to extend the French colony's boundaries in the Upper Ubangi. Under the 1887 Franco-Congolese protocol, this should give France the territory north of 4° latitude north running through Les Abiras at the Ubangi confluence of the M'Bomu and Uele rivers. The Belgians however did not prove malleable and, in the absence of sufficient concern in the Quai d'Orsay, presently concentrating on Lake Chad, they would encroach northwards cutting off French Congo from the Nile–Congo watershed. The young Duc d'Uzès would be a senior participant in a French Congo expedition in August 1892 directed to reinforce French influence in the now disputed Upper Ubangi, but disease had prevented it advancing beyond Les Abiras.

The appointment of Théophile Delcassé in January 1893 as French under-secretary for the colonies – part of the French ministry of marine, but with a Cabinet seat – and the approval of funds for an expedition across the Nile–Congo watershed marked the launch of serious French plans for a foot in the Upper Nile. Victor Liotard, a French naval doctor, would claim in October 1898 that in 1890 he had been charged by de Brazza to create in the Upper Ubangi a French region 'ayant une porte ouverte sur le Nil'. Professor Sanderson has pointed out that Liotard was not posted until late 1891 and then for purposes of guarding the flank of expansion towards Lake Chad, although de Brazza did that year canvass with Delcassé's predecessor, Eugène Étienne, the potential benefit of an occupation of the Upper Nile as a lever to open discussions with Britain on Egypt. Leopold meanwhile had sealed off the Nile–Congo divide against French penetration, and in December 1892 came within an ace of persuading the Quai d'Orsay to recognise latitude 6° 30′ north as the Upper Nile boundary between the French and the Congo Free State.[15]

French militant colonial opinion had become organised in 1890 with the formation of the Comité de l'Afrique Française, especially distrustful of any French diplomatic approach deemed over-conciliatory. Initially having concentrated on the Lake Chad region, the creation of the *'groupe colonial'* in the Chamber of Deputies in July 1892 led the next year to first priority being given to the Upper Nile and to sustained pressure for the dispatch of expeditions across the Nile–Congo watershed into Bahr el Ghazal. Delcassé like Étienne was a member of the *groupe* and became responsible on his appointment for moving the colonial under-secretary's office from the ministry of Marine to the Pavillon de Flore, then to become a separate ministry in March 1894.

When the new foreign minister, Develle, was pressurised in January 1893 to initiate a French Nile expedition, Delcassé, rejecting any association with Leopold's Upper Nile ambitions, in February 1893 telegraphed to de Brazza announcing his readiness to organise a mission to reinforce Liotard and penetrate the M'bomu river region, with a view to attaining the Nile Basin as quickly as possible. Delcassé had remarked the argument deployed by Alexandre Prompt, a French engineer in Egypt whose younger brother had been a fellow student at college of the French President, Sadi Carnot: in a speech the previous month Prompt had claimed that a barrage, constructed downstream from the junction of the White Nile and Sobat rivers, could create a reservoir, of great but measurable proportions, for local use and had the potential mortally to deny Egypt its irrigation needs. Patently however Prompt had not observed the unsuitable configuration of the site suggested for this initiative.

Monteil, 1898–94   Delcassé was determined that it should be *commandant supérieur* P. L. Monteil of Upper Ubangi, previously chosen by Étienne in 1890 to explore the Senegal-Lake Chad region, who should lead the Bahr el Ghazal expedition to the Nile. Overriding Monteil's protests of fatigue, he persuaded a sympathetic President Carnot to call Delcassé and Monteil to a meeting at the Elysée on 3 May 1893 and personally request Monteil to accept the commission, flourishing Prompt's speech as an imperative for the occupation of Fashoda, and declaring: 'Je veux rouvrir la question d'Égypte.'

Monteil loyally obeyed, instructing his second-in command already en route to Dakar to ascend the Congo river to the Ubangi confluence at Les Abiras (founded in 1891) whence the march to the White Nile confluence with the Sobat would commence. However by 14 August Monteil was pointing out the obstruction he might encounter from the Congo Free State military positions east of Les Abiras, and therefore the desirability of reaching an accord with the Belgians before heading for the Nile – a concern reinforced by news from de Brazza in October 1893, just as Monteil's second-in-command was leaving for the Ubangi, that the Belgians were denying the expedition's entry to Brazzaville and by de Brazza's recommendation of a postponement. The French foreign ministry, which had not been originally consulted about the Monteil expedition, agreed with Delcassé that reinforcements would indeed now be needed and that diplomatic pressure must be brought on Leopold.

In December 1893 that French government fell, the successor ministers proving unenthusiastic and dilatory regarding the Monteil expedition whose leader remained in Paris. Rosebery in London, shortly to succeed Gladstone as prime minister, was anxious to reach a swift agreement with King Leopold over recognition of the British sphere in the Nile, and in March 1894 he sent F. D. Lugard on an intelligence mission to Paris. Lugard reported that Monteil was planning to march on Lado or Fashoda with a major expedition. This development strengthened Rosebery's determination to press on towards an Anglo-Congolese agreement to preempt the current Franco-Congolese negotiations in Brussels – an objective realised by Britain in May 1894 in return for the grant to Leopold of a lease of territory west of the White Nile north to the 10° latitude. Despite the arrival of the advance party at Les Abiras, the Monteil mission was further interrupted, Monteil being warned to rein back his forces from penetrating the Nile basin while France sought, successfully, to wreck this Anglo-Congolese treaty. Even when that objective was accomplished on 14 August 1894 by the signing of the Franco-Congolese agreement, Monteil's expedition would nevertheless be diverted a week later by Delcassé, back in office since the end of May, just as Monteil was about to leave the Atlantic coast, in order to suppress a rebellion in the Ivory Coast.

Leopold had now been obliged by the French to renounce the implied lease of the Bahr el Ghazal granted to him by the British in May 1894, together with the Free State fortified posts in the Upper Ubangi, even if, as a consolation, he had gained French recognition of the 'Lado enclave' north to the latitude 5° 30′ and east of 30° longitude. The French route from Les Abiras to Fashoda could now securely be planned to run north of the newly limited lease of Belgian territory west of the White Nile.[16]

The Monteil expedition was not the only planned French mission to the Nile to prove abortive. Three weeks after his meeting at the Elysée in May 1893, President Carnot, who would be assassinated in July 1894, had sought to persuade Casimir Maistre, formerly prospecting the Niger river, to participate in a second Nile initiative – but unofficially, under the umbrella of the Comité de l'Afrique Française. Exploiting the quest for political support of Emperor Menilek of Abyssinia who was being threatened by Italian aggrandisement, Carnot's plan was for a pincer movement on the Nile in tandem with Monteil. Maistre would land at Obock and, with Menilek's backing, cross Abyssinia and then descend the Sobat river, to rendezvous at its mouth with Monteil. Pleading indifferent health and absence of local experience, Maistre declined. That strategy was not however dead. More than three years later, in December 1896, Léonce Lagarde, governor of Obock at the time of the Maistre plan, would be authorised to negotiate with Menilek a comparable Sobat mission to meet with Marchand on the White Nile.

Liotard 1894–98   Twin French plans for Nile basin occupation may have thus foundered by August 1894, yet the French approach line up the Congo to the Nile–Congo watershed had been secured and the Belgian military posts on the M'bomu river were to be evacuated.

Delcassé in October 1894, with the support of the new French President, Jean Casimir-Périer, had now nominated Victor Liotard, currently French commissioner for the Upper Ubangi, to be the leader of a new mission to the Nile. Delcassé, mistakenly apprehensive that Colonel Henry Colvile, the British acting commissioner in Uganda, would be setting out for Wadelai after his campaign against Kabarega, believed no time was to be lost. Although as a civilian Liotard had been passed over as leader in May 1893 in favour of Monteil, he had persevered patiently to establish good relations with the Zande *sultans* Zemio and Rafa'i. On his return to Les Abiras from leave in France, Liotard would now, with his team of French officers and Zande support, set about successfully evicting the Belgian agents from Zemio's base in July 1895; occupying Tambura, on the Sueh beyond the Nile watershed, in February 1896; and Deim Zubeir in April 1897.

With correspondence between Paris and Les Abiras taking six months and difficulties seemingly being encountered in Upper Ubangi, the arrival in Paris in August 1895 from the Ivory Coast of Monteil's chief of staff, well briefed on recent history by Monteil and eager to promote his own mission to the Nile, brought about a revised appraisal. Capitaine Jean-Baptiste Marchand submitted his personal report, 'Mission de Congo-Nil, le Bahr el Ghazal', to minister C. de Chautemps at the Colonies on 11 September 1895.

Since the departure of Liotard from France on 25 October 1894, Anglo-French tensions had increased in the wake of the Franco-Congolese agreement. On 28 February 1895 François Deloncle, a *groupe* colonial deputy, while acknowledging that the Upper Nile regions belonged to the Ottoman empire, had affirmed the legitimacy of French access directed 'pour prendre à revers certaines positions de nos rivaux'. This statement would on 11 March draw from Sir Edward Grey in the House of Commons on behalf of Rosebery's government the insistence that the spheres of influence of the Egyptian *and* the British together covered the whole course of the Nile, the latter (British) sphere publicly recognised by Germany, Italy and the Congo Free State. On 28 March 1895, questioned as to whether a French expedition had already left for the Nile valley, Grey discounted the credibility of such a rumour but warned – in what subsequently became known as the 'Grey Declaration' – that 'it must be perfectly well known to the French Government that it would be an unfriendly act, and would be so viewed by England'. For this unpremeditated wording Rosebery would later claim personal responsibility. Lord

Salisbury reaffirmed to Paris on 10 December 1897 that 'England must not be understood to admit that any other European Power than Great Britain has any claim to occupy any part of the valley of the Nile'. Where in Grey's statement the Egyptian sphere might end and the British sphere begin would never be clarified, if only because the French declined to discuss the matter. It might have seemed that in order to occupy the Upper Nile from Uganda it would be a British expedition, while from the north – in the name of the Khedive – it would be Egyptian, a reconquest claim superior to that of the French. By July 1898 the issue would anyway be academic. Meanwhile, on 27 December 1895, the 1896 advance to Dongola would be discussed by Salisbury with the French ambassador as the 'premier objectif', while the Quai d'Orsay was scrupulously informed on 12 March 1896, in the aftermath of the Battle of Adwa, that in response to a request by the Egyptian government the advance of Egyptian troops had now been sanctioned.[17]

Marchand 1896–98   Marchand's plan was for an expedition of seven French officers, four NCOs, five technicians and 150 Senegalese troops. They would proceed over thirty months across Africa via Loango on the Atlantic coast and the Upper Ubangi to Deim Zubeir and to the Bahr el Humr, an affluent of the Ghazal; thence to the White Nile. They would adopt a pacific profile, seeking settlement by consent of the Mahdist rulers, so creating a buffer between the latter and the Anglo-Egyptians. Thus Britain's prolonged and illegal occupation of Egypt would be ended, and France safeguarded from the expulsion from Africa which she had suffered from Canada a century earlier. The discussions with the French foreign and colonial ministries were protracted but Marchand's mission would be approved in principle by Marcelin Berthelot at the Quai d'Orsay on 30 November 1895. According to his biographer, J. Delebeque, Marchand's personal papers, as did his formal instructions, disappeared. In the course of the extended discussions, the concept of a simultaneous expedition via Abyssinia was revived.

Marchand's first formal instructions appear to have been issued by M. Guieysse, now at the Pavillon, in February 1896 coinciding with those to Liotard who was presently ignorant of Marchand's initiative. Liotard was assured that Marchand intended his mission to be 'exclusivement pacifique', aiming for Fashoda via the Bahr el Ghazal, but falling back if encountering any unmistakable Mahdist hostility.

Marchand's expedition would be wholly under Liotard's command and a copy of Marchand's own instructions was enclosed. Another change of government in June 1896 led to the dispatch of revised instructions from André Lebon at the Pavillon to Liotard, promoted governor, dated (23 June) two days before Marchand's departure for Loango on 25 June. Again Marchand's mission was to be no military enterprise and good relations had to be sought with the Mahdists. Marchand's mission 'sous votre [Liotard's] direction, votre collabora-teur immédiat... votre adjoint temporaire et auquel, s'il se trouve éloigné de vous, vous laisserez des ordres précis pour le service dont il aura la responsabilité directe.' There is no copy attached of any revised instructions to Marchand and the inference would have been that these still accorded with those of Liotard.

Before his departure however Marchand had an interview with Gabriel Hanotaux back at the Quai d'Orsay at which the latter allegedly told Marchand: 'Vous allez tirer un coup de pistolet sur le Nil: nous en acceptons toutes les conséquences' – hardly reconcilable with an expedition instructed to avoid hostilities, its behaviour 'exclusive-ment pacifique', or indeed Hanotaux's acclaimed belief, in an earlier speech to the Senate in April 1895 that 'quand l'heure sera venue de fixer les destinées de ces contrées lointaines... deux grandes nations sauront trouver les formules propres à concilier leurs intérèts et à satis-faire leurs communes aspirations vers la civilisation et le progrès.' Of the Mission Marchand, London was told nothing. It was secret.[18]

Marchand would take a year to ascend the Congo and Ubangi rivers and thence, via the M'bomu, to arrive on 24 July 1897 at Tambura (Fort Hossinger) on an affluent of the Sueh. He had been obliged to hire a steamer from the Belgian governor at Leopoldville, leaving in January 1897 and, having himself reached the navigable limits of the Ubangi, to proceed on foot with porters. Requisitioning and twice disassembling the abandoned Congolese steamer *Faidherbe*, the expedition hauled the component parts on wooden rollers over 200 kilometres across the watershed to join Marchand on 22 November 1897.

Already, as he made his way along the M'bomu by canoe, Marchand had received a letter (dated April) from Liotard counselling him, because of the porter problems *inter alia*, to abandon his plan to proceed north to Deim Zubeir in order to approach the Nile via the Bahr el Humr, and instead to divert to the Sueh and thence the Ghazal. Liotard was already in the proximity of Deim Zubeir and anxious that Marchand should not risk a clash with the Mahdist Baqqara Arabs to the north. Such contact

Mission Marchand Front row: *Capitaine Largeau, Dr Émily,*
Capitaine Germain, Interprète militaire Landeroin, Capitaine Baratier,
Commandant Marchand, Enseigne de vaisseau H. Dyé
Second Row: *Sergent Venail, Lieutenant Fouqué,*
Sergent Dat, Capitaine Mangin
En route to Djibouti, 1899

would be certain to awaken the suspicions of the Azande whose support Liotard had so successfully wooed. Marchand complied but, having reached Tambura in July 1897 three months before the *Faidherbe,* he was able to reconnoitre Rumbek and then Wau, entering into good relations with the Dinka and Jur in preparation for the French advance. Unluckily, however, despite the reassembly of the *Faidherbe* fifty miles south of Tambura, the fall in the level of the Sueh prevented her negotiation of the rapids, half-way to Wau, in December. The expedition was therefore compelled to advance down the Sueh – without the *Faidherbe* – to Wau (Fort Desaix) and there await the rise in the water level. Not until 4 June 1898 did it set out thence to Fashoda. Capitaine Albert Baratier pronounced the delay 'une désastre'.

There had been a further important variation in Marchand's supposed instructions delivered in Paris in early 1896. When in October

Marchand was returning to Tambura from a reconnaissance, he received a message from France – *'lettre officielle no. 126'*: 'Request Liotard by the quickest means activate Marchand towards the Nile to link up with Clochette.' Marchand commented: 'I have received a letter from the *"haut protecteur"* of the Mission. At long last! Occupation of Fashoda decided by France.' Baratier certainly reported on 14 November 1897 a local message from Marchand that France approved the creation of Fort Desaix (Wau). In any event Glenn Brown affirms that Marchand dispatched a letter at once to Liotard: 'I am assuming the command of Mission with all the risks which that entails.' Marchand headed the letter 'Phase Three', and signed it 'Le Capitaine Marchand, chef de la Mission Congo-Nil'.

Toutes les conséquences. Had this development been canvassed in his discussion with Hanotaux? Conceivable but unlikely. The immediate authority for this directive, the *'haut protecteur'*, may be presumed to be Gustave Binger, former Governor-General of the Ivory Coast and now director of the Bureau d'Afrique; or alternatively Colonel Louis Archinard, under whom Marchand had served in the French Soudan in 1888–93, winning the Cross of the Légion d'Honneur. Archinard was now head of the military Direction de la Défense at the Pavillon (Marchand's *'mon maître'*) – noted for his contemptuous arrogance towards government ministers. The personal responsibilities of Binger and Archinard for the Fashoda débacle must be deemed substantial.

The reference to the 'link-up with Clochette' stems from the instructions of the Pavillon to Lagarde in Abyssinia in December 1896, to seek the acceptance of the Emperor Menilek for the dispatch of two expeditions to the White Nile, respectively under Clochette and Bonvalot, the latter to be swiftly succeeded by his deputy, the Marquis de Bonchamps. By March 1897 Menilek had agreed a White Nile Convention recognising a French mission on the west bank and Abyssinian occupation on the east. Marchand had himself written to Lagarde on arrival at Brazzaville at the end of 1896 alerting him to his own expected arrival at Fashoda not later than January 1898. In the event Clochette never got beyond the upper Sobat while de Bonchamps, authorised to plant Abyssinian and French flags either side of the White Nile at Sobat mouth, would, after a false start due to illness, arrive with his Abyssinian guides at this destination sixteen days before Marchand. The latter however, like the Reth of the Shilluk days before him, would find the flags already vanished, while de Bonchamps had returned up the Sobat within hours. So much for

Marchand's expected reinforcements. Approaching Mahdist-occupied territory, Marchand was becoming increasingly vulnerable.

In the past months the Abyssinian Negus had cooled towards his détente with the French. He now placed much greater value on his improved relations with the Khalifa Abdallahi than on the White Nile Convention. Moreover pressure, albeit limited, was being exerted on him by the British, not only through the Rennell Rodd/Wingate mission of May 1897 but also a British expedition simultaneously planned to the east bank of the White Nile under J. R. L. Macdonald (successor to Colvile as commissioner of the Uganda Protectorate) 'to make friends with the tribes before the French get there from the west... the ostensible reason for despatch will be to explore the source of the Juba'(river). Because of a major insurrection in Uganda, the departure of the Macdonald expedition was delayed until April 1898 and by November had been forced to turn back at Torit. A second expedition under Major Martyr, however, would join the Congolese at Rejaf and assist in the expulsion that November of Arabi Dafa'allah from Bor.[19]

Authority to move on Fashoda reached Marchand from the Pavillon, with or without the sanction of the Quai d'Orsay, at the end of October 1897, presumably having been dispatched in March or April. As late as 18 July 1898 a departmental note of the Quai d'Orsay affirmed officials' confidence that, with Marchand master of Fashoda and the White Nile intersections with the mouths of the Sobat and Bahr el Ghazal, 'nous pourrons attendre, munis d'un excellent gage, l'heure des pourparlers.' Yet even by April 1897 the commencement, under Sir Hebert Kitchener, of the trans-Atmur desert railway from Wadi Halfa to Abu Hamed and Berber was a clear indication that the Anglo-Egyptian move on the Sudan was not going to stop at Dongola and Merowe.

The British for their part had been alerted from Loango in June 1896, the month of Marchand's departure from Marseilles, of a new French Congo expedition, even if its destination remained uncertain. By August Liotard's movements on the Tambura area were recorded, leading to a British intelligence recommendation that the reconquest of Khartoum be expedited, though this must be contingent on the completed construction of the trans-Atmur desert railway.

By February 1897 the British Cabinet had been advised that Marchand 'was going in', although he would then have only just left Brazzaville for the Upper Ubangi. Abu Hamed, then Berber, would fall to Kitchener's army in August 1897 but the main armies of the Khalifa at Metemma and Omdurman were as yet uncommitted to battle, while the Anglo-Egyptian supply lines had been greatly extended.

Marchand in August 1897 had just reached Tambura, but the news filtering through of his progress, which would likewise be delayed by the elements, did not much alarm London. The Grey Declaration had expressly defined a French expedition to the Nile to be an unfriendly act. The last dispatch to Marchand from Paris with news about Abyssinia reached Marchand at Wau mid-December 1897, to be followed that month by instructions to Liotard to guard Marchand's flank from the north. Seemingly no further news from him had reached Paris by September 1898, although Marchand had sent advice of his impending departure to Fashoda through the *sudd* on 27 March 1898 – both via Brazzaville and Abyssinia. Likewise Kitchener, in March about to fight the battle of the Atbara, would only gain his first firm news of Marchand's whereabouts after Omdurman in September.

The French government was not fazed by the absence of news, optimistically content to await the establishment of a French encampment on the Nile which would trigger off a bilateral negotiation. Moreover Egyptian nationalist leaders like Mustafa Kamil were in close touch with Paris, even 'for a long time… knew more about [Marchand's venture] than the British and gave Marchand as much information as they could about the Mahdists in the Sudan'. However for the French, their first indirect news of Marchand's arrival would only reach Alexandria on 10 September 1898 through the capture of the Mahdist *Tawfiqia* at Khartoum three days before. Earlier in June Britain and France had signed a Convention regarding the Niger river and Lake Chad, a détente quickly followed by the fall of the Mélines government. Hanotaux, until then at the Quai d'Orsay, would subsequently but disingenuously contend that, because of the Convention's limited scope, France had lost her chance to settle the Upper Nile question with Britain well before the British encounter with Marchand's expedition. France was unprepared for the ferocity of the British response.

The Fashoda Incident The Mahdist threat to the Anglo-Egyptian expedition at Atbara fort in February 1898 brought about the dispatch of a British brigade from Cairo backed by British finance. The subsequent defeat of this Mahdist army on 8 April would open the way to Kitchener's advance, already sanctioned by London in January, on the Khalifa's army at Omdurman at the close of the hot summer months. Salisbury had decided in October 1897 that Omdurman should not be the final destination of the expedition. French occupation of Fashoda, if it proved a reality, would not be tolerated. And with the April victory at the Atbara, British public opinion had been stirred, memories of Gordon at Khartoum reawoken.

By June 1898 the British government had re-thought its policy on the Sudan. The Mahdist state had extended from the second cataract to Wadelai and was deemed to have extinguished the Ottoman imperial claim. Equally the Sudan's reconquest from the Khalifa would invalidate the concept of Egyptian (north) and British (south) spheres. To symbolise the new political regime the flags of the two conquerors, British and Egyptian, would fly side by side. British Cabinet instructions were drafted for Cromer on 25 July 1898. In response to Cromer's own anticipation of the need on the morrow of victory over the Khalifa to reconnoitre with gunboats both the Blue Nile, which might result in an encounter with the Abyssinians; and the White Nile, where correspondingly a French expedition was suspected, these operations were approved. The White Nile flotilla would be commanded by Kitchener himself, and be accompanied by Wingate whose intervention in the event at Fashoda, in insisting on flying the Egyptian flag only, would calm potential animosity on the part of the 'European Expedition at Fashoda' which was led, Delcassé was claimed to have insisted, by 'an emissary of civilisation'. Instructions as to how Kitchener was to respond in the event of the arrival of Marchand were contained in a sealed package delivered to Kitchener in the first week of August, to be opened immediately following the capture of Khartoum, on 3 September 1898.[20]

Kitchener's report of the Fashoda encounter dated 21 September was telegraphed to London from Cairo on the 29th, preceded by a telegram on the 24th, to form the basis for an aide-mémoire handed by Sir Edmond Monson to Delcassé in Paris on 27 September. Delcassé, already challenged by the new minister Trouillot at the Pavillon on 4 July as to what instructions to give Marchand when he reached Fashoda, had played for time, eventually noting on 7 September that with the fall of Omdurman the situation had become fluid and communication impracticable, but that Marchand should desist from advancing northwards and strengthen his lines to Liotard. Now, on receipt of the aide-mémoire, Delcassé volunteered to telegraph Marchand via the British Residency Cairo and Khartoum, inviting the earliest dispatch of an officer to Cairo with his report, while insisting to the British that he could not order evacuation. Capitaine Baratier reached Cairo with

Slatin Pasha via Khartoum on 20 October and left at once for Paris by boat with Marchand's dispatches of 10 July–27 September. Baratier was then followed to Cairo, to Delcassé's anger, by Marchand himself who arrived there on 3 November – the day on which Delcassé instructed Baron de Courcel, his London ambassador, to inform Lord Salisbury verbally that the French government had decided to leave Fashoda due to the mission's state of health. Marchand, incensed by this diplomatic excuse, threatened to refuse to withdraw from Fashoda and to tender his resignation as an officer. However, by 6 November, following Baratier's return from Paris where he had done his best to mobilise the support of the Comité against Delcassé, Marchand acquiesced. He and Baratier would return to Fashoda by steamer on 13 November, thence to evacuate the mission via Abyssinia and Djibouti.

Both Marchand and Baratier would serve with distinction at general rank in the First World War, but neither they nor Dr Emily would surpass the military reputation of their colleague Charles Mangin, the zealous *exécutant* of General Robert Nivelle, French commander-in-chief 1916–17, then General.

On 27 October Salisbury, having previously on 9 September affirmed that all Egyptian territories were now Anglo-Egyptian by right of conquest, had warned the French ambassador that no negotiation could be entertained regarding the Sudan so long as the French flag continued to fly at Fashoda. This was the apogee of the crisis. On 18 October the French naval attaché in London, sending details of departures of British home fleet vessels, had expressed his opinion that England was bent on war. On 24 the British reserve squadron was manned and on 29 October part of the Channel fleet was ordered to Gibraltar, and then the Mediterranean fleet from Corfu to Malta. A British cruiser squadron and destroyers were left to guard the Channel, the French northern fleet blockaded while, undetected, part at least of the French Mediterranean fleet steamed past Gibraltar for Cherbourg. The French fleets were however outnumbered and France was unable to look to her Russian ally for assistance, the Russian fleet in any case being in winter ports. Nevertheless the British fleet would remain at war stations throughout November 1898.

Yet the French newspaper headlines since September had been concentrating not on Omdurman and Fashoda, but on the latest development of the Dreyfus Affaire in the wake of Emile Zola's letter 'J'accuse' – namely the arrest of Commandant Henry of military intelligence *deuxième bureau*, charged with forging documents to incriminate Dreyfus. Premier Brisson's attention had become increasingly monopolised by the Affaire, which generated daily demonstrations in Paris, a nationwide rail strike, the fear of a military coup and, on 25 October, the resignation of the government. While the British and French fleets were mobilised, the Quai d'Orsay and the Pavillon remained at loggerheads over the Fashoda evacuation issue.

Delcassé was persuaded to remain on at the Quai d'Orsay, working in close liaison with his President, Félix Faure, and was successfully pressed by the latter to announce the evacuation on 3 November. Faure would affirm: 'Il rendit compte et je pris la responsabilité de l'acte' and conclude: 'Nous avous été comme des fous en Afrique – entrainés par des gens irresponsables qu'on appelle les coloniaux... Notre action dépasse tout à fait notre force maritime.'

The Anglo-French rapprochement which followed would be sealed by the Entente Cordiale in 1904, France finding compensation for her reverse on the Nile in Morocco.[21]

Epilogue

The Anglo-Egyptian Condominium Agreement of 1899 identified international boundaries for the largest political territory within the Nile region, the present Republic of the Sudan – boundaries which have endured with little variation over the past 100 years. The lease of the Lado Enclave on the White Nile expired with the death of King Leopold of Belgium in 1910; and, in a British preemptive strike to thwart suspected Turkish subversion, the Sultanate of Darfur, hitherto tributary of the Condominium, in 1916 became an integral part of the Sudan. Other modifications, as to the boundaries with Abyssinia, Uganda and Kenya and with French Equatorial Africa, were comparatively minor, if protracted – that relating to the Ilemi Triangle on the Sudan-Kenya-Abyssinia border, as demonstrated by Professor Robert Collins, still unresolved to this day.

The previous 400 years, ushered in with the foundation of the Kingdom of Sennar, following the victory of Amara Dunqas at the Battle of Arbagi about 1504 and extending north of 12° latitude, saw in contrast many changes in the political boundaries of what was originally known vaguely as *Bilaad el Sudan*. In 1699, 200 years before the Battle of Omdurman, Charles Jacques Poncet, had noted: 'The kingdom of Sudan lies westward of that of Sennar. The merchants of Egypt trade thither for gold and slaves. The kings of Sudan and Sennar are almost continually at war.' And 100 years later William G. Browne wrote of his journey to Darfur: 'Nothing can well be more vague than the use of the word Soudan or Sudan... It is used equally in Darfur to express the country to the West, but on the whole seems ordinarily applied to signify that part of the land of the Blacks nearest Egypt.'

The Kingdom of Sennar contributed increased stability to its part of the Nile region. The boundaries would indeed fluctuate, progressively expanding at least in the earlier part of its existence of 320 years; then disintegrating in the last forty odd years – until extinguished following the conquest by Mohammed Ali in the name of the Ottoman Sultan in 1821. The Abdullab *sheikhs*, defeated in 1504 at Arbagi, extended the Nile heartland of the new Kingdom between Gerri and Arbagi north to create a permanent frontier with Ottoman Egypt above the third cataract in 1584; east to dominate the fertile Butana country as far as the Atbara river; and, beyond, to absorb the territory of the Beja peoples of Taka. In their provincial capacity the Abdullab would exercise their authority through officials with the titles of *ajib, arbab* and *manjil,* all vassals of the Fung King whose capital was probably first at Gallabat (Lamul) and then Sennar.

The Fung influence *west* of the Nile was less enduring. If not *manjils,* there were evidently Fung *sheikhs* in Kordofan in the late seventeenth century prior to their eviction by the Musaba'at in 1734 – a province to be recaptured in 1755 and ruled in the name of Sennar until conquered by the Sultan of Darfur in 1786. Mohammed Ali's son-in-law, the Defterdar, was authorised to conquer Kordofan in 1821, thus becoming *seraskir* of a new entity, 'the Sudan and Kordofan', and then 'the provinces of the Sudan'. Darfur however was to be left alone - since, in the Viceroy's words, 'we have never seen these lands, know nothing about them, and... cannot know how to govern them' - until its annexation in 1874 in the name of the Khedive Ismail and, ten years later, occupation by the Mahdi and his Khalifa. After this brief incorporation in the Sudan of twenty-five years, Darfur would not become an integral part of the Condominium until 1916.

Thus by 1899 the Fung heartlands of the Nile and its principal affluents had experienced a distinct unity of government, compelling the general, if reluctant, consent of the governed, which had stretched over some 400 years. To them had been joined the Taka of the Beja – if less radically integrated – for 300 years; while Kordofan had now in all been part of this newly identified Sudan for over 100 years, the last 80 of which were an uninterrupted continuum.

This historical core of the modern Sudan had disparate roots among its component parts. Thus the Beja long predated the Arabs in their occupation of territory; spoke their own language; had adopted over the centuries a plurality of religions, until embracing Islam following their subordination by the Abdullab; but had maintained ancient trade communications to the Nile. The proximity of the Arab settlers west of Beja lands over very many generations resulted in the forging of progressively amicable relations. If in contrast the political unification of Kordofan had been of considerably more recent origin, yet here the ethnic, linguistic and religious links with the dwellers on the Nile were stronger.

With this earliest core of territories of the Sudan would, in the course of the nineteenth century, be joined (but not comparably integrated) three further regions: for a brief period the province of Hamasein, the Red Sea littoral, and Harar – all on the periphery of Abyssinia; for the last twenty-five years of that century, the Sultanate of Darfur; and finally, most extensive in area, the territories of the Upper Nile basin stretching roughly south of the thirteenth latitude North. The first of these three groups would quickly revert to Abyssinia, and to modern Eritrea and Somalia.

The second, Darfur, occupied by the Khedive only in 1874, presented a more difficult choice for the new rulers of the Sudan in 1898 as between inclusion and exclusion. Notwithstanding its medieval links with Wadai and Kanem (Bornu) to the west, whither its best communications lay, Darfur had at least from the early seventeenth century become a coherent polity looking progressively east, for the pilgrim route across Sennar to Mecca; and north, to Assiut and Cairo, for the annual caravan by the Darb el Arba'in. Remote from the Nile Arabs, in origin ethnically and linguistically distinct, the Fur had come to embrace both Islam and the Arabic language. The decision in 1898 was to recognise the restoration of the independent Sultanate but as a tributary of the Condominium Sudan, a decision reversed when the Sultan's hostility towards Khartoum in the First World War led to Darfur's full incorporation in the Sudan – if at the end of a long line of communication; a province Moslem and Arabic speaking whose peoples shared grazing country with the Kordofan Baqqara Arabs.

The future of the Upper Nile territories, the third group, was to prove far more complex. Their long-established inhabitants comprised numerous tribes. Numerically the largest of them were the Dinka and the Nuer who by the sixteenth century would have been joined by the Luo migration from the lacustrine areas of Equatorial Africa – notably the Shilluk, Anuak and Jur. Other major peoples were the Azande migrants from across the Congo watershed; and the Bari and the Latuka from the east. The Shilluk were the people to press furthest north and, in Fung times, were raiding at the confluence of the White and Blue Niles. Meanwhile the Nuba and the Ingessana maintained themselves in their *jebel* fastnesses in southern Kordofan and Fazughli, the principal source of recruitment for the renowned Fung cavalry.

The southern peoples were wholly different from the general population of Sennar and, more so, from its conquerors of 1821 – ethnically, linguistically and religiously. With the exceptions of the Shilluk and the

Azande, organised political structures among the southern tribes were lacking. With the overthrow of the Fung kingdom, they found themselves increasingly targeted by Turkish-led slave *razzias*, initially for army recruitment but commercially to supply the slave markets of Cairo, Khartoum, Shendi, Suakin and Massawa, and Jedda. The first recorded Turkish raids on the Nilotics took place in 1827–8, but until riverain exploration had successfully penetrated the *sudd* barrier in 1840 the Shilluk were strong enough to bar the Turkish invaders' progress up the White Nile. Once that barrier had fallen, and access gained by the Khartoum traders also to the Bahr el Ghazal ten years later, the long years of slave *razzias* had begun, scarcely to be mitigated in the 1860s by the establishment of government stations and patrols on the Upper Nile south of the effective frontier at Kaka – at least until the appointments of the worthy Ja'afar Mazhar, of Samuel Baker and of Charles Gordon. As for the mightily oppressed peoples of the Bahr el Ghazal, in the period 1860–86 they gained only the briefest of respites through the intervention of Gordon and Romolo Gessi.

Ismail Pasha Ibrahim on his accession to the Viceroyalty in 1863 would embark upon the creation of an African empire, one ostensible purpose of which under European pressure would be the suppression of the slave trade, a purpose at least partially accomplished in his name by Baker and Gordon. The bid for empire however would be short-lived, foundering in consequence of Khedivial bankruptcy and thereafter military insurrection in 1881.

In 1869, with the opening of the Suez Canal, a new, vastly shortened international waterway between Europe and Asia focused attention on the Red Sea littoral and the Horn of Africa. Within that next decade the nationalist ambitions of rival European powers had been awakened towards the whole African continent, and Ismail's defeated armies would be superseded in eastern Africa by expeditions to promote the respective interests of King Leopold of the Belgians, the First German Reich, the recently unified Kingdom of Italy, and the French Third Republic, even if denied access to an independent Sudan wrested from Egypt by armed rebellion.

Nevertheless the enhanced international strategic importance of Egypt, now under British hegemony, and her dependence on the Nile waters led to a fresh appraisal by European governments of the value of the headwaters of the Nile region and, progressively, to a political struggle to dominate the lands of the Upper Nile valley, notwithstanding their geographical remoteness and inhospitality.

Britain for her part, custodian of a country from whom the armies of the Mahdist theocratic state had seized its Sudan province, had historically no more ambition to seize these inaccessible, seemingly valueless, areas adjacent to the Nile–Congo watersheds than she had to occupy many other regions of the African continent. Her mercantile interests, guarded by the British fleet, were initially to be satisfied by denying claims to the territories, and certainly to their occupation by potentially hostile rival powers – until the pressures of these rivals would by the 1890s render that policy unviable. The Mahdist state had meanwhile relinquished its brief establishment of control over the Bahr el Ghazal after 1886 and would only reassert its presence, uncertainly, on the Bahr el Jebel itself at Rejaf after 1888.

Most acute of these overseas challenges to control of the headwaters of the White Nile would be that of France after 1893, directed towards the seizure of Fashoda below the confluence of the Bahr el Jebel, Bahr el Ghazal and Sobat rivers, and towards an understanding with Abyssinia whereby the latter would occupy the east bank and the French the west bank of the White Nile, leaving the Belgians a foothold on the upper reaches at Lado. The British were persuaded that the Anglo-Egyptian army of reconquest must, after the recapture of Omdurman, in the interests of Egypt's security proceed to the reoccupation of the whole of the former Turkish-Egyptian Sudan, the Lado lease excepted, notwithstanding in many parts the uneven and limited duration of that occupation.

Thus for reasons of *force majeure*, all the territories of the Upper Nile were included in the Condominium, irrespective of the election of their diverse peoples – whose opinions at that moment of history were not a matter of international concern, even had they been in practical terms ascertainable. Had the French never launched the Marchand mission to Fashoda, the occupation of the Sudan might have been halted at Omdurman: or, granted the cooperation of Abyssinia against the Mahdists, at the twelfth or thirteenth parallel of latitude. The future of the peoples of the southern Sudan in the twentieth century could have been very different.

The Sudan would gain her sovereign independence from the Anglo-Egyptian Condominium of 1899 on 1 January 1956. The circumstances, especially the inadequacies of the consultation arrangements, swiftly generated opposition on the part of the ethnically diverse peoples of the south, leading to a brutal civil war which, with the brief exception of the years 1872–83, extended until the Sudan Peace Agreement signed on 9 January 2005. The event was overshadowed by the more recent but continuing civil conflict in Darfur.

Under that Agreement, the peoples of the south will become an autonomous part of the Sudan for six years commencing July 2005 and will then vote whether to remain part of the Sudan or become independent. The history of the region traced in these two volumes of *The Nile in Darkness 1504–1899* illustrates the besetting problems which will underlie that decision.

El Sayyid Sir Abdel Rahman El Mahdi, KBE, 1930

*General Gordon: artist's sketch by Miss Catherine Ouless of portrait
to hang in Governor-General's Palace, Khartoum, 1910*

LEFT *The author's mother and Slatin Pasha, Khartoum, November 1926*
RIGHT *Sheikh Babikr Bedri 1861–1954; presented to author's father*

The author and Reth Kur Fafiti of the Shilluk, Kodok, 1953

Wingates, Udals (author on left, his father on right) and Sayyid Siddiq Abdel Rahman El Mahdi, visiting London Zoo, May 1937

Appendices

Ottoman Sultans 1451–1922

Mehemmed II	1451–1481
Bayazid II	1481–1512
Selim I	1512–1520
Suleyman I, *Kanuni*, alias 'the Magnificent'	1520–1566
Selim II	1566–1574
Murad III	1574–1595
Mehemmed III	1595–1603
Ahmed I	1603–1617
Mustafa I	1617–1618; 1622–1623
Othman II	1618–1622
Murad IV	1623–1640
Ibrahim	1640–1648
Mehemmed IV	1648–1687
Suleyman II	1687–1691
Ahmad II	1691–1695
Mustafa II	1695–1703
Ahmad III	1703–1730
Mahmoud I	1730–1754
Othman III	1754–1757
Mustafa III	1757–1774
Abdel Hamid I	1774–1789
Selim III	1789–1807
Mustafa IV	1807–1808
Mahmoud II	1808–1839
Abdel Majid I	1839–1861
Abdel Aziz	1861–1876
Murad V	1876
Abdel Hamid II	1876–1909
Mehemmed V	1909–1918
Mehemmed VI	1918–1922

Turkish-Egyptian Rulers of the Sudan 1863–85

Ottoman Sultan	Khedive/Viceroy	Governor-General
1861–76	(*Wali*) 1863–79	(*Hakimdar*)
Abdel Aziz	Ismail Pasha Ibrahim	1862–5 Musa Pasha Hamdi
		1865–6 Ja'afar Pasha Sadiq
		1866–71 Ja'afar Pasha Mazhar

1871–

1873–77 Ismail Pasha Ayub

1876–1909		1877–79 Charles Gordon Pasha
Abdel Hamid II	1879–92	
	Mohammed Tawfiq Pasha	
	Ismail	1880–2 Mohammed Ra'uf Pasha

1882–3 Abdel Qadir Pasha Hilmi
Resident Minister of the Sudan
<u>Central Sudan</u>

1883 Ala el Din Pasha Siddiq
Hakimdar

Subordinate *Hakimdars*
<u>West Sudan</u>
Mohammed Sa'id Pasha Wahbi
1882–3

<u>East Sudan</u>
Ala el Din Pasha Siddiq   1882
Rashid Kamil Pasha   1883
Sulieman Pasha Niyazi   1883

1884–5 Charles Gordon Pasha

1884
1884–

General-Governor (*Mudir 'Umum*) or Cairo-dependent provincial governor (*mudir*)	Governorate/Province
1870–3 Sir Samuel Baker Pasha	Equatoria
1870–1 Ahmed Mumtaz Bey	Red Sea Littoral
1870–1 Hussein Bey Khalifa (*mudir*)	Berber
1870–3 Sir Samuel Baker Pasha	Equatoria
1871–2 Ahmed Mumtaz Pasha	South Sudan
1872–3 Ismail Bey Ayub	South Sudan
1871–3 Hussein Pasha Khalifa	Berber and Dongola
1871–3 Ala el Din Bey Siddiq (*mudir*)	Taka
1871–3 Werner Munzinger Bey (*mudir*)	Massawa
1871–3 Abdel Wahhab Bey (*mudir*)	Kordofan
1873–4 Zubeir Bey Rahma Mansur (*mudir*)	Bahr el Ghazal
1873–5 Werner Munzinger Pasha	Eastern Sudan
1875–7 Ala el Din Pasha Siddiq	Eastern Sudan
1874–6 Charles Gordon Pasha	Equatoria
1875–8 Mohammed Ra'uf Pasha	Harar
1878–80 Radwan Pasha	Harar
1879–80 Romolo Gessi Pasha	Bahr el Ghazal and Equatoria
1880–82 Mohammed Nadi Pasha	Harar
Ali Rida el Tubji Pasha	Harar
Mahmoud Bey Ahmedani (*mudir*)	Khartoum
Busati Bey Madani (*mudir*)	Sennar
? ?	Berber
Mohammed Bey Shukri	Fashoda
Emin Bey	Equatoria
Rudolf Slatin Bey	Darfur
Ali Bey Sharif	Kordofan
Frank Lupton Bey	Bahr el Ghazal
Mustafa Yawar Bey	Dongola
Rashid Kamil Bey	Taka
Firhad Muhhib Bey	Massawa and Suakin
Mohammed Tawfiq Bey	Massawa and Suakin
Valentine Baker Pasha	East Sudan
Emin Pasha	Equatoria

Table of Mahdist Rulers of the Sudan 1883–98

The Sudan	Kordofan	Darfur	Taka
	The Mahdi 1883–4		
The Mahdi 1884–5	Mahmoud Abdel Qadir 1884–5	Mohammed Khalid 1884–5	Osman Abu Bakr Digna 1884–
Khalifa Abdallahi Mohammed Turshain 1885–98	Hamdan Abu Anja 1886–7	Sultan Yusef Ibrahim 1886–8	Osman Abu Bakr Digna –1898
	Osman Adam 1887–90	Osman Adam 1888–90	,,
	Mahmoud Ahmed 1890–7	Mahmoud Ahmed 1890–7	

Northern, including Dongola 1885–	Sennar/Gedaref	Bahr el Ghazal	Equatoria
Mohammed el Kheir Abdallah Khojali 1884–5	Mohammed el Tayyiib el Basir 1884–5	Karamallah Mohammed Kurqusawi 1885–6	Karamallah Mohammed Kurqusawi 1885–6
Abdel Rahman el Nejumi 1886–8	Yunus el Dikaim 1886–7	–	Omer Salih 1888–93
Yunus el Dikaim 1889–90	Hamdan Abu Anja 1887–9		Mohammad Osman Abu Qarja 1893
Mohammed Khalid 1890–1	El Zaki Tamal 1889–93		Arabi Dafa'allah 1893–97
Yunus el Dikaim 1892–5	Ahmed Ali Ahmed 1893		–
Mohammed Bushara (Dongola) 1895–6 Mohammed el Zaki Osman (Berber) 1895–6	Ahmed Fadil 1894–8		
Yunus el Dikaim (Berber) 1896–7 Mahmoud Ahmed 1897–8			

Reths of the Shilluk from 1545

		Village		Reign/ Yrs, about	
1	Nyikango Okwa Mot	Nyilwal	1545–75	30	
2	Cal Nyikango Okwa	Dinyo	1575–90	15	
3	Dak Nyikango Okwa	Palo	1590–1605	15	
4	Nyidoro Dak Nyikango	Nyiliac	1605–1615	10	
5	Ocollo Dak	Ditang	1615–1635	20	
6	Diwad Ocollo Dak	Malakal	1635–1650	15	
7	Bwoc Diwad Ocollo	Paoro	1650–1660	10	
8	Abudhok Bwoc Diwad	Thworo	1660–1670	10	
9	Dhokodh Bwoc Diwad	Watajuok	1670–1690	20	
10	Tugo Dhokodh Bwoc	Nyimongo	1690–1710	20	
11	Okon Tugo Dhokodh	Pabur	1710–1715	5	
12	Nyeduay Tugo Dhokodh	Dibworo	1715–1745	30	
13	Mugo Nyeduay Tugo	Pabo	1745–1750	5	
14	Wakk Nyeduay Tugo	Biu	1750–1760	10	
15	Tyelgot Nyeduay Tugo	Paeodo (Fashoda)	1760–1770	10	
16	Kudit Okon Tugo	Malakal	1770–1780	10	
17	Nyakwaci Kudit Okon	Kyjo	1780–1820	40	
18	Aney Nyakwaci Kudit	Nywudo	1820–1825	5	
19	Atwot Nyakwaci Kudit	Ogod	1825–1835	10	
20	Awin Nyakwaci Kudit	Opat (Nyigir)	1835–1840	5	
21	Akoc Atwot Nyakwaci	Ayago (Ogod)	1840–1845	5	
22	Nyidhok Nyakwaci Kudit	Padwal	1845–1863	18	
23	Kwatker Akwot Nyakwaci	Ogod	1863–67/ 1870–75	7	
24	Ajiyang Nyidhok Nyakwaci	Pacodo	1870–1875	5	Executed
25	Kwickon Kwatker Akwot	Ogod	1875–1882	7	Killed
26	Yor Akoc Akwot	Bappi (Kodok)	1882–1892	10	
27	Kur Nyidhok Nyakwaci	Gollo	1892–1903	11	
28	Fadiet Kwatker Akoc	Wau	1903–1917	14	
29	Fafiti Yor Akoc	Wau	1917–1944	25	
30	Anei Kur Nyidhok	Ganawat	1944–1945	1	
31	Dak Fadiet Kwatker	Kujjo	1945–1951	6	
32	Kur Fafiti Yor Akoc	Ywodo (Kodok)	1951–1974	23	
33	Ayang Anei Kur	Omikyel (Fashoda)	1974–1992	18	Killed
34	Kungo Dak Fadiet	Fanyidwai	1992–		

Emperors of Abyssinia 1508–1913

Lebna Dengel, Wanad Segued I	1508–1540
Galawadewos or Claudius	1540–1559
Minas, Wanad Segued II	1559–1563
Sarsa Dengel, Malak Segued I	1563–1597
Yakob, Malak Segued II	1597–1603
Za Dengel Asnaf, Segued II	1603–1604
Socinios, Malak Segued III	1605–1632
Fasilidas, Alam Segued	1632–1665
John I, Kadus	1667–1682
Jasous I, Tallac (the Great), or Adyam Segued II	1682–1706
Tecla Haimanout I	1706–1708
Tewoflos, Asrav Segued	1708–1711
Justus, Tahai Segued	1711–1716
David III, Adbar Segued	1716–1721
Bacuffa	1721–1730
Jasous II, Adyam Segued II	1730–1755
Joas I, Adyam Segued III	1755–1769
John, Yohannes II	1769
Tecla Haimanout II	1769–1777
[Anarchy - competing Ras's]	1777–1855
Theodore (Tewodros) II, Kassa	1855–1868
Tecla Giyordis II (not anointed)	1868–1872
John, Yohannes IV	1872–1889
Menilek II	1889–1913

Lacustrine Kings, East Africa c. 1850–99

BUGANDA	*Kabaka*	M'tesa	1856–85
		M'wanga	1885–92
BUNYORO	*Mukama*	Nyamtoucara	?–1860
		Mougeria	?–1860
		Kamrasi	c.1860–70
		Kabarega	c.1871–99
KARAGWE		Dagara	?–1853
		Rumanika	c.1853–76

Source Notes

CHAPTER ONE

1 McCoan, J. C., *Egypt under Ismail*, 1889, pp. 19–20.
Vatikiotis, P. J., *The History of Egypt from Muhammad Ali to Sadat*, 1980, p.75.
F.O. 78/916, priv. Murray to Earl Granville, 16.1.52; Murray to Stratford de Redcliffe, no. 14, 18.5.52.
2 McCoan, J. C. op. cit., pp. 23–5.
F.O. 78/1754, Colquhoun to Earl Russell, no. 29, 20.2.63; no. 39, 13.3.63.
3 De Lesseps, Ferdinand, *The Suez Canal: Letters and Documents 1854–6* (trans. N. d'Anvers), 1876, pp. 97, 145, 250, 256.
Cameron, D. A., *Egypt in the Nineteenth Century*, 1898, p.241.
McCoan, J. C., op. cit., pp. 27–9, 98, 103.
F.O. 142/27, Colquhoun to Earl Russell, 15.5.64.
Douin, Georges, *Histoire du Règne du Khédive Ismail*, vol. I, 1933.
Chapters 2–7 give a blow by blow account of the negotiations.
4 Douin, Georges, op. cit., vol. III, part 1, 1936, pp.142–54.
Sabry, M. *Episode de la Question d'Afrique 1863–79*, 1933, p. 108.
Holt, P. M., *Egypt and the Fertile Crescent 1516–1922*, 1966, p. 203.
Cameron, D. A., op. cit., pp. 249–51.
McCoan, J. C., op. cit., pp. 30, 71.
Chirol, Sir Valentine, *The Egyptian Problem*, 1920, pp. 27–32.
Cromer, Earl of, *Modern Egypt*, 1908, vol. I, pp. 26–7.
F.O. 78/2284, Vivian to Earl Granville, no. 24, 2.8.73.
5 McCoan, J. C., op. cit., pp. 38–40, 50, 64.
Vatikiotis, P. J., op. cit, pp. 74–5.
F.O. 142/27, Colquhoun to Earl Russell, 25.5.64.
F.O. 78/1925, Stanton to Earl of Clarendon, no. 42, 16.4.66.
F.O. 78/2092, Stanton to Earl of Clarendon, tel. 8.8.69.
Douin, Georges, op. cit., vol. I, 1933, pp. 207–14.
6 McCoan, J. C., op. cit., pp. 58, 61.
Vatikiotis, P. J., op. cit., p. 76.
7 Douin, Georges, op. cit., vol. III, part 1, 1936, p. 63; vol. I, p.vii.
8 Ibid., vol. III, part 1, pp. 61–3, 65, 110.
F.O. 78/1675, Colquhoun to Earl Russell, no. 77 of 8.6.62

Jackson H. C., *Black Ivory and White*, 1913, p. 115.

9 Douin, Georges, op. cit., vol. III, part 1, 1936, pp. 62–9.

10 Ibid., pp. 103–4, 108–31.

11 Ibid., pp.115–18.

Garnier, F.-B., Letter to M. Outrey: *Correspondance Politique Egypte*, vol. 36, fol. 88 r à 104 v, no. 7, 5.5.65, pp. 98–9 in *Archives Diplomatiques Ministère des Affaires Etrangères*; ibid., to Tastu, vol. 37 fol. 144 r à 156 v, no.14, 28.10.65, pp.148–9.

12 Douin, Georges, op. cit., vol. III, part 1, 1936, pp. 57, 62, 114, 118.

F.O. 401/1 Cameron to Earl Russell, no. 802, 31.10.62; no. 826, 31.3.63.

Dufton, Henry, *Narrative of a Journey through Abyssinia in 1862–3*, 2nd edn, 1867, pp. 187–8, 246–7.

13 Douin, Georges, op. cit., vol. III, part 1, 1936, pp. 74–8.

Du Bisson, Comte R., Account of Expedition to Frontiers of Abyssinia in *Nouvelles Annales des Voyages*, 6 série, vol. IV, 1864, pp. 342–3.

F.O. 401/1, Colquhoun to Bulwer, no. 854, 11.11.63.

14 Douin, Georges, op. cit., vol. III, part 1, pp. 78–80.

Du Bisson, Comte R., op. cit., pp. 344–5.

15 Dufton, Henry, op. cit., pp. 157, 188.

Douin, Georges, op. cit., vol. III, part 1, pp. 80–2, 121–2.

Lejean, G., *Voyage en Abyssinie 1862–4*, 1870, pp. 19–21, 33–6.

16 Douin, Georges, op. cit., vol. III, part 1, 1936, pp. 81, 83–5, 90–6, 129, 219, 339–40.

Cumming, D. C., 'History of Kassala and the Province of Taka', in *Sudan Notes and Records*, vol. XXIII, part I, 1940, pp. 33–9.

F.O. 142/27, Colquhoun to Earl Russell, 17.3.64.

Du Bisson, Comte R., op. cit., pp. 349– 51.

Rassam, Hormuzd, *Narrative of the British Mission to Theodore, King of Abyssinia*, vol. I, 1869, p. 45.

17 Douin, Georges, op. cit, vol. III, part 1, pp. 231, 238–42, 267–9, 274–7.

18 Ibid., pp. 103–8, 135, 202.

Baker, Samuel White, *Albert N'yanza, Great Basin of the Nile*, vol. II, London, 1866, pp. 299–300, 335.

F.O. 84/1181, Colquhoun to Earl Russell, no. 3, 6.6.62.

Heuglin, Theodor von, *Reise in das Gebiet des Weissen Nil*, 1869, p. 242.

Heuglin, Theodor von, 'Travels in the Sudan in the Sixties', etc., in *SNR*, vol. XXIV, 1941, p. 151.

Hill, R. L., *History of Egypt in the Sudan, 1820–81*, 1959, pp. 103–4, 107, 109.

Hill, R. L., 'Rulers of the Sudan', in *SNR*, vol. XXXII, part 1, 1951, p. 94.

Lejean, G., op. cit., p. 64, 138.

19 Douin, Georges, op. cit., vol. III, part 1, 1936, pp. 33–4, 98–102.

Elles, R. J., 'Kingdom of Tegali', in *SNR*, vol. XVIII, part 1, 1935, p. 22.

MacMichael, H. A., *Tribes of Northern and Central Kordofan*, 1912, p. 34.

Munzinger, Johann Albert Werner, *Ostafrikanische Studien*, 2nd edn., 1883, pp. 555–6.

20 MacMichael, H. A., *A History of the Arabs in the Sudan*, vol. II, part 4, 'Ta'arikh', D.7, Cambridge, 1922, p. 403.

F.O. 141/36, Petherick to Green, 28.11.58.

Douin, Georges, op. cit., vol. III, part 1, 1936, p.133.

Stiansen, Endre, 'Overture to Imperialism, European Trade and Economic Trade in the Nineteenth Century', unpublished doctoral thesis, Bergen University, 1993.

21 MacMichael, H. A., op. cit., D.7, p. 403.

Heuglin, Theodor von, 'Travels in the Sudan in the Sixties', etc., in *SNR*, vol. XXIV, 1941, p.151.

Douin, Georges, op. cit., vol. III, part 1, 1936, p.139.

Du Bisson, Comte R., op. cit., p. 346.

22 Douin, Georges, op. cit., vol. III, part 1, 1936, p.103.

Baker, Samuel White, op. cit., vol. I, 1866, p. 29.

F.O. 141/54, Petherick to Colquhoun, 29.2.64.

23 Déhérain, Henri, *Le Soudan Égyptien sous Mehemet Ali*, 1898, p.182.

Melly, George MP, *Khartoum and the Blue and White Niles*, vol. II, 1851, p.121 (his figures are more credible than those of his father, André).

Hamilton, James, *Traveller in Africa: Sinai, the Hedjaz and Soudan*, 1857, pp. 381–2.

Petherick, John, *Egypt, the Soudan and Central Africa*, 1861, pp. 130, 245.

F.O. 141/57, Petherick to Colquhoun, 17.3.65.

Hill, R. L., *History of Egypt in the Sudan 1820–81*, 1959, p. 107.

24 Garnier, F.-B., op. cit., Letter to M. Outrey, no. 7, 5.5.65, pp. 100–1.

Petherick, John and Petherick, Katherine Harriet, *Travels in Central Africa and Explorations of the White Nile Tributaries*, vol. II, London, 1869, pp. 51–2.

25 F.O. 78/1871, Colquhoun to Earl Russell, no. 78, 28.6.65.

Baker, Samuel White, op. cit., vol. II, 1866, pp. 337–42.

Douin, Georges, op. cit., vol. III, part 1, 1936, p. 108.

F.O. 84/1246, Bulwer to Earl Russell, no. 17, 10.2.65, enclosing Joyce letter, Khartoum 10.11.64; Colquhoun to Earl Russell, no. 7, 10.7.65.

26 Cumming, D. C., op. cit., pp. 41–5.

Douin, Georges, op. cit., vol. III, part 1, 1936, pp. 184–6.

27 Hill, R. L., and Hogg, Peter, *A Black Corps d'Elite*, 1995, pp. 81, 87.

Douin, Georges, op. cit., vol. I, 1933, pp. 319–49; vol. III, part 1, 1936, pp. 186–90.

Cumming, D. C., op. cit., pp. 45–8.

28 Ibid, pp. 48–9.

Douin, Georges, op. cit., vol. III, part 1, 1936, pp. 186–7, 200.

Hill, R. L., and Hogg, Peter, op. cit., pp. 82–4.

F.O. 78/1871, Stanton to Earl Russell, no. 36, 2.11.65.

29 Douin, Georges, op. cit., vol. III, part 1, 1936, pp. 194–200.

Cumming, D. C., op. cit., pp. 50–1. Ismail Bey Ayub was to become Governor-General 1873–6.

30 Douin, Georges, op. cit., vol. III, part 1, 1936, pp. 177–80, 198–202, 206–9, 212.

F.O. 78/1871, Colquhoun to Earl Russell, no. 65, 2.6.65; no. 75, 19.6.65; no. 84, 17.7.65; no. 87, 4.8.65.

F.O. 84/1246, Colquhoun to Earl Russell, no. 7, 10.7.65.

Cumming, D. C., op. cit., p.52.

Hill, R. L., and Hogg, Peter, op. cit., p. 87 fn.

31 Douin, Georges, op. cit., vol. III, part 1, 1936, pp. 201–2.

Rassam, Hormuzd, op. cit., pp. 136–8.

F.O. 78/1926, Stanton to Earl of Clarendon, no. 89, 15.9.66; no. 90, 1.10.66.

CHAPTER TWO

1 Sabry, M., *Episode de la Question d'Afrique etc.*, 1863–79, 1933, p. 14. Douin, Georges, *Histoire du Règne du Khédive Ismail*, vol. III, part 1, 1936, pp. 177–80.

2 Douin, Georges, ibid., pp. 212–13, 220–3, 226–8. Schweinfurth, Georg, *The Heart of Africa: Three Years' Travels 1868–71* (trans. Ellen Frewer), vol. I, 1873, p. 78.

3 F.O. 141/28, Petherick to Bruce, 19.3.55. Douin, Georges, op. cit., vol. III, part 1, pp.110–13, 140, 218, 224. Hill, R. L., *Egypt in the Sudan 1820–81*, 1959, p. 107.

4 Douin, Georges, op. cit., vol. III, part 1, pp. 218–22, 226–8, 298–9, 418–22.

5 Douin, Georges, ibid., pp. 213–14, 218, 228, 443–4.

6 Schweinfurth, Georg, op. cit., vol. I, p. 44. Baker, Sir Samuel White, *Albert N'yanza: Great Basin of the Nile*, vol. II, 1866, p. 356. Douin, Georges, op. cit, vol. III, part 1, pp. 289, 302, 414–16; part 2, p. 468. Hill, R. L., op. cit., p. 113–14, 126–8. MacMichael, H. A., *A History of the Arabs in the Sudan*, vol. II, (4), D. 7, 1922, 2nd imp. 1967, p. 404.

7 Douin, Georges, op. cit., vol. III, part 1, pp. 222, 413, 443, 442–6; part 2, p. 483.

8 Ibid., vol. III, part 1, pp. 315–17, 446–8.
Schweinfurth, Georg, op. cit., vol. I, pp. 79–80, 100–1.
Hill, R. L., op. cit., p. 114.

9 Douin, Georges, op. cit., vol. III, part 1, pp. 317–27.
Hill, R. L., op. cit., p. 134.

10 Douin, Georges, op. cit., vol. III part 1, pp. 346–9, 369, 413, 436.
Hansard, House of Commons, *Prorogation of Parliament Speech*, 21.8.67, col. 1635.
Hansard, House of Commons, *Supply. The Abyssinian Expedition*, 26.11.67, Benjamin Disraeli, cols. 181–93; Lord Stanley, cols. 206–21.
Hansard, House of Lords, *Queen's Speech*, 19.11.67, col. 3.

11 Douin, Georges, op. cit., vol. III, part 1, pp. 140, 420, 433–4.

12 Vatikiotis, P. J., *The History of Egypt from Muhammad Ali to Sadat*, 1980, pp. 75–6, 85–6.
McCoan, J. C., *Egypt under Ismail*, 1889, pp. 28–9, 58, 61, 65.
Cameron, D. A., *Egypt in the Nineteenth Century*, 1898, pp. 240, 250–2.
Cumming, D. C., 'The History of Kassala and the Province of Taka', in *Sudan Notes and Records*, vol. XXIII, part 2, 1940, p. 262.

13 Douin, Georges, op. cit., vol. III, part 1, pp. 435–42.
Schweinfurth, Georg, op. cit., vol. I, pp. 41–4; vol. II, pp. 470, 483–5.
Baker, Sir Samuel White, *Ismailia*, 2nd edn., 1895, p.11.

14 Douin, Georges, op. cit., vol. III, part 1, p. 439.
MacMichael, H. A., op. cit., p. 404.
Hill, R. L., op. cit., p.117.

15 Douin, Georges, op. cit., vol. III, part 1, pp. 148–52, 206–8, 215–16, 230–1, 290–6, 309–14, 422–8.
Hill, R. L., op. cit., pp. 130–3.
Cumming, D. C., op. cit., pp. 256–9.

16 Douin, Georges, op. cit., vol. III, part 1, pp. 423–8; vol. III, part 2, pp. 435–7.
Hill, R. L., op. cit., p. 116.
Marno, E., *Reisen im Gebiete des Blauen und Weissen Nil 1869 bis 1873*, 1874, p. 133.

17 Douin, Georges, op. cit., vol. III, part 1, pp. 306–9, 314–15, 332–40, 428–9.
Schweinfurth, Georg, op. cit., vol. II, p. 481.

CHAPTER THREE

1 Sabry, M., *Episode de la Question d'Afrique, etc.*, 1863–79, 1933, pp. 14, 30.

Hansard, House of Commons, *Supply. The Abyssinian Expedition*, 26.11.67: Benjamin Disraeli, cols. 181–93; Lord Stanley, cols. 206–21.

Sykes, Sir Percy, *History of Persia*, 1921, vol. II, pp. 333, 357; *History of Afghanistan*, 1920, vol. II, p. 8.

2 Douin, Georges, *Histoire du Règne du Khédive Ismail: L'Empire Africain*, vol. III, part 2, 1938, pp. 197–207, passim.

Waterfield, Gordon, *Layard of Nineveh*, 1963, pp. 301–3.

F.O. 78/1870, Earl Russell to Stanton, no. 17, 10.10.65.

F.O. 142/29, Stanton to Earl Russell, no. 35, 21.10.65.

Mathew, David, *Ethiopia, the Study of a Polity 1540–1935*, 1947, pp. 123, 181–2.

Zewde, Bahru, *A History of Moslem Ethiopia 1855–1874*, 1991, pp. 24, 30.

3 Dufton, Henry, *Narrative of a Journey through Abyssinia in 1862–3*, 2nd edn., 1867, p. 148.

F.O. 401/1, Colquhoun to Lord John Russell, no. 641, 2.5.60; Cameron to Lord John Russell, no. 660, 3.12.60; Lord John Russell to Lord Cowley, no. 661, 5.12.60; Lord John Russell to Cameron, nos. 668 and 669, 2.2.61; Colquhoun to Lord John Russell, nos. 684, 28.2.61, and 685, 1.3.61; Baroni to Lord John Russell, no. 712, 8.9.61; James Murray to Lord John Russell, no. 713, 16.11.61; Cameron to Lord John Russell no. 714, 16.11.61.

4 F.O. 401/1, Cameron to Earl Russell, nos. 804, and 805, 1.11.62; Earl Russell to Cameron, no. 818, 22.4.63; James Murray to India Office, no. 819, 5.5.63; Hertslet memo, no. 820, 16.5.63; Cameron to Earl Russell, no. 826, 31.3.63 and no. 831, 18.5.63; Cameron to Colquhoun, no. 833, 20.5.63.

House of Commons Blue Book, *Correspondence Respecting Abyssinia, 1846–68*, Jan. 1868. Plowden to Earl of Clarendon, no. 284 of 25.11.57; Cameron to Earl Russell, no. 349, 1.1.63; Colquhoun to Earl Russell, no. 355, 25.6.63; Cameron to Earl Russell, no. 362, 20.5.63.

House of Commons Blue Book, *Papers Relating to British Captives in Abyssinia*, June 52 to 10.8.66: Earl of Clarendon to Plowden, no. 6, 27.11.55; Earl Russell to Stanton, no. 14, 5.10.65.

Hansard, House of Commons paper, *Abyssinia – The Foreign Office*, cols. 606–36.

5 Lejean, Guillaume, *Voyage en Abyssinie, 1862–4*, 1870, pp. 8–9, 16, 21, 34–6.

F.O. 401/1, Earl Russell to Cameron, no. 837, 8.9.63.

House of Commons Blue Book, *Correspondence Respecting Abyssinia, 1846–68*, Jan. 1868, Beke to Lord Stanley, no. 836, 22.11.67.

6 Henty, G. A., *March to Magdala*, 1868, pp. 14–15.

F.O. 141/54, Petherick to Colquhoun, 4.1.64, 26.3.64.

F.O. 142/27, Colquhoun to Earl Russell, nos. 13–68, 23.1.64 –10.5.64, passim.

F.O. 141/53, Earl Russell to Colquhoun, 9.3.64; 15.6.64;16.6.64.

Hansard, House of Commons, 3.6.64, Layard, col. 1145–6.

7 F.O. 142/27, Reade to Earl Russell, nos. 5–16, 30.6.64–22.7.64, passim.

F.O. 141/53, Earl Russell to Colquhoun, 16.6.64; Earl Russell to Reade, 19.7.64.

F.O. 142/29, Colquhoun to Earl Russell, no. 82, 13.7.65; Stanton to Earl Russell, no. 16, 6.9.65; Stanton to Earl of Clarendon, sep. 10.11.65.

Rassam, Hormuzd, *Narrative of the British Mission to Theodore, King of Abyssinia*, vol. I, 1869, pp. 2, 5–6, 41, 66, 98–9.

Dufton, Henry, op. cit., pp. 254–5.

House of Commons Blue Book, *Correspondence Respecting Abyssinia, 1846–68*, Jan. 1868, nos. 435, 451, 488, 491, 498, 503, 504.

Buckle, E. E., ed., *Letters of Queen Victoria*, second series, vol. I, *1862–9*, 1926, pp. 249–50.

8 Rassam, Hormuzd, op. cit., vol. I, pp. 98–114, passim.

Dufton, Henry, op. cit., pp. 268–73.

F.O. 78/1871, Stanton to Earl Russell, no. 4, 22.8.65; no. 15, 6.9.65.

House of Commons Blue Book, *Correspondence Respecting Abyssinia, 1846–68*, Jan. 1868, nos. 523, 524, 528, 529, 541, 721.

9 Douin, Georges, op. cit., vol. III, part I, 1936, pp. 345–48, 356.

House of Commons Blue Book, *Correspondence Respecting Abyssinia, 1846–68*, Jan. 1868, nos. 712, 716, 721, 793, 796, 801.

House of Commons Blue Book, *Further Correspondence Relating to British Captives in Abyssinia, 1865–7*, no. 91.

Munzinger, Johann Albert Werner, *Ostafrikanische Studien*, 2nd edn., 1883, p. 3.

10 F.O. 142/30, Reade to Lord Stanley, no. 25, 3.9.67; no. 35, 8.10.67; Stanton to Lord Stanley, no. 11, 11.1.68; no. 21, 25.1.68.

House of Commons Blue Book, *Correspondence Respecting Abyssinia, 1846–68*, Jan. 1868, nos. 799, 824, 828.

House of Commons Parliamentary Paper 4260, 1867, *Papers Connected with the Abyssinian Expedition*, no. 161.

Douin, Georges, op. cit., vol. III, part I, pp. 350–5, 370–1, 378–82.

11 House of Commons Blue Book, *Correspondence Respecting Abyssinia, 1846–68*, Jan. 1868, nos. 764, 775, 833.

House of Commons Parliamentary Paper 4260, 1867, *Papers Connected with the Abyssinian Expedition*, nos. 32, 95.

Cumming, Duncan, *The Gentleman Savage*, 1987, pp. 160–1.

12 Douin, Georges, op. cit., vol. III, part I, pp. 383–404, passim, 410.

Rassam, Hormuzd, op. cit., vol. II, passim.
Mathew, David, op. cit., p. 204.
F.O./142/30, Stanton to Elliot, no. 18, 27.4.68.
F.O. 142/32, Stanton to Lord Stanley, no. 62, undated, June 68; no. 137, 29.10.68; no. 155, 20.11.68.
Daily Telegraph, 27.3.1998, p. 3; 11.4.1998, p. 23; 30.5.2000, p. 17.
Moorehead, Alan, *The Blue Nile*, 1962, p.273.

CHAPTER FOUR

1 F.O. 84/1246, Sharif–Bulwer, 18.3.65.
 Douin, Georges, *Histoire du Règne du Khédive Ismail*, vol. III, part 1, pp. 340, 376, 437–8.
2 Douin, Georges, op. cit., vol. II, pp. 32–3; vol. III, part 1, pp. 358–74 passim, 382, 410.
 F.O. 142/30, Reade to Lord Stanley, no. 39, 25.10.67.
 F.O. 142/32, Stanton to Earl of Clarendon, no. 89, 12.8.68; no. 34, 16.4.70; no. 42, 12.5.70; no. 51, 25.5.70. Stanton to Earl Granville, no. 84, 16.7.70.
3 Gray, Richard, *History of the Southern Sudan 1839–1889*, 1961, p.170.
 Douin, Georges, op. cit., vol. III, part 2, pp. 197-9, 436.
4 Ibid., pp. 228–40, 248–53, 266, 435–6.
5 Ibid., vol. II, pp. 722–9; vol. III, part 2, pp. 266–79, 285, 358, 358–62, 387, 396–8, 409–11.
 F.O. 78/2284, Vivian to Earl Granville, no. 54, 18.10.73.
 Gray, Richard, op. cit., p.180.
6 Douin, Georges, op. cit., vol. III, part 1, pp. 374–6, 404–9; part 2, pp. 282–91, 296, 301–10.
 F.O. 78/2041, Munzinger to Stanton, no. 98, 28.8.68; Lord Stanley to Stanton, no. 55, 7.12.68.
 F.O. 142/32, Stanley to Earl of Clarendon, 4.6.69; Stanton to Earl of Clarendon, 17.9.69, 16.10.69.
 Cumming, Duncan C., 'History of Kassala and the Province of Taka', in *Sudan Notes and Records*, vol. XXIII, part 1, 1940, p.24 fn.
7 Douin, Georges, op. cit., vol. III, part 2, pp. 310–20, 324–8, 333–5.
8 Ibid., pp. 335–48, 365, 373–81.
9 Ibid., pp. 365, 382–95, 399–409, 416–17.
 Cumming, Duncan C., op. cit., pp. 25–7.
 F.O. 142/35, Stanton to Earl Granville, nos. 72, 75, 77, 94–8, Sept.–Dec. '72.
10 Douin, Georges, op. cit., vol. III, part 2, pp. 396–8, 417–20, 428–33.
 Boutros Ghali, Mirrit, *Mémoires de Nubar Pasha 1825–79*, 1983, p. 428.

CHAPTER FIVE

1 Douin, Georges, *Histoire du Règne du Khédive Ismail*, vol. III, part 1, 1936, pp. 446–8; part 2, 1938, pp. 726–7.
Schweinfurth, Georg, trans. Ellen Frewer, *The Heart of Africa: Three Years' Travels 1868–71*, 1873, vol. I, p. 101.

2 Ibid, pp. 78–9, 92–5.
Douin, Georges, op. cit., vol. III, part 1, pp. 448–50, 453–4.

3 Baker, Sir Samuel White, *Ismailia*, 2nd ed., 1895, p. 16.
Douin, Georges, op. cit., vol. III, part 1, pp. 472–4, 479–83; part 2, p. 374.

4 Baker, Sir Samuel White, op. cit., pp. 42–50, 58–60, 64, 73–6, 82, 91.
Baker, Sir Samuel White, 'Journal 1869–73', unpublished manuscript deposited at Royal Geographical Society, vol. 3, 20.4.70, 1.5.70, 5.5.70, 1.7.70; letter to Sharif Pasha, 3.12.70; to Khedive, 15.6.70, 28.12.70; vol. 4, 19.4.70, 20–24.4.70, 3 –5.5.70.
Gray, Richard, *A History of the Southern Sudan, 1839–89*, 1961, p. 93 fn.

5 Douin, Georges, op. cit., vol. III, part 2, pp. 10–22, 26, 725–32, 735–6.
Baker, Sir Samuel White, op. cit., p. 460

6 Douin, Georges, op. cit., vol. III, part 2, pp. 458–61.
Schweinfurth, Georg, op. cit., vol. II, pp. 395, 474–9.

7 Douin, Georges, op. cit., vol. III, part 2, 1938, p. 561, fn 3; part 3, 1941, p. 24, 1130–1.
Marno, E., (I) *Reisen im Gebiete des Blauen und Weissen Nil 1869 bis 1873*, 1874, pp. 330–1, 392.
Baker, Sir Samuel White, op. cit., pp. 458–61.
Murray, T. Douglas and White, A. Silva, *Sir Samuel Baker, A Memoir*, 1895, p. 177.

8 Baker, Sir Samuel White, *Ismailia*, 2nd ed., 1895, p. 3.
Baker, Sir Samuel White, *The Albert N'yanza*, 1866, vol. II, 1866, pp. 310–15.
Gray, Richard, op. cit., 1961, pp. 167–8.
Douin, Georges, op. cit., vol. II, 1934, p.107; vol. III, part 1, 1936, p. 226.
British Parliamentary Papers 4260 of 1867: Baker to Lord Stanley no. 885 of 27.10.67; no. 932 of 31.10.67.
The Times, 21.11.67.
Murray, T. Douglas and White, A. Silva, op. cit., pp. 124, 130.
F.O. 142/29, Colquhoun to Earl Russell, no. 43, 6.4.65.

9 Boutros Ghali, Mirrit (ed.), *Mémoires de Nubar Pasha 1825–79*, 1983, pp. 333, 337–8, 438–9.
Baker, Sir Samuel White, *Ismailia*, 2nd ed., 1895, p. 5.

10 Russell, W. H., *A Diary in the East during the Tour of the Prince and Princess of Wales*, 1869, p. 384.
Douin, Georges, op. cit., vol. II, pp. 107–13.
F.O. 84/1246, Earl Russell to Bulwer, no. 1, 22.2.65.
F.O. 142/29, Colquhoun to Earl Russell, no. 43, 6.4.65.
F.O. 142/32, Stanton to Earl of Clarendon, no. 40, 2.4.69.
F.O. 78/2092, Earl of Clarendon F.O. internal memo, 12.4.69 and 14.4.69.
Gordon Mss., Moffitt Collection, 51295, 20.4.79.

11 F.O. 142/32, Stanton to Earl of Clarendon, no. 40, 2.4.69, no. 49, 22.4.69, no. 56, 3.5.69, no. 62, 5.5.69.
Murray, T. Douglas and White, A. Silva, op. cit., pp. 149–51.
Douin, Georges, op. cit., vol. III, part 1, pp. 433, 479–83.
Baker, Sir Samuel White, *Ismailia*, op. cit., p. 4.
Shukry, Mohammed Fuad, *Equatoria under Egyptian Rule 1874–6*, 1953, pp. 22–3.

12 Douin, Georges, op. cit., vol. II, p. 324; vol. III, part 1, p. 483.
Hill, Richard L., *Biographical Dictionary of the Sudan*, 2nd ed., 1967, p. xiii.
Hill, Richard L., 'Rulers of the Sudan 1820–85', in *Sudan Notes and Records*, vol. XXXII, part 1, June 1951, p. 90.
Murray, T. Douglas and White, A. Silva, op. cit., p. 153.

13 Douin, Georges, op. cit., vol. III, part 1, pp. 479–82, 485–6; part 2, pp. 1–2, 435–6.
Gray, Richard, op. cit., pp. 89, 90 fn.
Murray, T. Douglas and White, A. Silva, op. cit., pp. 150–3.
Baker, Sir Samuel White, *Ismailia*, op. cit., pp. 5–10, 13, 42, 79.
Baker, Anne, *Morning Star*, 1972, pp. 42–7.
F.O. 142/29, Colquhoun to Earl Russell, no. 84, 17.7.65.

14 Baker, Sir Samuel White, *Ismailia*, op. cit., pp. 13, 72.
Douin, Georges, op. cit., vol. III, part 1, pp. 453–6, part 2, p. 3.
Gray, Richard, op. cit., p. 90 fn.

15 Douin, Georges, op. cit., vol. III, part 1, pp. 111 fn, 196, 211, 419, 453, 471; part 2, pp. 3–6.
Baker, Sir Samuel White, *Ismailia*, op. cit., pp. 12–14, 18, 34, 89, 95.
Baker, Sir Samuel White, 'Journal 1869–73', unpublished manuscript, deposited at the Royal Geographical Society, vol. 3: letter to Sharif Pasha, 12.1.70; vol. 4: 8.2.70, 11.3.70, 9.4.70.
Berlioux, E. F., *La Traite Orientale*, 1870, pp. 113–15.
Schweinfurth, Georg, *The Heart of Africa*, trans. Ellen Frewer, vol. II, 1873, p. 485.

16 Douin, Georges, op. cit., vol. III, part 2, pp. 22–5.
Baker, Sir Samuel White, *Ismailia*, op. cit., pp. 72–9, 91–6, 107, 120–1.

Baker, Sir Samuel White, 'Journal 1869–73', op. cit. vol. 3, letter to Sharif Pasha, 3.12.70; to Khedive, 28.12.70; vol. 4, 18.5.70, 17.6.70, 1.10.70, 9/10.10.70, 25.10.70, 20.12.70.

17 Baker, Sir Samuel White, *Ismailia*, op. cit., pp. 108, 114, 136–9, 152–4.
Baker, Sir Samuel White, 'Journal 1869–73', op. cit., vol. 4, 12.6.71, 22.9.71.
Douin, Georges, op. cit., vol. III, part 2, pp. 37–41, 43, 51–2.

18 Douin, ibid., pp. 44–52.
Baker, Sir Samuel White, *Ismailia,* op. cit., pp. 42, 175, 192–3, 218–19.
Baker, Sir Samuel White, 'Journal 1869–73', op. cit., vol. 3, letter to Khedive, 15.6.70; to Sharif Pasha, 3.12.70; to Khedive, 8–17,10.71; to Sharif Pasha, October (undated); to Ja'afar Pasha Mazhar, 6–19.10.71; vol. 4, 27.12.71.
Murray, T. Douglas and White, A. Silva, op. cit., pp. 173, 178.
Baker, Anne, op. cit., pp. 94–6.
Beaton, A. C., 'A Chapter in Bari History' in *SNR*, vol. XVII, part 2, 1934, pp. 189–99.
F.O. 78/2186, Stanton to Earl Granville, no. 58, 6.12.71; no. 61, 22.12.71.
F.O. 78/2229, Stanton to Earl Granville, no. 5, 21.1.72.
The Times, 30.1.72, p. 6g.

19 Baker, Sir Samuel White, *Ismailia,* op. cit., pp. 193, 216–17.
Baker, Sir Samuel White, 'Journal 1869–73', op. cit., vol. 4, 27–29.1.72, 6.3.72–23.5.72 passim; vol. 3, letter to Ja'afar Pasha Mazhar, 18.5.72.
F.O. 78/2284 Vivian to Earl Granville, no. 22, 2.8.73 enclosing Baker to Stanton 13.8.72.
Beaton, A. C., op. cit., p.180.
Douin, Georges, op. cit., vol. III, part 2, pp. 59, 66–70.

20 Douin, Georges, ibid., pp. 48 fn, 70–88, 97.
Baker, Sir Samuel White, *Ismailia,* op. cit., pp. 377–454 passim.
Baker, Sir Samuel White, 'Journal 1869–73', op. cit., vol. 4, 19.5.72–1.4.73 passim.
F.O. 78/2283, Stanton to Earl Granville, no. 37, 17.5.73 and no. 39, 19.5.73.

21 Douin, Georges, op. cit., vol. III, part 2, pp. 88–96.
F.O. 78/2138, Earl of Clarendon to Stanton, no. 19, 22.4.70.
F.O. 78/2139, Stanton to Earl of Clarendon, no. 43 of 12.5.70, no. 56, 27.5.70, no. 66, 14.6.70.
F.O. 78/2218, Elliot to Earl Granville, no. 81 of 2.7.72.
F.O. 78/2229, Stanton to Earl Granville, no. 99, 7.12.72, no. 102, 14.12.72.

Shukry, Mohammed Fuad, op. cit., p. 25.

Baker, Sir Samuel White, *Ismailia*, op. cit., p. 460.

22 Ibid., pp. 457–9, 461–3.

Baker, Sir Samuel White, 'Journal 1869–73', op. cit., vol. 4, 16.5.73, 19–20.6.73.

Douin, Georges, op. cit., vol. III, part 2, pp. 97–105.

Boutros Ghali, Mirrit (ed.), op. cit., p.440.

F.O. 78/2229, Stanton to Earl Granville, no. 69, 6.9.72, no. 102, 14.12.72.

F.O. 78/2283, Stanton to Earl Granville, no. 23, 5.3.73; tel. 25.4.73; no. 37, 17.5.73, no. 39, 19.5.73; Vivian to Earl Granville, tel. 30.6.73; conf. of 1.7.63; no. 11, 4.7.73; no. 13, 10.7.73.

F.O. 84/1871, Vivian to Earl Granville, no. 8, 25.7.73, no. 10, 28.7.73, no. 17 most conf., 6.9.73, no. 19, 22.9.73.

F.O. 78/2284, Vivian to Earl Granville, no. 29 of 16.8.73, no. 32 of 22.8.73, no. 38 of 25.8.73, no. 52 of 10.10.73.

23 Gray, Richard, op. cit., pp. 68–9.

F.O. 84/1371, Stanton to Earl Granville, no. 7, 25.4.73.

Baker, Sir Samuel White, *Ismailia*, op. cit., p. xii.

F.O. 84/1371, Stanton to Earl Granville, no. 7, 25.4.73; Vivian to Earl Granville, no. 17 most conf., 6.9.73, no. 14 of 30.8.73.

F.O. 78/2284, Vivian to Earl Granville, no. 22, 2.8.73 enclosing Baker to Stanton, 19.4.73, tel., 30.8.73, no. 48, 4.10.73; Earl Granville to Vivian, tel. 29.9.73.

CHAPTER SIX

1 Douin, Georges, *Histoire du Règne du Khédive Ismail*, vol. III, part 1, 1936, pp. 317–27, 450–2.

Schweinfurth, Georg, trans. Ellen Frewer, *The Heart of Africa 1868–71*, vol. II, pp. 330, 365.

2 Douin, Georges, op. cit., vol. III, part 1, pp. 15–19, 453–6.

Schweinfurth, Georg. op. cit., vol. II, pp. 265–6.

Berlioux, E. F., *La Traite Orientale*, 1870, pp. 113–15.

3 Jackson, H. C., *Black Ivory and White: The Story of El Zubeir Pasha, Slaver and Sultan as Told by Himself*, 1913, pp. 33–6.

Douin, Georges, op. cit., vol. III, part 2, 1938, pp. 148–51.

Schweinfurth, Georg, op. cit., vol. II, pp. 265–6, 304, 330–1.

4 Schweinfurth, Georg, op. cit., vol. II, pp. 329–31, 351, 356–7, 363–4.

Jackson, H. C., op. cit., pp 39–41.

Douin, Georges, op. cit., vol. III, part 2, pp. 151–4.

5 Ibid., pp. 156, 165, 167, 473–4.

Jackson, H. C., op. cit., pp. 41–7, 49.

F.O. 78/2284, Vivian to Earl Granville, no. 22, 2.8.73, enclosing Baker to Stanton, priv. 19.4.73.

6 Schweinfurth, Georg, op. cit., vol. II, pp. 3–4, 427; vol. I, pp. 186, 200, 258–60.
Douin, Georges, op. cit., vol. III, part 2, pp. 108–12.
Seligman, C. G., and Seligman, Brenda Z., *Pagan Tribes of the Nilotic Sudan*, 1932, pp. 501–2.
Gray, Richard, *A History of the Southern Sudan, 1839–1889*, 1961, pp. 14–16.

7 Junker, Wilhelm, trans. A. H. Keane, *Travels in Africa 1875–86* , vol. III, 1892, pp. 31, 262–5.
Schweinfurth, Georg, op. cit., vol. II, pp. 36, 82–4, 365.
Gray, Richard, op. cit., pp. 65–6.
Wyld, J. W. G., 'Recollections of Two Zande Chiefs', in *Sudan Notes and Records*, vol. XLII, 1961, pp. 127–31.

8 Schweinfurth, Georg, op. cit., vol. I, pp. 320 (but cf p.175), 466–7; vol. II, pp. 307–11, 318, 365–6, 417.
Junker, Wilhelm, op. cit., vol. I, 1890, p. 304.
Jackson, H. C. op. cit., pp. 25–32, 37–9, 98.
Brown, Robert, *The Story of Africa and Its Explorers*, 1893, vol. II, pp. 139–40.

9 Douin, Georges, op. cit. vol. III, part 2, p. 159.
Schweinfurth, Georg, op. cit., vol. II, pp. 305, 358–60, 427.

10 MacMichael, H. A., *History of the Arabs in the Sudan*, 1922, 2nd imp. 1967, vol. I, pp. 221–2; vol. II, p. 118.
Jackson, H. C., op. cit., pp. 8–32 passim, 49–55.
Schweinfurth, Georg, op. cit., vol. II, pp. 84, 361, 429–30.
Gray, Richard, op. cit., pp. 53, 68.
Junker, Wilhelm, op. cit., vol. III, p. 262.
Douin, Georges, op. cit., vol. III, part 2, pp. 161, 165.

11 Ibid., pp. 161–5, 568–70, 589.
Jackson, H. C., op. cit., p. 49.

12 Douin, Georges, op. cit., vol. III, part 2, pp. 166–70.
Jackson, H. C., op. cit., pp. 55–61.
Lampen, G. D., 'History of Darfur', in *SNR*, vol. XXXI, part 2, 1950, pp. 188–9.
Junker, Wilhelm, op. cit., vol. I, p. 170.
F.O. 84/1305, Francis to Earl of Clarendon, no. 36, 1.12.69.
O'Fahey, R. S., 'The Conquest of Darfur 1873-1882', in *SNR*, New Series no. 1, 1977, pp. 53–5.

CHAPTER SEVEN

1 Douin, Georges, *Histoire du Règne du Khédive Ismail,* vol. III, part 1, 1936, pp. 361–74, 440; part 2, 1938, pp. 435–41, 456–8, 477.
   Hill, R. L., *Egypt in the Sudan 1820–1881,* 1959, p.116.

2 Douin, Georges, op. cit., vol. III, part 2, pp. 322, 445–501, 471–3.
   MacMichael, H. A., *History of the Arabs in the Sudan,* 2nd imp. 1967, vol. II, D.7; *Ta'arikh,* p. 404.
   Cox, Frederick J., 'Munzinger's Observations on the Sudan 1871: The Little America of Africa', in *Sudan Notes and Records,* vol. XXXIII, part 2, 1952, pp. 189–200.

3 Douin, Georges, op. cit., vol. III, part 2, pp. 453–7, 498.
   Cumming, D. C., 'The History of Kassala and the Province of Taka' in *SNR,* vol. XXIII, part 2, 1940, pp. 253–4.

4 Douin, Georges, op. cit., vol. II, 1934, pp. 589–613 passim; vol. III, part 2, 1938, pp. 475–6, 498–9, 503–4, 524–5, 537–8, 569–71.

5 Murray, T. Douglas and White, A. Silva, *Sir Samuel Baker: A Memoir,* 1895, p. 177.
   Douin, Georges, op. cit., vol. III, part 2, pp. 480–91 passim, 492–4, 496–8, 600–1.
   Hill, R. L., *A Biographical Dictionary of the Anglo-Egyptian Sudan 1820–81,* 2nd ed., 1967, pp. 27, 397.
   MacMichael, H. A., op. cit., vol. I, pp. 257, 261.

6 Douin, Georges, op. cit., vol. III, part 2, pp. 567–73, 581–2, 599; vol. III, part 3, 1941, pp. 1100–1, 1104.
   MacMichael, H. A., op. cit., vol. II, D.7, pp. 404–5.
   Marno, E., *Reisen im Gebiete des Blauen und Weissen Nil 1869 bis 1873,* 1874, p. 330.

7 Douin, Georges, op. cit., vol. III, part 1, p. 24 fn; vol. III, part 2, pp. 365, 401–2, 571–5, 577–8, 581–2, 591–8.
   Marno, E., op. cit., p. 307.
   Schweinfurth, Georg, trans. Ellen Frewer, *The Heart of Africa: Three Years' Travels 1868–71,* vol. II, 1873, pp. 479–80.
   Newbold, D., 'The History of Gallabat', in *SNR,* vol. VII, part 1, 1924, pp. 96–8.

8 Douin, Georges, op. cit., vol. III, part 2, pp. 582–6, 589, 601.

9 Ibid., pp. 475–6, 502–3, 506, 510–25 passim, 529.
   Paul, A., *A History of the Beja Tribes of the Sudan,* 1954, p. 104.

10 Douin, Georges, op. cit., vol. III, part 2, pp. 450 fn, 525–6, 542–3.
   Cumming, D. C., op. cit., part 2, pp. 254–5.
   F.O. 78/3554, Malet to Earl Granville, no. 154, 14.5.83, enclosing Stewart, 18.4.83.

Cox, Frederick, J., op. cit., pp. 189–201.
11 Douin, Georges, op. cit., vol. III, part 2, pp. 337–44, 352–4, 358–60.
Cumming, D. C. op. cit., part I, pp. 17–21.
British Library, Moffitt Collection, Gordon Mss. 51295, 12.10.79.

CHAPTER EIGHT

1 Cameron, D. A., *Egypt in the Nineteenth Century*, 1898, pp. 233, 252–5.
Holt, P. M., *Egypt and the Fertile Crescent 1516–1922*, 1966, p. 208.
McCoan, J. Carlisle, *Egypt under Ismail*, 1889, pp. 69–70.
Chirol, Sir Valentine, *The Egyptian Problem*, 1920, pp. 25–6.
F.O. 78/2284, Vivian to Earl Granville, no. 24, 2.8.73; no. 50, 4.10.73.
F.O. 78/2342, Stanton to Earl of Derby, no. 39, 28.5.74.
2 McCoan, J. Carlisle, *Egypt As It Is*, 1877, pp. 125–7, 138.
Boutros Ghali, Mirrit (ed.), *Mémoires de Nubar Pasha 1825–79*, 1983, pp. 338, 441, 443, 451–5, 461–7.
Chirol, Sir Valentine, op. cit., pp. 28–32.
Cromer, Earl of, *Modern Egypt*, 1908, vol. I, p. 26.
Creasy, Sir Edward S., *History of the Ottoman Turks*, revised edn., 1877, p. 548.
Dicey, Edward, *The Story of the Khedivate*, 1902, pp. 101–3, 138–9.
F.O. 78/2403, Earl of Derby to Stanton, no. 69, 18.11.75; no. 88, 29.11.75; no. 97, 6.12.75.
F.O. 78/2404, Stanton to Earl of Derby, no. 105, 30.10.75.
F.O. 78/2405, Stanton to Earl of Derby, no. 110, 6.11.75; no. 140, 27.11.75; no. 173, 17.12.75; no. 181, 23.12.75; no. 183, 29.12.75.
F.O. 78/2498, Earl of Derby to Stanton, no. 66, 17.3.76.
3 Cromer, Earl of, op. cit., pp. 11–15; 26–7.
Holt, P. M., op. cit., pp. 208–9.
McCoan, J. Carlisle, *Egypt As It Is*, 1877, Appendix G.
F.O. 78/2498, Earl of Derby to Stanton, no. 29, 10.2.76; no. 58, 13.3.76; no. 63, 15.3.76; no. 77, 24.3.76; no. 81, 27.3.76; no. 101, 13.4.76; no. 106, 21.4.76.
F.O. 78/2499, Earl of Derby to Stanton, no. 109, 5.5.76; no. 116, 11.5.76; no. 125, 23.5.76; no. 129, 26.5.76.
F.O. 78/2501, Stanton to Earl of Derby, no. 80, 14.3.76; no. 97, 26.3.76; no. 113, 31.3.76; no. 123, 6.4.76; no. 128, 8.4.76.
F.O. 78/2502, Stanton to Earl of Derby, no. 161, 26.4.76.
F.O. 78/2503, Stanton to Earl of Derby, no. 187, 13.5.76; no. 205, 27.5.76;
Cookson to Earl of Derby, no. 215, 7.6.76.

4 F.O. 78/2503, Vivian to Earl of Derby, no. 12, 27.10.76.
F.O. 78/2504, Vivian to Earl of Derby, no. 27, 11.11.76; no. 62, 28.12.76.
F.O. 78/2631, Vivian to Earl of Derby, no. 1, 1.1.77.
Boutros Ghali, Mirrit (ed.), op. cit., pp. 472–3.
Chirol, Sir Valentine, op. cit., pp. 24–5.
Jerrold, Blanchard (ed.), *Egypt under Ismail Pasha,* 1879, pp. 199–200, 207.
Crabités, Pierre, *Ismail the Maligned Khedive,* 1933, pp. 243–8.
Dicey, Edward, op. cit., pp. 144–62 passim.
Cameron, D. A., op. cit., pp. 259–60.

5 Douin, Georges, *Histoire du Règne du Khédive Ismail,* vol. III, part 2, 1938, pp. 601–2; part 3, 1941, pp. 1099–1109, 1251–2.

6 Ibid., vol. III, part 3, pp. 1–3, 1111–20.

7 Ibid., pp. 1096–7, 1122–3, 1129–30.

8 Ibid., pp. 543–5, 1149, 1160–73.

9 Ibid., pp. 505–6, 509–23.

10 Douin Georges, op. cit., vol. III, part 2, p. 561; part 3, pp. 260–3, 1130–1.
Allen, Bernard M., *Gordon and the Sudan,* 1931, pp. 29, 54–7.

11 Douin, Georges, op. cit., vol. III, part 2, p. 598; part 3, pp. 122–3, 263, 1131–6, 1140.
Pumphrey, M. E. C., 'The Shilluk Tribe', in *Sudan Notes and Records,* vol. XXIV, 1941, p. 4.
Gessi, Romolo, ed. Felix Gessi, *Seven Years in the Sudan,* London, 1892, p. 23.

12 Douin, Georges, op. cit., vol. III, part 3, pp. 1144–53.

13 Ibid., 1141–3.
O'Fahey, R. S., 'The Conquest of Darfur 1873–1882', in *SNR,* New Series, no. 1, 1997, pp. 56–7.

14 Douin, Georges, op. cit., vol. III, part 2, pp. 606–16, 628–9; part 3, pp. 1282–6.

15 Douin, Georges, op. cit., vol. III, part 2, pp. 631–44; part 3, p. 1258.
O'Fahey, R. S., op. cit., pp. 61–2.

16 Douin, Georges, op. cit., vol. III, part 3, pp. 1258–75.
O'Fahey, R. S., op. cit., pp. 62–3.

17 Douin, Georges, op. cit., vol. III, part 3, pp. 1275–82.
O'Fahey, R. S., op. cit., p. 65.

18 Douin, Georges, op. cit., vol. III, part 2, pp. 644–6, 650–1; part 3, pp. 1286–1315 passim.
Hill, Richard L., *Egypt in the Sudan: 1820–81,* 1959, pp. 130–1.

19 Douin, Georges, op. cit., vol. III, part 3, pp. 352 fn 1, 354, 358–60, 370.
Jackson, H. C., *Black Ivory and White,* pp. 60–1 .

20 Douin, Georges, op. cit., vol. III, part 2, p. 586; part 3, pp. 364–9.
21 Boutros Ghali, Mirrit (ed.), *Mémoires de Nubar Pasha 1825–79, 1983*, pp. 445–6.
   Douin, Georges, op. cit., vol. III, part 3, pp. 370–80.
   Jackson, H. C., op. cit., pp. 61–5.
22 Ibid., pp. 62–72.
   Douin, Georges, op. cit., vol. III, part 3, pp. 370–94, 397–401, 410–12, 462.
23 Ibid., pp. 410, 413–23.
24 Ibid., pp. 423–37, 480–7, 489.
   Jackson, H. C., op. cit., pp. 72–9.
25 Ibid., pp. 75–6.
   Douin, Georges, op. cit., vol. III, part 3, pp. 441–4, 462–80, 501, 503.
26 Ibid., pp. 503–6, 523–34.
   Crabités, Pierre, *Americans in the Egyptian Army*, 1938, p. 59.
27 Douin, Georges, op. cit., vol. III, part 3, pp. 508–14, 523, 535–45.
   Murray, Douglas, and White, A Silva, *Sir Samuel Baker: A Memoir*, 1895, p. 233.
   Crabités, Pierre, op. cit., p. 64.
28 Douin, Georges, op. cit., vol. III, part 3, pp. 484–503.
   Jackson, H. C., op. cit., pp. 78–81.
   British Library, Moffitt Collection, Gordon Mss. 51294, 8.5.77.

CHAPTER NINE

1 Douin, Georges, *Histoire du Règne du Khédive Ismail*, vol. III, part 2, 1938, pp. 365, 396–7, 401–2, 557–60; part 3, 1941, pp. 699–701, 1195–1212, 1244.
   Newbold, D., 'The History of Gallabat' in *Sudan Notes and Records*, vol. VII, part 1, 1924, p. 98.
   Cumming, D. C., 'The History of Kassala and the Province of Taka', in *SNR*, vol. XXIII, part 1, 1940, pp. 17–21.
2 Douin, Georges, op. cit., vol. III, part 3, pp. 1210–30.
   Cumming, D. C., op. cit., *SNR*, vol. XXIII, part 2, 1940, pp. 236–43.
3 Ibid., pp. 239–43, 267–8.
   Douin, Georges, op. cit., vol. III, part 2, pp. 538–41.
4 F.O. 78/2342, Stanton to Earl of Derby, no. 50, 17.6.74.
   F.O. 78/3188, Marquess of Salisbury to Earl of Derby, nos. 86–8, 23.3.75; Stanton to Earl of Derby, memo 5.7.75.
   Gray, Richard, *A History of the Southern Sudan 1839–1889*, 1961, p. 180.
   Douin, Georges, op.cit., vol. III, part 3, pp. 549–50, 555–99 passim.
5 Ibid., pp. 583–7, 602–14, 618–27, 706–15, 718–19.

Boutros Ghali, Mirrit (ed.), *Mémoires de Nubar Pasha 1825–79*, 1983, pp. 443–5.
F.O. 78/2405, Stanton to Earl of Derby, no. 112, 11.11.75.

6 Boutros Ghali, Mirrit (ed.), op. cit., pp. 447–8.
Douin, Georges, op. cit., vol. III, part 3, pp. 601, 645, 721–3, 726, 731–6.

7 Ibid., pp. 792–823 passim.
Thesiger, Wilfred, *The Life of My Choice*, 1987, pp. 107, 120, 150, 157.

8 Douin, Georges, op. cit., vol. III, part 3, pp. 601, 724–31.

9 Ibid., pp. 738–46.

10 Ibid., pp. 745–56.
F.O. 78/2403, Earl of Derby to Stanton, no. 17, 26.2.75
F.O. 78/2404, Stanton to Earl of Derby, no. 25, 11.2.75; Cookson to Earl of Derby, conf. no. 88, 11.8.75; conf. no. 95, 27.9.75.
F.O. 78/2632, Vivian to Earl of Derby, no. 137, 19.5.77.
Boutros Ghali, Mirrit (ed.), op. cit., pp. 446–8.
Hill, Richard and Hogg, Peter, *A Black Corps d'Élite*, 1995, pp. 130–2.

11 F.O. 78/2405, Stanton to Earl of Derby, no. 117, 14.11.75.
Douin, Georges, op. cit., vol. III, part 3, pp. 756–73 passim.

12 Ibid., pp. 773–92 passim.

13 Ibid., pp. 789, 813–28.
Hill, George Birkbeck, *Colonel Gordon in Central Africa 1874–1879*, 2nd edn., 1885, repr. 1969, pp. 423–4.
F.O. 78/2403, Earl of Derby to Stanton, no. 121, 17.12.75.
F.O. 78/2405, Stanton to Earl of Derby, no. 142, 27.11.75; no. 183, 29.12.75.
Boutros Ghali, Mirrit (ed.), op. cit., p. 449.

14 Douin, Georges, op. cit., vol. III, part 3, pp. 836–902 passim.

15 Ibid., pp. 902–63 passim.
British Library, Moffit Collection, Gordon Mss. 51294, 15–18.3.77.

16 Douin, Georges, op. cit., vol. III, part 3, pp. 971–81.

17 Ibid., pp. 993, 999–1002, 1007–10.
F.O. 78/2503, Stanton to Earl of Derby, no. 170, 6.5.76; no. 188, 13.5.76; Cookson to Earl of Derby, no. 235, 7.8.76; Vivian to Earl of Derby, no. 17, 3.11.76.
Boutros Ghali, Mirrit, (ed.), op. cit., p. 466.

18 Douin, Georges, op. cit., vol. III, part 3, pp. 1010–94 passim.
F.O. 78/2503, Vivian to Earl of Derby, no. 6, 20.10.76.
F.O. 78/2504, Vivian to Earl of Derby, no. 31, 17.11.76; no. 42, 2.12.76; no. 60, 26.12.76.
F.O. 78/2631, Vivian to Earl of Derby, no. 18, 23.1.77.
Zewde, Bahru, *A History of Modern Ethiopia 1855–74*, 1991, pp. 52–4.

CHAPTER TEN

1 Boutros Ghali, Mirrit (ed.), *Mémoires de Nubar Pasha, 1825–79,* 1983, p. 440.
Douin, Georges, *Histoire du Règne du Khédive Ismail,* vol. III, part 2, 1938, pp. 47, 88; part 3, 1941, pp. 1–6.
Elton, Lord, *General Gordon,* 1954, pp. 142–3, 146–9.
F.O. 78/2218, Elliot to Earl Granville, no. 81 of 2.7.72.
F.O. 78/2284, Stanton to Earl Granville, no. 52 of 20.12.73.
British Library, Moffit Collection, Gordon Mss. 51291, 9.11.73; 51292, 2.9.74; 51305, Baker to Gordon, 8.7.75.
Murray T. Douglas and White, A. Silva, *Sir Samuel Baker, a Memoir,* 1895, pp. 219–20.
Dicey, Edward, *The Story of the Khedivate,* 1902, p. 93.
2 F.O. 78/2342, Stanton to Earl of Derby, no. 19 of 24.2.74.
Douin, Georges, op. cit., vol. III, part 3, pp. 12–21.
Allen, Bernard M., *Gordon and the Sudan,* 1931, pp. 14–15, 86–7.
Elton, Lord, op. cit., pp. 157–60.
Pollock, John, *Gordon, the Man behind the Legend,* 1993, pp. 134–8.
Hill, George Birkbeck (ed.), *Colonel Gordon in Central Africa 1874–79,* fourth edition, 1969, pp. 4–6.
Stanton, Colonel E. A. (ed.), 'Unpublished Letters of Charles George Gordon to General Sir E. Stanton' in *Sudan Notes and Records,* vol. X, 1927, pp. 3–4.
Gordon Mss., op. cit., 51292, 14.3.74, 17.3.74.
3 Stanton, Colonel E. A. (ed.), op. cit, p. 4.
Hill, George Birkbeck (ed.), op. cit., pp. 8–14.
Gordon Mss., op. cit., 51292, 17.3.74, 4.4.74, 5.4.74, 10.4.74.
Douin, Georges, op. cit., vol. III, part 3, pp. 22–5.
4 Ibid., pp. 25–8.
Stanton, Colonel E. A. (ed.), op. cit., pp. 15–16.
Gordon Mss., op. cit., 51295, 17.4.78.
5 Hansal, Martin, *Austrian Geographical Journal,* Vienna, 1874, p. 380.
Douin, Georges, op. cit., vol. III, part 3, pp. 16, 28–37.
6 Ibid., pp. 37–48, 53–60, 487.
Stanton, Colonel E. A.(ed.), op. cit., p. 8.
Hill, Richard (ed.), *The Sudan Memoirs of Carl Christian Giegler Pasha 1873–1883,* 1984, pp. 34–5.
7 Douin, Georges, op. cit., vol. III, part 3, pp. 49–53, 60–6.
8 Ibid., pp. 66–73, 142.
Hill, George Birkbeck (ed.), op. cit., pp. 39–40.
9 Ibid., p. 42.

Douin, Georges, op. cit., vol. III, part 3, pp. 74–87, 142.

Stanton, Colonel E. A. (ed.), op. cit., pp. 6–9, 15–16.

Murray T. Douglas and White, A. Silva, op. cit., pp. 221–2.

Gordon Mss., op. cit., 51294, 18.5.77.

10 Hill, Richard, and Hogg, Peter, *A Black Corps d'Élite*, 1995, pp. 142, 171.

Douin, Georges, op. cit., vol. III, part 3, p. 76, 105–11, 114–16.

11 Ibid., pp. 106–8, 110–11, 124–8, 145–56 passim.

Stanton, Colonel E. A. (ed.), op. cit., pp. 10–11, 13, 16.

Allen, Bernard M., op. cit., pp. 82–101.

Junker, Wilhelm, trans. Keane, A. H., *Travels in Africa 1875–78*, 1890, vol. I, pp. 480–1.

Gessi, Romolo, ed. Felix Gessi, *Seven Years in the Soudan*, 1892, pp. 355–7.

12 Douin Georges, op. cit., vol. III, part 3, pp. 50–2, 62–3, 109–10, 122–4, 128–9, 138–9.

Stanton, Colonel E. A. (ed.), op. cit., p. 19.

13 Ibid., pp. 9–17.

Hill, George Birkbeck (ed.), op. cit., pp. 65–6, 151.

Collins, Robert O., *The Nile*, 2002, p. 12.

Douin, Georges, op. cit., vol. III, part 3, pp. 133–6, 140–3, 155 fn, 201–5.

14 Ibid., pp. 117–18, 125–6, 137, 156, 159, 210–17, 246–52 .

15 Ibid., pp. 156–69 passim, 195.

16 Ibid., pp. 169 –87 passim.

Schweinfurth, Georg (ed.), trans. Mrs R. W. Felkin, *Emin Pasha in Central Africa*, 1888, p. 129.

17 Douin, Georges, op. cit., vol. III, part 3, pp. 190–1, 198, 206–7, 210, 246.

Allen, Bernard M., op. cit., pp. 43–5, 50–2.

Hill, George Birkbeck (ed.), op. cit., pp. 85, 93.

Gordon Mss., op. cit., 41340, 11.7.75.

18 Douin, Georges, op. cit., vol. III, part 3, pp. 161, 202, 210–14, 217–23, 230–8, 242, 246–59, 264–5 fn.

Wallis, C. A., ed. Douglas H. Johnson, *The Upper Nile Province Handbook*, 1995, p. 180 fn.

Hill, George Birkbeck (ed.), op. cit., p. 93.

Stanton, Colonel E. A. (ed.), op. cit., p. 28.

Allen, Bernard M., op. cit., pp. 58–9.

Gordon Mss., op. cit., 51293, 20.9.75.

19 Gray, Richard, *A History of the Southern Sudan 1839–1889*, 1961, pp. 175–7.

Douin, Georges, op. cit., vol. III, part 3, pp. 246–52, 255, 265–6, 629–45.

20 Ibid., pp. 629–72 passim.

F.O. 78/2403, Earl of Derby to Stanton, nos. 91–3 of 3.12.75.
F.O. 78/2405, Stanton to Earl of Derby, no. 135 of 25.11.75.
F.O. 78/3188, Stanton to Earl of Derby, 11.11.75, 14.11.75, 5.12.75; no. 160 of 9.12.75.

21 Douin, Georges, op. cit., vol. III, part 3, pp. 251–2, 268, 270, 289, 335, 687–97.
Gordon Mss., op. cit., 51293, 18.1.76, 12.3.76.

22 Ibid., 8.9.75, 20.9.75, 3.1.76, 13.1.76, 24.1.76, 30.1.76, 3.3.76, 9.3.76.
Douin, Georges, op. cit., vol. III, part 3, pp. 270, 272, 276–7.

23 Ibid., pp. 278, 280–3, 286–8, 290, 297.
Gordon Mss., op. cit., 51293, 24.1.76, 28.1.76, 24.2.76, 13.8.76.

24 Ibid., 2.8.76, 4.11.76.
F.O. 78/2502, Stanton to Earl of Derby, no. 172, 6.5.76.
Douin, Georges, op. cit., vol. III, part 3, pp. 276–8, 284–6, 293–300, 306, 310, 314, 326.

25 Ibid., pp. 276–7, 288–91, 293–6.
Stanton, Colonel E. A. (ed.), op. cit., p. 40.
Gordon Mss., 51293, op. cit., 12.3.76, 27.5.76, 29.7.76, 13.8.76.

26 Ibid., 29.7.76, 2.8.76, 11.8.76, 13.8.76, 18.8.76, 20.8.76, 23.8.76, 9.9.76, 11.9.76, 15.9.76.
Stanton, Colonel, E. A. (ed.), op. cit., p.50.
F.O. 78/2503, Vivian to Earl of Derby, no. 10, 21.10.76.
Douin, Georges, op. cit., vol. III, part 3, pp. 273, 309, 318–21, 328–32.

27 Ibid., pp. 322–5, 326–8, 332–37.
Gordon Mss., op. cit., 51293, 18.8.76, 23.8.76, 22.9.76, 23.9.76, 29.9.76.

28 Douin, Georges, op. cit., vol. III, part 3, pp. 176, 300–1, 322–3, 338–42.
Hochschild, Adam, *King Leopold's Ghost*, 1998, pp. 42–5.
Sanderson, G. N., *England, Europe and the Upper Nile 1882–1899*, 1965, p. 9.

29 Douin, Georges, op. cit., vol. III, part 3, pp. 343–9, 484–5.
Gordon Mss, op. cit., 51293, 19.10.76, 25.10.76, 29.11.76, 2.12.76.
Stanton, Colonel E. A. (ed.), op. cit., pp. 52–3.
Allen, Bernard M., op. cit., pp. 106–7.
Boutros Ghali, Mirrit (ed.), *Mémoires de Nubar Pasha 1825–79*, 1983, pp. 474–5.
Junker, Wilhelm, op. cit., pp. 229, 253.

CHAPTER ELEVEN

1 Elton, Lord, *General Gordon*, 1954, pp. 233–6.
Allen, Bernard M., *Gordon and Sudan*, 1931, pp. 106–7.
FO 78/2504, Vivian to Earl of Derby, no. 60, 26.12.76.
FO 78/2630, Earl of Derby to Vivian, no. 8, 30, 77.

Shukry, Mohammed Fuad, *The Khedive Ismail and Slavery in the Sudan 1863–79*, doctoral thesis, University of Liverpool, 1935, pp. 419–21.
Letters of General Gordon to His Sister, M. A. Gordon, 1888, pp. 136–7 fnn.
British Library, Moffit Collection, Gordon Mss. 51294, 19.3.77, 17.7.77; 51295, 11.7.78.
Hill, George Birkbeck, ed., *Colonel Gordon in Central Africa 1874–79*, fourth edition, 1969, pp. 210–11.
Moore-Harell, Alice, *Gordon and the Sudan, Prologue to the Mahdiyya, 1877–80*, 2001, pp. 89 –90.

2 Hill, George Birkbeck, op. cit., pp. 203–4, 207–8.
Gordon Mss., op. cit., 51294, 27.2.77, 8.3.77, 21.3.77, 23.3.77, 30.3.77.
FO 78/2632, Vivian to Earl of Derby, no. 89, 7.4.77; no. 98, 16.4.77; no. 112, 2.5.77.

3 FO 78/2630, Earl of Derby to Vivian, no. 85, 15.6.77.
FO 78/2633, Vivian to Earl of Derby, no. 159, 3.6.77; no. 183, 19.6.77; no. 232, 24.7.77.
FO 78/2851, Earl of Derby to Vivian, no. 5, 11.1.78.
Gordon Mss., op. cit., 51294, 25.6.77, 23.10.77, 4.11.77, 10.11.77, 22.11.77, 11.12.77–5.1.78 passim.
FO 78/2634, Vivian to Earl of Derby, no. 324, 1.12.77; no. 345, 22.12.77.

4 Gordon Mss., op. cit., 51295, 20.5.78, 19.6.78, 25.7.78, 22.12.78, 19.6.78, 9.1.79, 22.3.79, 12.2.79, 25.4.79, 30.4.79, 9.7.79, 23.8.79, 31.8.79, 2.9.79, 6.9.79, 11.9.79–23.9.79 passim.
Hill, George Birkbeck, ed., op. cit., pp. 410–25.

5 FO 78/2633, Vivian to Earl of Derby, no. 211, 12.7.77.
FO 78/2634, Vivian to Earl of Derby, no. 276, 5.9.77; no. 288, 14.9.77; no. 331, 7.12.77; no. 337, 14.12.77.
FO 78/2853, Vivian to Earl of Derby, no. 16, 23.1.78; no. 17, 25.1.78.
Gordon Mss op. cit., 51295, 25.1.78, 15.2.78, 7.3.78.

6 FO 78/2853, Vivian to Earl of Derby, no. 24, 30.1.78; no. 27, 2.2.78; no. 45, 23.2.78; no. 60, 8.3.78; no. 61, 8.3.78; no. 64, 11.3.78; no. 70, 14.3.78.
Gordon Mss., op. cit., 51295, 16.3.78, 31.3.78, 17.4.78, 18.10.78.
Allen, Bernard M., op. cit., p.133.
Elton, Lord, op. cit., pp. 252–4.
Roberts, Andrew, *Salisbury, Victorian Titan*, 1999, p. 228.
Cromer, Earl of, *Modern Egypt*, 1908, vol. I, chapters 3–8 passim.
Dicey, Edward, *The Story of the Khedivate*, 1902, pp. 162–3, 172–218 passim.
Gray, Richard, *A History of the Southern Sudan 1839–89*, 1961, p. 137.
Owen, Roger, *Lord Cromer*, 2004, pp. 100–5.

Waterfield, Gordon, *Layard of Nineveh*, 1963, pp. 412–17.

7 Gordon Mss., op. cit., 51294, 3.4.77, 9.4.77, 20.4.77, 24.10.77, 6.12.77; 51295, 21.5.78, 26.5.78, 23, 31.3.79.
FO 78/2634, Vivian to the Earl of Derby, no. 345, 22.12.77.
Bredin, G. R. E., 'The Life Story of Yuzbashi Abdallah Adlan', in *Sudan Notes and Records,* vol. XLII, 1961, p. 41.
Hill, Richard, ed., *The Sudan Memoirs of Carl Christian Giegler Pasha 1873–83,* 1984, p. 135.

8 Gordon Mss., op. cit., 51294, 28.9.77, 19.10.77, 23.10.77; 51295, 11.4.78, 16–17.4.78, 12.12.78.
FO 78/2631, Vivian to Earl of Derby, no. 37, 15.2.77.
FO 78/2630, Lord Tenterden to Vivian, letter 31.8.77.
FO 78/2853, Vivian to Lord Tenterden, letter 5.1.78.
Murray, T. Douglas, and White, A. Silva, *Sir Samuel Baker, A Memoir,* 1895, pp. 239, 241.
Sabry, M., *L'Empire Égyptien sous Ismail et L'Ingérence Anglo-Française 1863–1879,* 1933, pp. 423–4.
Moore-Harell, Alice, op. cit., pp. 184–90.

9 Junker, Wilhelm, trans. A. H. Keane, *Travels in Africa During the Years 1875–86,* 1890, vol. I, pp. 174–8.
Gessi, Romolo, ed. Felix Gessi, *Seven Years in the Sudan,* 1892, pp. 180–3.
Gordon Mss., op. cit., 51294, 16.5.77, 7.6.77, 22.11.77; 51295, 28.1.78, 20.4.78, 24.4.78, 3.6.78.

10 Hill, Richard (ed.), op. cit. [Giegler], pp. xxx–i, xxxiv.
Moore-Harell, Alice, op. cit., pp. 95–102.
Gordon Mss., op cit., 51295, 1.7.78, 11.7.78, 15.8.78, 23.9.78, 23–27.10.78, 6.11.78, 24.1.79, 19.2.79, 5.3.79.

11 Gordon Mss., op. cit., 51294, 11.4.77, 23.10.77, 1.11.77, 6.11.77; 51295, 26.2.78, 7.3.78, 23–27.10.78, 7.3.79, 9.3.79, 30.3.79.

12 Gordon Mss., op. cit., 51293, 18.10.75; 51294, 16.5.77; 7.9.77, 26.11.77; 51295, 7.7.78, 8.8.78, 26.8.78, 25.9.78, 27.10.78, 13.11.78, 15.11.78, 27.11.78, 29.1.79, 3.3.79, 4.3.79, 10.3.79, 15.3.79.
Hill, George Birbeck (ed.), op. cit., pp. 398–9.
Werner, Roland; Anderson, William; Wheeler, Andrew, *Day of Devastation, Day of Contentment,* 2000, pp. 173–8, 181–3.
Hill, Richard (ed.), op. cit. [Giegler], p. 139.
Wylde, A. B., '83–'87 in the Soudan, 1888, pp. 124, 129–6.

13 FO 84/ 1370, Elliot to Earl Granville, nos. 12–13, 12.7.73.
FO 84/1371, Stanton to Earl Granville, no.7, 25.4.73; no. 10, 19.5.73; Elliot to Earl Granville, no. 14, 30.10.73.
FO 78/2284, Vivian to Earl Granville, no. 32, 22.8.73.
Shukry, Mohammed Fuad, op. cit., pp. 405–14.

14 Gordon Mss., op. cit., 51294, 28.7.77, 31.7.77, 12.8.77, 7.9.77, 11.9.77, 17.9.77, 27.9.77.

15 Ibid., 27.5.77, 7.6.77, 10.6.77, 15.6.77, 29.6.77, 1.7.77, 2.7.77, 13.7.77, 5–15.8.77, 22.8.77 p.s., 31.8.77, 29.5.79, 31.5.79.
O'Fahey, R. S., 'The Conquest of Darfur 1873-82', in *SNR*, New Series, no. 1, 1997, pp. 66–7.

16 Gordon Mss., op. cit., 51294, 28.7.77, 31.7.77, 30.8.77–17.9.77 passim; 51295, 15.2.78, 3.6.78, 7.7.78, 15.11.78, 30.4.79.
Letters of C. G. Gordon to His Sister, op. cit., p. 147.
Slatin, Rudolf C., Pasha, trans. Major F. R. Wingate, *Fire and Sword in the Sudan*, 1896, pp. 9–13, 57–8.
Gordon to Sir Richard Burton, letter, Berber, 24.10.77 (Bloomsbury Auction Catalogue, 11.11.1999, no. 48).
McLynn, Frank, Burton: *Snow upon the Desert*, 1990, pp. 302–3.
Zaghi, Carlo, *Gordon, Gessi e la Riconquista del Sudan*, 1947, p. 262.
Shukry, Mohammed Fuad, op. cit., p. 440.
Murray, T. Douglas, and White, A. Silva, op. cit., p. 242.
Hill, George Birkbeck (ed.), op. cit., pp. 248–9.

17 Zaghi, Carlo, op. cit., pp. 227–9, 262, 317. The dates do not match with Gordon Mss. 51295.
Gessi, Romolo, op. cit., pp. 175, 180–2.
Gordon Mss., op. cit., 51295, 7.7.78; Misc. Papers, 47609, 16.2.80.
Murray, T. Douglas, and White, A. Silva, op. cit., p. 257.
Junker, Wilhelm, op. cit., pp. 283–5, 505–6, 513–16.
Slatin, Rudolf C., Pasha, op. cit., pp. 13–16.
Sabry, M., op. cit., pp. 529, 533–8.
Wilson, C. T., and Felkin, R.W., *Uganda and the Egyptian Soudan*, 1882, vol. 2, p. 152.

18 Zaghi, Carlo, op. cit., pp. 227–69 passim.
Gessi, Romolo, op. cit., pp. 206, 227–43 passim.
Gordon Mss., op. cit., 51295, 20.11.77, 1.7.79; Misc. Papers, 47609, 16.2.80.

19 Zaghi, Carlo, op. cit., pp. 270–306 passim, 364–68.
Gessi, Romolo, op. cit., pp. 245–71 passim.

20 Zaghi, Carlo, op. cit., pp. 313, 348–53, 380, 384, 396, 414.
Gordon Mss., op. cit., 51295, 24.1.79, 11.4.79, 25.4.79, 12.10.79.
Gessi, Romolo, op. cit., p. 303.
Moore-Harell, Alice, op. cit., p. 233 re Gordon Mss., op. cit., 51303, 24.4.79.

21 Gessi, Romolo, op. cit., pp. 319–23, 329–30.
Zaghi, Carlo, op. cit., pp. 396–404.
Sabry, M., op. cit., p. 546.
Slatin, Rudolf C., Pasha, op. cit., pp. 22–30.

Gordon Mss., op. cit., 51295, 25.4.79, 24.5.79, 21.7.79, 24.7.79, 1.8.79, 12.10.79, 13.10.79.

Wilson, C. T., and Felkin, R. W., op. cit., p. 202.

22 Junker, Wilhelm, op. cit., pp. 249, 253, 284, 490–4, 503, 513.

Gordon Mss., op. cit., 51295, 10.10.77, 23.10.77, 28.1.78, 15.3.78, 31.3.78.

Douin, Georges, *Histoire du Règne du Khédive Ismail,* vol. III, part 3, 1941, p. 348.

Schweinfurth, Georg (ed.), trans. Mrs R. W. Felkin, *Emin Pasha in Central Africa,* 1888, pp. 4, 15, 25–6, 28–31, 49–52, 58–69 passim, 128–9, 136–7.

23 Junker, Wilhelm, op. cit., pp. 373, 417–18, 432, 501.

Zaghi, Carlo, op. cit., pp. 211–13.

Gessi, Romolo, op. cit., pp. 187–200.

24 Gordon Mss., op. cit., 51295, 23.9.78, 25.9.78, 27.11.78, 30.11.78, 17.1.79, 11.4.79, 25.12.79.

Murray, T. Douglas, and White, A. Silva, op. cit., pp. 253–5.

Hill, Richard (ed.), op. cit. [Giegler], p. xxxi.

25 Gray, Richard, op. cit., p. 138.

Schweinfurth, Georg (ed.), op. cit., pp. xv–xvi.

Zaghi, Carlo, op. cit., pp. 405, 424.

26 Gordon Mss., op. cit., 51295, 31.3.79, 17.4.79, 10.5.79, 1.7.79, 2.7.79, 21.7.79, 1.8.78, 19.8.78, 31.8.79, 14.9.78.

Hill, George Birkbeck (ed.), op. cit., p. 427.

Hake, A. Egmont (ed.), *The Journals of Major-Gen. C .G. Gordon C.B. at Kartoum,* 1885, pp. 425, 559.

CHAPTER TWELVE

1 Hill, Richard (ed.), *The Sudan Memoirs of Carl Christian Giegler, 1873–83,* 1984, pp. 149–50, 154, 158, 160–1, 164–5, 174, 184.

FO 78/3553, Malet to Earl Granville, no. 71, 6.3.83, enclosing Stewart, 20.2.83.

British Library, Moffitt Collection, Gordon Mss., 47609, 26.11.80, C. H. Allen of Anti-Slavery Society to Gordon.

Shibeika, Mekki, *British Policy in the Sudan 1882–1902,* 1952, p. 24.

Murray, T. Douglas, and White, A. Silva, *Sir Samuel Baker, a Memoir,* 1895, pp. 227–8.

2 Hill, Richard, *Egypt in the Sudan 1820–1881,* 1966, pp. 149, 154–6.

Hill, Richard, ed., op. cit. [Giegler], pp. 155–6, 161–3.

Paul, A., *The Beja Tribes of the Sudan,* 1954, p. 106.

Stewart, Lieutenant-Colonel J. D. H., *Report on the Soudan 1883;* Egypt, no. 11, 1883, British Command Paper C. 3670, Stewart to Malet, 9.2.83.

Hill, George Birkbeck (ed.), *Colonel Gordon in Central Africa 1874–79*, 1969, pp. 390, 392.

3 Zaghi, Carlo, *Gordon, Gessi e La Riconqista del Sudan 1874–81*, 1947, pp. 405–9, 423–36, 439–43, 459–61, 466–76, 486–7.

Gessi, Romolo, ed. Felix Gessi, *Seven Years in the Soudan*, 1892, pp. 347–58, 359, 364, 366, 380–9, 406, 409, 415, 419, 424–33 passim, 513–15, 516–48 passim.

Emily, Dr J., *Mission Marchand, Journal de Route*, 1913, pp. 55, 64, 111–22.

Junker, Dr Wilhelm, trans. A. H. Keane, *Travels in Africa 1879–83*, vol. 2, 1881, pp. 19–23, 38, 53, 58–64, 70–1, 81, 100–1, 148–9.

Hill, Richard, ed., op. cit. [Giegler], op. cit., pp. 155, 158–63.

Schweinfurth, Georg (ed.), trans. Mrs R. W. Felkin, *Emin Pasha in Central Africa*, 1888, p. 513.

4 Ibid., pp. xxii, 258–9 fn, 269, 408–14 passim, 421–6, 434.

Macro, E., 'Frank Miller Lupton', in *Sudan Notes and Records*, vol. XXVIII, 1947, pp. 50–2.

Gray, Richard, *A History of the Southern Sudan 1839–89*, 1961, pp. 134, 148–50, 156.

Holt, P. M., *The Mahdist State in the Sudan 1881-1898*, 2nd edn, 1970, pp. 76–9.

Santandrea, Father S., 'An Account of the Indri, Togoyo, Feroge etc.', in *SNR*, vol. XXXIV, part 2, 1953, pp. 236–8.

Hill, Richard, ed., op. cit. [Giegler], pp. 200, 202.

5 Slatin, Rudolf C., Pasha, trans. Major F. R. Wingate, *Fire and Sword in the Sudan 1879–95*, 1896, pp. 73, 85, 88, 96, 101–11 passim, 126, 132–4, 137–9.

Ohrwalder, Father Joseph, trans. and abridged Major F. R. Wingate, *Ten Years' Captivity in the Mahdi's Camp 1882–92*, 12th edn, 1895, pp. 1–3, 9.

Hill, Richard (ed.), op. cit. [Giegler], pp. 167–8.

Holt, P.M., op. cit., pp. 49–50, 53–4, 74.

6 Ibid., pp. 45–56 passim.

Slatin, Rudolf C., Pasha, op. cit., pp. 122–32 passim.

Theobald, A. B. *The Mahdiya, A History of the Sudan 1881–99*, 1951, pp. 28–9.

L. W. A. Raven, District Commissioner Kodok, later Kosti, told the author that the posthumous surviving son of the Mahdi, El Sayyid Sir Abdel Rahman, believed his father originally asked permission of the Shilluk to settle on Aba Island; that the Shilluk *jago* (chief) refused (Arabic, *'aba'*); and that the Mahdi ignored the refusal, (letter L. W. A. Raven to John O. Udal, 13.9.1999).

Trimingham, J. Spencer, *Islam in the Sudan*, 1965, p. 94 fn.

El Hasan bin Talal, Prince, *Continuity, Innovation and Change, Selected Essays*, 2001, p. 34.

7 Holt, P. M., op. cit., pp. 53, 58–65, 118–19.
Holt, P. M., 'The Place in History of the Sudanese Mahdia', in *SNR*, vol. XL, 1959, p. 109.
Trimingham, J. Spencer, op. cit., pp. 152–6.
FO 78/3552, Malet to Earl Granville, no. 20, 20.1.83.
Ismail Abdel Qadir el Kordofani, trans. Ha'im Shaked, *The Life of the Sudanese Mahdi*, 1978, pp. 63–5, 73–81.
Hill, Richard, ed., op. cit. [Giegler], pp. 169–73, 175–7.
Slatin, Rudolf C., Pasha, op. cit., pp. 135–9.
Theobald, A. B., op. cit., pp. 30–5.
Shibeika, Mekki, op. cit., pp. 14–15.
Murray, T. Douglas, and White, A. Silva, *Sir Samuel Baker, a Memoir*, 1895, pp. 292–5.

8 Shibeika, Mekki, op. cit., pp. 30–2.
FO 78/3552, Malet to Earl Granville, no. 20, 20.1.83.
Hill, Richard (ed.), op. cit. [Giegler], pp. 170, 173, 178–82, 184, 196.
Murray, T. Douglas, and White, A. Silva, op. cit., pp. 295–6.
Holt, P. M., op. cit., pp. 54–7.
Ismail Abdel Qadir el Kordofani, op. cit., pp. 90–2.

9 Ibid., pp. 93–9.
FO 78/3443, Malet to Earl Granville, no. 796 conf., 6.11.82.
FO 78/3552, Malet to Earl Granville, no. 20, 20.1.83.
Hill, Richard (ed.), op. cit. [Giegler], pp. 182–99, 205–6, 210.
Holt, P. M., op. cit., pp. 57–8, 66–8.
Murray, T. Douglas, and White, A. Silva, op. cit., pp. 296–304.
Shibeika, Mekki, op. cit., pp. 34–40.
Slatin, Rudolf C., Pasha, op. cit., pp. 146–7.

10 Shibeika, Mekki, op. cit., pp. 41–3, 60–7.
Ismail Abdel Qadir el Kordofani, op. cit., pp. 100–18 passim.
Holt, P. M., op. cit., pp. 60–5.
Ohrwalder, Father Joseph, trans. and abridged Major F. R. Wingate, op. cit., pp. 11–14, 60–1, 64–5, 71.
Slatin, Rudolf C., Pasha, op. cit., pp. 141–7, 153, 162–3, 183–207 passim, 321.
FO 78/3443, Malet to Earl Granville, no. 796, conf. 6.11.82.
FO 78/3552, Malet to Earl Granville, no. 20, 20.1.83.
FO 78/3442, Malet to Earl Granville, no. 740, 26.10.82; no. 744, 28.10.82.

11 Cromer, Earl of, *Modern Egypt*, vol. I, 1908, pp. 89–100, 174–345 passim.
Cameron, D. A., *Egypt in the Nineteenth Century*, 1898, p. 264.

Colvin, Sir Auckland, *The Making of Modern Egypt,* 1906, pp. 16, 21–30, 36.

Dicey, Edward, *The Story of the Khedivate,* 1902, pp. 227–33, 250–315 passim, 321, 325–35.

Stewart, Lt-Colonel J. D. H., *Report on the Soudan 1883,* op. cit.

FO 78/3433, Earl Granville to Malet, no. 375, 26.10.82; no. 386, 29.10.82.

FO 78/3442, Malet to Earl Granville, no. 725, 21.10.82.

Granville Papers, Kew Public Record Office, 30/28/166, 13.11.82.

Wright, Patricia, *Conflict on the Nile,* 1972, p. 25.

Lane-Poole, Stanley, *Watson Pasha,* 1919, pp. 121–30.

Chirol, Sir Valentine, *Fifty Years in a Changing World,* 1927, p. 34.

Lyall, Sir Alfred, *The Life of the Marquis of Dufferin and Ava,* 1905, vol. 2, pp. 35, 38.

12 Shibeika, Mekki, op. cit., pp. 42–3, 46–51, 53–4, 56–8.

FO 78/3433, Earl Granville to Malet, no. 368, 23.10.78; no. 387, 30.10.82; no. 393, 2.11.82; no. 402, 4.11.82.

FO 78/3442, Malet to Earl Granville, no. 659, 2.10.82; no. 740, 26.10.82; no. 744, 28.10.82; no. 749, 28.10.82.

FO 78/3444, Malet to Earl Granville, no. 836, 16.11.82.

FO 78/3452, Malet to Earl Granville, no. 581, 4.11.82; no. 590, 8.11.82; no. 603, 15.11.82; no. 615, 10.12.82; no. 621, 18.12.82; no. 625, 20.12.82; no. 626, 22.12.82.

Granville Papers, PRO 30/29/166, 5.12.82, 30.1.83; 30/29/168, 17.11.82.

Stewart, Lt-Colonel J. D. H., *Report on the Soudan 1883,* op. cit.

Hill, Richard (ed.), op. cit. [Giegler], pp. 210, 215–16.

13 FO 78/3452, Malet to Earl Granville, no. 550, 26.10.82; no. 557, 28.10.82; no. 590, 8.11.82.

Hill, Richard (ed.), op. cit. [Giegler], pp. 215–16.

FO 78/3553, Malet to Earl Granville, no. 71, 6.3.83.

FO 78/3562, Malet to Earl Granville, no. 10, 6.3.83; no. 14, 28.4.83.

14 Stewart, Lt-Colonel J. D. H., *Report on the Soudan 1883,* op. cit.

FO 78/3442, Malet to Earl Granville, no. 659, 2.10.82.

FO 78/3553, Malet to Earl Granville, no. 83, 13.3.82; no. 88, 20.3.83.

FO 78/3554, Malet to Earl Granville, no. 154, 14.5.83.

Bjorkelo, Anders, 'The Territorial Unification and Administrative Divisions of Turkish Sudan, 1821–1885', in *SNR,* New Series, vol. 1, 2000, pp. 37–41.

15 Shibeika, Mekki, op. cit., pp. 69–78, 141.

Hill, Richard (ed.), op. cit. [Giegler], pp. 211–18, 222.

Holt, P. M., op. cit., pp. 68–9.

FO 78/3442, Malet to Earl Granville, no. 659, 2.10.82.

FO 78/3443, Malet to Earl Granville, no. 780, 3.11.82; no. 816, 11.11.82.

FO 78/3452, Malet to Earl Granville, no. 626, 22.12.82.

FO 78/3552, Malet to Earl Granville, no. 33, 30.1.83; no. 55, 19.2.83; no. 57, 20.2.83.

FO 78/3553, Malet to Earl Granville, no. 659, 2.10.82; no. 71, 6.3.83 enclosing Stewart 9.2.83; no. 83, 13.3.83 enclosing Stewart 13.2.83.

FO 78/3667, no. 215, Baring to Earl Granville, 20.2.84 enclosing Hicks 13.3.83.

16 Hill, Richard (ed.), op. cit. [Giegler], pp. 212–13.

Slatin, Rudolf C., Pasha, op. cit., pp. 194, 210–23, 233, 244–5, 251–6, 263, 270, 274–5.

Macro, E., op. cit., pp. 52–3.

Junker, Dr Wilhelm, op. cit., vol. III, 1892, p. 357.

Wingate, F. R., *Mahdiism and the Egyptian Soudan*, 1891, pp. 97–9.

Schweitzer, George, *Emin Pasha, His Life and Work*, vol. I, 1898, pp. 147–8.

FO 78/3553, Malet to Earl Granville, no. 88, 20.3.83 enclosing Stewart 28.1.83.

Holt, P. M., op. cit., pp. 74–6.

Schuver, Juan Maria, ed. Wendy James, Gerd Baumann and Douglas H. Johnson, *Travels in North East Africa 1880–1883*, 1996, pp. 227–38, passim.

17 Wingate, F. R., op. cit., p. 74.

Cromer, Earl of, *Modern Egypt*, vol. I, 1908, p. 354.

FO 78/3433, Earl Granville to Malet, no. 387, 30.10.82; no. 402, 4.11.82.

FO 78/3553, Cartwright to Earl Granville, no. 105, 31.3.83.

FO 78/3554, Malet to Earl Granville, no. 177, 24.5.83.

Hill, Richard (ed.), op. cit. [Giegler], pp. 213–15, 219–21.

Shibeika, Mekki, op. cit., pp. 79–84.

18 Ibid., pp. 83–92.

FO 78/3554, Malet to Earl Granville, no. 176, 22.5.83; no. 179, 24.5.83 with memos of Childers and Earl Granville.

FO 78/3555, Malet to Earl Granville, no. 210, 5.6.83 and memos; no. 232, 12.6.83; no. 245, 21.6.83; no. 271, 1.7.83.

FO 78/3562, Malet to Earl Granvile, no. 37, 5.6.83 and memos; no. 92, 18.8.83.

FO 78/3667, Baring to Earl Granville, no. 215, 20.2.84 enclosing Hicks 31.5.83; 1.6.83; 23.7.83; 31.7.83; 3.8.83; 19.8.83.

Lyall, Sir Alfred, *The Life of the Marquis of Dufferin and Ava*, 1905, p. 344.

19 Ali Gulla, 'The Defeat of Hicks Pasha', in *SNR*, vol. XL, 1959, pp. 119–20.

Abbas Bey Hilmi, 'The Diary of Abbas Bey', in *SNR*, vol. XXXII, part 2, pp. 181–96 passim.

FO 78/3555, Malet to Earl Granville, no. 254, 23.6.78; no. 271, 1.7.83.

Shibeika, Mekki, op. cit., p. 106.

Wingate, F. R., op. cit., pp. 84–91, 107.

20 Ismail Abdel Qadir el Kordofani, *The Life of the Sudanese Mahdi, 1888*, trans. Ha'im Shaked, 1978, pp. 119–26, 128–33, 222.

Shibeika, Mekki, op. cit., pp. 165, 180–6, 190–4.

Holt, P. M., op. cit., pp. 71–3, 81–5.

Theobald, A. B., *The Mahdiya, A History of the Sudan 1881–99*, pp. 50–66 passim.

Slatin, Rudolf C., Pasha, op. cit., p. 289.

Paul, A., *A History of The Beja Tribes of the Sudan*, 1954, pp. 3, 21, 106–9.

Paul, A., 'Tawfiq Bey', in *SNR*, vol. xxxv, part 1, 1954, pp. 132–5.

FO 78/3559, Baring to Earl Granville, no. 507, 12.11.83; no. 527, 19.11.83; no. 533, 21.11.83.

FO 78/3560, Baring to Earl Granville, nos. 605–6, 14.12.83; no. 628, 17.12.83; no. 631, 18.12.83.

FO 78/3562, Baring to Earl Granville, no. 139, 29.10.83; no. 148, 12.11.83; no. 160, 18.11.83.

FO 78/3667, Baring to Earl Granville, no. 171, 11.2.84; Stewart's diary, 24.1.84; 29.1.84.

Granville Papers, PRO, 30/29/127, Gladstone to Earl Granville, private, 12.12.83.

CHAPTER THIRTEEN

1 Cromer, Earl of, *Modern Egypt*, 1908, vol. I, p. 366.

Zetland, 2nd Marquess of, *Lord Cromer*, 1932, p. 93.

FO 78/3551, Earl Granville to Baring, no. 279, 15.11.83.

FO 78/3561, Earl Granville to Baring, no. 99, 20.11.83; no. 102, 22.11.83; no. 103, 22.11.83; no. 104, 25.11.83; no. 105, 25.11.83.

FO 78/3562, Baring to Earl Granville, no. 172, 23.11.83; no. 175, 25.11.83.

FO 78/3559, Baring to Earl Granville, no. 542, 23.11.83; no. 547, 24.11.83; no. 553, 26.11.83; no. 560, 26.11.83.

PRO 30/29/133, Lord Wolseley to Marquess of Hartington, 23.11.83.

PRO 30/29/161, Earl Granville to Baring, 6.9.83; Baring to Earl Granville, 9.10.83, 29.10.83.

PRO 30/29/127, Gladstone to Earl Granville, 24.11.83, 12.12.83, 24.12.83.

Shibeika, Mekki, *British Policy in the Sudan 1882–1902*, 1952, pp. 110–19.

2 Cromer, Earl of, op. cit., vol. I, pp. 399–404.

Holt, P. M., *The Mahdist State in the Sudan 1881–1898*, 2nd edn, 1970, p. 85.

Wingate, F. R., *Mahdiism and the Egyptian Sudan*, 1891, p. 107.

FO 78/3560, Baring to Earl Granville, no. 577, 3.12.83; no. 592, 10.12.83.

FO 78/3551, Earl Granville to Baring, no. 321, 13.12.83.

FO 78/3665, Baring to Earl Granville, no. 2, 1.1.84.

PRO 30/29/161, Baring to Earl Granville, private, 10.12.83, 16.12.83, 17.12.83.

PRO 30/29/127, Gladstone to Earl Granville, 12.12.83.

3 FO 78/3551, Earl Granville to Baring, no. 331, 20.12.83.

FO 78/3560, Baring to Earl Granville, no. 636, 20.12.83.

FO 78/3562, Baring to Earl Granville, no. 234, 22.12.83.

FO 78/3662, Earl Granville to Baring, no. 5, 4.1.84.

FO 78/3665, Baring to Earl Granville, no. 2, 1.1.84; no. 7, 1.1.84; no. 11, 2.1.84; no. 21, 6.1.84; no. 27, 8.1.84; no. 35, 9.1.84; no. 46, 11.1.84.

Shibeika, Mekki, op. cit., pp. 125–40 passim.

Bell, Charles F. Moberly, *Life and Letters of C. F. Moberly Bell*, 1927, p. 91.

4 Shibeika, Mekki, op. cit., pp. 136–7, 143–4.

FO 78/3665, Baring to Earl Granville, no. 35, 9.1.84; no. 44, 11.1.84; no. 47, 11.1.84; no. 52, 14.1.84.

PRO 30/29/162, Baring to Earl Granville, private, 14.1.84.

The Times, 14.1.84, p. 11; 15.1.84, p. 9.

5 Allen, Bernard, M., *Gordon and the Sudan*, 1931, pp. 220–4.

Gordon, Sir Henry, *Events in the Life of Charles George Gordon*, 1886, pp. 305–6.

FO 78/3665, Baring to Earl Granville, no. 43, 11.1.84

FO 78/3562, Baring to Earl Granville, no. 198, 2.12.83.

British Library, Moffitt Collection, Gordon Mss., 51298, 17.1.84, 10 a.m.

Fitzmaurice, Lord Edmond, *Life of Lord Granville*, vol. II, 1905, p. 381.

6 FO 78/3662, Earl Granville to Baring, no. 31B, 15.1.84.

FO 78/3665, Baring to Earl Granville, no. 58, 16.1.84.

Cromer, Earl of, op. cit., vol. I, p. 426.

Gordon, Sir Henry, op. cit., p. 319.

Allen, Bernard, M., op. cit., p. 224 fn.

Watson, Sir Charles M., *The Life of Major-General Sir Charles William Wilson*, 1909, pp. 259–60.

Wood, Sir Evelyn, *From Midshipman to Field Marshal*, 2nd edn., vol. II, 1906, pp. 161–4.

Owen, Roger, *Lord Cromer*, Oxford, 2004, pp. 191–2.

Hill, Richard, *A Biographical Dictionary of the Sudan*, 1967, pp. 13–14.

Wingate, F. R., *Mahdiism and the Egyptian Soudan*, 1891, p. 108.

Dicey, Edward, *The Story of the Khedivate*, 1902, p. 345.

PRO 30/29/161, Baring to Earl Granville, private, 21.1.84.

7 Allen, Bernard, M., op. cit., pp. 225–35.

Gordon Mss., Moffitt Collection, op. cit., 51298, 17.1.84; 18.1.84; 19.1.84.

FO 78/3662, Earl Granville to Baring, no. 28, 14.1.84.

Owen, Roger, op. cit., pp. 193–5.

8 FO 78/3662, Earl Granville to Baring, no. 40, 18.1.84.

FO 78/3665, Baring to Earl Granville, no. 60, 17.1.84; no. 66, 18.1.84; nos. 76 and 79, 19.1.84.

FO 78/3685, Baring to Earl Granville, no. 54, 19.1.84.

9 Gordon Mss., Moffitt Collection, op. cit., 51301, Colonel Watson's Report, January 1884, 19.1.84; 25.1.84; 26.1.84.

Gordon Mss., Bell Collection (British Library), 52408, Colonel Stewart's Diary, 18.1.84–26.1.84; 13.2.84.

Wood, Sir Evelyn, op. cit., p.164.

Gordon, Sir Henry, op. cit., pp. 337–9.

Hake, A. Egmont (ed.), *The Journals of Major-General C. G. Gordon at Kartoum*, 1885, pp. 309, 552.

Wingate, F. R., *Private Diaries*, Durham University Library Sudan Archive, 17 –18.1.84.

FO 78/3685, Baring to Earl Granville, no. 76, 1.2.84.

Owen, Roger, op. cit., pp. 195-7.

10 Gordon Mss., Bell Collection, op. cit., 52408, 26.1.84–17.2.84 passim.

Gordon Mss., Moffitt Collection, op. cit., 51301, 1.2.84.

Pollock, John, *Gordon, The Man Behind the Legend*, 1993, pp. 280–4.

Murray, T. Douglas, and White, A. Silva, *Sir Samuel Baker: A Memoir*, 1895, p. 330 fn.

Holt, P. M., op. cit., pp. 92–5.

FO 78/3683, Earl Granville to Baring, no. 58, 4.2.84.

FO 78/3685, Baring to Earl Granville, no. 81, 5.2.84; no. 100, 9.2.84; no. 117, 13.2.84.

FO 78/3744, Gordon to Baring, no. 40, 20.2.84.

11 Gordon Mss., Bell Collection, op. cit., 52408, 17.2.84–23.2.84.

Gordon Mss., Moffitt Collection, op. cit., 51301, 22.2.84; 51300, 29.11.86; 512981, 15.3.84.

Allen, Bernard, M., op. cit., pp. 272–304 passim, 310–15, 341 fn.

Gordon, Sir Henry, op. cit., pp. 352–4.

Zetland, 2nd Marquess of, op. cit., pp. 115–17.

Owen, Roger, op. cit., pp. 197–202.

Cromer, Earl of, op. cit., vol. 1, pp. 488–558 passim.

Lyall, Sir Alfred, *The Life of the Marquis of Dufferin and Ava*, vol. II, 1905, pp. 57–8.

FO 78/3662, Earl Granville to Baring, no. 179, 22.3.84; no. 182, 25.3.84; no.184, 26.3.84; no. 191, 28.3.84.

FO 78/3669, Baring to Earl Granville, no. 319, 17.3.84; no. 323, 17.3.84; no. 340, 22.3.84; no. 345, 22.3.84; no. 347, 24.3.84; no. 350, 24.3.84; no. 362, 26.3.84.

FO 78/3685, Baring to Earl Granville, no. 177, 28.2.84; no. 155, 19.2.84; no. 192, 4.3.84; no. 203, 8.3.84; no. 213, 13.3.84; no. 217, 14.3.84.

FO 78/3744, Gordon and Stewart to Nubar and Baring, no. 95, 27.2.84; no. 104, 29.2.84; no. 36, 5.3.84; no. 52, 7.3.84.

12 Ismail Abdel Qadir el Kordofani, *The Life of the Sudanese Mahdi*, 1888, trans. Ha'im Shaked, 1978, pp. 127, 160–5, 176–9.

Holt, P. M., op. cit., pp. 100–1.

Allen, Bernard M., op. cit., pp. 316–20.

Hake, A. Egmont (ed.), op. cit., pp. 27, 62.

Ohrwalder, Father Joseph, trans. Major F. R. Wingate, *Ten Years' Captivity in the Mahdi's Camp*, 12th edn, 1895, pp. 140–2.

FO 78/3744, Gordon to Nubar and Baring, no. 11, 1.3.84.

13 Slatin, Rudolf C., Pasha, trans. Major F. R. Wingate, *Fire and Sword in the Sudan 1879–1895*, 1896, pp. 271, 275, 376, 411.

Macro, E., 'Frank Miller Lupton', in *Sudan Notes and Records*, vol. XXVIII, 1947, pp. 53–60.

Wingate, F. R., op. cit., pp. 137–8.

FO 78/3560, Baring to Earl Granville, no. 592, 10.12.83.

FO 78/3665, Baring to Earl Granville, no. 79, 19.1.84.

Holt, P. M., op. cit., pp. 78–80, 135.

Junker, Dr Wilhelm, trans. A. H. Keane, *Travels in Africa 1882–6*, vol. III, 1892, pp. 357, 365, 379, 381–3, 389.

14 Junker, Dr Wilhelm, op. cit., pp. 299–300, 363, 366–7, 395–6, 400, 419–21, 425–6.

Johnson, Douglas H., 'Prophecy and Mahdism in the Upper Nile', in *British Journal of Middle Eastern Studies*, 1993, vol. 20, no. 1, p. 48.

Schweitzer, Georg, *Emin Pasha: His Life and Work*, vol. I, 1898, pp. 147–8, 165–7, 171.

Gray, Richard, *A History of the Southern Sudan 1839–1889*, 1961, pp. 155–60 passim.

Wingate, F. R., op. cit., pp. 103–4.

Collins, Robert O., *The Southern Sudan, 1883–98: A Struggle for Control*, 1962, p. 32.

Ryle, John, *Warriors of the White Nile: The Dinka*, 1982, pp. 20, 28.

15 Schweinfurth, Georg (ed.), trans. Mrs R. W. Felkin, *Emin Pasha in Central Africa*, 1888, pp. 425–6, 463–71, 484, 487–8, 490, 495, 505, 510–11.
Junker, Wilhelm, op. cit., pp. 378, 505, 509, 515–17.
Slatin, Rudolf C., Pasha, op. cit., pp. 411–14.
Wingate, F. R., op. cit., pp. 260–2.
FO 78/3665, Baring to Earl Granville, no. 79, 19.1.84.
Holt, P. M., op. cit., pp. 153, 216.
Collins, Robert O., op. cit., pp. 50–3.
16 FO 78/3665, Baring to Earl Granville, no. 47, 11.1.84; no. 52, 14.1.84.
Allen, Bernard M., op. cit., pp. 265–7, 270–1, 294.
Shibeika, Mekki, op. cit., pp. 189–212 passim.
Holt, P. M., op. cit., pp. 85–7.
Moberly-Bell, E. H. C., op. cit., pp. 93, 98–9.
Ismail Abdel Qadir el Kordofani, op. cit., pp. 134–8, 143–5.
Cromer, Earl of, op. cit., vol. I, pp. 410, 536–47; vol. II, pp. 52–4.
Paul, A., *The Beja Tribes of the Sudan,* 1954, pp. 110–12.
Sanderson, G. N., *England, Europe and the Upper Nile,* 1965, pp. 19–22.
Paul, A., 'Tewfiq Bey', in *SNR,* vol. XXXV, part 1, 1954, pp. 132–7.
17 FO 78/3665, Baring to Earl Granville, no. 66, 18.1.84; no. 81, 19.1.84.
FO 78/3685, Baring to Earl Granville, no. 199, 6.3.84.
FO 78/3662, Baring to Earl Granville, no. 193, 29.3.84.
Ismail Abdel Qadir el Kordofani, op. cit., pp. 139–41, 149–51.
Holt, P. M., op. cit., pp. 166–9.
Hake, A. Egmont, op. cit., pp. 214, 219, 517–18.
Zewde, Bahru, *A History of Modern Ethiopia 1855–1974,* 1991, pp. 54–5.
Matthew, David, *Ethiopia, The Study of a Polity 1540–1935,* 1947, pp. 215–16.
Wingate, F. R., op. cit., pp. 152, 244–52.
Cromer, Earl of, op. cit., vol. II, pp. 56–8.
Sanderson, G. N., 'Conflict and Cooperation between Ethiopia and the Mahdist State, 1884–1898', in *SNR,* vol. L, 1969, p. 22.
Bredin, G. R. F., 'The Life-Story of Yuzbashi Abdallah Adlan', in *SNR,* vol. XLII, 1961, pp. 41–3.
18 Ismail Abdel Qadir el Kordofani, op. cit., pp. 155–7, 174–5.
Holt, P. M., op. cit., pp. 98–9, 101–2.
Allen, Bernard, op. cit., pp. 328–30, 365–9, 373–4, 413–14, 450–1.
Wingate, F. R., op. cit., pp. 122–8.
Ohrwalder, Father Joseph, op. cit., p. 74.
Slatin, Rudolf C., Pasha, op. cit., p. 303.
FO 78/3671, Egerton to Earl Granville, no. 459, 23.4.84.
FO 78/3672, Egerton to Earl Granville, no. 505, 10.5.84.
FO 78/3676, Egerton to Earl Granville, no. 742, 27.7.84.

FO 78/3678, Baring to Earl Granville, no. 871, 10.9.84.

Shibeika, Mekki, op. cit., pp. 259–73 passim.

Gordon, M. A., *The Letters of General Gordon to His Sister*, 1888, p. 383.

Maurice, Sir F., and Arthur, Sir George, *Life of Lord Wolseley*, 1924, pp. 194–5.

19 Ismail Abdel Qadir el Kordofani, op. cit., pp. 159, 165–72, 175–82.

Holt, P. M., op. cit., pp. 92–6, 99–104.

Allen, Bernard, op. cit., pp. 277–8, 321, 357, 363, 430–2, 450–5.

Gordon, Sir Henry, op. cit., pp. 386–7.

Watson, Colonel Sir Charles M., op. cit., pp. vii, 267–9, 282–6, 294–9, 313–17.

Theobald, A. B., *The Mahdiya*, 1951, pp. 109, 113, 119–21.

Gordon Mss., Moffitt Collection op. cit., 51301, p. 183, 3.11.87.

Bedri, Babikr, trans. Bedri, Yousef and Scott, George, *Memoirs...*, vol. I, 1969, pp. 28–30.

Ohrwalder, Father Joseph, op. cit., pp. 154–62.

Wingate, F. R., op. cit., pp. 158–72 passim.

Hake, A. Egmont (ed.), op. cit., pp. 224, 307–8, 536.

20 Ismail Abdel Qadir el Kordofani, op. cit., pp. 186–8, 188–91, 191–6.

Shibeika, Mekki, op. cit., pp. 301–8.

Holt, P. M., op. cit., pp. 124, 141–3, 166, 186-7.

Theobald, A. B., op. cit., pp. 124–34.

Hake, A. Egmont (ed.), op. cit., pp. 121–3.

Paul, A., *A History of the Beja Tribes of the Sudan*, 1954, pp. 113–14.

CHAPTER FOURTEEN

1 Holt, P. M., 'The Archives of the Mahdia' in *Sudan Notes and Records*, vol. XXXVI, part 1, June 1955, pp. 71–80.

Holt, P. M., *The Mahdist State in the Sudan 1881–98*, 2nd edn., 1970, pp. 105–32 passim, 210.

Trimingham, J. Spencer, *Islam in the Sudan*, 1965, pp. 155–6.

FO 78/3669, Baring to Earl Granville, no. 319, 17.3.84.

Mohammed Omer Beshir, 'Abdel Rahman Ibn Hussein and his book, "History of the Mahdi"', in *SNR*, vol. XLIV, 1963, pp. 136–9.

2 Holt, P. M., op. cit. pp. 113, 122–4, 133–40.

3 Ibid., pp. 141–6, 175–9.

Slatin, Rudolf C., Pasha, *Fire and Sword in the Sudan*, 1896, pp. 386, 394–9.

4 Ohrwalder, Father Joseph, *Ten Years of Captivity in the Mahdi's Camp 1882–92*, 12th edn, 1895, pp. 2, 62, 73, 198–9, 206, 219, 249–52.

Holt, P. M., op. cit., pp. 147–55.

Slatin, Rudolf C., Pasha, op. cit., pp. 411–17.

5 Trimingham, J. Spencer, op. cit., p. 153.

Holt, P. M., op. cit., pp. 155–65.

Ohrwalder, Father Joseph, op. cit., pp. 232, 252–6.

Slatin, Rudolf C., Pasha, op. cit., pp. 427–8, 442–4.

6 Holt, P. M., op. cit., pp. 152, 169–74.

Theobald, A. B., *The Mahdiya,* 1951, pp. 146–7.

Zewde, Bahru, *A History of Modern Ethiopia 1855–1974,* 1991, p. 59.

Wingate, F. R. *Mahdiism and the Egyptian Sudan,* 1891, pp. 369–72.

Sanderson, G. N., 'Conflict and Cooperation between Ethiopia and the Mahdist State, 1884–1898', in *SNR,* vol. L, 1969, pp. 19–25, 27–34.

Slatin, Rudolf C., Pasha, op. cit., pp. 422–7.

Ohrwalder, Father Joseph, op. cit., pp. 258–63, 268–9.

7 Wingate, F. R., op. cit., pp. 269–70, 345, 406, 413, 422, 432.

Holt, P. M., op. cit., pp. 175–83, 195.

Theobald, A. B., op. cit., pp 158–64.

Slatin, Rudolf C., Pasha, op. cit., pp. 451–3.

Ohrwalder, Father Joseph, op. cit., pp. 277–88, 330–6.

Bedri, Babikr, trans. Yousef Bedri and George Scott, *Memoirs,* vol. I, 1969, pp. 42–4, 58, 73.

8 Sanderson, G. N., op. cit., pp. 26–8.

Paul, A., *A History of the Beja Tribes of the Sudan,* 1954, pp. 114–17.

Ohrwalder, Father Joseph, op. cit., pp. 289–90.

Slatin, Rudolf C., Pasha, op. cit., pp. 433, 473–4.

Holt, P. M., op. cit., pp. 186–92.

Magnus, Philip, *Kitchener, Portrait of an Imperialist,* 1958, pp. 70–3.

Theobald, A. B., op. cit., pp. 165–9.

Holt, P. M., 'The Archives of the Mahdia', op. cit., p. 72.

Wingate, F. R., op. cit., pp. 297, 353.

9 Ibid., pp. 326–8, 549.

Holt, P. M., *The Mahdist State in the Sudan,* op. cit., pp. 213, 216–22.

Ohrwalder, Father Joseph, op. cit., pp. 292–6.

Perham, Margery, *Lugard, The Years of Adventure 1858–98,* 1956, pp. 275–6.

Gray, Richard, *A History of the Southern Sudan 1839–89,* 1961, pp. 162–3.

Collins, Robert O., *The Southern Sudan 1883–98: A Struggle for Control,* 1962, pp. 63–91 passim, 111–14.

White, Stanhope, *Lost Empire on the Nile,* 1969, pp. 235–58 passim.

Gleichen, Lt-Colonel Count A. E. W. (ed.), *The Anglo-Egyptian Sudan,* vol. I, 1905, pp. 259–61.

Beaton, A. C., 'A Chapter in Bari History', *SNR*, vol. XVII, part 2, 1934, p. 181.

10 Holt, P. M., *The Mahdist State in the Sudan*, op. cit., pp. 193, 209.

Sanderson, G. N., *England, Europe and the Upper Nile, 1882–1899*, 1965, p. 42.

Frost, John Warner, 'A History of the Shilluk of the Southern Sudan', unpublished doctoral thesis, University of California, Santa Barbara, 1974, pp. 234–7.

Kwawang, K. G. A., 'Government and Community in a Modern State: A Case Study of the Shilluk and their Neighbours', unpublished doctoral thesis, Wolfson College, Oxford, 1982, pp. 223–6.

Pumphrey, M. E. C., 'The Shilluk Tribe', in *SNR*, vol. XXIV, 1941, pp. 4–5.

Johnson, Douglas, H., 'Prophecy and Mahdism in the Upper Nile', in *British Journal of Middle Eastern Studies*, vol. 20, no. 1, 1993, p. 54.

Collins, Robert O., op. cit., pp. 111–12.

Slatin, Rudolf C., Pasha, op. cit., pp. 471–2.

Ohrwalder, Father Joseph, op. cit., p. 308.

11 Ibid., pp. 228–33, 254–6, 264, 337–43, 379.

Slatin, Rudolf C., Pasha, op. cit., pp. 457–60, 475, 505–6.

Holt, P. M., op. cit., pp. 121, 146, 193–5, 199, 207–10, 257, 261–3.

Theobald, A. B., op. cit., pp. 175, 181–3, 187.

Holt, P. M., 'The Archives of the Mahdiya', in *SNR*, vol. XXXVI, part 1, pp. 75–7.

12 Holt, P. M., *The Mahdist State in the Sudan 1881–98*, 2nd edn, op. cit., pp. 188–9, 195–203, 209–10.

Slatin, Rudolf C., Pasha, op. cit., pp. 473, 475–83, 487, 500–2, 574–5.

Ohrwalder, Father Joseph, op. cit., pp. 287–8, 389, 399–405, 417.

Rosignoli, Father C., ed. and trans. F. Rehfisch, 'Omdurman during the Mahdiyya', in *SNR*, vol. XLVIII, p. 40.

Theobald, A. B., op. cit., pp. 174–6.

Collins, Robert O., op. cit., p. 111.

13 Theobald, A. B., op. cit., p. 176.

Holt, P. M., op. cit., pp. 212–15.

Slatin, Rudolf C., Pasha, op. cit., pp. 496, 502–9, 537.

14 Ohrwalder, Father Joseph, op. cit., p. 384.

Collins, Robert O., op. cit., pp. 90–1, 100–10, 115–20, 125–35 passim, 156–8.

Holt, P. M., op. cit., pp. 216–21.

Sanderson, G. N., op. cit., 1965, p. 106.

15 Collins, Robert O., op. cit., pp. 141–55 passim.

Santandrea, Father S., 'The Belgians in the Western Bahr el Ghazal', in *SNR*, vol. XXXVI, part 2, 1955, pp. 188–91.

Slatin, Rudolf C., Pasha, op. cit., pp. 509–11, 537–8, 628–9.

Holt, P. M., op. cit., pp. 221–2.
16 Theobald, A. B., op. cit., pp. 177–80.
Slatin, Rudolf C., Pasha, op. cit., pp. 535–7.
Holt, P. M., op. cit., pp. 207–9, 244–66 passim.
Collins, Robert O., op. cit., p. 158.

CHAPTER FIFTEEN

1 Sanderson, G. N., *England, Europe and the Upper Nile 1882–1899*, 1965, pp. 79–80, 242–6.
Shibeika, Mekki, *British Policy in the Sudan 1882–1902*, 1952, pp. 322–3, 327–31, 352–5.
Sanderson, G. N., 'Conflict and Cooperation between Ethiopia and the Mahdist State', in *Sudan Notes and Records*, vol. I, pp. 30–3.

2 Holt, P. M., *The Mahdist State in the Sudan*, 2nd ed., 1970, pp. 230–1.
Sanderson, G. N., *England, Europe and the Upper Nile*, op. cit., p. 252.
Shibeika, Mekki, op. cit., pp. 371–2, 376.
Holt, P. M., 'The Archives of the Mahdia', in *SNR*, vol. XXXVI, part 1, 1955, p. 71.
Theobald, A. B., *The Mahdiya*, 1951, pp. 204–7.
Churchill, Winston, *The River War*, 1899 (3rd ed., 1933), pp. 142–6, 154–61.

3 Ibid., pp. 162–200 passim.
Theobald, A. B., op. cit., pp 212–4.
Holt, P. M., *The Mahdist State in the Sudan*, op. cit., pp. 231–8.
Shibeika, Mekki, op. cit., pp. 373–81.
Magnus, Philip, *Kitchener, Portrait of an Imperialist*, 1958, pp. 108, 115.

4 Holt, P. M., op. cit., pp. 235–8.
Shibeika, Mekki, op. cit., pp. 381–9.
Theobald, A. B., op. cit., pp. 220–1.
Magnus, Philip, op. cit., pp. 115–16, 121.
Sanderson, G. N., 'Conflict and Cooperation ...', op. cit., pp. 32–40 passim.

5 Collins, Robert O., *The Southern Sudan 1883–98: A Struggle for Control*, 1962, pp. 156–75 passim.
Sanderson, G. N., *England, Europe and the Upper Nile*, op. cit., pp. 263, 306–7.
Holt, P. M., op. cit., pp. 239–43.
Theobald, A. B., op. cit., pp. 222–8, 234–6, 256–7.
Steevens, G. W., *With Kitchener to Khartoum*, 1898, pp. 282–3.
Holt, P. M., 'The Archives of the Mahdia', op. cit., pp. 72–3.
Bredin, G. R. F., 'The Life Story of Yuzbashi Abdallah Adlan', in *SNR*, vol. XLII, 1961, pp. 50–1.

6 Emily, Dr J., *Mission Marchand, Journal de Route*, 1913, pp. 9, 20–1, 27–8, 63–5, 152–3, 156–60, 167–71, 175–6.
Sanderson, G. N., op. cit., pp. 294–6.
Baratier, A. E. A., *Souvenirs de la Mission Marchand*, vol. 2, *Vers le Nil*, 1925, 14.12.97–27.3.98; vol. 3, *Fachoda*, 1941, 16.5.98–11.12.98 passim.
Bates, Darrell, *The Fashoda Incident of 1898, Encounters on the Nile*, 1984, pp. 111–24 passim.
7 Magnus, Philip, op. cit., pp. 112, 138–41.
Sanderson, G. N., op. cit., pp. 332–9, 369–71.
Baratier, A. E. A., op. cit., vol. 3, 16.9.98–10.10.98.
Emily, Dr. J., op. cit., pp. 177–93, 198–9, 203–4, 227, 359.
Wingate, Ronald, *Wingate of the Sudan*, 1955, pp. 117–21.
Jackson, Sir H. W., 'Fashoda, 1898', in *SNR*, vol. III, 1920, pp. 4–7.
Keown-Boyd, Henry, *A Good Dusting*, 1986, pp. 212–43 passim.
Churchill, Winston, op. cit., pp. 306–7, 314–23.
Bates, Darrell, op. cit., pp. 125–76 passim.
Gleichen, Lt-Colonel Count A. E. W., ed., *The Anglo-Egyptian Sudan*, vol. I, 1905, pp. 266, 283–5.
Boyle, Clara, *Boyle of Cairo*, 1965, pp. 76–8.
Daly, M. W. *Empire on the Nile*, 1986, pp. 73, 136–7.
8 Theobald, A. B., op. cit., 236–7, 249–56.
Holt, P. M., op. cit., pp. 242–3.
Gleichen, A. E. W., op. cit., pp. 267–8.
Wingate, Ronald, op. cit., pp. 125–7.
Magnus, Philip, op. cit., pp. 152–3.
Arthur, Sir George, *Life of Lord Kitchener*, 1920, vol. i, pp. 260–3.
Hill, Richard, *Slatin Pasha*, 1965, pp. 68–9.
Mohammed Omar Beshir, 'Abdel Rahman Ibn Hussein el Jabri and His Book "History of the Mahdi"', in *SNR*, XLIV, 1963, p. 138.
Churchill, Winston Spencer, *The River War*, vol. 2, 1899, vol. 2, pp. 212–13.

CHAPTER SIXTEEN

1 Vatikiotis, P. J., *The History of Egypt*, 2nd ed., 1980, pp. 42–5.
Lytton Bulwer, Sir Henry, *Life of Viscount Palmerston*, vol. II, 1871, p. 145, quoting Palmerston to Sir William Temple 21.3.33.
2 Douin, Georges, *Histoire du Règne du Khédive Ismail*, vol. III, part 3, 1941, pp. 340–1.
Sanderson, G. N., *England, Europe and the Upper Nile, 1882–1899*, 1965, pp. 10–11.
Hallett, Robin, *Africa since 1875*, 1974, pp. 129–30, 430–1.

Hochschild, Adam, *King Leopold's Ghost*, 1999, pp. 42–6.

3 Sanderson, G. N., op. cit., pp. 21–3, 41, 48, 115–16.
Miller, Charles, *The Lunatic Express*, 1971, pp. 157–8.
Colvin, Sir Auckland, *The Making of Modern Egypt*, 1906, pp. 128–30, 143–58 passim.
Dicey, Edward, *The Story of the Khedivate*, 1902, pp. 406–18 passim.
Cecil, Lady Gwendolen, *Life of Robert, Marquis of Salisbury*, vol. IV, *1887–1892*, 1932, pp. 138–9.
Milner, A., *England in Egypt*, 11th edn., 1904, pp. 117–24.

4 Pakenham, Thomas, *The Scramble for Africa*, 1991, pp. 143–63 passim.
Sanderson, G. N., op. cit., pp. 117, 123.

5 Pollock, John, *Gordon, the Man Behind the Legend*, 1993, pp. 175–6, 182, 206, 263–4.
Allen, Bernard M., *Gordon and the Sudan*, 1931, pp. 211–12, 308, 446–9.
Pakenham, Thomas, op. cit., pp. 316–35 passim.
Miller, Charles, op. cit., pp. 182–9.
FO 84/1775, Marquis of Salisbury on Consul Holmwood to Earl of Iddesleigh, no. 173,23.9.86.
Sanderson, G. N., op. cit., pp. 37–40, 89–90.
Gray, Richard, *A History of the Southern Sudan*, 1961, pp. 197–203.
Boulger, Demetrius C., *Life of Gordon*, 1896, vol. II, pp. 92–3.
Hochschild, Adam, op. cit., pp. 108–12, 119–21, 162–4, 177–81.

6 Sanderson, G. N., op. cit., pp. 90–7, 110, 128–9.
Collins, Robert O., *The Southern Sudan 1883–98: A Struggle for Control*, 1962, pp. 141–55.

7 Collins, Robert O., *Land Beyond the Rivers: The Southern Sudan, 1898–1918*, p. 222.
Sanderson, G. N., op. cit., pp. 94–100, 112–13, 138–9, 162–87 passim.

8 Ibid., pp. 24–5.
Pakenham, Thomas, op. cit., pp. 253–4, 332–4, 444–5.
Miller, Charles, op. cit., pp. 153–70 passim.
Hallett, Robin, op. cit., pp. 433, 564–5.

9 Perham, Margery, *Lugard, The Years of Adventure 1858–1898*, 1956, pp. 447–56.
Sanderson, G. N., op. cit., pp. 34, 44–5, 52–63.
Pakenham, Thomas, op. cit., pp. 351–7, 413–15.
Miller, Charles, op. cit., pp. 189–201 passim, 209–16.
Gale, H. P., *Uganda and the Mill Hill Fathers*, 1959, pp. 48–56.

10 Miller, Charles, op. cit., pp. 257–86 passim.
Pakenham, Thomas, op. cit., pp. 431–3.
Gale, H. P., op. cit., pp. 59–61, 73–8.

11 Sanderson, G. N., op. cit., pp. 34, 41, 67, 152–3.

Mathew, David, *Ethiopia, the Study of a Polity 1540–1935*, 1947, pp. 215–23.

Zewde, Bahru, *A History of Modern Ethiopia 1855–1974*, 1991, pp. 75–6.

Pakenham, Thomas, op. cit., pp. 471–3.

12 Sanderson, G.N., op. cit., pp. 70–87 passim, 156.

Shibeika, Mekki, *British Policy in the Sudan 1882–1902*, 1952, pp. 319–32 passim.

13 Pakenham, Thomas, op. cit., pp. 473–4, 477–8, 484–6.

Mathew, David, op. cit., pp. 230–4.

14 Hallett, Robin, op. cit., p.130.

Sanderson, G. N., op. cit., pp. 242–51.

Shibeika, Mekki, op. cit., pp. 351–63.

15 Sanderson, G. N., op. cit., pp. 118–24, 128–33.

Stengers, Jean, 'Aux Origines de Fachoda: L'Expédition Monteil', in *Revue Belge de Philosophie et d'Histoire*, vol. 36, 1958, pp. 442–3.

Rouard de Card, E., *Les Territoires Africains et Les Conventions Franco-Anglaises*, 1901, pp. 121–2.

16 Brown, Roger Glenn, *Fashoda Reconsidered*, 1969, pp. 18–27.

Stengers, Jean, op. cit., pp. 444–9.

Cocheris, Jules, *Situation Internationale de l' Egypte et du Soudan*, 1903, pp. 425–31.

Sanderson, G. N., op. cit., pp. 144–51, 162–4.

Documents Diplomatiques Français 1871–1914, first series, 1929, vol. XI, no. 65, 7.3.94 fn 1; no. 191, Delcassé to Monteil 13.7.94.

17 Sanderson, G. N., op. cit., pp. 144, 152–4, 206, 213, 239, 293.

Maistre, Casimir, 'Le Président Carnot el Le Plan Français d'Action sur Le Nil en 1893', in *Bulletin du Comité de l'Afrique Français*, March 1932, pp. 156–7.

Cocheris, Jules, op. cit., pp. 414, 454–5.

Grey of Fallodon, Viscount, *Twenty-Five Years 1892–1916*, 1925, vol. I, pp. 19–21.

Taylor, A. J. P., 'Prelude to Fashoda: The Question of the Upper Nile 1894–5, in *The English Historical Review*, vol. LXV, no. 254, January 1950, pp. 78–9.

FO 78/4893, Marquess of Salisbury to Marquess of Dufferin, no. 30, 12.3.96.

Hanotaux, G., *Le Partage d'Afrique: Fachoda*, 1909, pp. 106, 108.

FO 27/3336, Marquess of Salisbury to Monson, no. 406, 9.12.97.

18 Brown, Roger Glenn, op. cit., pp. 36–40.

D.D.F. 1871-1914, op. cit., vol. XII, no. 312, Guieysse to Liotard, 24.2.96; no. 411, Lebon to Liotard, 23.6.96.

Journal Officiel 1895, Débats parlementaires, Sénat, pp. 388ff.

Delbeque, J., *Vie du Général Marchand*, 1936, pp. 63, 76–8.

19 *D.D.F. 1871-1914*, op. cit., vol. XIII, no. 365, Liotard-Lebon to Hanotaux, 22.11.97.

Bates, Darrell, *The Fashoda Incident of 1898, Encounter on the Nile*, 1984, pp. 50–71, 84–95 passim.

Emily, Dr J., *Mission Marchand, Journal de Route*, 1913, pp. 14–88 passim.

Baratier, A. E. A., *Souvenirs de la Mission Marchand*: vol. 2, *Vers Le Nil*, 1925, pp. 72–95 passim; vol. 3, *Fachoda*, 1941, 8.7.98, 10.7.98.

Brown, Roger Glenn, op. cit., pp. 46–51.

Gifford, Prosser, and Louis, William Roger, *France and Britain in Africa*, 1971, pp. 313, 315, 317–18, 321–3.

Sanderson, G. N., op. cit., pp. 255–60, 285–9, 293–6.

20 Ibid., pp. 254–6.

Baratier, A. E. A., op. cit., vol. 2, *Vers le Nil*, 14.12.97, 26.3.98.

D.D.F., Affaires du Haut Nil et du Bahr el Ghazal 1897–8, Yellow Book, 1898, no. 5n.

D.D.F. 1871–1914, op. cit., vol. XIV, no. 258, 18.7.98.

Faure, Félix, 'Fachoda (1898)', in *Revue d' Histoire Diplomatique*, vol. LXIX, Jan– Mar 1955, p. 34.

Hanotaux, G., op. cit., p. 122.

Tignor, Robert L., *Modernisation and British Colonial Rule in Egypt 188–1914*, 1966, p. 268, quoting Mudhakkirat Khidiri, Al Misri, May 1951.

21 Sanderson, G. N., op. cit., pp. 265–8, 332–3, 337–54 passim.

Shibeika, Mekki, op. cit., pp. 392–403, passim.

Magnus, Philip, *Kitchener, Portrait of an Imperialist*, 1958, pp. 138–40.

Bates, Darrell, op. cit., pp. 160–2.

D.D.F. 1897–8, op. cit., Delcassé to Geoffray, no. 12, 27.9.98; no. 13, 28.9.98.

D.D.F. 1871–1914, vol. XIV, no. 246, 4.7.98; no. 329, 7.9.98; no. 440, 18.10.98; no. 442, 20.10.98; no. 445, 21.10.98; no. 459, 27.10.98.

Baratier, A. E. A., op. cit., vol. 3, *Fachoda*, pp. 207–19.

Marder, Arthur J., *The Anatomy of British Seapower, 1880–1905*, 1940, pp. 321–8.

Faure, Félix, op. cit., pp. 35–8.

Brown, Roger Glenn, op. cit., pp. 80–6, 90, 98, 101–10.

Roberts, Andrew, *Salisbury, Victorian Titan*, 1999, pp. 705–7.

Glossary

abd (el) (Arab.):	slave (of)
abu (Arab.):	father (of)
agha (Turk.)	Honorary title below *bey*
ahl (Arab.):	family
'ama (Arab):	turban
'alim (Arab.):	scholar, jurist (pl. 'ulemá)
'amil (Arab.):	*amir* designated for Mahdist responsibility (after 1883)
amin (Arab.):	secretary (in authority)
amir (Arab.):	commander, prince (pl. amara)
Ansar (Arab.):	followers of the Prophet Mohammed; and of the Mahdi.
arbab (Fung):	title, dignitary
Arnaout (Turk.):	Albanian
atmur, atamur (Arab.):	sand dunes
bab (Arab.):	door, gateway
bashi-buzouq (Turk.):	irregular troops esp. cavalry
bazinqir (Turk.):	Black armed militia
bey (Turk.):	title, second to Pasha
bimbashi (Turk.):	battalion commander
bint, pl. *banāt* (Arab.):	daughter, girl
da'ira (Arab.):	household, circle
damuria (Arab.):	woven cloth
dar (Arab.):	homeland
defterdar (Turk.):	accountant-general
deim (Arab.):	settlement
dejach, dejazmach (Abyss.):	senior dignitary
dhahabiya (Arab.):	large sailing boat
diwan (Arab.) *divan* (Turk.):	council
dura (Arab.):	sorghum
effendi (Arab.):	learned person
eid (Arab.):	festival
faqi (Arab.):	Islamic teacher (pl. *fuqãra*)

fariq (Arab.):	general of division (*firqa*)
fatwa (Arab.):	Islamic ruling
feddan (Arab.):	acre (approx)
fellah (Arab.):	Egyptian peasant
geiger (Arab.):	trench/rampart
ghazwa (Arab.):	raid (*razzia*)
haj (Arab.):	Moslem pilgrimage
hākim (Arab):	ruler
hakimdar a'am (Arab.):	governor-general
hatti-i-sharif (Turk.):	irrevocable decree or *proclamation* by Ottoman Sultan
hijra (Arab.):	flight (of the Prophet from Mecca to Medina)
ibn (*bin*) (Arab.):	son (of)
idara (Arab.):	administration, organisation
imam (Arab.):	Islamic leader
jallaba (Arab.):	merchant (lit. weaver of foot-length shirt)
Jarkas (Arab.):	Circassian
jebel (Arab.):	hill, mountain
jibba (Arab.):	patched smock worn by *Ansar*
jihad (Arab.):	Moslem holy war
kabaka (Ganda)	king (of Buganda)
kashif (Arab.):	district officer (arch.)
khalifa (Arab.):	caliph, supreme successor
khalwa (Arab.):	mosque school
khor (Arab.):	water-course
khedive (Turk.):	title, second to Ottoman Sultan
kinj (Turk.):	junior
kuchuk (Turk.):	junior
kurbaj (Arab.):	whip
lewa (Arab.):	brigade, brigadier
Maghreb (Arab.):	Moorish, western African
maqdoum (Arab.):	Darfur provincial governor
mamur (Arab.):	commander of district (*mamuria idara*)
majlis (Arab.):	council, tribunal
malik (Arab.):	*lit.* king

manjil (Fung):	ruler
mek (Arab.):	kinglet
meshra (Arab.):	upstream landing pace
miralai (Turk.):	regimental (brigade) commander
mu'awin (Arab.):	military rank between *bimbashi* (Turk.) and *yuzbashi* (Turk.)
mudir (Arab.):	province governor
mudir 'Umum (Arab.):	general-governor of province(s)
mufettish (Arab.):	inspector
mufti (Arab):	senior Islamic judge
muhafiz (Arab.):	province commissioner
mukama (Nyoro):	king (of Bunyoro)
mulazim (Arab.):	military lieutenant
mushir (Arab.):	marshal
mut'amad (Arab.):	senior political representative
na'ib (Arab.):	deputy
nazir (Arab.):	head of important tribe
negus (Abyss.):	king; *negus'a, nagest*, emperor
nuggar (Arab.):	sailing barge
nyireth (Shilluk):	son of a *reth*
omda (Arab.):	ruler of tribal section, village group or town
omodor (Arab.):	town ruler
pasha (Turk.):	title senior to *bey*, four grades
piastre (ghyrsh, Arab.):	100 *piastres* = £E1
Porte (Turk.):	government of Ottoman empire
qadi (Arab.):	judge
qa'id (Arab.):	commanding officer
qa'immaqam (Arab.):	lieutenant-colonel, senior to *bimbashi*
qapudan (Turk.):	sea-captain
qism (Arab.):	district, department (pl. *'aqsam*)
ras (Abyss.):	most senior dignitary after *negus*
ras (Arab.):	head, leader, headland
ratib (Arab.):	formulary of prayers, esp. of the Mahdi
razzia (ghazwa, Arab.):	raid esp. for slaves
reth (Shilluk):	hereditary king
sagh qol aghasi (Turk.):	major

sagia (Arab.):	water-wheel
sanjak (Turk.):	squadron commander irregular cavalry (province governor)
sayyid (Arab.):	religious title
seraskir (Arab.):	commander-in-chief
shaduf (Arab.):	hand-operated instrument for raising water
shahada (Arab.):	witness (of faith)
shari'a (Arab.):	Islamic law
sharīf (Arab.):	descendant of the Prophet
shartai (Fur):	district ruler
shawish (Turk.):	sergeant
sheikh el masheikh (Arab.):	senior (federal) tribal ruler
sirdar (Arab.):	Egyptian commander-in-chief
sudd (Arab.):	vegetation blockage, dam
ta'arikh (Arab.):	history, chronicle
tariqa (Arab.):	religious brotherhood
tuki (Arab.):	thatched round hut
umm (Arab.):	mother of
umma (Arab.):	community
vizir (Turk.):	minister
wadi (Arab.):	large river bed
wakil (Arab.):	deputy, agent
walad, or *wad* (Arab.):	son of, (pl. *awlad*)
wali (Arab.):	Ottoman provincial governor
wazir (Arab.):	minister
yuzbashi (Turk.):	captain
zariba (Arab.):	protective thorn fence, fortified camp
zuhur (Arab.):	revelation

Bibliography

MANUSCRIPTS AND OFFICIAL PUBLICATIONS

Public Record Office, Kew, London
  FO 78 Turkey (Egypt)
  FO 84 Slave Trade
  FO 141 Cairo Agency Archives
  FO 142 Egypt Consulates
  PRO Granville Papers. 30/29: 127, 133, 146, 160–2, 166, 168, 199, 200, 221
British Library Gordon Manuscripts: Moffitt Collection; Bell Collection
Durham University Library, Sudan Archive: Wingate papers
British Parliamentary Papers, London
House of Commons Blue Books
House of Commons Hansard
Archives Diplomatiques Ministère des Affaires Étrangères, Paris
Documents Diplomatiques Français, 1871–1914 First Series vols. XI–XIV, Paris, 1929
'Affaires du Haut Nil et du Bahr el Ghazal 1897–98', Yellow Book, Paris, 1898
Journal Officiel, Débats Parlementaires, Sénat, Paris
Baker, Sir Samuel White, 'Journals 3 and 4, 1869–73', unpublished mss. deposited Royal Geographical Society, London
Frost, John Warner, 'A History of the Shilluk of the Southern Sudan', unpublished doctoral thesis, University of California, Santa Barbara, 1974
Kwawang, K. G. A., 'Government and Community in a Modern State: A Case Study of the Shilluk and Their Neighbours', unpublished doctoral thesis, Wolfson College, Oxford, 1982
Stiansen, Endre, 'Overture to Imperialism', unpublished doctoral thesis, Bergen University, 1993

PRINTED SOURCES

Abbas Bey Hilmi, 'The Diary of Abbas Bey', in *Sudan Notes and Records*, vol. XXXII, part 2, 1951, Khartoum
Allen, Bernard M., *Gordon and the Sudan*, London, 1931
Anderson, Dorothy, *Baker Pasha: Misconduct and Mischance*, Norwich, 1999

Andrew, Christopher, *Théophile Delcassé and the Making of the Entente Cordiale*, Cambridge, 1968

Arthur, Sir George, *Life of Lord Kitchener*, 3 vols., London, 1920

Arthur, Sir George, and Maurice, Sir F., *Life of Lord Wolseley*, London, 1924

Asad, Talal, *The Kababish Arabs*, London, 1970

Baker, Anne, *Morning Star*, London, 1972

Baker, Sir Samuel White, *Albert N'yanza, Great Basin of the Nile*, 2 vols., London, 1866

——, *Ismailia*, 2nd edn., London, 1895

Baratier, A. E. A., *Souvenirs de la Mission Marchand*, vol. 2, *Vers le Nil*, Paris, 1925; vol. 3, *Fachoda*, Paris, 1941

Bates, Darrell, *The Abyssinian Difficulty: the Emperor Theodorus and the Magdala Campaign, 1867–68*, Oxford, 1979

——, *The Fashoda Incident of 1898*, Oxford, 1984

Beaton, A. C., 'A Chapter in Bari History', in *Sudan Notes and Records,* vol. XVII, part 2, 1934, Khartoum

Beattie, John, *Bunyoro, An African Kingdom*, New York, 1960

Bedri, Babikr, trans. Bedri, Yousef, and Scott, George, *Memoirs of ...*, vol. I, Oxford, 1969

Bell, Charles F. Moberly, *Life and Letters of C. F. Moberly Bell*, London, 1927

Berlioux, E. F., *La Traite Orientale*, Paris, 1870

Beshir, M. O., 'Abdel Rahman Ibn Hussein and His Book "History of the Mahdi"', in *Sudan Notes and Records*, vol. XLIV, 1963, Khartoum

——, 'Nasihat Al Awam', in *Sudan Notes and Records*, vol. XLI, 1960, Khartoum

Bjørkelo, Anders, 'The Territorial Unification and Administrative Divisions of Turkish Sudan 1821–1885', in *Sudan Notes and Records*, New Series, vol. I, 1997, Khartoum

Boulger, Demetrius C., *Life of General Gordon*, 2 vols., London, 1896

Boutros Ghali, Mirrit (ed.), *Mémoires de Nubar Pasha 1825–79*, Beirut, 1983

Boyle, Clara, *Boyle of Cairo*, Kendal, 1965

Bredin, G. R. E., 'The Life Story of Yuzbashi Abdallah Adlan', in *Sudan Notes and Records*, vol. XLII, 1961, Khartoum

Brown, Robert, *The Story of Africa and its Explorers,* 2 vols, London, 1893

Brown, Roger Glenn, *Fashoda Reconsidered*, Baltimore, 1969

Bulwer, Sir Henry, *Life of Henry John Temple, Viscount Palmerston*, 3 vols., 3rd edn., London 1871–4

Burleigh, Bennet, *Desert Warfare: the Eastern Soudan Campaign*, London, 1884

Cameron, D. A., *Egypt in the Nineteenth Century*, London, 1898

Cecil, Lady Gwendolen, *Life of Robert, Marquis of Salisbury 1887–1892*, vol. IV, London, 1932

Chenevix Trench, Charles, *Charley Gordon, An Eminent Victorian Reassessed*, London, 1978

Chirol, Sir Valentine, *The Egyptian Problem*, London, 1920

——, *Fifty Years in a Changing World*, London, 1927

Churchill, Winston Spencer, *The River War*, 1st edn., 2 vols., London, 1899; 3rd edn., London, 1933

Cocheris, Jules, *Situation Internationale de l'Egypte et du Soudan*, Paris, 1903

Collins, Robert O., *The Southern Sudan 1883–98: A Struggle for Control*, New Haven and London, 1962

——, *Land Beyond the Rivers, The Southern Sudan 1898–1918*, New Haven and London, 1971

——, *The Nile*, New Haven and London, 2002

——, 'The Ilemi Triangle', paper delivered to Sudan International Conference, Georgetown University, Washington D.C., 2003

Colvin, Sir Auckland, *The Making of Modern Egypt*, London, 1906

Cox, Frederick J., 'Munzinger's Observations on the Sudan 1871: The Little America of Africa', in *Sudan Notes and Records*, vol. XXXIII, part 2, 1952, Khartoum

Crabités, Pierre, *Ismail the Maligned Khedive*, London, 1933

——, *Americans in the Egyptian Army*, London, 1938

Creasy, Sir Edward S., *History of the Ottoman Turks*, revised edn., London, 1877

Cromer, Earl of, *Modern Egypt*, 2 vols., London, 1908

——, *Abbas II*, London, 1915

Cumming, D. C., 'History of Kassala and the Province of Taka', in *Sudan Notes and Records*, vol. XX, part I, 1937; XXIII, parts 1 and 2, 1940

Cunnison, Ian, *Baggara Arabs: Power and the Lineage in a Sudanese Nomad Tribe*, Oxford, 1966

Daly, M. W., *Empire on the Nile*, Cambridge, 1986

Daly, M. W., and Holt, P. M., *The History of the Sudan*, 3rd edn., London 1979

De Card, E. Rouard, *Les Territoires Africains et Les Conventions Franco-Anglaises*, Paris, 1901

Dehérain, Henri, *Le Soudan Égyptien sous Mehemet Ali*, Paris, 1898

Delbeque, J., *Vie du Général Marchand*, Paris, 1936

De Lesseps, Ferdinand, *The Suez Canal: Letters and Documents 1854–6*, trans. N. d'Anvers, London, 1876

Dicey, Edward, *The Story of the Khedivate*, London, 1902

Douin, Georges, *Histoire du Règne du Khédive Ismail*, vol. I, *Les Premières Années du Règne 1863–67*, Rome, 1933; vol. II, *L'Apogée 1867–73*, Rome, 1934; vol. III, *L'Empire Africain, partie 1 1863–69*, Cairo, 1936; *partie 2, 1869–73*, Cairo, 1938; *partie 3 i and ii, 1874–76*, Cairo 1941

Du Bisson, Comte R., 'Account of Expedition to Frontiers of Abyssinia', in *Nouvelles Annales des Voyages*, 6 série, vol. IV, Paris, 1864

Dufton, Henry, *Narrative of a Journey through Abyssinia in 1862–3*, 2nd edn., London, 1867

Elles, R. J., 'Kingdom of Tegali', in *Sudan Notes and Records*, vol. XVIII, part I, 1935, Khartoum

Elton, Lord, *General Gordon*, London, 1954

Emily, Dr J., *Mission Marchand, Journal de Route*, Paris, 1913

Faure, Félix, 'Fachoda', in *Revue d' Histoire Diplomatique*, Paris, 1955

Felkin, Dr R. W., and Wilson, Rev'd C. T., *Uganda and the Egyptian Soudan*, London, 1882

Fitzmaurice, Lord Edmond, *Life of Earl Granville*, 2 vols., London, 1905

Gale, H. P., *Uganda and the Mill Hill Fathers*, London, 1959

Garnier, F. B., letter in *Archives diplomatiques Ministère des Affaires Etrangères*: Correspondance politique Egypte, vols. 36, 37, Paris

Gessi, Romolo, ed. Felix Gessi, *Seven Years in the Sudan*, London, 1892

Giffen, Morrison B., *Fashoda, The Incident and Its Diplomatic Setting*, Chicago, 1930

Gifford, Prosser, and Louis, William Roger, *France and Britain in Africa: Imperial Rivalry and Colonial Rule*, New Haven, 1971

Gleichen, Lieutenant-Colonel Count A. E. W. (ed.), *The Anglo-Egyptian Sudan*, 2 vols., London, 1905

Gordon, Sir Henry, *Events in the Life of Charles George Gordon*, London, 1886

Gordon, M. A., *Letters of General Gordon to His Sister*, London, 1888

Gray, Richard, *History of the Southern Sudan 1839–1889*, Oxford, 1961

Grey of Fallodon, Viscount, *Twenty-Five Years 1892–1916*, 2 vols., London, 1925

Gulla, Ali, 'The Defeat of Hicks Pasha', in *Sudan Notes and Records*, vol. XL, 1959, Khartoum

Hake, A. Egmont (ed.), *The Journals of Major-General C.G. Gordon at Kartoum*, London, 1885

Hallett, Robin, *Africa Since 1875*, Michigan, 1974

Hamilton, James, *Traveller in Africa: Sinai, the Hedjaz and Soudan*, London, 1857

Hanotaux, G., *Le Partage d'Afrique; Fashoda*, Paris, 1909

El Hassan Bin Talal, HRH Prince, *Continuity, Innovation and Change, Selected Essays*, Amman, 2001

Hansal, Martin, in *Austrian Geographical Journal*, Vienna, 1874

Henderson, K. D. D., 'A Note on the Migration of the Messiria Tribe into South West Kordofan' in *Sudan Notes and Records*, vol. XXII, part I, 1939, Khartoum

Henty, G. A., *March to Magdala*, London, 1868

Heuglin, Theodor von, *Reise in das Gebiet des Weissen Nil*, Leipzig and Heidelberg, 1869

——, 'Travels in the Sudan in the Sixties etc', in *Sudan Notes and Records*, vol. XXIV, 1941, Khartoum

Hill, George Birkbeck, *Colonel Gordon in Central Africa 1874–1879*, 4th edn. 1885, rep. New York, 1969

Hill, Richard L., *Egypt in the Sudan 1820–81*, Oxford, 1959

——, 'Rulers of the Sudan', in *Sudan Notes and Records*, vol. XXXII, part I, 1951, Khartoum

——, *Biographical Dictionary of the Sudan*, 2nd edn., Oxford, 1967

——, *Slatin Pasha*, Oxford, 1965

—— (ed.), *The Sudan Memoirs of Carl Christian Giegler Pasha, 1873–1883*, London and Oxford, 1984

——, and Hogg, Peter, *A Black Corps d'Élite*, Michigan, 1995

Hochschild, Adam, *King Leopold's Ghost*, London, 1999

Holt, P. M., *Egypt and the Fertile Crescent 1516–1922*, London, 1966

——, *The Mahdist State in the Sudan 1881–98*, 2nd edn., Oxford, 1970

——, 'The Archives of the Mahdia', in *Sudan Notes and Records*, vol. XXXVI, part I, 1955, Khartoum

——, 'The Place in History of the Sudanese Mahdia', in *Sudan Notes and Records*, vol. XL, 1959, Khartoum

——, and Daly, M. W., *The History of the Sudan*, 3rd edn., London, 1979

Ismail Abdel Qadir el Kordofani, 1888, trans. Shaked, Ha'im, *The Life of the Sudanese Mahdi*, New Jersey, 1978

Jackson, H. C., *Black Ivory and White: The Story of El Zubeir Pasha*, London, 1913

Jackson, Sir H. W., 'Fashoda, 1898', in *Sudan Notes and Records*, vol. III, 1920, Khartoum

Jerrold, Blanchard (ed.), *Egypt under Ismail Pasha*, London, 1879

Johnson, Douglas H., 'Prophecy and Mahdism in the Upper Nile', in *British Journal of Middle Eastern Studies*, 1993

Junker, Wilhelm, trans. A. H. Keane, *Travels in Africa during the Years 1875–1886*, 3 vols., London, 1890

Keown-Boyd, Henry, *A Good Dusting*, London, 1986

——, *Soldiers of the Nile, 1882–1925*, Thornbury, 1996

Lampen, G. D., 'History of Darfur', in *Sudan Notes and Records*, vol. XXXI, part 2, 1950, Khartoum

Lane-Poole, Stanley, *Watson Pasha*, London, 1919

Lejean, G. *Voyage en Abyssinie 1862–4*, Paris, 1870

Lienhardt, Godfrey, *Divinity and Experience: The Religion of the Dinka*, Oxford, 1961

Lyall, Sir Alfred, *The Life of the Marquis of Dufferin and Ava*, London, 1905

McCoan, J. Carlisle, *Egypt As It Is*, London, 1877

—, *Egypt under Ismail*, London, 1889

McLynn, Frank, *Burton: Snow Upon the Desert*, London, 1990

MacMichael, H. A., *Tribes of Northern and Central Kordofan*, London, 1912

—, *A History of the Arabs in the Sudan*, 2 vols., Cambridge, 1922; 2nd imp., London, 1967

Macro, E., 'Frank Miller Lupton', in *Sudan Notes and Records*, vol. XXVIII, 1947, Khartoum

Magnus, Philip, *Kitchener,Portrait of an Imperialist*, London, 1958

Maistre, Casimir, 'Le Président Carnot et Le Plan Français d'Action sur Le Nil en 1893', in *Bulletin du Comité de l' Afrique Française*, 1932, Paris

Marder, Arthur J., *The Anatomy of British Seapower*, New York, 1940

Marno, E., *Reisen in Gebiete des Blauen und Weissen Nil, 1869 bis 1873*, Vienna, 1874

Mathew, David, *Ethiopia, the Study of a Polity, 1540–1935*, London, 1947

Matthew, H. C. G., *Gladstone 1875–1898*, Oxford, 1995

Maurice, Sir F., and Arthur, Sir George, *Life of Lord Wolseley*, London, 1924

Melly, George, *Khartoum and the Blue and White Niles*, London, 1851

Middleton, Dorothy, *Baker of the Nile*, London, 1949

Miller, Charles, *The Lunatic Express*, London, 1971

Milner, Alfred, *England in Egypt*, 11th edn., London, 1904

Moore-Harell, Alice, *Gordon and the Sudan: Prologue to the Mahdiyya, 1877–1880*, London, 2001

Moorehead, Alan, *The White Nile*, London, 1960

—, *The Blue Nile*, London, 1962

Munzinger, Johann Albert Werner, *Ostafrikanische Studien*, 2nd edn., Schaffhausen, 1883

Murray, T. Douglas, and White, A. Silva, *Sir Samuel Baker: A Memoir*, London, 1895

Newbold, D., 'The History of Gallabat', in *Sudan Notes and Records*, vol. VII, part I, 1924, Khartoum

Neillands, Robin, *The Dervish War:Gordon and Kitchener in the Sudan 1880–1898*, London, 1996

Nicoll, Fergus, *The Sword of the Prophet: The Mahdi of Sudan and the Death of General Gordon*, Stroud, 2004

O'Fahey, R. S., 'The Conquest of Darfur, 1873–1882', in *Sudan Notes and Records*, New Series, vol. I, 1997, Khartoum

—, and Spaulding, Jay L., *Kingdoms of the Sudan*, London, 1974

—, *State and Society in Darfur*, London, 1980

Ohrwalder, Father Joseph, trans. and abridged Major F. R. Wingate, *Ten Years' Captivity in the Mahdi's Camp, 1882–92*, 12th edn., London, 1895

Owen, Roger, *Lord Cromer*, Oxford, 2004

Pakenham, Thomas, *The Scramble for Africa*, London, 1991

Paul, A., *A History of the Beja Tribes of the Sudan*, Cambridge, 1954

——, 'Tewfiq Bey', in *Sudan Notes and Records*, vol. XXXV, part 1, 1954, Khartoum

Perham, Margery, *Lugard, The Years of Adventure 1858–98*, London, 1956

Petherick, John, *Egypt, the Soudan and Central Africa*, Edinburgh and London, 1861

——, and Petherick, Katherine Harriet, *Travels in Central Africa and Explorations of the White Nile Tributaries*, 2 vols., London, 1869

Pollock, John, *Gordon, the Man behind the Legend*, London, 1993

Prouty, Chris, and Rosenfeld, Eugene, *Historical Dictionary of Ethiopia*, London, 1981

Pumphrey, M. E. C., 'The Shilluk Tribe', in *Sudan Notes and Records*, vol. XXIV, 1941, Khartoum

Rassam, Hormuzd, *Narrative of the British Mission to Theodore, King of Abyssinia*, 2 vols., London, 1869

Roberts, Andrew, *Salisbury, Victorian Titan*, London, 1999

Rosenfeld, Eugène, and Prouty, Chris, *Historical Dictionary of Ethiopia*, London, 1981

Rosignoli, Father C., 'Omdurman During the Mahdiyya', in *Sudan Notes and Records*, vol. XLVIII, extract from *I Miei Dodici Anni di Prigionia 1898*, Khartoum

Russell, W. H., *A Diary in the East during the Tour of the Prince and Princess of Wales*, London, 1869

Ryle, John, *Warriors of the White Nile: The Dinka*, Amsterdam, 1982

Sabry, M., *Episode de la Question d'Afrique 1863–79*, Paris, 1933

——, *L'Empire Égyptien sous Ismail et L'Ingérence Anglo-Française 1863–79*, Paris, 1933

Sanderson, G. N., 'Contributions from African Sources', in *Journal of African History III (I)*, 1962, London

——, 'Foreign Policy of the Negus Menilek', in *Journal of African History V*, 1964, London

——, *England, Europe and the Upper Nile, 1882–1899*, Edinburgh, 1965

——, 'Conflict and Co-operation Between Ethiopia and the Mahdist State, 1884–1898, in *Sudan Notes and Records*, vol. L, 1969, Khartoum

Santandrea, Father Stefano, 'An Account of the Indri, Togoyo, Ferroge etc.', in *Sudan Notes and Records*, vol. XXXIV, part 2, 1953, Khartoum

——, 'The Belgians in the Western Bahr el Ghazal', in *Sudan Notes and Records*, vol. XXXVI, part 2, 1955, Khartoum

——, *Ethnography of the Bahr el Ghazal (Sudan)*, Bologna, 1981

Schuver, Juan Maria, ed. Wendy James, Gerd Baumann and Douglas H. Johnson, *Travels in North East Africa 1880–1883*, Hakluyt Society, 1996

Schweinfurth, Georg., (trans. Ellen Frewer), 2 vols., *The Heart of Africa*

Three Years Travels in the Unexplored Regions of Central Africa, *1868–71*, London, 1873

——, and others (ed.), trans. Mrs R. W. Felkin, *Emin Pasha in Central Africa,* London, 1888

Schweitzer, George, *Emin Pasha, His Life and Work*, 2 vols., London, 1898

Seligman, C. G., and Seligman, Brenda, *Pagan Tribes of the Nilotic Sudan*, London, 1932

Shannon, Richard, *Gladstone, Heroic Minister 1865–1898*, London, 1999

Shibeika, Mekki, *British Policy in the Sudan 1882–1902*, Oxford, 1952

Shukry, Mohammed Fuad, *The Khedive Ismail and Slavery in the Sudan*, *1863–79*, doctoral thesis University of Liverpool, 1935; Cairo, 1938

——, *Equatoria under Egyptian Rule 1874–6*, Cairo, 1953

Slatin, Rudolf C., Pasha, trans. F. R. Wingate, *Fire and Sword in the Sudan,* *1879–1895*, London, 1896

Spaulding, Jay L., and O'Fahey, R. S., *Kingdoms of the Sudan*, London, 1974

Stanton, Colonel E. A., ed., 'Unpublished Letters of Charles George Gordon', in *Sudan Notes and Records*, vol. X, 1927, Khartoum

Steevens, G. W., *With Kitchener to Khartoum*, London, 1898

Stengers, Jean, 'Aux Origines de Fachoda: L'Expedition Monteil', in *Revue Belge de Philosophie et d'Histoire*, 1958, Brussels

Stevens, E. S., *My Sudan Year*, London, 1912

Stewart, Lieutenant-Colonel J. D. H., 'Report on the Soudan 1883', Cmd 3670, Egypt no. 11, British Parliamentary Paper, London

Sykes, Sir Percy, *History of Persia*, 2 vols., London, 1920

Taylor, A. J. P., 'Prelude to Fashoda: The Question of the Upper Nile 1894–5', in *The English Historical Review*, vol. LXV, 1950, London

Thesiger, Wilfred, *The Life of My Choice*, London, 1987

Theobald, A. B., 'The Khalifa Abdallahi' in *Sudan Notes and Records*, vol. XXXI, part 2, 1950, Khartoum

——, *The Mahdiya: A History of the Anglo-Egyptian Sudan, 1881–1899*, London, 1951

Tignor, Robert L., *Modernisation and British Colonial Rule in Egypt 1882–1914*, Princeton, 1966

Trimingham, J. Spencer, *Islam in the Sudan*, Oxford, 1965

Udal, John O., *The Nile in Darkness: Conquest and Exploration,* *1504–1862*, Norwich, 1998

——, 'Ja'afar Pasha Mazhar: A Worthy Governor-General', in *Sudan Studies*, no. 26, 2001, Durham

——, 'Equatoria – An Indian Ocean Outlet?', in *Sudan Studies*, no. 31, 2003, Durham

Vatikiotis, P. J., *The History of Egypt from Muhammad Ali to Sadat*, 2nd edn., London, 1980

Velay, Étienne, 'Les Rivalités Franco-Anglaises en Égypte 1876–1904', doctoral thesis, University of Nîmes, 1904

Wallis, C. A., ed. Douglas H. Johnson, *The Upper Nile Province Handbook*, Oxford, 1995

Waterfield, Gordon,. *Layard of Nineveh*, London, 1963

Watson, Sir Charles M., *Life of Major-General Sir Charles William Wilson R.E.*, London, 1909

Werner, Roland; Anderson, William; Wheeler, Andrew, *Day of Devastation, Day of Contentment*, Nairobi, 2000

White, Stanhope, *Lost Empire on the Nile*, London, 1969

Wilson, Rev'd C. T., and Felkin, Dr R. W., *Uganda and the Egyptian Soudan*, London, 1882

Wingate, F. R., *Mahdiism and the Egyptian Sudan*, London, 1891

Wingate, Ronald, *Wingate of the Sudan*, London, 1955

Wood, Field Marshal Sir Evelyn, VC, *From Midshipman to Field Marshal*, 2 vols., 2nd edn., London, 1906

Wright, Patricia, *Conflict on the Nile*, London, 1972

Wyld, Major J. W. G., 'Recollections of Two Zande Chiefs', in *Sudan Notes and Records*, vol. XLII, 1961, Khartoum

Wylde, A. B., *'83–'87 in the Soudan*, London, 1888

Yacoub Pasha Artin, trans. George Robb, *England in the Sudan*, London, 1911

Yusuf Fadl Hasan, *The Arabs and the Sudan*, Edinburgh, 1967

Zaghi, Carlo, *Gordon, Gessi è la Riconquista del Sudan 1874–81*, Florence, 1947

Zetland, 2nd Marquess of, *Lord Cromer*, London, 1932

Zewde, Bahru, *A History of Modern Ethiopia 1855–1974*, London, 1991

Ziegler, Philip, *Omdurman*, London, 1973

PERIODICALS

Bulletin du Comité de l' Afrique Française, 1932, Paris
The Daily Telegraph, London
The English Historical Review, 1950, London
Nouvelles Annales des Voyages, 6 série, Paris
Journal of African History, London
Revue Belge de Philosophie et d'Histoire, 1958, Brussels
Sudan Notes and Records, Khartoum
Sudan Studies, SSSUK, Durham
The Times, London

Index

Figures in **bold type** refer to the number of the relevant map

413, 414–15, 418, 430, 462; arrival in Khartoum, 411–13; El Obeid expedition, 420, 531, 540 (defeat and annihilation of, 408, 415, 440, 444, 472); requests more troops, 412; troops seized by Karamallah, 446

Higginbotham, Edwin, Sir Samuel Baker's chief engineer, 120, 122, 133; death of, 138

hijra: of Mohammed Ahmed the Mahdi, 377, 378; of Rizeiqat, 480

Hilali expedition *see* Mohammed el Hilali

Hill, Dr Richard Leslie, historian, 34, 46, 59, 111, 173, 193, 332; *Biographical Dictionary*, 430

Hillelson, S., Arabist, author, 471

Hodges, Colonel, British consul-general Cairo, 84

Hogg, Peter, author, Sudan administrator, 34

Holled Smith Pasha, Charles, *lewa*, *hakimdar* Suakin, 489, 491

Holt, Professor P.M., author, 376, 377, 454, 472, 473, 496, 508; 'The Archives of the Mahdia', 471; *The Mahdist State in the Sudan 1881–98*, 470; view of Khalifa Abdallahi, 511

Holy Cross mission, Bahr el Jebel, 266

hospitals, Sudan, 47; building of, 240

Hufrat el Nahas, Dar Fertit, 121, 142, 151, 163, 232, 505; Congolese expedition to, 547; copper deposits, 145, 146, 155 [4]

Humr, Baqqara, 151 [6] Hunter, Sir Archibald, *lewa*, Kitchener's senior British officer, 514, 527

Hunter, Major (Indian Army), 454

El Hussein, son of the Khalifa Ali Abu Talib (*q.v.*), 470

Hussein Ibrahim el Zahra, *Qadi el Islam*, 496

Hussein Kamel Ismail, Prince, 192, 211, 318; minister of finance, 201

Hussein Pasha Khalifa el Ababda, 48, 120, 172, 178, 179–80, 365, 435, 455, 516; captured, 455; *mudir* Berber, 48; general-governor Berber and Dongola, 203; possible successor to Gordon, 436; reinstated as general-governor, 456; submission of Bisharin, 434, 452

Hussein el Majdi, Khartoum *sheikh* (?Hussein el Mohamedi), 465

Hussein Pasha Mazhar, *lewa*, chief of staff, Hicks, 414

Hussein Bey Sadiq, *mudir* Sennar, 380, 422

Hussein Pasha Wasif Sirri, *mudir*, Khartoum, 403, 414, 419, 422, 426; deputy *hakimdar*, 403; replaced by de Coëtlogon, 434

Husseiniya, steamer, 463

Ibrahim Effendi, chief clerk to Ahmed Agha, i/c Hilali's troops, 148

Ibrahim Bey Adam Mahallawi, *mudir*, Taka, 21, 24, 33

Ibrahim Adlan (*amin beit el mal*), 477, 497–8, 509; criticised by Khalifa Abdallahi, 498; executed, 498

Ibrahim Fawzi, *pasha* and *lewa*, 272, 276, 292, 301, 308, 352, 353, 433, 436, 463; appointed *mudir* of Bahr el Ghazal, 335, 345, 354; Gordon's personal assistant, 434; *mudir* Bor and Rohl, 303; promoted *qa'immaqam*, 307; taken prisoner in Omdurman, 466

Ibrahim (Garad) Mohammed Hussein, Fur *sultan*, 160, 207, 219, 224, 227, 230, 444, 478; death of, 225, 226

Ibrahim Haidar Pasha, *seraskir*, 422, 426, 436

Ibrahim el Khalil Ahmed, commandant Omdurman *jihadiya*, 524

Ibrahim Lutfi Bey, *mudir*, Taka, 40, 42

Ibrahim Mohammed Gurguru Agha, *mamur*, Makaraka, 445, 446, 447

Ibrahim Musa, *sheikh* Hadendoa tribe, 48

Ibrahim Bey Tawfiq, head of Sudan department, Cairo, 411, 417

Ibrahim Pasha el Wali, Viceroy, 7, 41, 84, 98, 112

Ibrahimiya canal, 12

Ibrahimiyya (Dufile), 133 [7]

Ibrahimiyya frigate, 36, 39

Idris Bey Abtar, *mamur*, *mudir* Bahr el Ghazal, 327, 345–6, 354

Ilyas Ahmed Umm Birair, *pasha*, *mudir* of Shakka, 372; joins *Ansar*, 381, 382

Imperial British East Africa Company (IBEAC), 504, 544, 545, 551, 552; abolition recommended, 553; agreement with Leopold II, 547; extension of lease, 552

India: communications with, 536; French threat to, 535–6; Government of, 91; route to, 192

Indian Ocean: littoral expedition, 294–300; outlet to, 336 [10]

India Office, 77, 81, 240, 241, 454

Indian troops, use of, 393

indigo, cultivation of, 64

Inflexible, HMS, 389